CW01338255

ELGAR COMPANION TO ADAM SMITH

Elgar Companion to Adam Smith

Edited by

Jeffrey T. Young

A. Barton Hepburn Professor of Economics, St Lawrence University, Canton, New York, USA

Edward Elgar
Cheltenham, UK • Northampton, MA, USA

© Jeffrey T. Young 2009

All rights reserved. No part of this publication may be reproduced, stored in a retrieval system or transmitted in any form or by any means, electronic, mechanical or photocopying, recording, or otherwise without the prior permission of the publisher.

Published by
Edward Elgar Publishing Limited
The Lypiatts
15 Lansdown Road
Cheltenham
Glos GL50 2JA
UK

Edward Elgar Publishing, Inc.
William Pratt House
9 Dewey Court
Northampton
Massachusetts 01060
USA

A catalogue record for this book
is available from the British Library

Library of Congress Control Number: 2009936735

Mixed Sources
Product group from well-managed
forests and other controlled sources
www.fsc.org Cert no. SA-COC-1565
© 1996 Forest Stewardship Council
FSC

ISBN 978 1 84542 019 2

Printed and bound by MPG Books Group, UK

Contents

List of figures and tables	vii
List of contributors	viii
Acknowledgements	x
Introduction by Jeffrey T. Young	xi
Table of Smith's primary works by Brendan Long	xxiii
Smith's life and major works by Brendan Long	xxv

PART I ADAM SMITH'S SYSTEM AND ITS ANTECEDENTS: PHILOSOPHICAL CONCERNS

1	Adam Smith, the last of the former virtue ethicists Deirdre McCloskey	3
2	Adam Smith and Aristotle Gloria Vivenza	25
3	Agency and discourse: revisiting the Adam Smith problem Vivienne Brown	52
4	Adam Smith's theism Brendan Long	73
5	Smith's philosophy and economic methodology Sheila C. Dow	100
6	The moral philosophical frame of Adam Smith's economic thought Jerry Evensky	112

PART II ADAM SMITH'S SYSTEM AND ITS ANTECEDENTS: ANALYTICAL ECONOMICS

7	Adam Smith, the Physiocrats and Turgot Peter Groenewegen	135
8	Wants versus needs: a Smithian model of general equilibrium Amos Witztum	141
9	Stochastic demand and the extent of the market: another piece of the Smith puzzle James M. Buchanan and Yong J. Yoon	173
10	Smithian answers to some puzzling results in the experimental literature Maria Pia Paganelli	181

PART III APPLICATIONS AND POLICY ANALYSIS

11	The invisible hand Warren J. Samuels	195

12	Adam Smith and economic development *Salim Rashid*	211
13	'In the heat of writing': polemics and the 'error of Adam Smith' in the matter of the corn bounty *Glenn Hueckel*	229
14	The mercantile system *Andrew S. Skinner*	261
15	Jeremy Bentham and Adam Smith on the usury laws: a 'Smithian' reply to Bentham and a new problem *Samuel Hollander*	277
16	'Only three duties': Adam Smith on the economic role of government *Steven G. Medema and Warren J. Samuels*	300
17	Adam Smith on the standing army versus militia issue: wealth over virtue? *Leonidas Montes*	315
18	Adam Smith and the place of faction *David M. Levy and Sandra J. Peart*	335
19	Adam Smith and the Chicago School *Steven G. Medema*	346

Index   359

Figures and tables

Figures
1.1	The seven virtues	6
4.1	Divine names (Nature included)	85
4.2	Divine names (Nature excluded)	86
8.1	Technological set-up	149
8.2	Own surpluses and net surpluses	151
8.3	The exchange box	152
8.4	Net-surplus and maximum growth	154
8.5	Growth	155
8.6	Expansion paths	157
8.7	Price and conditional expansion paths	160
8.8	Multiple equilibria	161
8.9	A unique equilibrium: present enjoyments take precedence	162
8.10	Demand with fixed current needs and wants	165
8.11	Partial and general equilibrium	167
10.1	Ultimatum Game	185
10.2	Dictactor Game	186

Tables
4.1	References to scripture in the Smithian corpus	75
15.1	Year and estimated effective yield	292

Contributors

Vivienne Brown, Professor of Intellectual History, Faculty of Social Sciences, The Open University, Milton Keynes, UK.

James M. Buchanan, Advisory General Director, Center for the Study of Public Choice, George Mason University, Fairfax, Virginia, USA.

Sheila C. Dow, Professor of Economics, University of Stirling, Stirling, UK.

Jerry Evensky, Professor of Economics and Meredith Professor for Teaching Excellence, Syracuse University, Syracuse, New York, USA.

Peter Groenewegen, Professor Emeritus of Economics, University of Sydney, Sydney, Australia.

Samuel Hollander, University Professor Emeritus, University of Toronto, currently affiliated with Ben Gurion University of the Negev, Israel.

Glenn Hueckel, Adjunct Professor of Economics, Pomona College, Claremont, California, USA.

David M. Levy, Research Associate Center for the Study of Public Choice and Professor of Economics, George Mason University, Fairfax, Virginia, USA.

Brendan Long, Political Adviser, Minister for Human Services, Canberra, Australia.

Deirdre McCloskey, Distinguished Professor of Economics, History, English, and Communication, University of Illinois at Chicago, Chicago, Illinois, USA; Extraordinary Professor of Economics and English, University of the Free State, Bloemfontein, South Africa; Professor of Social Thought, Academia Vitae, Deventer, The Netherlands

Steven G. Medema, Professor of Economics, University of Colorado Denver, Denver, Colorado, USA.

Leonidas Montes, Dean, School of Government, Universidad Adolfo Ibáñez, Santiago, Chile.

Maria Pia Paganelli, Assistant Professor of Economics, Yeshiva University and Adjunct Associate Professor of Economics at New York University, New York, USA.

Sandra J. Peart, Dean, Jepson School of Leadership Studies, University of Richmond, Richmond, Virginia, USA.

Salim Rashid, Professor of Economics, University of Illinois, Champaign-Urbana, Illinois, USA.

Warren J. Samuels, Professor Emeritus, Michigan State University, East Lansing, Michigan, USA.

Andrew S. Skinner, Adam Smith Professor Emeritus, Glasgow University, Glasgow, UK.

Gloria Vivenza, Professor of Economic History and History of Economic Thought, University of Verona, Verona, Italy.

Amos Witztum, Professor of Economics, London Metropolitan University, London, UK.

Yong J. Yoon, Associate Professor in Economics and Senior Research Scholar at the Center for the Study of Public Choice, George Mason University, Fairfax, Virginia, USA.

Jeffrey T. Young, A. Barton Hepburn Professor of Economics, St Lawrence University, Canton, New York, USA.

Acknowledgements

I wish to acknowledge the kind support of the professional staff at Edward Elgar. They first approached me almost five years ago with the idea of editing their Smith Companion. I must also mention the group of authors I have assembled here. It has been my pleasure to work with them, and the strength of the volume lies in the excellent contributions they have made.

An earlier version of Deirdre McCloskey's chapter appeared as 'Adam Smith, the last of the former virtue ethicists', *History of Political Economy*, 2008, **40** (1), 43–71.

Samuel Hollander's chapter on the usury laws was previously published in the *European Journal of the History of Economic Thought*, **6** (4), 523–51 (1999). I am pleased to reprint it here with the permission of the publisher: http://www.tandf.co.uk/journals. Excerpts from the *Glasgow Edition of the Works and Correspondence of Adam Smith, The Theory of Moral Sentiments* and *An Inquiry into the Nature and Causes of the Wealth of Nations* are used by permission of Oxford University Press, especially in Chapters 3, 6, 13 and 14.

Brendan Long kindly provided the 'Table of Smith's primary works' and time line of Smith's life, which I have thought useful to reproduce here.

Lastly, I must acknowledge the support of my department and my family. Two unforeseen illnesses have delayed this publication. My colleagues in the Economics Department at St Lawrence University have gone above and beyond the call of duty in helping to carry my professional responsibilities through these times. Judy VanKennan provided invaluable assistance in preparing the manuscript for publication. And, of course, the love and support of my wife, Cherry, has been indispensable. I have been truly blessed.

Introduction
Jeffrey T. Young

'A *kind* of Smith *renaissance seems* to be in progress' (Recktenwald, 1978, p. 56; emphasis on 'renaissance' in original, the rest added). So wrote Horst Claus Recktenwald in his survey of the bicentennial literature on Adam Smith. We are now in the second generation of Smith scholarship since the publication of Recktenwald's survey, and we may now safely revise the guarded tone of his claim. To keep up with the scholarly output survey articles are multiplying (West, 1978; Brown, 1997; Tribe, 1999; Vivenza, 2004; Labio, 2006; Brewer, 2007), there is now an International Adam Smith Society, and the fourth volume of its *Adam Smith Review* is in press at the time of writing. There is already an Adam Smith *Companion* (Haakonssen, 2006), so this volume adds another, as well as new collections of essays on Smith (Montes and Schliesser, 2006; Cockfield et al., 2007). There were more new editions of the *Wealth of Nations* (WN) published in the 1990s than in the 1890s, and more in the 1890s than in the 1790s (Tribe and Mizuta, 2002, p. 49). Smith scholarship is very much a growth industry.

How can we account for Smith's enduring and growing appeal among scholars? Recktenwald gives us no less than seven features of Smith's work that may account for this: 'catholicity' of his work, timelessness of subject matter, foundational role of self-interest, development of both positive and normative economics, realism and attention to facts, use of modelling, and lastly his personal integrity (1978, pp. 57–8). Without denying the validity of any of these claims, I would suggest that Smith has provided a set of principles, which still allow us to tell a compelling story of the formation and evolution of social life; one which still resonates with the latest thinking in economics. Indeed the contributions in the present volume give testimony to the richness and enduring appeal of Smith's principles and wisdom.

Andrew Skinner in his masterly expositions of Smith has taught us to think in terms of Smith's 'system', a coherent, consistent, multifaceted body of social science (1996). In considering the nature of his system recall that Smith himself outlined a projected system of law and government erected on the foundations set out in the *Theory of Moral Sentiments* (TMS). In the concluding paragraphs of TMS he introduces natural jurisprudence as an offshoot of his theory of justice:

> Every system of positive law may be regarded as a more or less imperfect attempt towards a system of natural jurisprudence, or towards an enumeration of the particular rules of justice. As the violation of justice is what men will never submit to from one another, the public magistrate is under a necessity of employing the power of the commonwealth to enforce the practice of virtue. Without this precaution, civil society would become a scene of bloodshed and disorder, every man revenging himself at his own hand whenever he fancied he was injured. (TMS VII. iv.36)

Grotius was the first to produce a systematic treatment of natural jurisprudence, and Smith concludes with his intention to do the same:

I shall in another discourse endeavour to give an account of the general principles of law and government, and of the different revolutions they have undergone in the different ages and periods of society, not only in what concerns justice, but in what concerns police, revenue, and arms, and whatever else is the object of law. (TMS VII.iv.37)

Smith added an 'Advertisement' to the sixth edition of TMS, the last piece Smith prepared for publication before he died in which he explained his decision not to delete the above paragraph from the work. Moreover, he explains that, 'In the *Enquiry concerning [sic] the Nature and Causes of the Wealth of Nations*, I have partly executed this promise; at least so far as concerns police, revenue, and arms' (TMS Advertisement.2). Contrary to the as yet to be discovered Adam Smith problem, Smith has told us at least one thread that runs through his work from the virtue of justice in TMS to police, revenue and arms in WN via natural jurisprudence.

However, Smith never finished the project, and the material, which undoubtedly would have been his third treatise on natural jurisprudence, was burned at his insistence shortly before he died. We now have two sets of student notes, dated 1762–63 and 1766, which were originally published in 1978 and 1896, respectively. These give us a pretty good idea of what the missing treatise would have contained. The earlier report, which has only been available to scholars for a short time, is much more detailed, and as such it allows us to see important connections between jurisprudence and moral philosophy, which are only superficially treated in the report of 1766.

We now have a much better idea of the systematic character of Smith's work as a consistent social theory worked out in three overlapping discourses: moral philosophy, natural jurisprudence and what we now call economics. Each of these traces the nature and evolution of social order in that aspect of it that pertains to the particular discourse. Thus, we see in Smith parallel accounts of the coevolution of the virtue of justice embodied in certain enforceable rules, the concept of property embodied in the laws of property and contract, and the division of labour, money and exchange embodied in the market. The starting point for Smith is his conjectural history of the 'early and rude state of *society*' (WN I.vi.1; emphasis added). Smith was a harsh critic of contract theory, which tended to posit a pre-social state of nature. Smith always assumed that people were to be found only in society, never a pure state of nature. While the first accounts of property and exchange in the *Lectures on Jurisprudence* (LJ) and the *Wealth of Nations* (WN), respectively, are explicitly stated to pertain to the early state, the account of justice in TMS has a timeless quality about it, in that no specific state of human development is specified. This gives it a certain universality across all social states, including the early one.

However, a short introduction to the present volume is not the place to expound my own views on how we should fit the pieces of Smith's system together into a coherent account of social evolution from the 'savage' state to the 'civilized' state, to use politically incorrect eighteenth-century language. My purpose has been to suggest that the systematic character of Smith's work, coupled with its foundations in moral philosophy, lend it a richness and breadth which continues to inspire scholars from around the world and from many different political persuasions, as represented, for example, by the contributors to this volume. Samuel Fleischacker observed toward the end of his recent book that there is a 'left' and a 'right' Adam Smith (Fleischacker, 2004, p. 265). Those on the left find a fellow traveller in Smith's commitment to human equality, coupled with his distaste for the rich and powerful and compassion for the labouring poor. While those on the right champion his love of liberty and scepticism toward government and politicians. The 'catholicity' of Smith and the systematic character of his work are amply reflected in the diverse contributions to this volume.

The contributions
In this age in which academic output continues to grow exponentially, product differentiation takes on added significance. Why another collection of chapters on Smith? Why another *Companion to* when Knud Haakonssen has already assembled a fine *Companion* for Cambridge University Press (2006)? There has been no collection of papers on Smith, to my knowledge, written exclusively by economists since the Skinner and Wilson bicentennial volumes (1975, 1976). My guiding principle, then, was to assemble a volume of contributions written primarily, if not exclusively by economists. However, in the intervening 30-odd years the history of economic thought has developed into a subdiscipline, regrettably outside the mainstream of the economics profession. The reading of Adam Smith remains alive primarily among economists who specialize in the history of the discipline. And, of course, there are those of us within the subdiscipline who specialize in Smith. This is a collection of chapters written by economists, some of whom are noted as primarily historians of economics and some of whom are noted as Smith specialists. I am also pleased to be able to include contributions from some outstanding contemporary economists, James Buchanan and Deirdre McCloskey, who continue to draw inspiration from reading the Smithian corpus.

Unlike the *Cambridge Companion*, which is primarily philosophical in its outlook, the present volume is oriented around the concerns of historians of economics. Moreover, the content was essentially dictated by what these scholars wanted to write about Smith than by a desire on my part to cover all the Smithian bases, to use an American sports allusion. The result is that this *Companion* tells us a lot about the current state of scholarship among historians of economics; what they find interesting and compelling in Smith's work. Among current scholars there are three main trends, which are broadly reflected in the three-part division of the book. First, compared to about 30 years ago interest in Smith's philosophical thought in general and TMS in particular has grown significantly. This is true among historians of economics just as much as it is among philosophers and others. There is growing interest in TMS, and it may not be too far off to suggest that it has or will eclipse WN in the scholarly assessment of Smith's thought. The first two contributions by Deirdre McCloskey and Gloria Vivenza, respectively, remind us of the classical Greek and Christian ancestry of Smith's ethics.

As McCloskey argues, Smith's moral philosophy must be seen as a culmination of classical virtue ethics. She maintains that Smith, in sharp contrast to his great contemporaries in ethical theorizing (Kant and Bentham), was a virtues man, a half-conscious follower of Plato and Aristotle and therefore of Aquinas, and also of the Stoics in emphasizing a system of multiple virtues. Of the seven Aquinian virtues (courage, temperance, justice, prudence, faith, hope and love) she finds five in Smith; faith and hope, the transcendent virtues are missing.

She goes on to argue that modern ethical thinking, in which she includes modern normative economics, falls into three sorts of errors, which Smith's virtue ethics avoided.

Modern ethical theories run into problems of quality (the reduction of ethics to taste), quantity (too many or too few virtues), and object (other selves, not God or self, are the only objects toward which ethical behaviour applies). Modern economics fits this pattern as it embraces a prudence-only ethic, and it reduces ethics to taste. Moreover, it is entirely secular, so the transcendent virtues of faith and hope are lost completely, which is true of Smith also. McCloskey, then, concludes with a plea not only for economists to move beyond prudence, embracing the other four Smithian virtues of justice, self-command, courage and beneficence, but also to reaffirm the transcendent, being herself a practising Anglican Christian.

Gloria Vivenza follows this with a more detailed and nuanced assessment of the Aristotelian influences on Smith. She notes that such an assessment is complicated by the fact that Aristotle's philosophy itself underwent substantial changes during the Middle Ages and the modern era, and by the well-known influence of other classical authors on Smith. Moving beyond the commonplace observation that Smith's concept of propriety embraced Aristotle's golden mean, she finds some significant analogies between the two authors in concepts such as the gradation of affections from the nearest relations to the farthest, the importance of feeling (rather than reason) in determining the right degree of virtuous behaviour, and the fact that every man, or head of the family, should be left perfectly free to decide how to administer his money and estate. She, then, concludes that Smith's overall perspective on human, social and political relationships is articulated and complex, a point that is quite understandable in light of McCloskey's argument that Smith has five virtues, not just prudence, operating in his ethical universe.

From virtue ethics we next turn our attention to the famous 'Adam Smith problem' – the question of the consistency of TMS and WN. Despite the insistence of the editors of the *Glasgow Edition of The Theory of Moral Sentiments* that it is merely a 'pseudo problem' arising from a simple misunderstanding of the TMS, the problem continues to draw scholarly attention (Raphael and Macfie, 1976, p. 20). As indicated above, Smith did provide at least one broad road map of his overall plan, of which TMS and WN were both parts. However, he never completed the intended work on jurisprudence, which many believe would have supplied at least one link between the two. Moreover, neither work contains a single reference to the other (except for the 'Advertisement' to the sixth edition of TMS, quoted above) and, significantly, the central concepts of TMS, sympathy and the impartial spectator, make no appearance in WN.

In her chapter Vivienne Brown revisits the Adam Smith problem, although consistency *per se* is no longer the main issue in examining differences between the texts. Building on her earlier work on Smith she examines issues of agency in TMS and WN, by arguing that the emphasis, in debates about the so-called 'Adam Smith problem', on construing questions about human nature in terms of 'motives to action' begs a more fundamental question about the metaphysics of agency and the model of action in these two texts. Her chapter argues against what appears to be the current consensus that in the TMS Smith conceived of motives to action in a causal sense (howsoever the notion of causality is construed). Rather she concludes that in the TMS the model of action presupposes causal independence as well as, or rather as necessary for, the normative functioning of the social embeddedness of human life. The impartial spectator thus presupposes freedom of action. This she contrasts with the analytic conception of economic agency in the WN which is given by the requirements of Smith's causal analysis of economic relations, including the causal determinants of the exchangeable value of the annual produce. The problem of consistency is illuminated by her argument that we must view the two works as employing different conceptions of agency and causality appropriate to the differing analytical purposes of the two books.

Closely associated with the Adam Smith problem is the role, or lack thereof, of Smith's theological beliefs in shaping his moral and economic theory. The trend in recent years has been to treat Smith as a wholly secular thinker, thus setting aside the references to God, nature and related terms found primarily in TMS. However, there has been a revival of interest in the theological aspects of TMS and their role in his theory. Brendan Long's chapter is in this revivalist tradition. Examining both biographical and textual evidence he provides evidence in favour of a theistic reading of Smith. While Smith's earlier works attest to a more traditional Christian perspective, later writings pivot in the direction of a moderate Christian Stoicism. Still, the predominately Christian references to the divine names and scriptural references are simply too numerous to be ignored. Long concludes that a moderate Christian theistic position seems a reasonable reading of Smith's position.

The last two chapters of the first part of the book move in a different direction. Sheila Dow investigates Smith's economic methodology, while Jerry Evensky gives an overview of Smith's system taken as a whole. As such it provides a convenient bridge to a consideration of Smith's economics. The purpose of Dow's contribution is to focus on Smith's distinctive approach to economic methodology. She explores its underpinnings in the epistemology of the Scottish Enlightenment and the particular Scottish interpretation of Newton's experimental method. The discussion focuses on his analytical historical approach, his notion of system, and the nature and role of principles within that system. Yet Smith is often seen as the inspiration of general equilibrium theory, which employs a very different methodological approach. The possibility is explored that a significant element of differences in the interpretation of Smith is itself methodological, including a lack of appreciation for the distinction between theory formulation and rhetoric.

Jerry Evensky's contribution rounds off the first part of the book. In an edited volume such as this that begins with Smith's philosophical concerns, focuses on his economic analysis, and traces that analysis into the realm of policy, it seems valuable to have a frame within which to contextualize these contributions. This chapter examines the full dimensionality of Adam Smith's moral philosophy in order to contribute that frame. He shows, what many scholars now accept, that TMS is the foundational work in Smith's system.

A second trend in Smith scholarship forms the unifying principle of Part II. This is the nature of contemporary interest in Smith as an analytical economist. While Smith continues to be highly regarded, the nature of this regard has changed considerably. No one today is much interested in Smith's price theory. Issues of measure versus cause of value are no longer much discussed, especially among the broader discipline. Neither are earlier conundrums, such as the distinction between productive and unproductive labour, given much attention. While Smith's theory of growth is still of interest, it is his perceived contribution to endogenous growth theory, not the old classical model of capital accumulation, which inspires contemporary thought. And as economists have increasingly discovered TMS, Smith has inspired modern experimental and behavioural economists. It is testimony to Smith's analytic power and commonsense observation of human life that he continues to influence and foreshadow contemporary developments in economics, even as those developments evolve in new directions. However, discussion of the theoretical aspects of Smith's economics has certainly faded into the background. This is reflected in the fact that this is the shortest part of the book, and by the fact that the only purely theoretical chapters in the book (Witztum, and Buchanan and Yoon) are more concerned with developing Smithian concepts, rather than with interpreting them.

Proceeding in chronological order Peter Groenewegen revisits the question of French influence on Smith. Since we now have copies of students' notes, which contain the economic portions of his lectures in jurisprudence, we now know the profound impact of Smith's trip to France, 1764–66, and his encounter with the Physiocrats. The evidence suggests that prior to the trip Smith had no knowledge of Physiocracy and its doctrines. Groenewegen examines the similarities between Smith's economics and that of the Physiocrats and Turgot. He does so by looking at what Smith had to say on these topics, before assessing the importance of these French writers as authorities for Smith, including enumerating the presence of their works in his library. The entry concludes that Smith adapted a number of Physiocratic terms, including 'distribution', 'productive and unproductive labour', 'annual produce', 'capital' and 'employment of capitals', the use of which considerably enriched the contents of his treatise. The model of capital accumulation and general interdependence developed in Book II of WN, therefore, owes much to the Physiocratic model of the circular flow.

In a very ambitious chapter Amos Witztum takes up Smith's approach to general interdependence and proposes a general equilibrium model, one that brings to the fore the fundamental differences between Smith and neoclassical economics. These differences as Witztum sees them stem from differences both in their research agendas and in the way they depict the relative position of agents in the system. The economic problem at the heart of neoclassical economics is that of reconciling insatiable wants with scarcity. That of Smith is the circumstances most conducive to growth maximization.

In the Smithian context not everybody has the same position in the system in the sense that they can equally affect the outcome. Although workers may influence wages (and thus, cost of production) in a multisectoral context this may not seriously affect the plans of the surplus owners (that is, the capitalists). It is conceivable that it may have no influence at all on their plans for luxurious consumption. On the other hand, the wish of the surplus owners will always affect the ability of workers to satisfy their needs. *Contra* Hollander's one-paradigm interpretation of the history of economic thought, Witztum places Smith squarely in the surplus tradition of Ricardo, Marx and Sraffa.

Given that in Smith the conditions of labour are an important component in what produces growth, and that workers' productive powers are influenced either by their own wages or by the provision of capital, growth in an economy is entirely in the hands of the few. What will determine growth, therefore, is the coincidence of wants among the capitalists. This, in turn, may or may not generate growth according to how their plans to balance the passions for present enjoyment, and the desire to 'better their condition', coincide. The upshot of the model demonstrates how precarious the position of individuals is when they forgo their independence and move into an interdependent existence in the pursuit of social approbation. It makes sense of Smith's ambiguous attitudes towards the working of natural liberty while building on the fundamentals of his description of how commercial societies operate.

There is an unfortunate tendency to associate general equilibrium with Walrasian models of utility maximizers, market clearing, perfect competition, and knowledge. However, Witztum shows that there is more than one way to model general interdependence in a market-oriented private economy. Seeing Smith as a proto-Walrasian, as Sheila Dow points out in her chapter, certainly offends against Smith's historical, institutional and empirical approach. However, when it came to analysing the interconnections of a commercial society at a given stage of development and with given institutions, Smith uses the analytical tools available to him, one of which, of course, was the Physiocratic circular flow model of interdependence between the sectors of the economy. Such models readily lend themselves to mathematical forms of expression, so it is not surprising that modern mathematical modellers, such as Witztum, are able to apply their tools to Smith's analytics, and to move beyond them.

One of the enduring qualities of Smith among contemporary scholars has been the ability of his writing to inspire both sides (and the middle) of the political spectrum. It is not at all odd or unusual that ideological opposites such as Witztum and James Buchanan trace what they consider to be important insights back to Smith. While Witztum is concerned with bringing out the analytical implications of inequality of position between wage earners and capitalists, James Buchanan and Yong Yoon in the next contribution try to solve the puzzle of increasing returns within the neoclassical model of competitive equilibrium. Allyn Young referred to Smith's theorem that the division of labour is limited by the extent of the market as 'one of the most illuminating and fruitful generalisations which can be found anywhere in the whole literature of economics' (Young, 1928, p. 529). As is well known, this commonsense proposition sits very uncomfortably with the competitive organization of markets. Alfred Marshall famously developed the concept of externalities to explain how the progressive division of labour could continually lower long-run average costs, while maintaining individual firms small enough relative to the market to prevent the monopolization of the industry. Adam Smith's theory of economic progress is summarized by Smith's theorem that the division and specialization of labour depends on the extent of the market. Buchanan and Yoon show that the neoclassical paradigm, inevitably, finds difficulty in reconciling competitive market structures with the presence of increasing returns implied in Smith's theorem. Their contribution briefly surveys various insights into the problem including Marshallian external economies, preferences for diversity and monopolistic competition, and market interaction networks. They claim that there is more to Adam Smith's theorem than these models suggest. The presence of stochastic demand, they argue, may be seen as yet another example of how Smith's theorem operates in a competitive market environment. As an example, if a potential buyer is assumed to have a 1 per cent chance of placing a value above opportunity cost on a non-storable good, then there must be at least 100 such potential buyers in the trading network for the good to be produced. The larger the extent of the market, the more goods with stochastic demand properties will be produced, thus extending the division of labour. They conclude that Smith's theorem needs to be more systematically incorporated into our whole conception of market processes.

Behavioural and experimental economists represent another group who currently draw inspiration from Smith, especially TMS (see for example, Ashraf et al., 2005). Maria Pia Paganelli draws attention to the increased use and usefulness of Adam Smith with regards to the experimental economic literature. She notes that the Ultimatum Game, Dictator Game and Trust Game are three of the most commonly used environments in economics experiments. In contrast to the predictions of standard rational choice theory, these games generate results that do not show the exclusive presence of self-regarding preferences motivating subjects' behaviour. Adam Smith's attention to both self-regarding and other-regarding preferences, and in particular to the role of resentment, love of praiseworthiness and hate of blameworthiness, provides plausible explanations for these experimental results.

The third, and final, trend among contemporary historians of economics is that there remains substantial interest in Smith's analysis of economic policy and the proper role of government in the economy. Marxist pronouncements aside, this interest is remarkable for its largely non-ideological bent. Smith as the prophet of laissez-faire capitalism is gone from the specialist literature. Rather than enlisting Smith in support of this or that political agenda, modern scholars see Smith as a much more eclectic advisor with complex, nuanced views on the policy issues of his day. While Smith was certainly sceptical of the possibility of the political system with which he was familiar to improve upon market allocations of resources, he did nonetheless prescribe a broad role for government, and left open the possibility that virtuous legislators could be entrusted with more responsibility over economic affairs.

Thus, while there has been a definite waning of interest in Smith's theoretical economics taken as a whole, the same cannot be said of his policy analysis, broadly the subject matter of Books IV and V of WN. Part III, the longest in the book, examines various aspects of Smith's criticisms of current policy and of his positive recommendations for government involvement in economic affairs. The section begins with a piece taken from Warren Samuels's monumental work on the invisible hand. This chapter is not concerned with what Smith 'really meant' by the invisible hand, nor the correctness of the interpretations and usages made since Smith, nor solving the problems raised by usage, nor taking a position on key issues. It is devoted to understanding the concept's multiple usages by Smith and others, identifying problems with those usages, and fostering clear thinking about the concept, for example, the topics on which assumptions must be made to reach conclusions. Whatever Smith may have meant by the phrase, it has taken on a life of its own, a life which Samuels shows is highly ambiguous and fraught with difficulty.

In the next chapter Salim Rashid, a well-known critic of Smith and debunker of Smith's stature in the history of economics, examines Smith as a development economist. He notes that situating Adam Smith as a development economist requires both a definition of what constitutes economic development as well as some idea of what contemporaries were thinking about such issues. If economic development is defined to include a vision of continuous economic growth as well as the equitable distribution of such economic gains, then the Irish can be said to have founded the first school of economic development in the 1730s. By comparison, Adam Smith is seen to possess less sympathy for the poor than the Irish and to be more reluctant to admit the many particular problems that beset economic growth in any country. As to the vision of continuous economic growth, this was clearly set out by the Rev. Josiah Tucker, but Smith ignored Tucker's arguments altogether. Rashid concludes that Adam Smith can be said to have a broad conception of economic development only when contrasted with some of his followers, but not when compared with the best ideas of his contemporaries, a theme reminiscent of older debates in value theory, which asserted that Smith's cost of production theory was a setback to the development of a sound (defined as the subjective marginal utility theory) theory of value in economics.

The next two chapters consider aspects of Smith's critique of what he called the 'mercantile system'. Glenn Hueckel focuses on a single piece of policy analysis, namely Smith's claim that an export subsidy to corn produces no stimulus to output. Hueckel argues that this peculiar claim loses its paradoxical air when it is read within the larger context of his theory of economic development. Derived as an element in his attack on the mercantilist identification of economic growth with specie accumulation and inflation, Smith's dictum that the 'price of corn regulates that of all other commodities' is defined only within a strictly static framework. Because his contemporary critics failed to grasp the limited, static nature of his principle, their objections fell wide of the mark, explaining Smith's much remarked 'equanimity' in the face of those objections.

Smith's analysis of the American crisis, which was unfolding as he was attempting to complete the first edition of WN, is perhaps the centrepiece of his critique of mercantilism. Andrew Skinner, in the next chapter, gives a careful exposition of Smith's analysis as he raises the question why the material on America remained in the book well after the crisis had been resolved. He reminds us that Smith was acutely aware of the fact that the connection with America had brought the mercantile system a degree of 'splendour and glory which it could never otherwise have attained to' (WN IV.vii.c.81). Thus, it would be seen as an important test case for his principles. If the fallacies of the system could be exposed here they could be exposed anywhere, because it was in America that the system of political economy seemed to be well on the way toward enriching the sovereign and the people. Writing in the early 1770s up to publication in 1776, Smith was seeking to persuade, and he was on the offensive. However, by 1783 he could write as if his case had been confirmed by events, and with a degree of confidence which would have been inappropriate ten years earlier when he was in London. America, Skinner concludes, had acquired the status of an experiment which 'confirmed' Smith's theses; one which could be allowed to remain in *The Wealth of Nations* as a kind of permanent exhibit.

Legal maximum rates of interest was one form of specific government regulation which Smith endorsed in WN, although it fell outside of his systematic treatment of the public sector in Book V. A famous exchange ensued with Jeremy Bentham who argued against such regulations. In Chapter 15 Samuel Hollander revisits this debate. He notes that Smith's justification for a legal maximum interest rate in some respects resembles modern arguments (Joseph Stiglitz for one) in favour of credit rationing, which turn on the hypothesis that bankers cannot stipulate (at least not costlessly) all the actions of a borrower that might affect the return of the loan, and consequently formulate the terms of the contract – including the interest rate – to the end of maximizing the expected return. Such terms function as a screening mechanism in favour of those most likely to repay the loan. These arguments have a Smithian flavour to them in that he ascribes to lenders faced by an excess demand a concern to select low-risk borrowers and a capacity to ration loans effectively, which prevents upward pressure on the interest rate. Smith, similarly associates the willingness to pay high interest specifically with rash 'projectors'. Hollander concludes that the deliberation with which Smith sets out his position makes it doubtful that he would have been convinced by Bentham's objections. There is however, a remaining problem in that Smith's specific recommendation for the legal rate was already obsolete in 1776, but Smith left his argument unchanged through all three editions of WN. While Skinner in the previous chapter faces a similar interpretive problem, he proposes a plausible solution; Hollander leaves his problem as an open question.

As just mentioned above, Smith's considered views on the proper role of government are set out in Book V, which follows the famous general pronouncement concluding Book IV:

> According to the system of natural liberty, the sovereign has only three duties to attend to; three duties of great importance, indeed, but plain and intelligible to common understandings: first, the duty of protecting the society from the violence and invasion of other independent societies; secondly, the duty of protecting, as far as possible, every member of the society from the injustice and oppression of every other member of it, or the duty of establishing an exact administration of justice; and thirdly, the duty of erecting and maintaining certain public works and certain public institutions, which it can never be for the interest of any individual, or small number of individuals, to erect and maintain; because the profit could never repay the expence to any individual or small number of individuals, though it may frequently do much more than repay it to a great society. (WN IV.ix.51)

Steven Medema and Warren Samuels maintain that a thoroughgoing assessment of Smith's views on this score requires attention to the complexity of Smith's system – beginning with his tripartite model of society: the formation of moral rules (as elaborated in *The Theory of Moral Sentiments*), the operation of the market (in *The Wealth of Nations*), and the operation of government and the formation of legal rules and rights (in *Lectures on Jurisprudence*). The fact of three domains permits, even engenders, analysis in one domain that disregards the operation of and interaction with the other domains – for example, the freedom of the 'free market' vis-à-vis social control through moral and legal rules. The fact of these multiple paradigms explains how it is possible not only to give a coherent account of Smith's theory taken as a whole, but several such accounts, each grounded on some combination and interpretation of the foregoing.

Their chapter examines Smith's view of the role of the state, including the legal system, in economic affairs, paying close attention to the ideas set forth by Smith in both *The Wealth of Nations* and his *Lectures on Jurisprudence*. From there they take up the different interpretations attributed to Smith. Among the rivals to the market-plus-framework approach to the interpretation of Smith are interpretations which portray a more activist economic role of government; some of which suggest not a strict laissez-faire approach by Smith but a laissez-faire-with-exceptions approach, in which the exceptions are very important and sometimes rather broad-based; and the minimalist interpretation, which claims that Adam Smith stands for the themes of laissez-faire, non-interventionism and minimal government – a dominant theme in economics and elsewhere, including among those critical of the laissez-faire position. These latter are particularly hard to sustain when set against the corpus of Smith's writings. They arise out of partial readings of Smith and, as the other contributions in this book testify, they are seriously out of touch with contemporary scholarly opinion on Smith.

McCloskey argued in the first chapter that as a virtue ethicist Smith identified moral goodness with the proper balancing of several virtues (she argues for five) in a person's thoughts and actions. Smith's outline of the three duties of the sovereign highlight justice, the prevention of injury (first and second duties), and prudence, the maximization of public utility (third duty). However, Smith felt the sovereign should be concerned about the level of virtue among the people and that those who would participate in the political process should themselves be highly virtuous. The next two chapters, by Leonidas Montes, and David Levy and Sandra Peart, take up two aspects of this that concerned Smith. Montes looks at Smith's position on the militia compared to a standing army, while Levy and Peart examine Smith's thinking on factions, a potent source of the corruption of the moral sentiments in public life.

Montes's chapter is the only one of the volume that confronts the civic humanist (or classical republicanism) versus natural jurisprudence debate in Smith scholarship by looking at the militia issue in the Scotland of Smith's day. Smith's actions and writings on the issue are a fertile ground for examining the tension between these two political paradigms in Smith. Montes begins with a brief analysis of classical republicanism and the importance of the militia for this set of political ideas. He then discusses how the militia debate was brought about in Scotland, and goes on to investigate why and how Adam Smith apparently changed his mind on the standing army–militia debate, tracking the context and some possible reasons for this supposed change of mind. Smith's position on the militia, ranging from his Correspondence, LJ, and his published legacy in TMS and WN, is discussed in some detail. Montes argues that although Smith clearly supported a professional army in WN, traces of civic humanism can still be found throughout his narrative. Thus, he concludes that if the father of economics might represent the twilight of a republican tradition, he does not preclude some crucial aspects of civic humanism in his concern for public virtue.

This theme is also reflected in Smith's deep concern for the powerful role that factions played in contemporary British politics. He blamed the merchant faction, for example, for burdening the British (and colonial) economies with a system of political economy that he believed failed to promote the public interest. In their chapter Levy and Peart examine the nature and role of factions in Adam Smith's work. They place his analysis into the context of his general theory of social cohesion to show how Smith moved from a recognition and appreciation of cooperative behaviour, to the realization that cooperation might produce deleterious results, as in the case of 'masters of men'. For Smith, cooperation is a natural outcome for men who come together desiring approbation; deleterious outcomes are the result not so much of the sentiments of men as the institutions that frame their actions. If the actions which are approved result in deleterious outcomes, this is a sign that the institutions are in need of reform. Smith's denunciation of the mercantile system, therefore, can be seen as operating on multiple levels.

Among modern economists, the so-called Chicago School has been most closely associated with the name and perceived ideas of Adam Smith. The relationship of Smith's thought to the ideas of the Chicago School are the subject of the last chapter in the book. In this chapter Steven Medema examines perhaps the most fertile use in the twentieth century of a set of ideas ostensibly taken from Smith: that undertaken by the Chicago School. The standard caricature of the Chicago approach is that it seizes on two aspects of Smith's thought – the efficacy of the system of natural liberty and the dim view of the abilities of the state to improve on the outcomes associated with natural liberty – and pushes them to the limit in its elaboration of a model of a competitive market system in which government is an impediment to, rather than a facilitator of, economic efficiency.

Like most caricatures, this one has elements of truth to it. However, the Chicago

School's discussion and use of Smith is not homogeneous; indeed, it is emblematic of the problem of multiple interpretations. These differences are reflected in the Stigler–Friedman and Coase wings of the Chicago School – the former, a-institutional, and the latter more overtly attuned to the import of what Coase has called 'the institutional structure of production' and the role played by government within that structure. This distinction is perhaps nowhere more evident than in the meanings attributed to 'the problem of social cost' by Coase and by Stigler, both of whom see themselves working squarely in the tradition of Smith.

One of the implications of this association of Smith, especially with the Stigler–Friedman wing of the Chicago School, has been a severe narrowing of the wider economics profession's view of Smith. Thus, recovering Smith's lost legacy has become a recurring theme among historians of economic thought. However, as Medema shows, even in Chicago there was a broader view of Smith, which was inspired by his analysis of the emergence and evolution of social institutions. It is my hope that this volume will in some way contribute to this project of recovery. The richness, breadth and insightfulness of Smith's thought deserve such treatment.

References

Ashraf, Nava, Colin Camerer and George Lowenstein (2005), 'Adam Smith, behavioral economist', *Journal of Economic Perspectives*, **19** (3), 131–45.
Brewer, Anthony (2007), 'Let us now praise famous men: assessments of Adam Smith's economics', *Adam Smith Review*, **3**, 161–87.
Brown, Vivienne (1997), '"Mere inventions of the imagination": a survey of recent literature on Adam Smith', *Economics and Philosophy*, **13**, 281–312.
Cockfield, Geoff, Ann Firth and John Laurent (eds) (2007), *New Perspectives On Adam Smith's The Theory of Moral Sentiments*, Cheltenham, UK and Northampton, MA, USA: Edward Elgar.
Fleischacker, Samuel (2004), *On Adam Smith's Wealth of Nations: A Philosophical Companion*, Princeton, NJ: Princeton University Press.
Haakonssen, Knud (ed.) (2006) *The Cambridge Companion to Adam Smith*, Cambridge: Cambridge University Press.
Labio, Catherine (2006), 'The solution is in the text: a survey of the recent literary turn in Adam Smith studies', *Adam Smith Review*, **2**, 151–78.
Montes, Leonidas and Eric Schliesser (eds) (2006), *New Voices on Adam Smith*, London: Routledge.
Raphael, D.D. and Alec Macfie (1976), 'Introduction', *The Glasgow Edition of the Works and Correspondence of Adam Smith: The Theory of Moral Sentiments*, Oxford: Oxford University Press, pp. 1–52.
Recktenwald, Horst Claus (1978) 'An Adam Smith Renaissance Anno 1976?' *Journal of Economic Literature*, **16** (1), 56–83.
Scott, William R. (1965), *Adam Smith as Student and Professor*, New York: Augustus M. Kelley.
Skinner, Andrew S. (1996), *A System of Social Sciences: Papers Relating to Adam Smith*, 2nd edn, Oxford: Clarenden Press.
Skinner, Andrew S. and Thomas Wilson (eds) (1975), *Essays on Adam Smith*, Oxford: Oxford University Press.
Skinner, Andrew S. and Thomas Wilson (eds), (1976), *The Market and the State: Essays in Honour of Adam Smith*, Oxford: Oxford University Press.
Smith, Adam (1784), *An Inquiry into the Nature and Causes of the Wealth of Nations*; R.H. Campbell, A.S. Skinner and W.B. Todd (eds) (1976), *The Glasgow Edition of the Works and Correspondence of Adam Smith*, Oxford: Oxford University Press.
Smith, Adam (1790), *The Theory of Moral Sentiments*; D.D. Raphael and A.L. Macfie (eds) (1976), *The Glasgow Edition of the Works and Correspondence of Adam Smith*, Oxford: Oxford University Press.
Tribe, Keith (1999), 'Adam Smith: critical theorist?' *Journal of Economic Literature*, **37** (2), 609–32.
Tribe, Keith and Hiroshi Mizuta (eds) (2002), *A Critical Bibliography of Adam Smith*, London: Pickering & Chatto.
Vivenza, Gloria (2004), 'Reading Smith in the light of the classics', *Adam Smith Review*, **1**, 107–24.
West, Edwin G. (1978), 'Scotland's resurgent economist: a survey of the new literature on Adam Smith', *Southern Economic Journal*, **45** (2), 343–69.
Young, Allyn A. (1928), 'Increasing returns and economic progress', *Economic Journal*, **38** (152), 527–42.

Table of Smith's primary works

Date	Code	Abbreviated title	Notes on referencing and dating assumptions
1740–44	ES	*External Senses*	There is some evidence that Smith wrote this before he had access to Hume's critique of Berkeley suggesting a dating of some time towards the beginning of his studies at Balliol, say 1740–44.
1746	HA	'History of Astronomy'	This was Smith's only unpublished work not ordered destroyed. Raphael believes it was completed a little before the first edition of TMS, but it was probably earlier as Smith could not have been 'juvenile' at the age of 36 (C137 – correspondence item no.137). He could have begun work on this piece at Balliol when he read Hume's *Treatise of Human Nature* and it was probably worked on some time thereafter. The majority of the work could have been in place by the time he left Balliol in 1746 at the age of 23.
1746–51	PH	*Physics*	See LM below.
1746–51	LM	*Logic and Metaphysics*	This was probably started after HA. Scott believes it relates to the Edinburgh period (Scott, 1965, p. 53). If he is right it could have been written some time after 1746. The work was completed before Smith became Professor of Moral Philosophy at Glasgow.
1751–59	AT	Atonement manuscript	This was probably part of lecture notes (now lost) relating to his early courses on ethics at Glasgow.
1755–56	LE	Letter to the *Edinburgh Review*	
1759	C40	Early draft to TMS, most added in 2nd edition	This was included in a letter to Gilbert Elliot and probably reflects Smith's response to concerns Elliot raised with him.
1759–90	TMS	Theory of Moral Sentiments	Smith published six editions in his life time, with the sixth of 1790 containing substantial revisions. There was a seventh edition, but Smith had no hand in this and so is not relied upon.
1761–69	FA	1st fragment on the division of labour	Scott believes this relates to the Edinburgh period; however Raphael and Meek suggest that it relates to the 1760s.
1761–69	FB	2nd fragment on the division of labour	Scott believes this relates to the Edinburgh period; however Raphael and Meek suggest that it relates to the 1760s.
1762–63	LJA	*Lectures on Jurisprudence*	Lecture notes taken by a student in class, dated 1762–63.
1762–63	LRBL	*Lectures on Rhetoric and Belles Lettres*	The text is the collaborative work of a number of note takers, probably students.

xxiii

Table (continued)

Date	Code	Abbreviated title	Notes on referencing and dating assumptions
1763	ED	Early draft of WN	
1766	LJB	*Lectures on Jurisprudence*	Lecture notes taken by a student in class of a more summary nature than LJA, dated 1766.
1776–90, 6 editions	WN	*Wealth of Nations*	There were six editions, but changes to edition 1 were cosmetic only. What are of greater import are the early material ED, FA and FB.
1777	IM	*On the Imitative Arts*	In EPS 171–3 the likely position is that Smith either wrote this in 1777 or he wrote much of it long before (perhaps 1764) and edited it over the next 14 or so years.
	EPS	*Essays on Philosophical Subjects*	Includes HA, PH, LM, LE and others. Published posthumously.

Source: Courtesy of Brendan Long.

Smith's life and major works

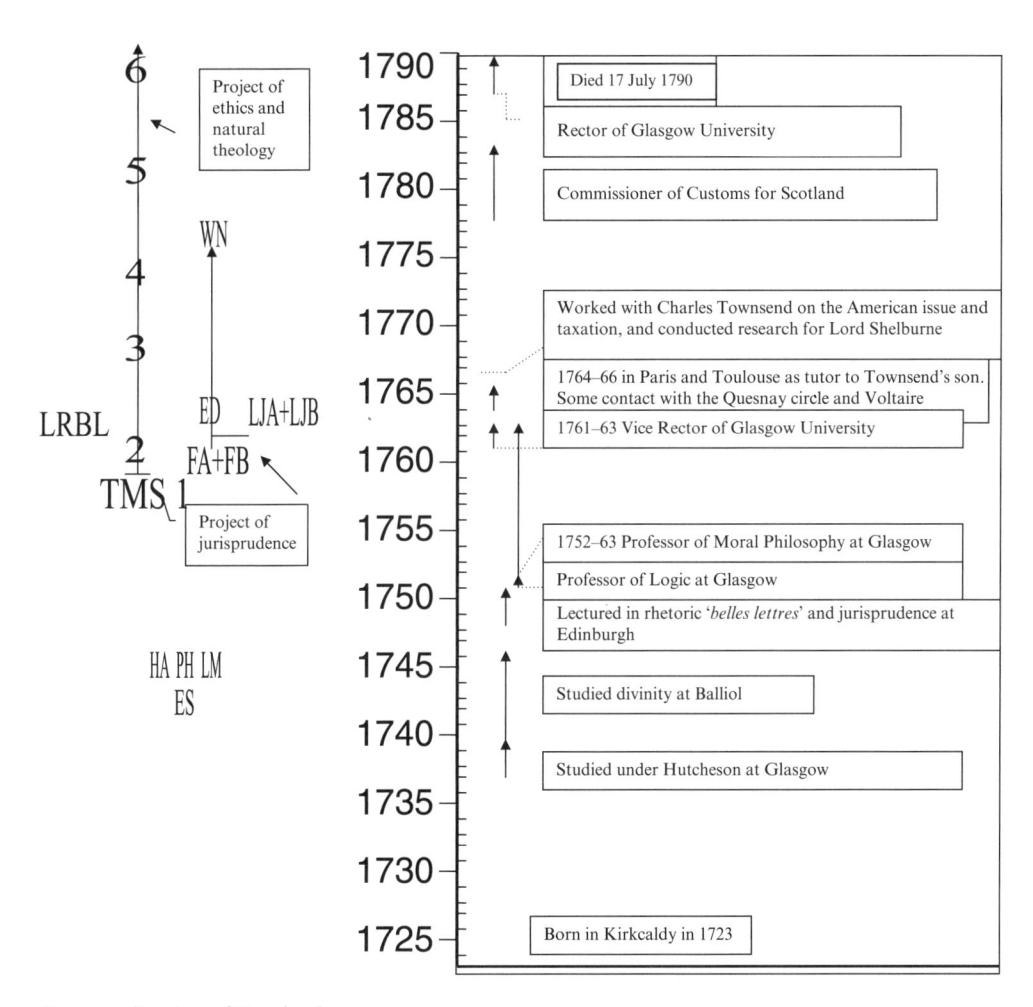

Left axis	Year	Right axis
6 — Project of ethics and natural theology	1790	Died 17 July 1790
5	1785	Rector of Glasgow University
WN	1780	Commissioner of Customs for Scotland
4	1775	
3	1770	Worked with Charles Townsend on the American issue and taxation, and conducted research for Lord Shelburne
LRBL ED LJA+LJB	1765	1764–66 in Paris and Toulouse as tutor to Townsend's son. Some contact with the Quesnay circle and Voltaire
2 FA+FB	1760	1761–63 Vice Rector of Glasgow University
TMS 1 Project of jurisprudence	1755	1752–63 Professor of Moral Philosophy at Glasgow
	1750	Professor of Logic at Glasgow / Lectured in rhetoric 'belles lettres' and jurisprudence at Edinburgh
HA PH LM ES	1745	Studied divinity at Balliol
	1740	Studied under Hutcheson at Glasgow
	1735	
	1730	
	1725	Born in Kirkcaldy in 1723

Source: Courtesy of Brendan Long.

PART I

ADAM SMITH'S SYSTEM AND ITS ANTECEDENTS: PHILOSOPHICAL CONCERNS

1 Adam Smith, the last of the former virtue ethicists
*Deirdre McCloskey**

Smith was mainly an ethical philosopher. The recent literature from Knud Haakonssen (1981) through Charles Griswold (1999) and Samuel Fleischacker (2004, pp. xv, 48–54) says so, against the claim by the economists, believed for a long time, that he was mainly an economist in the modern, anti-ethical sense. Taking ethics out of Smith began immediately after his death, in the reactionary era of the French Revolution. Perhaps to assure the British authorities and British public opinion that political economy was not subversive, ethics was omitted. The Cold War inspired similar omissions, and it may be that during the American conquest of the field of economics a fear of radicalism supported the anti-ethical reading of Smith.

But another reason the economists' claim was accepted for so long, against the textual and biographical evidence, is that Smith practiced what was considered for a long time after him an obsolete sort of ethical philosophy, known as 'virtue ethics'. Virtue ethics somewhat mysteriously disappeared from academic circles after the sixth and final and substantially revised edition of Smith's own favorite of his two published books, *The Theory of Moral Sentiments* (TMS) (1759, 1790 [1976, 1982]). Since 1790 most ethical theory as practiced in departments of philosophy has derived instead from two other books published about the same time, one by Immanuel Kant (1785 [1993]; for example Frankfurt, 2004) and the other by Jeremy Bentham (1789 [1948]; for example Singer, 1993). A third and older tradition of natural rights, which influenced Smith too, by way of Locke and Pufendorf, finds favor nowadays among conservative and Catholic intellectuals (Leo Strauss, 1953; John Finnis, 1980; cf. Hont and Ignatieff, 1983; but then see Fleischacker, 2004, pp. 221–6). And the new contractarian theories of Rousseau, Locke and Hobbes, to which Smith paid no attention, has provided in our time a fourth, related, stream of narrow ethics paired with grand political theory (Buchanan and Tullock, 1962; Rawls, 1971; Nussbaum, 2006).

But the fifth and by far the oldest and broadest stream is the virtue-ethical one. It flowed from Plato and from Aristotle, meandered through the Stoics, was mapped by Cicero (44 BC), and was channeled into Christianity by Aquinas (*c.* 1269–72). As I say, in the late eighteenth century this ethics of the virtues, viewed until then by most Europeans as the only sensible way to think about good and bad character, was pushed underground, at least in the academic theories of philosophers, re-emerging only in 1958 (Anscombe, 1958 [1997]; Foot, 1978; MacIntyre, 1981; Nussbaum, 1986; Hursthouse, 1999).

The 170-year reign of ethical theories new in the Enlightenment lasted until the frailties of logic without context became clear, in the later Wittgenstein, for example, and in numerous other post-positivist thinkers. Before then, 'the notion that the mathematical method could be applied to ethics, rendering it a demonstrative science', writes Father Copleston of the proliferation of new ethical theories *circa* 1710, following the examples of Hobbes and Spinoza, 'was . . . common . . . partly because of the prestige won by

3

mathematics through its successful application in physical science and partly because it was widely thought that ethics had formerly depended on authority and needed a new rational basis' (Copleston, 1959, p. 251). By 1950 the Enlightenment program was in this respect looking frayed, though quite a few decades passed before the news began to reach fields like economics or evolutionary biology. As Isaiah Berlin noted in his very last paper on analytic philosophy, 'no abstract or analytic rigour exists out of all connection with historical, personal thought . . . Every thought belongs, not just somewhere, but to someone and is at home in a context . . . which is not purely formally described' (Berlin, 1950 quoted in Ignatieff, 1998, p. 88).

Though Immanuel Kant, to speak of a historical and personal context of thought, knew and appreciated the 1759 edition of TMS in its German translation, Smith even in 1790 knew nothing of Kant's ruminations in far-off Köningsberg about the duty to follow generalizable ethical maxims. D.D. Raphael and A.L. Macfie note that 'the extent to which Smith was influenced by other moral philosophers of his time' was 'remarkably small' (1976 [1982], p. 10). But Smith did know, and sharply opposed, the reduction of what is good to what causes pleasure, that is, utilitarianism, if not quite in the form of the 'chaos of precise ideas' in Bentham's *A Fragment on Government, with an Introduction to the Principles of Morals and Legislation*, published in the year before Smith's death. The utilitarian stream began earlier than Bentham, of course – for example in the writings of Smith's great friend David Hume, though it also has ancient predecessors in the Epicureans, and it had modern ones in figures like Bernard Mandeville (1714), in the extreme form of 'license', or for that matter Niccolò Machiavelli, in the extreme form of the *virtú* of the prince. Smith opposed these. 'In the opinion of [Epicurus, Hume, and the like],' Smith noted, 'virtue consists in prudence' (TMS, p. 267):

> That system . . . which makes virtue consist in prudence only, while it gives the highest encouragement to the habits of caution, vigilance, sobriety, and judicious moderation, seems to degrade equally both the amiable [Hutchesonian] and respectable [Stoic] virtues, and to strip the former of all their beauty, and the latter of all their grandeur. (TMS, p. 307)

Since Bentham, however, and especially since the anti-ethical turn in twentieth-century economics (associated with Pigou, Robbins, Samuelson and Friedman), the economists have interpreted Smith's praise of the virtue of prudence to mean what the economists meant by virtue, that is: you do uncontroversial good only by doing well. As the economist Frank Knight wrote in 1923, 'the nineteenth-century utilitarianism was in essence merely the ethics of power, "glorified economics" . . . Its outcome was to reduce virtue to prudence' (Knight, 1923 [1935, 1997], p. 62). The turn towards prudence-only was renamed in the 1930s the 'new' welfare economics, attempting to build judgments about the economy on the supposition that virtue consists in prudence, with justice taken as sheer taste. If all are benefited, or could be benefited, the proposed policy is good. That is all ye know of ethics, and all ye need to know (see Brown 1994, pp. 165–6 and footnotes for a discussion of such an 'overly economistic' readings of *The Wealth of Nations* (WN); and Evensky, 2005, Chapter 10, on the 'Chicago Smith' versus the 'Kirkaldy Smith').

Smith did praise prudence as a virtue, especially in his book on prudence. For example: 'what is prudence in the conduct of every private family can scarce be folly in that of a great kingdom' (WN, IV.ii, p. 457). But in his other published book one can find hundreds of pages in praise also of other virtues, especially temperance; or of justice, in the unpublished lecture notes taken by his students in 1762–63 and 1766. And even in WN, unless one is precommitted to seeing its implied hero as merely a confused precursor to Karl Marx's Mister Money Bags or Paul Samuelson's Max U, one can find a good deal of ethical judgment more grown-up than 'prudence suffices' or 'greed is good'.

The actual, 'Kirkaldy', Smith assumed a person with all the needful virtues – in his accounting, five of them, namely, love, courage, temperance, justice and self-interested prudence, too. From about 400 BC to about 1790 AD the moral universe was described in Europe as composed of the Seven Primary Virtues, resulting by recombination in hundreds of minor and particular virtues. The seven are a jury-rigged combination of the four 'pagan' or 'cardinal' virtues (courage, temperance, justice and prudence) and the three 'Christian' or 'theological' virtues (faith, hope and love, 'these three abide').

Jury-rigged or not, they are a pretty good philosophical psychology. The tensions among the seven, and their complementarities too, can be expressed in a diagram (Figure 1.1).

Minor though admirable virtues such as thrift or honesty or purity can be described as combinations of the primary seven. A vice is a notable lack of one or more of them. The seven are in this sense primary colors. They cannot be derived from each other. Blue cannot be derived from red. Contrary to various attempts since Hobbes to do so, for example, justice cannot be derived from prudence only. And the other, minor colors can be derived from the primaries. You cannot derive red from maroon and purple. But blue plus red does make purple, blue plus yellow make green. The Romantic virtue of honesty, for example, is justice plus temperance in matters of speech, with a dash of courage and a teaspoon of faithfulness.

Aquinas was the master of such analyses of virtues and vices. He provides scores of examples in showing that the seven are primary, or in his word 'principal'. 'The cardinal virtues,' he declares, 'are called more principal, not because they are more perfect than all the other virtues, but because human life more principally turns on them and the other virtues are based on them' (Aquinas, *c.* 1269–72 [1999], Art. 1, p. 112). Courage plus prudence yields enterprise, a virtue not much admired by Adam Smith, who recommended instead safe investments in agriculture (Brown, 1994, pp. 7, 53, 177). Temperance plus justice yields humility, prominent in Smith's theorizing and in Smith's own character, Fleischacker argues, accounting for his principled modesty in social engineering (Fleischacker 2004, pp. 34–5, 97, 99). Temperance plus prudence yields thrift, which Smith came to believe, erroneously, was the spring of economic growth.

You can persuade yourself in various ways that the Aquinian Seven are a pretty good philosophical psychology. For example, you can examine each in turn, noting its importance in human flourishing (McCloskey, 2006). Plato did, finding the four in balance in the good person or the good *polis*. 'His own distinctive contribution', writes the classicist Helen North, 'is the theory that all virtue depends on the orderly arrangement of faculties within the soul, a condition achieved by the practice of *sōphrosynē*' (North, 1973–74, Vol. 4, p. 369), that is, temperance, just as in *The Theory of Moral Sentiments*. Prudence is the executive function, and especially when pursued alone can be thought of as self-interest or rationality in attaining ends. Justice is the social balance answering to the personal balance of temperance. Thus Plato and the Stoic tradition.

Courage is the characteristically male interest, and it is no wonder therefore that the

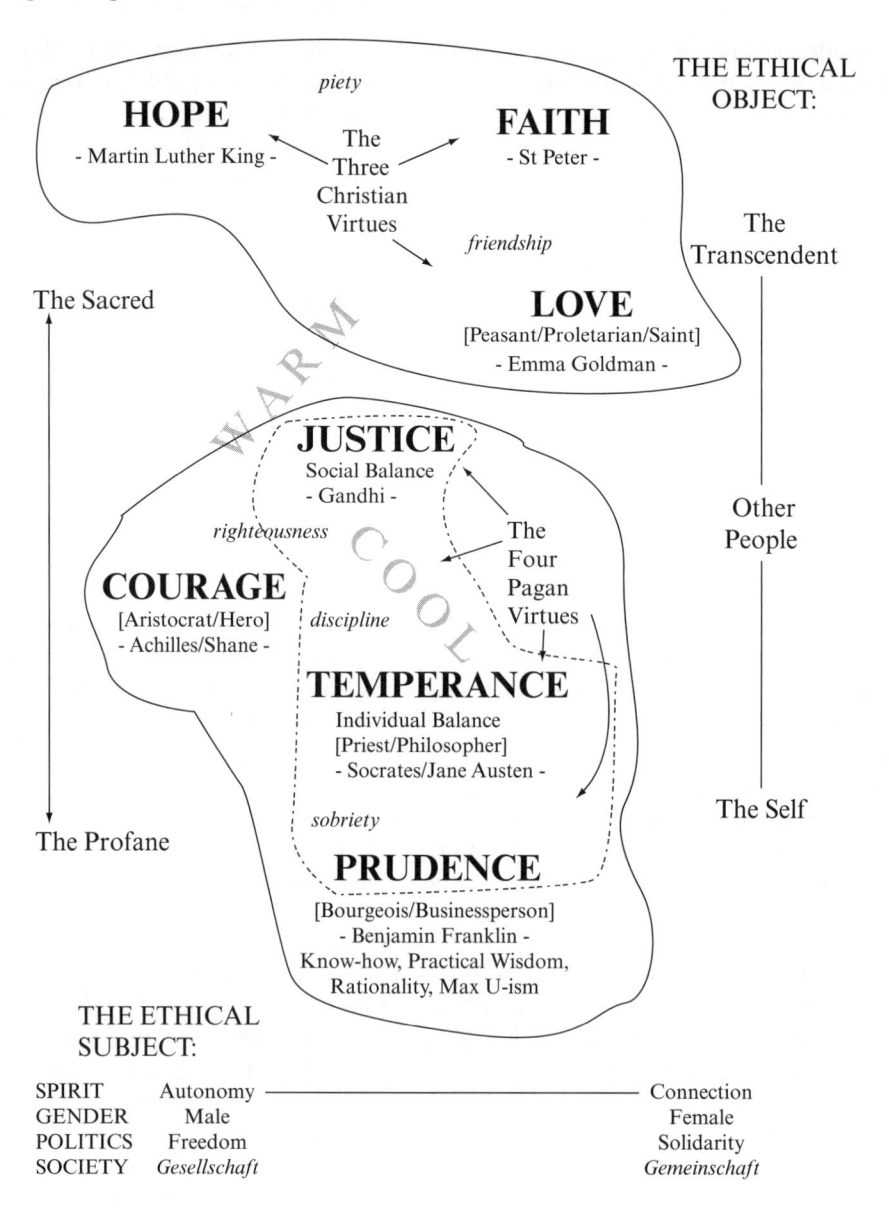

Figure 1.1 The seven virtues

THE ETHICAL OBJECT:

- **HOPE** – Martin Luther King –
- **FAITH** – St Peter –
- **LOVE** [Peasant/Proletarian/Saint] – Emma Goldman –

piety, *friendship*

The Three Christian Virtues

WARM

- **JUSTICE** Social Balance – Gandhi –
- **COURAGE** [Aristocrat/Hero] – Achilles/Shane –
- **TEMPERANCE** Individual Balance [Priest/Philosopher] – Socrates/Jane Austen –
- **PRUDENCE** [Bourgeois/Businessperson] – Benjamin Franklin – Know-how, Practical Wisdom, Rationality, Max U-ism

righteousness, *discipline*, *sobriety*

The Four Pagan Virtues

COOL

The Sacred ↕ The Profane

The Transcendent / Other People / The Self

THE ETHICAL SUBJECT:

SPIRIT	Autonomy	Connection
GENDER	Male	Female
POLITICS	Freedom	Solidarity
SOCIETY	*Gesellschaft*	*Gemeinschaft*

pagan four elevated it high. The Christians elevated love to primacy, and it is therefore construed as feminine. The other Christian additions, hope and faith, are at first puzzling, but less so when hope is understood in secular terms as the forward-looking virtue of imagination, and faith as the backward-looking virtue of imagination. In other words, hope is the virtue of having a human project. Faith is the virtue of having a human identity. They do not have to be theological. But they do constitute, along with the higher form of love (what the Greeks called *agape*) the 'transcendent'.

Or you can imagine the miseries of a human life without one of the seven, a life without courage, cowering in the corner; or a life without faith, without identity; or a life without hope, left abruptly this afternoon with a bullet to your head.

Or you can ask people how they feel about the virtues. Alan Wolfe found in his surveys and interviews about American ethical views in the 1990s that 'virtue', singular, means little to ordinary Americans, except to arouse irritation at the conservative churches and their recent obsession with sex, sex, sex. But to Wolfe's Americans the particular named virtues, plural, mean a great deal, provoking calm yet committed discussion. Americans admire, for example, loyalty, that blend of the theological and pagan virtues. And especially they admire honesty – justice and temperance with a dash of courage and a teaspoon of faith. In a broader sense 'honesty' is used to mean a bourgeois blend of all the virtues (Wolfe, 2001, pp. 23ff).

Or you can note that the seven virtues figure in the stories of our culture. The historian of rhetoric Robert Hariman argues that in answering the question of what is to be done you can stand with some of the philosophers such as Kant or Bentham, and 'look for rules'. Smith did not like such rule books. Or you can stand with Sophocles, Thucydides, Adam Smith and the sophists up to Jane Austen and Iris Murdoch, and 'look for exemplars', that is, human models of prudence or justice or love (Hariman, 2003, p. 7). Smith favored the humanistic teaching of ethics. For example, Plutarch (most of whose ample surviving work is ethical theorizing) was in his *Lives* steadily ethical, inspiring medieval saints' lives and modern mythologies of national heroes, William Tell to the Blessed John Fitzgerald Kennedy. We are still writing the particular virtues, filming them, singing them, retelling the stories in the women's gossip about relationships, with its focus on the virtue of love, and the men's instant replay. It is not merely the abstract, Aquinian analysis of, say, courage that forms an ethical tradition of resistance to fear. It is the stories of particular courages, in our particular faiths.

Or again you can compare the seven with virtues in other traditions, such as the Confucian. The characterization by Bryan Van Norden of the ethical theory of 'the Second Sage' in the Confucian tradition, Mencius (372–289 BC), is startlingly similar to the Smith of TMS. Mencius's grounds for opposing utilitarianism, for example, were identical to Smith's:

> Suppose someone suddenly saw a child about to fall into a well: everyone in such a situation would have a feeling of alarm and compassion – not because one sought to get in good with the child's parents, not because one wanted fame among their neighbors and friends, and not because one would dislike the sound of the child's cries'. (2A6 in Mencius, quoted in Van Norden, 2004, p. 159)

The 'sprout' of such feeling, to use Mencius's vocabulary, would be the 'moral sentiment' posited by Smith. Moral sentiments in Smith, like Mencius's sprouts, are few but powerfully generative of the mature impartial spectator. Van Norden calls the growth of a mature ethical character the 'affective extension' (p. 150) of the Confucian sprout. The sprout of benevolence, then, is the beginning of a moral sentiment of benevolence à la Smith. 'Affective' extension is to be contrasted with what Van Norden calls the 'cognitive extension', seen in Kant and Bentham and the like. The focus on affect rather than cognition, I am saying, is very Scottish of Mencius. Again, 'righteousness' (*yi*) in Mencius is 'what is appropriate', strikingly similar to the notion of neo-Stoic and Ciceronian 'propriety' elaborated in Smith (Van Norden, 2004, p. 150). Indeed 'propriety' is often paired with 'righteousness' in the translations from the Chinese. And so forth. We are in a different ethical universe from a Kantian or utilitarian one, but not all that different from virtue ethics in the West.

Or yet again you can predict that if Aquinas's Seven are good places to start a philosophical psychology, then they should show up in the works of psychologists. They do. A recent book published under the auspices of the American Psychological Association, edited by Christopher Peterson and Martin E.P. Seligman, *Character Strengths and Virtues: A Handbook and Classification* (2004), lends empirical support to the Seven, at any rate within the European tradition in which they were theorized. It seeks, as the philosopher Peter Danielson says in another connection, the 'ethical genome'. In 644 big-format text pages, using 2300 citations to the technical literature in clinical and social psychology and related fields, the 40 drafters of the chapters (which Peterson and Seligman then rewrote) present a 'manual of the sanities', that is, the 'positive psychology' of healthy people. These are not mere assertions but findings, summarizing a gigantic scientific literature, though a literature dealing chiefly with modern Europeans and Americans, not Chinese or Bantu.

What is most relevant here is that the 24 species of strengths they detect are clustered into the encompassing genuses of courage, humanity, justice and so forth – that is to say, precisely the 'virtues . . . the core characteristics valued by [Western] philosophers and religious thinkers' (Peterson and Seligman, 2004, p. 13). The authors number them as six rather than seven, but this is mainly because they lump hope and faith together in one virtue named transcendence, that is, 'strengths that forge connections to the larger universe and provide meaning' (p. 30). Five of their 'High Six' virtues lay down with ease on the classical Seven – transcendence (that is, faith and hope), courage, humanity (that is, love, which appears in their classification as a 'character strength' within what they view as the wider virtue), justice and temperance. Smith, it appears, was on to something.

From the Seven Primary Virtues, I say, Adam Smith chose five to admire especially. He chose all four of the pagan and Stoic virtues of courage, temperance, justice and prudence. To these he added, as virtue number five, a part of the Christian virtue of love, the part which his tradition – such as that of his teacher at Glasglow, Francis Hutcheson (1725, 1747) – called benevolence (though it must be admitted, as Gloria Vivenza points out to me, that Hutcheson's 'lay benevolence' has transcendent features beyond *eros* and *philia*). In exposing Plato's system, for example, Smith enumerates the pagan four, 'the essential virtue of prudence', the 'noble' virtue of courage (TMS, p. 268), 'a word [*sōphrosynē*] which we commonly translate temperance', and 'justice, the last and greatest of the four cardinal virtues' (TMS, p. 269). In exposing Stoicism he repeats the four, also with approval, speaking of virtue as 'wise [that is, practically prudent: Greek *phronesis*], just, firm [that is, courageous], and temperate conduct' (p. 282). And then a triad of prudence, benevolence, justice: 'Concern for our own happiness recommends us to the virtue of prudence; concern for that of other people, the virtues of justice and beneficence', 'the first [prudence] . . . originally recommended by our selfish, the other two [justice and human love] by our benevolent affections' (p. 262). An impartial spectator develops in the breast which 'in the evening . . . often makes us blush inwardly both for our . . . inattention to our own happiness, and for our still greater indifference and inattention, perhaps, to that of other people' (p. 262).

Smith particularly admired what Hume had called the 'artificial' virtues, the three on which any society must rest, namely, temperance, prudence and justice. His admiration shows in his life plan to write a great, thick book about each: temperance is the master virtue of TMS, prudence of WN, and justice (though 'not only': TMS, p. 342) was to be that of a treatise on jurisprudence, never completed.

The other two virtues of the Smithian five were courage in, say, entrepreneurship and love in, say, family arrangements. These stood apart from Smith's central concerns for temperance, prudence and justice. Contrary to what the men in Adam Smith ties believe, Smith detested buccaneer capitalism, with its emphasis on manly but imprudent courage. And as feminist students of the matter have noted, Smith did not much emphasize family love. Although he expected his dinner from the regard to their self-interest of the butcher, the brewer, or the baker, Smith neglected to observe that he expected it, too, from the love of Mrs Smith the elder in arranging to cook it.

Smith made his virtue-ethical approach clear enough in his works generally and in TMS even in its 1759 edition. But he made it most clear at the end of his life, in a Part VI added 31 years after the first edition. 'I have inserted', he wrote on 2 February 1789 to his publisher, apologizing for delays, 'a complete new sixth part containing a practical system of morality, under the title of the Character of Virtue' (Smith, 1977, p. 320). Section I of the new part is an encomium to the 'Prudent Man' – thus prudence. Section II is an analysis of benevolence in an expanding circle outward from self to country, taken of course, as was natural at the time, from the male point of view – thus a limited and secular form of love.

And then Smith embarks on a concluding, climactic Section III, 'Of Self-Command', which has always been the master virtue in his book. 'The man who acts according to the rules of perfect prudence, of strict justice, and of proper benevolence [love, that is] may be said to be perfectly virtuous' (p. 237). That accounts for three of the seven primary virtues – prudence, justice and love. But suppose the man in question knows that he should act with prudence, justice and love, but can't bring himself to do it? 'The most perfect knowledge, if it is not supported by the most perfect self-command, will not always enable him to do his duty.' 'Extravagant fear and furious anger', to take one sort of passion, '[are] often difficult to restrain even for a single moment' (p. 238). The 'command' of fear and anger was called by the ancients 'fortitude, manhood, and strength of mind', which is to say the cardinal pagan virtue of courage. 'The love of ease, of pleasure, of applause, and other selfish gratifications . . . often mislead us.' The ancients called the command of these 'temperance, decency, modesty, and moderation', that is to say, the cardinal virtue of temperance, so very much admired by the Stoics (pp. 338–9; cf. pp. 268f, 271).

Smith then elaborates on the virtues of courage (pp. 238–40), temperance (p. 240), a combined courage and temperance (self-command again, pp. 241–3), love briefly (p. 243), cowardice and courage again (pp. 243–6), and then discusses at length mere vanity as against proper self-esteem, figured repeatedly as temperance in judging oneself (pp. 246–62). He asserts at the beginning of the section that 'the principle of self-estimation may be too high, and it may likewise be too low' (p. 246) and ends the section by praising 'the man who esteems himself as he ought, and no more than he ought' (p. 261).

Such an analysis of temperance is no great advance on Aristotle's golden mean. But Smith did not seek striking originality in his ethical theory. He was building an ethics for a commercial society, but on the foundation of ethical thought in the West, not on some novelty circa 1710 or 1785 or 1789. Smith's main contribution to ethical theory in his own estimation was the notion of the impartial spectator: 'reason, principle, conscience, the inhabitant of the breast, the man within, the great judge and arbiter of our conduct' (TMS, pp. 294, 137). (Smith's use of dynamic theatrical metaphors such as the 'spectator', by the way, has been emphasized by David Marshall, 1986 and especially by Charles Griswold, 1999). The argument shows in the book's outline. Smith begins with his own theory in Part I, 'Of the Propriety of Action', to which merit (Part II), duty (III), utility (IV) and custom (V) are subordinated. The spectator is formed at first by upbringing and social pressure but at last evolves into a conscience – what was much later to be called 'inner direction'.

Though well expressed, it was a routine piece of virtue ethics. The alternative and novel systems of prudence-only, or of love-only, or of anything-only, as Smith noted, did not work very well. Specializing a theory of ethics down to merely one of the seven virtues – the economist specializing in prudence only, for example, the theologian in love only – does not do the ethical job. Smith declares himself on the issue early, indeed in the very first clause of his book. 'How selfish soever man may be supposed', he begins, and then proceeds to show in the next 330 pages that a specialized selfish account, like the one nowadays so popular with economists and evolutionary psychologists, does not suffice. On the fifth page he attacks prudence-only again: 'Those who are fond of deducing all our sentiments from certain refinements of self-love think themselves at no loss to account' for sympathy. The supposed egoist rejoices in expressions of approval of his projects, and is downcast by expressions of disapproval, 'but both the pleasure and the pain are always felt so instantaneously, and often upon such frivolous occasions [for example in a theatre for the characters portrayed, as he later notes; or in an account of some courageous act in ancient times], that it seems evident that neither of them can be derived from any such self-interested consideration' (TMS, pp. 13–14). And so repeatedly throughout.

Smith is sometimes viewed as a Stoic in the mold of Epictetus (Fitzgibbons, 1995; Raphael and Macfie, 1976 [1982], pp. 5–10). But such a view, though importantly true in part, tends to specialize him down to temperance-only. As Raphael and Macfie themselves put it, 'Smith's ethical doctrines are . . . a *combination* of stoic and Christian virtues – or, in philosophical terms, a *combination* of stoicism and Hutcheson . . . who resolved all virtue into . . . a philosophical version of the Christian ethic of love' (TMS, 'Introduction', p. 6, emphasis added). Smith certainly admired the 'manly' character of Stoicism, and he famously remarked in a letter that the atheist Hume faced death 'with more real resignation . . . than any whining Christian ever died with pretended resignation to the will of God' (*Correspondence*, Letter 163, 14 August 1776). And I have said that Smith spent a third of his life's creative effort inquiring into the master virtue of TMS, the self-command or temperance-plus-courage so characteristic of a successful Stoic. In the old Part VII of TMS, dating from his lectures in the 1750s and included in the first edition, in which he surveys the ancient and a very few of the modern systems of ethics, he spends a mere 4½ pages on Plato and Aristotle together, 5 on Hutcheson recommending benevolence-only, 5½ on Epicurus (really on Hume) and 8 on Mandeville recommending prudence-only. But he spends fully 21 pages on Stoicism according to Zeno, Epictetus, Cicero, Seneca and Marcus Aurelius, 9½ of which are a disquisition on the Stoic attitude towards suicide added to the sixth edition, apparently in reply to a notorious essay by Hume.

What Smith mainly took from his readings in Stoicism, however, was the system of the virtues. That is, Smith was a virtue ethicist who learned his trade in a Stoic school (from which, Fleischacker argues – 2004, p. 112 – in 1759 he graduated; contrast Raphael and Macfie, 1976 [1982], p. 18: 'Smith had [by 1790] acquired an even warmer regard for stoicism'). His admiring pages on Stoicism are gathered in the sixth edition into the chapter of section VII entitled 'Of those Systems which make Virtue consist in Propriety', that is, those attending like his own system to a set of virtues instead of merely to one. And in the section VI added in 1790 he argues against the specialized excesses of Stoic insensibility, or what we would now call Buddhist disengagement from the world. He recommends instead an active virtue, 'that keen and earnest attention to the propriety of our own conduct, which constitutes the real essence of virtue' (p. 244).

A man following propriety shows in a temperate way all the primary virtues. That is to say, he shows a balance of all them, or selects the subset appropriate to the occasion. Not temperance-only. The virtues are not cloistered, but take place in the *vita activa*. In church on Sunday morning the virtuous person exercises chiefly the virtue of spiritual love, on the dance floor on Saturday night the virtue of self-asserting courage, at her job in the bank Monday through Friday the virtue of careful prudence.

Such, I am claiming, was the ethically plural theme of Smith's very last published writing. His very first, 'To the Memory of Mr William Crauford, Merchant of Glasgow', praised

> that exact frugality, that downright probity and plainness of manners so suitable to his profession, [which] joined a love of learning . . . an openness of hand and a generosity of heart . . . and a magnanimity that could support . . . the most torturing pains of body with an unalterable cheerfulness of temper, and without once interrupting, even to his last hour, the most manly and the most vigorous activity in a vast variety of business . . . candid and penetrating, circumspect and sincere. (Smith, 1980, p. 262)

This is Stoicism, perhaps, but in a distinctly virtue-ethical key, admiring frugality, probity, plainness of manners, love of learning, generosity of heart, great-heartedness, enduring courage, cheerfulness, candor, penetration, circumspection and sincerity. It admires in short the bourgeois virtues, all of them, together in a system, just as virtue ethicists recommend.

Vivienne Brown, who supports the notion that Smith thinks as I say in terms of the virtues in TMS, argues that in WN by contrast he cannot be seen as ethical at all. She declares especially that the book 'cannot be read as an endorsement of "liberal capitalism"' (1994, p. 53). She argues that the highly 'dialogic' character of TMS makes it an ethical work (pp. 188, 195). The two texts are seen as emphasizing two different sets of so-called virtues, in a hierarchy denying in fact the lower set any true ethical standing. 'The truly moral virtues of beneficence and self-command in TMS', she writes, 'are those that define the moral agent as engaged in a dialogic encounter with the self, a moral process of internal debate that is represented by the metaphor of the impartial spectator.' In her reading, 'the other virtues of justice and prudence' – the main subjects of WN as against TMS – 'are therefore denominated as second-order . . . [eliciting] a certain esteem . . . [but not] truly moral virtues' (p. 208).

It is Brown, not Smith, I would reply, who thus 'denominates' prudence and justice as second-order, in aid of downplaying Smith's evident approval of the economic parts of 'the liberal plan of equality, liberty, and justice' (WN, p. 664). Brown's ingenious application of Bakhtin's notion of dialogic as against monologic discourse certainly does illuminate the rhetoric of the two books. But speaking of rhetoric, WN was written to influence policy under the control of men who fancied themselves as prudent above all. To be effective rhetorically the book had to follow Smith's own advice about anger and indignation in TMS – 'before resentment . . . can become graceful and agreeable it must be . . . brought down below that pitch to which it would naturally rise than almost every other passion' (TMS, p. 34). A book on 'police' would do so.

Nonetheless, Smith's indignation regularly broke out in WN, as Brown admits (Brown, 1994, p. 190). WN, as Griswold (1999, pp. 260–61) and Fleischacker (2004, throughout) argue, is an ethical book. One can agree with Brown that ethics depends on 'a moral process of internal debate'. But justice and prudence in Smith are not in fact treated non-dialogically, as Brown to the contrary asserts. In both books Smith gives hundreds of instances of the impartial spectator staging an internal debate about even these 'second-order' virtues.

I noted the revival of virtue ethics after Elizabeth Anscombe's essay in 1958, 'Modern moral philosophy'. (The revival, by the way, has been led notably by women; ethics is the only part of academic philosophy with a substantially feminine voice, heard with growing volume since the 1950s.) The revival directed attention to the desirability of talking about a set of virtues directly, rather than talking in Enlightenment style only of one allegedly universal principle. 'It would be a great improvement', wrote Anscombe, 'if, instead of "morally wrong," one always named a genus such as "untruthful," "unchaste," "unjust"'(Anscombe, 1958 [1997], p. 34).

But where does one stop in listing the virtues of, say, truthfulness, chastity, justice and the like? A list of 170 virtues would be so broad as to be useless. The point is worth stressing here because Smith's definite five virtues, and his emphasis on the joint cultivation of the five by the impartial spectator, puts him solidly in the older tradition of virtue ethics. Some post-1958 virtue ethicists, by contrast, seem to have no definite list in mind, or an embarrassingly long one, a fault which the classical virtue ethics of Plato, Aquinas and Smith avoided.

Modern ethical philosophy has indeed two opposite faults of quantity. The one is to let virtues thus proliferate, leaving us to struggle with the 170 words for 'virtues' in the main headings of 'Class Eight: Affections' of Roget's *Thesaurus* (edition of 1962). It would be like recommending as an ethical system the 613 commandments of orthodox Judaism, Hillel's count. The study of Kant and Bentham (or indeed of the Torah) imposes a healthy discipline on such proliferation. But so does the study of Aquinas and the rest of the virtue-ethical tradition, which narrows the list to the Seven Primaries.

And the study of Kant or Bentham or Locke leads, alas, to the other fault of quantity, acknowledging too few virtues to fit the stories of our lives – for example, one virtue only, The Good, or the categorical imperative, or the greatest happiness, or the contract behind a veil of ignorance. It chooses one of the seven, such as prudence or love or justice, to stand for all. Smith's better plan is to stop as Epictetus or Aquinas did with a definite yet reasonably comprehensive list of a moderate number of the primary virtues. That way you know better what you are talking about. Five or seven, after all, is a mean among $N = 1$ and $N = 170$ or 613, if not a particularly golden one.

The clerisy nowadays views Aquinas as Catholic dogma, and therefore as something unnecessary for us Protestant or anti-clerical intellectuals to read. And so the divine doctor's seven do not get much of a hearing in secular discussions, even by virtue ethicists. The pioneer Philippa Foot on the contrary argued in 1978 that '*Summa Theologica* is one of the best sources we have for moral philosophy, and moreover . . . St Thomas' ethical writings are as useful to the atheist as to the . . . Christian believer' (1978, p. 2). She and Alasdair MacIntyre are among the handful of ethical philosophers to realize how very useful Aquinas is, and to take Aquinas's numbering of the virtues seriously. Foot for instance wrote that 'nobody can get on well if he lacks courage, and does not have some measure of temperance and wisdom [her word for what Smith and I call prudence], while communities where justice and charity [her word – referring to the King James Bible – for what I call secular love and Smith calls benevolence] are lacking are apt to be wretched places to live, as Russia was under the Stalinist terror, or Sicily under the Mafia' (1978, pp. 2–3). That is five out of the seven virtues, counting from the bottom of the diagram – just the five that Smith selected.

Athol Fitzgibbons regards Smith as an enemy of Aristotelianism and of fundamentalist religion (which two Fitzgibbons tends to merge), and claims with considerable justice, I have noted, that Smith was a 'Ciceronian Stoic'. My claim is that Smith, if a Stoic, was willy-nilly therefore the last of a tradition of virtue ethics dating from Aristotle and perfected by Aquinas and practiced by the casuists, whom Pascal and other single-virtue theorists began to assault in the seventeenth century (Toulmin and Jonsen, 1987). The one characterization of Smith emphasizes his Stoicism. The other emphasizes the wider technique of ethical pluralism of which St Thomas Aquinas, the follower of Aristotle, in turn was the student of Plato, is a sophisticated version. Both characterizations can be true.

This is not to say that Smith was a close student of Aquinas or of other Christian thinkers. He does not appear to have read them much. About Jesuit casuistry he was scathing, in a passage added in 1790: 'Books of casuistry . . . are generally as useless as they are commonly tiresome', because they do not change people's dispositions. 'With regard to one who is negligent in his [duty], the style of those writings is not such as is likely to awaken him to more attention' (TMS, p. 339). In Smith's time St Thomas had nothing like the prestige he has acquired from the neo-Thomism initiated in the late nineteenth century by Pope Leo XIII. In 1759 in a Protestant country even a scholar of Smith's quality was liable to suppose that little could be learned from the 'scholastics', which was in the Enlightenment of course a term of contempt. He scorns 'a scholastic or technical system of artificial definitions, divisions, and sub-divisions; one of the most effective expedients . . . for extinguishing whatever degree of good sense there may be in any moral or metaphysical doctrine' (TMS, p. 291). In the one place where Smith might have noted, if he had known it, that Aquinas unlike the lesser theorists of 'the benevolent system' gives full weight also to the secular and pagan virtues, he does not (TMS, p. 301). He leaps from 'many ancient fathers of the Christian church' – which pointedly leaves out Aquinas, who was medieval, born eight centuries after the death of the last of the 'ancient fathers', the last at any rate in Western Christendom, St Augustine – right to the Reformation, in which the benevolent system 'was adopted by several [Protestant] divines of the most eminent piety and learning', and then by Hutcheson, 'the most philosophical . . . the soberest and most judicious'.

Smith appears to have read mere summaries of 'the schoolmen', as he called them impatiently, for example using in discussing courage and temperance the Aquinian distinction between the 'irascible' emotions (that is, hot, angry emotions; TMS, p. 268) and the 'concupiscible' (that is, appetitive; recent English translations of Aquinas's Latin prefer instead 'concupiscent'). Smith never quotes or refers to Aquinas or any other schoolman directly by name, and a doctrinal influence is untraceable. The power of such evidence, admittedly, is low, since Smith does not quote anyone much at all. Even David Hume, whose doctrinal influence is palpable, is not actually quoted in Smith, though often replied to. But anyway Smith, in common with some recent writers – who at this date should perhaps know better – skips over the Aquinian and later Christian syntheses of Stoic and theological virtues, courage–temperance–justice–prudence plus faith–hope–love, adding up to seven. Nor was Smith even, to speak of the acknowledged root of Aquinas's tradition, a self-conscious Aristotelian. As Fleischacker observes, for example, Smith's egalitarianism and his suspicion of philosophical experts implies a virtue of humility that Aristotle would have found very strange indeed (Fleischacker, 2004, p. 74). In Smith's summary history of ethics in TMS the philosopher gets only two pages, and those pages are focused not on Aristotle's somewhat rambling listing of the virtues but on the doctrine of the golden mean, so suitable to an impartial spectator.

I am merely arguing that Smith, in sharp contrast to his great contemporaries in ethical theorizing, was a virtues man, a half-conscious follower of Plato and Aristotle and therefore of Aquinas, and also of the Stoics (though they, I repeat, can be accused of a monism of temperance only), in emphasizing a system of multiple virtues – and indeed precisely five of the seven Aquinian virtues. That is to say, he was indeed the last of the former virtue ethicists. Smith puts Plato (in parts), Aristotle, the Stoics, and in shadowy form the schoolmen into the tradition of 'propriety' as against prudence-for-self or love-for-others:

> If virtue . . . does not consist of propriety [which is to say the balance in the soul recommended by Plato, Aristotle, some of the Stoics, Aquinas and Smith himself], it must consist either in prudence [thus Smith's friend Hume] or in benevolence [thus Smith's teacher Hutcheson]. Besides these three, it is scarce possible to imagine any other account can be given of the nature of virtue. (TMS, p. 267)

All ethics in Smith was divided into these three: propriety, prudence and benevolence/love. In choosing the first, the multiple virtues of propriety, he chose to stand with the tradition of Aristotle and Epictetus and Aquinas against the monism of some of Plato's Stoic followers (reducing justice and prudence and courage and temperance to The Good) or of Hobbes and early Hume (reducing The Good to prudence only) or of Hutcheson in a late and literally sentimental version of Christianity (reducing all the virtues to love only).

As a virtue ethicist Smith disliked all such reductions. 'By running up all the different virtues . . . to this one species of propriety [namely, 'the most real prudence'], Epicurus indulged a propensity', Smith noted, 'which philosophers . . . are apt to cultivate with a peculiar fondness, as the great means of displaying their ingenuity . . . to account for all appearances from as few principles as possible' (TMS, p. 299). It is Ockham's Razor, with which so many male philosophers have cut themselves shaving. Parsimony, after all, is not the only intellectual virtue. In his very method Smith recommends a balance of the virtues, historical relevance balanced with parsimony, justice in summarizing other philosophers balanced with hope in going beyond them. And therefore in substance he avoided the utilitarian pitfall, into which Hume gazed fondly and into which Bentham enthusiastically leapt, of reducing all other virtues to prudence only.

Love was one of the Smithian virtues, but balanced with pluralism. In TMS the 'amiable' Christianity of Hutcheson came in for criticism chiefly because it tended to suppose that 'the mixture of any selfish motive, like that of a baser alloy . . . took away altogether the merit that would otherwise have belonged to any action' (TMS, p. 302). According to the system of love-only, 'self-love was a principle which could never be virtuous in any degree or in any direction' (TMS, p. 303). Such a specialized version of Christian love violated the propriety of a balanced set of virtues. Smith would have already known that Aristotle admired *philautia* – proper regard for oneself. And he would have discovered had he looked into Aquinas, love-only violated Christian orthodoxy, too. Hutcheson's false lemma, Smith noted, implies that 'virtue must consist in pure and disinterested benevolence alone' (TMS, p. 302). The same fault infects Kant, with justice put in the place of love. Smith was a virtue ethicist, not like many of his contemporaries an ethical reductionist.

Smith's confining of attention to five virtues, then, avoided the dual errors of quantity in modern ethical thinking – too many virtues or too few. The other two errors are of quality and of object. Smith's obsolete virtue-ethical system avoided them as well.

The most prevalent error is that of quality, the reduction of ethics to taste, or rather to 'mere' taste, viewed as analogous to a taste for chocolate ice cream. Though ancient, found for example in some Platonic characters, it has in recent times been articulated most insistently by the logical positivists and their descendents. The theory is called officially 'emotivism', 'the doctrine that all evaluative judgments and more specifically all moral judgments are *nothing but* expressions of preference' (MacIntyre, 1981, p. 11). Or as Hobbes wrote in 1651, 'Good and evil are names that signify our appetites and aversions' (1651 [1914], I, Chapter 15, p. 82; and I, Chapter 6, p. 24). Most academics and other intellectuals nowadays, without giving it much thought, adhere to the emotivist, chocolate-ice-cream theory. They view the ethical person as maximizing their utility function with respect to the doing of good deeds, just as he or she does in the eating of ice cream. No duty, love, faith or persuasion carried weight. The sort of amiable, casuistic reasoning together that the virtue-ethical and rhetorical tradition recommends, the trading of 'more or less good reasons', as the literary critic Wayne Booth put it, such as the stories of good or bad lives ranging from the Hebrew Bible and Plutarch to the latest movie, is spurned. No persuasion, please: we're positivists.

Economists in the centuries after Smith, and especially in the twentieth century, led the attack by the secular clerisy against preaching the virtues. The economist Mark Blaug, for example, in many other respects a surprisingly sensible member of his profession, asserted in 1980 that: 'There are no . . . methods for reconciling different normative value judgments – other than political elections and shooting it out at the barricades' (1980, pp. 132–3). By 'methods for reconciling' he appears to mean air-tight proofs such as the Pythagorean theorem, not the reasonable discourse of impartial spectators, what Smith called the 'faculty of speech' by which 'every one . . . is practicing oratory on others thro the whole of his life' (WN, p. 25; *Lectures on Jurisprudence* (1762–63), p. 352; cf. TMS, p. 336). The economist Joseph Schumpeter of Vienna and Harvard had earlier expressed an ethical philosophy and a trivialization of language similar to Blaug's: 'We may, indeed, prefer the world of modern dictatorial socialism to the world of Adam Smith, or vice versa, but any such preference comes within the same category of subjective evaluation as does, to plagiarize Sombart, a man's preference for blondes over brunettes.' Thus also Lionel Robbins of the London School of Economics: 'If we disagree about ends it is a case of thy blood against mine – or live and let live, according to the importance of the difference, or the relative strength of our opponents . . . If we disagree about the morality of the taking of interest . . . then there is no room for argument' (Robbins, 1932, p. 134).

The central dogma of modernism, Wayne Booth noted, is 'the belief that you cannot and indeed should not allow your values to intrude upon your cognitive life – that thought and knowledge and fact are on one side and affirmations of value on the other' (1974, p. 13). Booth instances Bertrand Russell as one in whom 'passionate commitment has lost its connection with the provision of good reasons' (p. xi and Chapter 2). (Note by the way the self-refutation embodied in such a rule of method, that one should not say 'should'. As Russell himself found in another connection, self-reference leads to cycling self-contradiction. 'All Cretans are liars', quoth the Cretan.)

Russell claimed to not allow values to intrude upon his cognitive life, which meant that he indulged his values without the check of good reasons. And so the mathematical philosopher applied low and sometimes no standards to his opinions about ethics and politics and economics. His friend Santayana describes Russell during the Great War exploiting his retentive memory without ethical reasoning:

> This information, though accurate, was necessarily partial, and brought forward in a partisan argument; he couldn't know, he refused to know everything; so that his judgments, nominally based on that partial information, were really inspired by passionate prejudice and were always unfair and sometimes mad. He would say, for instance, that the bishops supported the war because they had money invested in munitions works. (Santayana, 1943–53 [1986], p. 441)

We cannot have reasonable ethical lives, the virtue ethicists like Smith claim, if we depend only on a narrow definition of reason. 'But though reason is undoubtedly the source of the general rules of morality', Smith noted, without much optimism that 'general rules' were themselves worth having, 'it is altogether absurd and unintelligible to suppose that the first perceptions of right and wrong can be derived from reason' (TMS, p. 320). Such taste, however, is not 'mere' in Smith, to be determined without education or reflection. It is rather the providing of good reasons, yielding 'reason, principle, conscience, the inhabitant of the breast, the man within, the great judge and arbiter of our conduct' (TMS, p. 137).

The other characteristically modern error in thinking about ethics is an error of object. The error is more technical than the chocolate ice cream theory just described, and is committed especially by analytic philosophers venturing into ethics. It reduces ethics to matters of how you treat other people. That might seem to be no error. Surely ethics is about altruism? No, it is not, not only. Look back at Figure 1.1, and note the ethical objects of self, of others and of the transcendent. The good life will involve all three. A triple perfection, one might say.

For example, the philosopher Susan Wolf in a well-known essay, 'Moral saints', adopts an exclusively public, social, altruistic definition of 'virtue' (1982 [1997], p. 80, 'improving the welfare of others or of society as a whole', among many other places – four times on p. 80, for example; on p. 81; p. 85; taken back on p. 93, but then, 'This approach seems unlikely to succeed'). In the style of many Anglophone philosophers she leaves out privately self-interested prudence as a virtue, and so lets her moral saints behave badly towards themselves. Showing its badness is Wolf's point, by a reduction to absurdity: moral saints are objectionable precisely because they care nothing for themselves. 'If the moral saint is devoting all his time to feeding the hungry', Wolf observes, 'then necessarily he is not reading Victorian novels, playing the oboe, or improving his backhand . . . A life in which *none* of these possible aspects of character is developed may seem a life strangely barren' (Wolf, 1982 [1997], p. 81).

It's the Jewish-mother version of goodness: 'Oh, don't bother to replace the bulb. I'll just sit here in the dark.' But the mother, after all, is God's creature, too, and her benevolence therefore should include a just benevolence towards herself. Being wholly altruistic, and disregarding the claims of that person also in the room called Self, about whose needs the very Self is ordinarily best informed, is making the same mistake as being wholly selfish, disregarding the claims of that person called Other. Smith of course agreed. It is the characteristically anti-paternalistic feature of his thought to assert that Self is best informed about Self's needs. Fleischacker observes: 'That ordinary people could be trusted with their own decisions about what . . . to consume was one of the least acceptable propositions of *WN*, to the intellectuals and politicians of its day, and at the same time one of its most important . . . insofar as it robbed merchants of a prime argument for government control' (2004, p. 89)

The ethical error is to ignore someone. Oddly, selflessness – note the word – is unjust, inegalitarian. 'There is a manifest negligence in men of their real happiness or interest in the present world', said Bishop Joseph Butler in 1725. People are 'as often unjust to themselves as to others' (Butler, 1725, Sermon I, p. 371). The more optimistic Earl of Shaftesbury took in 1713 an evolutionary line to arrive at praise for such prudence:

> the affection toward private or self-good, however selfish it may be esteemed, is in reality not only consistent with public good but in some measure contributing to it . . . [It is] for the good of the species in general . . . So far as being blamable in any sense . . . it must be acknowledged absolutely necessary to constitute a creature good. . . . No one would doubt to pronounce so if he saw a man who minded not any precipices which lay in his way, nor made any distinction of food, diet, clothing or whatever else related to his health and being. (Shaftesbury, 1713, 1732 [2001], Vol. II, pp. 13f; cf. Vol. II, p. 18, 'if the affection be . . . .')

Prudence within a set of cultivated virtues is not self-centeredness.

Even very sensible philosophers want nowadays to deny such an obvious truth by reducing every virtue to improving the welfare of others or of society as a whole. In his last book Robert Nozick, who was most famous for his attempt to bring libertarian ideas traceable in part to Smith into political philosophy, tried to argue that 'ethics exists because at least sometimes it is possible to coordinate actions to mutual benefit' (2001, p. 244). This is the economist's all-ye-need-to-know, the new welfare economics of the 1930s. Or: 'Ethics arises when frequently or importantly there are situations offering opportunities for mutual benefit from coordinated activity' (p. 246) And a utilitarian, which Nozick tried not to be, would say that: 'since cooperation to mutual benefit is the function of ethics, the only thing that matters is . . . the size of the social pie' (p. 256).

But after 64 closely reasoned pages Nozick is left worrying that ethics must have something more. The reason he gets into trouble is that he makes that characteristically modern philosophical error of simply defining ethics as 'concerning interpersonal relations' (2001, p. 248). In other words, his main argument has no place for the virtues of self-improvement or of devotion to a transcendent. It is a middle-level ethics, neither at the hope–faith–transcendent-love top or the temperance–self-interested–courage bottom, but aimed at a shallow conception of justice-only implemented with prudence. It is entirely about economics; that is to say, about 'Pareto optimality', about mutually beneficial deals in the middle range. The ethical objects are the other people in the deal, not ever oneself or God.

But I said Nozick was sensible. And it is hard to imagine a more intellectually honest person. So occasionally he breaks into praise for the alternative ethical objects, as though realizing uneasily that his reduction to prudent but procedurally just deals has not sufficed. He distinguishes four 'levels or layers of ethics', referring to a treatment in his semi-popular book of 1989, *The Examined Life* (2001, p. 280; 1989, pp. 212–15). The first, or lowest, is the mutual benefit on which Nozick spends most of his analytic effort in the 2001 book, Pareto optimality, the ethic of respect. The next is an ethic of responsibility, discussed also in his 1981 book, *Philosophical Explanations* (pp. 499–570). The next is an ethic of caring, Nozick's version of love, though again 'caring' only about other people, not about oneself or God. And the fourth and highest is an ethic of 'Light', 'truth, goodness, beauty, holiness', or in other words the ethics of faith, hope and transcendent love (1989, pp. 214f).

Nozick admits that he has no account of how the levels relate, or why he should always call the ethic of respect 'basic' – except on the not unreasonable political grounds that it is the least controversial. He does not know the virtue ethicists. They are never mentioned by this most ethically obsessed of the analytic philosophers. The two references to Bernard Williams in *Invariances* (2001) are on matters of metaphysics, not ethics. Aristotle as an ethical theorist is discussed only briefly; Aquinas is not mentioned in any work of Nozick; nor are any other virtue ethicists (1981, pp. 515ff). Though he thinks his social ideas originate in Smith, he appears not to have read TMS with care. His 2001 book speaks of Smith's book on one occasion, as holding a theory of the 'ideal observer', a misquotation placed in quotation marks – the phrase, dear Robert, is the 'impartial spectator'. (Note the shift registered in the error, by the way, between a humanistic metaphor of theater to an antihumanistic metaphor of observational science.) And the passage construes the notion in Smith as being about 'moral' matters having to do with other people, not the self-shaping temperance that is the chief theme of TMS (2001, p. 288).

James Otteson has tried to place Smith in an evolutionary frame, a version of prudence-only along Nozickian lines, in which 'over time, people find that they can better satisfy their interests if they cooperate in certain ways' (2002, p. 295). 'Rules about propriety and contracts are those that have proved to satisfy human interests most efficiently' (p. 296). 'The goal whose attainment these exercises make more likely is mutual sympathy of sentiments' (p. 294). This seems to come at it the wrong way. Moral sympathy in Smith is the input, not the output, as can be judged from the organization of TMS: it starts with sympathy, sharply distinguishing it from selfishness. The output is the ethical person, for his or her own sweet sake, not for the sake of 'better satisfying [his or her] interests'.

Interests are good, says Smith, since poverty is bad, and it was surely part of Smith's project to 'detoxify the pursuit of wealth', as Griswold puts it (1999, p. 265). But in both TMS and (even) WN, Smith roundly attacks the better-satisfying of interests as a final end of living.

Smith is also very fierce against rules and maxims, even 'rules about propriety and contracts', unless the strict rules of procedural justice, as though he knew about Professor Kant's theorizing in far away Köningsberg, and had a low opinion of it. I have noted his attacks on casuistry, which he understood as the giving of rules (Toulmin and Jonsen, 1987 give it a more sympathetic reading). He says elsewhere that 'the general rules of almost all the virtues . . . are in many respects loose and inaccurate . . . and require so many modifications that it is scarcely possible to regulate our conduct entirely by regard to them' (TMS, p. 174).

One is reminded (and so is Otteson: 2002, p. 268, n. 20) of the most extreme of the evolutionary psychologists nowadays, such as Steven Pinker. Listen to Pinker in 1997 on the rationality of friendship: 'now that you value the person, they should value you even more . . . because of your stake in rescuing him or her from hard times . . . This runaway process is what we call friendship' (Pinker, 1997, quoted in Fodor, 1998).

No, Steven, it is what we call self-absorption. The cognitive philosopher Jerry Fodor remarks of Pinker's one-factor theory:

> A concern to propagate one's genes would rationalize one's acting to promote one's children's welfare; but so too would an interest in one's children's welfare. Not all of one's motives could be instrumental, after all; there must be some things that one cares for just for their own sakes. Why, indeed, mightn't there be quite a few such things? Why shouldn't one's children be among them? (Fodor, 1998)

He quotes Pinker on the evolutionary explanation for why we humans like stories; namely, that they provide useful tips for life, as for example to someone in Hamlet's fix: 'What are the options if I were to suspect that my uncle killed my father, took his position, and married my mother? Good question.' Startlingly, Pinker does not appear to be joking here. It is funny, this 'scientific' attempt to get along without sheer love, or sheer courage, or to get along without the aesthetic pleasure of stories reflecting faith and hope. The output, I say, is the ethical hero, the human with a conscience, the Human Within, not pleasures or interests that would satisfy a cat.

All right. Smith analyses good and bad not as a specialized prudence or justice or temperance but as a proper balance among five of the seven Aquinian virtues. We will not grasp his argument if we insist on making it lie down on a Kantian or a utilitarian or a natural-rights or even a social-contractual bed, as analytic philosophers amateur and professional have long tried to do. Smith was a virtue ethicist first and last.

But something is missing. In choosing his five virtues, Smith drops the two transcendent virtues of hope and faith, with the transcendent version of love going beyond love for people, *agape* as against the *philia* or *eros* in the precise Greek. There is no question that Smith realized what he was doing. He knew perfectly well that hope and faith and *agape* were primary virtues in Christian thought – this would have been clear even in the secondary descriptions of scholastic thought – though as I have said he may have lacked a direct understanding of Aquinas's role in the construct. But if someone lacks 'strengths that forge connections to the larger universe and provide meaning', in Peterson and

Seligman's words, they do not have a fully human life (Peterson and Seligman, 2004, Table 1.1). That cat again. Or as the Anglican theologian Richard Hooker put it in 1593:

> Man doth seek a triple perfection: first a sensual . . . then an intellectual . . . Man doth not seem to rest satisfied . . . For although the beauties, riches, honours, sciences, virtues [which means 'power' here], and perfections of all men living, were in the present possession of one; yet somewhat beyond and above all this there would still be sought and earnestly thirsted for' (Hooker, 1593 [1907], First Book, IX, 4, pp. 205–6).

The reason Smith neglected hope and faith and *agape* is not obscure. He shared with Enlightenment figures such as Hume and Voltaire an aversion to any alleged 'virtue' that could be seen as conventionally religious. Hope and faith looked to advanced thinkers in the eighteenth century horribly conventionally religious, and anyway dispensable. Let us build a new world free from religious superstition, they cried, free from the wars of sects, free from the meddling of priests and dominies. Let us dispense with 'hope' and 'faith,' and establish a new . . . uh . . . faith on the . . . uh . . . hopes for reason and propriety.

The Christianity that Smith opposed was the rigid Calvinism still influential in Scotland at the time, no longer ascendant but able (with some help from the benevolent Francis Hutcheson) to keep atheists like Hume out of the universities. And he opposed too Catholicism that could in France still warrant the conviction of a Protestant, Jean Calas, alleged on slender evidence in 1762 to have murdered his suicidal son to prevent the son's conversion to Catholicism. Such religious fanatics, with which Scotland had recently had so much experience, impute 'even to the great Judge of the universe . . . all their own prejudices . . . Of all of the corrupters of moral sentiments . . . faction and fanaticism have always been by far the greatest' (TMS, p. 156). Smith wanted, as did Hume and Kant and Bentham and Locke for that matter, to bring ethics down to earth: 'The most sublime speculation of the contemplative philosopher can scarce compensate the neglect of the smallest active duty' (TMS, p. 237). One can hear him including the theologian and other advocates for the transcendent in that phrase 'contemplative philosopher'. Compare Hume's sneering at 'divinity or school metaphysics' and the 'monkish virtues'. Thus Hobbes without God, Spinoza without God, Vico without God, Hume without God, Kant without God. No monkish virtues of hope and faith, please: we are Enlightenment philosophers.

In their official Christian vestments, that is, hope and faith were often unwelcome in the clubs and salons of the *philosophes* and, later, especially after 1848, in the ateliers and universities of the European and especially the Continental intelligentsia. So still. Even the excellent Rosalind Hursthouse seems embarrassed by the Transcendent Two. Her lucid exposition of virtue ethics in 1999 mentions in its index the virtue of love 90 times under various headings: benevolence, charity, compassion, generosity, kindness, loyalty, friendship (Hursthouse, 1999, index; I am counting multiple pages at their total: thus 'benevolence, Humean, 99–102' counts as four pages). Loyalty and friendship have perhaps an element of faith in them, though note the absence of the transcendent part of love itself, *agape*. The virtue of justice, the male philosophical obsession, she mentions 28 times. Temperance (and self-control), 18. Courage, 24 (more male obsession). Moral wisdom, that is, *phronēsis*, that is, prudence, which in Aquinas's analysis underlies all the virtues, 26 times. The typically modern and bourgeois philosopher's virtue of honesty (out of justice, temperance, courage and faith), 22 times. That covers the Smithian pentad.

But where are the other two, sacred hope and sacred faith, and the transcendent part of love? Hursthouse ends her book with an appeal: 'Keep hope alive.' Her only other mention of hope and faith is a page attacking the so-called virtue of piety, which combines them, as irrational, not characteristically human, 'based on a complete illusion' from an atheist's point of view (Hursthouse, 1999, pp. 232f; cf. p. 218: 'But what could this fifth end be?'). One wonders, though: is the physicist's pious but entirely atheistic faith in the orderliness of nature, which Smith and Hume and Kant buried in their magic adjective 'natural', and which Hursthouse elsewhere notes is essential for a scientific world view, therefore also 'irrational'? Is science, then, as religious faith is in her account, 'based on a complete illusion'? Hursthouse's own project – based on the pious hope that the virtues can be justified piecemeal from within a cultural set of them – is likewise undercut.

We humans cannot get along without transcendence, which is faith in a past, hope for a future, love for an ideal, justified by larger considerations. If we do not have faith, hope and love for God, we will substitute art or science or national learning. If we do not have art or science or national learning or Anglicanism we will substitute fundamentalism or the Rapture. If we don't have fundamentalism or the Rapture or the local St Wenceslaus parish we will substitute our family or the rebuilt antique car. Faith, hope and transcendent love are a consequence of the human ability to symbolize, a fixture of our philosophical psychology.

We might as well acknowledge transcendence in the way we talk and think about ethics, if only to keep watch on it and prevent it from doing mischief, as did once a Russian hope for the socialist Revolution and as does now a Saudi Arabian faith in an Islamic past. In the century after Smith and during the Romantic Era the virtues of hope, faith and transcendent love came back into the Western discussion with a vengeance, in the form of a forward-looking hope for socialism and in the form of a backward-looking faith in nationalism, justified by a self- and other-sacrificing love for the transcendent. Whence the First World War and the Russian Revolution and National Socialism and all our woe. The Bulgarian-French critic, Tzvetan Todorov, warns that 'democracies put their own existence in jeopardy if they neglect the human need for transcendence' (2000 [2003], p. 32). Michael Ignatieff put it well: 'The question of whether . . . the needs we once called religious can perish without consequence . . . remains central to understanding the quality of modern man's happiness' (1984 [2001], p. 21). Evidently the answer is no. There are consequences and there will be more. That is not a reason to return to the older sureties, although I do warmly recommend progressive Episcopalianism. But it is a reason to take seriously the transcendent in our imagined lives. Adam Smith's error was the error, and the glory, of the Enlightenment, trying to liberate us from transcendence.

But anyway the hope and faith and transcendent love slip back into Smith, as into Kant and the rest, although by the back door unobserved. The impartial spectator, or the Kantian or even the Benthamite equivalent, are not merely behavioral observations about how people develop ethically. They are recommendations. Recommendations depend on faith and hope and transcendent love, articulated from the identity of an urbane resident of Edinburgh, for example, hopeful for a rather better society, loving sweetly the imagined result. As Fleischacker notes: 'When we ask after the "nature" of human beings we are looking for what human beings "really" want, beneath the surface trappings ... Human nature always includes what people aspire to, for Smith; it is never reduced [as in the economist's version of utilitarianism] to the desires they merely happen to have' (2004, pp. 61, 63).

And how was this faithful and loving hope, this aspiration to full humanity, to be achieved? Through cultivating the seven virtues – or Smith's five, with hope and faith and transcendent love knocking at the back door.

Note
* With thanks to Gloria Vivenza of the University of Verona for her comments on an earlier draft.

References

Anscombe, G. Elizabeth M. (1958), 'Modern moral philosophy', *Philosophy*, **33**, 1–19; reprinted as pp. 26–44 in Roger Crisp and Michael Slote (eds) (1997), *Virtue Ethics*, Oxford: Oxford University Press.

Aquinas, St Thomas (*c.* 1270), *Treatise on the Virtues* [*Summa Theologiae*, First Half of the Second Part, questions 49–67], John A. Oesterle (ed.) (1984), Notre Dame, IN: University of Notre Dame Press.

Aristotle (*c.* 330 BC), *Nicomachean Ethics*, H. Rackham (ed.) (1934), Cambridge, MA: Harvard University Press.

Bentham, Jeremy (1789), *A Fragment on Government, with an Introduction to the Principles of Morals and Legislation*; W. Harrison (ed.) (1948), Oxford: Basil Blackwell.

Blaug, Mark (1980), *The Methodology of Economics: Or, How Economists Explain*, Cambridge: Cambridge University Press.

Booth, Wayne C. (1974), *Modern Dogma and the Rhetoric of Assent*, Chicago, IL: University of Chicago Press.

Brown, Vivienne (1994), *Adam Smith's Discourse: Canonicity, Commerce, and Conscience*, London: Routledge.

Buchanan, James and Gordon Tullock (1962), *The Calculus of Consent*, Ann Arbor, MI: University of Michigan Press.

Butler, Joseph, Bishop (1725, 1736), *Fifteen Sermons*; in *The Analogy of Religion and Fifteen Sermons*, reprinted (n.d.), London: Religious Tract Society, pp. 335–528.

Cicero, Marcus Tullius (44 BC), *De officiis* (Concerning Duties), trans. W. Miller (1913), Cambridge, MA: Harvard University Press.

Copleston, Frederick (1959), *A History of Philosophy*, Vol. V, *Modern Philosophy: The British Philosophers from Hobbes to Hume*, London: Burns & Oates.

Evensky, Jerry (2005), *Adam Smith's Moral Philosophy: A Historical and Contemporary Perspective on Markets, Law, Ethics, and Culture*, Cambridge: Cambridge University Press.

Finnis, John M. (1980), *Natural Law and Natural Rights*, Oxford: Clarendon Press.

Fitzgibbons, Athol (1995), *Adam Smith's System of Liberty, Wealth, and Virtue: The Moral and Political Foundations of The Wealth of Nations*, Oxford: Clarendon Press.

Fleischacker, Samuel (2004), *On Adam Smith's Wealth of Nations: A Philosophical Companion*, Princeton, NJ: Princeton University Press.

Fodor, Jerry (1998), 'The trouble with psychological Darwinism' (review of *How the Mind Works* by Steven Pinker and *Evolution in Mind* by Henry Plotkin), *London Review of Books*, **20** (2), available at http://humanities.Uchicago.edu/faculty/Goldsmith/CogSciCourse/Foder.htm and http://www.homestead.com/flowstate/files/fodor.html.

Foot, Philippa (1978), 'Virtues and Vices', *Virtues and Vices and Other Essays in Moral Philosophy*, Berkeley and Los Angeles, CA: University of California Press.

Frankfurt, Harry (2004), *The Reasons of Love*, Princeton, NJ: Princeton University Press.

Griswold, Charles L., Jr. (1999), *Adam Smith and the Virtues of Enlightenment*, Cambridge: Cambridge University Press.

Haakonssen, Knut (1981), *The Science of a Legislator: The Natural Jurisprudence of David Hume and Adam Smith*, Cambridge: Cambridge University Press.

Hariman, Robert (2003), 'Theory without Modernity', in Robert Hariman (ed.), *Prudence: Classical Virtue, Postmodern Practice*, University Park, PA: Pennsylvania State University Press, pp. 1–32.

Hobbes, Thomas (1651), *Leviathan*; Everyman Edition (1914), London: J.M. Dent and New York: E.P. Dutton.

Hont, Istvan and Michael Ignatieff (1983), 'Needs and justice in the *Wealth of Nations*', in I. Hont and M. Ignatieff (eds), *Wealth and Virtue*, Cambridge: Cambridge University Press, pp. 339–443.

Hooker, Richard (1593), *On the Laws of Ecclesiastical Polity*, Vol. I (Books I–IV); Everyman Edition (1907), London: J.M. Dent.
Hursthouse, Rosalind (1999), *On Virtue Ethics*, Oxford: Oxford University Press.
Hutcheson, Francis (1725), *Inquiry into the Original of our Ideas of Beauty and Virtue, in Two Treatises*; A. Garrett (ed.) (2002), Indianapolis, IN: Liberty Fund.
Hutcheson, Francis (1747), *A Short Introduction to Moral Philosophy in Three Books, containing the Elements of Ethics and the Law of Nature*; W. Leidhold (ed.) (2004), Indianapolis, IN: Liberty Fund.
Ignatieff, Michael (1984), *The Needs of Strangers*; reprint (2001), New York, USA and London, UK: Viking Penguin Books.
Ignatieff, Michael (1998), *Isaiah Berlin: A Life*, New York: Metropolitan.
Kant, Immanuel (1785), *Grounding for the Metaphysics of Morals*; trans. James Ellington (1993), Indianapolis, IN: Hackett.
Knight, Frank (1923), 'The ethics of competition', *Quarterly Journal of Economics*; reprinted in Frank Knight (1935), *The Ethics of Competition*, reprinted (1997) New Brunswick, NJ: Transaction Publishers, pp. 33–67.
MacIntyre, Alasdair (1981), *After Virtue: A Study in Moral Theory*, Notre Dame: University of Notre Dame Press.
Mandeville, Bernard (1705, 1714, 1723, 1728), *The Fable of the Bees*; F.B. Fay (ed.) (1924), Oxford: Clarendon Press; reprinted (1988), Indianapolis, IN: Liberty Fund.
Marshall, David (1986), *The Figure of Theater: Shaftesbury, Defoe, Adam Smith, and George Eliot*, New York: Columbia University Press.
McCloskey, Deirdre N. (2006), *The Bourgeois Virtues: Ethics for an Age of Commerce*, Chicago, IL: University of Chicago Press.
North, Helen F. (1973–74), 'Temperance (*Sōphrosynē*) and the canon of the cardinal virtues', in P.P. Wiener (ed.), *The Dictionary of the History of Ideas: Studies of Selected Pivotal Ideas*, Vol. 4, New York: Charles Scribner's Sons, pp. 365–78.
Nozick, Robert (1981), *Philosophical Explanations*, Cambridge, MA: Harvard University Press.
Nozick, Robert (1989), *The Examined Life: Philosophical Meditations*, New York: Simon & Schuster.
Nozick, Robert (2001), *Invariances: The Structure of the Objective World*, Cambridge, MA: Harvard University Press,
Nussbaum, Martha (1986), *The Fragility of Goodness: Luck and Ethics in Greek Tragedy and Philosophy*, Cambridge: Cambridge University Press
Nussbaum, Martha C. (2006), *Frontiers of Justice: Disability, Nationality, Species Membership*, Cambridge, MA: Harvard University Press.
Otteson, James R. (2002), *Adam Smith's Marketplace of Life*, Cambridge: Cambridge University Press.
Peterson, Christopher and Martin E.P. Seligman (2004), *Character Strengths and Virtues: A Handbook and Classification*, Oxford: Oxford University Press.
Raphael, D.D. and A.L. Macfie (1976), 'Introduction', Adam Smith, *The Theory of Moral Sentiments*, Glasgow Edition, D.D. Raphael and A.L. Macfie (eds), Oxford: Oxford University Press; reprinted (1982), Indianapolis, IN: Liberty Classics.
Rawls, John (1971), *A Theory of Justice*, Cambridge, MA: Harvard University Press.
Robbins, Lionel (1932), *The Nature and Significance of Economic Science*, London: Macmillan.
Santayana, George (1943–53), *Persons and Places*; Vol. 1 of *The Works of George Santayana* (1986), Cambridge, MA: MIT Press.
Shaftesbury, Anthony Ashley Cooper, 3rd Earl (1713, 1732), *Characteristics of Men, Manners, Opinions, Times*, 6th edn; D. Den Uyl (ed.) (2001), Indianapolis, IN: Liberty Fund.
Singer, Peter (1993), *Practical Ethics*, 2nd edn, Cambridge: Cambridge University Press.
Smith, Adam (1759, 1790), *The Theory of Moral Sentiments*, Glasgow Edition, D.D. Raphael and A.L. Macfie (eds) (1976), Oxford: Oxford University Press; reprinted (1982), Indianapolis, IN: Liberty Classics.
Smith, Adam (1776), *An Inquiry in to the Nature and Causes of the Wealth of Nations*, 2 vols, Glasgow Edition, R.H. Campbell, A.S. Skinner and W.B. Todd (eds) (1976), Oxford: Oxford University Press; reprinted (1981), Indianapolis, IN: Liberty Classics.
Smith, Adam (1977), *Correspondence of Adam Smith*, Glasgow Edition, E.C. Mossner and I.S. Ross (eds), Oxford: Oxford University Press.
Smith, Adam (1980), *Essays on Philosophical Subjects*, Glasgow Edition, W.P.D. Wightman and J.J. Bryce (eds), Oxford: Oxford University Press.
Strauss, Leo (1953), *Natural Right and History*, Chicago, IL: University of Chicago Press.
Todorov, Tzvetan (2000), *Hope and Memory: Lessons from the Twentieth Century*; trans. David Bellos (2003), Princeton, NJ: Princeton University Press.
Toulmin, Stephen and Albert Jonsen (1987), *The Abuse of Casuistry: A History of Moral Reasoning*, Berkeley and Los Angeles, CA: University of California Press.

Van Norden, Bryan W. (2004), 'The virtue of righteousness in Mencius', in Kwong-Loi Shun and David B. Wong (eds), *Confucian Ethics: A Comparative Study of Self, Autonomy, and Community*, Cambridge: Cambridge University Press, pp. 148–82.
Wolf, Susan (1982), 'Moral saints', *Journal of Philosophy*, **79**, 419–39; reprinted in Roger Crisp and Michael Slote (1997), *Virtue Ethics*, Oxford: Oxford University Press, pp. 79–98.
Wolfe, Alan (2001), *Moral Freedom: The Search for Virtue in a world of Choice*, New York and London: Norton.

2 Adam Smith and Aristotle
Gloria Vivenza

In this chapter I will return to and expand upon certain aspects of the relationship between Adam Smith and the classical philosophers, dedicating particular attention to Aristotle, one of the classical authors with whom we so often have to deal.

It is generally considered that Adam Smith was indebted principally to the Hellenistic philosophies. This view need not necessarily be disputed: the Hellenistic philosophies, or rather their seventeenth-century revival, effectively played a significant role by supplying arguments and instruments to the beginnings of modern science, as well as to political and moral philosophy of course. The scientific revolution as well as the political theories were greatly influenced by the revival of the Hellenistic philosophies. Nevertheless the end result was distinctly modern: the ancient philosophers served principally to aid modern thinkers in developing new ideas.[1]

Aristotle did not disappear entirely from the scene however. Numerous scholars have emphasized the enduring presence of his thought in the modern age, despite its being regarded as fundamentally anti-Aristotelian.

Here I will endeavour to highlight just how much Smith owes to the Aristotle that survived in studies of the philosophy of praxis, the Aristotle that outlived other influences which may nevertheless have altered his original spirit,[2] at least in part. This is not the metaphysical, scholastic Aristotle that we find between the lines in Adam Smith. It is a rather different Aristotle, the Aristotle of the texts on ethics that shares certain remarkable similarities with Smith's thought, such as certain criteria identifiable by feeling rather than reason, for example.

Aristotle after the Middle Ages

Modern science was born under the sign of anti-Aristotelianism, and for a long time appeared as a reaction against the Middle Ages and against scholasticism, which placed 'the philosopher' at the basis of every inquiry. This misconception was rectified long ago, and Aristotle's fundamental role in the Renaissance both in Italy and elsewhere in Europe has been acknowledged.

As stated in H.C. Lohr's brief but effective summary, the 'monolithic' medieval Aristotle survived only in the Catholic Church.[3] Nevertheless a more 'secular' Aristotle was also to be found in Italy at least, where research in the medical and scientific fields was breaking free from theological methods.[4] France, Great Britain, the Netherlands and Germany maintained in their school curricula the Aristotelian encyclopaedia,[5] open to the new subjects which had aroused interest in the sixteenth century: mathematics, mechanics, rhetoric, poetics and even Platonism itself, as C.B. Schmitt has shown. We are also grateful to Schmitt for his illuminating account of how Renaissance Aristotelianism, far from being a rigid and inflexible system, was crossed by an eclectic current and even inspired by neo-Platonic elements.[6] Even the Jesuits, who wrote a series of highly authoritative commentaries at the University of Coimbra which influenced not only the Catholic universities but also many Protestant environments, showed an interest in mathematics and astronomy alongside their Aristotelian curricula. As a result many of their interpretations were closer to the 'revolutionary' Galileo than to traditional scholastic positions.[7] At least a mention should also be made of the finest sixteenth-century editions of Aristotle: at the time the wealth of Italian bibliography was spreading throughout Europe, and the *antiquae translationes* were being published alongside the humanistic translations, allowing the medieval Aristotle, the Aristotle retrieved by the humanists and the commentaries of Averroés and Leonardo Bruni to be reunited, with great critical awareness.[8]

It is therefore perfectly legitimate to speak of 'Aristotelianisms' in the plural to indicate the various ways in which European educational reform endeavoured to address the new forms with ancient tools;[9] this demonstrates the great versatility and vigour with which the Stagirite's philosophy not only survived but was highly influential in schools and universities at least until the end of the seventeenth century.

Lohr's intuition that this multiform Aristotle closely resembles the real Aristotle, and much more so than the medieval Aristotle, who was confined to a clerical mould, is rather relevant. Aristotle's philosophy was underpinned by a spirit of free research, and however paradoxical it may seem, it was this very spirit that brought about the end of theological synthesis and traditional authority in scientific methods.[10]

Neither the revolt against scholasticism nor the success of other ancient philosophies opposed to Aristotelianism should induce us to overlook the startling expansion of Aristotelian studies between 1500 and 1650,[11] partly the result of efforts made by the universities to adapt traditional structures to the new circumstances.

Undoubtedly Latin played an important role, just as it had done for the medieval Aristotle. Despite the humanistic-Renaissance interest in Greek, commentaries were in Latin; furthermore Latin translations abounded alongside compendia, anthologies, synoptic tables and many other tools which allowed works to be committed to memory regardless of whether the original Greek text had been consulted directly.

In particular, Aristotle's works on ethics, which had already been translated into Latin in the Middle Ages and edited with commentary by philosophers of the calibre of Albert the Great, St Thomas and Buridan (not to mention other lesser but nevertheless authoritative scholars) were retranslated into the elegant, humanistic Latin and edited by Leonardo Bruni of Arezzo. This paved the way for the fruitful interaction between the Aristotelian philosophy of praxis[12] and the themes of the so-called civic humanism.[13]

The diffusion of Aristotle's works on ethics not only outlived his scientific synthesis[14] but also reached far more widely in Northern Europe than in Italy; the widely accepted explanation for this can be found in the school, or rather university, curricula. The northern universities were more oriented towards theology and hence towards questions of a moral nature than the Italian universities, which specialized in science.[15] The *Nichomachean Ethics* was printed more than any other Aristotelian text in the sixteenth century.[16]

The particular attention dedicated to the philosophy of praxis, or rather to how to behave in the concrete situations of life, also emphasized the economic aspects of Aristotle's thought. Here I am not referring to the studies which were prevalent in the Middle Ages on just price or on usury, or to medieval intuitions on the concept of value, but rather to the copious series of sixteenth-century treatises inspired by behaviour which implied attention to worldly things, to sound household management and to the search for wealth in order to use it for good causes and for the benefit of oneself, one's family and the state. As we know, this literature derived from classical works such as Xenophon's *Oeconomicus* and the pseudo-Aristotelian *Oikonomikà*, or the Latin treatises *De Re Rustica*.

This thread of thought consists of a number of arguments relating to public life, and hence to the social and political status of the head of the household within the town or state: to what we now call the paradigm of civic humanism. In my opinion the most Aristotelian aspect is that of independence: it is well known that Aristotle did not seek wealth for its own sake, but as a way to achieve the self-sufficiency of the family or the *polis*. It is this aspect that in modern times was theorized, following the principle that the economic independence of the 'republican' citizen guaranteed his political independence.[17] Another important Aristotelian influence, endorsed by Cicero, was the idea that property guaranteed the personality of the individual.[18]

Another important principle has been inferred from modern studies of sixteenth-century treatises on economics: the rehabilitation of types of economic activity other than agriculture, as a reaction to the Franciscan ideal of poverty. This approach, supported by the leading scholars of humanism (H. Baron, E. Garin) has recently been challenged:[19] also because in Italy, from the turn of the fifteenth century to the 'long' sixteenth century and seventeenth century, there was a shift towards an aristocratic elite which turned its back on mercantile values.[20]

This brief and inadequate introduction serves to clarify an underlying question. It is well known that the Hellenistic philosophies (Stoicism, Epicureanism, Scepticism) had the lion's share in modern times, probably because they combined a greater attention to the complexities of individual behaviour with a lesser attention to the organization of the city-state. The latter had already been superseded by the Hellenistic *koiné*, although the language and fundamental concepts of politics had already been established (the fact that recently the urge was felt to write a book on the City of the Stoics (Schofield, 1999) and that attempts have often been made to understand more about their behaviour in politics[21] is not sufficient to erase the fact that for the Stoics, politics was not a primary issue in the same way as it was for the great classical philosophers).

The aim of these brief remarks is to recall that from the Renaissance onwards, Aristotle not only had not disappeared from scholarship, but on the contrary provided the fundamental structures with which to analyse behaviour at a personal, household, social and, in part, political level.

Aristotle and Middle Stoicism

In 1985 F.H. Sandbach wrote a brief essay entitled *Aristotle and the Stoics*, principally concerned with the early Stoa, despite a short section on Panaetius and Posidonius, which argued that contacts between Stoicism and Aristotelian philosophy were non-existent, or virtually so.

I entirely agree that the two doctrines were radically opposed. Nevertheless it is also true that 'philosophers cannot escape their intellectual environment',[22] which may make it seem strange that the early Stoa showed no interest in Aristotle's philosophy, as Sandbach[23] argues. I agree with those who believe that if indeed one of the two 'greats' of Greek philosophy can be likened to the Stoics, it is Plato,[24] whose views were markedly more radical than Aristotle's.

The middle Stoa's relationship with Aristotle was less antagonistic than that of the early Stoa; this is what we intend to consider here. The great transmitter of moderate Stoicism in modern times was of course Cicero in De Officiis, whose declared source was Panaetius. Other authors, perhaps closer to the original Stoa, were read and loved rather than actually followed (Seneca, Marcus Aurelius, Epictectus, Diogenes Laertius),[25] while the De Officiis served as a manual for the education of the ruling classes throughout Europe: its influence was undeniable and highly pervasive.

Panaetius, who inspired the De Officiis, was well acquainted with both Aristotle and Plato; Cicero himself attests his high consideration of both men in the passage in which he laments the excessive rigour of the Stoics. Cicero also asserts that in Panaetius's writings there is a clear and constant presence of less 'extreme' philosophers than the Stoics (as well as Plato and Aristotle, Cicero mentions Xenocrates, Theophrastus and Dicaearcus).[26]

The so-called middle Stoa probably developed precisely because the basic concepts of the original doctrine were impossible to apply to concrete social life, and in particular to social life in Rome, which not by chance was the principal 'user' of moderate Stoicism. In fact it would have been impossible to adhere to the original doctrine, which tended to break up hierarchies: the paradox, quoted by Smith (TMS VII.ii.1.40), that killing a cock or one's own father were equally reproachable would have been inconceivable in a state in which the *paterfamilias* had so many rights over things and persons that it was impossible not to be dependent upon him. The original Stoicism was anti-hierarchical and egalitarian:[27] a position intrinsically opposed to the structure of Roman society. It is hardly surprising that Stoicism had to tone down this characteristic in order to take hold in Rome.

This is certainly not the only paradox to emerge from the history of a philosophy which started out in a radical form and ended as the emblem of a conservative and somewhat class-ridden establishment.[28] We should also bear in mind that all available sources on Stoic philosophy spring from the period of Roman supremacy, even if they are in Greek – which may have partially influenced the reception of the doctrine.[29]

This is not the place for a thorough treatment of the issue. However I would briefly like to say that the initially rigoristic attitude of Stoic philosophy (as well as equality, other fundamental characteristics were the absence of gradation of the scale of values, and the qualification only of virtue as 'good') began to become more moderate as early as the second century BC; or rather, a part of Stoicism distanced itself from the rigoristic positions. It was this part that moved towards the emergent power of Rome, after the extremist ideology of the Stoics had played an important role in the so-called 'Spartan revolution' in the third century BC.[30]

Panaetius of Rhodes was in perfect harmony with the circle of the Scipios and the conservative attitudes of the Roman *nobilitas* connected with the hierarchical and timocratic constitution, while more traditionalist exponents of the doctrine such as Blossius of Cumae inspired the opposition movement of the Gracchans.[31] Panaetius as a source for Cicero has obviously attracted a great deal of attention in modern times. The fact that numerous studies have been dedicated to him is singular for an author none of whose texts have survived. We are interested in elements alien to the early Stoa in his work, such as his interest in legal justice and its contrast with the concept of *aequitas*;[32] but above all his conviction that it was right for those unable to govern themselves to be governed by others.³³ This is clearly an Aristotelian, rather than a Stoic, concept and it would be superfluous to point out how perfectly suited it was to the Roman legal system in which only a (very small) part of the population was *sui iuris*.

The issue was by no means exclusively, or prevalently, political: Aristotle had already drawn a parallel between relationships of authority within the family and within the state,³⁴ which on account of its size could be defined as a set of families. This argument sanctioned a hierarchical structure within the family and the state, with the addition of moralistic Stoic themes such as the analogy between institutional and figurative slavery (the non-virtuous are 'slaves' to their own errors) which, thanks to the mediation of Christian thinkers,³⁵ added value to the concept of subordination, that had been absent in the early Stoa.

From the Middle Ages onwards, the triad God–sovereign–head of the family established an analogy between divine, regal and paternal authority,³⁶ justified by the supposed advantage it brought to the subordinate. In modern times we are repeatedly told that it is in the interest of man to be governed by God, in the same way that subjects are ruled by their king, and children by their parents:³⁷ an argument tailor-made for feudal society.

This type of subordination, which naturally implies the classification of a whole series of rights and duties depending on the individual's role in the family, the society and the state, is the result of re-elaboration of classical principles, from the categories of Aristotelian ethics to the sum of powers of the Roman *paterfamilias*. However it does not correspond to the principles of the early Stoa, in which only the wise man can govern himself, and no one in the world can govern him. The fact that at the time of Panaetius Stoicism was oriented in the opposite direction, or at least had highlighted the fact that since not all men are wise,³⁸ those who are not should be governed by others, made it possible for this doctrine to be happily accepted in Rome, a city in which radical and egalitarian principles would never have taken hold. It also explains how *this* Stoa was welcomed triumphantly in modern times, when society was structured in such a way that all men, except the sovereign, had to accept subordination to a superior level in the hierarchy.³⁹ Only a few understood that true Stoicism was radically different in character.⁴⁰

This explains the well-known criticism related by Cicero that the Stoics and Peripatetics differed more in their words than in their concepts.⁴¹ Panaetius was a Stoic, yet he derived some of his principles from Aristotle:⁴² presumably his readers were able to distinguish for themselves.

Probably between the seventeenth and eighteenth centuries even the well-educated moderns required no further explanation: although this was a topic for specialized philosophers, it was not necessary to specify that an element adopted by the middle Stoa was actually of Peripatetic derivation, since it was well known by all. Francis Hutcheson deemed it unnecessary to cite his sources since: 'The learned will at once discern how much of this compound is taken from the writings of others, from Cicero and Aristotle'.⁴³ However uncustomary this may seem today, it perfectly reflected the situation in the eighteenth century.

And today? It is apparently well known that the Stoics transmitted by the Latin authors lost the rigour of the old school, but we generally forget that this 'toning down' came about thanks to the Peripatetic elements which contrasted with the original Stoic positions.⁴⁴ I think it is obvious that if the middle Stoa adopted an Aristotelian principle, then it remained such even when it became part of Stoicism, and even more so when the principle was effectively the opposite of that proclaimed by the early Stoa.[45] In other words I believe it is appropriate to adhere as closely as possible to the original doctrine of a philosophy. I certainly do not intend to underestimate the middle Stoa, which was of great historical importance even in modern times; however, given the long-standing complexity of the relationship between the ancients and the moderns, today a wealth of principles are described as 'Stoic', as I have already had the occasion to mention.[46]

In conclusion a little clarity is required when theories can be attributed to both schools. If after a couple of centuries the Stoics embraced the theory that human relationships are graded by their intensity from the closest to the most distant (and with it the relevant duties), we should not forget that this theory was originally expounded by Aristotle. The Stoics derived it from Aristotle, hence it is an Aristotelian theory; neither should we forget that the original Stoic theory stated exactly the opposite.[47]

Smith and Aristotle

At first sight, the relationship between Smith and Aristotelian philosophy would appear to be one of conflict, at least judging from the following evidence: in terms of method, Smith declares a preference for Newtonian methodology (LRBL ii.133–4); the fact that Aristotle subdivided his already unintelligible dialectics into logic and metaphysics created more problems than it solved (HALM 1); even the structure of his writing, whether on ethics or other themes, is considered by Smith to be so burdened with divisions, classifications and so forth as to appear confused and disorganized. Smith concludes his assessment with a characteristic observation: 'that they produce the very effect he intended to have avoided by them Viz. Confusion' (LRBL ii.130).

There is also a degree of reservation in Smith's comment: 'Aristotle, who seems in many things original, and who endeavoured to seem to be so in all things' (HALM 8);[48] and in the slightly surprised observation that Aristotle included in his catalogue of virtues 'even jocularity and good humour' (TMS VII.iv.5), earning himself the label 'that indulgent philosopher' which I believe not many have attributed to Aristotle.

The fact that the celestial spheres move everything without knowing or wanting to reminds us singularly of the invisible hand,[49] but in early essays this is defined as a 'not very philosophical' prejudice (HAPh 10) since the revolutions of the skies presuppose some sort of divine intelligence – one of Smith's rare forays into theological issues.

If we now turn our attention to the positive aspects and leave aside questions of a 'technical' nature,[50] we should remind ourselves of Smith's observation in the *Theory of Moral Sentiments* (TMS VII.ii.1.17): 'The Peripatetics allowed of some degree of perturbation as suitable to the weakness of human nature, and as useful to so imperfect a creature as man', which sounds rather like implicit support of this vision of human nature in contrast to Stoic apathy.[51]

A further element which Smith acknowledges to have derived from Aristotle, this time explicitly, is the well-known passage on the 'propriety of conduct' which I have already treated on a previous occasion.[52] Here it is perhaps worthwhile investigating how much Smith derived from Aristotle and how much from Plato, since he notes an analogy with his concept of 'propriety' in both authors. (Here I would like to open a parenthesis and reiterate that when Smith claims to derive his concept from one of the ancients, we should take him seriously. I am inclined to think that he was capable of recognizing that his 'propriety' derived from Aristotle rather than from the Stoics, and that it was not necessary to wait for some much less learned twentieth and twenty-first-century classicist for the correct diagnosis. I remain convinced that when Smith states that his 'propriety' resembles an Aristotelian concept, that 'every man keeps to his own place' resembles a Platonic concept, and that the Stoic system should not be followed – TMS VII.ii.1.11;12;43 – we should pay heed to his words.)

As far as the phrase in TMS VII.ii.1.11 is concerned, it is preceded by a summary of Platonic theory drawn principally from *The Republic* (*Rep.* IV). After touching on the three parts of the soul and the four cardinal virtues, Smith digresses on the subject of justice, which according to Plato is respected when 'each of those three faculties of the mind confined itself to its proper office, without attempting to encroach upon that of any other' (VII.ii.1.9). This is precisely what Plato defines '*to ta tou autou prattein*' (*Rep.* 433A), in short to stay at one's own place and not encroach on others' competence. In sum, 'that of all the things in the city each man should take care of the one most suited to his nature' (ibid.). Plato's phrase is clearly an invitation, supported by *Rep.* 434 B–C, not to switch between categories. In other words, if an individual was born to work, he should work and not expect to govern the city or perform other activities not suited to him. This passage has often been singled out[53] as an example of the archaic view of the economy and the social rigidity in Plato's ideal city.

Smith indeed attributes to lack of time, and not to 'natural' differences among men, the necessity of specializing the professions, including politics.[54] His interpretation of ancient history is in accordance with the principle, both Platonic and Aristotelian, that working people should not be involved in politics; the right to vote that ancient constitutions gave indiscriminately to all citizens was considered by Smith an institutional flaw.

Smith's digression on justice (TMS VII.ii.1.10), based on Aristotelian and Scholastic concepts as well as theories of natural law, centres on the distinction between commutative and distributive justice. To avoid repetition of what I have written elsewhere,[55] here I will only say that in modern times distributive justice came to mean some sort of legitimization of the social hierarchy and its inherent duties and rights. Indeed *this* type of justice also includes 'proper beneficence' (ibid.), namely the generous behaviour that should be implicit in the status of the superior classes. Hence the element of 'propriety' which Smith declares to have derived from Plato is the appropriate use of each virtue in relation to one's station in life, and as such the perfection of each type of virtue.

It is no coincidence, in my view, that in the two very similar phrases with which Smith connects his 'propriety' with Aristotle and Plato (TMS VII.ii.1.11 and 12) there is a very significant difference: he claims to derive only 'propriety' from Plato, and both 'propriety and impropriety' from Aristotle. In fact Smith derives from Aristotle the more technical aspect of propriety, the one that I have already compared to Aristotle's *mesotes*. A straightforward comparison between the *Nicomachean Ethics* and TMS is sufficient to demonstrate that there are too many coincidences to deny that Smith's 'propriety' is connected to the golden mean. Clearly I am not referring to the passage in which Smith openly summarizes Aristotle (TMS VII.ii.1.12–14), but rather to the one in which he speaks for himself (TMS I.ii.intro.1–2). As I have already observed,[56] Smith's doctrine of sympathy is an integral part of the passage, so it would not be appropriate to say that 'propriety' corresponds exactly to Aristotle's golden mean; however if we look at the constituent elements of the golden mean, these are exactly the elements we find in Smith.[57]

As for the term 'mediocrity' which Smith uses in the above passage, one scholar recently preferred the Latin *medietas* or *mediocritas* to the English (and the Italian, as a matter of fact), precisely to avoid the negative connotation[58] of the word 'mediocrity'. Indeed we can never stress sufficiently that in this case Smith's 'mediocrity', just like Aristotle's 'mediocrity', is not a compromise but the perfection of the virtue, the maximum attainable.[59]

To my mind the most significant difference between Smith and Aristotle is that Smith considers this attitude essential to the sympathetic reaction. In other words he never leaves relational situations aside: even when his spectator is a figment of the imagination, he is still an indispensable, structural figure who is, however, distinct from the subject in a number of ways. He is a 'double', a witness and a judge; but he must also be emotionally involved ('go along with', TMS I.ii.intro.1). This alone should be sufficient to demolish any hypothesis of a Stoic origin.

The spectator in TMS also has something of the Aristotelian 'man of practical wisdom' (*phronimos*) in the sense that the 'point of propriety' cannot be measured with rational tools such as laws, rules and reasoning: something that depends upon 'sense and feeling' cannot be subjected to reason and casuistic rules. The fact that it must be evaluated by a wise man means that no scientific measure can offer the same results as the intuition of a virtuous man.[60] Even Aristotle, despite offering an almost mathematical image as an example – bearing witness to the intellectualism of classical Greek morality – argues that 'Prudence (*sc. phronesis*)[61] deals with the ultimate particular things which cannot be apprehended by scientific knowledge, but only by perception: not the perception of the special senses, but that sort of intuition whereby we perceive that the ultimate figure in mathematics is a triangle' (NE 1142a27–29, Rackham's transl.); and, 'Yet to what degree and how seriously a man must err to be blamed is not easy to define on principle. For in fact no object of perception is easy to define; and such questions of degree depend on particular circumstances, and the decision lies with perception' (NE 1109b20–23).[62] See also NE 1126b2–4 for similar wording which inevitably reminds us of TMS VII.iii.2.7.

It is nevertheless clear that this measurement, obtained thanks not to reasoning but rather to the sensibility and judgement of a wise man, is by no means arbitrary or subjective. In its own way it is a precise measure,[63] and this is what allows both Aristotle and Smith to say that *meson* is the perfection of virtue, the highest that can be attained.

It is this that gives Smith's man of virtue, supported by the satisfied spectator, the strength to go against everyone and everything when he knows he is right. For a philosophy which is so attentive to the social aspects of human life, the existence of a *vox populi* ('the man without', TMS III.2.32) which condemns certain types of behaviour should not be underestimated. After all these are the same common people, the majority of mankind, who abide by the rules of conventional virtue which cannot be achieved by complying with 'propriety' but by respecting a given code, formulated by means of reasoning and experience, and expressed in term of rules supported by social consensus – a behaviour which Smith certainly does not disdain, although he considers it imperfect.[64] Yet if behaviour judged honest by the 'man within' meets with the disapproval of the majority of society, then the honest man can, indeed should, disregard such a judgement (TMS III.2.32). He acted according to true 'propriety' and it is the others who are wrong.

In my opinion this behaviour cannot be reconciled with *decorum*, which from Waszek onwards is singled out as the most likely classical precedent of Smith's 'propriety'.[65] As I have already suggested, *decorum* is surely an aesthetic concept, relating to outward appearances. Naturally this does not necessarily involve relying only upon appearances or hypocritical behaviour. On the contrary, the true meaning of *decorum* is the reflection on the outside of an inner state of perfect equilibrium. Since inner equilibrium and harmony shun excesses, a certain overlap is comprehensible between *decorum* and *medietas*. However the similarity is achieved by an instrumental use of the golden mean. Behaviour is regulated in order to avoid extremes, stopping somewhere in the middle to respect the ideal of balance and harmony, which is assumed to be present on the inside, given that it is visible on the outside. Clearly such behaviour is *ex post*: perfect equilibrium is not reached by intuition, but by behaving in a manner considered excellent by the social conscience.

Rather than the perfection of sensibility and virtue, this is the best way to give a good impression of oneself, a constructed technique. It is rather significant that Smith alludes to *decorum* only in relation to artistic works, or social conventions in everyday life, and that *decorum* was often connected to the value of conversation.[66] Examples of the first type can be found in TMS I.ii.1.11; III.5.11; LRBL ii.93 (associated with propriety); of the second in TMS V.2.10; IV.i.10; VII.iv.21.

Since the times of W.R. Scott there has been a tendency to parallel Smith's 'propriety' to the Greek *prepon*, translated in Latin as *decorum* (Cicero Or. 21, 70–72), so it would perhaps now be appropriate to trace the history of this concept.

Decorum and behaviour

Quite rightly Cicero is considered an important source of transmission of the concept of *decorum* to modern times. Cicero defined *decorum* in the *De Officiis*,[67] and a source of ambiguity may be the fact that Cicero included *decorum* as part of temperance (*De Off.* I, 93–151), a virtue opposed to excesses and thus connected with the 'middle way' that shuns excess.

Cicero's *decorum* corresponds to the concept I outlined above. It is the exterior representation of 'moral beauty' (perceived in gestures, manner and behaviour in general), what the Greeks termed *kalon* and Cicero translated with the term *honestum*. We should already be on the alert here, as the words themselves are significant.[68] Cicero could have chosen the translation *pulchrum*, but avoided it, unlike a seventeenth century commentator.[69]

As we have already said, it is not just a matter of appearances. Nevertheless *decorum* focuses unmistakeably on the exterior: 'orderly' behaviour requires rigorous self-control,[70] allowing no emotional urges. Even subtle changes in behaviour have moral significance insofar as they offer exterior evidence of interior harmony.[71]

The great revival of interest in Cicero in the sixteenth century, when court treatises were inspired by the *De Officiis*, is well known. It has been observed that Cicero did not intend to establish a code of conduct for the noble classes, as became the case in the Renaissance. Indeed it would be more appropriate to liken the *De Officiis* to Erasmus's *De Civilitate* than to Castiglione's *Cortegiano*[72] as usual. The *decorum* of Panaetius and Cicero, which set out to establish the propriety of conduct of various figures in a variety of circumstances, actually became an integral part of sixteenth century treatises on behaviour. We cannot stress sufficiently the importance of the philosophy of praxis from humanism onwards, from which a whole series of codes of conduct derive. The time has come to examine a literary genre which has only recently been appreciated and considered within the realms of political economy, in Italy at least, but which is vital to our understanding of how things really stood at the time. The principal characteristics of the numerous treatises on family and civil life were: (1) an Aristotelian hierarchy of family relationships (to which I referred above[73] when I alluded to the tripartition of family relationships in *Pol.* 1253b6–7), which of course in modern times constituted the starting point for social and political hierarchies, not to mention religious ones; (2) a classical basis for the care of oneself and family property, which for the families belonging to the ruling class extended to the government of the *respublica*:[74] here Roman as well as Greek thought is significant, since the census structure of ancient Rome was fundamental, and it was necessary to preserve family property in order not to lose the right to political office;[75] (3) the exercise of virtues and moral values, of classical origin but profoundly transformed by Christianity, in private and public activity. Here fundamental virtues were justice and prudence.[76] The overall importance of this literature was that it preserved the status and role of the ruling classes in the *ancien régime*, at the same time as respecting all the competences and hierarchical functions.

This is the core of the extensive literature on behaviour (of which Castiglione's celebrated *Cortegiano* is only the best-known example). It had a precise importance, which was far from secondary as we might be led to believe, in establishing codes of conduct for every member of society, whether big or small. It also set out the rights and duties of those who commanded and those who obeyed, within the family, within society and in the various institutions such as the court, the nobility and the church. Beyond the apparently frivolous rules of precedence, of dress and so forth, were the real relationships of power. Every act was codified and represented the role of the individual who performed it within civil society. Every man had to maintain his status and not surpass the limits assigned to him (a gentleman fought only with his equal).

At this point it would be appropriate to consider Plato's *ta tou autou prattein*; however, as I have mentioned on previous occasions, the influence of the classical philosophers inspired modern culture in a variety of ways. What I would like to underline in this context is that there is some degree of overlap between *decorum* (predictably a protagonist in these treatises) and *mediocritas*, both in public and in private spheres.

The practical virtue which put abstract rules into practice by applying them to single cases was, of course, prudence. The behaviour of both the head of the household and the sovereign who ruled over a state[77] had to be typically prudent and, inevitably, calculating, rather than rash or excessive, or disproportionate to the status of the individual. Here *mediocritas* in the sense of awareness of limits came into play: every man was bound by the limits of his status to respect the constitutive principle of the *ancien régime* society. That principle was proportionality, clearly derived from the Aristotelian concept of distributive justice, yet appropriately modified to preserve authority at all levels of the hierarchy. Thus the Aristotelian base was broadened: Aristotle was concerned with the head of the household in his triple role of father, husband and master, namely in his 'private' aspect; but the social, political and religious structure of the modern age (from the Middle Ages onwards, in reality) called for a much more complex hierarchy, both private and public: so it became necessary to use a different type of prudence for each category, public or private.[78]

Note also that a relationship of sorts is evident between prudence and *mediocritas* in the true sense of 'mediocrity': the prudent-calculating individual never bites off more than he can chew, and his unrelenting weighing up of pros and cons ensures that he sticks to a moderate course of action, avoiding all extremities. This indeed is true 'mediocrity', certainly not the perfect point of equilibrium between the two excesses which constitutes the golden mean.

Adam Smith's 'mediocrity'
I think we can be certain that Smith was in favour of the type of social stability described above. Despite his frequent expressions of sympathy and solidarity towards the less fortunate classes and the sincere desire to see their lot bettered, we know that Smith considered this possible only by means of better organization of labour, capital and resources, and not through changes in the social structure, which Smith respected in terms of justice, as I have commented elsewhere.[79]

What interests me here is the extent to which Aristotelian themes are present in Smith, more in terms of the private virtue of the individual than in terms of civic humanism.[80] Arguments of an economic nature have recently been analysed in Smith's work as examples of *medietas*,[81] but even if we restrict ourselves to moral philosophy this is a complex matter. Clearly the idea of *meden agan* (no excess), again of Greek origin, lends itself to a whole host of interpretations relating to a wide range of subjects. On the other hand, as I mentioned above, the Ciceronian link between *decorum* and temperance may have fostered some degree of overlap, since both concepts stem from a sense of restraint, intended as moderation.

Finding one's bearings in the vast wealth of modern literature is no easy task, particularly when arguments relating to behaviour, virtue, and the rights and duties of a man's status were constantly re-elaborated and expanded upon. What I have been able to observe, obviously from a limited survey, is that Aristotle and Cicero were frequently used to explain the relationship between *decorum*, *honestum*, moderation, moral beauty and good.[82] Cicero was explained via Aristotle and vice versa; or rather, their concepts were incorporated to complete what was unsaid, or inadequately explained in the original text. Comparisons were made between *decorum*, *honestum* and *modus* (moderation), and even *meson* (the golden mean).[83] *Mediocritas* was related to geometrical proportion; and *decorum*, which was connected with *honestum* on the basis of Cicero, somehow became a relative concept: it was no longer equal for all, but differed according to people, places, ages and circumstances.[84] It is impossible to convey just how much debate surrounded these interpretations, and equally hard to know just how much of this complex reasoning found its way into the moral philosophy of the various modern authors.

The humanistic and Renaissance passion for the classics meant that the ancients were studied meticulously. Efforts were made to 'reconstruct' their world, as well as to explore their relationship with the Christian faith, particularly in terms of morals. Indeed one of the texts I have consulted is entitled *Ethica Aristotelica, ad Sacrarum Literarum normam emendate* (Crell, n.d.), which was followed by *Ethica Christiana*.

A further, and rather different aspect to consider is the complexity of Aristotle's text, which was certainly not straightforward to translate, and provoked countless commentaries, discussions and interpretations. Let us now attempt to determine which elements in Smith's work can be attributed with certainty to Aristotle, following the indications of

Smith himself. Indeed Smith speaks both of 'mediocrity' and *decorum*: I am convinced that he uses the terms appropriately.

First and foremost, there is nothing to suggest that he confuses or superimposes them. On the contrary, 'mediocrity' appears in TMS only twice, if I am not mistaken, and on one occasion (TMS VII.ii.1.12) Smith speaks on behalf of Aristotle.[85] So we are left with the introduction (TMS I.ii.intro.1): 'The propriety of every passion excited by objects peculiarly related to ourselves, the pitch which the spectator can go along with, must lie, it is evident, in a certain mediocrity.'

The presence of the spectator clearly indicated that Smith had rendered his own the Aristotelian principle, but Aristotle is clearly visible in his words: the 'objects peculiarly related to ourselves' corresponds exactly to 'the mean relative to us' of NE 1107a1, for example. This concept was subsequently taken further in the texts mentioned above, and a distinction was made between a mean relative to us, to others and in absolute terms.[86] Obviously these were medieval elaborations based on Aristotle's text (for instance NE 1106a24–1106b7) and there is no room for further consideration here. It must be underlined, however, that the expression 'relating to ourselves' represents a principle of personal choice, a self-regulated conduct of life, not imposed from outside, therefore not conventional or dependent on 'rules'.

Even Smith's clarifications remind us of Aristotle: 'Grief and resentment [. . .] may be too high [. . .] they may likewise [. . .] be too low' (ibid.). Aristotle's individual can 'feel desire or anger or pity' (1106b18) which may be excessive or not enough: at least one of the examples is analogous. Smith subsequently defines two negative extremes, which recapitulate the concepts that Aristotle treats at greater length in NE, Chapters 7 and 8 (1107a28–1109a19), where he describes numerous virtues and their corresponding vices.

Also the pitch, or degree of propriety, the term Smith uses to indicate the involvement of the spectator (TMS I.i.4.7–10) – a factor considered difficult to perceive in precise terms – reminds us of the typical Aristotelian example (a well-executed work is that which requires nothing to be added or taken away; NE 1106b9–10). One influential scholar recalls that the golden mean is between two extremes which are not values, but excesses. The golden mean is:

> defined inductively, starting from the excesses themselves. This doctrine, which may seem ethically scandalous, must be understood from the standpoint of how to find the right reaction in actual cases. It is immediately clear when one overreacts, i.e. when an emotional reaction is too strong or too weak; it is more difficult to decide when the emotional reaction is right.[87]

Other aspects shared by Aristotle and Smith are the admissibility of a slight deviation from perfection[88] and the difficulty of identifying the *meson* (NE 1109a22–4), something that comes naturally only to the man of excellence.

The latter has been likened, and not only by myself,[89] to the impartial spectator. I repeat once again that I likened the two figures on the grounds of their common function, namely to judge the point of propriety or golden mean. The two figures do in fact differ significantly: Smith's spectator, as we know, participates, while in Aristotle's more intellectualist approach, the wise man is more detached in his judgement, which is not, however, exclusively theoretical but also concerns practical behaviour.

This inevitably brings us to Fleischacker's book of 1999, which links Adam Smith to Aristotle on the basis of the virtue known as *phronesis* in Greek, which however Fleischacker interprets rather curiously. He identifies Aristotle's *phronesis* with Adam Smith's 'judgment', considering the latter as important as the self-interest which is a key concept in the WN. Fleischacker considers judgement and *phronesis* to be so closely related that he uses the adjective 'phronetic' to describe activities inspired by good judgement and common sense. There is certainly an Aristotelian ring to the word, if not to the meaning. In this way morals, far from being excluded from WN, play an important role, since every man must develop his own *phronesis* so that 'government non-interference with human actions can itself be a way to help people develop their characters' (p. 120). Why this type of policy in general, namely non-interference, is considered Aristotelian is not entirely clear. Fleischacker does point out the main difference between the two authors, of whom Aristotle is in favour of hierarchy while Smith, according to his interpretation, is egalitarian. He maintains, however, that Aristotle's ethics could be 'open to egalitarian uses', therefore Adam Smith's *Wealth of Nations* 'lays out an egalitarian, and non-teleological, version of Aristotle' (p. 119). In short, we ought to search for egalitarianism in Aristotle's various *Ethics*, rather than in the *Politics*, and from Aristotelian ethics Smith would have derived his egalitarianism. Fleischacker concludes that Smith 'turned Aristotle to nonteleological and egalitarian uses' (p. 120). I do not wish to dwell on the extent to which Smith himself was non-teleological and egalitarian: such issues are difficult to ascertain with certainty and I agree with parts of Fleischacker's analysis; nevertheless, despite Fleischacker's numerous arguments, I do not consider Smith completely egalitarian, although his celebrated comparison of the philosopher with the porter is certainly meaningful and 'open to egalitarian uses'. It is certainly true that some of Smith's basic arguments, for instance the principle of sympathy, speak in favour of a 'horizontal' relationship, so to say, rather than a hierarchical one of power and subordination. Something similar may be said, perhaps, of Smith's frequent expressions of solidarity towards the lower classes. As a matter of fact, however, he maintains that the orders of society are given and must be respected (TMS VI.ii.2.7–18); and that the distinction of ranks, which involves the subordination of one category of men to another, must be carefully maintained because peace and order in society are grounded on it (TMS VI.ii.1.20) – and it is *nature* which has wisely established this distinction. No necessity to relieve the distress of the poor is more important than the safeguarding of that order.

There is nothing new in the principle, widely circulating at the time, that social order is based on inequality; but I think that this principle could not be without consequences on Smith's 'egalitarian' inclinations, although I too think that Smith was in favour of a growing independence of the labourer, which would give to the latter more dignity. But I cannot say whether he did foresee that in the future this independence would spread more and more.[90]

I think also it is difficult to believe in Aristotle's quasi-egalitarian ethics: differently from Smith he did believe in natural differences among men. To my mind, the similarity between the two authors, in this particular case, lies in the fact that both were persuaded that differences in job could influence the individual's personality and attitudes.

This is beside the point. What I wish to underline is an argument that Fleischacker does not mention, or at least does not examine on both sides. In Adam Smith's thought, it is certainly true that labour promotes the labourer's independence, as Fleischacker points out, and this is an argument in favour of Smith's more 'democratic' attitude towards the differences of status inherent in the feudal system. But there is no mention of the fact that for Aristotle, as well as for many other classics, the exact opposite was true: to be obliged to work meant dependence, and the worst of all dependencies, namely to depend on another man. It was, in fact, like being a slave, who cannot choose what to do but must carry out the work ordered by the master. We find this attitude spread during all ancient times: from Aristotle's well-known observation that the main difference between a slave and a free worker is that the former has only one master whilst the latter has many (*Pol.* 1278 a 11–13), through Cicero's definition of wages as *auctoramentum servitutis* (the pay of slavery, *De Off.* I, 150), till the Digest's statement that wage-earners are *personae loco servorum* (persons in the position of slaves, *Dig.* VII, 8, 4).

I think it impossible to overlook this basic difference, because it explains one of the greatest gaps between ancient and modern thought: for the ancient labourer it was impossible to exercise even moral faculties, let alone political ones, because of his necessity to spend his time on work instead of nobler activities like science, philosophy or politics. Even if we were willing to concede that Aristotle's ethics was open to egalitarian uses, I think this is not enough to cancel this basic difference which renders the concept of labour (and the position of the labourer) radically different in the two authors.

Aristotle's concept of *phronesis* has been the subject of numerous more or less accurate interpretations,[91] but its historical development demonstrates beyond doubt that it was construed, from St Thomas to Adam Smith, as practical wisdom, that is, the ability to choose the means to an end.

Like others, Smith called this virtue prudence. Some preferred to compare the *phronimos* to Adam Smith's prudent man rather than to the impartial spectator.[92] I do not wish to embark upon the subject of prudence here, which I have already treated elsewhere.[93] Briefly, I agree that Smith's prudent man may have classical reminiscences, but from a different point of view.

Cicero transmitted to medieval and modern culture the Aristotelian dichotomy between practical and theoretical knowledge. He translated the words *sophia* and *phronesis* into Latin, so *sapientia/prudentia* (*De Off.* I, 153) went down in posterity as the first cardinal virtue, or rather, to use Cicero's terminology, the first of the four parts of the *honestum*. This helps us to understand the association of *phronimos* with the prudent man, but in fact it is the result of a subsequent interpretation rather than the true meaning of Aristotle's *phronimos*. Prudence as a form of practical wisdom was certainly related to some form of shrewdness, or if we wish to use a Ciceronian term, foresight (*provideo*, *De Leg.* I, 60).[94] It would be superfluous to add that this perfectly fits the praiseworthy behaviour of a wise and prudent man; indeed the impartial spectator supports him (TMS VI.i.11), which of course means that the two do not coincide.

Of course we do not need this simple observation to be certain that Aristotle's *phronimos* was something quite different. He needed only to determine the golden mean, which, as we have seen, certainly did not mean mediocrity, which is the virtue so to speak of the prudent man who, according to Smith, earns himself dispassionate respect rather than affection or admiration.

The fact that Smith uses the term 'mediocrity' does not help us to place the passage within an Aristotelian context. The well-known concluding phrase of WN, in which the term is used disparagingly, certainly does not help us either. The word has been used for its twofold meaning since the times of Horace's *aurea mediocritas* (*Odes* II, 10, v.5–6), and the fact that so many efforts have been made to distinguish between 'mediocrity' and the golden mean confirms that there is indeed a risk of relating one to the other.[95]

In this case I think that when Smith refers to 'mediocrity' as a salient feature of the propriety of passions, there are sufficiently strong Aristotelian connotations for us to be quite sure that Smith intends the golden mean as a correct measure of the intensity of sentiments coming from 'sense and feeling' rather than from servile obedience to external rules. A recent interpretation of Smith suggests that an alternative type of 'mediocrity' related more to behaviour than to judgement also exists, a mere approximation to propriety[96] which is typical of the lesser virtues.

The political 'model'
In seventeenth-century philosophy of politics, the Aristotelian family model [97] provided a naturalistic basis for and legitimized relationships of power. In the name of a natural hierarchy, such as that of the father over his offspring, for example, the patriarchal model proclaimed the divine right of the royal ruler, whose authority was exactly comparable to the father–son relationship. Theories of natural law on the other hand were based on contract, or consent, but in reality they were closer to the 'true' Aristotle. Indeed patriarchal theories transferred to the state a model which Aristotle applied only to the family. In the mind of the Greek philosopher political society originated in the family, or in a set of families that congregated in villages and towns. The family and political society nevertheless have different aims: although both are natural institutions, the difference is essentially qualitative. Aristotle affirms that:

> Those then who think that the natures of the statesman, the royal ruler, the head of an estate and the master of a family are the same, are mistaken; they imagine that the difference between these various forms of authority is one of greater and smaller numbers, not a difference in kind . . . as if there were no difference between a large household and a small city. (*Pol.* 1252 a 7–13, Rackham's translation)[98]

Both modern theories derived from Aristotle. The theory of natural law was more accurate and followed Aristotle more closely, by refusing to homologize family and state, although ultimately it moved political society away from nature, basing it on consent.[99] The patriarchal approach was a distortion, since it demanded to rule both the state and the family in the name of the 'naturalness' of relationships of authority, which were therefore unavoidable. It is no coincidence that one of the most frequently used texts was the one in which Aristotle states that some are born to rule and others to obey, by nature (*Pol.* 1252 a 28–30).[100] The only element common to both the theory of natural law and patriarchalism was the conviction that a relationship existed between the family as the original unit of the state, and the state itself. This type of historical-anthropological approach was substantially accepted by both parties and effectively derived from Aristotle.[101]

It is generally accepted that modern political economy derived, at least initially, from the classical household model, despite certain complexities; for example, the fundamental problem, identified by Bodin, that the authority of the state should have stopped before the equally absolute authority of the head of the family within his household. A number of solutions to this problem have been provided which we need not go into here.[102]

What should be stressed is that the so-called Aristotelian model (and we have seen how much caution is required in applying such a label) was still very much alive in Smith's time, and used by Smith's contemporary Steuart, with whom Smith did not see eye to eye, as we know. In the introduction to Book IV of WN, Smith expressly defines the subject of political economy as 'the science of a statesman or legislator'. This is sometimes considered slightly at odds with his thought, since it peculiarly resembles Steuart's, which reveals Aristotelian tendencies in proposing a household model of state management.[103] The latter model shares many elements with the 'domestic' literature mentioned above. Smith is generally considered a stranger to this model, probably because the 'statesman or legislator' should be left out, with some exceptions, from the field of economics at least.

It is not easy to understand whether something of the Aristotelian model is present in Smith's political and economic suggestions.[104] We must be wary of interpreting too literally certain phrases, especially in *Lectures on Jurisprudence* (LJ), which are essentially colloquial. So a phrase such as, 'to give anything without a reward is always generous and noble, but to barter one thing for another is mean' (LJB 301) is not enough to claim that Smith was against trade. Similarly I am not convinced that a phrase such as, 'What is prudence in the conduct of every private family, can scarce be folly in that of a great kingdom' (WN IV.ii.12), which apparently leans in favour of the household model, constitutes evidence of Smith's patriarchal stance. He certainly speaks out against the social contract and the state of nature; in a renowned phrase of the TMS he speaks out against the right of resistance,[105] but not even this is sufficient to count him among the supporters of divine right. Sovereign power, according to Smith, is grounded on authority and utility (LJA v.119–22, 129–32; LJB 12–14, 93), rather than on an absolutist idea of political power.

Apart from genuine political theory, what interests us here is the administrative aspect of government activity. Political and economic theories which consider the head of the household's responsibility for management analogous to that of the state foresee first and foremost a ruling monarchy, but also a form of guardianship for the subjects. This implies that economic activities must also be decided and directed by the central authority, a position which hardly seems congenial to Smith. It has been recognized from Viner onwards that the state may intervene to a greater extent than that established in WN IV.ix.51, but this is not sufficient to change things. In Smith's theory factors of production, means of circulation and individual economic enterprises all perform better when left alone, without any form of intervention. In this way every man is free to manage economic matters as he thinks best.

Perhaps we should remind ourselves that for the classical philosophers the economy was an entirely private concern, indeed this was its fundamental characteristic. Naturally I do not intend to claim that Smith derived this aspect from the classical thinkers. Far from it. However since it seems evident that his political economy did not welcome excessive intrusion of central power in the 'obvious and simple system of natural liberty' (WN IV.ix.51), it is appropriate to remember that the custom of ancient world, as expressed in the philosophers' works, but also in the political constitutions and in the Roman law, assumed that every man governed himself and his property.[106]

Conclusions
Aristotle's influence on Adam Smith should be viewed globally, rather than in detail. In general terms it can be traced back to the philosophy of praxis. Here we are interested

in ethics, since the politics of Adam Smith have been eminently analysed, and as far as his thinking on economics is concerned, very little of what may be considered economic thought in Aristotle is reflected in Adam Smith, particularly considering the Stagirite's well-known 'anti-economic' stances.[107]

A further factor to bear in mind, and perhaps more so than has been the case up to now, is that Cicero's *De Officiis*, which influenced Smith and all the other cultured Europeans of his day, takes a Stoic approach although it contains many elements which are clearly not Stoic. Some of the more sensitive scholars realized this long ago: there was nothing particularly Stoic about Cicero's definition of *honestum* in Book I. 'The gradation of the goods, the norm of moderation, the inclusion of instincts among the relevant faculties of man, and the strong preference of justice as the virtue par excellence are redolent of Aristotelianism'.[108] All the commentaries to Cicero's *De Officiis* from the sixteenth century onwards make frequent reference to Aristotelian principles, and, as we have already seen, the converse also occurred: there are modern editions of Aristotle's *Ethics* which draw numerous elements from Cicero.

The passage from Marcia Colish cited above gives a precise indication of the Aristotelian elements in the *De Officiis*. I would add what I have discussed in this chapter: the hierarchy in family and social relationships which provides the structure par excellence for all reasoning on human, social and political relationships by clearly defining the authority in each field.

So all this points towards a very general outline, an overall background which is however of the utmost importance. Smith certainly accepts the Aristotelian type of family structure which permeated all discussions of civic society in modern times. We can also be certain that the original Stoic position advocating undifferentiated *philanthropia* to all mankind was not to his liking because the most impelling familiar and social bonds (and duties) were watered down. Since Smith was not a man of extremes he maintained an Aristotelian approach to relationships with man and society. He describes relationships in terms of family or social bonds, and also describes an innate difficulty in putting oneself in another man's place, particularly when that person is far removed, without the aid of a third person 'who judges with impartiality' (TMS III.3.3). By nature, the death of millions of people in distant China leaves us more indifferent than a 'paltry misfortune' (III.3.4) which befalls us. This is a complex argument, and emphasises that thanks to our conscience ('the man within', who incidentally is in good company with 'reason' first and foremost, and then with the 'principle, conscience, the inhabitant of the breast', ibid.) we feel ashamed to feel so little for others and so much for ourselves. Of the two ways to contrast this '*natural* inequality' (TMS III.3.11, emphasis added), that is, heighten our sensibility towards others and diminish that towards ourselves, Smith opts for the second, which is Stoic. However he cites the example of Epictetus, namely that of one's 'neighbour'.

This argument forms part of the principle that man should prefer the good of all to his own good, and Smith, like many of his contemporary moralists, praises the 'propriety of resigning the greatest interest of our own for the yet greater interests of others' (TMS III.3.4).[109] However it is highly significant that he goes on to say that this implies that: 'the poor man must neither defraud nor steal from the rich, though the acquisition might be much more beneficial to the one than the loss could be hurtful to the other' (TMS III.3.6). This is a principle which later refers to the well-known Stoic formula taken straight from Cicero, that stealing from another man for whatsoever reason is against nature (ibid.). The Stoic formula can clearly be used as an argument against theft.

It seems fairly clear to me that Smith retains the elements of Stoic philosophy which are most congenial to him. Above all the 'rest of mankind' is appropriately redefined as 'neighbour' (to whom, despite being neither a relative nor a friend, it is obvious that we feel closer than to the millions of inhabitants of China).

The passage goes on to reveal that it is simply natural to feel stronger sentiments for the members of our family: our offspring, of course, but also our parents, siblings and friends. It concludes not by chance with harsh criticism for the Stoic apathy which generates insensitivity towards such sentiments (TMS III.3.14).

Smith's position is therefore much less radical than that of a true Stoic, something of which he is clearly well aware and deeply convinced. This is quite evident from the passionate tone he uses to describe one of the most radical Stoic doctrines: good is either absolute or non-existent, and to move away even slightly from good is equivalent to siding with evil (TMS VII.ii.1.39–40). Smith chooses two well-known paradoxes to illustrate this: the man who drowns whether his head is under water by a few centimetres or many metres; and the unmotivated killing of a cock or one's own father, mentioned above. On the first example Smith merely comments that it 'should appear sufficiently violent' without contesting it; while the second is 'too absurd to deserve any serious consideration' (VII.ii.1.41). Perhaps the second paradox is considered much graver than the first because it goes against family relationships, indeed against the most important relationship of all: the respect due to the authority of the father.

Naturally I do not wish to suggest that this is an exclusively Aristotelian principle: too many influences, from Roman law to Christianity, have intervened to make this type of authority inviolable. However what I do find significant is the fact that in this part of TMS, after having duly (and succinctly) alluded to the *media officia* – probably because he realized that he could not suppress the most moderate part of Stoic philosophy – Adam Smith returns to his original assessment, stating that 'the plan and system which Nature has sketched out for our conduct, seems to be altogether different from that of the Stoical philosophy' (TMS VII.ii.1.43). He subsequently reverts to the 'natural' (Aristotelian) gradation of affections: 'ourselves, our friends, our country'. He concludes with further criticism (after TMS VI.ii.3.5–6) of the Stoic tendency to contemplate, and reiterates his conviction that man should lead an active life.

It is not my intention to evaluate to what extent Smith is indebted to Aristotle simply by belittling what he owes to the Stoics. I have already demonstrated[110] that Stoicism was based at least in part on principles opposed to the philosophy of Smith, but this does not prevent me from recognizing that significant Stoic elements are present in his thought. I think however that there are plenty of Aristotelian elements which I have also considered elsewhere, so here I would like to conclude with a few comments on the deeper aspects.

Firstly, within the field of moral judgement, Aristotle also left plenty of room for feelings, specifically affirming that it is not reasoning, but rather sensation, which determines the golden mean. I do not wish to draw a parallel with Aristotle's *aisthesis* (on which a vast bibliography exists), but it is inevitable that this denigration of 'reasoning' and 'science' in favour of 'perceptions'[111] brings to mind the 'sense and feeling' (TMS VII.iii.2.8) of Adam Smith. This is yet another departure from Stoicism, which did not deviate from its perfect reason.

Generally speaking, both Aristotle and Adam Smith acknowledge that virtuous behaviour is better determined by feeling than by reason; and that it is a balanced behaviour, characterized by a sense of limit – not so extreme as the Stoics would suggest. The *phronimos*'s virtue, *phronesis*, is instrumental for identifying the exact point of virtue; but it is also, in its modern meaning of prudence, the virtue which constitutes a sort of *trait-d'union* between the excellence of the golden mean and the middling quality of *decorum*.

In fact, an additional element to be found in sixteenth- and seventeenth-century literature on behaviour, which I mentioned above, involves some degree of overlap between the concepts of *decorum* and *medietas*. Indeed the essence of this literature lies in the exercise of the appropriate virtues in relation to one's status. Here Aristotle appears indirectly through the *De Officiis*, providing an opportunity to discuss and comment on the most important virtues; there may well also have been a direct influence through the abundant literature mentioned in the first section of the chapter.

It seems, however, that about one more point Smith was on Aristotelian ground: private management cannot be transferred to the public field; in other words, he is not favourable to applying the household (economic) model to political economy, if this means committing all decisions to the head of the state. Economic affairs must be run by each individual according to his own interest; in other words, everybody can, and should, behave like the ancient *paterfamilias* as regards his economic choices. On the other hand, if this equal ability in judging about one's own interests is one of the reasons why recent scholarship attributes egalitarian principles to Smith,[112] I think that this kind of egalitarianism is far from being Aristotelian, since the philosopher of Stageira would never have admitted that a man of excellence could be in equality with a *banausos* even only as regards identifying the material interests of his everyday life.

Notes

1. Modern scientists, as M. Boas (1962) recalls in the concluding sentence of Chapter 1, trying to find in nature what Greek authors had seen in it, ended by seeing what really was there.
2. R. Sorabji very appropriately entitled the volume he edited on the ancient commentaries of Aristotle *Aristotle Transformed* (Sorabji, 1990). The same may be said for the Aristotle who was transformed by the Renaissance commentators and the wealth of modern exegesis.
3. Lohr (1974), pp. 229–30; see also Schmitt (1983), pp. 87–91.
4. Kristeller (1972), p. 136; Id. (1974), p. 43; Copenhaver and Schmitt (1992), 11–12; Lohr (1999), p. 288.
5. Lohr (1974), p. 229; Mcconica (1979), pp. 309, 313, 316; Schmitt (1985), pp. 86–8.
6. Schmitt (1983), pp. 92–8. This transformation of Aristotle with Platonic and Platonizing elements goes much further back, see Gottschalk (1987), p. 1102; id. (1997), p. 115; Kessler (1999), p. 2.
7. Schmitt (1983), pp. 104–5.
8. Garin (1983), p. 42.
9. Schmitt (1985), p. 86; see Copenhaver and Schmitt (1992), pp. 31–2; 74–6; Schmitt (1983), pp. 111–12.
10. Lohr (1974), p. 230.
11. Lohr (1974), p. 228.
12. Bruni translated *Ethics*, *Politics* and *Economics* (which was then thought to be by Aristotle), that is, all three arguments of the philosophy of praxis.
13. Frigo (1995), pp. 30–34; 43.
14. Which faded with the scientific revolution, as we know, while the ethical influence was bound to last considerably longer, see Schmitt (1983), p. 107.
15. Schmitt (1985), pp. 60–68; Kristeller (1972), p. 136; id. (1974), p. 43; Copenhaver and Schmitt (1992), pp. 11–12.
16. Twenty-five editions, see Schmitt (1983), p. 38.
17. Pocock (1968), pp. 179–83; id. (1983), pp. 235–6. For recent discussion, see Winch (2002).
18. Michel (1976), p. 93; Pesante (1995), p. 174.
19. Pesante (2000).

20. Frigo (1988), pp. 81–3.
21. Schofield (1999). On Stoic political thought see, among others, Erskine (1990), Brunt (1975), Manning (1989).
22. Gottschalk (1997), p. 112.
23. Sandbach (1985), p. 55.
24. Long (1997), p. 21. This fact had already been acknowledged in the ancient world, often by the Stoics themselves (Frede, 1999, p. 783; see Arnold, 1911, pp. 94–5, 109–10).
25. Gottschalk (1997), p. 115.
26. Cicero, *De Fin.* IV, 79. Sandbach uses this passage (Sandbach, 1985, p. 58) to state that despite this in Panaetius there is very little of Aristotle. Here I would tend to disagree.
27. Erskine (1990), pp. 26, 30, 120.
28. I use this term exclusively to refer to the classes of the Roman census.
29. Erskine (1990), pp. 1–2, 4, 207.
30. On the influence of the Stoic Sphaerus of Borysthenes in events in Sparta see Erskine (1990), Chapter 6.
31. There is a tendency to tone down this interpretation today, although it is well-founded. See Erskine (1990), p. 166.
32. Erskine (1990), p. 156.
33. Erskine (1990), pp. 181–2; 193–9. See also Narducci (1990), pp. 912–13.
34. The father–son relationship is monarchical; the husband–wife relationship is aristocratic; the relationship between siblings is a type of timocracy; democracy is to be found in the family with no head, or where the head is so weak that the other members can do what they please. *NE* 1160b24–1161a9.
35. St. Augustine particularly underlined by Erskine (1990), p. 193.
36. Lambertini (1985), p. 67; Frigo (1985), pp. 201–7.
37. See for example the comment of Amerbachius on Cicero's *De Officiis* III, 34 in Cicero (1550), p. 128.
38. Erskine (1990), p. 55.
39. See the interesting article of Radcliffe (1993) on the eighteenth-century debate about universal benevolence as an antidote to local and personal affections in dealing with the problem of small groups in a larger society.
40. Mentioned in Vivenza (2001b), p. 210. See also Monsarrat (1984), pp. 64, 73; Salmon (1989), pp. 221–3.
41. In *De Nat. Deor.* 3, 41 and *Tusc.* 5, 120; this opinion was taken up and spread in philosophy manuals in the modern age. See for example Brucker (1767), p. 899.
42. Erskine (1990), pp. 197, 199; Gottschalk (1987), *passim*.
43. This phrase can be found in the introduction to *Moral Philosophy*, dedicated 'To the Students in Universities', cited in Taylor (1965), p. 25.
44. Naturally they also made copious use of Plato, see Arnold (1911), p. 55; but since Aristotle was further from their positions, at this moment I give precedence to him. See also Gottschalk (1987), p. 1143.
45. Narducci (1990), p. 917.
46. Vivenza (2001b), p. 204.
47. Here I would like to clarify a point recently criticized by L. Montes. I mentioned *oikeiosis* in Vivenza (2001b), pp. 204–6, explaining the reasons why I think that the origin is more likely to be Aristotelian in this sense; however I will not digress because Montes does not agree (he limits his discussion to 'I believe she is wrong', Montes, 2004, p. 41n48), or on the fact that he is non-specific (he claims that I only include Marcus Aurelius among the texts consulted by Smith to gain an insight into the concept of *oikeiosis*, ibid., when it is evident that on p. 204n62 of Vivenza, 2001b I was referring to Grotius and not Smith).

The problem is that it was not appropriate even for me to dwell on the concept of *oikeiosis* because it became popular, and above all was considered Stoic, *after* Smith. He may well have read Stobaeus with the famous example of Hierocles and his concentric circles, but we should remember that Hierocles was not acknowledged as a Stoic before Praechter's monograph in 1901; previously he had been confused even by Zeller (in the mid-nineteenth century (1844–52)) as a Neoplatonist. The theory of *oikeiosis* was considered Peripatetic from Antiochus of Ascalon onwards, and even in the texts available to Smith the well-known passage 'parents–brothers–cousins–friends–countrymen' was generally classified under friendship (even when reference is made to *oikeiosis*, see Stanley, 1701, pp. 317–19), which is equivalent to putting it in the hands of Aristotle. So even if Smith had read Hierocles in Stobaeus, he would have considered him, if anything, Peripatetic or Neoplatonic rather than Stoic (recently P. Barney also linked a passage in TMS with the Stoic concept of *oikeiosis*; see Barney, 2003, pp. 326–30).

I am nevertheless grateful to L. Montes for having signalled a chronological slip of the pen (I wrote seventeenth instead of eighteenth century). So after expiating for having placed my author in the incorrect century, I continue to believe his appreciation of the grading of human relationships (parents, brothers, cousins, friends, countrymen) is an Aristotelian argument.

I wish to clarify that my discussion centred on this aspect, considered in isolation from the main body of the theory which cannot be treated briefly. Here I would add that even if *oikeiosis* was born after Aristotle (indeed the scholars who emphasize its Peripatetic aspect refer back to Theophrastus), the fact remains that the famous image of Hierocles's 'concentric circles' has a rather similar precedent in Aristotle, observed by Inwood (1983, p. 198), Brink (1955–56, p. 126), Baldry (1965, pp. 178–9), Whitlock Blundell (1990, p. 228), Magnaldi (1991, p. 34), Grilli (1992, p. 119) and probably others. Certainly Aristotle does not speak of circles, and above all in this passage deals with *philia* and not *oikeiosis*. But what I wish to underline is not so much the similarity of the two sequences of relationships (Aristotle: parents, children, brothers, cousins, other relatives, friends, fellow disciples, in NE 1161b16–1162a32; Hierocles: parents, offspring, brothers, uncles, grandparents, cousins, other relatives, fellow citizens, Stob in SVF, 1905, pp. 61–2), as the fact that this sequence introduces a hierarchy into the relationships themselves, a hierarchy that early Stoicism did not contemplate: for the early Stoics father, brother or a complete stranger were the same thing. One of the difficulties of the issue is the clarification of the transition from personal to social *oikeiosis*; now as far as Stoic sources are concerned we have, in the words of Inwood, 'an extension from the relationship one has to oneself and one's parts, to one's offspring, and thence to all other humans' (Inwood, 1983, p. 195; see also Brink, 1955–56, pp. 138–40; Mingay, 1972, p. 269; Inwood, 1984, p. 179; Isnardi Parente, 1989, pp. 2222–3, 2226; Annas, 1990, pp. 91–2).

Thus the most genuinely Stoic position would imply bypassing all the family and social hierarchies to reach an undifferentiated sentiment towards all mankind, with no intermediate degrees: sentiment for one's offspring is functional to their survival, see Plutarch, *Soll. An.* 962 A–B; and precisely for this reason it goes in one direction only. It was Aristotle once again who suggested that offspring reciprocate the affection received from their parents (NE 1161b18–27), but for the Stoics this reciprocal relationship did not exist, see Gorgemann (1983, p. 182) and Inwood (1983, p. 197). Modern authors often underline Hierocles's conclusions on his hierarchy of relationships: 'a good man should try to bring all these circles as close as possible'. This is generally construed as an invitation to iron out any differences: 'ideally therefore there should be no difference between his (i.e. the good man's) attitude to himself and his attitude to everyone else' (Erskine 1990, p. 116; see Mingay, 1972, pp. 270–71; Pembroke, 1971, p. 124; Inwood, 1984, p. 181; Whitlock Blundell, 1990, p. 226; Reydams-Schils, 2002, p. 242). So it is evident that the truly Stoic position is that of undifferentiated relationships between oneself and the rest of mankind; it is likewise equally clear that the concept of varying degrees of intensity of such relationships is not Stoic, or at least not of Stoic origin. It is the concept linked to the aristocratic socio-political structure, and related to the 'natural' sociality of man: the first element is the family, then friends, and various other relationships, and fellow citizens or fellow countrymen are always present. We should bear this in mind before we take up drastic stances in favour of Stoic or Peripatetic philosophy: the most balanced and scientifically valid positions are those which underline the links between the two theories, see for example Brink (1955–56), Isnardi Parente (1989), Magnaldi (1991), Levy (1992, pp. 381–7), Gorgemann (1983), Inwood (1983).

48. On the lack of originality, see also HA III.6: Plato and Aristotle supposedly took almost everything from the Pythagoreans.
49. 'they were causes who neither knew nor intended the effects which they produced' (HAPh, 10); see 'and thus without intending it, without knowing it, [they] advance the interest of the society' (TMS IV.i.1.10); 'He generally, indeed, neither intends to promote the publick interest, nor knows how much he is promoting it' (WN IV.ii.9).
50. One example for all: the tripartition upon which 'domestic law' (father–son, husband–wife, master–servant) is based (LJA iii.1; LJB 101) is taken from Aristotle, *Pol.* 1253b6–7. But it has been echoed infinitely in modern times by other authors, without a trace of citation.
51. Vivenza (2001b), p. 74. Smith recognized the total independence of the Stoic wise man, who became wise by eradicating, rather than controlling, his passions (TMS VII.ii.1.46). But in the original Stoic doctrine, the wise man does not even experience the wrong desires: he feels no such desire, because thanks to his perfect reason he overcomes the division of the soul into rational and irrational (Erskine, 1990, pp. 31, 195).
52. Vivenza (2001b), p. 192: here I stated Smith's claim that his 'propriety' bears affinity with both Plato and Aristotle.
53. Fabris (1982), p. 25; Vegetti (1976), p. 49.
54. Vivenza (1990), pp. 596–601.
55. Vivenza (2001b), pp. 198–202. I have treated justice and beneficence, which derive from Cicero, in Vivenza (1995), p. 511; (2001a), pp. 210–17; (2001b), p. 198; (2001c), pp. 130–31; (2004), p. 513. See now Fleischacker (2004), pp. 20–22.
56. Vivenza (2001b), p. 47.
57. I mention this below.
58. Paganelli (2000), p. 424n. 9; Paganelli (2003), p. 24n7.

59. For Aristotle, see Evrigenis (1999), pp. 396–7; see TMS I.ii.intro.1–2.
60. Berns (1994), pp. 77–8. Griswold (1999), p. 190. It has been impossible to take Temple-Smith (2007) into account.
61. *Phronesis* is not always translated with 'prudence' (see for instance 'intelligence' by T. Irwin); but to my mind the best translation remains 'practical wisdom' (Ross).
62. Here again I use Rackham's translation which gives 'perception' for *aisthesis*. I would prefer 'sense perception' or 'sensation' (Liddell Scott, *s.v.*). See Natali (2001), p. 74 with note 47, p. 85; and Hanley (2006), p. 20.
63. Vivenza (2001b), pp. 48, 193–4.
64. TMS I.i.5.9; VI.iii.23; see Vivenza (2001b), pp. 190–91.
65. Waszek (1984); Montes (2004), p. 124. According to Cummings (1969), Vol. II, p. 25, Smith derived the concept from a Platonizing version of Stoicism.
66. Let us make it quite clear that Cicero also connected *decorum* with the art of conversation in *De Off.* I, 134–7. See Cicu (2000), p. 141.
67. Not an entirely shrewd definition, as has been observed (Narducci (1999), p. 45).
68. Berns (1994), p. 80, is not wrong when he observes that certain ethical judgments made by Smith (and also Hume) may seem more aesthetic than moral, while the problem did not exist for Aristotle because 'one and the same word *kalon*, whose basic meaning is beautiful, in ethical contexts is almost always translated differently, translated as noble'. See also Owens (1981), pp. 264–9.
69. Crell (n.d.), p. 43.
70. Lotito (1981), pp. 111–18.
71. Labowski (1934); see also Narducci (1984)
72. Narducci (1994), p. 47. See Hampsher-Monk (2002), pp. 86–7 for the antithesis between courtly and republican manners.
73. See n. 50 *supra*. Although in different ways, wife, children and servants are subordinated to the husband/father/master, according to Aristotle's text. In Roman law, however, the kind of subordination was identical: the wife was *loco filiae*, and the only way to distinguish between children and slaves was to call the children *liberi*, because the father's authority was identical over both.
74. As we know, the classical political model in its most prestigious form contemplated collegiate management of power by a group of individuals, generally with equal rights, except in times of tyranny or government by one individual. Family life, on the other hand, was governed by one individual. So the 'head of the household' model was adapted to modern monarchies but did not fit the classical political model. The principle that governing the *polis* was similar to governing the family, apart from the difference in size, was Greek and already controversial (Natali 1995, pp. 28–9). See here, p. 39 with n. 98.
75. Gabba (1988).
76. Both qualified with a virtually infinite series of attributes. Here we will only say that justice was perceived both in its corrective and 'distributive' aspects (see n. 55 *supra* and related text), and prudence, which was often confused with the first cardinal virtue, roughly meant wisdom applied to actions, to concrete choices.
77. I will leave aside God, who needed no instructions to perform his task of governing the universe.
78. As I have already noted in Vivenza (2001b), p. 196.
79. Vivenza (2001b), p. 200.
80. I take this opportunity to clarify that I do not intend to judge Smith in general terms, for example by establishing whether he followed this paradigm or that of natural law; or if his morals led him to take up deontological or utilitarian positions. My interest is in his relationship with the classical authors. Naturally some general trends emerge, but these are only consequential.
81. Paganelli (2003) pp. 23, 27.
82. This division also depends on the fact that Cicero himself related *decorum* to *honestum* (*De Off.* I, 93–4), which he used to translate the Greek *kalon*, losing however the ideal relationship between good and beauty which constitutes the well-known Greek principle of *kalokagathia*. Cicero focuses more on the relationship between *honestum* and *utile*.
83. Perionio (1540), pp. 86–7. Also between the first century BC and the second AD Aristotelian ethics included both the doctrine of the mean and that of the passions which must be moderated, not eradicated (Gottschalk, 1987, pp. 1144, 1147).
84. Crell (n.d.), pp. 41–3.
85. The editor's note on p. 270 notes, quite rightly in my opinion, that the final version with which Smith illustrates the Aristotelian principle ('habit of "mediocrity"') is less precise than that used in the first edition of TMS: 'habitual "mediocrity" of the affections'. The expression 'golden mean' is used in TMS V.2.7, about the relativity of the 'sentiments concerning the exact propriety of character' in the different circumstances.
86. *Medium rei ipsius, absolute sumptae; medium rei ad alia; medium ad nos relatum*, Crell (n.d.), p. 42 (a

theme already present in Buridan and again in Stanley (1701), p. 263. It was the elaboration of the concepts expressed by Plato and Aristotle in *Euthydemus*, *Politicus*, *Eudemian Ethics* and *Nichomachean Ethics* see Natali (1989), pp. 47–53 (unfortunately deleted in the English translation).
87. Natali (2001), p. 35. Recently the connection between Smith's propriety and Aristotle's mean has been stressed by Tugendhat (2004), pp. 93, 99.
88. 'One's behaviour may be praiseworthy not only if one grasps exactly the right amount of emotion between excess and defect, but also if one comes close to it' (Natali, 2001, p. 37; see Aristotle NE 1109b18–23 and Smith, TMS I.i.5.8).
89. See recently Griswold (2001).
90. That Smith 'both hoped and expected' that owners of stock could lose their hold over the labourers is what Fleischacker thinks, perhaps on good grounds (Fleischacker, 1999, p. 182); but that 'Nature has wisely judged that the distinction of ranks, the peace and order of society, would rest more securely on the plain and palpable difference of birth and fortune, than upon the invisibile and often uncertain difference of wisdom and virtue' (TMS VI.ii.1.20) is what Smith actually wrote.
91. To understand the true nature of Aristotelian *phronesis* see Natali (2001).
92. Scott (1940), p. 89.
93. Vivenza (2001b), pp. 54–7, 196–7; Vivenza (2004), pp. 113–14.
94. Vivenza (2001b), p. 57.
95. Urmson (1973), p. 225; Evrigenis (1999), pp. 396–7; Natali (2001).
96. Zanini (1995), p. 33.
97. See note 50 *supra*.
98. 'Those . . . who think' in this way were Plato and Xenophon. See Natali (1995), p. 29.
99. Bobbio (1989), p. 4; Fagiani (1986), p. 143.
100. Neri (1986), pp. 132–4.
101. Fagiani (1986), pp. 142–3. On the medieval formulation of the concept see Nedermann (1991).
102. Fagiani (1986), p. 144.
103. Tribe (1978), pp. 84, 107; Kelly (1986), pp. 256–7.
104. According to Tribe it is, but only in words (Tribe, 1978, chap.5).
105. 'That kings are the servants of the people, to be obeyed, resisted, deposed, or punished, as the public conveniency may require, is the doctrine of reason and philosophy; but it is not the doctrine of Nature' (TMS I.iii.2.3). In LJ, however, Smith shows an attitude more inclined to 'the doctrine of reason and philosophy', see LJA v. 124–7; LJB 94–6.
106. If I am not mistaken, this is what Fleischacker means with 'judgment' in the sense that every human being, according to Smith, is able to judge of his own interest and to direct his affairs (household included) if left without impediments (Fleischacker, 1999, p. 139). I wish to recall, however, that in the ancient world this was not simply a problem of leaving people free to exercise their judgement in economic matters. It was intended, by Aristotle as well as other classical authors, in terms of a *right* naturally possessed by the heads of the families in force of the law, with power juridically exercised over persons and things.
107. Naturally I allude to his hostility towards trade as a source of wealth beyond basic needs, and his suspicion towards all activities which involve the handling of money.
108. Colish (1985), p. 148. See Skinner (2002), p. 11.
109. In general terms the issue behind this moral precept is how the individual can recognize what is the good of mankind, in order to promote it instead of his own. The argument (by R. Cumberland, but also J. Tucker and F. Galiani) is that man, although willing to further the common good, is unable to know the means to achieve it, this being the task of divine Providence. In other words, it is impossible for men to make choices about too distant objects (see Radcliffe, 1993, p. 224 on Hume's and Smith's position). The only 'means' man knows are those which promote his own good; and, as Providence is assumed to be benevolent, he has only to follow his own interest in order to advance that of mankind. See Vivenza (1996a), p. 34 and Vivenza (1996b), p. 41.
110. Vivenza (2001b).
111. See n. 62 *supra*.
112. Fleischacker (1999), p. 139.

References

Adam Smith's works are quoted in the usual abbreviations:
TMS, *The Theory of Moral Sentiments*, D.D. Raphael and A.L. Macfie (eds) (1976), Oxford: Clarendon Press.
WN, *An Inquiry into the Nature and Causes of the Wealth of Nations*, R.H. Campbell and A.S. Skinner (eds) (1976), Oxford: Clarendon Press.

LJA and LJB, *Lectures on Jurisprudence*, R.L. Meek, D.D. Raphael and P.G. Stein (eds) (1978), Oxford: Clarendon Press.
HA, *The History of Astronomy*, in *Essays on Philosophical Subjects*, W.P.D. Wightman, J.C. Bryce and I.S. Ross (eds) (1980), Oxford: Clarendon Press.
HAPh, *The History of Ancient Physics*, in *Essays on Philosophical Subjects*, W.P.D. Wightman, J.C.Bryce and I.S. Ross (eds) (1980), Oxford: Clarendon Press.
HALM, *The History of Ancient Logics and Metaphysics*, in *Essays on Philosophical Subjects*, W.P.D. Wightman, J.C.Bryce and I.S. Ross (eds) (1980), Oxford: Clarendon Press.
LRBL, *Lectures on Rhetoric and Belles Lettres*, J.C. Bryce (ed.) (1983), Oxford: Clarendon Press.

References to the classics are from the Teubner, Oxford or Paris Belles Lettres editions, when it comes to locating the text. If an English translation is given, it is usually from the Loeb's edition. Abbreviations:
De Fin. = Cicero (1967), *De Finibus*, Cambridge, MA and London, UK: Harvard University Press.
De Leg. = Cicero (1994), *De Legibus*, Cambridge, MA and London, UK: Harvard University Press.
De Nat. Deor. = Cicero (1968), *M. Tulli Ciceronis De natura deorum*, A. Stanley Pease (ed.), Darmstadt: Wissenschaftliche Buchgesellschaft.
De Off. = Cicero (1968), *De Officiis*, Cambridge, MA and London, UK: Harvard University Press.
Dig. = *Digesta*, in *Corpus juris civilis*, first part, editio stereotipa (1833–34), Leipzig: Sumptibus Baumgartneri.
NE = Aristotle (1994), *Nicomachean Ethics*, Cambridge, MA and London, UK: Harvard University Press.
Liddell Scott = H.G. Liddell and R. Scott (1968), *A Greek–English Lexicon*, Oxford: Clarendon Press.
Odes = Horace (1998), *Odes*, Oxford: Clarendon Press.
Or. = Cicero (1962), *Orator*, Cambridge, MA and London, UK: Harvard University Press.
Pol. = Aristotle (1990), *Politics*, Cambridge, MA and London, UK: Harvard University Press.
Rep. = Plato (1963), *The Republic*, Cambridge, MA and London, UK: Harvard University Press.
Soll. An. = Plutarch (1995), *De Sollertia Animalium*, Venice: Marsilio.
SVF = *Stoicorum Veterum Fragmenta*, J. von Arnim (ed.) (1905), Stuttgart: Teubner.
Tusc. = Cicero (1966), *Tusculan Disputations*, English trans. by J.E. King, London, UK and Cambridge, MA: Harvard University Press.

Annas, J. (1990), 'The hellenistic version of Aristotle's ethics', *The Monist*, **73**, 80–96.
Arnold, E.V. (1911), *Roman Stoicism*, Cambridge: Cambridge University Press.
Baldry, H.C. (1965), *The Unity of Mankind in Greek Thought*, Cambridge: Cambridge University Press.
Barney, R. (2003), 'A puzzle in Stoic ethics', *Oxford Studies in Ancient Philosophy*, **24**, 303–40.
Berns, L. (1994), 'Aristotle and Adam Smith on justice: cooperation between ancients and moderns?' *Review of Metaphysics*, **48**, 71–90.
Boas, M. (1962), *The Scientific Renaissance 1450–1630*, London: William Collins Sons & Co.
Bobbio, N. (1989), *Thomas Hobbes*, Turin: Einaudi.
Brink, C.O. (1955–56), '*Oikeiosis* and *Oikeiotes*. Theophrastus and Zeno on Nature in moral theory', *Phronesis*, **1**, 123–45.
Brucker, J. (1767), *Historia critica philosophiae*, Leipzig: Weidemann et Reichl.
Brunt, P.I. (1975), 'Stoicism and the Principate', *Papers of the British School at Rome*, **43**, 7–35.
Cicero (1550), *M.T. Ciceronis de officiis libri III. Cum copiosissimis viri longe doctissimi commentariis, & cum Viti Amerbachii commentariolis, Annotationibus Erasmi Roter., Philippi Melanch. & Disquisitionibus aliquot Caelij Calcagnini*, Paris: apud Thomam Richardum.
Cicu, L. (2000), 'Cicerone e il *prepon*', *Paideia*, **55**, 123–62.
Colish, M. (1985), *The Stoic Tradition from Antiquity to the Early Middle Ages, I: Stoicism in Classical Latin Literature*, Leiden: E.J. Brill.
Copenhaver, B.P. and C.B. Schmitt (1992), *Renaissance Philosophy*, Oxford, UK and New York, USA: Oxford University Press.
Crell (n.d.), *I. Cirelli Germanici Ethica Aristotelica, ad Sacrarum Literarum normam emendata*, Selenoburgi.
Cummings, R.D. (1969), *Human Nature and History. A Study of the Development of Liberal Political Thought*, Chicago, IL and London, UK: University of Chicago Press.
Erskine, A. (1990), *The Hellenistic Stoa*, Ithaca, NY: Cornell University Press.
Evrigenis, I.D. (1999), 'The doctrine of the mean in Aristotle's ethical and political theory', *History of Political Thought*, **20**, 393–416.
Fabris, G. (1982), 'Economia di sussistenza, rapporti di scambio e istituzioni politiche. Un'indagine su Platone', in L. Ruggiu (ed.), *Genesi dello spazio economico*, Naples: Guida Editori.
Fagiani, F. (1986), 'Dimensioni sociali ed economiche della critica giusnaturalistica del patriarcalismo', in F. Fagiani and G. Valera, *Categorie del reale e storiografia. Aspetti di continuità e trasformazione nell'Europa moderna*, Milan: Franco Angeli, pp. 140–65.

Fleischacker, S. (1999), *A Third Concept of Liberty: Judgment and Freedom in Kant and Adam Smith*, Princeton, NJ: Princeton University Press.
Fleischacker, S. (2004), *A Short History of Distributive Justice*, Cambridge MA and London, UK: Harvard University Press.
Frede, M. (1999), 'Epilogue', in K. Algra, J. Barnes, J. Mansfeld and M. Schofield (eds), *The Cambridge History of Hellenistic Philosophy*, Cambridge: Cambridge University Press, 771–97.
Frigo, D. (1985), *Il padre di famiglia. Governo della casa e governo civile nella tradizione dell' 'economica' tra Cinque e Seicento*, Rome: Bulzoni.
Frigo, D. (1988), 'La "civile proportione": ceti, principe e composizione degli interessi nella letteratura politica d'antico regime', in C. Mozzarelli (ed.), *Economia e corporazioni. Il governo degli interessi nella storia d'Italia dal Medioevo all'età contemporanea*, Milan: Giuffrè, pp. 81–108.
Frigo, D. (1995), 'Amministrazione domestica e prudenza "oeconomica": alcune riflessioni sul sapere politico d'ancien régime', *Annali di storia moderna e contemporanea*, **1**, 29–49.
Gabba, E. (1988), 'Ricchezza e classe dirigente romana fra III e I sec. a.C.', in: *Del buon uso della ricchezza. Saggi di storia economica e sociale del mondo antico*, Milan: Guerini e associati, pp. 27–44.
Garin, E. (1983), *Il ritorno dei filosofi antichi*, Naples: Bibliopolis.
Gorgemann, H. (1983), '*Oikeiosis* in Arius Didymus', in W.W. Fortenbaugh (ed.), *On Stoic and Peripatetic Ethics: The Work of Arrius Didymus*, New Brunswick, NJ and London, UK: Rutgers University Studies in Classical Humanities, Vol. I, pp. 165–89.
Gottschalk, H.B. (1987), 'Aristotelian philosophy in the Roman world from the time of Cicero to the end of the second century AD', *Aufstieg und Niedergang der römischen Welt*, **36** (2), Berlin: De Gruyter, 1079–1174.
Gottschalk, H.B. (1997), 'Continuity and change in Aristotelianism', in R. Sorabji (ed.), *Aristotle and After*, London, *Bulletin of the Institute of Classical Studies*, Suppl. 68, pp. 109–15.
Grilli, A. (1992), 'Studi paneziani', in *Stoicismo Epicureismo e letteratura*, Brescia: Paideia editrice, pp. 109–78.
Griswold, C.L. (1999), *Adam Smith and the Virtues of Enlightenment*, Cambridge: Cambridge University Press.
Griswold, C.L. (2001), 'Reply to my critics', *Perspectives on Political Science*, **30**, 163–7.
Hampsher-Monk, I. (2002) 'From virtue to politeness', in M. van Gelderen and Q. Skinner (eds), *Republicanism: A Shared European Heritage*, Cambridge: Cambridge University Press, Vol. II, pp. 85–105.
Hanley, R. (2006), 'Adam Smith, Aristotle and virtue ethics', in L. Montes and S. Schliesser (eds), *New Voices on Adam Smith*, London, UK and New York, USA: Routledge, pp. 17–39.
Inwood, B. (1983), 'Comments on Professor Gorgemanns' Paper' in W. Fortenbaugh (ed.), *On Stoic and Peripatetic Ethics. The Work of Arius Didimus*, New Brunswick, NJ and London, UK: Transaction Books, pp. 190–201.
Inwood, B. (1984), 'Hierocles: theory and argument in the second century AD', *Oxford Studies in Ancient Philosophy*, **2**, 151–83.
Isnardi Parente, M. (1989), 'Ierocle stoico. Oikeiosis e doveri sociali', *Aufstieg und Niedergang der römischen Welt*, II, **36** (3), Berlin: De Gruyter, 2201–26.
Kelly, P.H. (1986), 'Between politics and economics: concepts of wealth in English mercantilism in the seventeenth and eighteenth centuries', in F. Fagiani and G. Valera, *Categorie del reale e storiografia. Aspetti di continuità e trasformazione nell'Europa moderna*, Milan: Franco Angeli, pp. 235–262.
Kessler, E. (1999), 'Introducing Aristotle to the sixteenth century: the Lefèvre enterprise', in C. Blackwell and S. Kusukawa (eds), *Philosophy in the Sixteenth and Seventeenth Centuries: Conversations with Aristotle*, Aldershot: Ashgate, pp. 1–21.
Kristeller, P.O. (1972), *Renaissance Concepts of Man*, New York and San Francisco, CA: Harper & Row.
Kristeller, P.O. (1974), 'Thomism and Italian thought', in E.P. Mahoney (ed.), *Medieval Aspects of Renaissance Learning*, Durham, NC: Duke University Press, pp. 29–91.
Labowski, L. (1934), *Die Ethik des Panaitios. Untersuchungen zur Geschichte des decorum bei Cicero und Horaz*, Leipzig: Felix Meiner Verlag.
Lambertini, R. (1985), 'Per una storia dell'*oeconomica* tra alto e basso medioevo', *Cheiron*, **2** (4), 45–74.
Levy, C. (1992), *Cicero academicus*, Rome: Ecole française de Rome, coll.162.
Lohr, C.L. (1974), 'Renaissance Latin Aristotle Commentaries: Authors A–B', *Studies in the Renaissance*, **21**, 228–89.
Lohr, C.L. (1999), 'Metaphysics and natural philosophy as sciences: the Catholic and the Protestant views in the sixteenth and seventeenth centuries', in C. Blackwell and S. Kusukawa (eds), *Philosophy in the Sixteenth and Seventeenth Centuries: Conversations with Aristotle*, Aldershot: Ashgate, pp. 280–95.
Long, A.A. (1997), 'Stoic philosophers on persons, property-ownership and community' in R. Sorabji (ed.), *Aristotle and After*, London, *Bulletin of the Institute of Classical Studies*, Suppl. 68, pp. 13–31.
Lotito, G. (1981), 'Modelli etici e base economica nelle opere filosofiche di Cicerone', in A. Giardina and A.

Schiavone (eds), *Società romana e produzione schiavistica, III: Modelli etici, diritto e trasformazioni sociali*, Bari: Laterza, pp. 79–126.
Magnaldi, G. (1991), *L'oikeiosis peripatetica in Ario Didimo e nel De Finibus di Cicerone*, Florence: Le lettere.
Manning, C.E. (1989), 'Stoicism and slavery in the Roman Empire', *Aufstieg und Niedergang der roemischen Welt*, II, **36** (3), Berlin: De Gruyter, 1518–43.
Mcconica, J. (1979), 'Humanism and Aristotle in Tudor Oxford', *English Historical Review*, **94** (371), 291–317.
Michel, A. (1976), 'Philosophie grecque et libertés individuelles dans le "de officiis" de Cicéron, in *La filosofia greca e il diritto romano*, Rome: Acc. Naz. Dei Lincei, CCCLXXIII, quad. 221, 83–96.
Mingay, J. (1972), 'Coniunctio inter homines hominum. Cicero, de finibus V 65 and Related Passages', in S.M. Stern, A. Hourari and V. Brown (eds), *Islamic Philosophy and the Classical tradition*, Columbia, SC: University of South Carolina Press, pp. 261–75.
Monsarrat, G.D. (1984), *Light from the Porch: Stoicism and English Renaissance Literature*, Collection études anglaises 86, Paris: Didier.
Montes, L. (2004), *Adam Smith in Context*, London, UK and New York, USA: Palgrave Macmillan.
Montes, L. and S. Schliesser (eds) (2006), *New Voices on Adam Smith*, London, UK and New York, USA: Routledge.
Narducci, E. (1984), 'Il comportamento in pubblico. Cicerone, *de officiis* I, 126–94', *Maia*, **36** (3), 203–9.
Narducci, E. (1990), 'Pratiche letterarie e crisi della società. Oratoria, storiografia e filosofia nell'ultimo secolo della repubblica', in A. Momigliano and A. Schiavone (eds), *Storia di Roma*, Turin: Einaudi, Vol. II (1), pp. 885–921.
Narducci, E. (1994), 'Una morale per la classe dirigente', in Cicero, *I doveri*, Milan: Rizzoli, pp. 5–68.
Natali, C. (1989), *La saggezza di Aristotele*, Naples: Bibliopolis.
Natali, C. (1995), 'Introduzione', in Aristotele, *L'amministrazione della casa*, Bari: Laterza.
Natali, C. (2001), *The Wisdom of Aristotle*, Albany, NY: State University of New York Press.
Nedermann, C.J. (1991), 'Aristotelianism and the origins of "Political Science" in the twelfth century', *Journal of the History of Ideas*, **52**, 179–94.
Neri, D. (1986), 'Elementi di trasformazione del paradigma aristotelico nella filosofia politica del Seicento: Althusius e Hobbes', in F. Fagiani and G. Valera (1986), *Categorie del reale e storiografia. Aspetti di continuità e trasformazione nell'Europa moderna*, Milan: Franco Angeli, pp. 131–9.
Owens, J. (1981), 'The *kalon* in Aristotelian *Ethics*', in D.J. O'Meara (ed.), *Studies in Aristotle*, Washington, DC: Catholic University of America Press, pp. 261–77.
Paganelli, M.P. (2000), 'Adam Smith: il primo o l'ultimo?', *Annali di storia moderna e contemporanea*, **6**, 421–34.
Paganelli, M.P. (2003), 'In *Medio Stat Virtus*: an alternative view of usury in Adam Smith's thinking', *History of Political Economy*, **35** (1), 21–48.
Pembroke, S.G. (1971), 'Oikeiosis', in A.A. Long (ed.), *Problems in Stoicism*, London: Athlone Press, pp. 114–49.
Perionio (1540), *Ioachimi Perionii Benedict. Cormoeriaceni de optimo genere interpretandi commentarij*, Paris: apud Simonem Colinaeum.
Pesante, M.L. (1995), 'An impartial actor: the private and the public sphere in Adam Smith's *Theory of Moral Sentiments*', in D. Castiglione and L. Scarpe (eds), *Shifting the Boundaries. Transformation of the Languages of Public and Private in the Eighteenth Century*, Exeter: University of Exeter Press, pp. 172–95.
Pesante, M.L. (2000), 'Il commercio nella repubblica', *Quaderni storici*, **35** (3), 655–95.
Pocock, J.G.A. (1968), 'Civic humanism and its role in anglo-american thought', *Il pensiero politico*, **1**, 172–89.
Pocock, J.G.A. (1983), 'Cambridge paradigms and Scotch philosophers: a study of the relations between the civic humanist and the civil jurisprudential interpretation of eighteenth-century social thought' in I. Hont and M. Ignatieff (eds), *Wealth and Virtue. The Shaping of Political Economy in the Scottish Enlightenment*, Cambridge: Cambridge University Press, pp. 235–52.
Praechter, K. (1901), *Hierokles der Stoiker*, Leipzig: Dieterich'sche Verlags-Buchhandlung.
Radcliffe, E. (1993), 'Revolutionary writing, moral philosophy, and universal benevolence in the Eighteenth Century', *Journal of the History of Ideas*, **54** (2), 221–40.
Reydams-Schils, G. (2002), 'Human bonding and *oikeiosis* in Roman Stoicism', *Oxford Studies in Ancient Philosophy*, **22**, 221–51.
Salmon, J.H.M. (1989), 'Stoicism and Roman example: Seneca and Tacitus in Jacobean England', *Journal of the History of Ideas*, **50**, 199–225.
Sandbach, F.H. (1985), *Aristotle and the Stoics*, Cambridge: Cambridge Philological Society.
Schmitt, C.B. (1983), *Aristotle and the Renaissance*, Cambridge, MA and London, UK: Harvard University Press.
Schmitt, C.B. (1985), *La tradizione aristotelica: fra Italia e Inghilterra*, Naples: Bibliopolis.
Schofield, M. (1999), *The Stoic Idea of the City*, Chicago, IL and London, UK: University of Chicago Press.

Scott, W.R. (1940), 'Greek influence on Adam Smith', in *Etudes dediées à la mémoire d'André Andréadès*, Athens: Imprimerie Pyrsos S.A., pp. 79–100.
Skinner, Q. (2002), 'Classical liberty and the coming of the English Civil War', in M. van Gelderen and Q. Skinner (eds), *Republicanism: A Shared European Heritage*, Cambridge: Cambridge University Press, Vol. II, pp. 9–28.
Sorabji, R. (ed.) (1990), *Aristotle Transformed*, London: Duckworth.
Stanley, T. (1701), *The History of Philosophy*, London: Battersby.
Taylor, W.L. (1965), *Francis Hutcheson and David Hume as Predecessors of Adam Smith*, Durham, NC: Duke University Press.
Temple-Smith, R. (2007), 'Adam Smith's treatment of the Greeks in the *Theory of Moral Sentiments*: the case of Aristotle', in G. Cockfield, A. Firth and J. Laurent (eds), *New Perspectives on Adam Smith's The Theory of Moral Sentiments*, Cheltenham, UK and Northampton, MA, USA: Edward Elgar, pp. 29–46.
Tribe, K. (1978), *Land, Labour and Economic Discourse*, London, UK and Boston, MA: Routledge & Kegan Paul.
Tugendhat, E. (2004), 'Universalistically approved intersubjective attitudes: Adam Smith', *Adam Smith Review*, **1**, 88–104.
Urmson, J.O. (1973), 'Aristotle's doctrine of the mean', *American Philosophical Quarterly*, **10** (3), 223–30.
Vegetti, M. (1976), *Polis e economia nella Grecia antica*, Bologna: Zanichelli.
Vivenza, G. (1990), 'Lavoro e attività politica: motivi classici e moderni nel pensiero di Adam Smith', in G. Gaburro, R. Molesti and G. Zalin (eds), *Economia Stato e Società. Studi in memoria di G. Menegazzi*, Pisa: IPEM edizioni, pp. 581–611.
Vivenza, G. (1995), 'Origini classiche della benevolenza nel linguaggio economico (dall'evergesia del mondo antico alla "benevolence" della società commerciale)', in R. Molesti (ed.), *Tra economia e storia. Studi in memoria di Gino Barbieri*, Pisa: IPEM edizioni, pp. 497–529.
Vivenza, G. (1996a), 'Benevolenza pubblica, benevolenza privata e benevolenza reciproca. La virtù del dono e dello scambio dall'antichità al Settecento', *Studi storici Luigi Simeoni*, **46**, 15–37.
Vivenza, G. (1996b), 'Virtù aristocratiche ed etica commerciale', *Nuova Economia e Storia*, **2**, 33–56.
Vivenza, G. (2001a), 'The "Northern" Cicero. On the *fortuna* of the *De Officiis* in Central Europe', *Mésogeios*, **13–14**, 201–27.
Vivenza, G. (2001b), *Adam Smith and the Classics*, Oxford: Oxford University Press.
Vivenza, G. (2001c), 'Cicero und die traditionelle Wirtschaftsmoral in der Antike', in B. Schefold (ed.), *Marcus Tullius Ciceros de officiis. Vademecum zu einem klassiker des römischen Denkens über Staat und Wirtschaft*, Düsseldorf: Verlag Wirtschaft und Finanzen.
Vivenza, G. (2004), 'Renaissance Cicero: the "economic" virtues of *De Officiis* I, 22 in some sixteenth century commentaries', *European Journal of the History of Economic Thought*, **11** (4), 507–23.
Waszek, N. (1984), 'Two concepts of morality: a distinction of Adam Smith's ethics and its Stoic origin', *Journal of the History of Ideas*, **45**, 591–606.
Whitlock Blundell, M. (1990), 'Parental nature and Stoic *Oikeiosis*', *Ancient Philosophy* **10**, 221–42.
Winch, D. (2002), 'Commercial realities, republican principles', in M. van Gelderen and Q. Skinner (eds), *Republicanism: A Shared European Heritage*, Cambridge: Cambridge University Press, Vol. II, pp. 293–310.
Zanini, A. (1995), *Genesi imperfetta. Il governo delle passioni in Adam Smith*, Turin: Giappichelli.
Zeller, E. (1844–52), *Philosophie der Griechen, Eine Untersuchung über Character, Gang und Hauptmomente ihrer Entwicklung*, 3 vols, Tübingen: L.F. Fues.

3 Agency and discourse: revisiting the Adam Smith problem
Vivienne Brown[*]

I

The current consensus is that there is no inconsistency between the suppositions concerning human motivation, or motives to action, in Adam Smith's two great works, *The Theory of Moral Sentiments* (1759 [1976a]) and *An Inquiry into the Nature and Causes of the Wealth of Nations* (1776 [1976b]). In this sense the old 'Adam Smith problem' has been put to rest. But, as the continuing interest in the issue illustrates, newer versions of the 'problem' are concerned with the question of just how the two works relate to each other. This modern version of the Adam Smith problem may be construed in different ways, for example in terms of: how the suppositions about human nature presented in the *Moral Sentiments* relate to those which are presented in the *Wealth of Nations*; how different motives to action are (or are not) emphasized relatively more in one work rather than in the other; how Smith's moral philosophy relates to his economic analysis; and how each of the two works contributes to the larger yet unfinished (or even unfinishable) intellectual project on which Smith was engaged.

In earlier work I argued that the relation between the *Moral Sentiments* and the *Wealth of Nations* can be understood in terms of an overarching moral hierarchy, owing much to the Stoics in spite of Smith's formal rejection of central tenets of Stoicism, within which each of the works is differently positioned; important theoretical differences between the two works are thereby respected whilst not construing difference as implying inconsistency (Brown, 1991, 1994, 1997a). As part of this interpretation, I argued that the two works are characterized by different core conceptions of the 'agent', as 'moral agent' and as 'economic agent', and that these different conceptions are registered in the style and voice of the two texts. This is not to say that all the content of these two works can be subsumed under these particular approaches to conceptions of agency; there is too much diversity for that. But it is to suggest that these conceptions of the moral agent and economic agent are crucial for the central theoretical arguments and innovations of the two works.

In this chapter I further explore issues of agency in the *Moral Sentiments* and *Wealth of Nations* by questioning some widely shared presuppositions in scholarly debates about Smith's approach to 'motives to action'. I argue that the emphasis on construing questions about human nature in terms of 'motives to action' begs a more fundamental question about the metaphysics of agency in these two texts. When this is understood, it turns out that there are some systemic differences in the treatment of agency that have been overlooked, and that these differences are important for understanding the originality and distinctiveness of Smith's contribution to both moral philosophy and economics.[1]

II

The question of the relation between the *Moral Sentiments* and *Wealth of Nations* has been posed by many scholars in terms of whether Smith held inconsistent presuppositions about human 'motives to action'. Although the terms of the debate shift somewhat, the central issue has tended to be seen in terms of a series of binary pairs involving a basic dichotomy between other-regarding and self-regarding motives to action – pairs such as altruism–egoism, benevolence–self-interest, sympathy–selfishness – such that a fundamental question is whether other-regarding motives to action are assumed in the *Moral Sentiments* whereas self-regarding ones are assumed in the *Wealth of Nations*.

D.D. Raphael and A.L. Macfie in their Introduction to the Glasgow Edition of the *Moral Sentiments* (Raphael and Macfie, 1976, pp. 20–25) and Raphael (1985, esp. Ch. 5; 2007, esp. Ch. 13) have challenged this dichotomy of motives to action by arguing that it is wrong to counterpose self-interest to the virtues in the *Moral Sentiments*. According to this argument, Smith's account of the motives to action includes a variety of motives for virtuous action, including self-interest ('self-love' in eighteenth-century terms, to be contrasted with 'selfishness' which harms others). Although self-interest is the motive that 'comes to the fore' in the *Wealth of Nations*, they say, it also has its place in the *Moral Sentiments* where Smith defends it as 'a necessary element' in virtue. Building on the work of scholars such as August Oncken (1897; 1898 [2000]) and Walther Eckstein (1926 [2000]), Raphael and Macfie claim that there is therefore no inconsistency, or at least no 'radical inconsistency' (1976, pp. 24–5), between the two works. As Smith 'recognizes a variety of motives, not only for action in general but also for virtuous action' in the *Moral Sentiments*, they conclude that it is 'impossible to accept the view that there is any difference of substance between TMS and WN on self-interest as a motive' (p. 22).[2] According to this view the *Moral Sentiments* and *Wealth of Nations* comprise overlapping areas of investigation with shared presuppositions about the full range of human motives to action. Smith's argument against the egoism of Mandeville's system is thus seen as an attack on the exaggerated bifurcation of human motives that is represented by the basic dichotomy and which Mandeville exploited so powerfully in the *Fable of the Bees* (Mandeville, 1732 [1924, 1988]). As Samuel Fleischacker, for example, elaborates the point: 'the very presentation of human motivations as running between self-interest and benevolence is simplistic and narrow . . . the spectrum between self-interest and benevolence is not in fact Smith's only axis on which to locate human emotions' (Fleischacker, 2004, p. 67).

Raphael and Macfie's argument against the view that there is any dichotomy between other-regarding and self-regarding motives to action in Smith's two major works included a criticism of Henry T. Buckle who, in his *History of Civilisation in England* (1857, 1861), accepted the basic dichotomy but argued that the two different motives relate to different domains of investigation which taken together comprise 'a magnificent unity' (1861, vol. 2, p. 442).[3] The *Moral Sentiments* and *Wealth of Nations* are 'the two divisions of a single subject' because the classification of motives to action in terms of sympathy (in the *Moral Sentiments*) and selfishness (in the *Wealth of Nations*) is 'a primary and exhaustive division of our motives to action' (Buckle, 1861, Vol. 2, p. 433). Buckle's argument that Smith adopted a deductive approach, characteristic of eighteenth-century Scottish thinking, is hard to square with the evidence, but his interpretation of sympathy as a motive to action has elicited a mixed response. Raphael and Macfie have argued that

Buckle was mistaken in thinking that sympathy was a 'motive to action'; instead, they argue, 'sympathy is the core of Smith's explanation of moral *judgment*. The motive to action is an entirely different matter' (Raphael and Macfie, 1976, pp. 21–2). Raphael has since conceded that Smith is not entirely consistent in his use of the term 'sympathy', but he still maintains that the primary sense of 'sympathy' in the *Moral Sentiments* relates to moral judgement not motive to action (Raphael, 1985, pp. 29, 86–90; 2007, pp. 116ff.). Buckle was thus not only mistaken in thinking that sympathy and selfishness are contrasting motives to action in the *Moral Sentiments* and *Wealth of Nations* (also misconstruing self-interest as selfishness), but was more seriously in error in making the category mistake that sympathy is a motive to action. Other commentators, however, have challenged Raphael and Macfie on this, and have argued that sympathy is a motive to action (Khalil, 1990, pp. 256–7; Montes, 2004, esp. pp. 45–55).

Buckle makes a further point, however, that is also significant for his interpretation of Smith's method, that in a young science the exposure of the necessary regularities or 'social laws' sometimes requires focusing on 'ideal' rather than 'real' processes.[4] The 'simplifications' this entails are given theoretically, he argues, as science requires separating 'in speculation qualities which are inseparable in reality' (Vol. 2, p. 437). The different motives to action assumed in the *Moral Sentiments* and *Wealth of Nations* may thus be explained by the requirements of science. As an example of the implications of this requirement, Buckle argues that it is a misunderstanding of the science of political economy to reproach it for 'hardheartedness' because 'the science could not be constructed if it were necessary to take in the whole range of generous and benevolent affections' (Vol. 2, pp. 435–6). This is elaborated as follows:

> The political economist aims at discovering the laws of wealth, which are far too complicated to be studied under every aspect. He, therefore, selects one of those aspects, and generalizes the laws as they are exhibited in the selfish parts of human nature. And he is right in doing so, simply because men, in the pursuit of wealth, consider their own gratification oftener than the gratification of others . . .[5] But we must always remember, that political economy, though a profound and beautiful science, is only a science of one department of life, and is founded upon a suppression of some of the facts in which all large societies abound. It suppresses, or, what comes to the same thing, it ignores, many high and magnanimous feelings which we could ill afford to lose. We are not, therefore, to allow its conclusions to override other conclusions. We may accept them in science, and yet reject them in practice. (Buckle, 1861, Vol. 2, p. 436)

The laws of political economy thus hold only given its particular assumptions, so that other considerations come into play which might justify rejecting those laws in practice. Buckle provides two examples of this, both politically charged examples where the 'laws' of political economy had come in for criticism: the first concerns the question whether government should supply the working classes with employment, and the second whether it is wrong to relieve the poor with charity. Buckle argues that in both cases the laws of political economy state that the proposed measures would be ineffective, yet he also argues that other considerations (of public policy or the charitable impulse deriving from sympathy) might overrule those laws and justify taking the contrary action. In practice therefore Buckle did not hold that the two areas of human life are distinct. What are distinct are the theoretical requirements of different areas of inquiry. Furthermore, he emphasized that in practice the analysis of the young science of political economy is and should be overridden by broader issues of public policy and private morality, again illustrating that in practice the two aspects of human life – involving other-regarding and self-regarding motives to action – are not in fact separable.

Discussion about the motives to action in Smith's works has thus been concerned with *which* motives to action are assumed in different works of Smith (or different editions of those works) and whether *these* motives to action have some appropriate moral standing. Whatever other differences there might be between commentators, there is agreement that a core issue relates to the moral qualities of the different motives to action that are assumed in Smith's texts. Yet this is to beg a more fundamental question about the *theory of human agency* in Smith's texts – whether it should be construed in terms of motives to action and, if so, what is the relation between motives and action. These are fundamental issues in the metaphysics of agency, and they are huge and philosophically problematic. Characterizing the Adam Smith problem in terms of human motives to action, however, is to use terms that are already freighted with such issues.

III

A core question concerns the relation between motives to action and the subsequent action. In particular, is the relation a causal one such that the motive to action is the 'cause' of the subsequent action; and if so does this imply that the cause is sufficient for the action to take place, in which case an action is necessitated by the cause? Such questions in the metaphysics of agency involve long-standing philosophical problems and the eighteenth century proved no exception to their power to elicit lively debate. A root philosophical question is whether motives to action necessitate what an agent does or whether they merely influence the agent in deciding what to do. This is the old debate about whether a human agent is free to do otherwise or whether action is necessitated or determined by prior events so that it is not possible for an agent to act otherwise. This is also the debate about 'freedom of the will' and whether an agent's volitions as well as actions are necessitated.[6]

Against this background, David Hume's 'reconciling project' was to try to reconcile necessitarians and libertarians by showing that the debate between them derived from a misconception of 'necessary connexion' or causation. Hume's arguments have been much debated and are still the subject of philosophical disagreement;[7] but the standard interpretation has largely been that Hume redefined the notion of necessary connexion or causation in terms of the constant conjunction between events of different kinds and the inference of the mind in passing from what are thus taken to be causes and effects (together with temporal priority of the cause, and contiguity of cause and effect) (*Treatise*, 1739–40 [1978], 1.3.14; first *Enquiry*, 1748, 1777 [1975], 7). Necessity is thus not 'in nature': our idea of 'necessary connexion' among events, Hume argued, derives from the way we respond to, and try to make sense of, what we observe as the constant conjunction of events. Hume insisted, however, that given this understanding of necessary connexion, there is the same relation of cause and effect between motives and actions as there is between events in the physical world (*Treatise* 2.3.1; first *Enquiry* 8). According to Hume's argument, therefore, human actions are necessitated by motives to act just as physical events are necessitated by prior events:

> as the *union* betwixt motives and actions has the same constancy, as that in any natural operations, so its influence on the understanding is also the same, in *determining* us to infer the

existence of one from that of another. If this shall appear, there is no known circumstance, that enters into the connexion and production of the actions of matter, that is not to be found in the operations of the mind; and consequently we cannot, without a manifest absurdity, attribute necessity to the one, and refuse it to the other. (Hume, *Treatise* 2.3.1, p. 404; cf. first *Enquiry* 8)

Human liberty thus consists not of freedom of the will (an unintelligible notion, Hume argued) but the absence of impediments to action, a conclusion familiar to Hume's readers as one advocated by Thomas Hobbes (1660 [1996], Ch. 21), although Hume's account of causation ran against Hobbes's. Hume thus presented a new argument for the compatibilism of necessity and freedom, an argument that sparked off (or rather rekindled) an enduring philosophical debate not only about what can be understood by necessity and causation, but also about how actions are to be explained, whether the explanation of action takes the same form as explanation of physical events, and whether human freedom and moral responsibility are compatible with necessity and determinism.

Thomas Reid, who succeeded Adam Smith as Professor of Moral Philosophy at the University of Glasgow in 1764, was one of the philosophers who challenged Hume's account. In his *Essays on the Active Powers of Man* (1788 [1963, 1994]) he argued in favour of the freedom of the will in terms of what has come to be known as 'agent-causation', that human actions are caused by the agent, not by the agent's motives to action. Reid differentiates between motives and acts of will; the former provide the goals of action and the latter is the means of choosing. Motives to action are thus more like 'advice' that the agent takes into account in exercising free will, and are not the cause of action. The cause of action is thus rooted in the 'power' that an agent has to choose and act in one way rather than in another.

It might be thought that metaphysical questions about motivation and causality are far removed from the *Moral Sentiments*, yet there is some evidence that Hume and Reid, Smith's contemporaries, were not uninterested in what they took to be the metaphysical implications of the *Moral Sentiments*. In Hume's 'Abstract' of the *Moral Sentiments*, sympathy is described in a passing reference as 'this spring, this movement, this power, is the chief foundation of his [Smith's] system. By means of it he [Smith] hopes to explain all the species of approbation or disapprobation, which are excited by human action or behaviour' (Hume, 1984 [1997], p. 35), thus providing an interpretation of sympathy that is more like Buckle's. Reid, however, criticized Smith for basing his account of moral approbation on a person's feelings rather than actions, on the grounds that it is the latter which are subject to the will. According to Reid in his 'Sketch' on the *Moral Sentiments* no one can be 'a just object either of moral Approbation or disapprobation for what is not in his power' (Reid 1984 [1997], p. 77); for Reid actions are 'in a person's power' so that a person may, properly, be held responsible only for them. Although Reid notes that in the *Moral Sentiments* the nature of virtue is sometimes placed in 'an Effort to regulate our own Emotions so as that others may sympathize with them', such that this 'effort' may indeed be subject to 'an act of the will' and hence liable to moral appraisal, yet he argues that Smith's system is still vulnerable to his basic charge of misconstruing the proper object of moral evaluation (1997, p. 77). For Reid, a man's moral character 'depends not upon what he feels but how he acts' (p. 76).

In his *History* Buckle (1857, 1861) takes up Hume's account of causation. He does not engage in criticism of Hume, noting that: 'Among his speculative views, the most important are, his theory of causation as discarding the idea of power, and his theory of the laws of association' (Vol. 2, p. 460). He is, however, scathing of Reid's attempts in *Essays on the Active Powers of Man* to criticize 'the profound views of Hume respecting causation' (Vol. 2, p. 477). Given Buckle's characterization of sympathy and self-interest in terms of 'motives to action', it is not surprising to find that Buckle's historiographical stance is an adaptation of his Humean position on causality, according to which the possibility of a 'science of history' is based on the fact that the actions of men are necessitated by their motives:

> When we perform an action, we perform it in consequence of some motive or motives; that those motives are the results of some antecedents; and that, therefore, if we were acquainted with the whole of the antecedents, and with all the laws of their movements, we could with unerring certainty predict the whole of their immediate results. (Buckle, *History*, 1857, Vol. 1, p. 17)[8]

According to Buckle, 'social laws', which he argues are subject to statistical analysis, arise because the 'moral actions of men are the product not of their volition, but of their antecedents' (Vol. 1, p. 29). Buckle's view of the possibility of history is thus rooted in his causal account of human action. This is not to say that Buckle attributes Smith with Hume's theory of causation or with his version of necessitarianism; but it does illustrate the importance of debate about the significance of causal relations for the study of society and the science of political economy in which Buckle was interested.

Smith published the *Moral Sentiments* after Hume had published the *Treatise on Human Nature* and the *Enquiry into the Human Understanding*. If Smith accepted aspects of Hume's causal account of action then we might expect to find some evidence of that in the *Moral Sentiments*, or at least some indication of a causal approach to action, whether or not Smith concurred with Hume's reconceptualization of causation as constant conjunction. Indeed some scholars have subscribed to a causal account of action in the *Moral Sentiments*. According to D.D. Raphael (2007), Hutcheson and Hume argued that moral judgement is affective, in resting on feeling, and that 'the motive for acting upon that judgement must likewise be affective, since reason alone does not have the power to stir bodily movement' (2007, p. 6). Raphael seems to subscribe to a causal account of action in the *Moral Sentiments* when he writes that a judgement of propriety or impropriety is 'an assertion that an action is appropriate or inappropriate, suitable or unsuitable, to the cause that has prompted the agent to do it' (2007, p. 14). The editors of the Glasgow Edition of the *Wealth of Nations* comment that 'we may judge an action taken by ourselves or others, "first, in relation to the cause or object which excites it; and, secondly, in relation to the end which it proposes . . ."' (Campbell and Skinner, 1976, p. 5; citing TMS II.i.Intro.2). Here they seem to construe the anaphoric 'it' as referring back to 'action', so that a judgement is made concerning the cause or object which excites the action.[9] In both these interpretations, then, judgement seems to relate to the 'cause' of action, thus presupposing that Smith did have a causal theory of action. Fleischacker, like Raphael (1977), notes that in the 'History of Astronomy' (Smith, 1795 [1980], pp. 31–105) Smith uses language similar to Hume's in describing the way that the imagination 'creates connections between commonly associated impressions' (Fleischacker, 2004, p. 29). Fleischacker argues that although it is unclear whether Smith agreed with Hume in thinking that this 'is all there is to causality', nonetheless Smith 'clearly did share Hume's view that causality applies to human events in the same way that it applies to nonhuman ones' such that the relationship between physical causes and physical events is 'exactly on a level with the relationship between our motivations and our actions' (p. 29). In support of this position Fleischacker cites Hume's *Enquiry Concerning Human Understanding* (8.1; pp. 92–3) and he even suggests that this chapter of Hume's did influence Smith (2004, p. 287, n. 11). As noted above, Leonidas Montes argues, against Raphael and Macfie, that sympathy is a motive for action and so has motivational force, but he thereby accepts their assumption of a causal model of action. He argues that Smith works in terms of motives for action which have causal force, since both 'motives' and 'antecedent causes' are held to 'trigger our conduct'; and elsewhere he argues that it is 'the strong sense of propriety' which is 'the cause which excites an action' (Montes, 2004, pp. 53, 54, 107; cf. p. 108).[10]

Construing the Adam Smith problem in terms of motives to action is thus to adopt an interpretative framework that predisposes towards a causal interpretation of Smith's account of action in the *Moral Sentiments*, howsoever the difficult notion of 'causation' might be understood. Although this is a question in the metaphysics of agency rather than a question in moral philosophy, its answer turns out to be significant for the relation between the *Moral Sentiments* and the *Wealth of Nations*.

IV

A problem with this interpretative framework of the Adam Smith problem, however, is that Smith does not argue in terms of motives as 'causes' of action. Indeed in the *Moral Sentiments* there is no mention of the causes of actions at all. In spite of Smith's familiarity with Hume's argument on causality and action, the argument presented in the *Moral Sentiments* provides no echoes of Hume.

In the *Moral Sentiments* it is argued that we can form a conception of others' sentiments and affections by changing places in the imagination with them and imagining how they feel (for example, TMS I.i.1; VII.iii.1.4). Thus it is the exercise of the imagination, problematic though that might sometimes be,[11] that is held out as solving the problem, posed by Hume, that a person's sentiments or motives are unavailable to others. Thus in the *Moral Sentiments* the object of moral approbation and disapprobation is primarily the sentiment or affection from which the action proceeds. This is explained as follows in the first passage that introduces it:

> The sentiment or affection of the heart from which any action proceeds, and upon which its whole virtue or vice must ultimately depend, may be considered under two different aspects, or in two different relations; first, in relation to the cause which excites it, or the motive which gives occasion to it; and secondly, in relation to the end which it proposes, or the effect which it tends to produce. [para. 5]
>
> In the suitableness or unsuitableness, in the proportion or disproportion which the affection seems to bear to the cause or object which excites it, consists the propriety or impropriety, the decency or ungratefulness of the consequent action. [para. 6]
>
> In the beneficial or hurtful nature of the effects which the affection aims at, or tends to produce, consists the merit or demerit of the action, the qualities by which it is entitled to reward, or is deserving of punishment. [para. 7]
>
> Philosophers have, of late years, considered chiefly the tendency [that is, effects] of affections, and have given little attention to the relation which they stand in to the cause which excites

them. In common life, however, when we judge of any person's conduct, and of the sentiments which directed it, we constantly consider them under both these aspects. When we blame in another man the excesses of love, of grief, of resentment, we not only consider the ruinous effects which they tend to produce, but the little occasion which was given for them . . . [para. 8]

When we judge in this manner of any affection, as proportioned or disproportioned to the cause which excites it . . . [para. 9] (TMS I.i.3.5–9; see also TMS II.i.Intro.2)

The point of the passage is to differentiate between a judgement of propriety and a judgement of merit. Both judgements concern the feeling or sentiment from which the action proceeds, but the judgement of propriety is concerned with the feeling or sentiment in relation to 'the cause which excites it' (or, more or less equivalently, 'the motive which gives occasion to it'[12]), whereas the judgement of merit is concerned with the effects intended by that feeling or sentiment. This distinction thus answers to Hume's argument which focuses on the latter, the merit or effects, of the sentiment and action. This passage is the first one to explain that the virtue or vice of an action is given by an assessment of the sentiment or affection of the heart from which the action proceeds. It is the first mention of 'action' and 'motive' in TMS; it is also the first discussion in terms of 'cause and effect'. This raises a question of the relation between sentiment or affection, action and motive, and the role of the relation of 'cause and effect' here.

Crucially, the distinction between 'cause' and 'effect' does not refer to the relation between the sentiment or affection and the subsequent action. The word 'cause' refers to what causes the sentiment; it does not refer to the sentiment as the cause of the action. Raphael (2007, pp. 23–4) finds paragraph 5 'rather obscure' in trying to construe the anaphoric 'it' in the expression 'first, in relation to the cause which excites it'. Grammatically the backwards reference of the anaphoric 'it' here seems to be 'the sentiment or affection of the heart from which any action proceeds', not to 'any action'. This is made entirely clear in the following paragraphs 6, 8 and 9, since there the word 'action' does not make any appearance in advance of the anaphoric 'it' or 'them' which can therefore only refer back to sentiment or affection. This is also clearly seen in a later summary passage: 'upon the suitableness or unsuitableness, upon the proportion or disproportion, which the affection seems to bear to the cause or object which excites it, depends the propriety or impropriety, the decency or ungracefulness of the consequent action' (II.i.Intro.2; also VII.ii.1.48). It follows from this that the 'motive' in paragraph 5 is not a motive in relation to the action but in relation to the sentiment or affection. In the other summary passages of the judgement of propriety (for example TMS I.i.3.6, 8, 9; II.i.Intro.2; VII.ii.1.48) there is no further mention of 'motive' in relation to the sentiment or affection, perhaps because it adds little to the argument, but its inclusion in paragraph 5 led Raphael to misconstrue the anaphoric 'it' so that he concluded that the judgement of propriety is 'a judgment of the motive of action'. Similarly, Campbell and Skinner (pp. 5–6) also seem to have misconstrued the anaphoric 'it' at II.i.Intro.2 as referring to 'action' rather than 'affection' in saying, as noted above, that 'we may judge an action taken by ourselves or others, "first, in relation to the cause or object which excites it; and, secondly, in relation to the end which it proposes . . ."' (Campbell and Skinner, 1976, p. 5; citing TMS II.i.Intro.2).[13]

These interpretations of motives as causes to action are misleading for three reasons: first, they misplace the role of causality in presupposing that what is relevant is the cause of action, rather than the sentiment in relation to its causes; second, they misconstrue 'motive' as being in relation to action whereas here it is in relation to sentiment or affection; and third, they overstate the significance of 'motive' altogether. Smith's account here is not framed in terms of affections (or motives) as the causes of action. It therefore does not reproduce Hume's argument that the relation of 'cause and effect' is applicable to human actions.[14] Instead, the propriety and the merit of an action depend on the relation between the sentiment, its causes and the effects it aims at.

Indeed, as far as I can tell, the word 'cause' is never used in connection with action in the *Moral Sentiments*. In the passage just cited an action 'proceeds from' the sentiment or affection of the heart (also I.i.3.5; II.i.4.2–4; II.i.Intro.2; II.iii.Intro.1). Elsewhere other expressions include: the affections 'influence' the person's conduct (II.i.3.1; II.1.iv.1); an action is 'consequent' upon the affection (I.i.3.6; II.i.Intro.2); the sentiment 'gives occasion to' the action (also I.i.3.9; II.i.Intro.2; II.iii.Intro.1); the sentiments 'direct' a person's conduct (I.i.3.8). Terms such as these are consistently used instead of 'cause'. Similarly 'motive' is never said to be the cause of action. Mostly motive is used alongside sentiment or affection or as interchangeable with it as what is sympathized with, entered into and gone along with, and which influences action or from which action proceeds: 'wherever the conduct of the agent appears to have been entirely directed by motives and affections which we thoroughly enter into and approve of' (II.i.3.3); 'as our sense, therefore, of the propriety of conduct arises from what I shall call a direct sympathy with the affections and motives of the person who acts' (II.i.5.1; also II.i.5.4); 'when we entirely sympathize and go along with the motives of the agent' (II.i.4.1); 'If, upon placing ourselves in his situation, we thoroughly enter into all the passions and motives which influenced it, we approve of it' (III.1.2); 'when he views it in the light in which the impartial spectator would view it, he thoroughly enters into all the motives which influenced it' (III.2.5); 'wherever there seems to be no propriety in the motives which influenced his conduct' (II.i.3.2); 'When his passion is gratified, and he begins coolly to reflect on his past conduct, he can enter into none of the motives which influenced it' (II.ii.2.3); 'we either can or cannot entirely sympathize with the sentiments and motives which directed it [the conduct of another man]' (III.1.2); 'actions of a beneficent tendency, which proceed from proper motives' (II.ii.1.1; also II.ii.1.2); 'crimes should be punished, from whatever motives they proceed' (III.6.12); 'the motive from which he hurt him' (II.ii.2.1); and 'the man who, not from frivolous fancy, but from proper motives, has performed a generous action . . . when he looks backward to the motive from which he acted' (II.ii.2.4). Sometimes the motives which influence action are presented as a sense of duty, or as reverence for the rule of duty (III.5.1), or in terms of principles of action that provide guidance as to what to do, such as religious principles (III.6.1) or 'a regard to what is right and fit to be done' (VII.ii.4.10). Motives are never presented as the 'cause' of actions. Mostly they are treated as indistinct from sentiments and affections, and together with these they influence but do not cause actions.

The consistency of the distinction between 'cause' on the one hand and 'influence', 'proceed from', 'direct' and so on, is striking. Perhaps it might be thought that the latter terms are also causal but simply used in a weaker or looser sense of cause. Certainly these latter terms are weaker and looser than that of 'cause'. If a sentiment (or motive) 'influences' action then the action is not necessitated (howsoever 'necessity' might be construed) by the sentiment or motive. This implies that the action could have been otherwise than it is; or, in terms of causation as regularity, that the conjunction of events is not constant, so that the sentiment (or motive) is not regularly followed by the action that would otherwise be taken to be its effect. The consistency of the linguistic distinction that is being adhered to, however, suggests more than a weakening of a causal relation in respect of action.[15] Rather it suggests a challenge to the view that actions are to be understood causally (howsoever 'causality' is to be understood). It follows that it is also a challenge to the view that actions are to be understood by analogy with physical events.[16] Crucially what Smith's non-causal account of action allows for here is an independent role of some sort for the 'agent'. As an example, this non-causal account of action allows that, whatever the agent's sentiments, it is possible that the agent might not act in accordance with those sentiments.[17] Indeed in many situations the agent may be experiencing a range of sentiments and so it will be an issue of deliberation and judgement for the agent as to how to act.[18]

Smith's non-causal approach to action thus allows conceptual space for accommodating two different dimensions of human agency that might otherwise appear difficult to reconcile. On the one hand, throughout the *Moral Sentiments* it is emphasized that human beings are social creatures and that the making of moral judgements is a socialized process. The spectatorial model of moral judgement presupposes that people's awareness of themselves and their functioning as moral agents are the result of a lifetime process of habituation to and inculcation of social norms; and this seems to suggest a model of agency in which the process of socialization plays a large role in forming people for society. On the other hand, moral judgement presupposes that agents exercise some independent deliberation, and moral responsibility presupposes that behaviour is not simply given by social circumstances. In some cases agents have so great a degree of independence that they even engage in judgement and action that goes against the mores and practices of the society in which they live. This is particularly the case when agents engage with the impartial spectator as this requires the highest level of independent judgement and critical self-reflexivity. The moral exemplar here is the perfectly wise and just man who comes closest to identifying with the impartial spectator and who engages in the severest kind of self-reflexive moral judgement and dialogism of conscience; it is he who desires to be praiseworthy, not merely to be praised, and whose inner resources provide consolation and support at times when moral judgement is in conflict with the mores or practices of society. Even for the less morally elevated, however, who act decently according to the sense of duty or a reverence for the established rules of behaviour (III.4, 5), there would usually be some minimal degree of independence in selecting the relevant rules and adjusting behaviour so as to act in accordance with them. Indeed it is a characteristic of the rules of almost all the virtues that they are 'loose and inaccurate' and 'loose, vague and indeterminate' (III.6.9, 11; VII.iv.1), so they require some interpretation to ascertain what is prescribed in particular circumstances. It is only the virtue of justice whose rules specify 'with the greatest exactness every external action which it requires' (III.6.10). These rules are 'accurate in the highest degree, and admit of no exceptions or modifications, but such as may be ascertained as accurately as the rules themselves'. It follows from this that people are liable to punishment for their actions only, not their sentiments (II.iii.3.2). This does not mean that the observance of justice cannot be attended by the appropriate sentiments; when it is, it qualifies for moral approbation by the impartial spectator according to the judgement of propriety (II.ii.1). The perfectly wise and just man, for example, understands the reasons for and implications of the impartial spectator's approval of such rules and would no doubt act justly with appropriate feelings even in the absence of formal laws; but the safety and functioning of society is too important for it to have to rely on this more elevated moral engagement. Smith thus makes a distinction between acting justly (according to the exact rules of justice) and judgements of justice, such that it is the latter only that requires independent spectatorial deliberation.

Thus both socialization and deliberative independence are important for the model of human agency in the *Moral Sentiments*. The significance of Smith's non-causal account of action is that it is able to accommodate them both. The role of sentiments, together with motives such as a sense of duty, registers the social situatedness of the human agent, as well as the natural feelings that are common to all humanity, yet there are other factors that come into play in making judgements about action and what is the right course of action. The moral agent is one who is able to take the more independent stance required by moral judgement. This agent is always socially situated and the spectatorial mechanisms on which moral judgement is based derive from that essential sociality, yet the developed moral agent is also able to go beyond this social rootedness in exercising the independence that is required for moral judgement. The most independent moral agent of all is one who steadfastly engages with the impartial spectator. As I have argued elsewhere (Brown, 1991, 1994), the overarching moral hierarchy of Smith's moral system thus allows for different degrees of proficiency in this exercise of independent moral agency, but it is Smith's non-causal account of action that provides the metaphysical resources for it.

V

The *Wealth of Nations*, by contrast, is replete with arguments aimed at identifying and explaining causal relations. Indeed the title itself signals a shift towards a causal focus in including reference to the 'causes' of the wealth of nations. As early as the 'Introduction and Plan of the Work' it is stated that one of the main subjects of the first book of the *Inquiry* is that of the 'causes' of the improvement in the productive powers of labour (Intro. 5), and this is then reflected in the title of Book I. Thereafter, much of the economic analysis is conducted in terms of identifying the relevant 'causes' and 'effects'; and the frequent use of terms involving 'necessitation', terms such as 'must', 'necessary' and 'necessarily', leaves no doubt that these causes are held to necessitate their effects.

This may be seen from the frequent depiction of causal relations such as: 'The discovery of the abundant mines of America, seems to have been the sole cause of this diminution of the value of silver in proportion to that of corn [roughly between 1570 and 1640]' (I.xi.f.3); the rise of the price of cattle in Scotland 'has not only raised the value of all highland estates, but it has, perhaps, been the principal cause of the improvements of the low country' (I.x.l.3); 'The increase of the quantity of gold and silver in Europe, and the increase of its manufactures and agriculture, are two events which, though they have happened nearly about the same time, yet have arisen from very different causes' (I.xi.n.1); 'But the easy terms upon which the Scotch banking companies accept of repayment are, so far as I know, peculiar to them, and have, perhaps, been the principal cause, both of the great trade of those companies, and of the benefit which the country has received from them' (II.ii.44); 'The over-trading of some bold projectors in both parts of the united kingdom, was the original cause of this excessive circulation of paper money' (II.ii.57); 'Parsimony, and not industry, is the immediate cause of the increase of capital' (II.iii.16); 'It has been the principal cause of the rapid progress of our American colonies towards wealth and greatness, that almost their whole capitals have hitherto been employed in agriculture' (II.v.21); 'Overtrading is the common cause of it [scarcity of money]' (IV.i.16); 'a dearth never has arisen from any combination among the inland dealers of corn, nor from any other cause but a real scarcity' (IV.v.b.5); and 'The improvement and prosperity of Great Britain . . . may very easily be accounted for by other causes' (IV.v.b.43).

Sometimes the analysis is multicausal:

in the ordinary variations of the price of provisions, those two opposite causes [diminishing/increasing the demand for labour and high/low price of provisions] seem to counterbalance one another; which is probably in part the reason why the wages of labour are every-where so much more steady and permanent than the price of provisions. (I.viii.56)

The quantity of the precious metals may increase in any country from two different causes: either, first, from the increased abundance of the mines which supply it; or, secondly, from the increased wealth of the people, form the increased produce of their annual labour. The first of these causes is no doubt necessarily connected with the diminution of the value of the precious metals; but the second is not. (I.xi.e.31)

As the quantity of stock to be lent at interest increases, the interest, or the price which must be paid for the use of that stock, necessarily diminishes, not only from those general causes which make the market price of things commonly diminish as their quantity increases, but from other causes which are peculiar to this particular case. (II.iv.8)

Sometimes there are multiple effects:

The increase in the wages of labour necessarily increases the price of many commodities, by increasing that part of it which resolves itself into wages, and so far tends to diminish their consumption both at home and abroad. The same cause, however, which raises the wages of labour, the increase of stock, tends to increase its productive powers, and to make a smaller quantity of labour produce a greater quantity of work. (I.viii.57)

And, 'In such articles as bread and butcher's meat, the same cause, which diminishes apparent profit, increases prime cost' (I.x.b.37). Sometimes too these causal relations are expressed metaphorically: 'Gold and silver, like all other commodities, naturally seek the market where the best price is given for them . . . though the metals naturally fly from the worse to the better market . . .' (I.xi.e.34); and 'Gold and silver naturally resort to a rich country . . . It is the superiority of price which attracts them' (I.xi.i.2).

There is also a clear interest in the relation between the cause and its effect. For example, sometimes there is some characteristic of the effect that suggests a similar characteristic of the cause: 'The constancy and steadiness of the effect, supposes a proportionable constancy and steadiness in the cause' (I.v.40); and 'The suddenness of the effect can be accounted for only by a cause which can operate suddenly' (I.xi.g.19). In other places a different effect or a different cause from that which is commonly held is pointedly advanced: 'and what may seem extraordinary, the dearness of house-rent is the cause of the cheapness of lodging' (I.x.b.52); 'But this cheapness [of unmanufactured agricultural commodities] was not the effect of the high value of silver, but of the low value of those commodities' (I.xi.e.25); and '[that corn is always dearer in great towns than in remote parts of the country], however, is the effect, not of the real cheapness of silver, but of the real dearness of corn' (I.xi.e.37). And in many places there seems to be a delight in challenging established views about the direction of the causal relation: 'This difference, however, in the mode of their subsistence is not the cause, but the effect of the difference in their wages; though, by a strange misapprehension, I have frequently heard it represented as the cause' (I.viii.33); 'The liberal reward of labour, therefore, as it is the effect of increasing wealth, so it is the cause of increasing population. To complain of it is to lament over the necessary effect and cause of the greatest publick prosperity' (WN I.viii.42); 'Rent, it is to be observed, therefore, enters into the composition of the price of commodities in a different way from wages and profit. High or low wages and profit, are the causes of high or low price; high or low rent is the effect of it' (WN I.xi.a.8); 'the high price of the wine seems to be, not so much the effect, as the cause of this careful cultivation' (I.xi.b.31); 'But this inferiority of quality [of dairy in Scotland] is, perhaps, rather the effect of this lowness of price than the cause of it' (I.xi.l.11); 'The exportation of gold and silver is, in this case, not the cause, but the effect of its declension ... The increase of those metals will in this case be the effect, not the cause, of the publick prosperity' (WN II.iii.23–4); 'The carrying trade is the natural effect and symptom of great national wealth: but it does not seem to be the natural cause of it' (WN II.v.35); and 'It is thus that through the greater part of Europe the commerce and manufactures of cities, instead of being the effect, have been the cause and occasion of the improvement and cultivation of the country' (WN III.iv.18).

The comparative use of 'determine' in the *Moral Sentiments* and *Wealth of Nations* also illustrates this shift to a causal focus in the *Wealth of Nations*. In the *Moral Sentiments* the main uses of 'determine' are in the sense of 'come to a judgement', 'decide upon' or 'ascertain': for example 'when we are determining the degree of blame or applause which seems due to any action' (TMS I.i.5.9); 'nice and delicate situations in which it is hard to determine whereabouts the propriety of conduct may lie' (TMS VII.iv.17); and what a rule or principle implies ('There is, however, one virtue of which the general rules determine with the greatest exactness every external action which it requires' (TMS III.6.10)). As an adjective 'determined' means 'resolute': for example 'the most determined and cruel resolution' and 'the coolest and most determined courage' (TMS VI.iii.12). There is also a use of 'determined by nature': 'we, therefore, despise him; unjustly, perhaps, if any sentiment could be regarded as unjust, to which we are by nature irresistibly determined' (TMS I.iii.1.15). In the *Wealth of Nations* there is a corresponding use of 'determine' in the sense of 'ascertain' or 'work out': 'but in what proportion ... I shall not take upon me to determine' (WN I.viii.15); and 'We can, even in this case, seldom determine more than what are the most usual wages' (WN I.ix.3). There is also the sense of 'enact', 'decide upon' and 'settle upon': 'This question ... was at last determined by the 13th and 14th of Charles II' (WN I.x.c.47); and 'The seat of such manufactures, as they are generally introduced by the scheme and project of a few individuals, is sometimes established in a maritime city, and sometimes in an inland town, according as their interest, judgement or caprice happen to determine' (WN III.iii.19).

In the *Wealth of Nations*, however, there is a systematic use of 'determine' which seems to signify a causal relation. Sometimes this is in connection with establishing a causal rule or principle: for example: 'These rules determine what may be called the relative or exchangeable value of goods' (WN I.iv.12; cf. I.xi.c.29–30). This is in contrast to the sense in the *Moral Sentiments* in which rules determine what it is right to do. More often in the *Wealth of Nations* 'determine' is used straightforwardly in a causal sense to specify or explain a causal relation, for example: 'First, I shall endeavour to explain what are the circumstances which naturally determine the rate of wages . . . Secondly, I shall endeavour to show what are the circumstances which naturally determine the rate of profit' (WN I.vii.34–5); 'The demand for labour, according as it happens to be increasing, stationary, or declining, or to require an increasing, stationary, or declining population, determines the quantity of the necessaries and conveniencies of life which must be given to the labourer; and the money price of labour is determined by what is requisite for purchasing this quantity' (WN I.viii.52; cf. V.ii.i.1); and 'The quantity of money, therefore, which can be annually employed in any country must be determined by the value of the consumable goods annually circulated within it' (WN II.iii.23).

The word 'regulate' also suggests a similar causal meaning: 'It is in this manner that the rent of the cultivated land, of which the produce is human food, regulates the rent of the greater part of other cultivated land' (I.xi.b.34); 'In Europe corn is the principal produce of land which serves immediately for human food. Except in particular situations, therefore, the rent of corn land regulates in Europe that of all other cultivated land' (I.xi.b.35); and 'The proportion between the real recompense of labour in different countries, it must be remembered, is naturally regulated, not by their actual wealth or poverty, but by their advancing, stationary, or declining condition' (I.xi.e.35).

One of the primary concerns of the *Wealth of Nations* is thus to present and explain a particular conception of an economic 'system' by identifying and analysing the causal relations that constitute it.[19] In this it shares the same impulse as all scientific analysis or philosophical 'systems' of thought, according to Smith, in attempting to articulate the relevant 'connecting principles' of that system. This again raises the question, familiar from Hume, of whether those connecting principles refer to nature's 'real chains' or are instead only the imaginative constructs or inferences of the human mind as it endeavours to interpret and make sense of empirical objects and events in terms of philosophical systems of thought.[20]

A fundamental question here is how these causal relations of the economic system are to be interpreted at the individual level. How are we to interpret the analytic requirements of systemic economic causality in terms of individual actions? Precious metals do not 'fly' of their own accord to better-priced markets; prices do not 'gravitate' in the absence of human buyers and sellers who agree and/or set those prices; wages, rents and profits do not adjust without human adjustment of them; the carrying trade does not carry itself across the oceans; and so forth. This raises a question about the possible implications for the model of human action that is presupposed in the *Wealth of Nations*, and whether a difference between it and the *Moral Sentiments* is to be found in assumptions relating to human action.

In some instances in the *Wealth of Nations* what are being described are historical processes. For example in the second chapter, Smith writes that the division of labour is 'the necessary, though very slow and gradual consequence' of the 'propensity to truck, barter, and exchange one thing for another' (WN I.ii.1). A little later, on the use of metals as money, Smith writes: 'In all countries, however, men seem at last to have been determined by irresistible reasons to give the preference, for this employment, to metals above every other commodity' (WN I.iv.4). Here the terminology of what is 'necessary' and what is 'determined by irresistible reasons' is in contrast with that of the *Moral Sentiments*. This may perhaps be construed in terms of Smith's 'conjectural history' according to which, in Dugald Stewart's words: 'when we cannot trace the process by which an event *has been* produced, it is often of importance to be able to show how it *may have been* produced by natural causes' (1794 [1980], p. 293; original emphasis). Stipulating what was necessary to mankind's development is thus a form of hypothetical or theoretical explanation; that is, it is a form of conjectural history that attempts to show how an event or process must have been produced, given what is assumed or thought to be known about human nature. As a retrospective analysis of human development it thus provides a systemic account of how humans as intelligent beings respond to their varied contexts and develop the practices that are conducive to supplying their needs (such as the division of labour and the use of metals as money).[21]

This is different from the question of how the causal properties of an economic system might be construed analytically with respect to individual behavioural responses to patterns of incentives. One answer to this might be that the properties of the economic system are constituted in terms of the aggregate of actual individual actions. It might thus be thought that the *Wealth of Nations* is based on assumptions about what people tend to do, that is, on assumptions about what most people do most of the time.[22] But to interpret the *Wealth of Nations* in this way is to overlook the theoretical significance of the analytic structure of the new economic system that is being presented.

A core theoretical component of the economic analysis of the *Wealth of Nations* is a reconceptualization of the wealth of a nation in terms of the 'annual produce' (or the exchangeable value of the annual produce of the land and labour of a country), and an analytic account of how this annual produce is determined.[23] The notion of 'determination' here is analytic; it refers to causal relations between economic variables as specified within an analytic system or model. By specifying causal relations between economic variables of the system, the *Wealth of Nations* thus constructs both the concept of an economic system and the concept of 'economic agency' that is required for such an economic system. Economic agency is thus conceptualized in terms of the necessary effects of a proposed causal economic structure. Economic agency in the *Wealth of Nations* is thus not so much construed in terms of empirical persons who are, in general, motivated by self-interest in their economic dealings, but rather a conceptual construction whose characteristics are given analytically by the properties of the economic system. Empirical agents in the *Wealth of Nations* may indeed be influenced in their actions and responses by a range of motivations, including self-interest, as well as by ignorance, vanity and opportunism. But what is significant for understanding the system of causal relations that is its analytic core, is that the *Wealth of Nations* also constructs the concept of economic agency that is required by these causal relations.

One of the most famous passages in the *Wealth of Nations* occurs in Book II where it is stated that 'the desire of bettering our condition, a desire which, though generally calm and dispassionate, comes with us from the womb, and never leaves us till we go into the grave' (WN II.iii.28; also 31). This passage is frequently compared with passages in the *Moral Sentiments* where the desire to better one's condition is subject to some critical commentary (TMS I.iii.2, 3), yet in the *Wealth of Nations* the 'desire of bettering our condition' is reported as an apparently natural fact about human aspiration – 'our' desire which 'comes with us from the womb' – an apparently 'naturalized' category that applies to 'any man'. But this passage follows upon an argument about the economic significance of the proportion between what are termed 'capital' and 'revenue', such that increases in capital tend to increase the exchangeable value of the annual produce of the land and labour of the country, which is the real wealth and revenue of all its inhabitants (para. 13). Capitals, it is then explained, are increased by parsimony and diminished by prodigality (paras 14–18). This then leads into a diatribe against the prodigal who 'perverts' the fund for the maintenance of productive workers from its proper destination (paras 19–20), 'impoverishes his country' by 'feeding the idle with the bread of the industrious' (para. 20), and is 'a publick enemy' (para. 25). It is into this highly charged argument that individual 'interest' (para. 19) and 'the desire of bettering our condition' as 'the principle which prompts to save' (para. 28) are inserted. The point of the passage taken as a whole is to redefine 'saving' not as denial of consumption but as accumulation of 'capital', and to propound a causal relation between the accumulation of capital so defined and the growth of the annual produce. 'Frugality' and 'prodigality' are thus reconceptualized in terms of this causal relation so that frugality is now the cause of an effect that is economically beneficial whereas prodigality is the cause of an effect that is economically harmful. In this context the point of introducing the 'desire to better our condition' is not so much to make some empirical statement about the generality of the behaviour of 'any man', but to provide a conceptualization of a particular kind of 'economic agent' – a wealth owner as a proper owner of capital – whose function is to save from this capital and so enhance the fund for the employment of productive labour and increase the exchangeable value of the annual produce. Otherwise, he engages in 'perversion' and is a 'publick enemy'. Although in the passage on 'bettering our condition' it is stated that 'in the greater part of men, taking the whole course of their life at an average, the principle of frugality seems not only to predominate, but to predominate very greatly' (para. 28), what is important is not so much an empirical statement of a general desire that human beings have, but a conceptualization of a particular form of economic agency. The passage thus needs to be taken in theoretical context, which is to provide an account of the causal determinants of increases in the exchangeable value of the annual produce, thus providing an analytic means of upturning Mandeville's hierarchy of the relative economic advantageousness of prodigality and frugality.

Smith's analysis of the nature and causes of the wealth of nations comprises a reconceptualization of the 'wealth of nations' in terms of the exchangeable value of their annual produce, and this involves identifying a causal structure of economic relations according to which the size of that annual produce is analytically determined. But in order to render the system of economic relations determinate, there must be some principles for specifying how economic agents act; and the pursuit of economic self-interest answers to such a principle. What are conceptualized as forms of 'economic agency' are thus the economic behaviours, consistent with self-interest, that are implied by the system of causal relations. Those forms of economic behaviour that do not correspond with this are castigated; the perpetrators of such behaviour are 'publick enemies' who 'pervert' the course of the annual produce.

Another example of this may be seen in a discussion of the employment of money, where Smith writes: 'The interest of whoever possesses it [money], requires that it should be employed' (WN II.iii.23). Individual behaviour is here construed in terms of what economic interest requires a money possessor to do with the money thus possessed; that is, economic agency with respect to the ownership of money is conceptualized in terms of the necessity of putting it to appropriate use. The context here is the analytical relation that: 'the same quantity of money . . . cannot long remain in any country, in which the value of the annual produce diminishes', so that 'the quantity of money, therefore, which can be annually employed in any country must be determined by the value of the consumable goods annually circulated within it' (II.iii.23). The validity of this relation presupposes that money does not lie idle and that is why economic agency here requires that owners of money do put it to employment; that is, 'possessors of money' are conceptualized as economic agents in terms of the necessity of putting that money to employment. The argument is not conducted in terms of what individuals who own money in fact do; rather the economic analysis conceptualizes economic agency in terms of what is required by that analysis.

Smith also writes that: 'The consideration of his own private profit is the sole motive which determines the owner of any capital to employ it either in agriculture, in manufactures, or in some particular branch of the wholesale or retail trade' (WN II.v.37). In the *Moral Sentiments* 'motives' are never said to 'determine' action. Here, however, private profit is said to be the 'sole motive' which determines the investment behaviour of the owner of capital. Yet again, what the passage here is saying is not that people's behaviour is determined solely by the motive of making private profit, nor even that the investment behaviour of people who are owners of capital is determined solely by the motive of making private profit, but that the 'owner of capital' is conceptualized according to the economic theory as an agent whose investment behaviour is determined solely by considerations of private profit. As a matter of fact people who own capital may have many motivations (to adopt the language of motivations for a moment), even in their investment behaviour, not all of which are compatible with their acting according to the sole motive of making profit; but the analysis being put forward in the passage needs to construct as economic agent an owner of capital whose investment behaviour is (analytically) determined by private profit, because such an assumption is required for the analysis of the different employment of capitals to be determinate.

Thus it is the requirements of the economic analysis that stipulate particular conceptions of 'economic agency' in terms of behaviour that leads to determinate economic outcomes. If, faced with alternative possibilities of capital investment, owners of capital were not assumed to follow economic interests then there could be no determinate analysis of capital investment. If shopkeepers were assumed to sell their goods at prices other than the maximum which the market could bear (for example, according to some benevolent or humanitarian view of what they thought their customers' needs were), then there could be no determinate theory of market price. The construction of economic agency in terms of self-interest, such as the pursuit of profit, thus makes economic outcomes analytically determinate and so makes systematic economic analysis possible; and the theoretical significance of this is not diminished by the recognition that in practice actual outcomes might only ever approximate, as tendencies, to these analytically determinate outcomes.[24] Buckle picks up on something of this when he makes the point that one of Smith's achievements was to introduce 'the conception of uniform and necessary sequence into the apparently capricious phenomena of wealth' (Buckle, Vol. 2, 1861,

p. 454), although he interprets this in empirical terms as actual outcomes rather than as a theoretical requirement. The determinacy of these analytical solutions is, however, in contrast with the indeterminacy of the normative rules relating to most of the virtues in the *Moral Sentiments*; this indeterminacy is compatible with, indeed requires, some minimally independent exercise of judgement in interpreting or applying those rules, and even going beyond them in some cases. In the case of engagement with the impartial spectator, this indeterminacy is structural to it.

VI

Smith's theorization of 'agency' is central to his work as moral philosopher and economic theorist; and part of the power of his work derives from the way that it challenged contemporary understandings of the relation between subjectivity and intersubjectivity, and between individual action and social outcomes. Yet the accounts of 'agency' in his two most famous works are distinctively different, a difference that is also illustrated in the style and voice of the two texts. In previous work I offered an explanation of this difference in terms of the Stoic moral hierarchy within which both works are positioned. In this chapter I have argued that a further yet related explanation of this difference is to be found in the models of action applied in the two texts. In the *Moral Sentiments* the model of action presupposes the causal independence of action as integral to moral agency, and this is registered particularly in the dialogic qualities of moral deliberation although it is not absent from the rule-following that sustains much of social life. In the *Wealth of Nations*, however, conceptions of economic agency are constructed according to the requirements of a determinate analysis of causal relations postulated between economic variables.

This suggests that the search for something that might be termed 'human agency', or a unitary conception of 'human agency', across both texts is perhaps something of a false trail since the notion of 'agent' is constructed differently in the two discourses. The resulting differences relating to conceptions of agency are thus the product of different modes of theorizing which impose something of their own requirements on the conceptions of agency that are put to work. Again, the approach presented in this chapter suggests a means of understanding some of the distinctive differences between the *Moral Sentiments* and the *Wealth of Nations*, but without construing difference in terms of inconsistency.

Notes

* I am grateful to Anthony Brewer, Samuel Fleischacker, Christel Fricke, Gloria Vivenza, Donald Winch and Jeffrey Young for comments on earlier versions of this chapter. Thanks also to the audience at the History of Economic Thought conference, Queen's University Belfast, 2007.
1. For other recent contributions to debates about the Adam Smith problem see: Brewer (2007, esp. pp. 173–6); Darwall (1999), Dickey (1986), Dupuy (1993), Dwyer (2005), Griswold (1999, esp. pp. 29–39, 260–61, 310, 366–8), Evensky (2005, esp. pp. 20–23), Fleischacker (2004, esp. Chs 4, 5), Montes (2004, Ch. 2), Nieli (1986), Otteson (2002, Ch. 4), Peters-Fransen (2001), Raphael (1985, esp. Ch. 5; 1992; 2007, Ch. 13), Shinohara (1993), Skinner (1996, Ch. 3), Teichgraeber (1981), Tribe (2002, esp. pp. 120–23, 137–48), Wilson and Dixon (2006), Witztum (1998), Young (1997, esp. pp. 2–26). For a brief summary of the debate in the mid-1990s see Brown (1997b, pp. 296–300).
2. See also Raphael (1985) pp. 86–90.
3. Thus Buckle did not subscribe to the view that Smith changed his mind over human motivation (Buckle 1861, pp. 442–3); see also Montes (2004, esp. pp. 31–2) and Tribe (2002, esp. pp. 139–40).
4. Cf. Buckle's methodological discussion in (1857), Vol. 1, Chapter 1, and his discussion of Hume, following that of Smith (1861), Vol. 2, pp. 468–9.

5. The omitted sentence refers to the example of the geometer who blots out one part of his premises that he may manipulate the remaining part with greater ease; the example previously given is that a line is assumed to be one-dimensional, not two, even though in practice it is not possible to draw a line with literally no breadth.
6. See Harris (2005) for an account of the free will debate in eighteenth-century Britain.
7. See Read and Richman (2007) for a selection of papers relating to the 'new' Hume debate.
8. As part of his criticism of Reid's attempt to argue against Hume on causation, Buckle (1861) argues: 'we are moulded by the society which surrounds us . . . even our most vigorous actions are influenced by general causes of which we are often ignorant, and which few of us care to study' (Vol. 2, pp. 481–2).
9. See also 'his [Smith's] interest in the judgement of an action not merely in relation to the "cause or object which excites it" but also in relation to the end proposed or the effects produced' (Skinner 1996, p. 58).
10. Khalil too seems to subscribe to a causal model of action: 'Smith distinguishes between the judgements of the *propriety* of an action in relation to its cause and of the *merit* of an action in respect to its effect' (Khalil 1990, p. 257).
11. There are passages in the *Moral Sentiments* that cast doubt on the reliability of the imagination (for example, TMS I.iii.2.2, 8; IV.1.9).
12. In the later summary at II.i.Intro.2 this alternative wording is omitted.
13. The same misconstrual is repeated by Montes (2004, p. 101).
14. This is also clear from Hume's summary of TMS at this point: 'The sentiments and affections of others may be considered in two lights; either with a reference to their cause or their effect. When we consider them with reference to their cause, we approve or disapprove of them according as we find ourselves capable or incapable of sympathizing with them . . .' (Hume, 'Abstract', 1984 [1997], p. 42).
15. On some construals of 'cause' it makes no sense even to talk of weakening it, since 'cause' just is 'sufficient cause'.
16. This suggests that it is unwise to assume that Smith is engaged in a 'science of man' in exactly the same manner as Hume.
17. Importantly it also allows for the possibility that the agent has a degree of control over those sentiments, as in the virtue of self-command, so that the agent intervenes in the causal relation between events of the world and his or her sentiments. Some implications of this further extension of Smith's account of human agency are developed in Brown (2009).
18. Cf. Brown (1995, 2005).
19. Fleischacker remarks that in the *Wealth of Nations* Smith 'often seems to want a rather stronger notion of causality than one could get from Hume'; he suggests a reconciliation in terms of Hume's distinction between commonly and uncommonly conjoined events (2004, p. 29).
20. Cf. 'History of Astronomy' (in Smith, 1795 [1980]).
21. This conjectural historical approach should be differentiated from Smith's remarks about 'moral causes' (WN V.i.e.26; V.iii.5; see also IV.vii.c.107) in the case of specific actions (such as those of servants of the East India Company and government officers) where the individuals are acting on behalf of or as servants of a specific institution.
22. I thank Donald Winch for this suggested formulation.
23. See Brown (1994, Ch. 7).
24. Smith often recognizes the distance between analytically determinate solutions and what actually happens. For example, he cautions that the natural price is that to which actual prices are 'gravitating', thus making it clear that the natural price is an analytical abstraction, not necessarily an empirical reality (WN I.vii.15, 20).

References

Brewer, A. (2007), 'Let us now praise famous men: assessments of Adam Smith's economics', *Adam Smith Review*, 3, 161–86.
Brown, V. (1991), 'Signifying voices: reading the "Adam Smith Problem"', *Economics and Philosophy*, 7, 187–220.
Brown, V. (1994), *Adam Smith's Discourse: Canonicity, Commerce and Conscience*, London, UK and New York, USA: Routledge.
Brown, V. (1995), 'The moral self and ethical dialogism: three genres', *Philosophy and Rhetoric*, 28, 276–99.
Brown, V. (1997a), 'Dialogism, the gaze and the emergence of economic discourse', *New Literary History*, 28, 697–710.
Brown, V. (1997b), '"Mere inventions of the imagination": a survey of recent literature on Adam Smith', *Economics and Philosophy*, 13, 281–312.
Brown, V. (2005), 'Moralische Dilemmata und der Dialogismus von Adam Smiths *Theorie der moralischen*

Gefühle' (Moral dilemmas and dialogism in Adam Smith's *Theory of Moral Sentiments*), in C. Fricke and H.-P. Schütt (eds), *Adam Smith als Moralphilosoph*, Berlin: de Gruyter, pp. 190–213.

Brown, V. (2009), 'Intersubjectivity, objectivity and agency in Adam Smith's *Theory of Moral Sentiments*', revised version of the papers presented at the workshop on Adam Smith and Edmund Husserl, Centre for the Study of Mind in Nature, Oslo, September 2007, 2008.

Buckle, T.H. (1857, 1861), *History of Civilization in England*, 2 vols, London: Parker, Son & Bourn.

Campbell, R.H. and A.S. Skinner (1976), 'Introduction', in A. Smith, *An Inquiry into the Nature and Causes of the Wealth of Nations*, Oxford: Clarendon Press.

Darwall, S. (1999), 'Sympathetic liberalism: recent work on Adam Smith', *Philosophy and Public Affairs*, **28**, 139–64.

Dickey, L. (1986), 'Historicizing the "Adam Smith Problem": conceptual, historiographical, and textual issues', *Journal of Modern History*, **58**, 579–609.

Dupuy, J.-P. (1993), 'A reconsideration of *Das Adam Smith Problem*', *Stanford French Review*, **17**, 45–57.

Dwyer, J. (2005), 'Ethics and economics: bridging Adam Smith's *Theory of Moral Sentiments* and *Wealth of Nations*', *Journal of British Studies*, **44**, 662–87.

Eckstein, W. (1926 [2000]), 'Preface and introduction', in H. Mizuta (ed.), *Adam Smith: Critical Responses*, Vol. 5, London, UK and New York, USA: Routledge, pp. 12–49.

Evensky, J. (2005), *Adam Smith's Moral Philosophy: A Historical and Contemporary Perspective on Markets, Law, Ethics, and Culture*, Cambridge: Cambridge University Press.

Fleischacker, S. (2004), *On Adam Smith's Wealth of Nations: A Philosophical Companion*, Princeton, NJ: Princeton University Press.

Griswold Jr, C.L. (1999), *Adam Smith and the Virtues of Enlightenment*, Cambridge: Cambridge University Press.

Harris, J.A. (2005), *Of Liberty and Necessity: The Free Will Debate in Eighteenth-Century British Philosophy*, Oxford: Oxford University Press.

Hobbes, T. (1660), *Leviathan*, R. Tuck (ed.) (1996), Cambridge: Cambridge University Press.

Hume, D. (1739–40), *A Treatise of Human Nature*, L.A. Selby-Bigge (ed.), 2nd edn revised by P.H. Nidditch (1978), Oxford: Clarendon Press.

Hume, D. (1748), *Enquiry into Human Understanding*; reprinted as *An Enquiry Concerning Human Understanding* (1777 edn), in *Enquiries Concerning Human Understanding and Concerning the Principles of Morals*, L.A. Selby-Bigge (ed.), 3rd edn revised by P.H. Nidditch (1975) Oxford: Clarendon Press.

Hume, D. (1984), 'Hume's Abstract of Adam Smith's Theory of Moral Sentiments' (May 1759), in D. Raynor (ed.), *Journal of the History of Philosophy*, **22**, 65–79; reprinted as 'Hume's *Abstract*', in (1997) J. Reeder (ed.), *On Moral Sentiments: Contemporary Responses to Adam Smith*, London: Thoemmes Press, pp. 33–50.

Khalil, E.L. (1990), 'Beyond self-interest and altruism', *Economics and Philosophy*, **6**, 255–73.

Mandeville, B. (1732), *The Fable of the Bees or Private Vices, Public Benefits*, 2 vols, F.B. Kaye (ed.) (1924); reprinted (1988), Indianapolis, IN: Liberty Fund.

Montes, L. (2004), *Adam Smith in Context: A Critical Reassessment of some Central Components of His Thought*, New York: Palgrave Macmillan.

Nieli, R. (1986), 'Spheres of intimacy and the Adam Smith problem', *Journal of the History of Ideas*, **47**, 611–24.

Oncken, A. (1897), 'The consistency of Adam Smith', *Economic Journal*, **7**, 443–50.

Oncken, A. (1898 [2000]), 'The Adam Smith problem', in H. Mizuta (ed.), *Adam Smith: Critical Responses*, Vol. 5, London and New York: Routledge, pp. 84–105.

Otteson, J.R. (2002), *Adam Smith's Marketplace of Life*, Cambridge: Cambridge University Press.

Peters-Fransen, I. (2001), 'The canon in the history of the Adam Smith problem', in E.L. Forget and S. Peart (eds), *Reflections on the Classical Canon in Economics: Essays in honour of Samuel Hollander*, London, UK and New York, USA: Routledge, pp. 168–84.

Raphael, D.D. (1977) '"The true old Humean philosophy" and its influence on Adam Smith', in G.P. Morice (ed.), *David Hume: Bicentenary Papers*, Edinburgh: Edinburgh University Press, pp. 23–38; parts of this chapter are reproduced in 'General Introduction', Section 5, to Adam Smith, *Essays on Philosophical Subjects* (1980), Oxford: Clarendon Press, pp. 15–21; Liberty reprint, 1982.

Raphael, D.D. (1985), *Adam Smith*, Oxford: Oxford University Press.

Raphael, D.D. (1992), 'Adam Smith 1790: the man recalled; the philosopher revived', in P. Jones and A.S. Skinner (eds), *Adam Smith Reviewed*, Edinburgh: Edinburgh University Press, pp. 93–119.

Raphael, D.D. (2007), *The Impartial Spectator*, Oxford: Oxford University Press.

Raphael, D.D. and A.L. Macfie (1976), 'Introduction', *The Theory of Moral Sentiments*, Oxford: Clarendon Press, pp. 1–52.

Read, R. and K.A. Richman (eds) (2007), *The New Hume Debate*, Revised edition, London, UK and New York, USA: Routledge.

Reid, T. (1788), *Essays on the Active Powers of Man*, in Sir W. Hamilton (ed.), *The Works of Thomas Reid*, Vol. 2, 6th edn, Edinburgh (1963); reprinted (1994), London: Thoemmes Press.

Reid, T. (1984), 'Thomas Reid on Adam Smith's Theory of Morals', J.C. Stewart-Robinson and D.F. Norton, *Journal of the History of Ideas*, **45**, 310–21; reprinted as 'A Sketch of Dr Smith's Theory of Morals', in J. Reeder (ed.) (1997), *On Moral Sentiments: Contemporary Responses to Adam Smith*, London: Thoemmes Press, pp. 69–88.

Shinohara, H. (1993), 'The practical system of morality in Adam Smith', in H. Mizuta and C. Sugiyama (eds), *Adam Smith: International Perspectives*, New York: St Martin's Press, pp. 27–42.

Skinner, A.S. (1996), *A System of Social Science: Papers Relating to Adam Smith*, Oxford: Clarendon Press; 1st edn 1979.

Smith, A. (1759), *The Theory of Moral Sentiments*, 1st edn; variorum edition in D.D. Raphael and A.L Macfie (eds) (1976a), *Glasgow Edition of the Works and Correspondence of Adam Smith*, Vol. I, Oxford: Clarendon Press; Liberty reprint 1982.

Smith, A. (1776), *An Inquiry into the Nature and Causes of the Wealth of Nations*, 1st edn; variorum edition in R.H. Campbell and A.S. Skinner (eds) (1976b), *Glasgow Edition of the Works and Correspondence of Adam Smith*, Vol. II, Oxford: Clarendon Press, 1976b; Liberty reprint 1981.

Smith, A. (1795), 'History of Astronomy'; reprinted in W.P.D. Wightman (ed.) (1980), *Essays on Philosophical Subjects, Glasgow Edition of the Works and Correspondence of Adam Smith*, vol. III, Oxford: Clarendon Press; Liberty reprint 1982.

Stewart, D. (1794), 'Account of the Life and Writings of Adam Smith, LL.D', reprinted in W.P.D. Wightman (ed.) (1980), *Essays on Philosophical Subjects, Glasgow Edition of the Works and Correspondence of Adam Smith*, Vol. III, Oxford: Clarendon Press; Liberty reprint 1982.

Teichgraeber III, R.F. (1981), 'Rethinking *Das Adam Smith Problem*', *Journal of British Studies*, **20**, 106–23.

Tribe, K. (2002), 'The German reception of Adam Smith', in K. Tribe (ed.) and H. Mizuta (advisory ed.), *A Critical Bibliography of Adam Smith*, London: Pickering & Chatto, pp. 120–52.

Wilson and Dixon (2006), 'Das Adam Smith problem: a critical realist perspective', *Journal of Critical Realism*, **5**, 251–72.

Witztum, A. (1998), 'A study into Smith's conception of human character: Das Adam Smith problem revisited', *History of Political Economy*, **30**, 489–512.

Young, J.T. (1997), *Economics as a Moral Science: The Political Economy of Adam Smith*, Cheltenham, UK and Lyme, NH, USA: Edward Elgar.

4 Adam Smith's theism
Brendan Long

Smith's religious views

In the current literature the issue of Smith's theism and Christianity is usually side-stepped. Some commentators contend that this has led to an impoverishment in Smithian studies.[1] One cannot help but be puzzled that the question of Smith's religious views attracts such opposing conclusions. He is seen by some as a strong Christian, by others as a sort of Stoic pagan, or possibly a deist or even a convinced atheist. Certainly there is always room for pluralism of interpretation regarding nuances, influences and implications of a great thinker. However this confusion regarding a fundamental aspect of the thought of such an influential mind is concerning. It highlights a philosophical issue which needs to be properly resolved.

Was Smith an atheist?

The more atheistic readings of Smith take a strong position which needs to be examined critically. An important thinker in this interpretation is Joseph Cropsey. He sees Smith as a convicted atheist and hater of religion.[2] He believes Smith values only life in this world. Its preservation is all that matters and there is, according to this commentator, no higher virtue in Smith's eyes:

> Nature is the internal principle that establishes life as the supreme *desideratum*. There being no mention of any end beyond life, or of anything to which the possession of life is supposed to contribute, we must say that life appears as the highest good or the thing which is desired for its own sake and not for the sake of anything else. Polity or society is for the sake of the preservation of life, rather than, as was once supposed, for the perfection of life.[3]

Cropsey reads Smith as saying that there is no teleological view of the subject, Christian or pagan. Cropsey's rejection of Smith's Christianity relies on the interpretation he places on Smith's presentation of the golden rule: the Christian imperative to love one's neighbour as oneself. Smith says:

> that to feel much for others and little for ourselves, that to restrain our selfish, and to indulge our benevolent affections, constitutes the perfection of human nature; and can alone produce among mankind that harmony of sentiments and passions in which consists their whole grace and propriety. As to love our neighbour as we love ourselves is the great law of Christianity, so it is the great precept of nature to love ourselves only as we love our neighbour, or what comes to the same thing, as our neighbour is capable of loving us.[4]

Cropsey[5] interprets this to mean 'each person doing for himself as much as, but no more than, what is consistent with the self-preservation of others'. Cropsey thinks that Smith has reduced the perfectionist moral order of Christianity to mandating a full exercise of one's own rights within the limits imposed by respecting those equal rights of others. The result is the 'exclusion of benevolence as the principle of society'.[6] Cropsey believes that Smith despises the clergy and traditional religious institutions, in fact he argues that Smith treats religion as something that in large quantities is 'toxic'. He thinks that Smith sees civil freedom as undermining religious institutions: 'no polity except a secular one can remain free'. The clergy are a 'perpetual menace to the good order of society'. According to Cropsey, the 'violent dominion' of the influential Roman Catholic clergy 'Smith unfailingly condemns as superstition', and he is extremely anxious to banish it from society. Cropsey interprets Smith as saying that the proliferation of a large number of religious sects will do no harm and possibly some good.[7] He then takes this as clear evidence that doctrinal rectitude is not part of Smith's views on religion: 'Smith could not have desired even two to exist if he had believed in the verity of either'. So Smith is a secular, materialist, anti-cleric who does not believe in Christian doctrine.

Another strong atheistic reading is given by Minowitz. Minowitz holds the position that the *Wealth of Nations* (WN) is an anti-Christian and atheistic work through which Smith fights a war against Christianity. Through it Smith not only rejects the Christian God, but also unambiguously rejects the afterlife as a figment of the imagination,[8] and posits a godless universe.[9] In fact, Smith anticipates Marx's withering attack on religion[10] and seeks to secularize political economy.

Minowitz plays upon the divergence between WN and the *Theory of Moral Sentiments* (TMS) in the religious sphere.[11] Minowitz is right to raise this issue. There can be no doubt that TMS is replete with references to the divine as discussed hereafter. However WN does not treat this issue in any substantive way.[12] His solution to the puzzle is that Smith lost his faith in the period between working on TMS and WN. However this fails to appreciate that both works had a significant history in their development, a historics that in fact overlapped considerably. The same man with the same convictions was working on both pieces at the same time (TMS in the form of later editions and WN in the form of early drafts). Minowitz also argues that Smith makes few references to revelation in either TMS or WN and these are generally sarcastic. Minowitz simply ignores many of the scriptural references that Smith uses (see Table 4.1). His prejudices reveal themselves in his language:[13] 'From Smith's point of view, the biblical God represents theistic superstition, and one suspects the bad news (superstition) outweighs the good news (monotheism).'[14] 'Smith is so determined to deny the divine Jesus that he denies even the human Jesus.'[15]

This is indeed a strong claim. All that Minowitz offers as argument for this conclusion is that Smith fails to identify Christ's life and death as one of the three 'great revolutions in human history'.[16] Besides his simplistic bifurcation of Smith into a literary schizophrenic (the man of TMS and of WN), Minowitz also has the problem that his understanding of Christian theology is somewhat narrow. He has a very low notion of the biblical God, the God of the Fall and the Flood, who punishes unremittingly,[17] who continually and miraculously intervenes to keep the walls of the world from falling in. As a result Minowitz sees the Christian God as being inconsistent with the emphasis that Smith places on order in creation.[18] However most of the contemporaries of Smith making the argument for the existence of God from design were usually Christians. Minowitz has an explanation to cover some of the explicitly Christian references discussed in the rest of this paper. When Smith says that we are made in the image of God he is being 'insincere'.[19] When he says that happiness cannot be gained by one who believes in a fatherless world he is simply speaking in a 'tragic voice'. Minowitz says that the

Table 4.1 References to scripture in the Smithian corpus

Reference	Scripture	Summary	Notes
C54	e.g. Matt. 12:31	Sins of the Holy Ghost	The reference is not a substantive theological point, more of a whimsical comment to Strahan, but it reveals a strong comfortability with the discourse of a committed Christian.
LRBL, 13.167	Gen. .2	Eve leaving Paradise	This is a reference to Milton's Paradise Lost: xi268–85. It can be interpreted as a scriptural allusion, as the context shows Smith believed these to be historical events.
LRBL, 13.167	Gen. .2	Adam talking to God	See above: reference to Paradise Lost: xi215–29.
LRBL, 17.21	Gen. .2	Fall of Adam	Smith seems to believe this is an historical event.
LRBL, 6.65	I Chr. 16:32.	The fields rejoiced	Examples of metaphors.
LJA, iii.66 p. 166	Lev. 18:6–18	Consanguinity	Revelation is seen as consistent with nature and reason.
LJA, iii.67 p. 167	Lev. 18:18	Marriage	Scripture is here not seen as consistent with nature.
LJA, iii.99. p. 180	Gen. 15	Promises to Abraham	Indicates a strong O.T. background.
LJB, 166, p. 467	O.T. Generally		Generic reference to O.T. as a source of historical information about ancient probate practises.
LJB, 23, p. 405	Genesis	Abraham and Lot	Smith again uses scriptural examples to illustrate points of economic or jurisprudence.
LJB, 133, p. 451 and LJA, 3.99, p. 180	General O.T. reference	Messiah who was to come	The 1762/63 reference in LJA uses the words the 'messiah they [the Jews] say would be born'. In the 1766 adaptation, according to the notetaker, the meaning firms to the 'Messiah was to come'. If one assumes the notetaker was quite accurate here, there is some evidence of a firming in Smith Christian expression.
LR 6.65	Ps. 98:8	Floods clapped their hands	Examples of metaphors.
PH 11, p. 117	Rev. 21:1	New Heaven and New Earth	This is a reference to the book of Revelation.
T(1–5), 2.2.3.12, p. 91	Many refs	The mercy of God	This reference is typically Christian.
T1, 2.1.5.9, p. 77	Many refs	The wrath of God	Classical Protestant reference.
T, 1.1.1.5.5, p. 25 and T1, 3.6.1, p. 171	e.g. Luke 10:27	To love our neighbour as we love ourselves	The perfection in human nature comes from following the biblical rule of loving one's neighbour.

76 *Elgar companion to Adam Smith*

Table 4.1 (continued)

Reference	Scripture	Summary	Notes
T1, 2.2.1.1.10, p. 82	Lev. 24:19	As every man doth so shall it be done to him	
T1, 2.3.1.3, p. 95	Ex. 21:18	The ox that gores . . .	A reference to the Mosaic Law.
T1, 3.5.7, p. 166	James 4:4	Who shall be a true friend of the world shall be an enemy of God	By acting contrary 'to the dictate of our moral faculties' we seem to 'declare ourselves, if I may say so, in some measure the enemies of God'.
T1, 3.6.1, p. 171	Luke 10:27	Love the Lord our God with all your heart . . .	Central theological notion of Christianity.
T1, 3.6.13, p. 178	Matt. 5:39	Turning the other cheek	This is quoted by Smith as 'our Saviour's precept'.
T2, 5.2.31, p. 128, + 1759 draft in C40	Gen. 1	Created him after his own image	Central Christian concept.
T6, 2.2.3.12, p. 91	Many references	Widow and the fatherless	Reference to the classical notion of God vindicating the widow and the orphan.
T6, 3.3.13, p. 142	Ex. 34:28	Honour thy father and thy mother	The reference seems to assume a strong scriptural authority. The edit was included just prior to Smith's death.
WN 3.4.15, p. 421	Genesis	Esau	Esau exchanged his birthright for a mess of pottage.
WN 1.4, p. 41	Gen. 23:14–18	Abraham	Scriptural examples used in economics and jurisprudence.

Notes: References to God, the Almighty, Creator, providence are only indirectly scriptural and are therefore not included above. Smith's allusions are generally rendered from the King James Version. O.T. refers to the Old Testament.

impartial spectator takes the place of God. Minowitz seeks to exorcise any sense of the transcendent in Smithian thought.

Was Smith a lapsed Christian and a convert to Stoicism?
Some commentators explore a middle position that Smith lost his interest in Christianity in his later years, but remained committed to a strong natural religion. This position emerged with Eckstein's introduction to his German edition of TMS and seems to be partially endorsed by Raphael and Macfie in theirs. Eckstein believed that the T6 edition of TMS reveals a change in Smith's religious views, especially his omission of a famous defence of the traditional doctrine of the atonement that was based upon his own theory of human sentiments.[20] Raphael and Macfie conclude that Smith gradually tended towards a natural religion, as shown by his expanded discussion of Stoicism in T6.[21] This

position has the convenience of accounting for Smith's lack of any serious theological exposition in published form, his removal of the atonement section from T6 and his eulogizing of Hume (these are discussed below). Rae, Smith's most quoted biographer, also tantalizes us with an uncertain reference:

> Whatever may have been his [Smith's] attitude to historical Christianity, these words [on the comfort in religion and confidence in the divine judgement] written on the eve of his death, show that he died as he lived, in the full faith of those doctrines of natural religion which he had publicly taught.[22]

Smith finds elements of Stoic philosophy and theology very attractive. This was not that unusual in this period as his predecessors Joseph Butler and Hume refer to Epictetus.[23] The degree of Smith's dependence on his reading of the Stoics is well documented.[24] Raphael and Macfie acknowledge that 'Smith's ethical doctrines are in fact a combination of Stoic and Christian virtues',[25] but conclude, 'Adam Smith's ethics and natural theology are predominately Stoic.'[26] This is also a very strong claim.

Was Smith a Christian?

The traditional account of reading Smith emphasized the explicitly theological elements of his anthropology. Earlier interpretations of Smith emphasize the importance of theology for his project and its strongly spiritual flavour. In 1870, Leslie described Smith's theory of Nature as being given form by 'theology, political history and the acts of his own mind'.[27] According to this commentator Smith has blended speculation of the Greco-Roman world with Christian theology. Christian notions of the divine benevolence are fused with classical attention to order and harmony. Veblen (1899) makes Smith's theology the focal point of his interpretation of Smith. For Veblen, Smith's philosophical and theological inclinations are expressions of his devout optimism. He characterizes Smith's work as 'animistic'. Veblen does not mean to say that Smith believes that natural (including economic) phenomena in some way manifest a spiritual soul, but rather that they are impregnated with a providential and benign teleology. Smith showed a 'gently optimistic spirit of submission' as an economist who went 'to his work with the fear of God before his eyes'.[28] Jacob Viner, one of the more scholarly scholars of Smith, was more direct in his description of Smith's Christian faith. He states that: 'Smith definitely commits himself to the theism of his time'.[29] He is influenced by the 'optimistic theism' of Hutcheson and Shaftesbury.[30] His ethics is based upon 'a harmonious order in nature guided by God'.[31] 'Harmony and beneficence to be perceived in the matter of fact processes of nature are the results of the design and intervention of a benevolent God.'[32] This optimistic theism of Smith's day was unquestionably Christian. Viner concludes that to deny Smith his faith is to put on mental blinkers. It is poor scholarship.[33]

Another key commentator is Bitterman (1940), who endorses this interpretation of the centrality of theological assumptions to Smith's system, although he demurs on the question of Smith's specifically Christian theism. He notes the early work of Hasbach,[34] who first emphasized the influence of the theologies of Shaftesbury and Hutcheson on Smith's ethics. Quoting Leslie and Veblen he says that: 'With some variations these conclusions have been widely accepted'.[35] Bitterman sees that there are simply too many references to the Deity in TMS to suggest anything but a strong theological position in the Smithian corpus. Bitterman suggests that he has found 'little evidence that Smith believes in revelation', but his own citations do not support this. With the previous sentence he notes that Smith refers to the 'inspired writers' of the Old Testament and 'Our Saviour'.[36] This is hardly the language of a person uncommitted to the general Christian worldview. This theological reading of Smith is not without more recent support. Speigel in 1976 emphasized the continuity between Smith and a theological tradition of long standing, essentially the Christian tradition. Davis (1990) also notes Smith's theological leanings. For Davis, if one attempts to eliminate the religious elements once integral to economics one ends up with 'Hamlet without the Prince'.[37]

There are two ways to settle this issue. The first is to examine the life and writing of Smith to see if they conform to a faith broadly typical for the period. The second, and more demanding, task is to analyse Smith's natural theology in terms of Christian theology as then understood. This chapter seeks to approach the first question. The second issue is considered by Long in the *Adam Smith Review* (2006) and in detail in Long (2004).

Investigating Smith's theism biographically
There is some purely biographical evidence that Smith retained a Christian view, although none of this is absolutely conclusive. Certainly, it is difficult to identify any point at which it appears that Smith's Christian faith lapsed. That the young Smith was religious, if not prone to public displays of this, is established by the fact that he obtained a Snell scholarship to Oxford. Hutcheson was Smith's teacher at Glasgow and given Hutcheson's own strong Christian convictions it is not likely that he would have chosen a lukewarm believer. This would in fact have been irresponsible as the scholarship obliged the exhibitioner to take up orders. In addition, Smith's acceptance of the scholarship must then be seen as something of a statement of faith by him. Although most exhibitioners were not ordained, only a fool would enter such an arrangement (with specified sanctions for non-compliance) with no intention of seeking ordination. Smith's decision not to take religious orders is relevant for examining his theism, but is in no way decisive.

Smith's faith would have been the subject of some scrutiny in 1751 when he was appointed to the Logic Chair at Glasgow. It is likely that would not have succeeded if his orthodoxy was seriously suspected, as revealed by Hume's unsuccessful application to fill the same position. In either logic or moral philosophy professorships he would have a key influence on the future leadership of the Church in Scotland.

There are some anecdotal points that can be made in support of Smith's theism. Some of his close friends were senior churchmen.[38] He took the Westminster Confession before the Presbytery of Glasgow. He had religious duties at Glasgow which he seemed to take seriously.[39] He was strongly supportive of the Sunday School movement.[40] He prayed at the deathbed of his mother (who was deeply religious). At the end of his life his parting words to his friends were that 'this conversation will need to be adjourned to another place'.[41]

Some questions were raised about Smith's faith in theological circles. Rae implies that even when Smith was extremely popular in Glasgow there was 'a little' suspicion of him in the Church, and 'more than a little' in the case of certain individuals – Rae produces four witnesses. The first was John Ramsay of Ochtertyre who seems to have attended Robin Simson's Club with Smith[42] who accused Smith of being a friend of Hume the atheist, ominously reticent on religious subjects, did not conduct a Sunday class on Christian evidences, and petitioning the University Senatus to be excused from opening his class with prayers, but there is no record of the petition. What Ramsay reveals is that Smith must in fact have said prayers before his classes (otherwise this would not have been the allegation). The second witness is Smith's former pupil and friend the Earl of Buchan. Rae reports that he described Smith as being in many ways a 'chaste disciple of Epicurus'.[43] Surely, he must have meant Epictetus: Smith was never an Epicurean and tended more to Stoicism. Smith's Oxford friend Bishop Douglas wrote a book in the form of a letter to try to convince certain individuals of the truth of Christian miracles and Smith seems to have been a target.[44] The last cynic is Rae himself. He calls Smith a theist, but suggests that Smith probably did not believe in the miracles[45] We do not know what Smith thought on this point. These four accounts are purely hearsay.

The influence of Hutcheson
Hutcheson's strong influence needs to be considered, given the former's strong Christian theism. The judgement is put by Rae: 'If Smith is the disciple of anyone it is Hutcheson'.[46] Hutcheson believed that the will of the divine is visible through human sentiments, that goodness exists in benevolence apprehended via a moral sense. The first point accords with and may ground Smith's natural theology as discussed in Long (2004). Smith emphasized a broad empiricism and rejected the moral sense. To discover a new sense so late in human history seems to question the reliability of them all. Smith accepts Hutcheson's broad theological framework as a description of moral norms, but not as a description of fact. Smith does not reject benevolence as the final cause of human welfare, but as the only efficient cause. Although their ethics are divergent, the theological inspiration that grounds them is not.

Relationship with Hume
Accounting for Hume's influence is difficult. Still, this pivotal relationship with Hume becomes the litmus test of Smith's theism. Hume held the distinction of being one of the first to be seriously called an atheist whilst Smith's thought is inspired by strong theological premises. However they remained the closest of friends in life. The influence of Hume on Smith is discussed in detail in Long (2004). This analysis focuses on the major source of tension between the two minds: Hume's religious scepticism. There are four key episodes where Hume's religious views created difficulties for Smith:

1. Hume's nomination for the Logic Chair at Glasgow;
2. Smith acquiescing in the virtual ban on Hume contributing to the *Edinburgh Review*;
3. Smith's concerns over the *Dialogues* and his actions as Hume's literary executor; and
4. Smith's words at the time of Hume's death.

Smith's reservations over Hume's bid to fill the Logic Chair at Glasgow were religious in nature. This was a significant moment in Hume's life. It appears Smith was consulted on the prospective appointment. Rae notes that Smith 'expresses himself with great caution' when writing to Cullen, a professor at Glasgow, on the issue.[47] Rae however then suggests that Smith and Cullen acted in concert to support Hume, but notes that there is no decisive information either way. We should allow Smith to speak for himself: 'I should prefer David Hume to any man for the College, but I am afraid the public would not be of the same opinion, and the interest of the society will oblige us to have some regard to the opinions of the public.'[48] When he declared war on the Scottish Kirk, Hume made himself an enemy in the minds of the common people. This would have really worried Smith. Certainly Smith's reservations as written are more political than doctrinal. There is no evidence that he suspects Hume of atheism, just political inexpediency.

However there is more to it than this. Rae suggests that Smith energetically threw himself behind Hume's candidature as Cullen is reported to have done. This however seems wrong. Smith was then in good standing with the Kirk, and his support would have been very significant. Given his well-documented reticence on issues that excite religious opposition, it seems more likely that he would have refused to commit himself. It was a critical decision for Smith. The objections to Hume's application must have been firmly held for Smith to commit them to paper. That Smith would deny a man who was probably already his friend, and certainly one whom he held in great esteem, on the basis of religious sensitivities is significant for interpreting Smith's religious position. He simply believed that Hume's religious scepticism assured that his appointment was not in the public interest.

Hume appears to have been banned from the Scottish literary magazine the *Edinburgh Review* that was a special project of Smith's. Unfortunately, the journal died prematurely with only two numbers. The reason cited by Lord Woodhouselee[49] is that there was opposition from elements of religious fanaticism within the Scottish Kirk. It is difficult to judge this, but even if it were only a partial truth it would be enough to explain excluding Hume. Hume's *History of England* was one of the most recent publications to flow from a Scotsman's pen. However Hume was not asked to contribute to the *Review*, was not informed of the magazine at all prior to its publication, and was never referred to in any of the publications. This can only mean a deliberate policy of exclusion and one that Smith must have agreed with as one of its key proponents. In the end, not even this could save the *Review* from the zealots. As Rae notes,[50] it was still criticized on theological grounds and because Hume, the 'atheist', was suspected of being 'among their number'. Close friend or not, David Hume's insights must have been an embarrassment for Smith in such a tempestuous theological climate.

Their theological differences are most clearly seen in Smith's attitude to the *Dialogues*. Gaskin[51] believes that Hume worked on the *Dialogues* upon his return from Turin in 1748 and had all but the last section written by 1751. He then circulated the draft amongst his close friends. We do not know for certain that Smith was one of these select few.[52] Bitterman's view that Hume did send the *Dialogues* to Smith for comment needs to be balanced against the fact that Smith would have had much influence in the choice of his successor in the Logic Chair at Glasgow. Hume might not have wanted to put the draft before him at such a critical stage. Alternatively, perhaps this is exactly what did happen and helps explain Smith's reservation to Hume's cause. In any event, Hume did not consider publishing the work until his health deteriorated later in life. He added a codicil to his will making Smith his literary executor and specifically requesting him to publish the *Dialogues*. When Smith learned of this (probably by letter) he must have fallen off his chair.[53] Rae records that Smith informed Hume of his objections.[54] Always the gentleman, Hume did not hesitate to relieve Smith of the burden, even to the point of giving him permission not to publish the work at all. However Hume felt an especially strong attachment to this particular philosophical progeny and later asked his publisher Strahan to be his literary executor and imposed a deadline for the publication of the work (against Smith's advice). In the end, the work went to press after Hume died without a publisher's name (though sponsored by Hume's nephew and heir). Smith refused to have any part in the project whatsoever. Some of the basis of Smith's objections can be gleaned from his correspondence with Hume and Strahan on this point. Smith begged Strahan not to publish the account of Hume's life in the same volume as the *Dialogues*. He loved his friend tenderly and feared that the *Dialogues* risked infamy. Smith asked Hume to give him freedom to act as he willed in the matter of the *Dialogues*. Though telling him his scruples were groundless, Hume also informed Smith: 'I have become sensible that on account of the nature of the work and of your situation it may be improper to hurry on that publication.'[55]

Perhaps Smith feared what would become of him should he take on the task. Still, Hume acknowledges that the issues run deeper. In Rae's words Smith was opposed to the publication 'on general grounds and under any editorship whatsoever'.[56] In his letter[57] of September 1776 Smith admitted to Strahan that he had tried to persuade Hume to let him decide whether or not the works should ever be published. He goes on to say:

> I could have wished that the *Dialogues* had remained in manuscript to be communicated only to a few people. When you read the work you will see my reasons without my giving you the trouble of reading them in a letter. I once had persuaded him to leave it entirely to my discretion either to publish them at what time I thought proper or not to publish them at all. It would never have been published in my lifetime. I am resolved, for many reasons, to have no concern in the publication of the *Dialogues*.

This was extremely painful for Smith. He was torn between his affection for his friend, his admiration of the majority of his work, a desire to preserve a reputation for his own later work, and his religious beliefs. Smith does not explicitly tell Strahan what he objects to, as this is not his way. He was averse to putting to paper any comments that might cause religious division and he did not want to provide possible ammunition to Hume's enemies.

Smith must have found the content of the *Dialogues* most objectionable. These are Rae's 'general grounds' and Hume himself admits it. The caveats that Hume artfully draws under rationalist theology have been so well discussed that there is little to be gained from exploring them rigorously here. Some value might be added however by locating Smith within the tripartite dialogue in the work between Demea, Philo and Cleanthes. The character Demea probably refers to Samuel Clarke. Within the dialogue he is the weaker opponent whose position Philo seeks to undermine, probably with some success. Philo himself is almost certainly a philosophical self-portrait, as indicated in correspondence between Hume and Strahan.[58] The polite but withering scepticism of Philo is classically Humean. Cleanthes is probably Butler and emphasizes the argument for the existence of God from design. After reading TMS one might also suspect that Smith could also be part of the Cleanthes character. Philo takes Cleanthes to task about how, at best, a design argument suggests that the existence of God is only probable and says little about the nature of God. Although in the end Hume awards the debate to Cleanthes, Philo's argument contains a powerful critique of certain aspects of natural theology. One commentator notes that: 'how sceptical of natural theology Hume really was is not certain, and Smith apparently did not consider him a complete sceptic'.[59] Smith had already seen Hume's position in *Natural History*:

> Happily, the first question, which is the most important, admits of the most obvious, at least the clearest, solution. The whole frame of nature bespeaks an intelligent author; and no rational inquirer can, after serious reflection, suspend belief a moment with regard to the primary principles of a genuine theism and religion.[60]

Moreover, Philo in the *Dialogues* does not present an atheistic position. Although at times this is intimated, Philo's retraction is there in black and white: 'Thus all the sciences lead us insensibly to acknowledge a first intelligent Author; and their authority is so much the greater, as they do not posses that intention.' And a few pages later in the same section: 'here then the existence of the deity is plainly ascertained by reason'.[61]

The meaning of these phrases is still much disputed. Some suggest that Hume may have added such material to protect himself. Hume would not have accepted this. He was a man of conscience like Smith himself. To attempt such a ruse would have been beneath them both and would seem a cowardly approach from a man not known for such cowardice. To the contrary, he seems to have rejoiced in creating such religious ferment. This is exactly what must have irritated Smith. Smith lectured in natural theology. We know from Millar that his curriculum was quite typical containing arguments for the existence of God and the normal philosophical foundations of religion.[62] In effect, Hume was attacking one of the pillars of Smith's professional life. Smith's philosophy which ultimately also grounds his economics and jurisprudence is a strong application of the divine plan.[63] Hume was seeking to erode the apologetic grounds of Smith's faith and his whole philosophical system. So it is not surprising that Smith treats the *Dialogues* as something toxic.

Hume's death exacerbated the difficulties. In correspondence with Wedderburn of August 1776[64] Smith eulogized his departed friend in extremely provocative theological language: 'Poor David Hume is dying very fast, but with great cheerfulness and good humour and with more real resignation to the necessary course of things than any Whining Christian ever dyed with pretended resignation to the will of God.' He toned this down and excluded the 'Whining Christian' quote from the letter for publication for Strahan.[65] Smith thought Hume showed great virtue in adversity, greater indeed than the virtue he saw in those ecclesiastics whom he knew would have rejoiced over the death of his great friend. This sets the scene for his passionate eulogy of Hume that he amazingly allowed to be published. Perhaps Smith's grief was sufficient to allay his natural caution and fear of religious divisiveness. Perhaps it was a very deliberate challenge to Hume's ecclesiastical adversaries:

> Thus died our most excellent, and never to be forgotten friend; concerning whose philosophical opinions people will, no doubt, judge variously every one approving or condemning them, according as they happen to coincide or disagree with his own; but concerning whose character and conduct there can scarce be a difference of opinion . . . upon the whole, I have always considered him, both in his lifetime and since his death, as approaching as nearly to the idea of a perfectly wise and virtuous man, as perhaps the nature of human frailty will permit.[66]

Rae's analysis of the letter runs as follows:

> The letter to Strahan . . . excited a long reverberation of angry criticism. Smith had certainly in writing not thought of undermining the faith, or of anything more than speaking a good word for the friend he loved, and putting on record things that he considered very remarkable when he observed them, but in the ear of that age his simple words rang like a challenge to religion itself.[67]

Smith's comments were not well received at all. Boswell, the celebrated biographer of Samuel Johnson, calls it a piece of 'daring effrontery' and George Horne, President of Magdalen, Oxford, wrote a public letter to Smith on it.[68] The result was that Smith's good name was besmirched and in some measure attended with the nasty odour that accompanied the memory of Hume in theological circles.

Smith's resolve never to have a hand in the publishing of the *Dialogues* is very important for reading Smith's theism. Certainly, Smith was not comfortable with Hume's rejection of natural theology. In purely philosophical terms Hume's questioning of natural theology is not necessarily a rejection of Christian theism. Still, this natural theology was accepted widely by the Christian community. An attack on it was interpreted as an attack on Christianity, and it is this that Smith would have nothing to do with. The decision to stand against Hume for the Logic Chair, the issue of the *Edinburgh Review*, and the attitude to the *Dialogues* indicate the strength of Smith's commitment to a relatively orthodox, if progressive, theological worldview. In light of these events it is surprising that in some quarters there is still a tendency to interpret Smith's theology as if it were Hume's.[69] The above incidents suggest that this is at best simplistic and at worst negligent on crucial biographical details of Smith's life. Let us permit Hume to speak for himself on the question of Smith's theism: 'I doubt not, but you [Smith] are so good a Christian as to return me good for evil.'[70]

Reading Smith's theism from redaction of his written work

This analysis can now turn from a discussion of biographical aspects of Smith's life to a redaction of elements of his written work. Again it must be emphasized that this work does not attempt rigorous examination of Smith's theology *per se*.

Smith was no quasi-Humean sceptic. He was not an agnostic who suspended judgement. He not only calmly affirmed his theism, but looks on atheism as a curse. When discussing Aristotle's metaphysics he suggests that Aristotle understood 'all things below' as being characterized by 'disorder and confusion'. In a clearly pejorative reference Smith says that: 'this opinion saps the foundations of human worship, and may have the same effect on society as Atheism itself'.

In T6 he wrote:

> This universal benevolence, how noble and generous whatsoever, can be the source of no solid happiness to the man who is not thoroughly convinced that all the inhabitants of the universe, the meanest as well as the greatest are under the immediate care and protection of that great, benevolent and all wise being, who directs all the movements of nature; and who is determined by his own unalterable perfections, to maintain in it, at all times, the greatest possible quantity of happiness. To this universal benevolence, on the contrary, the very suspicion of a fatherless world, must be the most melancholy of reflections: from the thought that the unknown regions of the infinite and incomprehensible space can be filled with nothing, but endless misery and wretchedness.[71]

This quotation reveals the strength of Smith's theism in that even the hint of agnosticism is sufficient to condemn a person to unhappiness. The reference to the fatherless world is not really one of natural religion isolated from a Christian context. The Judaeo-Christian tradition is not completely singular in its use of the analogy of the eternal fatherhood of God. Still, there can be little doubt that what influenced Smith's reference is the central notion of God as the first person of the Trinity. It is not a reference cited from Stoic or other sources. Here we see Smith's particular brand of Christian theism. It is one heavily influenced by the analogy of the perfection and harmony of nature to the mind of the divine. That Smith chose such an amendment to TMS in T6 does not sit well with the view that he lost interest in Christianity just before the end.

The golden rule
The love of neighbour is one of the principal hinges on which Smith's ethical system turns.[72] This is the key component in the Christian ethical system. It is usually described as the golden rule of loving one's neighbour as oneself. Smith was keen to extend the traditional category of virtue beyond pure benevolence to include certain actions that appear to be in the interests of the individual and may be beneficial to society (see Long, 2004).[73] This innovation was never intended to denigrate the pre-eminent place of benevolence as the paradigm of virtue. Like his predecessor Hutcheson, Smith preserves benevolence as the supreme standard of ethics. He was also explicit that benevolence constitutes his vision of human perfection:

> to feel much for others and little for ourselves, that to restrain our selfish, and to indulge our benevolent affections, constitutes the perfection of human nature . . . As to love our neighbour as we love ourselves is the great law of Christianity, so it is the great precept of nature to love ourselves only as we love our neighbour, or what comes to the same things, as our neighbour is capable of loving us.[74]

Here what is natural coincides with Christian revelation.

> . . . I shall only observe, that we should not have expected to have found it [that the only basis of ethics is the observance of God's commandments] entertained by any sect, who professed themselves a religion in which, as it is the first precept to love the Lord our God with all *our* heart, with all *our* soul, and with all *our* strength, so it is the second to love our neighbour as ourselves; and we should love ourselves surely for our own sakes, not merely because we are commanded to do so.[75]

The emphasis Smith places on the golden rule provides somewhat firm conclusions on Smith's Christian commitment. In fact, the first quote puts a Christian stamp on Smith's whole system. His sense of human perfection is inescapably Christian. The rather unusual rider Smith places to this great commandment is very far from Cropsey's bizarre secularist interpretation. Smith is not saying that benevolence exists in serving oneself as long as one does not infringe another's rights. To the contrary, Smith places strong restraints on self-love. We should love ourselves no more than we can love our neighbour (a strong, but classically Christian injunction).[76] It is also significant that the second quotation uses the first person plural possessive when talking of God (the scriptural texts use the second person singular).[77] Smith accepts the commandment as coming from his God.

Adam Smith's theism 85

The divine names
If names given to the divine reveal the shape of a theology then the character of Smith's theism is consistently Christian. Every plausible divine reference, be it pagan, Christian or relating to a concept of pure natural religion outside of a Christian context has been identified and temporally plotted (see Figure 4.1). A total of 403 substantive references have been identified.[78]

There is inevitably a subjective element in analysis of this nature and an element of risk in any classification. The allocation is always forced and one would not expect every commentator to agree on every reference. The assumption of greatest sensitivity is the use of phrases containing the word 'Nature'. The basis for this theological reading of nature is established in another work.[79] Some references to nature are clearly theological, like the 'Author of Nature' and the 'great Physician of Nature'. However a secondary analysis has been included (Figure 4.2) to consider the case where no references to nature are considered as divine.

This analysis adopts five classifications of divine names. These groups are:

- E – containing references to God classified as explicitly Christian by virtue of the content of the expression or the context in which they are employed;
- I – a designator for the divine or mediated agency of the divine that is not explicitly Christian, but is sufficiently connected to Christian thought and usage to be interpreted as implicitly Christian. It includes nature as an efficient causality of a divine final cause (see Long, 2004);
- N – a pure concept of natural religion that is loosely connected with any Christian usage or understanding;

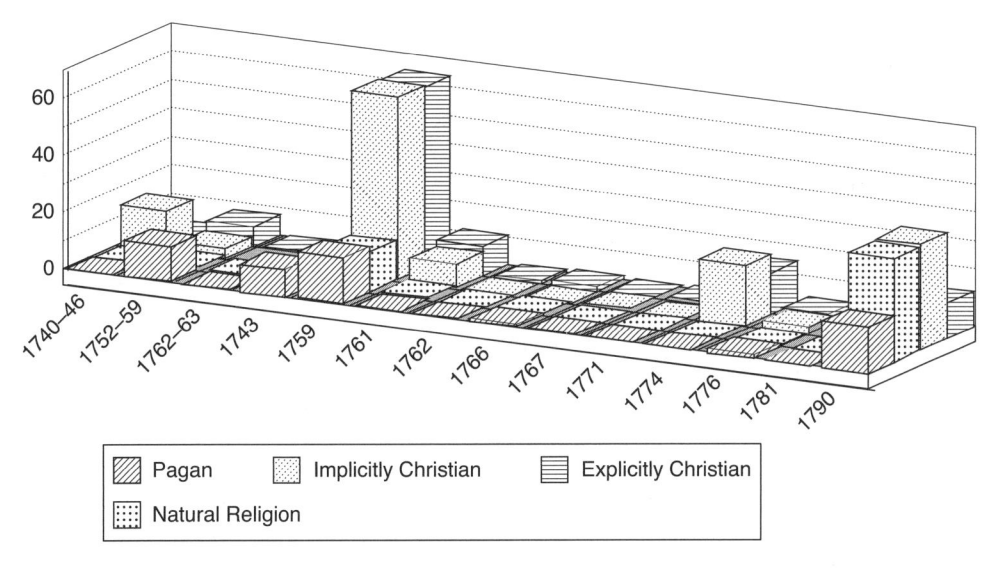

Note: The vertical axis identifies the number of references to devine names according to the concordance cited in Table 1 of Long (2006), p. 132.

Figure 4.1 Divine names (Nature included)

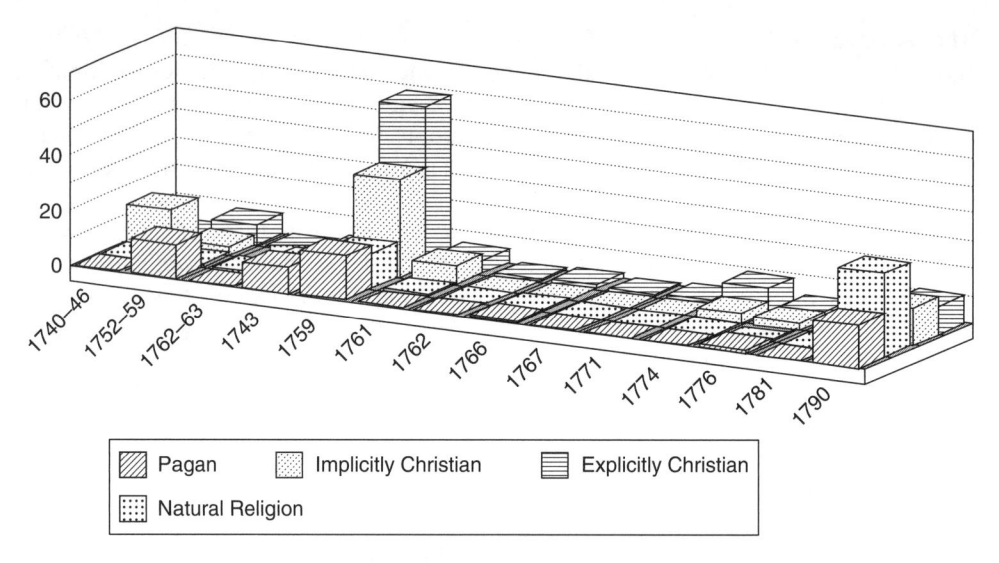

86   *Elgar companion to Adam Smith*

Note: As for Figure 4.1.

Figure 4.2   Divine names (Nature excluded)

- P – a descriptive reference to a pagan concept of God; and
- IN – an incidental reference with no real theological content or a quotation that is not cited in support of Smith's argument. They are not included in the Figures 4.1 and 4.2.

The key finding of the primary analysis in Figure 4.1 is that the majority of Smith's uses of the divine names are either implicitly or explicitly Christian. In aggregate, over all Smith's works approximately 30 per cent of the references are explicitly Christian and 39 per cent are implicitly Christian. Still, in many ways the more meaningful statistic is to ignore category P. The P references are simply descriptive and are not a vehicle of Smith's theological convictions. The explicitly Christian account for 35 per cent of the remainder with the implicitly Christian making up 46 per cent. Natural religion outside of the Christian concept was far from absent from Smithian thought (19 per cent of all references), but remains a minority element.

The primary analysis also detracts from the view that Smith moved towards a natural religion in his later years. For this to occur we would expect category N references to outweigh the E and I references over time. Figure 4.1 (and Figure 4.2) reveal an interesting increase in N references in T6. Those divine names present in T5 but removed with the atonement section in T6 are counted as N references.[80] Fifty-seven per cent of all the N references in Smith come from T6. This is of course an inevitable result of the greater attention he gives to Stoicism. One must conclude from this analysis the relative influence of Stoicism increased in Smith's last years. Still, the optimal word here is 'relative'. In absolute terms T6 actually includes more I references than N references. I and E references still make up 58 per cent of the changes in T6 (excluding P). Certainly the edits to T6 do not strengthen the explicitly Christian foundation of the work. Still, it needs to be remembered that the remainder of the work still stood and this in itself is sufficient to support a broadly Christian reading.

A cursory examination of the titles Smith employs supports this view. There are many extremely Stoic references: 'Author of Nature', 'Superintendent of Nature', 'great Conductor', 'great Director of the world'. The word 'Deity' was an acceptable Christian reference to God in this period and social setting. It did not then carry the strong connotation of deism that might be ascribed to it now.[81] This sort of theological language was acceptable within the progressive wing of the Christian environment of Smith's day. There are of course a number of clear Christian references that were not edited out at any time: 'The Lord our God', 'The Almighty', '[he who] created us in his own image'.

The secondary analysis appears to strengthen these conclusions. Here the use of Nature is not included as a divine referent. This reduces the implicitly Christian (I) factor and therefore increases the explicitly Christian references, in relative terms, to just under 50 per cent excluding P and N (see Figure 4.2).

The atonement

Those who prefer a materialist reading of Smith make much of his decision to delete the atonement section from T6 just prior to his death. T1–5 included a novel interpretation of the expiation from the perspective of Smith's own theory of moral sentiments. The argument is simply that natural sentiments teach us that our imperfections and real guilt are too great for anything but a divine atonement to reverse. Here are Smith's original words from T1 with amendments noted:

> That the Deity loves virtue and hates vice . . . because it promotes the happiness of society . . . 'tis not the doctrine of nature . . . but an artificial refinement of philosophy . . . If we consult our natural sentiments we are [T3–5 'even'] apt to fear [T2–5,] lest before the holiness of God, vice should appear to be more worthy of punishment than the weakness and imperfection of human nature can seem to be of reward . . . He thinks he can see no [this is T3–5, T1–2 uses a different construction] reason why the divine indignation should not be let loose without restraint, upon so vile an insect, as he is sensible [T3–5 'he imagines'] that he himself must be. If he would still hope for happiness, he is conscious [T3–5 'he suspects'] that he cannot demand it from justice, but that he must entreat it from the mercy of God. Repentance, sorrow, humiliation, contrition . . . are the sentiments that become him . . . He even distrusts the efficacy of these . . . Some other intercession, some other sacrifice, some other atonement, [T2–5 'he'] imagines, must be made for him, beyond what he himself is capable of making, before the purity of the Divine justice can be reconciled to his manifold offences. The doctrines of revelation coincide, in every respect, with those original anticipations of nature; and, as they teach us how little we can depend upon the imperfection of our own virtue, so they show us, at the same time, that the most powerful intercession has been made, and that the most dreadful atonement has been paid for our manifold transgressions and iniquities.[82]

Smith remained comfortable with these words for 30-odd years of his life and decided to delete them only a couple of months before his strength gave way.[83] The explanation given to some Edinburgh friends[84] was that the section was 'unnecessary and misplaced'. The sceptics read this 'unnecessary and misplaced' as code for 'I have now lost my faith'. The section is replaced with a singularly Humean invocation: 'In every religion, and in every superstition that the world has ever held, accordingly, there has been a Tartarus as well as Elysium, a place provided for the punishment of the wicked as well as one for the reward of the just.'[85]

Raphael and Macfie identify a number of amendments to this section in T3 where Smith seems to moderate the theological tone.[86] They cautiously imply that the moderation is due to dialogue with Hume. Still, the edits are generally very minor, as are the edits in T3 generally.

The mystery associated with the issue is deliciously enhanced by the discovery of a fragment of a lost manuscript. Rae records that in 1831 a W.B. Cunningham (husband to one of the inheritors of Smith's library) discovered a manuscript hidden for a generation in a work of Aristotle. Though written by an amanuensis, edits in Smith's own hand identify the work conclusively as his. The manuscript is essentially about the divine ground of justice and punishment. It is quite similar to the variant in T1, and is almost certainly derived from the early lecture series on ethics which eventually evolved into TMS itself. Smith ordered all his unpublished works destroyed (save 'History of Astronomy' (Smith, 1980)) close to the end of his life.[87] The manuscript was therefore included in the papers Smith ordered to be burnt. However by some providence or in Rae's words by some 'odd revenge for its suppression' it eluded the pyre. It gives us a powerful insight into the theology of the younger Smith. The reader can safely take the above-rendered quotation from TMS as an adequate presentation of the content of the manuscript on the question of the atonement, save for two points. There is the scriptural reference to orphans and widows that is present in the text of T1 that Smith decides to keep in T6 (it was never included in the manuscript) and Smith's vastly more universalist attitude to Christian salvation in T1. On the first caveat, for one familiar with the Old Testament (as Smith clearly was) the widows and orphans are often referred to as being vindicated by God: 'The justice of God . . . requires that he should hereafter avenge the injuries of the widow and the fatherless'.[88] One can forgive non-theologians like Macfie and Raphael for not stumbling upon this point, but it is not trivial. If the general position is that the deletion of the Christian content in T6 was more than editorial then why did he not also delete the scriptural reference in the line above? Surely, if he was no longer so keen on the whole Christian element, why bother with the Old Testament allusion?

The second point is more significant as it indicates a possible line of development in Smith's philosophy of religion. At the end of the manuscript Smith states: 'The Divine Justice we think cannot be satisfied without demanding some atonement, some expiation for the Offences of men, and Revelation teaches us that this atonement has not only been demanded, but has been paid for, at least, the more valuable part of mankind'.[89] Who is this more valuable part of mankind? Now it cannot mean simply the just, because Christian theology has consistently asserted that Christ's sacrifice was for all irrespective of the state of virtue of a person's past life. Within orthodox Christianity, noting that Smith is lecturing theology to Presbyterian theology students, the best fit seems to be a reference to the baptized. If we compare this to T1–5 we find two very interesting differences. The first is that here there is no reservation of this expiation for this 'more valuable part of mankind'. Rather the tone is universalist: 'The doctrines of revelation coincide, in every respect, with those original anticipations of nature', which all human beings must share. When Smith said that 'the most dreadful atonement has been paid for our manifold transgressions and iniquities', the 'our' is not restricted in any way. Here revelation and nature coincide to teach us of our need for expiation. So the essential theological interpretation of the human as requiring the mercy of God is established independently by both natural and revelatory theology. However in the manuscript there is no mention of this union. In fact, we have only revelatory theology. So this tendency to see human natural sentiments and Christian revelation as mutually reinforcing appears a natural progression in his thought. It embodies a more universalist understanding of revelation as being open to all persons, including the non-baptized as all have access to natural sentiments. This has implications that Smith did not really develop. Still, we know he toys with them as when he cites Voltaire's satirical verses questioning the damnation of the great men of antiquity:

> Vous y grillez sage et docte Platon,
> Divin Homère, éloquent Cicéron.[90]

Does this more progressive and universalist natural theology in T6 indicate a move to a denominationally uncommitted natural religion? Neither the new material in T6 nor any other later writings of Smith warrant this reading. Certainly Raphael and Macfie are too cautious to call for this conclusion from the atonement passage alone. Their argument appears to be that Smith deleted the passage because in his own mind it was not in the right spirit to end a chapter that essentially preserved his disagreement with his friend Hume. The chapter (and interestingly the manuscript as well) repudiated the view that justice is based on utility. Why end this chapter in a way that almost panders to the clerical conservatives who were so merciless to his dear friend? Why not end the piece with a short phrase in the spirit of Hume himself? At least this is the sort of reasoning Macfie and Raphael hypothesize. They could be right, but they seem unnecessarily speculative. A simpler answer presents itself from a holistic interpretation of Smith's life and work.

We know that Smith spoke his mind, but was cautious and measured in his words and hated to be a source of conflict particularly in religious matters. What evidence is there to doubt his own phrase that the words were 'unnecessary and misplaced'? His biographers seem to accept the clarification. In a sense this explanation is typically Smithian as it preserves his own paranoia about misinterpretation. The man was an obsessive editor. Six separate times in his life he edited his major work, tilling the same soil to the extent that he failed to leave himself enough time to complete the work on jurisprudence he had promised.[91] After his eulogizing of Hume he was under suspicion and he probably feared that if his theological work was posthumously published he would become the subject of criticism from the same set that attacked his friend. However while Hume loved to annoy the clerics Smith hated it. All this created some nervousness about the material and the next step would have been an easy one for the compulsive editor: 'if in doubt cross it out'. The deletion combined with the decision to burn his papers represents that sort of nervous and probably unwarranted yet understandable fear of a man sick near the end of his life. Smith's choice of the adjective 'unnecessary' for the deletion is therefore a reference to concern over the style rather than content of his previous presentation. It does not mean a change of heart about his Christian faith. In the end, the deletion itself caused more problems. A laissez-faire approach would have been better.[92]

Comparing TMS and WN

Smith's two major works are quite different. While the former never escapes the orbit of a theological naturalism (albeit one that maintained a critical and empiricist outlook) WN often seems largely an account of *homo economicus* in abstraction from Smith's philosophical theology. WN contains only six significant divine referents.[93] Although WN is almost three times as large as TMS, the latter uses references to the divine 45 times more frequently. Comparable ratios are also evident when we consider Smith's lectures on jurisprudence, his work on the imitative arts (hereafter IM). TMS was the theological grounding which he would apply to jurisprudence in his lectures and to economics in WN. In Smith's day an overarching theological worldview was almost universally held. To make it an explicit element of a work devoted to another topic entirely would have been somewhat peculiar, akin to stating one's commitment to arithmetic before using differential calculus. It was simply presumed. Newton was a noted believer, but did not feel the need to refer regularly to the divine in his scientific works. So the same applies for Smith in regard to his economics.

Minowitz has presented a strong version of the problem by suggesting that the divergence in theological content between TMS and WN suggests Smith lost his faith. The poverty of such a perspective is revealed by examination of what we know about when Smith started working on WN. There is not just WN itself to consider, but also manuscripts that contain the early draft to WN (ED), the first and second fragments (FA and FB) of the division of labour and LJA and LJB (*Lectures on Jurisprudence*). It is not clear that the younger Smith ever really intended to write an economic work. After completing his philosophical work his only real goal was the major work on jurisprudence. WN seems to have emerged as a partial attempt or first instalment of this work. ED appears to be an attempt to translate the more economic elements of LJA (1762–63) into book form. Meek, Raphael and Stein suggest this was shortly before April 1763.[94] Analysis by Meek and Skinner places FA and FB in the 1760s, later than Scott's attribution of the works to the Edinburgh period.[95] From correspondence we know that Smith was known to be working on WN in 1764[96] and had given a draft to the publisher in 1772 where it was edited and revised for four years until publication in late 1775 and early 1776.[97] In all a slow process of evolution taking some 14 or so years. However this was not all that Smith was doing. There is of course LJA and LJB, and also T3 (1767) and T4 (1774) and maybe even IM.

In light of this, the only way to interpret Minowitz's claim sensibly is that Smith gradually lost his faith over this period. However the evidence turns the other way. The theological references in these works have generally been classified as explicitly or implicitly Christian. Only five amendments have been tracked for T3. T4 is another interesting case. At this stage, WN was already at the publishers and close to being finalized. However T4 has been allocated 38 amendments to the divine names, of which 13 are explicitly Christian, and all but one of the remainder are implicitly Christian. Still, even if this is ignored, there are still a number of explicitly Christian references included after WN had been sent to the publisher. If Smith has lost his faith at about the time of WN, why did he not delete the Christian referents in T5? Finally, we see in T6 a number of new Christian referents to the divine (some are deleted as well). One of these is a reference to the Decalogue.[98] Smith thinks that by virtue of the Decalogue 'we are commanded to love our parents'. If the man had lost his Christian commitment, why would he bother about such a reference on the eve of his death? Figures 4.1 and 4.2 do not reveal any appreciable increase in N references which are at the expense of I and E references to God. T6 itself cannot be seen as providing any clear evidence of a move away from a Christian position, although it does show a great enthusiasm for certain aspects of natural religion. Overall, it appears there is no evidence to suggest a move away from the early Christian position before T6, and even in T6 there is no conclusive evidence of this either.

The question of revelation
An analysis of Smith's theism requires an interpretation of his attitude to Christian revelation. One must resist the temptation to read anything substantive into this decision to order most of his unpublished notes destroyed. That he did not publish a theological work is understandable given his temperament, the experiences of his friend Hume, and the explosive theological environment of his Scotland. As he intended that all the lectures be destroyed, not just those of natural theology, the decision to burn his papers at the end of his life does not tell anything about his religious convictions at that time.

It is also a false move to conclude that just because his work is not in the genre of a Christian theologian, his project is one of natural religion. It is more likely that his work is one of natural theology, seen as operating on a parallel track to revealed theology, supporting this theology, and serving it. In his 1762/63 Glasgow course on rhetoric Smith gave a lecture on Shaftesbury (hereafter LRBL). Shaftesbury is subtly derided by Smith, as is his system of natural religion. He was influenced by his father and his famous pedagogue Locke who were not committed to any particular religious tradition. Their strong emphasis on the liberty of conscience inclined them more to the puritans than any established church. Shaftesbury's temperament however was inconsistent with the puritans who showed 'grossness' and 'little decency' in the appearance of devotion. In time, this prejudiced him against all revealed religion and encouraged him to attempt to destroy these established systems and then try to build one of his own to replace them. This characterization of Shaftesbury may not be a fair one, but it is interesting that Smith chose to attack one of the leading lights of natural religion.

Smith clearly believed in Christian revelation. He refers to revelation explicitly five times[99] and more significantly employs (with varying degrees of emphasis) 29 scriptural quotations or allusions (see Table 4.1). Some of these biblical references like the 'ox that gores' only indicate a thorough knowledge of the scriptures and a predisposition to use them as didactic tools. Yet in other cases it is clear that Smith is using the scriptures to support his moral theory as in the case of the golden rule. Smith also seems to think that the scriptures are authoritative and normative for Christianity. Take again the reference to honouring our parents: 'In the Decalogue we *are commanded* to honour our fathers and our mothers'.[100]

Smith also uses the phrase 'inspired writers'. This formulation carries the connotation of some loyalty to the principle of biblical inspiration.[101] In LRBL Smith discusses the sentiments of Adam and Eve, as presented in Milton's *Paradise Lost*:

> The diversity of the same affection [grief] in different characters is finally instanced in the Sentiments of *our first Parents* on quitting Paradise – Eve she regrets Leaving the flowers and Walks and chief the Nuptial Bower – Adam in a very sublime passage the Scenes where he had conversed with God.[102]

Smith is going much further here than simply discussing Milton. He appears to believe that Adam and Eve were historical characters, as indeed any orthodox Christian of the day would have. The use of the adjective 'sublime' when talking of the discussion between Adam and God is more likely to be a spiritual reference than an aesthetic one.

In LRBL 8.115 he speaks against parodies of the scriptures. Many of the divine names are scriptural (for example the Lord our God, Messiah, Almighty).

In a number of places he emphasizes the consistency of his view of the human person with Christian revelation. In LJA he indicates that the laws of consanguinity, which have been borrowed from the Law of Moses, accord with nature and reason.[103] In T6, 3.3.13 (p. 142) the command to love our parents in revelation supports nature's edict that we love our children.

Smith's natural theology
Smith's natural theology is an important consideration for his theism which is presented in detail in other works (see Long 2004 and Long in the *Adam Smith Review*, 2006). The natural theology of TMS becomes the primary organizing principle of the whole corpus. It is not just the basis of Smith's ethics and jurisprudence, but is also the providentialist grounding of human sociality in economic affairs (broadly, the invisible hand doctrine). There are also strong (and sometimes overly strong) deist and Stoic influences. Still, Smith thinks that the natural theology arrives at broadly the same conclusions as Christian revelatory theology (to love one's neighbour as oneself) and is consistent with a moderate and balanced Christianity.

It is a natural theology of society. The final cause of God's creative action is a desire to produce a society of virtuous and happy persons. The efficient causality is nature, which is really human nature. Our natural sentiments are so artfully constructed by the Divine Architect that their combination in society is mutually correcting and enhancing, encouraging virtue, discouraging vice, and leading to reasonably just social and legal structures. An original desire for self-preservation (a Stoic notion) is developed to create a legitimate role for self-advancement and self-love. However this is almost always excessively strong and our perceptions of the adverse judgements of others ensure that we constrain it. In this way we act as vicegerents of God's divine authority in superintending each other's conduct. This spectatorial function is highly imperfect, so often we must rely on what our consciences tells us is worthy of praise. Potentially, we become an ideal spectator of our conduct in imitation of God, the paradigmatically impartial spectator. However even when we fail in this task the plan of the 'great Superintendent' is so ingenious that good will often eventuate. The social interaction of human sentiments seems to have some synergetic countervailing force that mitigates the impact of human imperfection. In the end, human sociality is invincibly benign. This providential underwriting of our relationships has implications on a broad front. Constrained self-love is not moral perfection, but is generally consistent with mutual welfare. Smith applies this to form an explanation of why commercial decisions (by individuals or corporations), which are usually motivated by constrained self-love rather than benevolence, can produce aggregate economic benefits. In the end, it is an extremely optimistic coherence theory of human nature.

Implications
The chapter has posed a single question: was Smith a theist? The analysis has essentially restricted itself to biographical and redactive methods. The conclusion is that Smith consistently held a moderate Christian theism. This assessment is pregnant with implications which are best posed here simply as questions. If Smith's theism was an enduring inspiration for his life then the whole Smithian corpus needs to be read in light of this, as

Adam Smith's theism 93

a basic hermeneutical principle. If Smith retained his loyalty to Christian thought when he wrote WN, how can this work not also embody a theological perspective? Surely, should not the Smithian corpus be interrogated to evaluate the impact of this theological perspective? If this is granted, then we must now remain open to the implications of Smith's Christian perspective for his economic writings.

Notes

1. This interpretation has been offered by Viner (1972), p. 82. and Davis (1990), p. 90.
2. The key work here was *Polity and Economy* (1957).
3. Ibid., p. 3.
4. T1, 1.1.5.5, p. 25.
5. Cropsey (1957), p. 19.
6. Ibid., p. 33.
7. See WN 5.1.g, pp. 792–3.
8. Minowitz (1993), p. 169.
9. Ibid., p. 9.
10. Ibid., p. 1 and Chapter 11.
11. Minowitz, p. 8.
12. This so-called 'Adam Smith problem' is addressed below.
13. For example, he thinks that Smith's reference to the phrase, 'As every man doth so shall it be done to him', T1, 2.2.1.1.10, p. 82 is simply a blind following of Locke in the *Second Treatise on Government* (1960). However it is really an independent reference to biblical revelation (Leviticus 24.19).
14. Minowitz (1993), p. 120.
15. Ibid., p. 158.
16. With Smith's classical inclinations it is not that surprising that Smith identifies these three revolutions as the fall of the Greek, Carthaginian and Roman empires.
17. Minowitz (1993), p. 196.
18. Ibid., p. 121.
19. Ibid., p. 192.
20. See Eckstein (1926) introduction to *Theorie der ethischen Gefühle*; this issue is explained below.
21. Chapter 6 of T6, which discusses the Stoics, is completely new.
22. Rae (1965), p. 430.
23. Butler takes his notion of the approving faculty of conscience from Epictetus (Note 1, Dissertation 2, *The Analogy of Religion*) (1987). Hume refers to Epictetus in the *Enquiry* (1998 [1751]), pp. 136, 181, 231, 248, and in section 5, Part 1 of *An Enquiry Concerning Human Understanding* (1993 [1748]).
24. See for example Heise (1995), Griswold (1999), Brown (1994).
25. TMS, p. 6.
26. Ibid., p. 10.
27. Leslie (1870), p. 17.
28. Veblen (1899), p. 130.
29. Viner (1972), p. 146.
30. Ibid., p. 144.
31. Ibid., p. 145.
32. Ibid., p. 146.
33. Ibid., pp. 79ff.
34. Hasbach (1891).
35. Bitterman (1940), p. 191.
36. Ibid., p. 221. The actual quote is 'Our saviour's precept', referring to the imperative to turn the other cheek (T1, 3.6.13, p. 178). Smith's language must be seen as implying some loyalty to Christian soteriology and christology.
37. Davis in Wood (1994), Vol. 7, p. 90.
38. See Scott (1965), p. 101 especially John Oswald and John Drysdale.
39. In C298 (Smith, 1977, p. 298) Smith asks a visitor, John Bruce, to delay his arrival at the university until he has finished his religious duties.
40. Rae (1965), p. 407.
41. Ibid., p. 435. Another reference also stated by Rae (p. 435) at Smith's deathbed is: 'I love your company Gentlemen, but I believe I must leave you to go to another world.'
42. Ibid., p. 97.

43. Ibid., p. 433 and see T1, 7.2.2.13, p. 298 when Smith says of Epicurus's system: 'this system is, no doubt, altogether inconsistent with what I have been endeavouring to establish'. Viner in the introduction to Rae cautions us not to place much reliance on the testimony of the Earl of Buchan who was thought to be quite eccentric (Rae 1965, pp. 22–3).
44. Ibid., p. 129.
45. Ibid.
46. Ibid., p. 11.
47. Ibid., p. 47.
48. C10 (Smith, 1977), pp. 5–6.
49. Rae (1965), p. 125. Woodhouselee was acquainted with the contributors.
50. Ibid., p. 125.
51. C19 (Smith, 1977), pp. 19–22. See Gaskin's editorial introduction to Hume's *Principal Writings on Religion* including *Dialogues Concerning Natural Religion* and *Natural History of Religion*.
52. We know that in 1754 Smith was asked to comment on the first edition of *Natural History of Religion* (hereafter *Natural History*). In the 1757 edition Hume followed Smith's advice to amend the work 'in point of prudence' so as not to increase the 'clamour' against him (see C22).
53. There is no definite record of the original correspondence (see Note 2, C156).
54. Rae (1965), p. 296.
55. C157 (Smith, 1977).
56. Rae (1965), p. 296.
57. Ibid., p. 172.
58. Ibid., p. 298.
59. Bitterman (1940), p. 194.
60. Hume (1993), *Natural History*, p. 134.
61. Ibid., *Dialogues*, Part XII.
62. Rae (1965), p. 54.
63. This is discussed in detail in Long (2004).
64. C163 (Smith, 1977).
65. Smith uses the 'whining' adjective in T6, long after Hume had died, to describe certain overly melancholic Christian thinkers (T2, 3.3.9, p. 139).
66. C178 (Smith, 1977).
67. Rae (1965), p. 311.
68. Ibid., p. 312.
69. Minowitz and Griswold are examples of authors who suggest that Smith was influenced by Hume's sceptical agnosticism or atheism.
70. The tone is jovial, but not sarcastic: C31 (Smith, 1977).
71. T6, 6.2.3.2, p. 235.
72. Long (2004) shows how the Golden Rule is implicated in the notions of sympathy and conscience so central to TMS.
73. Long (2004).
74. T1, 1.1.5.5, p. 25.
75. T1, 3.6.1, p. 171, emphasis added. The complex relationship between benevolence and self-love is also developed in Long (2004).
76. Smith's unusual rider to the quote is discussed below.
77. See for example Luke 10.27: you will love: Ἀγαπήσεις from *The New Interlinear Greek NT* (http://www.scripture4all.org/OnlineInterlinear/NTpdf/luk10.pdf).
78. Long (2004) presents each of these references in a detailed reference table.
79. Ibid.
80. See below for a discussion of this manuscript.
81. Hutcheson (1994) also prefers the word 'Deity' often instead of 'God'.
82. T1, 5:2.2.3.12, pp. 91–2. Gender specificity reluctantly preserved for clarity.
83. Stewart, V.9, suggests that T6 was sent to the publisher in the 'middle of the preceding winter' before 1790 so say January 1790. Rae indicates that by February Smith was very sick, his strength almost gone by March and he died on 17 July (see Rae 1965, pp. 432f). So there was only an interval of two months between the time he sent the work to the printers and when his health gave way.
84. Rae (1965) cites Sinclair (1837) here, *Life of John Sinclair*, i.40. There are no quotation marks in Rae's account.
85. T6, 2.2.3.12, p. 91.
86. TMS, p. 399; most of these are noted in the above quotation.
87. See Rae (1965), p. 434 and C137 (Smith, 1977) especially note 3.
88. T1 which in the reordering in T6 becomes 2.2.3.12, p. 91.

89. See TMS, pp. 383f.
90. 'You roast there wise and learned Plato, Divine Homer, eloquent Cicero.' Acutes and graves were not present in Smith's quotation from Voltaire: *La Pucelle d'Orléans, chant.* 5 T6, 3.2.35, referring to Besterman's (1968) translation of Voltaire's *Correspondence and Related Documents* as cited by D. Raphael and A.L. Macfie in Smith (1976 [1776–90]), p. 134.
91. See the Advertisement to T6.
92. Nobody noticed its absence for some time. In fact, 20 years after his death Archbishop Magee of Dublin praised Smith for such a sublime passage without realizing it had been deleted. He corrected himself with a haunting epitaph for Smith, one that history has not expunged: 'he was infected by David Hume's society'. However, Hume had been dead for 14 years by the time T6 was published.
93. 2 I, 2 E, 1 N, and 1 P reference (see Appendix to Long, 2004).
94. See ,Introduction' to ED. in LJ, p. 562.
95. Meck and Skinner (1973).
96. C84 (Smith, 1977). In 1764 Smith wrote to Hume while at Toulouse, mentioning the project that will become WN. From C85 we can see that Smith's friends knew he was working on the project in November 1764.
97. Rae (1965), pp. 255f.
98. T6, 3.3.13, p. 142.
99. The five references are:
    - the manuscript with the draft of the atonement passage: 'doctrine of revelation teaches us'.
    - the atonement section T1, 2.2.3.12, pp. 91–2: 'the doctrines of revelation show us'.
    - P9: 'The Divine revelation'.
    - LRBL, 11.14, Shaftesbury's rejection of revealed religion.
    - T2, 3.2.31. the reference to a 'fuller revelation of providence'.
100. T6, 3.3.13, p. 142.
101. T1, 2.1.5.09, p. 77.
102. LRBL 13.167 (hand b: a reliable addition reproduced by one of the scribes although absent from the other two), emphasis added.
103. LJA, 3.66, p. 166.

References and bibliography

Primary references for Adam Smith

The principal collection of Smith's relied upon in this analysis was *The Glasgow Edition of the Works and Correspondence of Adam Smith*, reprinted by Liberty Fund, Indianapolis, IN 1984–87, in six volumes comprising:

I   Smith, Adam [1776–90, 6 editions] (1976), *The Theory of Moral Sentiments*, reprinted in D.D. Raphael and A.L. Macfie (eds), *Glasgow Edition of the Works and Correspondence of Adam Smith*, Vol. 1, Oxford: Clarendon Press.
    Part I also includes the fragments on the 'Atonement' and on 'Justice'.
II Smith, Adam [1776–90, 6 editions] (1979), *An Inquiry into the Nature and Causes of the Wealth of Nations*, 2 vols, reprinted in D.D. Raphael and A.L. Macfie (eds), *Glasgow Edition of the Works and Correspondence of Adam Smith*, Oxford: Clarendon Press.
III Smith, Adam (1795), (1980), *Essays on Philosophical Subjects*, reprinted in W.P.D. Wightman and J.C. Bryce (eds), *Glasgow Edition of the Works and Correspondence of Adam Smith*, Oxford: Clarendon Press.
    Part III includes:
    'The History of Astronomy';
    'The History of Ancient Physics';
    'The History of Ancient Logics and Metaphysics';
    'Of the External Senses';
    'Of the Nature of that Imitation which takes place in what are called the Imitative Arts';
    'Of the Affinity between Music, Dancing, and Poetry';
    'Of the Affinity between English and Italian Verses';
    Contributions to the *Edinburgh Review* of 1755–56;
    Review of Johnson's *Dictionary*;
    A letter to the Authors of the *Edinburgh Review*; and
    Preface and Dedication to *William Mailton's Poems on Several Occasions*.
IV Smith, Adam [1762–63] (1983), *Lectures on Rhetoric and Belles Lettres*, reprinted in J.C. Bryce (ed.), *Glasgow Edition of the Works and Correspondence of Adam Smith*, Oxford: Clarendon Press.

Part IV also includes: 'Considerations Concerning the First Formation of Languages'.
V   Smith, Adam (1978), *Lectures on Jurisprudence*, reprinted in R.L. Meek, D.D. Raphael and P.G. Stein (eds), *Glasgow Edition of the Works and Correspondence of Adam Smith*, Oxford: Clarendon Press.
Part V also includes:
'Early draft' of part of the *Wealth of Nations*;
'First Fragment on the Division of Labour'; and
'Second Fragment on the Division of Labour'.
VI   Smith, Adam (1977), *Correspondence of Adam Smith*, reprinted in E.C. Mossner and I.S. Ross (eds) *Glasgow Edition of the Works and Correspondence of Adam Smith*, Oxford: Clarendon Press.

Early editions consulted:
The Theory of Moral Sentiments, 1st edn (1759), held at the National Library of Australia, printed by A. Millar.
An Inquiry into the Nature and Causes of the Wealth of Nations, 1st edn (1776), held in the Robinson Collection at the Australian National Library, printed by Strahan & Cadell, London.

Other primary sources

Hume, D. (1998 [1751]), *An Enquiry Concerning the Principles of Morals*, reprinted in T. Beauchamp (ed.), Oxford: Oxford University Press.
Hume, D. (1993 [1748]), *An Enquiry Concerning Human Understanding*, reprinted in E. Steinberg (ed.), Indianapolis, IN: Hackett.
Hume, D. (1987 [1777]), *Essays Moral, Political, Literary*, reprinted in E. Miller (ed.), Indianapolis, IN: Liberty Fund.
Hume, D. (1983 [1778]), *History of England from the invasion of Julius Caesar to the revolution of 1688*, reprinted in W. Todd (ed.), Indianapolis, IN: Liberty Fund.
Hume, D. (1993), *Principal Writings on Religion including Dialogues Concerning Natural Religion and Natural History of Religion*, J. Gaskin (ed.), Oxford: Oxford University Press.
Hume, D. (1992 [1739]), *Treatise of Human Nature*, Buffalo, NY: Prometheus.
Hutcheson, F. (1994), *Philosophical Writings*, R.S. Downie (ed.), London: Everyman.

Secondary references

Ahmad, S. (1990), 'Adam Smith's four invisible hands', *History of Political Economy*, **22** (1), 441–58.
Anderson, G. (1998), 'Mr Smith and the preachers: the economics of religion in the *Wealth of Nations*', *Journal of Political Economy*, **96** (5), 1066–88.
Anderson, G. (1989), 'The butcher, the baker and the policy-maker: Adam Smith in public choice', *History of Political Economy*, **21** (4), 641–59.
Baumol, W. (1986), 'Smith versus Marx on business morality and the social interest', in M. Szenberg (ed.), *Essays in Economics*, Boulder, CO: Westview Press, pp. 241–6.
Becker, C. (1946), *Heavenly City of the Eighteenth-Century Philosophers*, New Haven, CT: Yale University Press.
Bestermann, T. (1968), *Correspondence and Related Documents*, Toronto: University of Toronto Press.
Billet, L. (1976), 'The just economy: the moral basis of the *Wealth of Nations*', *Review of Social Economy*, **34** (3), 295–315.
Bitterman, H. (1940), 'Adam Smith's empiricism and the law of nature', *Journal of Political Economy*, **48** (4) August, 487–520, and October, 703–34.
Brown, V. (1994), *Adam Smith's Discourse: Canonicity, Commerce and Conscience*, London: Routledge.
Butler, J. (1987), *The Analogy of Religion*, London: Routledge.
Campbell, R. and A. Skinner (1982), *Adam Smith*, London: Croom Helm.
Campbell, R. and A. Skinner (1979), 'General Introduction to Adam Smith', in R. Campbell and A. Skinner (eds), *The Inquiry Into the Nature and Causes of the Wealth of Nations*, Oxford: Clarendon Press, pp. 1–66.
Campbell, W. (1967), 'Adam Smith's theory of justice, prudence and beneficence', *American Economic Review*, **57**, 571–7.
Cesarano, F. (1976), 'Monetary theory in Ferdinando Galiani's *Della Moneta*', *History of Political Economy*, **8** (3), 380–99.
Choi, Y. (1990), 'Smith's view of human nature: a problem in the interpretation of the *Wealth of Nations* and the *Theory of Moral Sentiments*', *Review of Social Economy*, **48** (3), 288–302.
Coase, R. (1976), 'Adam Smith's view of man', *Journal of Law and Economics*, **19** (3), 529–46.
Coats, A. (1975), 'Adam Smith's conception of self-interest in economic and political affairs', *History of Political Economy*, **7** (1), 132–6.

Cropsey, J. (1957), *Polity and Economy: An Interpretation of the Principles of Adam Smith*, The Hague: Martinus Nijhoff.
Davis, J.B. (1989), 'Smith's invisible hand and Hegel's cunning of reason', *International Journal of Social Economics*, **16**, 50–66.
Davis, J.R. (1990), 'Adam Smith on the providentialist reconciliation of individual and social interest: is man led by an invisible hand or misled by a sleight of hand?' *History of Political Economy*, **22** (2), 341–52.
Deane, P. (1978), *The Evolution of Economic Ideas*, Cambridge: Cambridge University Press.
Downie, R. (1992), 'Ethics and casuistry in Adam Smith', in P. Jones and A. Skinner (eds), *Adam Smith Reviewed*, Edinburgh: Edinburgh University Press, pp. 119–42.
Dunn, J. (1983), 'From applied theology to social analysis: the break between John Locke and the Scottish Enlightenment', in I. Hont and M. Ignatieff (eds), *Wealth and Virtue*, Cambridge: Cambridge University Press, pp. 330–46.
Dunn, W.C. (1941), 'Adam Smith and Edmund Burke: contemporary contemporaries', *Southern Economic Journal*, **7** (3), January, 330–46.
Eatwell, J. (ed.) (1989), *The Invisible Hand*, The New Palgrave Series, London and New York: Macmillan.
Eatwell, J., M. Milgate and P. Newman (eds) (1987), *The New Palgrave: A Dictionary of Economics*, 4 vols, London and New York: Macmillan.
Eckstein, W. (1926), *Theorie der ethischen Gefühle*, Leipzig: F. Meiner.
Fitzgibbons, A. (1995), *Adam Smith's System of Liberty, Wealth and Virtue*, Oxford: Clarendon Press.
Fleischacker, S. (1999), *A Third Concept of Liberty: Judgement and Freedom in Kant and Adam Smith*, Princeton, NJ: Princeton University Press.
Fry, M. (ed.) (1992), *Adam Smith's Legacy, his Place in the Development of Modern Economics*, London: Routledge.
Gill, E. (1976), 'Justice in Adam Smith: the Right and the Good', *Review of Social Economy*, **34** (3), 275–94.
Gramm, W. (1980), 'The selective interpretation of Adam Smith', *Journal of Economic Issues*, **14** (1), 119–42.
Gregg, S. (ed.) (1999), *In Praise of the Free Economy, Essays by Michael Novak*, Sydney: Centre of Independent Studies.
Griswold, C. (1999), *Adam Smith and the Virtues of Enlightenment*, Cambridge: Cambridge University Press.
Haakonssen, K. (1981), *The Science of a Legislator: The Natural Jurisprudence of David Hume and Adam Smith*, Cambridge: Cambridge University Press.
Hasbach, W. (1891), *Untersuchungen über Adam Smith und die Entwicklung der Politischen Ökonomie*, Leipzig: Duncker & Humblot.
Hausman, D. (ed.) (1994), *The Philosophy of Economics: An Anthology*, Cambridge: Cambridge University Press.
Hazlitt, H. (1984), *The Wisdom of the Stoics*, Lanham, MD: University Press of America.
Heilbroner, R. (1953), *The Worldly Philosophers*, New York: Simon & Schuster.
Heise, P. (1995), 'Stoicism in EPS: the foundations of Adam Smith's moral philosophy', in I. Rima (ed.), *Perspectives in the History of Economic Thought: The Classical Tradition in Economic Thought*, Aldershot, UK and Brookfield, VT, USA: Edward Elgar, Vol. XI, pp. 17–30, .
Henderson, J. and J.B. Davis (1991), 'Adam Smith's influence on Hegel's philosophical writings', *Journal of the History of Economic Thought*, **13** (2), 184–204.
Hollander, S. (1973), *The Economics of Adam Smith*, London: Heinemann.
Hont, I. and M. Ignatieff (eds) (1983), *Wealth and Virtue: the Shaping of Political Economy in the Scottish Enlightenment*, Cambridge: Cambridge University Press.
Jones, P. and A. Skinner (eds) (1992), *Adam Smith Reviewed*, Edinburgh: Edinburgh University Press.
La Nauze, J. (1945), 'A manuscript attributed to Adam Smith', *Economic Journal*, **55**, 218–19.
Landes, D. (1999), *The Wealth and Poverty of Nations*, London: Abacus.
Leslie, L. (1870), 'The political economy of Adam Smith', *Fortnightly Review*, **8**, 17–130.
Locke, J. (1960), *Two Treatises of Government*, Cambridge: Cambridge University Press.
Long, B. (2004), 'Adam Smith and Adam's sin', Doctoral dissertation, University of Cambridge.
Long, B. (2006), 'Adam Smith's natural theology of society', *Adam Smith Review*, **2**, 124–48.
Lukes, I. (1997), 'Moral thinking and the self-interest axiom in the history of economic analysis', Doctoral dissertation, University of Cambridge.
Macfie, A. (1971), 'The invisible hand of Jupiter', *Journal of History of Ideas*, **32** (4), 595–9.
McNulty, P. (1975), 'A note on the division of labour in Plato and Smith', *History of Political Economy*, **7** (3), 372–8.
Meek, D., D. Raphael and P. Stein (eds) (1978), 'Introduction', in A. Smith, *Lectures on Jurisprudence*, Oxford: Clarendon Press.
Meek, R.L. and A.S. Skinner (1973), 'The development of Adam Smith's ideas on the division of labour', *Economic Journal*, **83** (332), 1094–116.

Melitz, J. and D. Winch (eds) (1978), *Religious Thought and Economic Society, Four Chapters of an Unfinished Work by Jacob Viner*, Durham, NC: Duke University Press.
Milton, J. (1668), *Paradise Lost*, A. Fowler (ed.) (1976), London: Longmen.
Minowitz, P. (1993), *Profits, Priests and Princes: Adam Smith's Emancipation of Economics from Politics and Religion*, Stanford, CA: Stanford University Press.
Morrow, G. (1927), 'Adam Smith: moralist and philosopher', *Journal of Political Economy*, **35** (3), 321–42.
Morrow, G. (1969), *The Ethical and Economic Theories of Adam Smith*, New York: Kelley.
O'Brien, D. (1975), *The Classical Economists*, Oxford: Clarendon Press.
Pack, S. (1995), 'Adam Smith's unnaturally natural (yet naturally unnatural) use of the word "natural"', in I. Rima (ed.), *Classical Tradition in Economic Thought: Perspectives on the History of Economic Thought*, Vol. 11, Aldershot, UK and Brookfield, VT, USA: Edward Elgar, pp. 31–42.
Pears, R. (1990), *Hume's System*, Oxford: Oxford University Press.
Petrella, F. (1970), 'Individual group, or government: Smith, Mill, and Sidgwick', *History of Political Economy*, **2** (1), 365–74.
Pocock, J.G. (1983), 'Cambridge paradigms and Scotch society: a study of the relations between the civic humanist and the civil jurisprudential interpretation of eighteenth-century social thought', in I. Hont and M. Ignatieff (eds), *Wealth and Virtue*, Cambridge: Cambridge University Press, pp. 235–52.
Rae, J. (1965), *Life of Adam Smith*, New York: A.M. Kelley.
Raphael, D. (1975), 'The impartial spectator', in A. Skinner and T.Wilson (eds), *Essays on Adam Smith*, Oxford: Clarendon Press, pp. 83–99.
Raphael, D. (1992), 'Adam Smith 1790: the man recalled; the philosopher revived', in P. Jones and A. Skinner (eds), *Adam Smith Reviewed*, Edinburgh: Edinburgh University Press, pp. 93–118.
Raphael, D. (1969), 'Adam Smith and "the infection of David Hume's society"', *Journal of the History of Ideas*, **30**, 225–48.
Raphael, D. and A.L. Macfie (1976), 'Introduction', in A. Smith, *The Theory of Moral Sentiments*, Oxford: Clarendon Press, pp. 1–52.
Reisman, D. (1976), *Adam Smith's Sociological Economics*, London: Croom-Helm.
Rogers, K. (1997), *Self-interest, an Anthology of Philosophical Perspectives*, New York: Routledge.
Scott, W. (1965), *Adam Smith as Student and Professor*, New York: A.M. Kelley.
Sinclair, Revd John (Sir John Sinclair's son) (1837), *Memoirs of the Life and Works of the Late Right Honourable Sir John Sinclair, Bart*, 2 vols, Edinburgh: W. Blackwood and Sons.
Skinner, A. and T. Wilson (eds) (1975), *Essays on Adam Smith*, Oxford: Clarendon Press.
Skinner, A. (1979), *A System of Social Science: Papers Relating to Adam Smith*, Oxford: Clarendon Press.
Skinner, A. (1992), 'Adam Smith: ethics and self-love', in P. Jones and A. Skinner (eds), *Adam Smith Reviewed*, Edinburgh: Edinburgh University Press, pp. 142–67.
Speigel, H. (1976), 'Adam Smith's Heavenly City', *History of Political Economy*, **8** (4): 478–93.
Stewart, D. (1980 [1793]), 'Account of the life and writings of Adam Smith, LL.D', in W. Wightman (ed.), *Essays on Philosophical Subjects by Adam Smith*, Oxford: Oxford University Press, pp. 269–351.
Stigler, G. (1982), *The Economist as Preacher, and other Essays*, Chicago, IL: University of Chicago.
Stigler, G. (1989), 'The butcher, the baker and the policy maker: Adam Smith on public choice: a reply', *History of Political Economy*, **21** (4), 641–60.
Taylor, W. (1965), *Francis Hutcheson and David Hume as Predecessors of Adam Smith*, Durham, NC: Duke University Press.
Teichgraeber, R. (1986), *Free Trade and Moral Philosophy: Rethinking the Sources of Adam Smith's Wealth of Nations*, Durham, NC: Duke University Press.
Tobin, J. (1992), 'The Invisible Hand in Modern Macroeconomics', in M. Fry (ed.), *Adam Smith's Legacy, His Place in the Development of Modern Economics*, London: Routledge, pp. 117–29.
Veblen, T. (1899), 'The preconceptions of economic science', *Quarterly Journal of Economics*, **13**, 121–50.
Veblen, T. (1961), *The Place of Science in Modern Civilisation, and Other Essays*, New York: Russell & Russell.
Viner, J. (1927), 'Adam Smith and laissez faire', *Journal of Political Economy*, **35** (2), April, 198–232.
Viner, J. (1972), *The Role of Providence in the Social Order: An Essay in Intellectual History*, Philadelphia, PA: American Philosophical Society.
Viner, J. (1965), 'A guide to John Rae's *Life of Adam Smith*', in J. Rae, *Life of Adam Smith*, New York: A.M. Kelley.
Waszek, N. (1988), *The Scottish Enlightenment and Hegel's Account of 'Civil Society'*, Dordrecht: Kluwer Academic Publishers.
Werhane, P. (1991), *Adam Smith and His Legacy for Modern Capitalism*, Oxford: Oxford University Press.
West, J. (1969), *Adam Smith: the Man and his Works*, New York: New Rochelle.
Wightman, W. (1980), 'General introduction to Adam Smith', *Essays on Philosophical Subjects*, Oxford: Oxford University Press.

Wood, J. (ed.) (1983–84), *Adam Smith: Critical Assessments*, Vols 1–4, London: Routledge.
Wood, J. (ed.) (1994), *Adam Smith: Critical Assessments*, Vols 5–7, London: Routledge.
Young, J. (1990), 'David Hume and Adam Smith on value premises in economics', *History of Political Economy*, **22** (4), 643–58.
Young, J. (1997), *Economics as a Moral Science: the Political Economy of Adam Smith*, Cheltenham, UK and Lyme, NH, USA: Edward Elgar.

5 Smith's philosophy and economic methodology
Sheila C. Dow

Introduction

Adam Smith is a towering figure in the history of economic thought. While he was by no means the first to develop many of the ideas which underpinned the development of modern economics, nevertheless it is often the case that earlier thinkers are discussed in terms of the extent to which they anticipated Smith, or more directly influenced him. While others, such as Quesnay and Hutcheson, for example, developed ideas on the functioning of the macroeconomy and value respectively, there was something distinctive about the way in which Smith put his ideas together and communicated them which made such an impact on the development of economics. The purpose of this contribution is to put the focus on Smith's distinctive approach to economic methodology.

Just as Smith developed others' economic ideas, his methodology too has its own history. Smith's philosophical background, notably the Scottish Enlightenment and the work of his friend David Hume, is something I will explore first in order to understand the basis of his methodology. I will draw on his essay on the 'History of Astronomy' (Smith, 1795; hereafter HA), his *Lectures on Rhetoric and Belles Lettres* (Smith, 1762–63; hereafter LRBL) and the *Theory of Moral Sentiments* (Smith, 1759; hereafter TMS), for evidence of the philosophical background on which Smith drew. I will then consider three particular aspects of his methodology which arise from this philosophy: the analytical historical approach; the notion of system; and the nature and role of principles.

The nature of Smith's influence on the development of modern economics has been coloured by the ways in which his work has been interpreted. In particular, Smith has been widely seen as the inspiration for general equilibrium theory (Arrow and Hahn, 1971), an interpretation which has increasingly been challenged (for example by Winch, 1997). The possibility is explored in the concluding section that a significant element of such interpretive differences is methodological, including a lack of appreciation for the distinction between theory formulation and rhetoric.

Before I proceed, there is a reflexive need to be explicit about the interpretive approach being adopted in this chapter. The analysis of Smith's methodology owes much to the seminal work of Andrew Skinner (notably 1965, 1972, 1996). The particular historiographic approach that I adopt, further, is consistent with the Scottish historical approach. It has been developed most fully in modern discourse by Quentin Skinner (1969, 1988), who advocates a focus on the context of the author, and the author's intentions within that context. Thus the exploration of Smith's philosophical background is seen as a way of understanding why Smith approached his economic enquiries in the way that he did, as well as to understanding his methodology. It is to this exploration that I now turn.

Philosophical underpinnings

Smith's philosophical background in the Scottish Enlightenment is the subject of a vast literature (see most recently Broadie, 2003). Here I attempt only to draw out those features which seem to be of greatest relevance to Smith's methodology: those which influenced Smith's understanding of science, and those which influenced the emerging character of economics as a moral science. The influence of his mentors Francis Hutcheson and David Hume is evident throughout.

Scottish Enlightenment philosophy was the outcome of a range of influences within a particular context. Scotland's political distance from England until the Union of Parliaments in 1707 had encouraged strong connections with continental Europe. This had in turn encouraged the introduction of ideas from the Continent, both formally as a result of attendance at universities (such as Paris and Leiden), and informally, as a result of the convention of the European Tour.

But the blend of influences emerged as a distinctive philosophy in Scotland. This can be understood partly as a response to the needs of a small, relatively cohesive, society in the process of commercialization, grappling with the practical problems posed by new opportunities for economic development. In particular the union with England and the opening up of new territories in Central and North America created new trading opportunities, and thus a spur to capitalize on Scottish inventiveness. But in addition, the union with England posed challenges to the idea of Scottish nationhood and the involvement of Scottish thinkers in politics. Finally, there was an ongoing struggle for supremacy between Catholicism and Presbyterianism, which further raised issues of authority. Overall this context meant that practical issues were to the fore, and these were addressed with a perspective which had naturally absorbed a sense of 'otherness'; it was impossible for example, in adapting to the new political arrangements with England, not to be conscious that there was more than one perspective to be brought to issues, each of which could claim legitimacy. This was to foster a distinctive attitude to what was possible for science in terms of discovering truth.

Hume (1739–40 [1978]) took on the challenge addressed by the French Enlightenment of building a complete philosophy founded on reason. But he concluded that this was impossible without some proof of existence. While there were differences between Hume and the commonsense philosophy of Thomas Reid (1785 [1969]), both placed importance on belief derived from experience. For Reid, common sense was taken to mean something more than simply what is commonly known. It involved rather the argument that the mind brings an additional capacity to observation than the five senses. For Hume, belief in existence was a prerequisite for all knowledge, in particular being prior to reason. A theory of human nature was thus the foundation on which knowledge was to be built. He drew on natural law philosophy to identify belief (and conventions, including morals, more generally) as the outcome of a historical process. Common sense was thus to prove a key element of his philosophy, and in turn for Smith (Comim, 2006).

Hume's epistemology thus derived from his theory of human nature, with his emphasis on the human faculties of sentiment (or passion) and imagination, and their product, sympathy. These are required as the basis for building knowledge, together with experience; only then could reason be applied. The subject matter of science is too complex for us to be able to identify real causal mechanisms. But we have a starting point in that detailed observation of constant conjunctions of events gives us (through our imaginations) the idea of cause. We then bring this idea to our further observation, in order to begin to hypothesize about causation. These ideas are evident in Smith's study of the science of astronomy in HA, where he analyses the motivation for science ('philosophy') in terms of identifying a system for connecting the chains of events which we observe: 'Who wonders at the machinery of the opera-house who has once been admitted behind the scenes? In the Wonders of nature, however, it rarely happens that we can discover so clearly this connecting chain' (HA II.9).

Since we cannot directly access the underlying causal powers, no hypothesis about the real world can be demonstrated to be true. It followed that science could not be an exercise in uncovering truth in any absolute sense. Nevertheless practical (provisional) knowledge is possible, and indeed is necessary when addressing the practical problems of a nation facing new challenges and opportunities. There is scope for argument as to whether some knowledge is more or less true, but no mechanism for settling on an absolute judgement on the matter.

According to Smith, the motivation for the development of new knowledge itself arises from human nature. A sense of unease ('surprise' and 'wonder') is created by experience which is in discord with accepted knowledge. The mind becomes accustomed to particular conjunctions and is surprised when one event is not accompanied, as expected, by another. Drawing on his theory of human nature, and in particular the power of the imagination, Smith (HA) argues that what is being sought is the tranquility of mind which comes from a system of thought which incorporates the new, disturbing, experience in a satisfactory manner, where what is satisfactory may be determined by aesthetic judgement as much as by reason and experience. When the conjunction of two events which has caused a sense of unease is connected by a chain of imaginary intermediate events, then the mind is set at rest.

It is important that these intermediate events are grasped by means of the imagination. Thus the concept of gravity may satisfy our psychological needs and appeal to our imaginations, but this does not make it 'true' in any absolute sense. Further, the new explanation must be plausible; thus, for example, the notion of planetary motion applied to the earth was initially regarded as implausible until an explanation was offered which connected with experience, such as Descartes's theory of fluxion (even though it would later be displaced as a satisfactory explanation). Also, what is plausible to one may not be plausible to another. Smith contrasts the wonder experienced by an outside observer of an artisan's work, on the one hand, with the easy familiarity with a sequence of events which seems 'natural' to the artisan himself, on the other (HA II.11). Further, the scientist may be attracted more than others to novel explanations. In discussing Copernicus's reluctance to put forward his new ideas, Smith refers to 'that love of paradox, so natural to the learned, and that pleasure, which they are so apt to take in exciting, by the novelty of their supposed discoveries' (HA IV.34). This is contrasted with the 'natural prejudices of sense, confirmed by education' which Copernicus would have feared from his audience (HA IV.35).

What ultimately persuades others that a new theory is satisfactory is a matter of rhetoric; if theories could not be demonstrated to be true, then some other criteria must be applied (LRBL). Smith discussed rhetoric as an exercise in persuasion, as one of the methods of discourse. Again his approach was psychological; persuasion required that an argument be tailored to the audience, and make some connection with what was already taken as known. Further, Smith noted that attention to aesthetic criteria, such as elegance and simplicity, as well as the portrayal of a system, might persuade regardless of other criteria for accepting an argument (Comim, 2006). While, as we shall see further below, Smith did not share Descartes's deductivist methodology for formulating theory, he could nevertheless understand the psychological appeal of his work.

> It gives us a pleasure to see the phaenomena which we reckoned the most unaccountable as deduced from some principle (commonly a wellknown one) and all united in one chain . . . We need not be surprised then that the Cartesian Philosophy . . . tho it does not perhaps contain a word of truth . . . should nevertheless have been so universally received by all the Learned in Europe at that time. The Great Superiority of the method over that of Aristotle . . . made them greedily receive a work which we justly esteem one of the most entertaining Romances that has ever been wrote. (LRBL, p. 146)

Smith recognizes further that consciousness of the psychological, more than rational, basis for accepting or rejecting theories does not protect the philosopher from his own psychology:

> [E]ven we, while we have been endeavouring to represent all philosophical systems as mere inventions of the imagination, to connect together the otherwise disjointed and discordant phaenomena of nature, have insensibly been drawn in, to make use of language expressing the connecting principles of this one, as if they were the *real* chains which Nature makes use of to bind together her several operations. (HA IV.76, emphasis added)

Indeed, even within a discussion of the appeal of theories to the imagination, Smith had earlier implied that the Newtonian explanation for planetary motion had uncovered the 'real' causal mechanism: 'Thus the eclipses of the sun and moon, which once, more than all the other appearances of the heavens, excited the terror and amazement of mankind, seem now no longer to be wonderful, since the connecting chain has been found out which joins them to the ordinary course of things' (HA II.10).

This self-awareness on the part of Smith with respect to the central role of the imagination, and thus of psychology, in the rhetorical power of theoretical explanation is important for our understanding of Smith's later exposition of his economic ideas. It is even more important for the way in which they have been interpreted. I will develop below more fully the argument that an understanding of the role of rhetoric is critical to our understanding of Smith's methodology with respect to systems and the role of principles. It is important to consider separately the psychology of the philosopher, the method of building knowledge, and the psychology of the philosopher's audience.

Finally, Smith's major work in moral philosophy, TMS, offered a fuller expression of his theory of human nature, showing the influence of Hutcheson (Skinner, 2006). It was here that some germs of Smith's ideas on economics were first aired in print. Here he discussed the individual's self-interest in the context of society, and specifically the concept of sympathy (which he drew from Hume) as the mechanism by which society constrains individual behaviour. Here we see the roots of economic questions being pursued by the building up of a moral science (see further Young, 1997).

Further, just as the scientist does not have access to truth, neither does man in general (indeed Smith makes a point of arguing in HA that there is no fundamental difference, other than inclination and subsequent specialization, between the philosopher and others). Indeed man is capable of self-deception as to the consequences of his actions. Smith illustrates the point by discussing 'the poor man's son, whom heaven in its anger has visited with ambition' (TMS IV.1.8). Here we have an example of the workings of the invisible hand, a theme much more clearly evident in TMS than in WN. The invisible hand is a metaphor to capture the unintended consequences of human action, given the human incapacity to anticipate these consequences correctly. As Heilbroner (1986, p. 60) puts it: 'The Deity, when he created the world, gave to humankind a surer guide than reason. This was the call of its passions.' While the poor man's son is deceived in thinking that riches are the basis for happiness, his efforts to amass riches have the fortunate externality of generating growth in the economy. The faculty of imagination and the sentiment of the pursuit of happiness, combined with the human incapacity to know the future, can in turn provide a reasonable psychological explanation for self-deception. Thus Smith shows the limited role of the faculty of reason in an explanation of human behaviour, just as he (and Hume) showed the limitations to its role in science.

It is against this background of Smith's philosophy that I turn now to consider how this translated into the way in which he analysed economic questions.

Methodology

Analytical history
The way in which philosophy and science were used in Scottish society reflected both the nature of practical concerns and the nature of the education system (which undoubtedly were not independent factors). Students entered higher education in their early teens (Smith was 14 when he entered the University of Glasgow; Hume had entered university at age ten), and were exposed early to moral philosophy, which then provided a common background to the pursuit of all other subjects. Further, these subjects were approached from a historical perspective (Davie, 1961). Thus, for example, rather than learning only one mathematical system, students learned about a range of approaches to mathematics adopted over history.

This conventional historical perspective in Scottish education is thus clearly a reflection of the same philosophical background that I discussed above as providing a foundation for Smith's views on science and rhetoric. Knowledge was seen as being built using approaches which are psychologically appealing (in the light of prior conventional knowledge and experience), and no one approach could be demonstrated to be superior to others in any absolute sense. Further, the standards of judgement were relative to context. Thus it was important to be aware of a range of possibilities in order to form a view as to which was preferable in a particular context. (Indeed it can be argued that it was this which fostered the remarkable inventiveness of the period.)

This historically contingent approach to scientific knowledge is most evident in Smith's (HA) account of evolving ideas on astronomy. He discusses the growing search for scientific explanation rather than superstition (or reference to the actions of 'invisible beings') as society evolves beyond subsistence and with more order and security (HA III.3). What constitutes a satisfactory scientific explanation then itself evolves. In considering the sequence of ideas on astronomy, Smith discusses what we would now refer to as 'paradigm shifts' in the understanding of the physical workings of the universe, with an awareness of the context in which each understanding was sustained. In this historical account we find many of Smith's methodological views (especially about system, and the role of principles) made explicit, which I will explore further in the following two sections.

Against this background, it was therefore not surprising that Smith's approach to economics should also be historical, drawing on a massive range of examples from different times and places. The Scottish approach to science is often labelled 'empiricist' in direct contrast to French 'idealism'. But this is misleading, not least because of the commonsense view that additional capacities of the mind, drawing on past experience, are brought to observation. But more important, rather than being seen as mutually exclusive, in the Scottish approach, observation and analysis were complementary. Here we see the profound influence of Newton's experimental philosophy on the Scottish approach to science. Newton's experimental methodology was to combine analysis and synthesis: 'analysis consists in making Experiments and Observations, and in drawing general Conclusions from them by Induction . . . Synthesis consists in assuming the Causes discover'd, and establish'd as Principles, and by them explaining the Phaenomena proceeding from them' (Newton, 1979 [1704], pp. 404–5). Newton's scientific method of analysis and synthesis was first fully absorbed, applied and promoted in Scotland, notably by MacLaurin (1748). This method combined induction and deduction within one epistemological system, both being essential elements. It is notable that, in contrast to its ready reception in Scotland, Newton's philosophy of science was not well received in France, with its deductivist Cartesian tradition. As Montes (2006, p. 114) puts it: 'On the role of mathematics, the Scottish tradition interpreted Newton's underlying idea that mathematics is an instrument to describe nature, not a model of reality.'

This combination of induction and deduction is particularly evident in the Scottish Historical approach taken to history itself, which has been characterized as 'analytical history' (Skinner 1965). Historical facts themselves were organized in such a way as to aid analysis. Thus patterns emerging from detailed historical analysis would provide structure for future investigations, which in turn would suggest modifications to theory. Specifically, historical experience was organized into historical stages (the 'stadial approach'). This was of particular relevance to the development of an analysis of economic organization and behaviour at a time of tremendous change, notably in commercialization and the mode of production addressed to expanding markets. Smith first discussed the four historical stages in the *Lectures on Jurisprudence* (1762–63, 1766) (see further Skinner 1996, Chapter 4), identifying a different mode of economic organization (and mode of production) within each of the four stages: hunting, pasturage, farming and commerce. By understanding how these stages played out in different contexts (of time and place), Smith was able to infer some causal mechanisms at work in the development of civil society. Thus, the origins of property and authority are found in the first two stages, and the connection between economic organization and the changing nature of subordination are found in the third and fourth stages. Further, the progression through the stages was seen as a natural process. The fourth stage represented progress in the sense that natural liberty, which had been jeopardized in earlier stages, was regained with commercialization. But that development could still be eroded by the encroachment of government, and by the alienation brought on by the increasing specialization of work practices, with the progressive division of labour.

While Montesquieu was an important influence on the emphasis placed on historical evidence, it was in Scotland, and with Smith in particular, that history was used as a means of identifying causes (Skinner, 1965). On the basis of natural law philosophy and his theory of human nature, Smith drew these causal mechanisms out from actual historical experience: 'Natural history must concern itself with the problem of change in those conditions within which the constant principles of human nature operate' (Skinner, 1965, p. 5). Change in turn was the unintended consequence of human action. This contrasted with the rationalist approach associated with Hobbes and Locke, whereby civil society was seen as developing as the result of the imposition of rational principles. Indeed Smith's view was that the standards of judgement applied to analysis of historical episodes were relative to perspective, not the outcome of some process of pure reason.

The historical approach thus also influenced the way in which economic theories themselves were regarded, having been drawn from analysis of history. Theory itself was understood historically, as being developed in particular contexts to suit particular purposes. How far a theory was accepted depended on what appealed to the audience of the time, in particular what seemed both plausible and aesthetically appealing. Thus there was no expectation of identifying one theory which was 'best' in any absolute sense, but rather one which was more persuasive than others in a particular context. Reality was too complex to be sure of identifying 'true' causal powers.

But, further, changing circumstances often require changing theory. Thus for example, while Smith's analysis of market behaviour was expressed in terms of competitive markets, he did warn of the possibilities of processes which would limit competition – the tendency for self-interested producers to combine (WN I.viii.13). Indeed increasing returns would inevitably threaten the competitiveness of markets. Similarly, both Hume and Smith struggled to provide coherent accounts of the evolving systems of money and banking. Both found it difficult to accept the rise in importance of inside money (bank notes) relative to outside money (specie) which went along with the rapid (and generally highly successful) expansion of banking in Scotland in the eighteenth century. But they were not consistent on this, at times expressing appreciation for the positive role of paper money, or the expansion of banking (see Murphy, 2006; Wennerlind, 2006). Hume in particular understood that the value attached to specie was in fact a sign of value, rather than purely intrinsic value. But we could look to a psychological explanation, to put alongside their expressed, reasoned explanations, for their anxieties about paper money. Hume and Smith's own monetary theory was thus in a process of evolution in relation to a rapidly changing reality.

The notion of system
Implicit in the organization of historical evidence according to stages of history in Smith's thought is the notion of system, that is, that there is some underlying regularity arising from human nature which can provide the basis for such organization. In line with natural law philosophy, this embodies the view that natural processes promote economic organization, and this organization can be understood as a system. And indeed it was the depiction of an economy as a system which marked out the greatness of Smith's contribution, a point given great emphasis by Dugald Stewart. By providing a persuasive cohesive account of coordination in commercialized society, Smith was able to address any unease as to whether this relatively new system of economic organization was sustainable, just as Newton had addressed unease about the sustainability of the solar system. Smith in turn was a great admirer of Quesnay's system (Skinner, 1996, Chapter 6).

Smith built up his theory of economic organization by means of connecting principles:

'Philosophy is the science of the connecting principles of nature' (HA 45). As Loasby (2003) points out, a system is defined not only by its connections, but also crucially by its lack of connections. While the market provides connections, the principle of the division of labour provides a crucial mechanism for limiting connections. Without some limitation on interconnectedness, a system cannot function (Potts, 2000). The division of labour segments sets of ideas, of production, and indeed of economic organization in general, so that they constitute systems. In Smith's terms, a theory is an 'imaginary machine':

> Systems in many respects resemble machines. A machine is a little system, created to perform, as well as to connect together, in reality, those different movements and effects which the artist has occasion for. A system is an imaginary machine invented to connect together *in the fancy* those different movements and effects which are already in reality performed. (HA 19, emphasis added)

This was a metaphor which he used in a variety of contexts, as for example in discussing systems of moral approbation: 'Human society, when we contemplate it in a certain abstract and philosophical light, appears like a great, an immense machine, whose regular and harmonious movements produce a thousand agreeable effects' (TMS iii.1.2).

Smith wrote about the aesthetic appeal of systems in a variety of ways which suggest that he himself felt their profound psychological appeal at the level of ideas. For example when discussing the building up of natural philosophy in ancient times, he referred to '[t]he beauty of a systematical arrangement of different observations connected by a few common principles' (WN V.1.f). However we have seen above that he was aware of the dangers of seduction by aesthetic appeal, particularly of the type of formal, axiomatic, deductive system set out by Descartes. He warned particularly of treating intentional individual behaviour as being directed to market coordination, on grounds of aesthetic appeal of the theoretical system. He noted the tendency to ascribe causal power to human reason, when the consequences were in general unintended. 'We are very apt to imagine that to be the wisdom of man, which in reality is the wisdom of God . . . [T]he system of nature seems to be more simple and agreeable when all its different operations are in this manner deduced from a single principle' (TMS II.ii.3.5).

Others in the tradition of the Scottish Enlightenment too, such as Sir James Steuart, were wary of this phenomenon, which made deductive systems more persuasive. While also aiming to present a system, Steuart took care to emphasize the need to tailor theory to context; but inevitably the outcome is less aesthetically appealing as theory. Terence Hutchison (1988, p. 350) concluded that Steuart's stylistic faults were 'brought about by his intellectual virtues, and by his persistent resistance to oversimplification . . . It is easier to write clearly and engagingly when one has a simple system to expound.'

However aesthetics form only one element of persuasion. It is deductivist theory which appears to perform best on aesthetic grounds. But, particularly within a context where practical application (in such wide-ranging contexts as moral behaviour and mechanics) was seen as the purpose of knowledge, grounding in reality was also significant for persuasion. Thus, while Smith saw the aesthetic appeal of Descartes's purely abstract explanation for planetary motion, he found Newton's explanation more persuasive, based as it was on his experimental philosophy. Indeed Smith saw the persuasive role of grounding in reality more important for moral philosophy (including economic questions) than for natural philosophy. In his writing on rhetoric, Smith emphasized the persuasive importance of connecting arguments to what is already accepted by the audience as knowledge. Persuasion required the explanation to be plausible to an audience who had direct experience of moral life (including commercial activity). It was less likely, by implication, that a purely abstract explanation of economic behaviour, however aesthetically appealing, would persuade an audience as readily as a purely abstract explanation of something of which the audience did not have direct experience.

Nevertheless, in weighing up aesthetics relative to grounding in experience, the persuasive power of a theoretical system would suffer if the system required ad hoc adjustments in order to maintain consistency with experience (Skinner, 1972). Where the prevailing theoretical system fails satisfactorily to explain new anomalies other than by ad hoc adjustment, there is a strong motivation to develop a new explanatory system. Here we find Smith anticipating Lakatos as well as Kuhn.

The nature and role of principles
How we understand Smith's notion of system depends in turn very much on how we understand the nature and role of principles, and here again we see the influence of Newton. Given Smith's explicit debt to Newton's methodology, Newton's principle of gravitation can be interpreted in the same way as Smith's principle of the division of labour, in relation to their respective systems. But how these systems in turn are interpreted depends on what is meant by a principle, and requires further exploration.

In the natural sciences literal experimentation is possible (in the sense of constructing a closed system for the purpose of isolating a causal mechanism). But for Smith (and Hume), experimentation took the form of historical observation of concrete episodes, out of which emerged principles which could then be considered for their explanatory power in other historical contexts. And both considered themselves as aiming to establish the 'unchanging principles' of human nature, which would provide the foundation of all knowledge. These principles refer to the human faculties, as Hume and Smith identified them: the passions, imagination (and thus sympathy), observation and reason. Thus, for example, Smith discussed 'the Principle of Self-approbation and of Self-disapprobation', such that sympathy meant that the reason for self-approbation accorded with the reason for our approval of others (TMS III.1).

In economics, the principle of the division of labour is the core on which his theoretical system is built. In accordance with the Newtonian methodology for formulating theory, this principle was the outcome of Smith's identification of a pattern from his detailed studies of history, and observation of economic life. In communicating this principle, like his principles of moral life, Smith (in accordance with his own principles of rhetoric) expressed them in terms of familiar examples, as well as using examples from history. The rhetorical power of the pin factory metaphor, with which Smith begins the *Wealth of Nations*, is attested to by the way in which it has stuck in the collective imagination. Later examples from older or remoter contexts served to illustrate the generality of the principle, often in intriguing ways.

Smith thus starts the exposition of his system with the principle. In Smith's own words:

> in the manner of Sir Isaac Newton we may lay down certain principles known or proved in the beginning, from whence we count for the severall Phenomena, connecting all together by the same Chain. This latter which we may call the Newtonian method is undoubtedly the most

Philosophical, and in every science whether of Moralls or Natural Philosophy etc., is vastly more ingenious and for that reason more engaging than the other [Aristotle's]. (LRBL 145–6).

But if we take Smith's philosophy of science seriously, then we must take it that the principle of the division of labour is, like the principle of gravity, an appeal to the imagination rather than a 'real' phenomenon. For Newton, the principles on which the analysis is based were previously derived using the experimental method, and are thus provisional (Montes, 2006).

For Descartes, however, the principles on which analysis is based are axioms which, as in *cogito ergo sum*, are arrived at through contemplation aided by classical logic. Because Descartes takes his axioms as true, the conclusions arrived at by applying deductive logic to the axioms were also true. Smith's principles of human nature were quite different. They were established by the 'experimental method', which involved detailed study of history. Further, for Smith, the principles appealed to the imagination as a way of explaining the diversity of human behaviour in different contexts in time and space. This diversity could be systematized according to the stages approach to history. Nevertheless, the emphasis was on the different forms which human behaviour can take, in spite of the unchanging principles of human nature. This approach is particularly understandable when we take account of Smith's social environment, where Highlanders could be classed as savages, and Scots were working alongside aboriginal peoples in North America.

Similarly the principle of the division of labour can be thought of as a way of organizing thought about causal powers at work in commercialized society. This is quite different from the role of an axiom in classical logic. We have seen that Smith was quite explicit that, while it is appealing to explain human behaviour in terms of deduction from one principle (referring only to human reason), this does not reflect the basis for human behaviour more in the passions than reason. While a rationalist account of society lends itself to a deductive axiomatic system, the more complex Scottish account of human behaviour, its determinants and its consequences, all referring to the particularities of the context in relation to the historical system, cannot be captured in a deductive system. In any case, the method of applying principles to new contexts might always lead to an evolution of theory, and thus a new mode of expression of the principles. Indeed, John Rae made exactly that argument in proposing that Smith's principle of the division of labour started too far along the causal chain. Rae argued instead that the division of labour followed from the human capacity for invention, so that that should provide the starting point (Mair, 2006).

The only common element, therefore, between the deductivist methodology of the French Enlightenment and the 'experimental' approach of the Scottish Enlightenment was that axioms in the first and principles in the second held a special place as the basis for deductive reasoning. There the similarity ended. While axioms are 'self-evidently true' by introspection, principles are derived from detailed observation. While the deduction of propositions from the axioms was the end of the matter for the deductivist approach, this was only one further step for the experimental approach, requiring also adaptation to the observed characteristics of the domain of application, with the possibility always of revision of principles. Smith's system ultimately was a mental construct designed for psychological appeal, but also for plausibility in the light of experience.

Nevertheless an experimental system might be expressed in an abstract form similar to a deductivist system (albeit communicated with a wealth of examples from history, of daily experience). Smith had noted the aesthetic appeal of an axiomatic system. But, as Skinner (1996, p. 21) has noted, Smith also distinguished between the formulation of theory (by the experimental method) and its communication (which started with principles), while the deductivist approach is the same in formulation as in communication, that is, by means of deductive logic.

It could be argued that this is an important factor in understanding later interpretations of Smith as inspiring general equilibrium theory. Smith's influence was so great because he offered such an appealing system, based on common principles of humanity. From a deductivist perspective, it was natural to confuse principles with axioms, and to confuse Smith's rhetorical system as being the sum total of his theory (rather than the outcome of application of the experimental method). This involved ignoring Smith's ideas on rhetoric, and the psychology of science, as well as the implications of his principles of human nature for how economic behaviour should be depicted. It is not uncommon for an idea developed within one methodology to inspire new developments within another methodology. Indeed this is evidence of exactly the kind of connecting principle which Smith himself had seen as the core of new knowledge. Nevertheless the outcome was very different from Smith's own system.

Conclusion

We have seen that Smith's methodology took much of its distinctiveness from the philosophy of the Scottish Enlightenment. Yet, in his hands, that philosophy allowed the building of a system of social science which was so masterful that Smith became commonly regarded as the father of economics. It was his capacity for analytical history which allowed him to build up a theory of human nature and apply that to formulate a theory of the social system. By attempting to explain the workings of commercial society in comparison with earlier stages, Smith's system provided an account of market behaviour which drew on his understanding of human nature.

It is now conventional to note the disparity between Smith's system and references to it as the origin of general equilibrium theory. We have seen that this disparity can be understood in terms of the methodological differences between Smith's approach and the deductivism of general equilibrium theory. It has also proved important to be aware of Smith's distinction between the principles of discourse, where elegance and simplicity persuade, on the one hand, and the principles of scientific enquiry, on the other. Perhaps the way in which Smith's system was developed by others along deductivist lines can be understood partly as the result of later economists not taking this distinction on board. But this was just one consequence of discounting the significance of Smith's alternative methodology. That methodology in turn was founded on his theory of human nature, and its consequences both for economic theorizing and for the behaviour of economic agents. Consistent with that theory, the effect of Smith's ideas was unlikely to be what he had intended. As Hutchison (1988, p. 355) has noted, the unintended consequence of Smith's work was to establish political economy 'as a separate autonomous discipline'.

References

Arrow, K. and F.H. Hahn (1971), *General Competitive Analysis*, Edinburgh: Oliver & Boyd.
Broadie, A. (ed.) (2003), *The Cambridge Companion to the Scottish Enlightenment*, Cambridge: Cambridge University Press.
Comim, F. (2006), 'Adam Smith: common sense and aesthetics in the age of experiments', in A. Dow and S. Dow (eds), *A History of Scottish Economic Thought*, London: Routledge, pp. 123–45.
Davie, G. (1961), *The Democratic Intellect*, Edinburgh: Edinburgh University Press.
Heilbroner, R.L. (1986), *The Essential Adam Smith*, Oxford: Oxford University Press.
Hume, D. (1739–40), *A Treatise of Human Nature*, K.A. Selby-Bigge and P.H. Nedditch (eds) (1978), 2nd edn, Oxford: Clarendon Press.
Hutchison, T. (1988), *Before Adam Smith*, Oxford: Basil Blackwell.
Loasby, B.J. (2003), 'Closed models and open system', *Journal of Economic Methodology*, **10** (3), 285–306.
MacLaurin, C. (1748), *An Account of Sir Isaac Newton's Philosophical Discoveries*, London: Printed for A. Millar.
Mair, D. (2006), 'John Rae', in A. Dow and S. Dow (eds), *A History of Scottish Economic Thought*, London: Routledge, pp. 198–212.
Montes, L. (2006), 'Adam Smith: real Newtonian', in A. Dow and S. Dow (eds), *A History of Scottish Economic Thought*, London: Routledge, pp. 102–22.
Murphy, A. (2006), 'John Law', in A. Dow and S. Dow (eds), *A History of Scottish Economic Thought*, London: Routledge, pp. 9–26.
Newton, Sir I. (1979 [1704]), *Opticks: or, a Treatise of the Reflections, Refractions, Inflections and Colours of Light*, London: William Innys.
Potts, J. (2000), *The New Evolutionary Microeconomics*, Cheltenham, UK and Northampton, MA, USA: Edward Elgar.
Reid, T. (1785), *Essays on the Intellectual Powers of Man*, B.A. Brody (ed.) (1969), Cambridge, MA: MIT Press.
Skinner, A.S. (1965), 'Economics and history: the Scottish enlightenment', *Scottish Journal of Political Economy*, **12** (1), 1–22.
Skinner, A.S. (1972), 'Adam Smith: philosophy and science', *Scottish Journal of Political Economy*, **19** (3), 307–19
Skinner, A.S. (1996), *A System of Social Science: Papers Relating to Adam Smith*, Oxford: Clarendon Press.
Skinner, A.S. (2006), 'Francis Hutcheson, 1694–1746', in A. Dow and S. Dow (eds), *A History of Scottish Economic Thought*, London: Routledge, pp. 27–45.
Skinner, Q. (1969), 'Meaning and understanding in the history of ideas', *History and Theory*, **8**, 3–53.
Skinner, Q. (1988), 'A reply to my critics', in J. Tully (ed.), *Meaning and Context: Quentin Skinner and his Critics*, Oxford: Oxford University Press, pp. 231–58.
Smith, A. (1759), *The Theory of Moral Sentiments*, Glasgow edition, D.D. Raphael and A. Macfie (eds) (1976), Oxford: Oxford University Press (TMS).
Smith, A. (1762–63), *Lectures on Rhetoric and Belles Lettres*, J.C. Bryce (ed.) (1983), Oxford: Oxford University Press (LRBL).
Smith, A. (1762–63, 1766), *Lectures on Jurisprudence*, R.L. Meek, D.D. Raphael and P.G. Stein (eds) (1978), Oxford: Oxford University Press (LJ).
Smith, A. (1776), *An Inquiry into the Nature and Causes of the Wealth of Nations*, R.H. Campbell and A.S. Skinner (eds.) (1976), Oxford: Oxford University Press (WN).
Smith, A. (1795), 'The history of astronomy', in W.L.D. Wightman (ed.) (1980), *Essays on Philosophical Subjects*, Oxford: Oxford University Press (HA).
Wennerlind, C. (2006), 'David Hume as a political economist', in A. Dow and S. Dow (eds), *A History of Scottish Economic Thought*, London: Routledge, pp. 46–70.
Winch, D. (1997), 'Adam Smith's problem and ours', *Scottish Journal of Political Economy*, **44** (4), 384–402.
Young, J.T. (1997), *Economics as a Moral Science: The Political Economy of Adam Smith*, Cheltenham, UK and Lyme, NH, USA: Edward Elgar.

6 The moral philosophical frame of Adam Smith's economic thought
Jerry Evensky

On moral philosophy

In the largest sense, the frame through which Adam Smith envisioned the world was philosophy:

> Philosophy is the science of the connecting principles of nature. Nature, after the largest experience that common observation can acquire, seems to abound with events which appear solitary and incoherent with all that go before them, which therefore disturb the easy movement of the imagination ... Philosophy, by representing the invisible chains which bind together all these disjointed objects, endeavours to introduce order into this chaos of jarring and discordant appearances, to allay the tumult of the imagination, and to restore it, when it surveys the great revolutions of the universe, to that tone of tranquility and composure, which is both most agreeable in itself, and most suitable to its nature. (Smith, 1795 [1980], pp. 45–6)

The challenge of philosophy lay in representing these invisible connecting principles when in fact they are unobservable. What we can observe is the face of nature, the effects of these principles. The principles themselves, like the pins and wheels and springs of a clock, lie behind the face of nature. They guide the course of nature but we cannot see how they are arranged for they are out of sight. Smith suggests just this challenge as follows:

> Who wonders at the machinery of the opera-house who has once been admitted behind the scenes? In the Wonders of nature, however, it rarely happens that we can discover so clearly this connecting chain. With regard to a few even of them, indeed, we seem to have been really admitted behind the scenes. (Smith, 1795 [1980], pp. 42–3)

Nature's 'Truth' lies 'behind the scenes'. No philosopher has the privilege, as an opera patron might, of going behind the scenes to observe those 'concealed connections' (Smith, 1795 [1980], p. 51). But while we cannot 'see' the invisible, based on what we can observe we can imagine those invisible connecting principles that might be consistent with what we observe. And having imagined those principles, we can then represent them in our philosophical works. This was for Smith the work of philosophy: 'Philosophy, therefore, may be regarded as one of those arts which addresses themselves to the imagination' (Smith, 1795 [1980], p. 46). 'Philosophy ... [only] *pretends* to lay open the concealed connections that unite the various appearances of nature' (Smith, 1795 [1980], p. 51, emphasis added).[1]

In Smith's day the realm of philosophy was divided into two content fields: natural philosophy and moral philosophy.[2] Natural philosophy sought to represent the invisible connecting chains that underlie the 'chaos of jarring and discordant appearances' (Smith, 1795 [1980], pp. 45–6) that we observe in the natural world that surrounds us. Sir

Isaac Newton was for Smith and his contemporaries the gold standard of excellence in this realm of natural philosophy. As Smith writes:

> The superior genius and sagacity of Sir Isaac Newton . . . made the most happy, and, we may now say, the greatest and most admirable improvement that was ever made in philosophy, when he discovered, that he could join together the movements of the Planets by so familiar a principle of connection ['gravity'], which completely removed all the difficulties the imagination had hitherto felt in attending to them. (Smith, 1795 [1980], p. 98)

The subject of moral philosophy was that small, most intimate dimension of the universe that encompassed us – the human condition. That condition lent itself to a separation from natural philosophy because there was, it appeared, something unique about the human condition that distinguished it from the nature that surrounded it.

In that natural order that surrounds humankind the principles that guide the course of events seem to function unperturbed, for the elements that make up the natural order around us have no choice in the paths they follow. They simply follow the dictates of those principles embodied in their nature. Not so humankind. We humans have capacities that make our little corner of the universe unique, and thus the subject of a distinct dimension of philosophy: moral philosophy.

The human capacities that make it possible for us to affect the events of our realm and thus to effect the course of events in the human condition are our imagination, our ability to reason and our 'human frailty' (Smith, 1740 [1987], p. 221). Our imagination makes it possible for us to see possibilities for choice. Our reason makes it possible for us to choose, and thus affect the course of events. Our frailty gives rise to choices that are less than perfectly moral, choices that distort the natural, ideal path of human events. It is this unique human capacity for immorality and thus distortion of the natural that makes our little corner of the universe the unique subject of moral philosophy.

This nexus of imagination, reason and frailty lies at the heart of Smith's moral philosophical enterprise. He sought to do for moral philosophy what Newton had done for natural philosophy, to represent the invisible connecting principles that guide humankind's motion. But even as he sought to emulate Newton, he appreciated that his task was more complicated. While the motions of nature are very complicated and thus they appear to be chaotic to the untutored eye – for example, planets seemed to be wandering stars – there are principles that, when represented, seem to explain the appearances of nature in systematic ways with familiar concepts.

It is not so for moral philosophy. Assuming, as Smith did, that there is a natural order for human nature – an undistorted flow of human events – nevertheless that natural order is not directly observable. Due to human imagination and reason wedded to human frailty, the observed realm of human affairs is a distorted version of the natural order. Humankind's natural order is unobservable:

> Human society, when we contemplate it in a certain abstract and philosophical light, appears like a great, an immense machine, whose regular and harmonious movements produce a thousand agreeable effects. As in any other beautiful and noble machine that was the production of human art, whatever tended to render its movements more smooth and easy, would derive a beauty from this effect, and, on the contrary, whatever tended to obstruct them would displease upon that account: so virtue, which is, as it were, the fine polish to the wheels of society, necessarily pleases; while vice, like the vile rust, which makes them jar and grate upon one another, is as necessarily offensive. (Smith, 1790 [1976], p. 316)

It is therefore the challenge of moral philosophy to represent invisible connecting principles that would guide an undistorted humankind, to describe the conditions that give rise to an ideal human condition, when all we can observe is the distorted version. Smith met this conceptual challenge by constructing parallel analyses: the real and the ideal. He used the real course of humankind's history as his empirical base and from that history he culled those principles that seemed to be consistent with the broad contours of the flow of human events.

How Smith constructed his moral philosophical vision
Smith was not a historian but he was by necessity a student of history, for history provided the data that drove his analysis.[3] As Skinner writes:

> Smith and his contemporaries did not disregard the experience of ages and clearly accepted Aristotle's dictum that we can only understand what presently exists by first considering 'the origins from which it springs'. (Skinner, 1972, p. 317)

And Raphael notes:

> Smith's inclination in the study of any subject was to approach it historically in the first instance and then to form his own ideas from reflections on past history. (Raphael, 1997, p. 18)

Smith's historical strategy was as follows. From his reading of history, from his understanding of societal differences around the world based on reports of travelers, from his own personal experience, and from the ideas of his predecessors he adopted the view that humankind evolves through four stages: hunting and gathering, pasturage, agriculture, and finally commerce. He envisioned this evolution as a story of progress for he believed that the state of humankind in the advanced commercial societies of the world, the most advanced in his mind being his own Great Britain, was most desirable and the closest approximation of a real society to the ideal of the human condition.

Thus evolution became the macro frame through which he envisioned humankind.[4] It was an evolution in which, while individual societies emerged, progressed and declined, humankind had made progress. Progress implies a norm toward which this evolution was moving. For Smith this norm was an ideal limiting case: 'the liberal plan of equality, liberty and justice' (Smith, 1784 [1976], p. 664).

I would argue that this frame of evolution with its limiting case of the liberal plan reflects Smith's faith in a deity and his belief that the deity has made this liberal plan the human prospect. This is not a gift freely given, but a possibility that humankind can approach to the degree that humankind struggles with and learns to master its own frailties. I have made that case at length elsewhere (Evensky, 2005). I will not belabor it here because the logic of Smith's analysis is in fact independent of this deity. The source of Smith's belief that the humankind has the prospect of approaching this ideal is not central to the argument that Smith believed that there is such a prospect and that humankind has been evolving toward it.

To make the case for this evolutionary story, Smith tells two histories of humankind. One is a narrative history of humankind – history as we 'know' it. As Smith tells the story, we can cull general principles from humankind's narrative history because while in the course of that narrative individual societies have emerged, stagnated and declined, the overall flow of humankind's history is consistent with a natural, conjectural story: evolution through four stages and progress toward the limit.

Thus by this culling of general principles from the narrative of humankind's historical story, Smith represents a 'theoretical or conjectural history' (Stewart 1793 [1980], p. 293) that describes the undistorted course humankind's evolution which would naturally follow according to his principles.[5]

Then with these general principles in mind, Smith returns to the narrative history offering an analysis of the course of recorded history that explains why the unnatural twists, turns, stagnations and declines of societies occur. As he tells it, these do not represent violations of his general principles but rather reflect peculiar distortions of those principles caused by human frailty.

Jerry Muller describes Smith's use of history to imagine this dynamic very nicely. He writes that Smith's method:

> entailed an inductive attempt to discover regularities in social life through observation and comparison, for which history provided much of the raw data. Finally, it called for an examination of the ways in which human propensities were shaped and molded into particular character types by historically changing social, political, and economic structures. (Muller, 1993, pp. 48–9)

Smith's complementary use of theoretical and narrative history to mutually support one another is reflected quite clearly in Books I, II and III of *The Wealth of Nations*. In Books I and II Smith lays the foundation for and tells a theoretical story of the accumulation and diffusion of capital as an engine for growth of the wealth of nations that begins with agriculture in the countryside and expands into commerce of the towns. In Book III he offers a narrative history of the distortions in Europe during feudal times that impeded this natural course of events, causing the towns to lead rather than follow the progress of the countryside. He writes of this distorted case:

> Had human institutions . . . never disturbed the natural course of things, the progressive wealth and increase of the towns would, in every political society, be consequential, and in proportion to the improvement and cultivation of the territory or country . . . But though this natural order of things must have taken place in some degree in every . . . society, it has, in all the modern states of Europe been, in many respects, entirely inverted. (Smith, 1784 [1976], pp. 378, 380)

In this quotation we hear the key to mapping from the theoretical to the narrative of history: 'human institutions'. In Smith's moral philosophy, human institutions have an organic existence that maintains societal structures across time. To the degree that these institutions 'disturb . . . the natural course of things' society is a distorted version of the natural, ideal case of the liberal plan. But while existing institutions can and do distort the natural course of things, it is institutions that also make progress possible, for it is the evolution of institutions and the societal standards they embody that sustains the progress of the past.

In Smith's analysis there is a natural selection process at work. A more mature institutional structure, one that more closely approximates the natural ideal, is, *ceteris paribus*, a stronger structure and thus more capable of defending itself. So, *ceteris paribus*, there is a selection bias toward institutional maturation that leads to the progress of humankind.

But institutions are inherently inert. They justify themselves, and if challenged they defend themselves. So while institutions are essential for the maintenance of any progress that has been made by a given society, they are not the source of progress itself. That comes from the chance, circumstance, and the intended and unintended consequences of individual human action.

At the heart of Smith's story is the individual. Individuals are born into and shaped by the extant societal construct, but human imagination, reason and frailty lead to choices that affect that construct and effect change. Smith's analysis of humankind's evolution is therefore a story of the coevolution of individuals and societies: each shaping the other and in the process creating change.

The next section explores Smith's conception of individual motivation and socialization. We will then see how, given that human foundation, Smith describes the instrumental role of institutions in humankind's evolution through stages toward the limiting case.

The human foundation of Smith's moral philosophy
Smith envisions human beings as being guided by that balance of sentiments – self-love, justice and beneficence – which resides in the human breast. Self-love is the spring for human action, it is the motive force driving individuals to 'better their condition' (Smith, 1784 [1976], p. 405). Justice is that sentiment that can rein in our self-love when its pursuit would do injury to another (Smith, 1790 [1976], p. 79). Beneficence is that sentiment that motivates the goodness and kindness of friendship or generosity or charity (Smith, 1790 [1976], p. 79).

In an ideal world we would all embody a perfect balance of these sentiments: 'The man who acts according to the rules of perfect prudence, of strict justice, and of proper benevolence, may be said to be perfectly virtuous' (Smith, 1790 [1976], p. 237). A society of such perfectly virtuous individuals is the necessary and sufficient condition for the limiting case of the 'the liberal plan of equality, liberty and justice' (Smith, 1784 [1976], p. 664). These individuals would be driven by self-love to better their conditions through energetic and creative participation in the market nexus; they would have the beneficence to care for those who were not capable of great success in the race for wealth; and they would have the self-command to impose upon themselves the standards of behavior that ensure justice for all.

When all enjoy justice, liberty is a threat to no one. But in the absence of this universal commitment to justice, and indeed in the absence of a universal definition of the standards of justice, liberty is an invitation to chaos. For in the pursuit of bettering one's condition, there are many opportunities for what in the modern discourse is referred to as 'rent-seeking' (Buchanan et al., 1980), the pursuit of institutional advantages in order to generate a larger distributive share.

The human foundation Smith develops in the *Theory of Moral Sentiments* (TMS) is an essential foundation for the liberal economic story he will tell in *The Wealth of Nations*. For without this human foundation to explain the concept of, the human capacity for, and the emergence of justice, Smith leaves blank a page that Hobbes opened and that his contemporaries the Physiocrats tried to fill with a *despotisme legal*: how can a liberal society cohere when all are motivated by a desire to better their condition? What power can hold the destructive forces of rent-seeking chaos at bay?

Smith's analysis of justice begins by establishing that we have the capacity for justice. It is a sentiment that can be developed within our breast. But, when the 'coarse clay' (Smith, 1790 [1976], p. 162) that is our raw being has not yet been shaped for justice, there is no sense of justice in our breast. It must be instilled in our being. But even the best measure of justice we embody is never equivalent to that ideal that would be consistent with perfect virtue. As Waterman writes: '*The Theory of Moral Sentiments*... expounds a detailed psychology according to which human action is motivated by a less-than-perfect balance of 'sentiments': self-love, justice, and beneficence or benevolence' (Waterman, 2002, pp. 912–13). But while perfection is not possible, progress toward that ideal is:

> [In] situations which bear so hard upon human nature, that the greatest degree of self-government, which can belong to so imperfect creature as man, is not able to stifle, altogether, the voice of human weakness ... though it [one's behavior] fails of absolute perfection, it may be a much nearer approximation towards perfection than what, upon such trying occasions, is commonly either to be found or to be expected. (Smith, 1790 [1976], pp. 25–6)

The source of that progress is our desire for approbation, for it is this desire that gives society the power to shape our coarse clay, to socialize us:

> This natural disposition to accommodate and to assimilate, as much as we can, our own sentiments, principles, and feelings, to those which we see fixed and rooted in the persons whom we are obliged to live and converse a great deal with, is the cause of the contagious effects of both good and bad company. (Smith, 1790 [1976], p. 224)

We desire to be praised, we abhor the prospect of being ostracized, so there is a strong motivation in all of us 'to accommodate and to assimilate' the extant standards of community values, the 'golden mean' (Smith, 1790 [1976], p. 204) of talent and virtue.

> Every age and country look upon that degree of each quality, which is commonly to be met with in those who are esteemed among themselves, as the golden mean of that particular talent or virtue. And as this varies, according as their different circumstances render different qualities more or less habitual to them, their sentiments concerning the exact propriety of character and behavior vary accordingly. (Smith, 1790 [1976], p. 204)

This socialization process begins with our observation of the response we get from real spectators that populate our world – our parents, our friends, our acquaintances. We accommodate our behavior to our perception of their judgment of us, seeking their approbation and avoiding their disapprobation; the power of this judgment over us being directly proportional to the value we place in their judgment.

In time we get habituated to the standards of our society and those standards become our 'duty':

> Our continual observations upon the conduct of others, insensibly lead us to form to ourselves certain general rules concerning what is fit and proper either to be done or to be avoided...
>
> The regard to those general rules of conduct, is what is properly called a sense of duty, a principle of the greatest consequence in human life, and the only principle by which the bulk of mankind are capable of directing their actions...
>
> [U]pon the tolerable observance of these duties, depends the very existence of human society, which would crumble into nothing if mankind were not generally impressed with a reverence for those important rules of conduct. (Smith, 1790 [1976], pp. 159, 161–2, 163)

Our duty is initially inculcated and enforced upon us by the active observation of those whose approbation we desire, but over time that standard takes on an independent position in our breast. As we mature, it becomes a standard that we associate with our society as represented by an impartial spectator, any fellow citizen, and which we enforce upon ourselves by our own self-command. And so it is that the stability of a given society is maintained by individual adherence to commonly shared standards of justice that constrain our self-love:

> Though every man may, according to the proverb, be the whole world to himself, to the rest of mankind he is a most insignificant part of it. Though his own happiness may be of more importance to him than that of all the world besides, to every other person it is of no more consequence than that of any other man. Though it may be true, therefore, that every individual, in his own breast, naturally prefers himself to all mankind, yet he dares not look mankind in the face, and avow that he acts according to this principle. He feels that in this preference they can never go along with him, and that how natural soever it may be to him, it must always appear excessive and extravagant to them. When he views himself in the light in which he is conscious that others will view him, he sees that to them he is but one of the multitude in no respect better than any other in it. If he would act so as that the impartial spectator may enter into the principles of his conduct, which is what of all things he has the greatest desire to do, he must, upon this, as upon all other occasions, humble the arrogance of his self-love, and bring it down to something which other men can go along with. They will indulge it so far as to allow him to be more anxious about, and to pursue with more earnest assiduity, his own happiness than that of any other person. Thus far, whenever they place themselves in his situation, they will readily go along with him. In the race for wealth, and honours, and preferments, he may run as hard as he can, and strain every nerve and every muscle, in order to outstrip all his competitors. But if he should justle, or throw down any of them, the indulgence of the spectators is entirely at an end. It is a violation of fair play, which they cannot admit of. (Smith, 1790 [1976], pp. 82–3)

Duty is a coarse form that we impress on our coarse clay in order for social order to be possible, but we are capable of a more refined shape.[6] We have the capacity to step outside of ourselves and of our social milieu, to observe ourselves from the position of an impartial spectator who is entirely detached from the interests embodied in the extant societal construct and the associated community values. From that meta-position and given our human capacity for imagination, we can assess ourselves not by the current standards that win one the community's praise, but from a detached standard that we conceptualize as worthy of praiseworthiness. Furthermore, from that position we can, if we so choose, act on the extant societal standards to try to bring them into line with those to which we feel committed. In this way we act to reshape the very society that has shaped us.

Thus, in Smith's analysis, while the character of that balance of sentiments that first guides us originates in socialization, we each have a unique biography that forms our coarse clay into an autonomous being. So while we are at root a social being, we have the capacity to grow into sovereign beings: 'In the great chess-board of human society, every single piece has a principle of motion of its own[, a unique balance of sentiments – self-love, justice and benevolence]' (Smith, 1790 [1976], p. 234). And from that unique position we can, in turn, reshape our society.

It is this coevolution of individual and society, along with chance, circumstance and the unintended consequences of human actions, that drives humankind's evolution and makes human progress possible.

At each stage of humankind's development, the societal construct is consistent with the current means of producing the material goods of that society. In the hunting and gathering stage, the societal construct is very rudimentary because the requisites for the social cohesion of such a society are very simple. It is a very small society, so standards and enforcement can be accomplished by tribal meeting. As domestication of animals occurs, life gets more complicated for there are significant issues of ownership that transcend generations. And so, this more complex mode of production requires more complex societal constructions to ensure the security of individuals and in turn the cohesion of the society. When pasturage gives way to agriculture, the size of society, the degree of societal complexity, increases very significantly. Again, the emergence of this more advanced mode of production can only occur if it goes hand in hand with the evolution of societal constructs that ensure societal cohesion.

At every stage of Smith's story of humankind's evolution, the process of evolution is described as a dynamic transformation of a three-dimensional simultaneous system. Social, political and economic conditions are interdependent, no one dimension can progress any faster than the least mature of these dimensions allows. Smith's is not a story of economic determinism. It is not a story of wealth as the *raison d'être* of and the measure for progress. It is a story that values 'the liberal plan of equality, liberty and justice' (Smith, 1784 [1976], p. 664). This is the ideal end toward which Smith envisions humankind moving. This is the limiting case and he would like his moral philosophical work to contribute to the continued approximation of that end.

The last stage of humankind's progress is, in Smith's story, the commercial society. The fruitfulness of that mode of production holds out the prospect of wealth generation far beyond anything the world has ever known because the commercial system, when working properly, accumulates and allocates capital in a dynamic circuit of production that expands the wealth of society immensely. But the *raison d'être* of that accumulation is not wealth itself; it is consumption: 'Consumption is the sole end and purpose of all production; and the interest of the producer ought to be attended to, only so far as it may be necessary for promoting that of the consumer' (Smith, 1784 [1976], p. 660). And the ultimate standard of a successful liberal society was, for Smith, the level of consumption among the least of the working class:

> Servants, labourers, and workmen of different kinds, make up the far greater part of every great political society. But what improves the circumstances of the greater part can never be regarded as an inconveniency to the whole. No society can surely be flourishing and happy, of which the far greater part of the members are poor and miserable. It is but equity, besides, that they who feed, clothe, and lodge the whole body of the people, should have such a share of the produce of their own labour as to be themselves tolerably well fed, clothed, and lodged. (Smith, 1784 [1976], p. 96)

Smith believed that the liberal plan would bring this well-being to the working class because it produces the greatest wealth for the nation and it distributes that wealth most justly.

In a 'well governed society' the competition among capitals will drive up wages so workers would be 'tolerably well fed, clothed, and lodged', while at the same time driving down the rate of interest 'so low as to render it impossible for any but the very wealthiest people to live upon the interest of their money' (Smith, 1784 [1976], p. 113). 'Holland [which] ... in proportion to the extent of its territory and number of people, is a richer country than England ... seems to be approaching near to this state' (Smith, 1784 [1976], pp. 108, 113). 'But perhaps no country has ever yet arrived at this degree of opulence' (Smith, 1784 [1976], p. 111).

But it is not the freedom or the independency or the material fruits of the liberal plan that Smith values most. These are instrumental in approaching the ideal limiting case that he envisions: a society in which all citizens have the opportunity to enjoy a life of 'secure tranquility' (Smith, 1790 [1976], p. 215). Tranquility represents for Smith peace of mind, 'that equal and happy temper, which is so necessary to self-satisfaction and enjoyment' (Smith, 1790 [1976], p. 23).

The *sine qua non* of this ideal is justice, for it is justice that provides the security for capital accumulation and allocation that in turn provides for tolerable material wellbeing, and it is justice that ensures the security within which to enjoy tranquility. Much of Smith's analysis is focused on how in the course of this dynamic, three-dimensional evolution of humankind the standards of justice evolve, become institutionalized and are ultimately approximated by a common set of civic ethics shared by individual citizens and enforced by individual self-command.

The instrumental actors in Smith's telling of this evolutionary story are social and political institutions. These institutions play a constructive role in that evolution to the degree that they are solid enough to secure the progress of the past, while at the same time not being so inert as to preclude further progress. To the degree that these institutions evolve in progressive ways, the societal construction they embody is, *ceteris paribus*, more capable of sustaining itself, for with the progress of opulence that is one dimension of this evolution comes the material capacity necessary to defend the nation. This strength of progress, *ceteris paribus*, explains humankind's evolution through four stages toward the liberal ideal.

We now turn to Smith's story of institutional evolution. As Jerry Muller writes: 'While Smith explored the more or less constant passions of the individual, he was more concerned with the degree to which historically developed institutions channel those passions in directions which are morally desirable and adapted for social survival' (Muller, 1993, p. 115).

Humankind's evolution, the instrumental role of institutions[7]

The first stage in humankind's evolution was the rude state of hunting and gathering. In this rude state the powerful, shared experience of wonder at nature's regular and her apparently irregular events (for example, the passing seasons and eclipses respectively) gave birth to shared superstitions as a community response to the mysteries of nature. Superstition was in time institutionalized in the form of polytheistic religions that codified superstition by offering stories of gods' actions that served to demystify the mysterious – a plethora of gods codify a multitude of superstitions. This emerging institution of 'religion, even in its rudest form, gave a sanction to the rules of morality, long before the age of artificial reasoning and philosophy' (Smith, 1790 [1976], p. 164). So in the very first stage of humankind's evolution the first human institution, religion, emerged to provide a cement for social cohesion: rules of morality.

This nascent systematization of human understanding of nature and the associated institutionalizing, organizing and regulating of individual behavior that came with religion complemented a simultaneously emerging human activity: the division of labor. The division of labor is 'derived' from a 'propensity [in all individuals] to truck, barter, and exchange one thing for another' (Smith, 1784 [1976], p. 25). Clearly, only through exchange is it possible for individuals to enjoy the gains from trade that are the fruits of the division of labor. But as Smith emphasizes again and again, production for exchange requires a sense of security. To the degree that religion established and enforced rules that created that sense of security, it facilitated the division of labor.

As the division of labor progressed, mechanisms for and metrics of exchange emerged, and so too issues of ownership. This necessitated rudimentary legal systems to provide the terms that codified and the authority that enforced nascent concepts of private property and contract. Religion, by inculcating a moral framework for social intercourse, served to reinforce and complement legal definitions and sanctions. The security provided by this nexus of religious and legal institutions made possible accumulation. The emergence of accumulation is central to Smith's story for it is accumulation that provides the deepening pool of capital necessary for an ever finer division of labor.

The extension of the division of labor goes hand in hand with the accumulation of capital, for greater productivity gives rise to the surplus that can be accumulated, and its extension is made possible by that accumulation being poured back into the circuit of production. With this accumulation come new issues of property rights. As a consequence justice becomes a more complicated concept.

In the first stage of society, the unrefined or rude state, 'there can be very little government of any sort' (Smith, 1762–63, 1766 [1978], p. 201). Indeed there is little need for such because little is private beyond one's reputation. 'Among savages property begins and ends with possession, and they seem scarce to have any idea of anything as their own which is not about their own bodies' (Smith, 1762–63, 1766 [1978], p. 460). As a consequence, the range of potential reasons for dispute is narrow. Further, all live under the eye of all in such a small community, so adjudication of any disputes can be done by the community as a whole and can be enforced by that community.

As society moves from hunting and gathering to the shepherding stage, complexity grows. 'Among shepherds the idea of property is further extended' (Smith, 1762–63, 1766 [1978], p. 460). 'Those animalls which are most adapted for the use of man . . . are no longer common but are the property of certain individualls. The distinctions of rich and poor then arise' (Smith, 1762–63, 1766 [1978], p. 202). With the expansion of property and the emergence of property as a source of status, issues of property become more complex. 'Property makes it [government] absolutely necessary . . . [for property is] the grand fund of all dispute' (Smith, 1762–63, 1766 [1978], p. 208). Thus: 'The age of shepherds is that [stage] where government properly first commences' (Smith, 1762–63, 1766 [1978], p. 202). But even as government commences, there is still no systematic legal structure being developed:

> With regard to laws and the legislative power, there is properly nothing of that sort in this period. There must indeed be some sort of law as soon as property in flocks commences, but this would be but very short and have few distinctions in it, so that every man would understand it without any written or regular law. It would be no other than what the necessity of the state required. Written and formall laws are *a very great refinement of government*, and such as we never meet with but in the latest periods of it. (Smith, 1762–63, 1766 [1978], p. 213, emphasis added)

It is the evolution of humankind from shepherding to agriculture that goes hand in hand with the emergence of legislative government, because in that transition 'property receives its greatest extension' (Smith, 1762–63, 1766 [1978], p. 460). As it does, the complexity of issues related to property rights, issues of accession, prescription or succession, expand dramatically. This necessitates the establishment by government of a system of formal positive law.

Smith's story of humankind's evolution is a story of three-dimensional social constructions – social, political and economic – evolving as a simultaneous system. In these transitions just cited, at each transition from stage to stage the move from one mode of production to another can only be firmly established to the degree that the institutions for resolution of issues of commutative justice mature in tandem with the transforming mode of material production.

Where the structures of commutative justice meet the needs of the organization of material production, the progress of opulence unfolds. But even as that material progress unfolds it requires the continued maturation of the institutions that ensure commutative justice. In Smith's story of humankind's evolution there is no privileged dimension of humankind; progress depends on the harmonious simultaneous development of all dimensions.

> It is easy to see that in these severall ages of society, the laws and regulations with regard to property must be very different . . . [W]here the age of hunters subsists . . . [a]s there is almost no property amongst them . . . [f]ew laws or regulations will [be] requisite . . . But when flocks and herds come to be reared property then becomes of a very considerable extent . . . [so] there are many opportunities of injuring one another . . . In this state many more laws and regulations must take place . . . In the age of agriculture . . . there are many ways added [to theft or robbery] in which property may be interrupted . . . The laws therefore . . . will be of a far greater number than amongst a nation of shepherds. In the age of commerce, as the subjects of property are greatly increased the laws must be proportionally multiplied. The more improved any society is and the greater length the severall means of supporting the inhabitants are carried, the greater will be the number of laws and regulations necessary to maintain justice. (Smith, 1762–63, 1766 [1978], p. 16)

Thus, civil government emerges to establish and enforce laws that define and secure these property rights:

> Civil government supposes a certain subordination. But as the necessity of civil government gradually grows up with the acquisition of valuable property, so the principal causes which naturally introduce subordination gradually grow up with the growth of that valuable property. (Smith, 1784 [1976], p. 710)

Religious institutions establish the precedent of subordination, but this concept is confirmed in the minds of many by the very accumulation that must be protected by law. There is according to Smith a natural 'disposition of mankind, to go along with all the passions of the rich and the powerful . . . [While] [o]ur deference to their inclinations [is not] founded chiefly, or altogether, upon a regard to the utility of such submission, and to the order of society, which is best supported by it' (Smith, 1790 [1976], p. 52), there is nevertheless utility in this authority. It is instrumental in establishing order.

As we have seen, with the evolution of society through stages from hunting and gathering to pasturage and then into agriculture, the complexity of society in general and of property rights in particular requires that civil government takes on more responsibilities. As this occurs the authority of civil government becomes institutionalized. This institutional authority in turn plays an important instrumental role in shaping social norms, because the 'duty of allegiance seems to be founded [in part] on . . . the principle of authority' (Smith, 1762–63, 1766 [1978], p. 318).

> [I]t is very seldom that one has a distinct notion of the foundation of their duties, but have merely a notion that they have such and such obligations . . . [I]ndeed it will but seldom happen that one will be very sensible of the constitution he has been born and bred under; everything by custom appears to be right or at least one is but very little shocked at it. (Smith, 1762–63, 1766 [1978], pp. 321–2)

Thus the weight of the government's authority inculcates the standards embodied in its laws as personal standards among the citizens. That '[a]uthority [also serves as] . . . the foundation of that . . . utility or common interest' (Smith, 1762–63, 1766 [1978], p. 322) that establishes the virtue of the law among citizens, and so the laws of the civil government become a force in the inculcation of civic ethics. As Smith writes: '[W]hat forms the character of every nation . . . is the nature of their government' (Smith, 1784 [1976], p. 586). Ancient Rome is, according to Smith, indicative of this interdependence of positive law and civic ethics. He makes this point by contrasting Rome with Greece:

> The superiority of character in the Romans over that of the Greeks, so much remarked by Polybius and Dionysius of Halicarnassus, was probably owing to the better constitution of their courts of justice ['The attention, to practice and precedent, necessarily formed the Roman law into . . . [a] regular and orderly system'], than to any other circumstances to which those authors ascribe it. Romans are said to have been particularly distinguished for their superior respect to an oath. But the people who were accustomed to make oath only before some diligent and well-informed court of justice, would naturally be much more attentive to what they swore, than they who were accustomed to do the same thing before mobbish and disorderly assemblies. (Smith, 1784 [1976], p. 779)

And so, another dimension of the social construct that is evolving and securing the extant standards of commutative justice, that in turn secure the current level of the progress of opulence, are the standards of commutative justice embodied in the civic ethics of that society – those standards of duty Smith refers to as that society's 'golden mean'.

Smith weaves this story of positive law, civic ethics and the progress of opulence together most explicitly in the *Lectures on Jurisprudence* that he delivered to his students at Glasgow University. In those *Lectures* the central lessons Smith seeks to communicate to his students are:

- The central role of justice in a liberal system.
- How chance, circumstance, and intended and unintended actions of individuals have made Britain the world's best approximation of the liberal plan to date.
- The instrumental and essential role of government in that British evolution.
- The nexus just cited between mature government and mature citizens.

Smith begins his Wednesday, 23 February 1763 lecture on jurisprudence as follows:

> In the last lecture I endeavoured to explain to you more fully that form of government which naturally arises amongst mankind as they *advance in society, and in what manner it gradually proceeded*. (Smith, 1762–63, 1766 [1978], p. 214, emphasis added)

The dimension of 'advance' that he will explore in these lectures is the English judicial system. He clearly admires that system as it exists, but his purpose is not adulation, it is to demonstrate to his students how order and good government evolve through chance, circumstance, and the intended and unintended consequences of individual actions. And further, how this advance in government goes hand in hand with the maturation of the citizenry and the nation's progress of opulence. His subject is the 'advance in society, and in what manner it gradually proceeded'. It is a story of humankind's evolution, that evolution as progress, and the principles that guide that progress.

Smith's analysis of the evolution of the English judicial system is an exemplar of his larger conception of the 'oeconomy' of nature at work: individuals' pursuit of their particular utility (self-interest) in their specific geopolitical circumstances can result in unintended but desirable general outcomes – the maturation of justice and the progress of opulence.

Smith explores two dimensions of the English judicial system: the evolution of the structure of the court system and the evolution of the jury system. He writes of that jury system:

> The law of England, always the friend of liberty, deserves praise in no instance more than in the carfull provision of impartial juries . . . Nothing can be a greater security for life, liberty, and property than this institution. The judges are men of integrity, quite independent, holding their offices for life, but they are tied down by the law. The jurymen are your neighbours who are to judge of a fact upon which your life depends. (Smith, 1762–63, 1766 [1978], p. 425)

In the case of both the structure of the courts and the jury system, Smith describes a history in which particular interests, noble leaders, chance and circumstance led to a serendipitous result: a system of justice that is to be admired not only in its own right, but as a foundation for that individual security that is so essential for the accumulation of capital and the fluidity of movement of labor and capital that is in turn essential for the commercial stage of humankind's evolution to emerge and flourish.

But institutions of justice are not sufficient for a secure system of commutative justice to prevail in a nation. Smith appreciated that if justice is truly to provide the foundation for the relations among citizens, the average citizen must value and adhere to the standards of justice embodied in the positive law. So, hand in hand with the institutions of justice, for progress to occur the civic ethics of the citizenry must mature. And apropos of Smith's argument that the authority of a respected government nurtures civic ethics, Smith believed that this is precisely what had unfolded in England.

He cited the differences between England and France as indicative of this phenomenon, arguing that the maturity of the British system of law relative to that of France is reflected in the character of the nations' respective citizens. In particular he contrasts the safety of London and Paris, asserting that the necessity of police to ensure personal security in these two cities is not proportional to population but rather to the 'nature of the manners of the people' (Smith, 1762–63, 1766 [1978], p. 332).

In Paris the large number of 'retainers and dependents' there necessitates a large police force because:

Nothing tends so much to corrupt and enervate and debase the mind as dependency, and nothing gives such noble and generous notions of probity as freedom and independency. Commerce is one great preventive of this custom. ['The establishment of commerce and manufactures . . . brings . . . independency, [and] is [therefore] the best police for preventing crimes' (Smith, 1762–63, 1766 [1978], pp. 486–7).] . . . Hence it is that the common people of England who are alltogether free and independent are the honestest of their rank any where to be met with. (Smith, 1762–63, 1766 [1978], p. 333)

And hence it is that while in Paris 'hardly a night passes . . . without a murther or a robbery in the streets . . . in London there are not above 3, 4, or 5 murthers in a whole year' (Smith, 1762–63, 1766 [1978], p. 332).

In Smith's story of humankind's evolution through stages there is a duality of limits. There is the ultimate, ideal limit, the liberal society of independent beings enjoying perfect liberty, making the most for all, and doing well for the least. This is the reference point by which all real human progress is assessed. Then there is that artificial limit a society can impose on itself by 'the nature of its laws and institutions' (Smith, 1784 [1976], p. 111). For example:

China has been long one of the richest, that is, one of the most fertile, best cultivated, most industrious, and most populous countries in world. It seems, however, to have . . . long [ago] . . . acquired that full complement of riches *which the nature of its laws and institutions permits it to acquire* . . . But this complement may be much inferior to what, with other laws and institutions, the nature of its soil, climate, and situation might admit of. (Smith, 1784 [1976], pp. 89, 111, emphasis added)

The problem with the laws and institutions of China is that rather than enhance the sense of security among the citizens, they undermine it:

In a country . . . where, though the rich or the owners of large capitals enjoy a good deal of security, the poor or the owners of small capitals enjoy scarce any, but are liable, under the pretence of justice, to be pillaged and plundered at any time by the inferior mandarins, the quantity of stock employed in all the different branches of business transacted within it can never be equal to what the nature and extent of that business might admit. In every different branch, the oppression of the poor must establish the monopoly of the rich, who, by engrossing the whole trade to themselves, will be able to make very large profits. (Smith, 1784 [1976], pp. 111–12)

Institutions, ethics and *The Nature and Causes of the Wealth of Nations*

In Smith's story of *The Nature and Causes of the Wealth of Nations* (WN) it is capital that fuels the progress of opulence: 'The greatest improvement in the productive powers of labour, and the greater part of the skill, dexterity, and judgment with which it is any where directed, or applied, seem to have been the effects of the division of labour' (Smith, 1784 [1976], p. 13).

The accumulation of capital makes possible the division of labor, and it is the division of labor that in turn generates an expanding pool of capital. In WN, Book II Smith describes the role of capital in the progress of opulence as follows. Capital travels in a circuit of production. As capital is thrown into successive circuits it finances an ever finer division of labor and this in turn means that the nation's capital returns from each circuit are larger. So long as the participants are parsimonious, throwing their original capital and some share of the surplus back into successive circuits, this expanding circuit of capital fuels the progress of opulence.

According to Smith, in the course of that progress capital naturally flows first into agriculture because, with the cooperative labor of nature, agriculture is the most productive application of capital. As the capital stock in agriculture deepens, the rate of return in agriculture falls. In search of better opportunities, some capital spills out of agriculture and into manufacturing. As capital makes successive circuits in manufacturing, capital deepens and at some point it begins to spill out into the wholesale trade. *Ceteris paribus*, capital flows there last for this application 'has the least effect [is least productive] of any of the three' (Smith, 1784 [1976], p. 366).

Smith divides this wholesale trade into three categories:

- the home trade,
- the foreign trade of consumption, and
- the carrying trade. (Smith, 1784 [1976], p. 368)

The home trade is most secure and quickest, so this is the first circuit into which capital flows. But again, as capital deepens it spills into the successively less secure and slower circuits: foreign trade of consumption and the carrying trade:

> [T]he returns of the foreign trade of consumption are very seldom so quick as those of the home-trade. The returns of the home-trade generally come in before the end of the year, and sometimes three or four times in the year. The returns of the foreign trade of consumption seldom come in before the end of the year, and sometimes not till after two or three years. A capital, therefore, employed in the home-trade will sometimes make twelve operations, or be sent out and returned twelve times, before a capital employed in the foreign trade of consumption has made one. If capitals are equal, therefore, the one will give four and twenty times more encouragement and support to the industry of the country than the other. (Smith, 1784 [1976], pp. 368–9)

In sum, as capital stock of a country deepens it successively fills each of these circuits, and then spills into the next. This is good for the nation according to Smith: 'Each of these different branches of trade . . . is not only advantageous, but necessary and unavoidable, when the course of things without constraint or violence, naturally introduces it' (Smith, 1784 [1976], p. 372).

But these advantages are contingent on the presence of those laws and institutions that make the capital secure. The commercial stage would never have emerged, nor would it have flourished so much as it had in England, had it not been for the evolution of the system of justice and the civic ethics of the citizenry that provided the security that comes with mature institutions, political and social, of commutative justice:

> That security which the laws in Great Britain give to every man that he shall enjoy the fruits of his own labour, is alone sufficient to make any country flourish, notwithstanding these [mercantile impediments] and twenty other absurd regulations of commerce . . . The natural effort of every individual to better his own condition, when suffered to exert itself with freedom and security, is so powerful a principle, that it is alone, and without any assistance, not only capable of carrying on the society to wealth and prosperity, but of surmounting a hundred impertinent obstructions with which the folly of human laws too often incumbers its operations . . . In Great Britain [and the American colonies] industry is perfectly secure; and though it is far from being perfectly free, it is as free or freer than in any other part of Europe. (Smith, 1784 [1976], p. 540)

The evolution of Smith's vision

Smith's liberal vision and his hope for the human prospect never waned. But his optimism about the future of Britain did because he believed that the laws and institutions of Great Britain were being captured and manipulated for the benefit of the mercantile interests and to the detriment of the general citizenry.

This voice of concern emerges and grows more clear and strong in successive editions of the WN and the TMS. The first edition of the WN arrived at the publisher much later than Smith predicted. He arrived in London in 1773 ready to publish the WN, but it is not finally published until 9 March 1776 (Campbell and Skinner, 'The text and apparatus', 1976, p. 61). The delay seems to be due to work he did in addressing issues raised by a new awareness of mercantile political power that he did not entirely appreciate from the distant vantage of his mother's home in Kirkcaldy, Scotland where he had spent years writing the WN.

As we have seen in Smith's analysis of capital, when markets are free from distortions the best return is initially in the home-trade circuit. It is only when that circuit is full that capital will naturally spill into broader circuits. The mercantilists advocated protectionist policies that distort this natural flow:

> [M]erchants and manufacturers, who being collected in towns, and naturally accustomed to that exclusive corporation spirit which prevails in them, naturally endeavour to obtain against all their countrymen, the same exclusive privilege which they generally possess against the inhabitants of their respective towns. They accordingly seem to have been the original inventors of those restraints upon the importation of foreign goods, which secure to them the monopoly of the home-market. (Smith, 1784 [1976], p. 462)

Smith rejects the zero sum game mentality that underlies the mercantile self-serving 'sophistry' (Smith, 1784 [1976], p. 467), arguing that these policies are really a path toward a negative sum game in which the only winners are those very mercantile interests that advocate them. The best policy is free, fair, secure trade:

> Nothing ... can be more absurd than this whole doctrine of the balance of trade, upon which, not only these restraints, but almost all other regulations of commerce are founded. When two places trade with one another, this doctrine supposes that, if the balance be even, neither of them either loses or gains; but if it leans in any degree to one side, that one of them loses and the other gains in proportion to its declension from the exact equilibrium. Both suppositions are false. A trade which is forced by means of bounties and monopolies, may be, and commonly is disadvantageous to the country in whose favour it is meant to be established ... But that trade which, without force or constraint, is naturally and regularly carried on between any two places is always advantageous, though not always equally so, to both. (Smith, 1784 [1976], pp. 488–9)

Unfortunately:

> nations have been taught that their interest consisted in beggaring all their neighbours. Each nation has been made to look with an invidious eye upon the prosperity of all the nations with which it trades, and to consider their gain as its own loss. Commerce, which ought naturally to be, among nations, as among individuals, a bond of union and friendship, has become the most fertile source of discord and animosity. The capricious ambition of kings and ministers has not, during the present and the preceding century, been more fatal to the repose of Europe, than the impertinent jealousy of merchants and manufacturers. The violence and injustice of the rulers of mankind is an ancient evil, for which, I am afraid, the nature of human affairs

can scarce admit of a remedy. But the mean rapacity, the monopolizing spirit of merchants and manufacturers, who neither are, nor ought to be the rulers of mankind, though it cannot perhaps be corrected, may very easily be prevented from disturbing the tranquility of any body but themselves. (Smith, 1784 [1976], p. 493)

Here we begin to hear the anger in Smith's voice as he not only disagrees with, but he despises the self-serving motives of those who advocate for the mercantile system. The consequence of their sophistry is a Europe burdened by a system of restraints on trade that reduces the wealth of each nation and pits nation against nation.

The mercantile interests have been able to get their hands on the levers of power and distort policy to their own ends by sophistry and persuasion and, when those tools have failed, by intimidation:

> This monopoly has so much increased the number of some particular tribes of them, that, like an overgrown standing army, they have become formidable to the government, and upon many occasions intimidate the legislature. The member of parliament who supports every proposal for strengthening this monopoly, is sure to acquire not only the reputation of understanding trade, but great popularity and influence with an order of men whose numbers and wealth render them of great importance. If he opposes them, on the contrary, and still more if he has authority enough to be able to thwart them, neither the most acknowledged probity, nor the highest rank, nor the greatest publick services can protect him from the most infamous abuse and detraction, from personal insults, nor sometimes from real danger, arising from the insolent outrage of furious and disappointed monopolists. (Smith, 1784 [1976], p. 471)

In 1784, eight years after the initial publication of WN, Smith offers 'Additions and corrections' to those who have the original edition and a new edition for those who do not. The most significant of the additions is a new chapter, Book IV, Chapter VIII, 'Conclusion of the mercantile system'. In this new chapter Smith picks up where the strong criticism of mercantile system embodied in the original Book IV left off, and he sharpens that criticism into a scathing attack.

The mercantile interests were, Smith feared, on the verge of destroying the most advanced example of humankind's progress, the emerging liberal system embodied in Great Britain. They had distorted the entire system of trade by peddling self-serving sophistry in the guise of a philosophy that, for the sake of the wealth not of the nation but of the merchants and manufacturers, made production not consumption the national purpose. As we have seen, this, according to Smith, is backward:

> Consumption is the sole end and purpose of all production; and the interest of the producer ought to be attended to, only so far as it may be necessary for promoting that of the consumer. The maxim is so perfectly self-evident, that it would be absurd to attempt to prove it. But in the mercantile system, the interest of the consumer is almost constantly sacrificed to that of the producer. (Smith, 1784 [1976], p. 660)

Indeed, not only has the consumer not benefited, the consumer paid for these foolish policies indirectly in higher prices caused by prohibitions or restrictions, and directly in taxes levied as protections and in taxes necessitated by the huge debt that the defense of the mercantile system had generated:

> For the sake of that little enhancement of price which this monopoly might afford our producers, the home-consumers have been burdened with the whole expense of maintaining and

defending that empire. For this purpose, and for this purpose only, in the last two wars, more than a hundred and seventy millions have been contracted over and above all that had been expended for the same purpose in former wars. The interest on the debt alone is not only greater than the whole extraordinary profit, which, it ever could be pretended, was made by the monopoly of the colony trade, but than the whole value of that trade or than the whole value of the goods, which at an average have been annually exported to the colonies.

It cannot be difficult to determine who have been the contrivers of this whole mercantile system; not the consumers, we may believe, whose interest has been entirely neglected; but the producers whose interest has been so carefully attended to; and among this latter class our merchants and manufacturers have been by far the principal architects. (Smith, 1784 [1976], p. 661)

Smith was furious, and he was worried. The debt generated by the defense of the mercantile system could, he feared, sink the British experiment.

In WN Book V, Smith specifically addresses his concerns about the British public debt. This debt has been incurred on an adventure in pursuit of an illusion, the creation of a British mercantile empire. Smith writes: 'It has hitherto been, not an empire, but the project of an empire; not a gold mine, but the project of a gold mine' (Smith, 1784 [1976], p. 947). The whole enterprise, undertaken at immense public expense, has not been for the benefit of the people as consumers but rather for the mercantile interests as producers. It has been a foolish and potentially deadly enterprise for the nation:

It is surely now time that our rulers should either realize this golden dream, in which they have been indulging themselves, perhaps, as well as the people; or, that they should awake from it themselves, and endeavour to awaken the people. If the project cannot be compleated, it ought to be given up. If any of the provinces of the British empire cannot be made to contribute towards the support of the whole empire, it is surely time that Great Britain should free herself from the expence of defending those provinces in time of war, and of supporting any part of their civil or military establishments in time of peace, and endeavour to accommodate her future views and designs to the real mediocrity of her circumstances. (Smith, 1784 [1976], p. 947)

These are the closing words of Smith's *Inquiry into the Nature and Causes of the Wealth of Nations*. Note the role of the 'rulers': 'They should awake from it [this golden dream] themselves, and endeavour to awaken the people.' This hints at a theme that emerges fully in the revisions Smith makes to the TMS, revisions he makes at the very end of his life.

Classical liberal Smith turns to civic humanist leaders for hope
Adam Smith's vision is a classical liberal vision: 'the liberal plan of equality, liberty and justice' (Smith, 1784 [1976], p. 664). But Smith is one who appreciates that this classical liberal vision is an ideal, a limit. It is, he believes, the human prospect, an end toward which he believes humankind is evolving. But that evolution is not constant in direction or speed.

As Smith tells the story, in the course of humankind's history there have been periods of speedy progress, slow progress and retrograde motion. Much of this speed and direction is beyond our control, determined by chance, circumstance and the unintended consequences of the actions of individuals. But there are examples of individuals, and in particular individual leaders, making a positive difference in the direction and speed of a society's development. For example the story Smith tells his students in his *Lectures on Jurisprudence* highlights the very constructive role played by Henry II and Edward I, asserting: 'that Henry 2d . . . of all our kings excepting Edwd. Is. had the greatest legislative capacity', and of how they each moved the judicial system along its path of maturation.

This belief that statesmen can contribute to the progress of humankind becomes a focal point of the revisions Smith makes to the TMS in the last year of his life. The voice of Smith as classical liberal is not diminished, but it is complemented by a civic humanist voice.

As Jerry Muller writes: 'The design and the rhetoric of Smith's work reflect his intention not only to *instruct* legislators by enunciating general principles but to *motivate* them to pursue the common interest' (Muller, 1993, p. 54). As he becomes more and more concerned about the destructive impact of the powerful mercantile interests, Smith's sense of urgency for achieving this goal grows.

In order to inspire this 'motivation . . . [for] the common interest' Smith adopts a civic humanist voice extolling 'citizenship . . . as an active virtue' (Pocock, 1983, p. 235). He appeals to today's and tomorrow's leaders to resist the seduction and pressures of partial interests and to 'assume the greatest and noblest of all characters, that of the reformer and legislator of a great state; and, by the wisdom of his institutions, [to] secure the internal tranquility and happiness of his fellow-citizens for many succeeding generations' (Smith, 1790 [1976], p. 232).

Leadership is, Smith asserts, essential, but leaders must have vision, and if vision is to be persuasive and well founded it must be based on a thoughtful system of philosophy. This is where the moral philosopher plays a significant role. This is the role Smith believed he was playing in offering his moral philosophical vision: 'Some general, and even systematical, idea of the perfection of policy and law, may no doubt be necessary for directing the views of the statesman' (Smith, 1790 [1976], p. 234).

But even as he extolled the notion of a 'general . . . systematical, idea of perfection' he warned that system must be a guide not a blueprint. The worst of leadership comes from the 'man of system . . . wise in his own conceit' (Smith, 1790 [1976], p. 233):

> [T]o insist upon establishing, and upon establishing all at once, and in spite of all opposition, every thing which that idea may seem to require, must often be the highest degree of arrogance . . . It is to fancy himself the only wise and worthy man in the commonwealth, and that his fellow-citizens should accommodate themselves to him and not he to them. (Smith, 1790 [1976], p. 234)

Smith's appeal is to those leaders who will be strong but humble leaders:

- making policy based on general rather than particular interests; and
- guided by a moral philosophy but not a slave to any such system.

His model was Solon, 'one of the leading figures in the republican "myth"' (Winch, 1978, p. 160):

> The man whose public spirit is prompted altogether by humanity and benevolence, will respect the established powers and privileges even of individuals, and still more those of the great orders and societies, into which the state is divided. Though he should consider some of them

as in some measure abusive [as Smith did the mercantile powers and privileges], he will . . . accommodate, as well as he can, his public arrangements to the confirmed habits and prejudices of the people; and . . . [w]hen he cannot establish the right, he will not disdain to ameliorate the wrong; but like Solon, when he cannot establish the best system of laws, he will endeavour to establish the best that the people can bear. (Smith, 1790 [1976], p. 233)

Conclusion

This book represents a long overdue volume of high-quality, original chapters on Smith, concentrating primarily on his economics. Smith is clearly the parent of modern economic thought and there has been a great deal of excellent work on Adam Smith's economics since the last similar volume, *Essays on Adam Smith*, was published over 30 years ago (Skinner and Wilson, 1975). This volume, by refocusing our attention on this important topic, offers a significant contribution to the literature.

Part I has focused on Adam Smith the moral philosopher as a philosopher. Now in Part II we turn to that seminal contribution of Adam Smith, his economic analysis. Finally, in Part III we trace the thread of Smith's analytical economics into the realm of policy.

Notes

1. Smith writes: 'And even we, while we have been endeavouring to represent all philosophical systems as mere inventions of the imagination . . . have insensibly been drawn in, to make use of language expressing the connecting principles of this one, *as if* they were the real chains which Nature makes use of to bind together her several operations' (Smith, 1795 [1980], p. 105, emphasis added).
2. This followed '[t]he antient Greek philosophy [that] was divided into three great branches; physicks, or natural philosophy; ethicks, or moral philosophy; and logick. This general division seems to be agreeable to the nature of things' (Smith, 1784 [1976], p. 766). 'Logick . . . [was] the science of the general principles of good and bad reasoning' (WN, 770).
3. Macfie writes: 'To them [the eighteenth century writers including Smith] the history of society was a philosophy of history. They took the view, without questioning it, that a philosophy of society must in method be historical. For societies themselves were natural growths in their own unique environments, and interpreting that growth implied a theory of growth' (Macfie, 1967, p. 14).
4. 'Smith has an evolutionary view of history and economic and political development' (Werhane, 1991, p. 50).
5. 'The sequences narrated in conjectural history were deemed to be *typical* [natural], whereas the sequences of narrative documentary history were *unique* and *particular*' (Hopfl, 1978, p. 23). Hopfl offers a very nice analysis of the role of conjectural history in Smith's analysis.
6. Human nature is constant (we are not 'better' than our predecessors), but human character evolves along with human institutions and these have the capacity to mature toward the ideal.
7. Rosenberg (1960) is generally excellent on this, but I think he is wrong to dismiss the role of ethics.

References

Buchanan, James, R.D. Tollison and G. Tullock (eds) (1980), *Toward a Theory of A Rent-Seeking Society*, College Station, TX: Texas A&M University Press.
Campbell, R.H. and Andrew Skinner (1976) 'General Introduction' to Adam Smith (1776), *An Inquiry into the Nature and Causes of the Wealth of Nations*; reprinted in W.B. Todd (ed.), *The Glasgow Edition of the Works and Correspondence of Adam Smith*, Vol. 1, Oxford: Clarendon Press.
Evensky, Jerry (2005), *Adam Smith's Moral Philosophy: A Historical and Contemporary Perspective on Markets, Law, Ethics, and Culture*, Cambridge: Cambridge University Press.
Muller, Jerry (1993), *Adam Smith in His Time and Ours: Designing the Decent Society*, New York: Free Press.
Pocock, J.G.A. (1983), 'Cambridge paradigms and Scotch philosophers: a study of the relations between civic humanist and the civil jurisprudential interpretation of eighteenth-century social thought', in Istvan Hont and Michael Ignatieff (eds) *Wealth and Virtue*, Cambridge: Cambridge University Press, pp. 235–52.
Raphael, D.D. (1997), *Three Great Economists*, Oxford: Oxford University Press.
Rosenberg, Nathan (1960), 'Some institutional aspects of the *Wealth of Nations*', *Journal of Political Economy*, **68** (6), 557–70.

Skinner, Andrew (1972), 'Adam Smith: philosophy and science', *Scottish Journal of Political Economy*, **19** (3), 307–19.
Skinner, Andrew and Thomas Wilson (eds) (1975), *Essays on Adam Smith*, Oxford: Clarendon Press.
Smith, Adam (1740), *Correspondence of Adam Smith*; reprinted in E.C. Mossner and I.S. Ross (eds) (1987), *The Glasgow Edition of the Works and Correspondence of Adam Smith*, Vol. 5, Oxford: Oxford University Press.
Smith, Adam (1762–63, 1766), *Lectures on Jurisprudence*, reprinted in R.L. Meek, D.D. Raphael and P.G. Stein (eds) (1978), *The Glasgow Edition of the Works and Correspondence of Adam Smith*, Vol. 5, Oxford: Oxford University Press
Smith, Adam (1784), *An Inquiry into the Nature and Causes of the Wealth of Nations*, reprinted in W.B. Todd (ed.) (1976), *The Glasgow Edition of the Works and Correspondence of Adam Smith*, Vol. 2, Oxford: Oxford University Press
Smith, Adam (1790), *The Theory of Moral Sentiments*; reprinted in D.D. Raphael and A.L.Macfie (eds) (1976), *The Glasgow Edition of the Works and Correspondence of Adam Smith*, Vol. 1, Oxford: Oxford University Press.
Smith, Adam (1795), 'The principles which lead and direct philosophical enquiries; illustrated by the history of astronomy'; reprinted in W.P.D. Wightman and J.C. Bryce (eds) (1980), *Essays on Philosophical Subjects, The Glasgow Edition of the Works and Correspondence of Adam Smith*, Vol. 3, Oxford: Oxford University Press, pp. 33–105.
Stewart, Dugald (1793), 'Account of the life and writings of Adam Smith, LL.D.'; reprinted in W.P.D. Wightman and J.C. Bryce (eds) (1980), *Essays on Philosophical Subjects, The Glasgow Edition of the Works and Correspondence of Adam Smith*, Vol. 3, Oxford: Oxford University Press, pp. 269–351.
Waterman, A.M.C. (2002), 'Economics as Theology: Adam Smith's *Wealth of Nations*', *Southern Economic Journal*, **68** (4), 907–21.
Winch, Donald (1978), *Adam Smith's Politics: An Essay in Historiographic Revision*, Cambridge: Cambridge University Press.

PART II

ADAM SMITH'S SYSTEM AND ITS ANTECEDENTS: ANALYTICAL ECONOMICS

7 Adam Smith, the Physiocrats and Turgot
Peter Groenewegen

As Skinner (1999, p. 104) indicated in his article, 'Adam Smith and Physiocracy', when Smith was in France during 1764–66, the Physiocratic school was at the zenith of its power. By then its major works had been published. It is also well known that over these years Smith enjoyed the friendship of Quesnay, the personal acquaintance of Turgot, and that he admired the works of Physiocracy sufficiently to have acquired many of them for his library during his sojourn in France and thereafter. Smith's first biographer, Dugald Stewart (1980, Vol. III p. 12), recalled that 'Smith had once an intention (as he told me himself) to have inscribed to him [that is, Quesnay] his *Wealth of Nations*'. Moreover, the chapter which Smith devoted to an examination of Physiocratic doctrines, albeit highly critical of these doctrines in part, simultaneously praised them as being perhaps the most correct version of political economy which had been published so far (Smith, 1976 [1776], p. 678). As Cannan pointed out long ago in the introduction he had prepared for his edition of *Wealth of Nations*, Smith was indebted to them for at least four significant parts of his economic system (Cannan, 1937, pp. xxxviii–xxxix).

In addition, the similarity between much of Smith's economics and that of Turgot for long created the view that Smith was heavily indebted to his friend for much of his political economy.

This chapter examines the association between Smith on the one hand, and the Physiocrats and Turgot on the other. It will do so first of all by looking at what Smith himself had said on these topics. It will then look at the importance of Physiocratic and Turgot's works as authorities used in writing the *Wealth of Nations*, and the place, if any, these works had found in Smith's library. By way of conclusion, the chapter will then briefly summarize in what areas of economics it can be said that Smith may have been indebted to particular views expressed by his French, mid-century, economist contemporaries.

The views on the Physiocrats and on Turgot in Smith's *Wealth of Nations*
Smith's most extensive discussion of Physiocratic thought was Book IV, Chapter IX of the *Wealth of Nations*: 'Of the agricultural system, or of those systems of political oeconomy which represent the produce of land as either the sole or the principal source of the revenue and wealth of every country'. It described Physiocracy as essentially a reaction to Colbertism, the French form of mercantilism.

The chapter then carefully explained the Physiocratic three-class structure, together with the role assigned to each class in their economic system. Proprietors, or landlords, were responsible for expenditure (*dépenses foncières*) to improve the land (such as buildings, drains, fences) which indirectly contribute to greater output, a share of which goes to the landlords in the form of a higher rent. The farmers, or cultivators, called the 'productive workers' by the Physiocrats, contribute both 'original' and 'annual' expenses for cultivating the land. Original expenses are their fixed capital contributions, including farm equipment; cattle and seed, and wear and tear on their capital, together with their subsistence, comprise the annual expenses of this class. The product at the time of the harvest should be sufficient, Smith added, to reproduce the whole of the annual expense together with profits calculated at the ordinary rate. These are the absolutely essential expenses of cultivation, which cannot be encroached upon. The remaining agricultural produce goes to the landlords as their rent (net product).

The third Physiocratic class is the unproductive, or sterile, class consisting of 'artificers', manufacturers and merchants. Their labour replaces the 'stock' which employs them without a surplus, that is, it reproduces wages, materials and tools used in their work together with their profits calculated at an annual rate. Mercantile stock is considered by the Physiocrats to be equally barren and unproductive. The opportunity of these unproductive classes for adding to national wealth can come only from 'parsimony' or their saving. Merchants, manufacturers and artisans are therefore maintained by the other two classes of society, that is, by the cultivators and landlords, in return for the useful services they provide for them. Hence, there is a mutual dependence of the three classes, and it pays none of them to oppress the others. All classes of society secure the highest prosperity when they are in 'perfect liberty' including 'perfect freedom of trade' for their merchants and manufacturers.

Smith concluded that such perfect liberty likewise stimulated industry from the unproductive classes, thereby raising surplus produce He added that oppressing such trade is contrary to agricultural interests. It raises the price of manufactures, together with more profit, and thereby discourages agricultural production.

Smith discussed the distribution of the annual produce of the land by means of Quesnay's analysis in the *Tableau économique*. This indicated the transactions summarized in the two previous paragraphs and led to Smith's observation that:

> some speculative physicians seem to have imagined that the health of the human body could be preserved only by a certain precise regimen of diet and exercise . . . [and that Quesnay] entertained a notion of the same kind concerning the political body, and to have imagined that it would thrive and prosper only under a certain precise regimen, the exact regimen of perfect liberty and perfect justice. (Smith, 1976 [1776], pp. 673–4)

Smith then identified the Physiocratic system's 'capital error' as 'representing the class of artificers, manufacturers and merchants, as altogether barren and unproductive' (Smith, 1976 [1776], p. 674), demonstrating the validity of his critique by no less than five separate points (Smith, 1976 [1776], 674–8). Despite these errors, Smith described the system of the Physiocrats as 'perhaps the nearest approximation to the truth that has yet been published upon the subject of Political Economy' (Smith, 1976 [1776], p. 678).

Smith then named the Physiocratic 'sect's' major writers as Quesnay, Mercier de la Rivière and Mirabeau, quoting the last's extravagant claim that the three greatest inventions in the history of mankind, were 'writing', 'money' and the '*Tableau économique*' (Smith, 1976 [1776], p. 679). The remainder of the chapter provides an overview of the political economies of modern European nations, indicating that these are far more favourable to manufacturing and commerce than Physiocracy proposed, and that only China, and to a lesser extent ancient Egypt and Indostan, appeared to have been particularly 'attentive' to the 'interests of agriculture' (Smith, 1976 [1776], pp. 679–81). The ancient Greeks and Romans discouraged employment in trade and manufacturing without especially encouraging agriculture (Smith, 1976 [1776], pp. 683–4). A digression on slavery and on some historical examples of luxury consumption items leads to the concluding part of Smith's chapter on the agricultural system. This ends with a restatement of the Physiocrats' basic error, their failure to realize that encouraging trade between town and country is the best way to encourage agriculture. More generally, Smith posited, let capital move freely to its preferred sector, allow people to pursue their self-interest without restraint, and provide the necessary social infrastructure of good government, justice and essential public works, in order to encourage the national increase of wealth (Smith, 1976 [1776], pp. 687–8). Smith's main discussion of the Phyiocrats provides a sympathetic, but highly critical, account of their major doctrines.

Other parts of the *Wealth of Nations* fill in gaps of this account, or reiterate certain points. Most important of these gaps is Smith's critical discussion of Physiocratic tax incidence analysis, in which the burden of every tax is said by them to fall ultimately on the rent (net product) of the landlord. Smith noted that they therefore regarded land tax as the most equitable of taxes, but that their doctrine proclaiming that the incidence of all taxes falls ultimately on the land was erroneous (Smith, 1976 [1776], p. 830). Likewise, their doctrine that all taxation should be levied directly on the net product of land was regarded as practically impossible, because aggregate rents in a nation, even in an agricultural nation, are invariably less than the tax revenue requirements of the government (Smith, 1976 [1776], pp. 822–3).

Throughout the text, Smith drew attention to various other aspects of Physiocratic thought, often indirectly. Thus cattle are treated by Smith as part of fixed capital (Smith, 1976 [1776], p. 280); the importance of the distinction between productive and unproductive labour is discussed by Smith on different lines, as is his analysis of the circulation of capitals (Smith, 1976 [1776], pp. 330–31, 364–6).

It may be noted in this context that Turgot's work is never directly mentioned by Smith in his *Wealth of Nations*, even if, as shown in the next section, there are strong possibilities that Turgot's work, in particular his *Reflections on the Production and Distribution of Wealth* (1977 [1766]), may have influenced Smith on some points.

The Physiocrats' and Turgot's economic writings as authorities in the writing of the *Wealth of Nations*
The list of authorities included in the bicentennial edition of the *Wealth of Nations* (1976 [1776], pp. 1009–18) mentions a number of physiocratic texts. As shown in the previous section, Smith referred directly to Quesnay's *Tableau économique* without indicating which edition of this text he was using, as well as to two other major Physiocratic texts, Mercier de la Rivière's *L'ordre naturel et essential des sociétés politiques* (1767), and Miraubeau's *Philosophie rurale* (Smith, 1976 [1776], pp. 672, 679, 689). All of these also appear to have been in his library, together with some work by Du Pont de Nemours, including his edition of *Physiocratie* containing a collection of Quesnay's major Physiocratic essays; two other major books by Mirabeau (*Théorie de l'impôt* and *L'Ami des Hommes*) and a work by Le Trosne. Smith's library also appears to have held at least some of Turgot's work since he owned a three-year run (1766–69) of the *Ephémérides du Citoyen* in which the first two parts of Turgot's *Réflexions* were published (that is, the first 71 paragraphs, therefore up to and including § LXXI on 'the fifth employment of capital' (see Groenewegen, 1968 [2002], esp. pp. 383, 384).

Following Cannan (1937, pp. xxxviii–xxxix), Smith's direct indebtedness to the Physiocrats appears to have been confined to four items. In Cannan's own words, these can be enumerated as follows:

> The introduction of the theory of stock or capital and unproductive labour in Book II, the slipping of a theory of distribution into the theory of prices towards the end of Book I, chapter vi, and the emphasizing of the conception of annual produce. These ... do not make so much real difference to Smith's own work as might be supposed; the theory of distribution, though it appears in the title of Book I, is no essential part of the work and could easily be excised by deleting a few paragraphs in Book I, chapter vi, and a few lines elsewhere; if Book II were altogether omitted the other Books could stand perfectly well by themselves. But to subsequent economics, they were of fundamental importance. They settled the form of economic treatises for a century at least.

On the basis of comparing the contents of the *Wealth of Nations* with that of the then available text of the *Lectures on Jurisprudence*, Cannan argued that Smith's frequent emphasis on 'annual produce', his explicit description of his theories of wages, profits and rent (Book I, Chapters 8–11) as a 'theory of distribution' in the title of that book, and his discussion of a theory of capital, and of productive and unproductive labour in Book II (Chapters 1, 3 and 5) were directly attributable to Smith's acquaintance with the works and ideas of the Physiocrats. Although it is possible to argue over details (I myself doubt for example that leaving out Book II of the *Wealth of Nations* would leave no serious gap in the argument, as Cannan suggests in the remarks quoted above), Cannan's identification of these four aspects of Smith's work as derived from the Physiocrats still seems to stand up well as consistent with the evidence. This includes Cannan's concluding sentence and historical assessment of the importance of these influenced items after Smith, because terminologically these aspects became well-used parts of the language of British classical economics. In short, the Physiocrats considerably enriched Smith's economic vocabulary together with some aspects of his economic analysis, both a language and an analysis which Smith bequeathed to later generations of British economists. Smith did this despite his critical approach to Physiocratic doctrine as a whole (examined in the previous section) which, as explained there, was also highly sympathetic in acknowledging the skills with which the Physiocratic system was constructed. Even then, of the four items of economic vocabulary in question, that on productive and unproductive labour was very significantly altered in meaning in Smith's account of the matter.

The issue of Smith's possible indebtedness to Turgot's economics needs to be separated from that of the limited Physiocratic influence on his work. It has already been indicated that Turgot and Smith met each other in Paris on several occasions during 1766, the year Turgot wrote his major economic text, *Reflections on the Formation and Distribution of Wealth*. Furthermore, as mentioned at the start of this section, Smith's library included a little more than two-thirds of the text of Turgot's *Reflections* as published in three parts in the *Ephémérides du Citoyen*. A detailed study of Smith's association with Turgot (Groenewegen, 1969 [2002]) identified five specific matters on which similarity in their text may suggest the possibility of influence by Turgot on Smith. The most important of these similarities relates to the phrase, 'the various employments of capital', unusual terminology at the time, and used both by Turgot in his *Reflections* and by Smith in the *Wealth of Nations*. The relevant passages are as follows:

> A capital may be employed in four different ways: either, first, in producing the rude product annually required for the use and consumption of the society; or, secondly, in manufacturing and preparing that rude produce for immediate use and consumption; or, thirdly, in transporting either the rude or manufactured produce from the places where they abound to those where they are wanted; or, lastly, in dividing particular portions of either into such small parcels as suit the occasional demands of those who want them. In the first way are employed the capitals of all those who undertake the improvement or cultivation of lands, mines, or fisheries; in the second, those of all master manufacturers; in the third, those of all wholesale merchants, and in the fourth, those of retailers. (Smith, 1976 [1776], p. 360)
>
> I have reckoned five different methods of employing capitals or of profitably investing them. The first is to buy a landed estate ... The second is to invest one's money in agricultural undertakings ... the third is to invest one's capital in industrial or manufacturing undertakings, the fourth is to invest it in commercial undertakings, and the fifth to lend it to those who want it, in return for an annual interest. (Turgot, 1977 [1766], § 83, p. 85)

Although it should be recalled that § 83 of Turgot's *Reflections* was not part of the holdings of the *Ephémérides* in Smith's library, the terminology and individual mention of each of the five employments, were so included (in §§ 58, 59, 62, 66, 71). From that perspective, there is no impediment to suggesting that in this instance the use of the phrase, 'employment of capitals' together with the various examples of it given, is a case where Smith may have been specifically indebted to Turgot's language and terminology. Moreover, it should be pointed out that these passages are not only similar because they use the peculiar, and new, terminology of 'employment of capitals', but also because their classification of the various capital employments, which at first sight seems different, is fundamentally the same. The five employments of capital listed by Turgot are easily reconciled with those mentioned by Adam Smith.

Two paragraphs previous to the passage just quoted from Smith on the subject – but in another chapter – Smith (1976 [1776], pp. 358–9) mentioned two additional employments of capital, that is, buying land and lending at interest, which replicate Turgot's first and fifth employments exactly. Furthermore, in Turgot's discussion of his fourth employment of capital, that is, 'investing it in commercial undertakings', he clearly distinguished between 'wholesale merchants' and 'retailers' – Smith's third and fourth employments. Turgot grouped them together because they both 'buy to sell again' (Turgot, 1977 [1766], § 67, pp. 74–5; the passage is quoted in italics in the original).

It is also not difficult to demonstrate (see Groenewegen, 1969 [2002], pp. 370–73) that there are strong similarities between Smith and Turgot's economic systems as a whole, explicable in terms of the common sources on which they both drew. Part of this relevant common heritage came from Quesnay's work, influential in spurring Turgot to develop his own, much broader approach to the subject, but there were plenty of other economic writers, both French and British, who inspired them both. Finally, it may be noted that Smith and Turgot appear to have admired each other as persons, and not only for each other's work, an important aspect of their relationship which should not be forgotten.

Conclusion

This chapter has reiterated that Smith owed a significant, but not overwhelming, intellectual debt to the Physiocrats and Turgot. It was significant with respect to language, in connection with the phrases 'distribution', 'productive and unproductive labour', and the emphasis on 'annual produce'. It was more than significant in the context of capital, including the use of the phrase, 'employments of capitals', which illuminated a crucial part of Smith's economic system. After all, the argument of Book II of Smith's *Wealth of Nations* discusses the second major cause of the wealth of nations, that is, the accumulation of capital; the first cause, the effect of the division of labour on productivity, was dealt with at the start of its Book I.

References

Cannan, Edwin (1937), 'Introduction', to Adam Smith, *An Inquiry into the Nature and Causes of the Wealth of Nations*, New York: Modern Library edition.

Groenewegen, Peter (1968), 'A new catalogue of Adam Smith's library', *Economic Record*, **44** (108), 498–506; reprinted in Peter Groenewegen (2002), *Eighteenth Century Economics*, London: Routledge, pp. 379–87.

Groenewegen, Peter (1969), 'Turgot and Adam Smith', *Scottish Journal of Political Economy*, **16** (3), 271–87; reprinted in Peter Groenewegen (2002), *Eighteenth Century Economics*, London: Routledge, pp. 363–78.

Skinner, Andrew (1999), 'Adam Smith and Physiocracy', in Roger E. Backhouse and John Creedy (eds), *From Classical Economics to the Theory of the Firm: Essays in Honour of D.P. O'Brien*, Cheltenham, UK and Northampton, MA, USA: Edward Elgar, pp. 104–19.

Smith, Adam (1976 [1776]), *An Inquiry into the Nature and Causes of the Wealth of Nations*, R.H. Campbell and A.S. Skinner (eds), Oxford: Clarendon Press.

Stewart, Dugald (1980), 'Account of the life and writing of Adam Smith', I.S. Ross (ed), in W.P.D. Wightman and J.C. Bryce (eds), *Essays on Philosophical Subjects*, Oxford: Oxford University Press, pp. 269–332.

Turgot, A.R.J. (1977 [1766]), *Reflections on the Formation and Distribution of Wealth*, in Peter Groenewegen (ed.), *The Economics of A.R.J. Turgot*, The Hague: Martinus Nijhoff.

8 Wants versus needs: a Smithian model of general equilibrium
*Amos Witztum**

Introduction

The importance of general equilibrium in promoting the institutions of competition cannot be overstated. Together with the first and second welfare theorems it provides both the logical underpinning and an ethical justification for a market-based organization of social interaction.[1] In the eyes of many, this is the culmination of the intellectual efforts which went into the study of decentralized decision-making, specialization and economic interdependence since the days of Adam Smith.[2] By implication, it is also suggested that classical and neoclassical economics seem to share a common research agenda. Indeed, in spite of the clear neoclassical nature of general equilibrium theory, it is always Smith's 'invisible hand' metaphor which is used to provide the ethos behind it.

However, there is plenty of evidence to suggest that classical economists in general, and Smith in particular, were not as enthusiastic as one would expect about the working of natural liberty. While Smith clearly considered a system of decentralized decision making as superior to mercantilism, he was far from sure about the generality of its beneficence. Apart from the long-term degrading effects of intense division of labour (see the Rosenberg, 1990 and West, 1996 debate), there are the more immediate questions concerning the actual outcomes of competitive interaction. According to Smith, these may indeed include progress, but equally there are the possibilities for stagnation or regression.[3]

Many Smith scholars – who are rightly keen to emphasize the differences between Smith and modern economics – find the dealing with general equilibrium particularly difficult. It is as if the mere suggestion that there might be some form of general equilibrium in Adam Smith immediately implies that Smith was merely a precursor of modern economics. But in so doing they both overlook Smith's text and refuse to subject it to any kind of analytical scrutiny. They seem to condemn all forms of analytical reconstruction as 'Whiggism'. However, if this were true it would have meant that logic itself is time dependent and what logically holds true today is not the same as what would have been logically true in the past. Moreover, if indeed Smith's theory is original and different from what followed, why should it be denied the possibility of being developed and better understood? Naturally, developing his theory would possibly go beyond what he thought himself, but is it not part of our duties as economists (rather than historians) to explore all the insights which are buried in the complexity of the system Smith proposed?

It is, of course, right that when one uses modern economic constructs (like, say, the rational utility maximizer, or, the firm) to represent Smith's analysis, one is committing a 'Whiggish' act. But the mere use of mathematics, as a logical instrument, should be welcomed by anyone who has a broader interest in the history of economics than merely to uncover the historical details about those individuals who proposed theories in the past. Indeed, this really raises the question of whether the history of economic analysis should be focused more on the history of individuals or the history of theories.[4]

Whichever way we look at it, the fact remains that irrespective of what Smith considered the economics problem to be and what is the modern conception of it, both theories are about interdependence among individual members of society. As such, the problem of coordination lies at the heart of such a system. Naturally, this does not mean that coordination would necessarily come through the markets, or prices, nor does it have to be contemporaneous.

Equally, the notion of 'general equilibrium' – broadly conceived – is not a construct of neoclassical economics. It is simply a framework for the analysis of the coordinated actions of a complex machine. Moreover even Walrasian general equilibrium – the modern economic construct of general equilibrium – is not really a description of the economy, as it is a logical test of its coherence. No serious economist would claim that Walrasian general equilibrium describes the state of markets at any point in time. Or, for that matter, that it explains how the markets operate. Instead, it is a simple logical test where we investigate whether the neoclassical system leads, in principle, to a coordinated outcome. The test is conducted at the limit where the model is at its most abstract. It is therefore much detached from the work of anyone who wishes to describe the modern economy.

However, it is obvious that had there not been a proof of the existence of general equilibrium, the ability of economist to persuade themselves as well as others that a system of decentralized decision-making works would have been considerably diminished. In fact, to a great extent, the agenda of modern economics can be defined as the search for structures and institutions that would asymptotically bring us to the promised benefits of our coordinated actions.

Equally, it is quite true that as Blaug (1999, 2003, 2007), Hutchison (1999) and others claim, Smith's description of the economy does not resemble a model of general equilibrium. It certainly does not resemble any Walrasian notion of general equilibrium. Yet, Smith too could not have advocated any form of natural liberty had he not believed that such a system works. Given that his is also a system of interdependence, the only way such a system can work is through some form of coordination. Otherwise, it would mean that some individuals would never get what they wanted and would work against it.

Elsewhere (Witztum, 2010) I have written at length a defence of why the notion of general equilibrium is as relevant to Smith's economics as it is to modern economics. There, I follow Smith's textual description of how commercial societies develop and how interdependence becomes so important. I also provide textual support for the existence of two notions of 'general equilibrium'. One is the coordinating power of the 'invisible hand' of *The Theory of Moral Sentiments* (TMS), which ensures that by specializing (in order to better one's condition) we do not take a risk of losing our subsistence. The other is the coordinating power of the market, which in Smith's case does not always work. The analysis in that paper is focused on the exchange between equal individuals. However, as I argued elsewhere (Witztum, 2005), the position of individuals in Smith's analysis may not be symmetrical when they come to the market. In part, the purpose of this chapter is to expand on this extension.

The fact that in Smith we can find equilibria where coordination fails, suggests that the claim according to which one cannot apply general equilibrium to Smith because general equilibrium implies efficiency (see, for instance, Baumol and Wilson, 2001) does not really hold.

In fact, such a claim is mistaken even in modern economics but the reasons for the failure of coordinated actions in modern economics are very different from the Smithian ones. In modern economics, these are all forms of market failures, but in Smith, there is no need for market failure for the coordinated outcome to be deemed a failure. I did not discuss the reasons for the failure of coordinated actions in my previous paper on interdependence in Smith (Witztum, 2010) and the purpose of this chapter is to do just that.

Between modern and Smithian general equilibrium
One of the reasons why objections are raised against the application of notions of general equilibrium to Smith is that in Smith's system the effects of competition are not necessarily desirable. As I said before, there is the problem of the degrading effect of enhanced division of labour as well as the prospects of stagnation and regression as potential outcomes of natural liberty. Modern general equilibrium, on the other hand, seems to be associated with the success of competitive practices, that is, with efficiency.

On the face of it, this may seem to be a problem based on the distinction between dynamic and static analysis. The Walrasian notion of general equilibrium appears as a static model of contemporaneous simultaneity,[5] the Smithian model – with a clear time dimension in the production process – seems nothing like it. Consequently, the merits of a Walrasian equilibrium are not directly related to its dynamic consequences[6] whereas in Smith's analysis it is these consequences which are not directly linked to the existence of general equilibrium.[7] However, some may argue, the fact that each school of thought concentrated on a different aspect of economic organization does not mean that they are not two sides of the same coin.

Nevertheless, in spite of the growing current interest in growth theory we must bear in mind that the economic problem embedded in the core of neoclassical analysis is the problem of reconciling insatiable wants with scarcity. Even in an intertemporal context, the issue is not growth as such but rather the coincidence of wants when preferences are a priori defined over consumption at different points in time. As such it is in essence a static problem, and what the Walrasian notion of general equilibrium does is to demonstrate that a system of decentralized decision making comprised of rational agents can work in the sense that all rational plans (that is, wants) coincide, and that through trade no one is made worse off and at least someone is made clearly better off. The ongoing debate on the importance of income distribution to questions like growth has not really connected the problem of coordination with its dynamic consequences. Most of it is conducted within the boundaries of the first and second welfare theorems,[8] which means that we do not really question the ability of competitive institutions to bring about coincidence of wants and, which is even more important, we see in the coincidence of wants a necessary condition for whatever it is society may wish to achieve. Put differently, at stake are not the institutions of competition, only the allocations to which they give rise.

When we consider the more serious difficulties such as the problem of incomplete markets, it becomes even more evident that at the heart of neoclassical economics is the coincidence of wants. The inefficiency of incomplete markets is entirely based on the incompatibilities of wants in a world where wants are defined across states of nature. The implications of this problem for the concept of allocative efficiency have not fully been recognized. If in a world of uncertainty rational plans fail to coincide and if we cannot design a mechanism that will correct it, is the coincidence of wants something we should strive to achieve? Does the coincidence of wants really matter so much as to raise doubts over the functioning of one of the most competitive forms of economic organization: financial markets? If, on the other hand, we choose to reject the view of rationality where preferences are defined across states of nature, we may find it very difficult to sustain our belief in the meaning of allocative efficiency altogether.

The coincidence of wants as the prime object of social organization is a sustained agenda in neoclassical analysis for two main reasons. First, as wants and needs are indistinguishable, the coincidence of the former will take care of the latter. Of course, it is not the mere coincidence of wants which guarantees the satisfaction of needs as the set of Pareto-efficient allocations may include distributions where some agents have not fully satisfied their needs.[9] Instead, it is the notion that for any given initial position, coincidence of wants (if there is trade) will always provide universal improvement, and even if needs have not been fully satisfied, coincidence of wants will always bring us nearer to that point. Similarly, whenever needs have already been fully satisfied, coincidence of wants will always preserve that level of satisfaction.

The second reason why coincidence of wants is a sustainable objective in the debate on social organization is that it expresses the idea of individual sovereignty. As long as there is a single agent in the economy who feels that his, or her, rational plans have not materialized, the economy will not reach equilibrium. By implication, the existence of equilibrium and the coincidence of wants also mean that everyone accepts the outcome and is equally responsible for it. Hence, the predicament of any individual cannot be traced to the action, or will, of anyone else.

To argue that Smith's economics and neoclassical economics are manifestations of the same research agenda one would need to demonstrate that in Smith's system, coincidence of wants is as universally beneficial as it is in neoclassical analysis. One would also need to demonstrate that agents are equally sovereign and that responsibility for outcomes cannot be established. In what follows I will endeavour to show that this is not the case. I will argue that while it is true that interdependence is a fundamental feature in classical economics, coincidence of wants is not necessarily an ideal for social organization.

The economic problem of classical economics is that of output maximization and growth: 'to provide a plentiful revenue or subsistence for the people' (*Wealth of Nations*: WN IV.1). 'According therefore, as this produce . . . bears greater or smaller proportion to the number of those who are to consume it, the nation will be better or worse supplied with all the necessities and conveniences for which it has occasion' (WN Introduction and Plan of Work 2). Evidently, the test of a proposed system which resolves this economic problem cannot be the mere coincidence of wants. Instead, the test must be the ability of it to generate that plentiful of revenues.

Nevertheless, the notion of interdependence and the subsequent problem of coordination are very much part of the economic problem confronting Smith's economics. Unlike Walras, Smith's more empirically oriented epistemology does not direct him to seek the genus of value as the foundation upon which to construct his theory.[10] Instead, the principle upon which Smith's analysis is based is a behavioural-evolutionary one: the propensity to barter and exchange. It is this disposition which, over time, brought about the division of labour.[11] This division of labour – a natural feature of human behaviour – is on the one hand the origin of growth and on the other the essence of interdependence. But while this means that interdependence is essential for growth, does it also mean that coincidence of wants constitutes an important part of it? This is far from obvious.

According to Smith, the provision of wealth depends on 'the skill, dexterity, and judgement with which . . . labour is generally applied; and . . . [on] the proportion between the number of those who are employed in useful labour, and that of those who are not so employed' (WN Introduction 3). This means that there are two major issues in the organization of society which affect the provision of wealth: productivity of labour and savings. The two are not unrelated.

The productive powers of labour are a function of the wages of those productively employed (WN I.viii.44) as well as improvements in other means of production (WN II.iii.32). These, in turn, depend on the decisions made by the owners of what had been produced with regard to how much is directed to luxurious consumption (unproductive labour) and how much will be devoted to reproduction and growth. Put differently, the essence of growth lies in the proper use of the surplus; that produce which is above what is required for reproduction.

The proper, or improper, use of the surplus upon which growth depends is a subject of what some would call 'rational' behaviour. Rationality, or prudence, in classical economics is basically embedded in the wish to 'better our condition'. This is not at all the same as the more static notion of satisfying our wants. As I mentioned earlier, the introduction of time and uncertainty in modern general equilibrium theory have done very little to alter this static notion of rational behaviour. In the simplest form, the fact that our utility is defined over consumption at different points in time does not imply that we want to 'improve' our condition in the second, or third period. Quite to the contrary, by expanding Walrasian equilibrium into time and uncertainty we have completely trivialized rational behaviour by having some form of a priori preferences over time (and across states). This means that it is equally rational to want to have a good time in the present and a bad time in the future, as it is to want to 'improve our condition'.

But there is a very good reason why a Walrasian notion of general equilibrium is unaffected by the kind of preference which individuals have. It is the implied symmetry in the position of agents in the system. By symmetry I mean that all agents, in a Walrasian model, play all roles in the economic process. They are all consumers as well as suppliers, owners as well as workers. In contrast, in classical economics there is no such symmetry. There are two reasons for it. First, in the classical model there is a clearer association between individuals and their role in the economic process. Hence, the agents in the classical model are clearly named as either labourers, capitalists or landlords. The influence which each group of agents has on the system is very different indeed. Leaving the landlords aside we find that wages affect the behaviour of the labourers who create the surplus (hence, profit). In turn, the decision which the capitalists (and landlords) take with regard to the use of this surplus will affect wages and the productive powers of labour. On the face of it this may appear as symmetry: each group of agents affects the other one. Nevertheless, even if we said nothing more this is still a very different kind of symmetry from a situation where no one affects anyone.

However, this is not really asymmetry. When the capitalists decide on the wage fund, it is together with the number of workers that the wage level will be determined. While it is true that the number of workers is a decision variable of the workers (that is, whether or not they propagate), it cannot be considered an equivalent to the much more immediate decision regarding the use of one's surplus. Equally, when we say that the actions of workers determine surplus (and profit) this is not the whole story. How successful the workers are will depend on the provision of capital too. The latter is again a decision parameter of the capitalists. So we have a slightly one-sided mechanism to determine wages and a combined mechanism to determine surplus. Even without going into details it is fairly obvious that this is far from symmetry.

But there is the second reason why there is asymmetry in the Smithian model. Even if workers and capitalists were considered as equal in terms of their ability to influence the outcome of the system (that is, growth), the way by which Smith describes their behaviour suggests that there is a fundamental difference between the way in which capitalists decide about their surplus, and how workers respond to their wages. I have discussed this point elsewhere (see Witztum, 2005) and I will only say that while capitalists decide between savings (accumulation) and luxurious consumption, workers seem to be acting more by custom. Whenever wages are above subsidence they propagate (instead of save).[12] Obviously this does not mean that workers are uninterested in improving their conditions. But the fact that the means by which they propose to obtain it are so different presents an asymmetry which cannot be ignored. Indeed, it is in this asymmetry where the interesting relationship between coincidence of wants and growth become significant.

In Smith's *Theory of Moral Sentiments* we come across the 'invisible hand' for the first time. This invisible hand is quite different from the one so frequently quoted from the *Wealth of Nations* (WN). The original invisible hand is basically a trickle-down theory.[13] It represents Smith's view that the introduction of private ownership will not affect the distribution of life's necessities. The reason for it is simply that the stomach of the rich is not greater than that of the poor. Hence, rich people will use the surplus to buy services through which they will pass subsistence to everyone in society. If we consider subsistence to be the equivalent of needs, then according to Smith, as long as capitalists behave rationally (in the sense that they will not destroy their surplus), the needs in society will be satisfied. However, while this is true from a static point of view, Smith is still considering the possibilities of regression. Namely, situations where the fund available for productive workers is diminishing. In such a case, while initially all workers will get their subsistence (some by moving from productive to unproductive labour), in the next period there will be a smaller surplus. In this case, some workers will not be able to get their subsistence. The meaning of it is that the wants of the capitalists (which allocated the surplus between savings and luxurious consumption) will influence the provision of needs for the workers. Put differently, the coincidence of the wants of some people may affect the provision of needs for the others. This is a feature which is clearly missing from the Walrasian notion of general equilibrium.[14] It should be of interest to us because, conceptually, it seems to be much more relevant to today's problem than the Walrasian idea of symmetry.

In the next section I will set out my choice of model against the background of what has already been done in the field. Evidently, as at the heart of my analysis lies an asymmetry between agents, none of the models which have so far been used to model general equilibrium in classical economics will be suitable for the purpose.

Within the framework I chose I will first of all point out the possibility of equilibria points where in spite of possible coincidence of wants, the needs of workers may not be sustained for a long enough period and subsequently, growth too will be eroded. I call such circumstances a situation without beneficence.

In the following sections I discuss the structure of demand and the subsequent coincidence of wants. I propose that the distinction between needs and wants will manifest itself through a difference in how responsive is one's demand to changes in prices. I will follow here Smith's own discussion of 'effective demand' and market price equilibrium. It will be shown that an intriguing 'dilemma' emerges where 'bettering one's own condition' may have adverse effects on the ability of others to satisfy their needs.

The model

Generally speaking there were two approaches to the modelling of general equilibrium in classical economics. One approach is more neoclassical in nature and it takes the form of growth models with diminishing marginal productivity of land.[15] The focus of analysis in these types of models is the relative shares of wages and profits and their development over time. However, once a multisectoral analysis is introduced, everything becomes so complex to a degree of indeterminacy.[16]

The other type of approach is a more Sraffian one in the sense that the focus of analysis is the interdependence in production and its implications for the theory of value. On the face of it this seems an ideal setting to bring together the theory of value (and the solution to the problem of interdependence) and the theory of distribution and growth.[17] However, there are two problems with such an approach. Firstly, while it may produce a relationship between coordination and growth (through the rate of profit), the determinants of these parameters are technological in nature and are therefore not suitable to capture a theory where growth is the most important problem. Secondly, in such a system there exists a very peculiar relationship between agents (and subsequently, between distribution variables). The rate of profits (as well as growth) is determined, among other things, by wages. These, however, are determined by previous decisions made by the capitalists with regard to the wage fund. These decisions, and their coincidence, fall outside the domain of a Sraffian-type model of classical general equilibrium. Instead of coincidence of wants, we end up with a system which relates the coincidence of needs (in production and subsistence) with the rate of growth. This, of course, could be interesting in itself if we believed that the coincidence of wants has no bearing on the coincidence of needs.

Perlman (1994) offers a third approach which is nearest to the neoclassical model in that it ascribes symmetry to the agents' position in the economy. In his model, everyone's decision is equally dependent on price. Put differently, all is in the domain of wants and there is no meaningful distinction between the two. Consequently, it is not surprising that he reaches the conclusion that the wage-fund doctrine is inconsistent with other aspects of classical economics like full employment and the uniform rate of profit.

Many draw lines between classical economics and neoclassical economics by comparing the idea of a uniform rate of profit with the working of the Walrasian entrepreneur. There are two problems with this approach. Firstly, although many classical economists argued that the rate of profit will tend to uniformity, this is not the same as saying that it will be uniform. Both Smith and Mill discuss at some length the reasons for differential rates of profit. Secondly, as will be demonstrated below, there is no unique allocation associated with any particular price. Consequently, while a price which corresponds to the natural price may emerge, it may not reflect the highest rate of growth.

I will now proceed to propose a model of Smith's economics set in a general equilibrium framework. It is a model which is distinct from all previous expositions of general equilibrium in classical economics. In it, we shall see how the existence of equilibrium (that is, coincidence of wants) can be associated with serious failures in resolving the economic problem. We will see that with the more complex structures of human behaviour, curious dilemmas may arise. Notably, we shall demonstrate how market signals could lead agents to act in such a way that will endanger the beneficence of the system of natural liberty.

The model suggested here is based on Smith's observation that the heart of the economic system is the creation of surplus, and its exchange. This assertion is very simply derived from the meaning of the division of labour, which is the consequence of the propensity to barter and exchange:

> When the division of labour has been once thoroughly established, it is but a very small part of man's wants which the produce of his own labour can supply. He supplies the far greater part of them by exchanging that surplus part of the produce of his own labour, which is over and above his own consumption, for such parts of the produce of other men's labour as he has occasion for. (WN I.iv.1)[18]

The main characteristics of my model are that it is a two-sector model where commodities are produced by means of other commodities,[19] that it is a general equilibrium framework, and that it is a surplus approach. For simplicity's sake, I will drop rents from my analysis, and also I will ignore that which Smith called fixed capital. This is a model in real terms. Therefore prices will be measured in terms of other commodities: 'Every commodity besides, is more frequently exchanged for, and thereby compared with, other commodities than labour. It is more natural, therefore, to estimate the exchangeable value by the quantity of some other commodity than by that of the labour which it can purchase' (WN I.v.5).

Thus we are to construct an economy in which surpluses are exchanged and prices are measured in real terms. From the technological side we may follow the tradition of fixed proportions production processes. It is, however, important to note that the degree of the division of labour, which actually gives us the technological coefficients, depends not only on the extent of the market but also, and more importantly, on the accumulation of capital. Hence, if we are to say anything in the long run we must incorporate this feature of Smith's economy. However, the two-sector model will enable us to say something about the long run without incorporating an explicit relationship between capital accumulation and the technological coefficients. Quite a lot will depend on the relative dependence of each sector on the other, and this in turn does not have to change even when a greater division of labour affects the technological coefficients.

Let there be a two-sector closed economy where C, corn, represents the agricultural sector and I (iron) represents industry. A is the technology matrix as follows:

$$A = \begin{bmatrix} a_{cc} & a_{cI} \\ a_{Ic} & a_{II} \end{bmatrix}$$

A Smithian model of general equilibrium 149

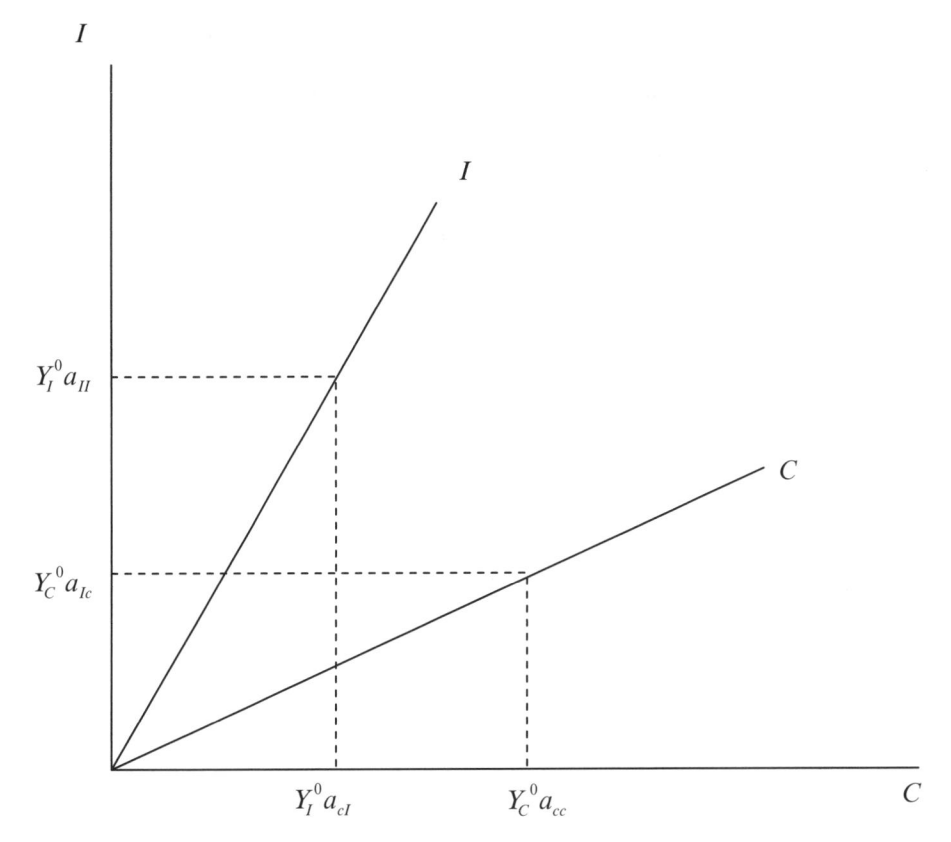

Figure 8.1 Technological set-up

where a_{ij} is the amount of commodity i required for the production of one unit of commodity j. A is productive. (That is, there is a vector x*, x* > 0, so that Ax* < x*, namely, that the total output in each sector is greater than the amount of it required for inputs.)

Figure 8.1 depicts the technology in the plane of the different levels of input, where Y_c^0 and Y_I^0 are the total (gross) outputs of each of the sectors.

The C and I rays depict the levels of input required for each level of gross output. Hence to produce Y_c^0 of C we need $Y_c^0 a_{cc}$ units of C and $Y_c^0 a_{Ic}$ units of I. In Smith's terminology, $Y_c^0 a_{cc}$ and $Y_c^0 a_{Ic}$ may be considered as the circulating capital of C. a_{cc} represents the amount of corn (or agricultural product as a whole) needed for the production of one unit of corn. This amount consists of materials (that is, the amount of seeds needed for the production of one unit of corn), as well as the amount of corn needed for the subsistence of the amount of labour required to turn those seeds into a unit of output. In the same manner, we can generalize with regard to all the coefficients. Iron here does not represent fixed capital but rather a kind of industrial output, which is consumed in the process of production of both iron and corn. This is indeed the way Smith regarded circulating capital: 'The circulating capital consists in this manner, of the provisions, materials, and finished work of all kinds' (WN II.i.22).

The circulating capital is in fact part of the total stock from which the capitalist will provide material and subsistence for his workers during the period of production. Surely, he will provide for himself as well as for his workers during the same period.[20] We may regard that part of his consumption which is at the level of his own subsistence, as part of that circulating capital which is represented by a_{cc}.

Obviously, every choice of inputs that is not depicted by the 'gross production' lines reflects inefficiency. The question, however, is what can we say about the choice of combinations between C and I. As the two sectors are interdependent, there must be some correlation between what is produced in one and what can be produced in the other. We may describe this interdependence by the following inequalities:

$$Y_c a_{cc} + Y_I a_{cI} \leq Y_c$$

$$Y_c a_{Ic} + Y_I a_{II} \leq Y_I$$

which also mean that:

$$Y_I a_{cI} \leq (1 - a_{cc}) Y_c$$

$$Y_c a_{Ic} \leq (1 - a_{II}) Y_I$$

The meaning of these inequalities is that the amount of one's sector product required by the other sector for reproduction cannot exceed what is left in that sector after what is needed for its own reproduction has been deducted.[21]

The right-hand expressions reflect what I shall call the 'own surplus' of the industries. They are depicted in Figure 8.2.

C^* and I^* are the lines of the 'own surplus'. At point A the two sectors produce $Y_i^0 i = C, I$. We shall measure their relative position by the input of their own product (the coordinates of A are $Y_c^0 a_{cc}$ and $Y_I^0 a_{II}$).

Point B depicts the 'own surplus' produced in that state. In order to continue and produce the same level of output sector I will need $Y_I^0 a_{cI}$ of C and sector C will need $Y_c^0 a_{Ic}$ of I. From the point of view of the economy as a whole the 'real net' is only that which is above what is needed for the reproduction of both industries. We can denote this 'real net' as:

$$NS^c = Y_c(1 - a_{cc}) - Y_I a_{cI}$$

$$NS^I = Y_I(1 - a_{II}) - Y_c a_{Ic}$$

where NS is the 'net surplus'.

The conditions for economic viability of the system are exactly that the above expressions will be positive. If one of the sectors produces no net surplus, there would be enough of this sector's output to reproduce the same level of output in both sectors but there would be no growth. It is, thus, a stationary state and according to Smith: 'The progressive state is in reality the cheerful and hearty state to all different orders of society. The stationary is dull; the declining, melancholy' (WN I.viii.43).

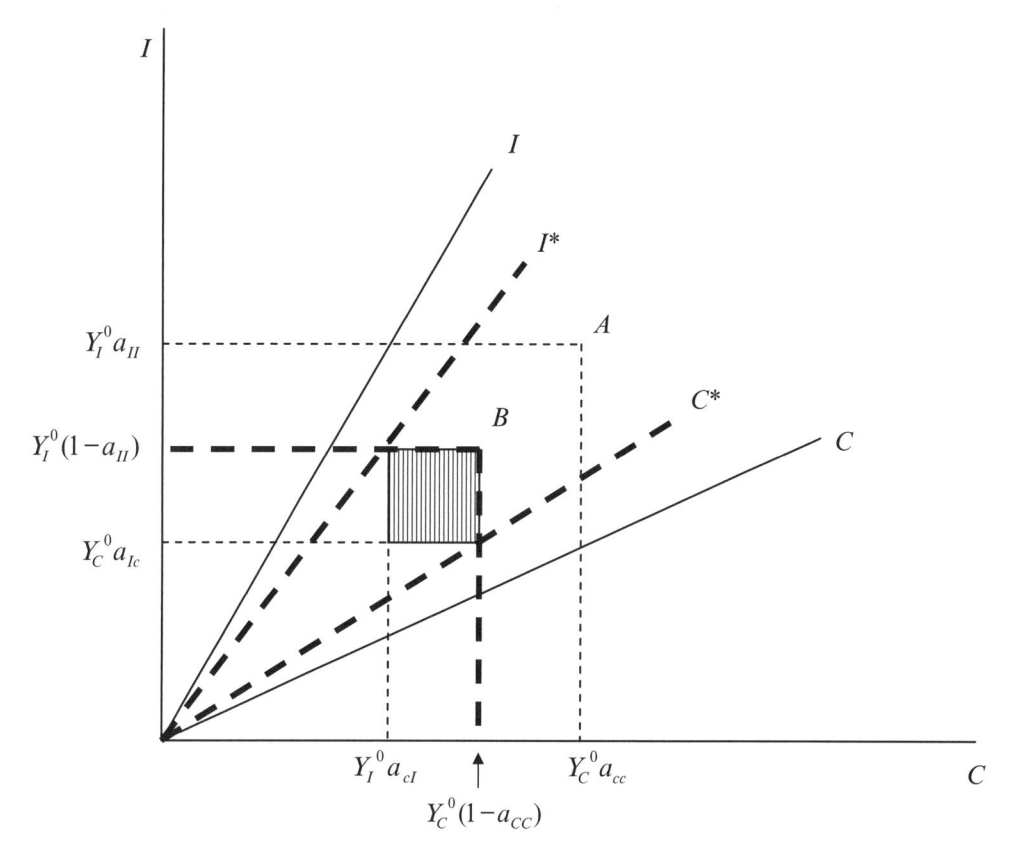

Figure 8.2 Own surpluses and net surpluses

The C^* and I^* lines enable us to see that viability prevails when the hatched area (in Figure 8.2) exists. The level of each sector's requirement for reproduction from the other sector must be smaller than its 'own surplus'.

The position of the 'own surplus' lines is determined by technology; namely, according to whether $(1 - a_{ii})$ is greater, equal or less than a_{ii}, $i = C,I$. For our purposes, at this stage, it is completely insignificant whether the 'own surplus' lines lie to the right, to the left, or even coincide, with the process lines. To a great extent, we will ignore the process lines altogether and only concentrate on the 'own surplus' lines.

The subject of some sort of rational considerations in this model is the 'own surplus', which for specific legal reasons, is owned by the capitalists. They will have to decide how much to consume and how much to save according to the balance they strike between the passions of today and the desire to better one's conditions. It is not because they legally own the surplus that they are different from labourers, it is because their reaction to the existence of surplus is different. Labourers too may find their wages above subsistence (hence surplus) but they cannot afford to deliberate its possible usages. Instead, they put it quite automatically to a given use.[22] Thus, by concentrating on the coincidence of wants among capitalists alone, I uphold the asymmetry between capitalists and labourers – which is reflected in the different

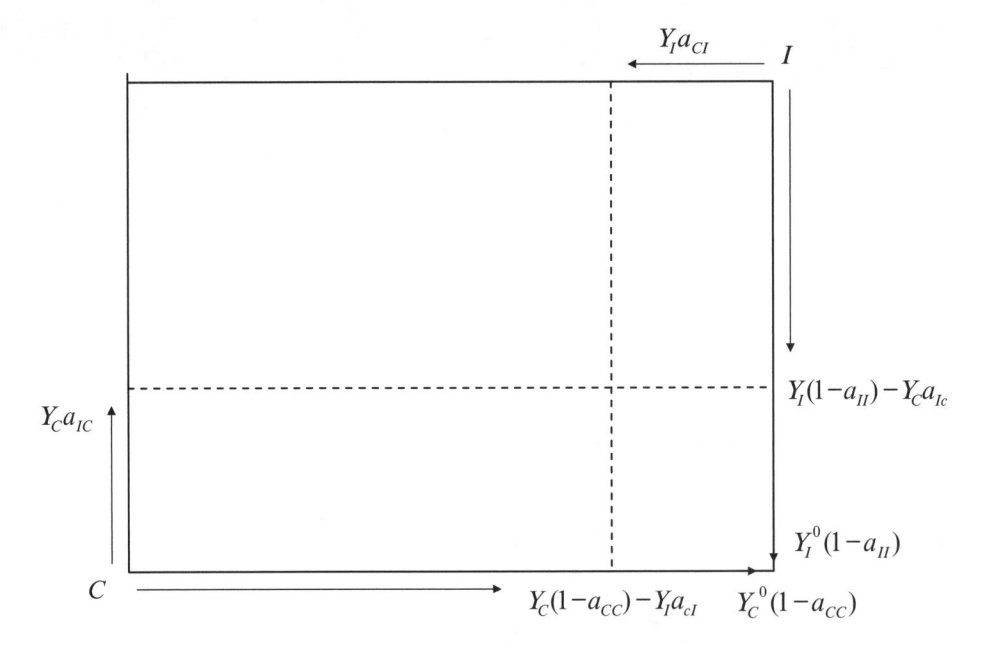

Figure 8.3 The exchange box

Labels on figure: $Y_I a_{CI}$, I, $Y_C a_{IC}$, $Y_I(1-a_{II}) - Y_C a_{Ic}$, $Y_I^0(1-a_{II})$, C, $Y_C(1-a_{CC}) - Y_I a_{cI}$, $Y_C^0(1-a_{CC})$

response to increase in earning – and I provide a less trivial meaning to the invisible hand.

In each sector, the capitalists will preserve for themselves that part of their own product which they need for reproduction, the rest they will bring to the market for exchange. Therefore, point *B* in Figure 8.2 defines the exchange box of the market.

In Figure 8.3 the exchange box from Figure 8.2 is presented in a manner of an Edgeworth box. The left bottom is the origin of sector *C* and the top right side, the origin of the *I* industry. The 'real net surplus', namely, the surplus that is left in the economy once that which is needed for the reproduction of the entire system has been put aside, becomes the upper left rectangle (it is the same as the hatched area in Figure 8.2). The size of the box depends on technology alone.[23]

In the mere fact that the economy can reproduce itself, there is no source of beneficence or success when the economic problem is that of growth maximization. In addition, there is the ethical element according to which beneficence will occur when at least someone of those who were acted upon improved their situation.[24] This can only happen if the real net surplus is positive, and accumulation takes place (that is, growth).

Accumulation can be manifested in two different ways. One is by an increase in productive labourers' wages, which will lead to an increase in their productivity. The other is by hiring more labourers to work with additional materials. Either way, the process lines remain the same. We know that a_{cc} denotes the amount of corn needed for the production of one unit of corn. When the labourers' productivity is higher due to the increase in wages, there might be a need for fewer workers to produce one unit of corn, but their wages (in real terms) are such that we cannot tell what will happen to a_{cc}. We might as well assume that it will remain unchanged together with other such coefficients.

A Smithian model of general equilibrium 153

If the entire net surplus is spent on unproductive labour (or 'luxurious consumption') all labourers will receive their subsistence and the economy can survive in such a stationary state for a long while. Only through accumulation of surplus does the possibility of a rise in wages arise. Only then does the chance of improved productivity and growth prevail. However, accumulation, as such, is not always beneficial. Obviously, if one sector accumulates its entire net surplus, and the other consumes it all, the sector that accumulated will not be able to fulfil its intentions and thus the economy will not progress. In other words, in our story there is something about which Smith did not write explicitly but which is a natural extension of his story.

Smith wrote at length about the balances between sectors. At one place he writes: 'It is thus that the same capital will in any country put into motion a greater or smaller quantity of productive labour, and add a greater or smaller value to the annual produce of its land and labour, according to the different proportions in which it is employed in agriculture, manufactures, and wholesale trade' (WN II.v.23).

But he also writes about the interdependence across sectors. I will quote him at some length:

> Without the assistance of some artificers, indeed, the cultivation of the land cannot be carried on, but with great inconveniency and continual interruption. Smiths, carpenters, wheel-wrights, and plough-wrights, masons and bricklayers, tanners, shoemakers, and tailors, are people, whose service the farmer has frequent occasion for. Such artificers too stand, occasionally, in need of the assistance of another . . . The inhabitants of the town and those of the country are mutually the servants of one another. The town is a continual fair or market to which the inhabitants of the country resort, in order to exchange their rude for manufactured produce. It is this commerce which supplies the inhabitants of the town both with the materials of their work, and the means of their subsistence. The quantity of the finished work which they sell to the inhabitants of the country, necessarily regulates the quantity of the materials and provisions which they buy. *Neither their employment nor subsistence, therefore, can augment, but in proportion to the augmentation of the demand from the country for finished work; and this demand can augment only in proportion to the extension of improvement and cultivation. Had human institutions, therefore, never disturbed the natural course of things, the progressive wealth and increase of the towns would . . . be consequential, and in proportion to the improvement and cultivation of the . . . country.* (WN III.i.4 emphasis added)

The country, in my story, is represented by the C sector, the town by the I sector. The meaning of proportional development here is that what both sectors tend to use for the hiring of new labour should be compatible.

To analyse the circumstances of a 'beneficial' accumulation let us first connect the distribution of the net surplus and the progress of the economy (see Figures 8.4 and 8.5).

In Figure 8.4 only the real net surplus box is depicted (the hatched area from Figure 8.2 or the upper left rectangle in Figure 8.3). Recall that the 'net surpluses' in the economy are:

$$NS_t^c = Y_c^t(1 - a_{cc}) - Y_I^t a_{cI}$$

$$NS_t^I = Y_I^t(1 - a_{II}) - Y_c^t a_{Ic}$$

where the index t denotes the period.

Let g_i, $i = C, I$ denote the rate of the net surplus that a producer decides to devote for

154 *Elgar companion to Adam Smith*

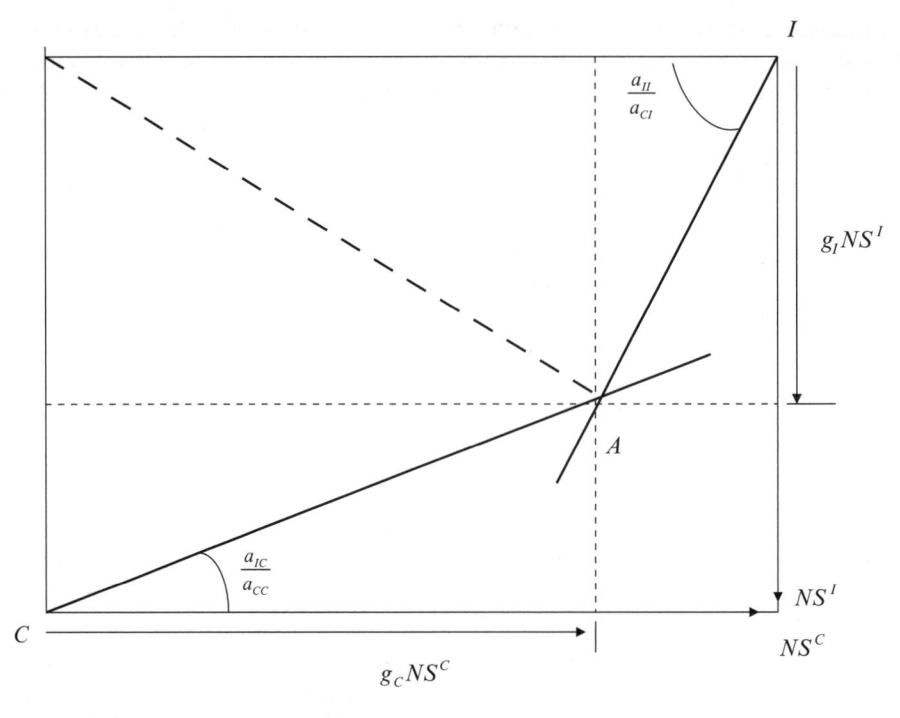

Figure 8.4   Net-surplus and maximum growth

accumulation. If $g_i NS^i$, $i = C,I$, is what each sector decides to accumulate it will have to accommodate that accumulation with the necessary amount of the other sector's product. To see this, I have introduced the process lines of each sector at its origin. The amount of the other sector product that each sector will need in order to achieve its own plans to accumulate will be $[g_i NS^i_t/a_{ii}]a_{ji}$, $i,j = C,I$. Clearly if a sector accumulates successfully the volume of its output in the next period will rise by: $g_i NS^i_t/a_{ii}$.

At point *A* in Figure 8.4 we can find a situation where the whole real net surplus was accumulated successfully. Namely, the plans of both sectors coincided. In the following period, therefore, the level of input of each sector will increase in exactly what they have accumulated, and the economy will progress from point *T* to point *L* in Figure 8.5 (note that these are the process lines and not the 'own surplus' lines).

The question now is whether this progress in the level of production is also an improvement in the levels of the real net surplus. It is, after all, the real net surplus from which the demand for more labour can spring and thus bring about progress and an increase in wages.

Recall that: 'The liberal reward of labour, therefore, as it is the necessary effect, so it is the natural symptom of increasing national wealth' (WN I.viii.27). Moreover, if anything, growth is closely associated with the improvement of the lot of the lower classes rather than with the objective of creating a lot of material wealth:

> Is this improvement in the circumstances of the lower ranks of the people to be regarded as an advantage or as an inconveniency to society? . . . No society can surely be flourishing and

A Smithian model of general equilibrium 155

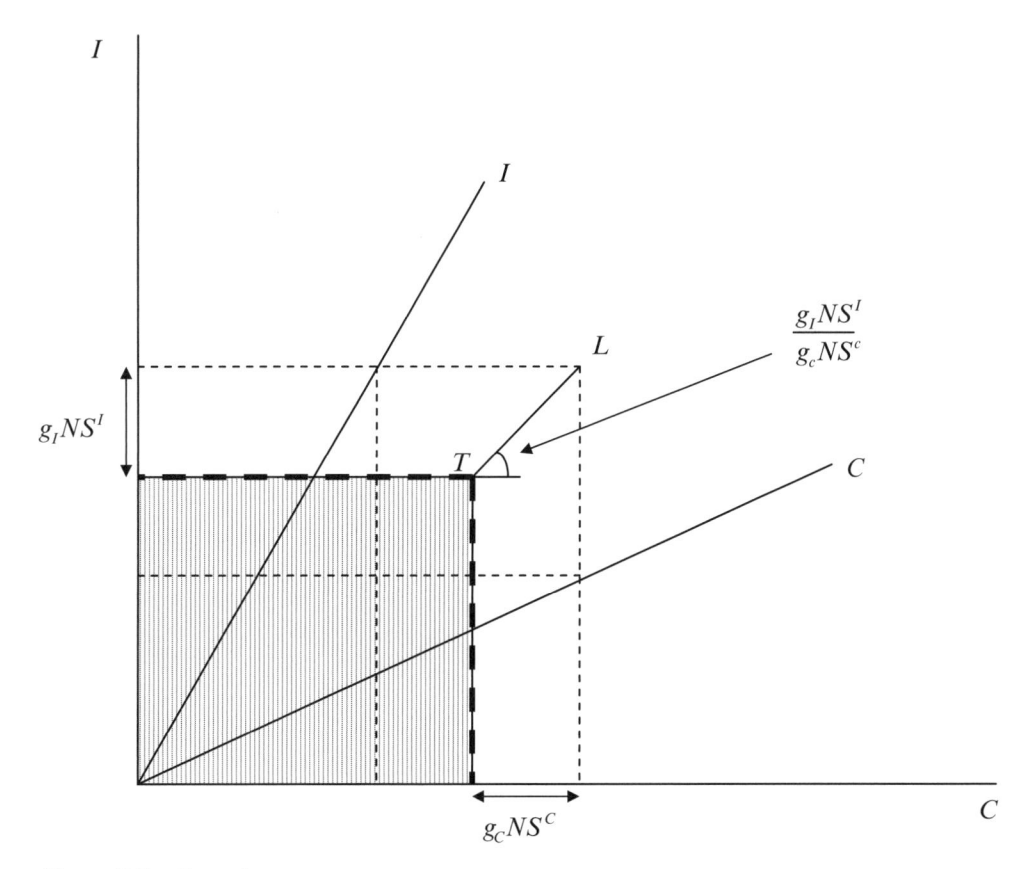

Figure 8.5 Growth

happy, of which the far greater part of the members are poor and miserable. It is but equity, besides, that they who feed, cloath and lodge the whole body of people, should have a share of the produce of their own labour as to be themselves tolerably well fed, cloathed and lodged. (WN I.viii.36)

Let us now examine the conditions for the real net surplus to improve. First, recall that the level of production at the second period will be:

$$Y_i^t + g_i \frac{NS_t^i}{a_{ii}} = Y_i^{t+1}$$

Thus, the net surplus of the second period will yield:

$$NS_{t+1}^i = \left(Y_i^t + g_i \frac{NS_t^i}{a_{ii}}\right)(1 - a_{ii}) - \left(Y_j^t + g_j \frac{NS_t^j}{a_{jj}}\right) a_{ij}$$

$$= Y_i(1 - a_{ii}) - y_j a_{ij} + g_i NS_t^i \frac{(1 - a_{ii})}{a_{ii}} - g_j NS_t^j \frac{a_{ij}}{a_{jj}} \quad (8.1)$$

as, $Y_i(1 - a_{ii}) - Y_j a_{ij} = NS_t^i$, (8.1) is reduced to:

$$NS^i_{t+1} = NS^i_t\left[1 + g_i\frac{(1-a_{ii})}{a_{ii}}\right] - g_iNS^j_t\frac{a_{ij}}{a_{jj}}$$

$$i,j = C, I.$$

In order for the real net surplus to increase, we should show the conditions for:

$$\frac{NS^c_{t+1}}{NS^c_t} \geq 1; \frac{NS^I_{t+1}}{NS^I_t} \geq 1 \qquad (8.2)$$

Substituting (8.1) into (8.2) will yield:

$$\frac{NS^c_{t+1}}{NS^c_t} = 1 + g_c\frac{(1-a_{cc})}{a_{cc}} - g_I\frac{NS^I_t}{NS^c_t}\frac{a_{cI}}{a_{II}} \geq 1 \qquad (8.3)$$

$$\frac{NS^I_{t+1}}{NS^I_t} = 1 + g_I\frac{(1-a_{II})}{a_{II}} - g_c\frac{NS^c_t}{NS^I_t}\frac{a_{Ic}}{a_{cc}} \geq 1 \qquad (8.4)$$

Dividing (8.3) and (8.4) with g_c and g_I respectively, and rearranging:

$$\frac{a_{II}}{a_{cI}}\frac{(1-a_{cc})}{a_{cc}} \geq \frac{g_I NS^I_t}{g_c NS^c_t} \qquad (8.3')$$

$$\frac{a_{Ic}}{a_{cc}}\frac{a_{II}}{(1-a_{II})} \leq \frac{g_I NS^I_t}{g_c NS^c_t} \qquad (8.4')$$

The right-hand expression is exactly the slope of the expansion path, in terms of inputs, which is depicted in Figure 8.5 between points T and L. a_{II}/a_{cI} is the slope of I's process line. In our example $(1 - a_{cc}) > a_{cc}$, hence for the condition to hold, the slope of the expansion path must be smaller than that of I's process line. At the same time, the slope of the expansion path must be greater than that of the C process line. I shall therefore maintain that conditions (8.3') and (8.4') delineate between those allocations where the net surplus of both sectors grows and those where at least one of them does not. The long-term implication of this is that sooner or later, there will not be enough of the lagging sector's surplus to sustain the growth of both sectors. In the end, this will lead to Smith's familiar story of stagnation and regression.

Figure 8.6 depicts possible expansion paths. Point A is the level of inputs employed in the first period. U is the correspondent exchange box, with the shaded area as the real net surplus box.

When all the net surplus was devoted to accumulation (as in Figure 8.4), the inputs of the next period will increase by the amount accumulated. The economy will progress from point A to point C, where D defines the relevant exchange box with the corresponding hatched box of the real net surplus. The expansion path, in terms of inputs, is the line connecting A and C. The slope of this line is exactly the right-hand expression in (8.3') and (8.4'). The expansion path of the real net surplus can be described as the line connecting U and D. This means that the combinations of own surplus must always lie between the two own surplus lines (C^* and I^*). As we move from U to D, the size of the hatched area (the real net surplus) is consistently increasing.

A Smithian model of general equilibrium 157

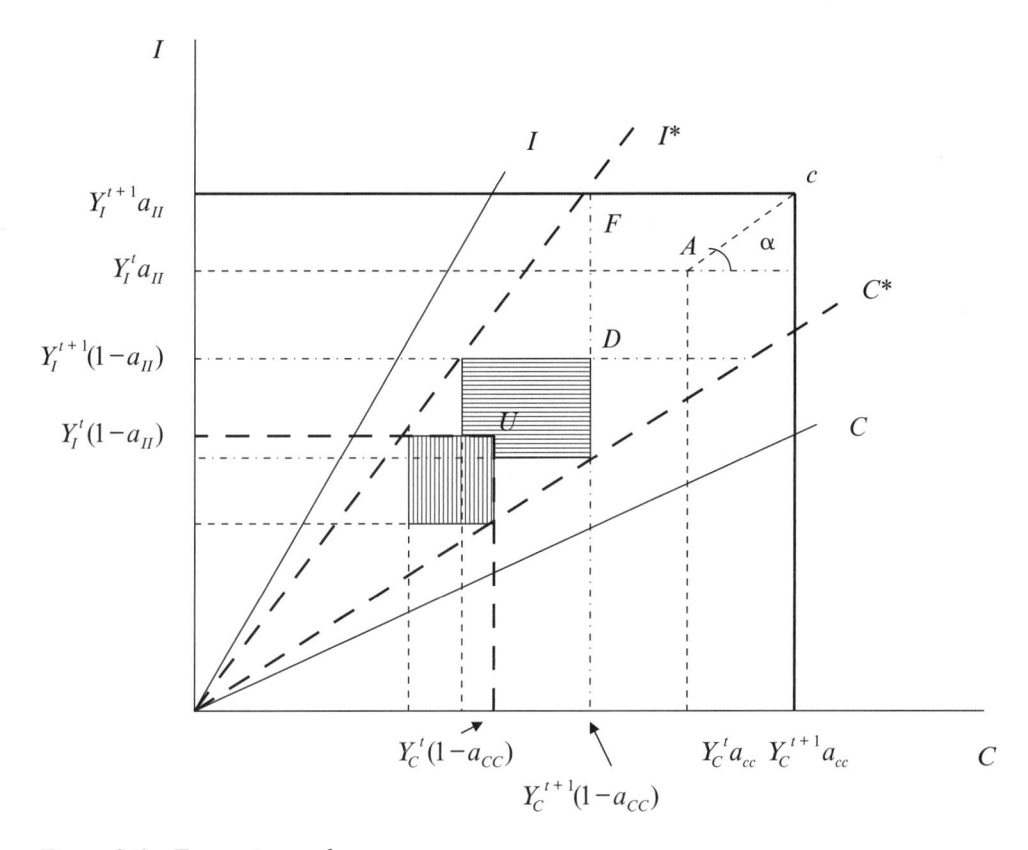

Figure 8.6 Expansion paths

However, if the expansion path of the real net surplus were to advance towards point *F* in Figure 8.6, it would mean that in one sector, no net surplus exists. Hence, the economy will not be able to accumulate any further due to technological interdependence. This, perhaps, corresponds to the uncontrolled growth of cities, in Smith's story, which is a result of human intervention.

To complete the picture let us examine now under which conditions the 'surplus expansion path' (the line connecting *U* and *D* in Figure 8.6) will not lead the economy to a point like *F*. Obviously the restrictions on the position of this expansion path with respect to the 'own surplus' lines are equivalent to those restricting the position of the total output expansion path.

The slope of the net surplus expansion line (between *U* and *D* for instance) is:

$$\frac{Y_I^{t+1}(1-a_{II}) - Y_I^t(1-a_{II})}{Y_c^{t+1}(1-a_{cc}) - Y_c^t(1-a_{cc})} \tag{8.5}$$

We already saw that:

$$Y_I^{t+1} = Y_I^t + g_I \frac{NS_t^I}{a_{II}}$$

and:

$$Y_c^{t+1} = Y_c^t + g_c \frac{NS_t^c}{a_{cc}}$$

Substituting into (8.5):

$$\frac{g_I NS^I (1 - a_{II}) a_{cc}}{g_c NS^c (1 - a_{cc}) a_{II}}$$

The corresponding slopes of the 'own surplus' lines are:

$$\frac{a_{Ic}}{(1 - a_{cc})}; \frac{(1 - a_{II})}{a_{cI}}$$

We would like to examine the conditions for the slope of the net surplus expansion path to be smaller than the I's own surplus line and greater than C's own surplus line:

$$\frac{a_{Ic}}{(1 - a_{cc})} \leq \frac{g_I NS^I (1 - a_{II}) a_{cc}}{g_c NS^c (1 - a_{cc}) a_{II}} \tag{8.6}$$

$$\frac{(1 - a_{II})}{a_{cI}} \geq \frac{g_I NS^I (1 - a_{II}) a_{cc}}{g_c NS^c (1 - a_{cc}) a_{II}} \tag{8.7}$$

By rearranging we get exactly (8.3') and (8.4') which represent the restriction on the 'own surplus' path.

Accumulation, therefore, is not enough to guarantee a beneficial outcome of the process of exchange. Even though we might find at certain stages the economy progressing (as well as a progressing net surplus), the fact that it is aiming towards a point similar to F in Figure 8.6, means that this progress is only temporary. Any rise in wages and population will inevitably be reversed once the economy reaches point F.

The important feature of the model is that for any allocation of surplus, it provides information about its long-term consequences if there is no change in those parameters which brought it about.[25] I will now move to demonstrate that allocations can easily fall within the domain of unsustained growth and that the responsibility for it lies with the one group alone: the capitalists.

Before we carry on I would like to point out another feature of the model which we must bear in mind: the effects of progress (or division of labour).[26] Improved productivity may not alter the position of the process lines but it will affect the conditions for sustained growth. When there is technological progress it should mean that the net surplus per unit in each industry should become greater. This means that $(1 - a_{ii})/a_{ii}$ will become greater in each sector. From equations (8.3')–(8.4') to (8.6)–(8.7) we can see that the implications would be that the domain of sustained growth in the net surplus box becomes greater. Admittedly, this seems to suggest that at the limit, this classical framework will be edging nearer to the neoclassical framework in the sense that all equilibrium outcomes are beneficent. However, this is not really the case. To complete the picture we must also ask what exactly is done with the surplus. If all of it is used for luxurious consumption, with or without improved technology there will be no growth. The long-term consequences of this for labourers could be devastating.

Equilibrium, demand structure and the role of prices

In this section I shall turn to analyse some of the mechanistic aspects of Smith's theory; namely, how a certain allocation of surplus is brought about. In Smith's discussion of the invisible hand in the *Theory of Moral Sentiments*, TMS IV.i.10, he is describing some kind of a trickle-down theory. The capitalists have to decide what to do with their surplus which is above what is needed for reproduction. In Smith's words, they have to decide between employing productive and unproductive labour. Thus, argues Smith, although there will be inequality in income distribution, at least there is an equal distribution (and satisfaction) of needs.

But this is only a partial description of the functioning of natural liberty. Add to it Smith's distinction between the calculated wants of the capitalist, the desperate needs of the labourer[27] and the interdependence between sectors, and the problem of the invisible hand changes significantly. Now it is not just the harmony between the capitalists and the labourers which should be considered. Also we have to consider: (1) the mechanism which harmonizes the rational wants of the capitalists; and (2) whether in the light of sectoral interdependence, the capitalists' wish to save is sufficient to generate needs satisfaction among the workers.

Obviously, the most important instrument in this mechanism is the price. However, while the price in a neoclassical system is a means of resource allocation through the coincidence of wants, in Smith, and probably in the classical school in general, prices are the tools of surplus distribution.

Let us now examine more carefully the exchange box presented in the previous section.

The producers enjoy the 'own surplus' of $Y_c(1 - a_{cc})$ and $Y_I(1 - a_{II})$ for C and I respectively. However, while they can simply put aside their own contribution for their reproduction (g_iNS^i, $i = C,I$), they still need the other sector's goods for reproduction ($g_iNS^ia_{ji}/a_{ii}$, $i = C,I$). This defines the upper left rectangle as the real net surplus. This net surplus will be used either for consumption or for accumulation, but unlike consumption, the decision on accumulation must be synchronized with the other sector's plans in order for it to be successful.[28] The process lines (leading to points like G) in the real net surplus rectangle show exactly how much of the other sector's good will be required for each decision of accumulation.

If sector C's capitalists decide to accumulate g_cNS^c, they will bring to the market only: $Y_c(1 - a_{cc}) - g_cNS^c$ which is also:

$$Y_I a_{cI} + (1 - g_c)NS^C$$

Thus, the actual exchange box is reduced to the box at the bottom right of G in Figure 8.7. If the I sector's plans coincide with those of C; namely that they bring into the market exactly what is required by C for reproduction and accumulation, and so does C (point G in Figure 8.7), the price in terms of commodities will necessarily become:

$$P = \frac{Y_c a_{Ic} + (1 - g_I)NS^I}{Y_I a_{cI} + (1 - g_c)NS^C}$$

Which is the price of C in terms of I, and is exactly the slope δ in Figure 8.7. That is to say that point G is an equilibrium if the price which prevails is δ.

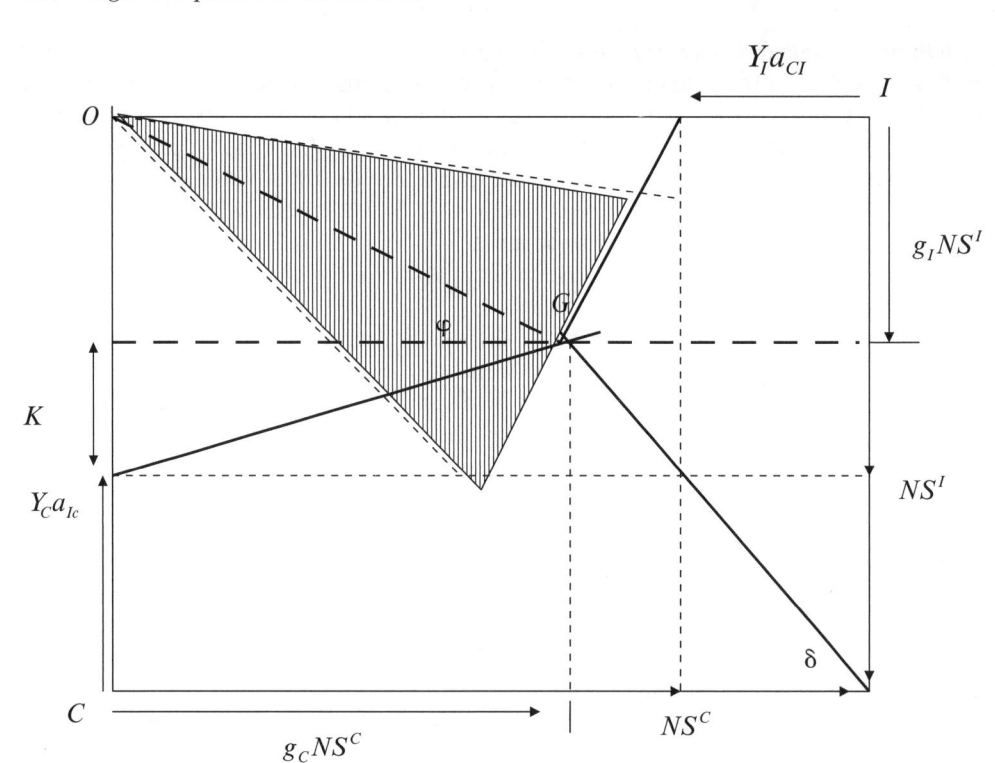

Figure 8.7 Price and conditional expansion paths

The slope of the diagonal in the far upper left rectangle that is created by G, $\varphi = g_I NS^I / g_c NS^c$, is exactly the slope of the conditioned expansion path of the previous section (equations 8.3' and 8.4'). The conditions for a growth in the net surplus of both sectors were (equations 8.5 and 8.6 in the previous section):

$$\frac{a_{Ic}}{a_{cc}}\left(\frac{a_{II}}{1-a_{II}}\right) \leq \frac{g_I NS^I}{g_c NS^c} \leq \frac{a_{II}}{a_{cI}}\left(\frac{1-a_{cc}}{a_{cc}}\right)$$

and they are depicted by the rays originating from O in Figure 8.7. The hatched area reflects allocations of accumulation which will yield not only an increase in production for one period, but also a continual increase in the real net surplus of the economy. At the same time, G is not the only equilibrium which is consistent with the price δ.

Let us examine point H in Figure 8.8. The two sectors have decided, separately, to accumulate, $g_i NS^i, i = C,I$ which is a smaller amount than that which had been designated in Figure 8.7. The exchange box now becomes the rectangle at the right-hand bottom of point H and the price will remain δ. The quantity of each product which will now be brought into the market will be substantially greater. Hence, it could obviously accommodate a decision for less accumulation.

Thus, once the exchange has been completed, each of the sectors finds itself with the other sector's goods that it did not need for accumulation. This could now be used for consumption. γ_I^c, γ_c^I denote those levels of consumption.

A Smithian model of general equilibrium 161

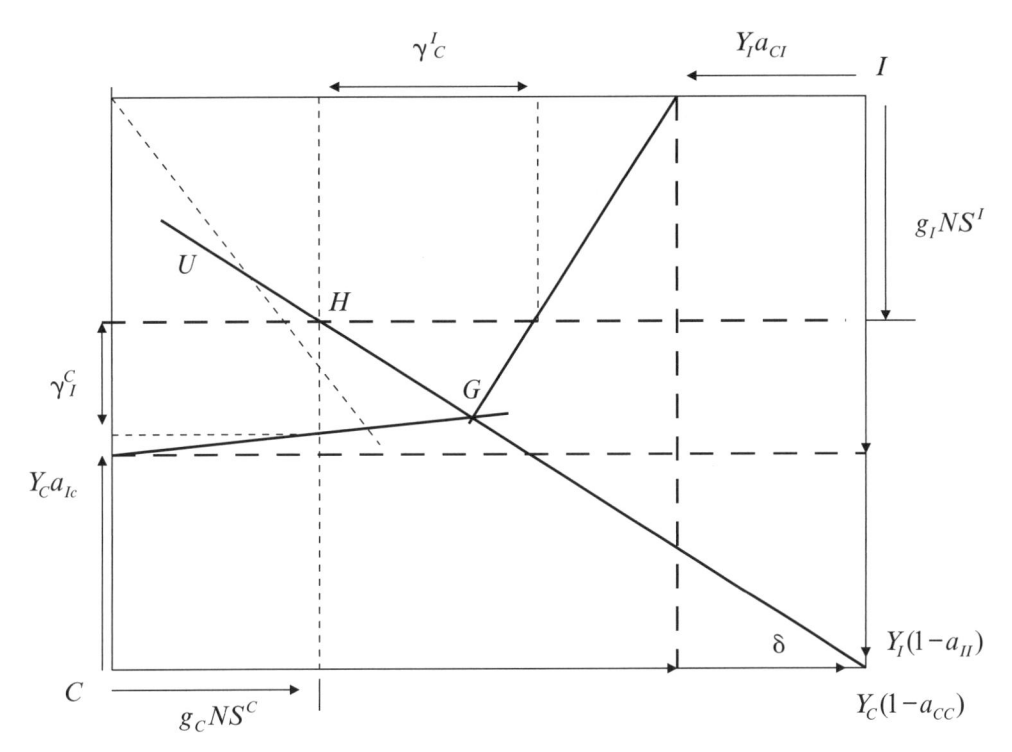

Figure 8.8 Multiple equilibria

Surely one will also use one's own surplus for superfluous consumption. This will influence the size of the exchange box. For the sake of brevity I neglect this aspect which could become more interesting as the decision for one's own product consumption, the demand for 'luxurious' consumption from the other sector, and the prices become related. However, this is a task for a separate investigation.

What we have at present is that the price δ supports many equilibria according to the initial decision to accumulate. We may observe that all the points along that line to the right of G represent dissonance of wants. Therefore they cannot constitute equilibria points and they represent points of excess demand where what is needed by each sector to support its own accumulation plans is more than what the other sector has brought into the market.

All the points along the price line that are to the left of G represent equilibria points if we assume that luxurious consumption is an implicit rather than explicit decision parameter. Another distinction that can be made, with regard to different equilibria supported by the same price, is the economy's general rate of growth. Clearly, this rate increases as we descend towards point G where it is the highest possible when the entire surplus is effectively directed for reproduction and accumulation. Notice too that the price itself does not guarantee a beneficial outcome as it would also support an equilibrium at a point like U. There, the condition for long-term growth would be violated and the economy would move towards a form of unbalanced growth which would lead to stagnation.

Throughout the above discussion I assumed that decisions were taken only with

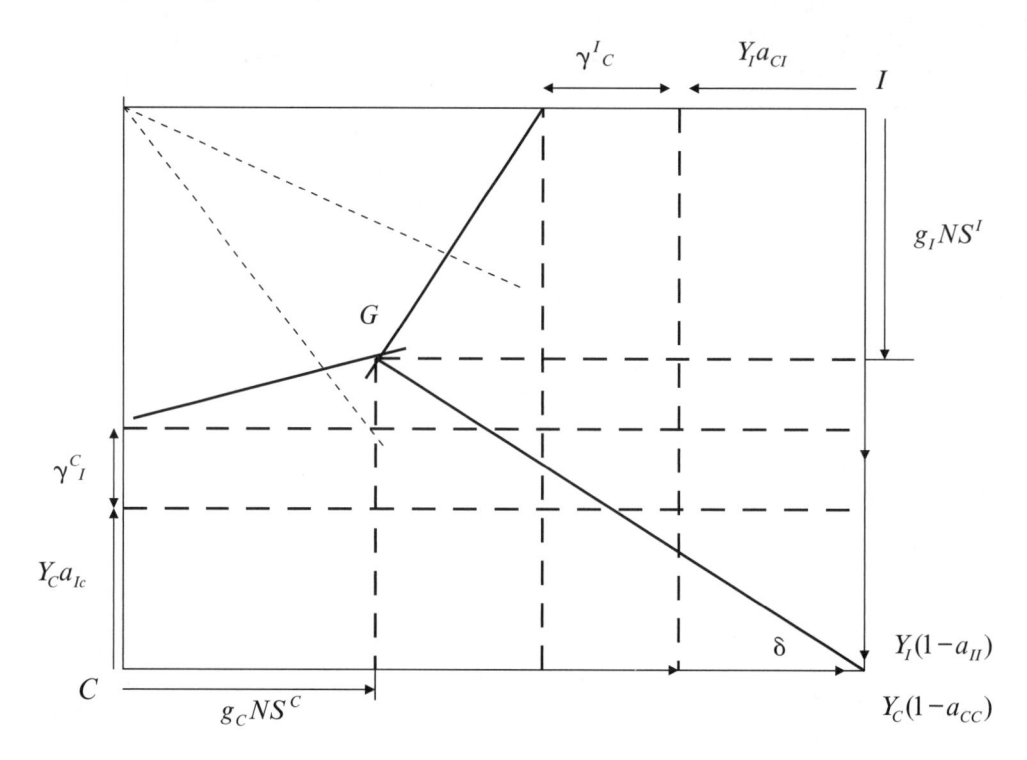

Figure 8.9   A unique equilibrium: present enjoyments take precedence

regard to reproduction and accumulation. 'Luxurious' consumption (that consumption which is above subsistence) became a residual. This, of course, is not the only way to look at the decision-making process by the capitalist. In fact, we shall soon see that Smith was much more explicit with regard to the structure of demand.

Meanwhile, allow me to examine the alternative approach where the pre-market decisions are made with regard to luxurious consumption. Figure 8.9 depicts the new circumstances.

Once the levels of luxurious consumption (γ^C_I, γ^I_C) are set, there is actually a unique equilibrium at point G. At any other point there will be no coincidence of wants. Every point on and above the process lines will yield excess supply; any point below, excess demand. So there is a unique equilibrium price, for any predetermined sets of demand for luxurious consumption. The long-term implications of this equilibrium are clearly dependent on the relative size of those predetermined levels of demand.

Constructing demand in Smith's analysis

Let me now devote some time to what can be understood as an assertion on demand. It is rather clear that Smith noticed the significance of demand in setting the price within the partial equilibrium framework of analysis. It is, however, less clear in the general context of his system.

There are three main usages (and thus, demands) for any surplus: reproduction, consumption and accumulation. If we look at the demand for C in our model it will take the form:

A Smithian model of general equilibrium 163

$$C^d = Y_I a_{cI} + g_I NS^I \frac{a_{cI}}{a_{II}} + \gamma_c^I$$

where $g_I NS^I a_{cI}/a_{II}$ represents the amount of C needed to accommodate the decision to accumulate $g_I NS^I$ of I.

Throughout the whole of the *Wealth of Nations*, reproduction is assumed to be crucial. Without loss of generality I will therefore assume that the demand for reproduction is always given and, which is most important, will be the last component of demand to be affected by market circumstances (that is, price). It is, in my view, not unreasonable to suppose that the demand for subsistence (of both workers and capitalists) needed to maintain current levels of existence will be inelastic. This could be the case either because the capitalists are fully aware of their own predicament if they fail to reproduce previous levels of surplus, or because the labourers themselves face even grimmer prospects if they fail to secure their demand.

We must therefore concentrate on the use of the real net surplus. This subject is extensively discussed in the chapter on the accumulation of capital (Chapter 3, Book 2). The distinction between luxurious consumption and accumulation is proposed through the employment of unproductive and productive labourers respectively.

What motivates demand, in Smith's theory, is a certain quality in human nature; a certain passion. The principle which 'prompts to expense, is the passion for present enjoyment . . . But the principle which prompts to save [namely, to accumulate or to employ productive labour], is the desire of bettering our condition' (WN II.iii.28).

Smith does not offer us a very accurate account of what regulates the relationship between these two contradicting features. However, he does maintain that they prevail together. No matter how pleased a person can be with a certain situation, he will always desire to better his conditions. Yet we must note that what drives luxurious consumption is passion while accumulation is driven by a desire. I feel that we will not be betraying Smith's general view of human nature by supposing that the passion, the uncalculated part of people's behaviour, is that aspect of demand which will be less dependent on external signals like prices. Indeed, in Smith's description of equilibrium in Book 1, he writes about equilibrium between 'effective demand' and supply. Effective demand, according to Smith, is the demand of those who can afford to buy the good at the given price. By implication, when the price changes, it is not that the same people will want to buy more or less of the good, but rather that more people will join or leave the market. Put differently, people have given needs (or wants) and these are not dependent on price. What does depend on the price is whether or not they will be able to fulfil their desires

Indeed, the inclination towards the momentary pleasures is spelt out when discussing the use to be made of the surplus by those who own it. 'They might . . . maintain indifferently either productive or unproductive hands. They seem however, to have some predilection for the latter. The expense of a great lord feeds generally more idle than industrious people' (WN II.iii.7).

There are, therefore, two main features in Smith's view of demand. Firstly, at least in part, it is motivated by passions which are not likely to be regulated by the system. Secondly, if we were to set the different components of demand in an order according to their dependence on the price, we may argue that Smith saw reproduction and luxurious consumption as least dependent on prices and accumulation – the calculated side of human behaviour – as a price-dependent residual.

164 *Elgar companion to Adam Smith*

It is, therefore, the second formulation of the general equilibrium solution which appears consistent with Smith's writings. In such a case the demand function for *C* as described before is a function of price in the following way:

$$C^d(P) = Y_I a_{cI} + g_I(P) NS^I \frac{a_{cI}}{a_{II}} + \gamma_c^I$$

Let us, now, descend from the general equilibrium level to the partial equilibrium framework to look more closely on the process of exchange in the light of the above observations. The analysis will differ somewhat from the exact analysis of Smith in Chapter 7 of Book 1; however, its spirit will prevail.

Figure 8.10 depicts the demand for *C* under the assertion that the fixed arguments of it are the demand for reproduction and luxurious consumption, and that a certain level of accumulation is planned but will be determined by prices. In other words, the needs and wants of the present take precedence over those of the future, the planning for which is left in the hands of market.

While it is implied that accumulation is essentially residual, it does not mean that there is no a priori notion of what is expected to be accumulated. In some respect we may even say that in Smith's analysis, there must be a hidden assumption about expectations. Before coming into the market, besides luxurious consumption and reproduction, there is bound to be a certain idea of what we would have liked to accumulate. This is reflected in the portion of our own product that we devote for accumulation. Hence, if the producers of *I* decided to accumulate $g_I^e NS^I$ of their product, they expect to get in the market $(g_I^e NS^I a_{cI})/a_{II}$ on top of what they want for reproduction ($Y_I a_{cI}$) and consumption (γ_c^I).

This pre-market formation of the demand is, in some respect, a similar idea to what Smith called the 'effectual demand'. It is a demand which is determined outside of the market and which, in parts, depends on technology (the demand for reproduction goods). Equilibrium price will then depend on how the quantities brought into the market relate to the preset demands.

The pre-market demand in Figure 8.10a is depicted by the segment *AK*. The actual demand will obviously depend on the price:

$$C^d(P) = Y_I a_{cI} + g_I(P) NS^I \frac{a_{cI}}{a_{II}} + \gamma_c^I$$

where $g_I' < 0$.

If the price that prevails is P_A, they will get exactly what they expected to get. If, however, the price of *C* in terms of *I* increases to $P_C(>P_A)$ then, for what they brought to the market they will get a smaller quantity than that which they expected to get (C^*). However, if they get less for accumulation they can reduce the quantity of their own product which they had put aside for it. This will cause an increase in their supply which, in turn, will lead the market to point *C*.

If the price is lower than what they have expected it to be they can always increase the level of accumulation (point *B*) by reducing the supply of their own product *I*. We can now draw that demand schedule in Figure 8.10b where the position of the curve depends on the level of consumption, and of the expected level of accumulation (g_I^e).

We can immediately derive the supply of *I* which corresponds to the behaviour of the

A Smithian model of general equilibrium 165

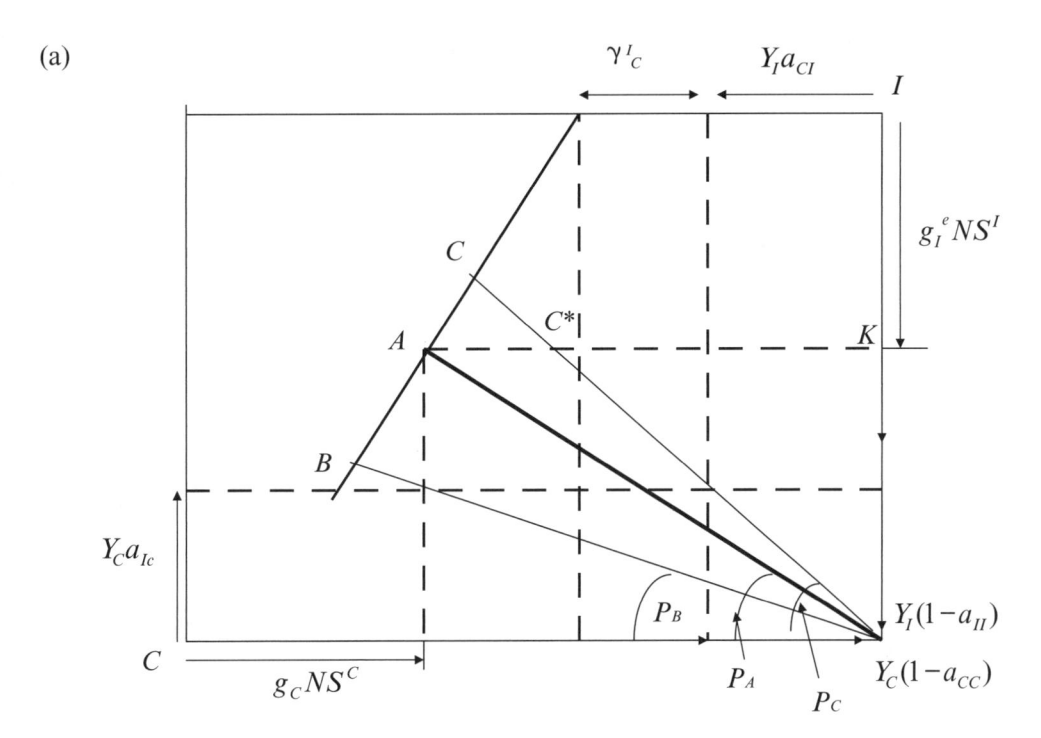

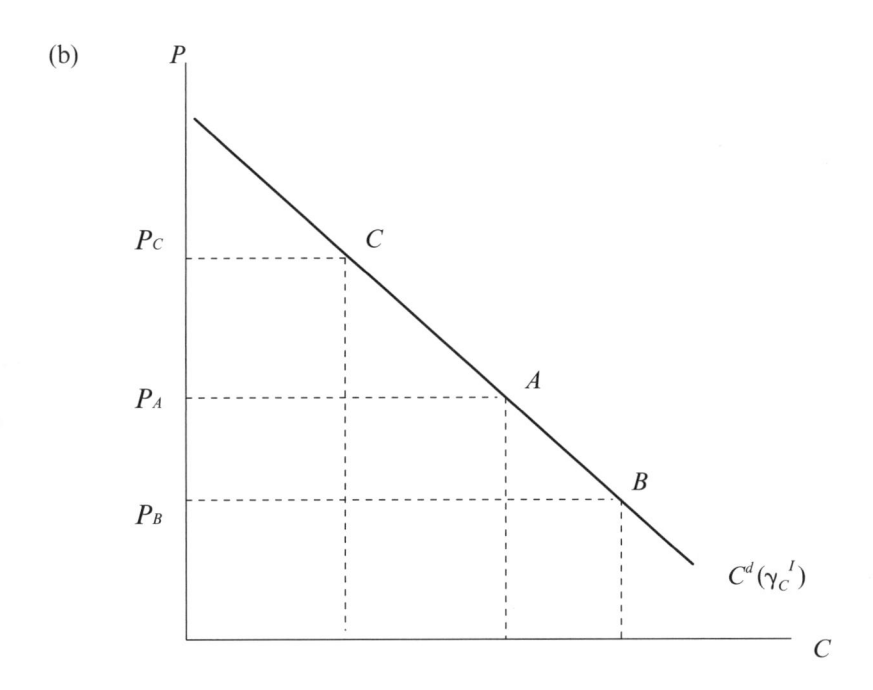

Figure 8.10 Demand with fixed current needs and wants

producers of *I* in the market for *C*. We saw that $g_I'(P) < 0$ and the supply of *I* will be their total surplus less that which they need for accumulation:

$$I^s(P) = Y_I(1 - a_{II}) - g_I(P)NS^I$$

as $g_I' < 0$, the supply of *I* is positively correlated with *P*.

In a similar way we can analyse the behaviour of the producers of *C* and get the following equations for their demand of *I* and supply of *C*:

$$I^d(P) = Y_c a_{Ic} + g_c(P)NS^c \frac{a_{Ic}}{a_{cc}} + \gamma_I^c$$

$$C^s(P) = Y_c(1 - a_{cc}) - g_c(P)NS^c$$

given that $g_c'(P) > 0$.

Figure 8.11a depicts the partial equilibrium settings in markets *C* and *I*. Clearly we can see that there might be a problem of stability in this model. As long as the supply schedules of *C* and *I* are steeper than the respective demand schedules, equilibrium will be stable. Without delving into the details of the problem, let us assume that the conditions for stability prevail. The existence of a unique general equilibrium is thus shown in conjunction with Figure 8.11b.

The process lines depict the demand and supply of each sector. At any point other than *G* wants do not coincide.

We can now write the equilibrium equations in the two markets:

$$C^d(P) = Y_I a_{cI} + \gamma_c^I + g_I(P)NS^I \frac{a_{cI}}{a_{II}} = Y_c(1 - a_{cc}) - g_c(P)NS^c = C^s(P)$$

$$I^d(P) = Y_c a_{Ic} + \gamma_I^c + g_c(P)NS^c \frac{a_{Ic}}{a_{cc}} = Y_I(1 - a_{II}) - g_I(P)NS^I = I^s(P)$$

which can be rewritten as:

$$NS^c - \gamma_c^I = g_c NS^c + g_I NS^I \frac{a_{cI}}{a_{II}}$$

$$NS^I - \gamma_I^c = g_c NS^c \frac{a_{Ic}}{a_{cc}} + g_I NS^I$$

Solving and assuming (for the Cramer method) that:

$$A = NS^c NS^I - \left(NS^c \frac{a_{Ic}}{a_{cc}}\right)\left(NS^I \frac{a_{cI}}{a_{II}}\right) \neq 0$$

we get the equilibrium growth rates:

$$g_c = \left[(NS^c - \gamma_c^I)NS^I - (NS^I - \gamma_I^c)NS^I \frac{a_{cI}}{a_{II}}\right]A^{-1}$$

$$g_I = \left[(MS^I - \gamma_I^c)NS^c - (NS^c - \gamma_c^I)NS^c \frac{a_{Ic}}{a_{cc}}\right]A^{-1}$$

A Smithian model of general equilibrium 167

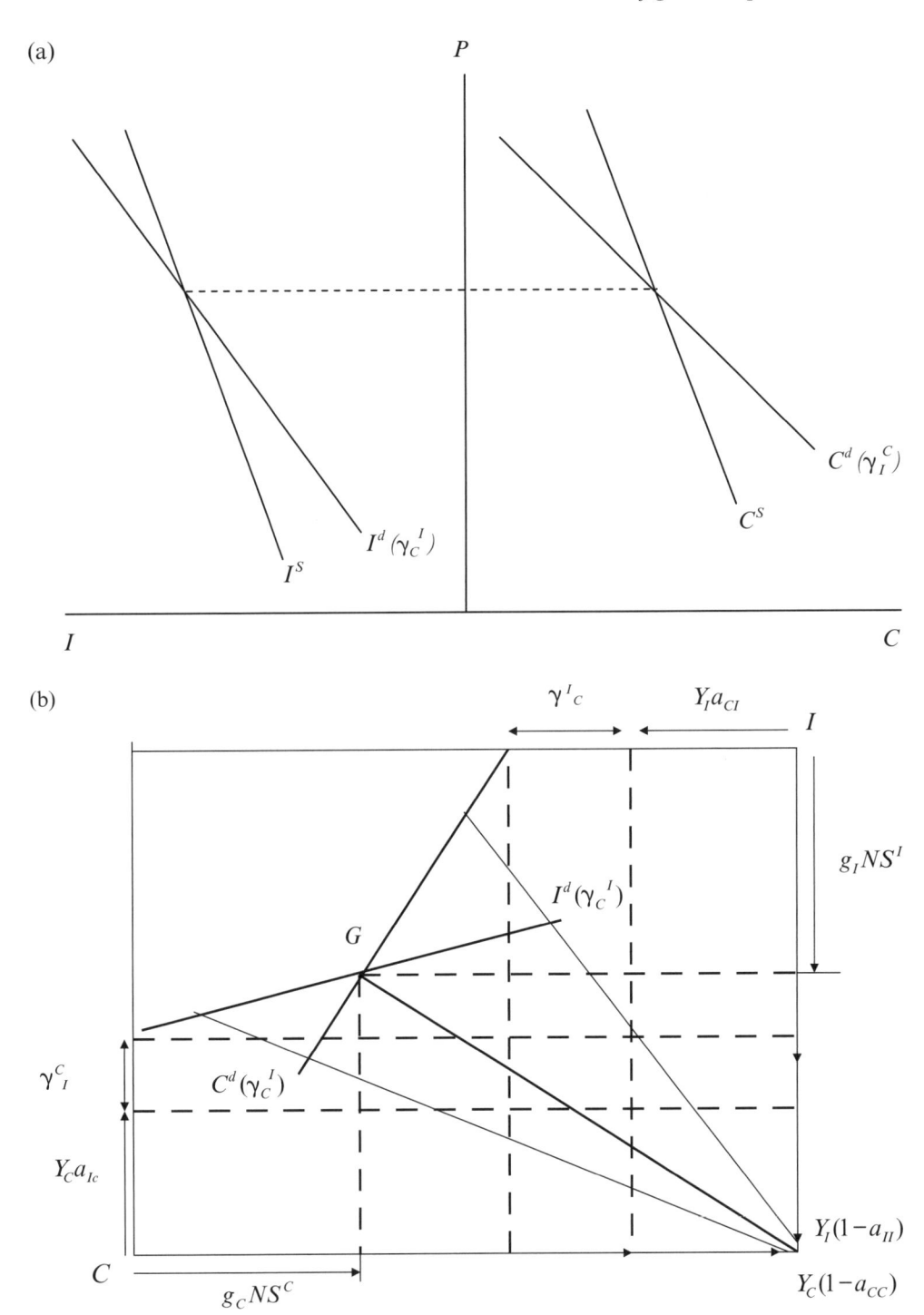

Figure 8.11 Partial and general equilibrium

By simple comparative statics we can see that the equilibrium growth rate of each sector is inversely related to the other sector's planned luxurious consumption and positively related to its own luxurious consumption. This means that what we have here is a serious problem for the beneficence of the coincidence of wants.

Given the above results it is clear that what we have here is a kind of a prisoner's dilemma. Each sector wants very much to consume luxurious goods but at the same time to better its conditions through accumulation. By increasing its demand for luxurious consumption (unproductive labourers) of the other sector's goods each sector can expect to enjoy both worlds: a higher luxurious consumption and a higher rate of growth. Performed simultaneously, they can drive the economy to a very low rate of growth which, in the end, will harm everybody. The effect of this on labourers is obviously catastrophic.

Conclusion

The purpose of this chapter was to propose a model of general equilibrium that will bring to the fore the more fundamental differences between Smith and neoclassical economics. I have tried to show that there is such a difference which stems from both the difference in their research agenda and the way they depict the relative position of agents in the system. The economic problem at the heart of neoclassical economics is that of reconciling insatiate wants with scarcity. That of Smith is the circumstances most conducive to growth maximization. While one may argue that the two are related, much of their relationship will depend on what exactly one considers as the engine of growth.

In a Walrasian context, growth is motivated by individuals' intertemporal preferences. Walras himself phrased it very much in the same manner: 'to increase the number of useful things which exist only in limited quantities . . . and to transform indirect utilities into direct utilities' (Walras, 1954. p. 73). A coincidence of wants, in the intertemporal sense, would mean that through the working of entrepreneurs growth will be directed by prices which represent the gap between utility and scarcity. As everyone in society has intertemporal preferences and as everyone's needs are part of these wants, the working of decentralized decision-making will always guarantee (in the long run) the satisfaction of needs.

In the Smithian context this is a slightly different affair. Not everybody has the same position in the system in the sense that they can equally affect the outcome. Although workers may influence wages (and thus, cost of production) in a multisectoral context this may not seriously affect the plans of the surplus owners (that is, the capitalists). It is conceivable that it may have no influence at all on their plans for luxurious consumption. On the other hand, the wish of the surplus owners will always affect the ability of workers to satisfy their need.

Given that in Smith the conditions of labour are an important component in what produces growth and that their productive powers are influenced either by their own wages or by the provision of capital, growth in an economy is entirely in the hands of the few. What will determine growth, therefore, is the coincidence of wants among the capitalists. This, in turn, may or may not generate growth according to how their plans to balance the passions for present enjoyment, and the desire to 'better their condition', coincide.

To some extent, one may argue that the Walrasian model is very much the limit of the Smithian model. At one point Walras claims that '[e]nfin je crois que c'est peu que la richesse sociale[29] soit produite abondamment, si elle n'est equitablement repartie entre tous les membres de la societe' (Walras, 1896, p. 31). This means, in the context of Smith, that had everyone owned an equal proportion of the stock of social capital, the coincidence of their wants is bound to guarantee needs satisfaction. But, as in Walras, it is not very clear whether this would also mean the highest rate of output and growth. The reason for it is that there are behavioural asymmetries in addition to the one we have already mentioned. These differences may not disappear even if social wealth were equally divided. In other words, the working of competitive institutions in Smith (and I believe in classical economics in general) is hindered by two major facts: (1) people do not have an equal position in the system; and (2) they do not have a uniform pattern of behaviour.

While it is quite evident that the model described in this chapter does not appear as such in Smith's writing, it does, in my view, capture the spirit of his tale. It demonstrates how precarious the position of individuals is when they forgo their independence and move into an interdependent existence in the pursuit of social approbation.[30] It makes sense of Smith's ambiguous attitudes towards the working of natural liberty while building on the fundamentals of his description of how commercial societies operate.

Notes

* I am in debt to M. Blaug, P. Bridel, A. Cot, M. DeVroy, J. Persky and J. Young for helpful comments on earlier drafts.
1. Notwithstanding the problems of incomplete markets in both certainty (externalities) and uncertainty formulations, the existence and stability of general equilibrium suggests that a system of decentralized decision-making can work among rational agents. The first and second welfare theorems suggest that it can also produce whichever outcome society prefers provided that we can agree on Pareto-efficiency as a necessary condition for the socially desirable allocation.
2. The lines between Smith and Walras were clearly drawn by Schumpeter (1954, p. 189), Jaffe (1977), Robbins (1935, pp. 68–9), Negishi (1985, p. 11) and Hicks and Hollander (1977).
3. See, for instance, Reid (1987), Witztum (1997, 2005) and Witztum and Young (2006) where the ethical need to defend those who might be adversely affected is discussed.
4. I do recognize that the individual circumstances matter to the understanding of ideas, but this should not preclude the attempts to take these ideas to their logical potential even if this has not been done by their inventor.
5. I hasten to say that when I say Walrasian I refer to the way Walras has been adopted by mainstream economics. This is not to suggest that I ignore the various criticisms with regard to such an interpretation of Walras' contribution (see, for instance, Jaffe 1980; Morishima, 1977; Walker, 1987, 1996; van Witteloostuijn and Maks, 1990). In any case, even those who believe in a 'temporary equilibrium' interpretation admit that Walras 'regarded the states of free competition and market clearing only as *ideal* rather than real' (van Witteloostuijn and Maks, 1990, p. 234). In addition, I would like to point out that I shall not be dealing with the debate on how true to Walras are the 'neo-Walrasian' interpretations of his work (see Walker, 1996; Costa, 1998). Personally, I do not believe that Walras's efforts in finding a real extension for his ideal makes any difference to his research agenda. This is, in my view, a reflection of his complex methodology. Due to space limitations I will have to leave this very important issue outside the present discussion.
6. For instance, the existence of general equilibrium is unaffected by, say, the Schumpeterian hypothesis. Put differently, the efficiency (both productive and allocative) of the equilibrium allocation is unaffected by whether there will be more or less research and development (R&D) (and thus growth) in the economy. Naturally, had the Schumpeterian hypothesis been confirmed, we might have questioned how meaningful is the efficiency of a Walrasian allocation. As things stand, there seems to be not enough evidence and very little theory to persuade us to abandon our beliefs in the merits of competitive structures as captured by the Walrasian notion of general equilibrium (see, for instance, Dasgupta and Stiglitz, 1980; Levin and Reiss, 1984; Sutton, 1998).
7. For instance, if we use the 'cost of production' approach to general equilibrium in classical economics, this will only prevail when there is a uniform rate of profit. However, while most scholars thought that there is a tendency of the rates of profit to uniformity, this was not a normal state of affairs. Nevertheless, the discussions about the implications for growth were in no way confined to circumstances when there is a uniform rate of profit.

170   *Elgar companion to Adam Smith*

8. I consider 'second-best' analysis as part of the same research agenda where we seek to direct competition to a certain desired distribution without questioning the institutions themselves.
9. However, this possibility may not be consistent with the rational depiction of human behaviour. This, perhaps, is the reason why the need arose to introduce the 'trade independence axiom' (TIA) in general equilibrium analysis. This axiom is relevant to the examination of whether general equilibrium – a situation in which everyone is believed to have at least not worsened their conditions is consistent with famine (see Coles and Hammond, 1986). It means that in the initial state people have enough endowment to ensure their survival. The intuition here is that if the TIA does not hold, then it is unlikely that individuals will behave in a rational manner. A desperate person is not necessarily rational, thus bringing down the entire idea of 'coincidence of wants'.
10. Some may argue that Smith too was concerned with the genus of value and that he found it in labour. This, of course, is quite true but the fact that scholars search for universals does not mean that they treat them, or use them, in the same manner. While Walras used this universal to construct an ideal upon which one can try to explain its numerous manifestation (the general equilibrium distribution of values), in Smith's analysis, labour values play no explanatory role except at the most primitive stages (which cannot be compared with abstraction).
11. This point is elaborated in Witztum (2010).
12. Workers would increase in number when wages are above subsistence mainly because a greater number of their children would survive. However, Smith did not see this as just a matter of luck: he considered the larger family to be the objective of the 'rational' poor: 'It is the sober and industrious poor who generally bring up the most numerous families, and who principally supply the demand for useful labour' (WN V.ii.k.7).
13. See a full discussion in Witztum and Young (2006).
14. Although Walras himself was very much concerned with distributional questions (in his *Economie Politique et La Justice*, 1860 and *Etudes d'Economie Sociale*, 1896) the logic of his reasoning (that is, from the truth of value in exchange – pure economics – to the 'art' and the 'ethics') suggests that the symmetrical abstraction of the pure theory remains unaffected.
15. Not surprisingly this approach is much more prevalent with respect to Ricardo (and Malthus) than it is in connection with Smith or Mill. See, for instance, Kaldor (1956), Blaug (1958), Pasinetti (1960, 1981), Caravale and Tosato (1980) and Casarosa (1985). A more general use of this approach to classical economics can be found in Eltis (2000 [1984]). There are, of course, those who believe that what is true to Ricardo is true to Adam Smith: for instance, Hollander (1979) and by implication Hicks and Hollander (1977) who deal with Ricardo's growth model should be relevant to Smith too. Samuelson (1977, 1978) is another example of someone who believes that modelling classical economics can be generalized in terms of Ricardo's corn model. Reid (1987) explores the fallacy behind Samuelson's vindication of Smith through the use of a kind of Ricardian corn model.
16. Also, the importance of the theory of value in such a context is not very clear. Kaldor (1956) and Pasinetti (1960) are quite explicit about the separation of the theory of value from that of distribution. Morishima (1989), on the other hand, is trying to combine the Sraffian approach (discussed below) with the theory of growth.
17. See, for instance, Morishima (1989), Roncaglia (1978), Sraffa (1960), Steedman (1977) and, to a limited extent, Walsh and Gram (1980).
18. A more systematic analysis of how the division of labour and interdependence develop can be found in Witztum (2010).
19. Some may find this Sraffian characteristic as not typical of classical economics. I agree that it might not have been characteristic to Ricardo but it certainly has been typical of Smith. I refer the reader to Smith's beautiful discussion of town and country relationship in Book 3, Chapter 1. Although the key issue here is balanced growth, the reasons for it are precisely the interdependence of the two sectors on one another.
20. Book 2, Chapter 1 of WN is devoted to discuss this division of an economy's stock.
21. In a more Smithian jargon, imagine the beaver and deer hunter when they choose to specialize. They will spend the whole day hunting only one animal (rather than the two if they were not specializing) and then bring to the market the surplus above what they would need from their own catch for their own subsistence. This process is described in detail and with full textual support in Witztum (2010).
22. I discuss the nuances of Smith's conception of rationality and its relevance to the different groups in society in Witztum (2005). The distinction, in part, is motivated by Smith's explicit assertion that the poor would respond to income above subsistence by propagating, while others would save, or accumulate.
23. In more general terms, the size of the box should be determined by $(1 - a_{ii} - \lambda_i)$, where λ_i is the luxurious consumption of one's own product. However, we shall assume without any loss of generality that $\lambda_i = 0$.
24. Smith's ethics and the theory of actions are developed in Witztum (2008).
25. In the context of Smith's ethical analysis, what we have here are the conditions for a system of actions to

be beneficial and to generate moral approval. Indeed they seem to be in line with Smith's emphasis on the importance of balanced growth to the advancement of opulence (see his discussion of it in WN III.i.1–6). On a more general note, the above kind of treatment of Smith allows us to deal with the cheerful and the dull states without having to commit ourselves to a Ricardian corn model. In the Ricardian model it was not really the question of interaction between the social classes which brings about the Smithian dull state. It was almost entirely due to the exogenous limitations of land. Here, as in Smith, the dull and cheerful states are seen as a result of particular interactions between the wants that prevail in society.

26. Recall that whether or not the division of labour is a source of increased productivity is a complex problem. As was pointed out by Rosenberg (1990) and West (1996), Smith deals with the effects of the division of labour differently in Books 1 and 5.
27. See a discussion in Witztum (2005).
28. This corresponds to the lengthy quote from WN III.i.4 where Smith describes the dependency between town and country.
29. By 'social wealth' Walras refers to personal faculties of individuals, land and capital, or produced wealth.
30. The point is elaborated in Witztum (2010).

References

Blaug, M. (1958), *Ricardian Economics: A Historical Study*, New Haven, CT: Yale University Press.
Blaug, Mark (1999), 'Misunderstanding classical economics: the Sraffian interpretation of the surplus approach', *History of Political Economy*, 31 (2), 213–36.
Blaug, Mark (2003), 'Rational vs historical reconstruction: a counter-note on Signorino's note on Blaug', *European Journal of the History of Economic Thought*, 10 (4), 607–8.
Blaug, Mark (2007), 'The fundamental theorems of modern welfare economics, historically contemplated', *History of Political Economy*, 39 (2), 185–208.
Baumol, W.J. and C. Wilson (eds) (2001), *Readings in Welfare Economics*, Cheltenham, UK and Northampton, MA, USA: Elgar Reference Collection.
Caravale G.A. and D.A. Tosato (1980), *Ricardo and the Theory of Value, Distribution and Growth*, London: Routledge & Kegan Paul.
Casarosa, C. (1985), 'The "New View" of the Ricardian theory of distribution and economic growth', in G.A. Caravale (ed.), *The Legacy of Ricardo*, London: Basil Blackwell, pp. 45–58.
Coles, J.L. and P.J. Hammond (1986), 'Walrasian equilibrium without survival: existence, efficiency and remedial policy', Technical Report no. 483, Stanford, CA: Institute for Mathematical Studies in the Social Sciences.
Costa, M.L. (1998), 'Walras and the NeoWalrasian diversion', *Journal of the History of Economic Thought*, 20 (1), 51–70.
Dasgupta, P. and J. Stiglitz (1980), 'Industrial structure and the nature of innovative activity', *Economic Journal*, 90, 266–93.
Eltis, W.A. (2000 [1984]), *The Classical Theory of Economic Growth*, 2nd edn, Basingstoke, UK: Palgrave.
Hicks, J, and S. Hollander (1977), 'Mr. Ricardo and the moderns', *Quarterly Journal of Economics*, 91 (3), 351–69.
Hollander, S. (1979), *The Economics of David Ricardo*, Toronto: University of Toronto Press.
Hutchison, T.W. (1999), 'Adam Smith and general equilibrium theory', in R.E. Backhouse and J. Creedy (eds), *From Classical Economics to the Theory of the Firm: Essays in Honour of D.P. O'Brien*, Cheltenham, UK and Northampton, MA, USA: Edward Elgar.
Jaffe, W. (1977), 'A centenarian on a bicentenarian: Leon Walras's *Elements* on Adam Smith's *Wealth of Nations*', *Canadian Journal of Economics*, 10 (1), 19–33.
Jaffe, W. (1980), 'Walras's economics as others see it', *Journal of Economic Literature*, 18 (2), 528–49.
Kaldor, N. (1956), 'Alternative theories of distribution', *Review of Economic Studies*, 23 (2), 83–100.
Levin, R.C. and P.C. Reiss (1984), 'Tests of a Schumpeterian model of R&D and market structures', in Z. Griliches (ed.), *R&D, Patents and Productivity*, Chicago: University of Chicago Press, pp. 175–208.
Morishima, M. (1977), *Walras's Economics: A Pure Theory of Capital and Money*, Cambridge: Cambridge University Press.
Morishima, M. (1989), *Ricardo's Economics: A General Equilibrium Theory of Distribution and Growth*, Cambridge: Cambridge University Press.
Negishi, T. (1985), *Economic Theories in a Non-Walrasian Tradition*, Cambridge: Cambridge University Press.
Pasinetti, L.L. (1960), 'A mathematical formulation of the Ricardian system', *Review of Economic Studies*, 27 (2), 78–98.
Pasinetti, L.L. (1981), *Structural Change and Economic Growth: A Theoretical Essay on the Dynamics of the Wealth of Nations*, Cambridge: Cambridge University Press.

Perlman, M. (1994), 'The inconsistency or redundancy of the wage fund doctrine in classical economics', *History of Political Economy*, **26** (3), 369–94.
Reid, G.C. (1987), 'Disequilibrium and increasing returns in Smith's analysis of growth and accumulation', *History of Political Economy*, **19** (1), 87–106.
Robbins, L. (1935), *An Essay on the Nature and Significance of Economic Science*, London: Macmillan.
Roncaglia, A. (1978), *Sraffa and the Theory of Prices*, Chichester: John Wiley & Sons.
Rosenberg, N. (1990), 'Adam Smith and the stock of moral capital', *History of Political Economy*, **22** (1), 1–18.
Samuelson, P. (1977), 'A modern theorist's vindication of Adam Smith', *American Economic Review*, **67** (1), 42–9.
Samuelson, P. (1978), 'The canonical classical model of political economy', *Journal of Economic Literature*, **16** (4), 1415–34.
Schumpeter, J.A. (1954), *History of Economic Analysis*, London: Allen & Unwin.
Smith, A. (1976), *The Theory of Moral Sentiments*, D.D. Raphael and A.L. Macfie (eds), Oxford: Oxford University Press (TMS).
Smith, A. (1976), *An Inquiry into the Nature and Causes of the Wealth of Nations*, R.H. Campbell, A.S. Skinner and W.B. Todd (eds), Oxford: Oxford University Press (WN).
Sraffa, P. (1960), *Production of Commodities by Means of Commodities*, Cambridge: Cambridge University Press.
Steedman, I. (1997), *Marx after Sraffa*, London: New Left Books.
Sutton, J. (1998), *Technology and Market Structure: Theory and History*, Cambridge, MA: MIT Press.
Walras, L. (1954), *Elements of Pure Economics*, Philadelphia, PA: Orion Editions.
Walras, L. (1896), *Etudes D'Economie Sociale (Theorie de la Repartition fe la Richesse Sociale)*, Lausanne: F. Rouge, Libraire-editeur.
Walras, L. (1860), *L'Economie Politique et La Justice*, Paris: Guillaumin.
Walker, D.A. (1987), 'Edgeworth versus Walras on the theory of Tatonnement', *Eastern Economic Journal*, **13** (2), 155–65.
Walker, D.A. (1996), *Walras' Market Models*, Cambridge: Cambridge University Press.
Walsh, V. and H. Gram (1980), *Classical and Neo-Classical Theories of General Equilibrium: Historical Origin and Mathematical Structure*, Oxford: Oxford University Press.
West, E.G. (1996), 'Adam Smith on the cultural effects of specialization: splenetics versus economics', *History of Political Economy*, **28** (1), 83–106.
Witteloostuijn, van A. and J.A.H. Maks (1990), 'Walras on temporary equilibrium and dynamics', *History of Political Economy*, **22** (2), 223–37.
Witztum, A. (1997), 'Distributive considerations in Smith's conception of economic justice', *Economics and Philosophy*, **13**, 241–59.
Witztum, A. (2005), 'Social circumstances and rationality: some lessons from Adam Smith', *American Journal of Economics and Sociology*, **64** (4), 1025–48.
Witztum, A. (2008), 'Unintended consequences and the ethics of interdependence: Smith's theory of actions and the moral significance of the invisible hand', *European Journal of the History of Economic Thought*, **15** (3), 401–32.
Witztum, A. (2010), 'Interdependence and equilibrium in Adam Smith', *History of Political Economy*, Spring, forthcoming.
Witztum, A. and J. Young (2006), 'The neglected agent: power, justice and distribution in Adam Smith', *History of Political Economy*, **38** (3), 437–96.

9 Stochastic demand and the extent of the market: another piece of the Smith puzzle
James M. Buchanan and Yong J. Yoon

Introduction
This chapter offers an interim progress report on a long-continued research program devoted to the unravelling of Adam Smith's theory of economic progress. The whole program is summarized in Smith's theorem that relates the division or specialization of labour, or other inputs, to the extent of the market, following the identification of specialization itself as the key element in the enhancement of value productivity.

The theorem itself has a curious history and place in economic discourse. Its validity is accepted without question in ordinary or commonsense discussions of market behaviour. Adam Smith's pin factory illustration graces the early chapters of many elementary textbooks, then and now. Yet, as presented, the relationship between market size and specialization is ignored in the more formalized and aesthetically elegant derivations of the conditions for economic equilibrium. At the heart of economists' apparent reluctance to explore Smith's theorem, as such, is the apparent contradiction between its implications for the organization of production and the observed reality of market competition. Dissonance has always been an element in the ongoing development of economic science, but the dominant neoclassical paradigm has continued to give Smith's principle little attention.[1]

In this chapter we sketch out the basic Smithean logic of trade or exchange, which is to be contrasted sharply with the dominant Ricardian logic, in which the Smith theorem on the extent of the market takes on trivial import.

We then summarize the neoclassical paradigm, with an emphasis on its welfare implications. The following sections examine the separate modern efforts to reconcile competitive market structures with the presence of increasing returns as implied in Smith's theorem. We then introduce the presence of stochastic demand as another possible source for the general validity of Smith's basic theorem. In the final section, we call attention to the implications of any incorporation of generalized increasing returns for the optimality properties of market equilibrium. We note, but do not formally examine, difficulties that arise in designing even idealized paths toward restoration of the familiar Paretian norms.

The origins of exchange
Why do persons specialize and trade? Economists locate their *raison d'être* in the explanatory response. Persons specialize and trade because, in so doing, they secure gains in value, as measured in their own judgmental rankings. Furthermore, and importantly, these gains are mutual. All parties to the production–exchange interaction find values enhanced; there are no losers. In modern terminology, the game is positive sum, and gains accrue to all participants.

To this point, no argument arises, regardless of any reference to motivational impetus that sets the whole process in being. But why is specialization and trade productive of net value? Response to this elementary, if secondary, question is twofold. A first response seems straightforward. Persons secure net value because they differ, one from another. This response, which we may describe as Ricardian, evokes the principle of comparative advantage. If persons should, perchance, be equally situated in all relevant descriptive dimensions, this motivation for specialization disappears. But so long as some differences exist, these may be increasingly exploited as the size of the overall potential interaction increases. Hence, Adam Smith's theorem seems to be corroborated so long as comparative advantage comes into play. This Ricardian motivational source for specialization and exchange implicitly informs the neoclassical analytical structure.

The point to be emphasized here, however, is that the comparative advantage model, introduced by Ricardo, was not the motivational source for specialization with Adam Smith as he derived the theorem concerning the extent of the market. In the Smithean setting, persons, prior to specialization, are roughly equal. Hence, there is no suggestion that specialization itself expresses a response to natural differences. For Adam Smith, persons would specialize and trade even if they were equal along all dimensions, both in capacities to produce value and in preferences among final products.

The persons who provide inputs in Adam Smith's familiar pin factory illustration are not initially different, one from another. The scale of the productive operation, which in turn depends on the size of the potential market, brings forth specialization as an emergent property. The existence of a potential demand for pins is a necessary determinant of the productivity of specialization. If this demand is sufficiently large, increasing differentiation among those who provide inputs to the joint effort becomes viable. The productivity of the enterprise increases disproportionately with the number of inputs applied.

Care must be taken to distinguish between the engineering and the economic logics of the scale economies. Measured outputs may increase disproportionately with increased measured inputs in some strictly quantitative sense, without reference to value. Economic meaning is given to scale economies only if values are assigned such that the value of outputs increases disproportionately with the increases in the value of inputs. The implication is that there must be sufficient demand for outputs to insure the economic viability of the scale of production required to generate those outputs. Exploitation of the economies of scale depends critically on the size or extent of the market.

In the Smithean model, illustrated by the pin factory, the economies of scale emerge from the intra-personal increases in dexterity made possible by specialization and hence concentration on particular tasks or shares in a joint production effort. If this feature is not present, there need be no net advantage over own or home production.

The neoclassical quandary
Adam Smith and his classical economics peers did not develop a satisfactory theory of distribution. Smith could, therefore, give a prominent place to the theorem relating specialization to the extent of the market without sensing any contradiction between this theorem and the implied organization of production. This contradiction, or quandary, emerges full-blown, however, in the more coherent neoclassical model of economic process. By completing the classical explanation so as to incorporate a theory of the distribution of valued end items, the neoclassical pioneers apparently felt it necessary to

introduce restrictions on the relationship between valued inputs and valued outputs in single organizational units.

If there are economies of scale, in a value sense, how extensive are they? If a productive unit or operation doubles in size, as measured by inputs, must the value of output more than double? If so, the logical consequence is that each good, or end item, will be most efficiently produced by a single organizational unit, or firm. If economies of scale extend without limit, the only constraints on rates of operation are imposed from the demand rather then the cost side of production. How, then, is competitiveness among separate producing units, whether existing or potential, at all viable in any inclusive model that generalizes Adam Smith's theorem on the extent of the market?

Some means of removing or solving the quandary or puzzle seems to be required by both empirical observation and logical coherence, as bolstered perhaps by normative inference. Industries seemed to be, for the most part and with relatively few exceptions, described by a multiplicity of producing units. A world of monopolies, as implied by models of increasing returns, seemed contrary to straightforward observation. Further, how is the theory of distribution to be made fully coherent? Any claim to the effect that this theory is complete must account for the payout of all value generated, with no surplus or deficit in the account. The value of final product must be precisely exhausted. Finally, how could the Marxian critique be contained?

The logical element was the easiest to resolve, with a solution that is also, admittedly, satisfying aesthetically. Euler's theorem, borrowed from mathematics, provided the key. If the production function exhibits constant returns, as the ratio between input and output values, then the payment to all input units at their measured marginal contributions will indeed precisely exhaust the total value of outputs produced. It is not surprising that the neoclassical economists seized the explanatory potential offered by Euler's theorem, but without concentrated attention on the implications of the constant returns presupposition. In the development of ideas, Smith's theorem on the relevance of the extent of the market was neglected, and this despite its near-universal commonsense acceptance.

But the puzzle remained. How could the neoclassical equilibrium, so beautifully laid out, be reconciled with everyday observation to the effect that industries show few signs of converging toward concentrations of production? Early response to this vexing question took the form of invoking offsetting elements of production that countered the presence of scale economies in the engineering sense. If the organization of production itself involves increasing costs, then competition among producing units seems viable. Firms are compelled to produce at output levels that minimize average costs, levels at which constant returns apply. By implication, the Smith theorem on the extent of the market does not hold. So long as the economy is modeled in this way, the extent of the market loses force as a determining variable in the generation of value.

Marshallian external economies

Alfred Marshall was unwilling to discard fully classical economists' ideas, and he was not satisfied with the conventional neoclassical response to the quandary sketched out in preceding sections. Marshall observed that increases in output in some industries did result in decreases in average costs, implying that aggregate production must take place under increasing returns. He also noted, however, that the relationship between production costs and industry output was not sensed by decision-makers for the firms in the industries involved.

Marshall's resolution became the origin of the concept of external economies. If the arguments in a firm's production function include the output of the industry as a whole quite apart from the firm's own output, and if the share of this firm in the total industry remains relatively small, the presence of the external effects will exert minimal influence on behaviour. In the limiting case, industry output is treated as a parameter in the single firm's choice of output level.

In this setting, increasing returns will characterize the relevant industries as the aggregate output of those industries increase. Adam Smith's basic theorem seems validated. And there is no conflict with observed competitive structures. Note, in particular, that in this Marshallian solution, the presence of increasing returns is concentrated in identified sectors rather then the inclusive economic nexus. The extent of the market, overall, is not the relevant variable.

The policy implications are clear. Increased economic value may be secured by some shift of resources from sectors that exhibit constant or decreasing returns to those sectors described by increasing returns, as generated by the externalities. And this result holds even if the overall or aggregate size of the economy remains unchanged.

The Marshallian resolution to the quandary posed by the juxtaposition between increasing returns and competitive organization resurfaced in important contributions made during the last decades of the twentieth century. Paul Romer (1990), especially, and Robert Lucas (1988), identified the knowledge industry as falling directly within the Marshallian explanatory model. Because any production of knowledge necessarily includes non-excludable elements, separate firms have little motivation to carry production to socially efficient limits. Further, no single firm confronts what appears to be potential monopoly advantage.[2]

Preferences for diversity

The modern revival of attention to increasing returns (Buchanan and Yoon, 1994) extended well beyond applications of Marshallian external economies. Economists had observed that trade among and between producing units in separate but similar political jurisdictions takes place, despite any apparent differences in factor endowments that might allow comparative advantage in some Ricardian sense to be exploited. At the same time, there seemed to be no basis for invoking the Marshallian explanatory model.

Paul Krugman (1979) and Wilfred Ethier (1982) introduced what has been referenced as the new theory of international trade as a means of explaining observed trading patterns. This theory incorporates increasing returns at the level of operation of individual firms, but it imposed a demand-side constraint that reflects consumer preferences for diversity. Building on earlier models of monopolistic competition, producing firms were modeled as operating under increasing returns (decreasing average costs), but each firm was limited in opportunities to exploit potential monopoly positions by the demand-side limits. Homogeneity in goods produced was accepted only within broad meaning. Consumer-buyers, whether of final products or intermediate goods, were modeled as expressing a preference for diversity, as such.

This structure of the production–exchange nexus insures that, in equilibrium, an increase in the size of the aggregate economy will generate disproportionate increases in value. Firms will, as demand increases, move further down the average cost functions, shifts in output that would not prove profitable prior to the aggregate demand change.

Market interaction networks
A further contribution to the modern renewal of interest in increasing returns was developed, almost single-handedly, by Xiaokai Yang (2001). He located economies of scale, as had Adam Smith, squarely in the productivity of the individual, whose creation of value is enhanced by intra-personal specialization.[3] Yang modeled an economic interaction network among equally situated persons who are simultaneously producers and consumers, each of whom, and for every good, confronts the choice between home or own production, with subsequent consumption, and production for the market, followed by exchange for desired final product.

In this stylized setting, given the intra-personal economies offered by specialization, generalized increasing returns to the size of the market are present. As the network expands, as measured roughly by the number of trading nodes, more and more persons specialize and shift goods from home to market production. As more goods become marketable, the aggregate value generated in the economy increases disproportionately with the extent of the network.

Yang's model differs from both the Marshallian external economies source of increasing returns and that source which reflects desires for diversity in its generality. There is no particular sector or industrial group or set of goods in which increasing returns are located or concentrated. Generalized increasing returns characterize the whole interaction process due to the inherent advantages of input specialization, as such. Hence, so long as more inputs face opportunities to specialize, the economy will operate under increasing returns. However, because the scale economies are limited to the productivity of the individualized input units, rather than to the scale of operation of some integrated team of units, as might be organized through a firm, there is no opportunity for potential monopolization.

Stochastic demand: another piece of the puzzle
Our aim in this chapter is neither to deny the presence of the possible sources for increasing returns sketched out in previous sections nor to relegate any of these to secondary explanatory status. Our claim is the more limited one to the effect that there may be an additional source for increasing returns applicable to the aggregate economy. In other words, we suggest that even if none of the previously discussed sources of increasing returns are present, an increase in the size of the economic nexus will disproportionately increase the value of output. In sum, there is yet more to Adam Smith's theorem than those models suggest.

Conventionally, economists give little attention to features of the goods upon which persons place value. It is plausible to suggest that there must always exist a 'sea of goods', either as final products or as intermediate inputs, upon which values may be assigned. These goods, as final products, become arguments in persons' utility functions. Only a finite number of these goods will be economically viable, whatever the size of the trading network. If all goods are partitionable among users, any goods that are valued above opportunity cost will be produced and distributed through the market, provided only that the demand remains stable over subsequent production–consumption periods.

We change the model only by the introduction of the plausible presupposition that, at least some of the goods upon which positive value is placed, a value that exceeds opportunity cost, exhibit stochastic rather than stable demands. Illustratively, think of a non-storable good that may be produced at an opportunity cost of $1 per unit, and assume that the market is fully contestable. A potential consumer-buyer places positive value on the good, but this value emerges only probabilistically. There is, say, only one chance in 100 that the good will be valued above opportunity cost in, say, any defined time period. Unless production is, quite literally, simultaneous with purchase, none of the good will be put on the market unless the size of the nexus extends to 100 or more potential equally situated customers. Clearly, the economic viability of the good in question depends on the extent of the market. Goods that remain below the threshold limit will not be produced. Adam Smith's principle applies over the whole range of goods that exhibit stochastic elements in demand.

Economists have neglected analyses of markets for these goods because of the implicit working presumption that the number and definition of potentially valued goods are fixed.

Competitive organization and increasing returns

Note that with the external economies explanatory model and also with the preferences-for-diversity model the neoclassical quandary is fully resolved. There is no inconsistency between these institutional structures and the emergence and maintenance of effective competition. No producing unit senses that a potential opportunity for monopolization exists.

The settings in both Yang's network model and in the one with stochastic demand presented above are somewhat different from those present in the more familiar models. In both cases, either a shift from home to market production or the production of a good with stochastic demand, the new good is available to all market participants. An initial producer might sense an opportunity to exploit a potential monopoly position. At best, however, any such exploitation is severely limited by the basic Smithean presumption that all persons are equally endowed. Hence, freedom of entry insures that all market opportunities are fully contestable. An overt effort by an initial specialized producing unit to secure monopoly rents would be met by expressed willingness of other producing units to enter the market. As the extent of the market increases, the overall competitive process is described by the presence of more and more specializations.

Pareto optimality and generalized increasing returns

The welfare implications of the presence of generalized increasing returns are in themselves interesting. Note that only if the source of increasing returns is located in some variant of Marshallian external economies is the stylized competitive equilibrium non-optimal in the conventional Pareto sense. If individual preference orderings are presumed to be exogenous, and hence beyond the purview for examination, then the stylized equilibrium attainable under preferences for diversity, for market versus home production, and for stochastic versus non-stochastic goods, meets criteria for Pareto efficiency.

Something seems amiss with such an evaluative judgment, however, since the presence of generalized increasing returns in itself implies that an expansion in the size or extent of the whole market nexus (Adam Smith's basic proposition) will disproportionately increase aggregate value. The critical question at issue is whether or not and in what circumstances the extent of the market can, in some meaningful sense, become a choice variable or, put differently, be treated as endogenous or exogenous.

Under constant returns, a shift in preferences carries no direct implications for aggregate evaluation and, by inference, for the welfare of participants, by their own standards. By contrast, under generalized increasing returns, specifically defined directional shifts in preference orderings can modify aggregate value. For example, in the models derivative from monopolistic competition equilibria, if persons, some or all, exhibit a shift toward acceptance of uniformity, everyone in the nexus may, conceptually, find utility enhanced. Similarly, in the home-versus-market model, if some or all persons shift toward production for the market, the adjusted equilibrium may be Pareto dominating. Essentially the same thing can be said about possible shifts toward preferences for goods with stochastic demands. (The welfare implications of any of the several sources of increasing returns depend, of course, upon acceptance of the presupposition upon which the whole analysis is based, namely that market evaluation is the basis for objective measures of welfare.)

As noted, except in settings in the presence of Marshallian externalities, there is no allocative shift of resources among sectors of the economy, among separate producers of well-defined goods, that will exploit opportunities for net value creation that seem to be offered by potential preference changes along several choice margins. So long as the presupposition of exogeneity in preference orderings is retained, there is no conceptually identifiable 'better' usage of existing resources.

There are, however, indirect implications of the presence of generalized increasing returns. In the absence of the conditions necessary to satisfy competitive equilibrium with optimality properties, possible changes in market constraints may take on enhanced importance. The effective extent of the market is affected by the institutional structure within which production and exchange take place, and any change in this structure, whether to add or remove barriers to exchange, modifies the potential for specialization. For example, the removal of a previously existing constraint on entry will increase the extent of the market, thereby creating the potential for gains over and beyond those that are conceptually measured by the 'excess burdens' (or welfare triangles) familiar in conventional models.

Much the same conclusion applies as macroeconomic considerations are incorporated into the analytical framework. To the extent that participants may, privately or collectively, effectively hoard or release apparent value represented by holding of non-producible 'goods', notably money or some equivalent store of value, the size of the aggregate production–trading network, measured by aggregate demand flow, may be changed. The previously existing allocation of resources is thereby disrupted and the restoration of equilibrium may involve adjustment lags. With generalized increasing returns, there are effects of macro-money disequilibria that are over and beyond the strictly temporal dislocations. If, for example, an unanticipated net hoarding acts to generate a reduction in aggregate demand on the market, the degree of specialization shrinks. Adam Smith's theorem comes into play to inaugurate secondary and cumulative allocative results which, in turn, makes return to any equilibrium more difficult.

In summation, Adam Smith's theorem must be more systematically incorporated into the way that economists conceptualize the whole market process. Properly understood, the theorem strengthens rather than weakens the normative argument for free and open exchange.

Notes

1. The central neoclassical postulate of constant returns has been challenged by many economists, and with varying degrees of success. For a volume that contains many of the contributions, see Buchanan and Yoon (1994). For a modern treatment of one of the several challenges, see Warsh (2006).
2. For a narrative account of this modern strand of analysis, see Warsh (2006).
3. Note should be made here of a much neglected paper by Houthakker (1956), which also concentrates on intra-personal scale economies.

Bibliography

Buchanan, James M. and Yong J. Yoon (eds) (1994), *The Return to Increasing Returns*, Ann Arbor, MI: University of Michigan Press.
Ethier, Wilfred J. (1982), 'National and international returns to scale in the modern theory of international trade', *American Economic Review*, **72** (3), 389–405.
Houthakker, Hendrik S. (1956), 'Economics and biology: specialization and speciation', *Kyklos*, **9** (2), 181–9.
Krugman, Paul R. (1979), 'Increasing returns, monopolistic competition, and international trade', *Journal of International Economics*, **9** (4), 469–79.
Lucas, Robert E., Jr. (1988), 'On the mechanics of economic development', *Journal of Monetary Economics*, **22**, 3–42.
Marshall, Alfred (1890), *Principles of Economics*, 9th variorum edn, C.W. Guillebaud, London: Macmillan, 1961.
Romer, Paul M. (1990), 'Endogenous technological change', *Journal of Political Economy*, **98** (5) (part 2), S71–102.
Smith, Adam (1776), *An Inquiry into the Nature and Causes of the Wealth of Nations*, edited by R.H. Campbell and A.S. Skinner, Oxford: Oxford University Press, 1976.
Warsh, David (2006), *Knowledge and Wealth of Nations*, New York: W.W. Norton.
Yang, Xiaokai (2001), *Economics: New Classical Versus Neoclassical Frameworks*, Oxford: Blackwell.
Yoon, Yong J. (2007), 'Stochastic demand, specialization, and increasing returns', manuscript.

10 Smithian answers to some puzzling results in the experimental literature
*Maria Pia Paganelli**

This chapter draws attention to the increased use of Adam Smith's work in the experimental economics literature. It also offers examples of how studying Adam Smith can help formulate possible answers to some otherwise counter-intuitive (if the intuition is based on the rational choice paradigm) experimental results. The first part of the chapter presents a short account of how, in recent years, the field has come to recognize the importance of considering other-regarding preferences as well as self-regarding preferences and how it is noticing the wealth of Adam Smith, who dealt with both. The central section of the chapter offers examples of how the Smithian apparatus can provide plausible explanatory stories for data from experimental games such as, but not limited to, the Ultimatum Game, the Dictator Game and the Trust Game, which usually cannot be explained using only strict rational choice. Smithian resentment, love of praiseworthiness and dread of blameworthiness, on the other hand, seem to be plausible explanations for the seemingly irrational punishment and generosity observed in these experimental games. Concluding remarks end the chapter.

Adam Smith is considered the father of economics. The concept of *Homo economicus*, the rational agent with self-regarding preferences, can be regarded as his most famous child, for good or bad. Adam Smith somehow generated *Homo economicus* with one sentence: 'it is not from the benevolence of the butcher, baker, brewer that we expect our dinner, but from their regard to their own interest' (WN I.ii.2). Of course, there is more in Smith than the self-interest of the 'baker, butcher, brewer'. But for some time not many economists bothered with it. Out of either shame or arrogance, most economists dismissed this embarrassing and/or uninteresting side of their old father's work. As a result, the other-regarding Smithian components fell into oblivion, leaving us with the lonely *Homo economicus*. But:

> Two implications of the standard model of self-regarding preferences are in strong conflict with both daily observed preferences and the laboratory and field experiments . . . The first is the implication that agents care only about the outcome of an economic interaction and not about the process through which this outcome is attained (e.g., bargaining, coercion, chance, voluntary transfer). The second is the implication that agents care only about what they personally gain and lose through an interaction and not what other agents gain or lose (or the nature of their intentions). Until recently, with these assumptions in place, economic theory proceeded like mathematics rather than natural science; theorem after theorem concerning individual human behavior was proven, while empirical validation of such behavior was rarely deemed relevant and infrequently provided. (Gintis et al., 2005, p. 6)

Recently something has changed. With experimental economics, the empirical validation of self-regarding behaviours has become feasible and it is so frequently provided that it can no longer be easily ignored. Results from experimental economics research cannot always be explained by self-regarding preferences alone, in their strict forms at least. Moreover, openness to multidisciplinary interaction is often required to interpret the complexity of human behaviours emerging from some of these experimental results.

In light of the development of some branches of experimental economics, a handful of economists is realizing at least two things about Adam Smith. First, that 'the butcher, baker, brewer' sentence is only one sentence in the almost 1500 pages that Smith published in his lifetime. And second, that Smith's analysis has such a deep and broad breadth that is often able to provide plausible explanations for some of the 'anomalies' reported in experimental results.

Adam Smith, and not just his 'economic' book, but the whole body of his work, is being increasingly read, even by economists. *The Theory of Moral Sentiments* (TMS), the 'other' book by Smith, the book that often embarrassed economists because of its strong other-regarding bent, is now the source of a relatively large literature. It is indeed that very TMS that today receives the applauses of economists, or at least of some of them. The same characteristics of Smith that were previously a source of dismissal, are now a source of interest, authority and appreciation. Today, with our hyper-specialization, we wonder at the beauty of the complexity of the human system described by one person. So we have Smith again – this time in his glory, with both *The Wealth of Nations* (WN) and TMS widely appreciated. A simple citation count in the economic journals of JSTOR alone shows that in the decade from 1945 to 1955, WN was cited 1267 times, but TMS only 98. In the decade 1995–2005, WN is counted about 40 per cent more times (1804 times), while the number of citations of TMS almost doubles over the same period of time, reaching 180. Nava Ashraf, Colin Camerer and George Loewenstein testify to this increasing usage of Smith with their 2005 article in the *Journal of Economic Perspectives*, where they show how well Adam Smith's analysis explains behavioural results. They motivate their work in the following way:

> Adam Smith's psychological perspective in *The Theory of Moral Sentiments* is remarkably similar to 'dual-process' frameworks advanced by psychologists . . . neuroscientists . . . and more recently by behavioral economists, based on behavioral data and detailed observation of brain functioning . . . It also anticipated a wide range of insights regarding phenomena such as loss aversion, willpower and fairness . . . that have been the focus of modern behavioral economics . . . The purpose of this essay is to draw attention to some of these connections. Indeed, as we propose at the end of the paper, *The Theory of Moral Sentiments* suggests promising directions for economic research that have not yet been exploited. (Ashraf et al., 2005, p. 132)

Ashraf et al., citing the literature for which TMS is relevant, list for example Kirkpatrick and Epstein (1992), Damasio (1994), Le Doux (1996), Sloman (1996), Panksepp (1998), Smith (1998), Metcaft and Mischel (1999), Benhabib and Bisin (2005), Bernheim and Rangel (2004), Camerer and Loewenstein (2004), Fudenberg and Levine (2004), and Loewenstein and O'Donoghue (2004).

Vernon Smith, 2002 Nobel Prize winner for his contribution to experimental economics (see Smith, 2003), opens the door to this new appreciation of the whole Adam Smith in his Southern Economic Society Distinguished Guest Lecture, published in the *Southern Economic Journal* in 1998. Here, Vernon Smith goes straight to the embarrassing part of Adam Smith. TMS and its other-regarding behaviours, the source of the infamous 'Adam Smith problem', should be considered seriously because, among other things, it does not contradict the book about self-regarding preferences; to the contrary, it is a complement to it. And so, using experimental results, Vernon Smith shows that the contradiction between the two books does not exist, as both books are about exchange, either material or intangible:

> [Adam] Smith had but one behavioral axiom, 'the propensity to truck, barter, and exchange one thing for another,' where the objects of trade I will interpret to include not only goods, but also gifts, assistance, and favours out of sympathy, that is, 'generosity, humanity, kindness, compassion, mutual friendship and esteem' . . . [Adam Smith's behavioral axiom] explains why human nature appears simultaneously self-regarding and other-regarding. It may also provide an understanding of the origin and ultimate foundation of property rights . . . Both social exchange and trade implicitly recognize mutual rights to act, which are conveyed in what we commonly refer to as 'property rights.' In what sense are such rights 'natural'? The answer, I think, is to be found in the universality, spontaneity, and evolutionary fitness value of reciprocity behavior. Reciprocity in human nature (and prominently in our closest primate relative, the chimpanzee) is the foundation of our uniqueness as creatures of social exchange, which we extended to include trade with nonkin and nontribal members long, long before we adopted herder and farmer life styles. (Smith, 1998, p. 3)

And while in 1998 Vernon Smith gives evolutionary and experimental evidence 'that trade can be hypothesized to have grown out of social or gift exchange' (p. 5), the previous year Jeffrey Young (1997) interpreted Adam Smith as saying exactly the same thing, as Ashraf et al. (2005) recognize. Vernon Smith states that:

> the key to understanding our long 'propensity to truck, barter, and exchange' is to be found, I think, in our evolved capacity for reciprocity, which formed the foundation for social exchange long before there was trade in the conventional economic sense. All humans, in all cultures, engage in the trading of favors. Although the cultural forms of reciprocity are endlessly variable, functionally reciprocity is universal. We do beneficial things for our friends, and implicitly we expect beneficial acts in kind from them . . . You invite me to dinner and two months later I invite you to dinner. (Smith, 1998, p. 4)

Jeffrey Young offers the argument he believes '[Adam] Smith would have made, to explain why voluntarily exchange emerges and why he viewed markets as essentially benign social institutions' in the following way:

> Market exchange is a social activity which depends for its origin on each person wanting both fellow-feeling and material goods. The other-regarding principles of human nature which bind people together in society are a necessary condition for the emergence of the exchange of surplus produce among neighbors. [Adam] Smith uses the moral side of human nature to help explain why voluntarily agreement and not violence takes place when these two hunters meet. Anti-social manifestations of self-love are ruled out on the ground that the offending individual would lose the concord of feeling which is agreeable in its own right. However, he would also lose the approbation of his neighbors (represented internally as the impartial spectator even when he is alone out in the woods) a prospect which is also disagreeable in itself, because of his human desire to be approved of. As a result he will eventually lose his dinner since the neighbors will cease bringing him gifts and/or no one will trade with him. No one would want to have the reputation of being ungrateful, that is, one who does not reciprocate gifts. (Young, 1997, p. 62)

Both Vernon Smith and Adam Smith, as here interpreted by Young, present the relevance of reciprocity, both positive and negative. Positive reciprocity is present when someone reciprocates a cooperative action with a cooperative action. Negative reciprocity is instead the willingness and ability to punish non-cooperation in a social exchange. In social exchanges, the (impartial) spectator withdraws his approbation if one does not cooperate, just like our neighbour withdraws his invitation for dinner if we are caught free-riding.

The relevance of negative reciprocity is also highlighted by what Adam Smith calls resentment, an emotion whose manifestation is captured in an experimental game known as the Ultimatum Game (Figure 10.1). In this game there are two human players, usually, but not always, undergraduate students. As in all economics experiments, subjects voluntarily come to the experiments and are paid in local currency the amount they earn by playing the experimental game. They read the instructions of the game and make their decisions either on sheets of paper or on computer terminals. For each experiment, the number of total participants is chosen so that the experimenter has enough observations to analyse the results statistically. In the standard Ultimatum Game players' anonymity is strictly preserved. Player 1 (Sender) receives an amount of dollars (usually $10 for undergraduate students in the US) and is asked to send any of those dollars to Player 2 (Receiver). Should the Receiver accept the Sender's offer, the $10 are divided according to the terms of the offer. If the Receiver rejects the offer, both the Receiver and the Sender do not earn anything.

The rational choice prediction is a sub-game perfect Nash equilibrium where Player 1 gives as little as possible and Player 2 accepts any amount.

When this game is played in experiments, the results persistently do not match the rational choice prediction. Even when conditions and pay-offs are changed, subjects tend to split the amount 50–50 and tend to reject offers that are less than 50 per cent (Guth and Tietz, 1990; Roth et al., 1991; Camerer and Thaler, 1995). So the question is: Why? Why do human subjects not behave like *Homo economicus*?

The explanation usually offered is a combination of two factors: fairness, and strategic behaviour due to fear of rejection. Fair behaviour under these conditions for US undergraduates is a 50–50 split. An offer of less than that may be rejected because it is perceived as unfair. Senders know this and decrease the risk of being punished by offering 50 per cent of the pie. Thus, rational choice theory may explain why Senders send 50 per cent. But what about the Receiver's rejections? These are one-shot games, so punishment with the aim of influencing future behaviour is not an option.

Receivers who reject offers, when asked, tend to explain their behaviour by saying that they wanted to punish unfair behaviour. Unfair Senders deserve to be punished, even at a personal cost. Indeed, if the Sender is a computer rather than a person, low offers are rarely rejected (Blount, 1995). Such results suggest that *Homo economicus* does not work well as an exclusive explanatory device.

Data from Trust (or 'gift exchange') Games mirror these results. Here, Player 1 can either keep a fixed sum of money or send part of it to Player 2, who will receive the amount sent multiplied by a predetermined factor. Player 2 can then take all of what they received and leave Player 1 with nothing, or send back some of the money. The rational choice prediction here is that Player 2 takes all that is sent to them and sends nothing back to Player 1. Because Player 1 is able to anticipate Player 2's behaviour, he or she initially sends nothing. Despite this prediction, a surprising amount of trust is usually observed, and the 'returns to trust' tend to be positive (Fehr et al., 1993; Berg et al., 1995).

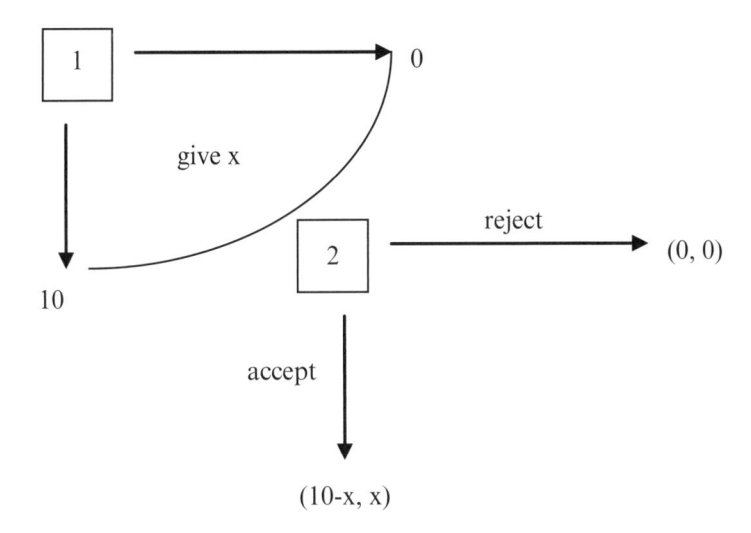

Figure 10.1   Ultimatum Game

Reciprocity seems to be a plausible explanation for these 'counter-intuitive' results. One rewards what is perceived as fair and kind, and one punishes what is perceived as a mean and intentional violation of fairness, even if punishment involves incurring a direct personal cost. Colin Camerer (1997) reminds us that formal models of these results are possible with the use of a utility function with '"sympathy coefficients" [which] were mentioned in Adam Smith' (p. 169) (see also Rabin, 1993). The recognition of Adam Smith is not just nominal.

Adam Smith indeed seems to provide explanations for why we tend to reject unfair offers in the Ultimatum Game if those offers come from another human player; for why we tend to accept low offers if they come from chance or from a machine; and for why we send money back in a Trust Game. We resent Player 1 in an Ultimatum Game if they do not split fairly the amount they receive, and we punish them as a consequence. We are grateful to Player 1 in a Trust Game, and we reciprocate the trust by sending some money back to them. But we do not think that a computer trusted us or was unfairly greedy toward us, so there is no need to reciprocate either positively or negatively. In Adam Smith's words:

> Before any thing, therefore, can be the complete and proper object, either of gratitude or resentment, it must possess three different qualifications. First, it must be the cause of pleasure in the one case, and of pain in the other. Secondly, it must be capable of feeling those sensations. And, thirdly, it must not only have produced those sensations, but it must have produced them from design, and from a design that is approved of the one case, and disapproved of in the other. It is by the first qualification, that any object is capable of exciting those passions: it is by the second, that it is in any respect capable of gratifying them: the third qualification is not only necessary for their complete satisfaction, but as it gives a pleasure or pain that is both exquisite and peculiar, it is likewise an additional exciting cause of those passions. (TMS II.iii.1.6)

From the results of the Ultimatum Game, one can hypothesize that a Receiver punishes out of resentment and that a Sender sends out of fear of that resented punishment.

```
        ┌───┐ ─────────────→ 0
        │ 1 │
        └───┘       give x
          │                  ┌───┐
          │                  │ 2 │
          ▼                  └───┘
         10                    │
                             accept
                               │
                               ▼
                            (10-x, x)
```

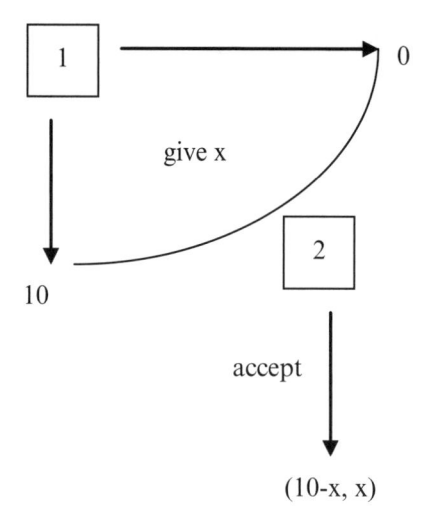

Figure 10.2 Dictator Game

But is that the end of the story? The answer is no. Experimentalists are aware that the design of the Ultimatum Game does not allow us to infer clearly the motivations of the Sender. One cannot completely discharge either fairness or strategic motivations. One can say that the self-regarding Sender gives to the Receiver because they do not want to be hated and punished. But one can also say that the other-regarding Sender gives to the Receiver because it is fair to do so. Do I give money to the beggar because I fear being attacked if I do not, or because I feel it is the right thing for me to do?

Experimentalists designed another experiment to control for the Sender's strategic behaviour and isolate fairness. This game is a modified Ultimatum Game, where the Receiver's ability to retaliate against an unfair Sender is eliminated, and it is known as the Dictator Game (Figure 10.2). In the Dictator Game, the Sender (Dictator) faces the same choice as in the Ultimatum Game: choose how much of the money given to them to send to their anonymously paired Receiver. But here, the Receiver cannot reject the offer of the Sender. The Receiver must take what the Dictator sends without any possibility of revenge. Thus, the game's dynamics imply that the choice of the Sender will not be motivated by strategic behaviour intended to decrease the risk of rejection. If a Sender sends a positive amount to the Receiver, he or she would be motivated only by other-regarding preferences. Given that there is no cost associated with this self-regarding action, the rational choice prediction is that the Dictator keeps everything and sends nothing.

But the experimental results of this game also do not conform with the rational choice prediction: 20–30 per cent of the Senders give 50 per cent, while 30 per cent of the Senders take the whole pot (Roth et al., 1991; Forsythe et al., 1994; Henrich et al., 2004). The average giving is around 30 per cent, significantly more than the rational choice prediction of zero. Although it is true that we do observe more aggressive low offers, which indicates that the fear of rejection does play a role in the giving of the Ultimatum Game, we also observe that strategic behaviour is not the whole story. Some fairness is present in these results.

Adam Smith, again, provides us a plausible explanation. Adam Smith would say that resentment does not come only from Player 2, or more generally from another person. Resentment comes also from the impartial 'inhabitant of our breast', from 'the man within' us. Indeed, Adam Smith writes:

> There can be no proper motive for hurting our neighbour, there can be no incitement to do evil to another, which mankind will go along with, except just indignation for evil which that other has done to us. To disturb his happiness merely because it stands in the way of our own, to take from him what is of real use to him merely because it may be of equal or of more use to us, or to indulge, in this manner, at the expence of other people, the natural preference which every man has for his own happiness above that of other people, is what no impartial spectator can go along with . . . Though it may be true, therefore, that every individual, in his own breast, naturally prefers himself to all mankind, yet he dares not look mankind in the face, and avow that he acts according to this principle . . . If he would act so as that the impartial spectator may enter into the principles of his conduct, which is what of all things he has the greatest desire to do, he must, upon this, as upon all other occasions, humble the arrogance of his self-love, and bring it down to something which other men can go along with . . . [The impartial spectator] readily, therefore, sympathize[s] with the natural resentment of the injured, and the offender becomes the object of [the impartial spectator's] hatred and indignation. He is sensible that he becomes so, and feels that those sentiments are ready to burst out from all sides against him. (TMS II.ii.11)

So for Adam Smith we do not 'indulge . . . at the expence of other people', not just because we fear their resentment but because we fear the resentment of the impartial spectator who voices from within us what is right and what is wrong.

The positive consequences of this self-directed resentment are described by Young (2005):

> Smith defines the laws of justice as those that guard a person against injury in the form of loss of life, health, possessions, estate, or personal rights (TMS, II.ii.2.2). Such injuries arouse the resentment of the impartial spectator and cause him to sympathize with the victim's desire for revenge. The sense of justice arises out of the unsocial passions: 'Resentment . . . is the safeguard of justice and the security of innocence' II.ii.1.4. (p. 95)

Adam Smith goes further in the analysis. He distinguishes between an action that is meant to generate a pay-off from another person, and an action with no external pay-off. Smith refers to pay-offs in terms of approbation, not in terms of monetary pay-offs as we observe in experimental games. Yet I believe his argument is strengthened, not weakened, by a monetary component. Adam Smith distinguishes between our willingness to be praised and to avoid blame – to receive a positive or negative pay-off from another person, even if in terms of approbation or disapprobation – and our willingness to be praiseworthy and not to be blameworthy – to do the right thing even if there is nobody there to praise or blame us.

He claims that we do the right thing, even in the absence of a threat of punishment from another person, because not only we love praise and dread blame, but we also love praiseworthiness and dread blameworthiness:

> Man naturally desires, not only to be loved, but to be lovely; or to be that thing which is the natural and proper object of love. He naturally dreads, not only to be hated, but to be hateful; or to be that thing which is the natural and proper object of hatred. He desires, not only praise, but praise-worthiness; or to be that thing which, though it should be praised by nobody, is,

however, the natural and proper object of praise. He dreads, not only blame, but blame-worthiness; or to be that thing which, though it should be blamed by nobody, is, however, the natural and proper object of blame. (TMS III.2.1, pp. 113–14)

The resentment of 'the man within' which makes an 'offender' the 'object of hatred and indignation' in the eyes of his conscience, and eventually generates justice in society, seems to be a plausible explanation for the Sender's giving which is observed in the experimental settings described above.

Adam Smith's analysis of the difference between praise and praiseworthiness offers us an additional point of reflection. Adam Smith seems to warn us against attempts to dress up explanations of self-regarding preferences as other-regarding behaviours when he says:

> The love of praise-worthiness is by no means derived altogether from the love of praise. These two principles, though they resemble one another, though they are connected, and often blended with one another, are yet, in many respects, distinct and independent of one another. (TMS III.2.2, p. 114)

The fairness observed in the experimental results may indeed have little to do with self-regarding preferences. Herbert Gintis, Samuel Bowles, Robert Boyd and Ernst Fehr, who begin their 2005 book stating that, 'The ideas presented in this book are part of a continuous line of intellectual inheritance from Adam Smith' (p. 3), say indeed that:

> if altruism is actually misapplied self-interest, we might expect altruistic behavior to be driven out of existence by consistently self-regarding individuals in the long run. If these arguments are correct, it would likely lead to the collapse of the sophisticated forms of cooperation that have arisen in civilized societies . . . Moreover, the alternative suggests that agents can use their intellect to 'learn' to behave selfishly when confronted with the results of their suboptimal behavior. The evidence, however, suggests that cooperation based on strong reciprocity can unravel when there is no means of punishing free-riders but that it does not unravel simply through repetition. (Gintis et al., 2005, pp. 25–6)

Furthermore, some contributions in their volume set out to demonstrate that:

> Strong reciprocity evolved because groups with strong reciprocators were capable of stabilizing prosocial norms that could not be supported using principles of long-term self-interest alone, because it is generally fitness-enhancing for an individual to punish only transgressions against the individual himself, and then only if the time horizon is sufficiently lengthy to render a reputation for protecting one's interests. On the other hand, the same mechanisms that have the ability to enforce prosocial norms can almost as easily enforce fitness-neutral and antisocial norms. (p. 30)

To one familiar with the work of Adam Smith, these results should not be surprising. David Levy (1992) notices that, although we observe rational choice utility-maximizing behaviour in experiments with animal subjects, we do not observe the more complex forms of cooperation more typical of human societies such as 'fair and deliberate exchange' (WN I.ii). We need more than just self-regarding preferences, as Adam Smith recognized. Young (2001) indeed notes that:

> the modern procedure of attempting to derive cooperation from the self-interest assumption alone is [not] a faithful representation of the way Smith actually thought about the problem . . .

Smith's theory is rooted in those characteristics of human nature which are on the benevolence side of the moral continuum . . . [In Smith there is] interdependence into each individual's utility function via the other-regarding impulses in human nature. (p. 99)

Given that complex forms of cooperation are distinctly human and are not easily explained with only self-regarding preferences, the question posed by Jerry Evensky becomes more salient: 'How does a society of autonomous individuals cohere?' (2001, p. 508). Or again: 'What cohesive force can hold liberal society together so that its potential – a good, secure life for each individual and the greatest possible wealth for the nation – can be realized? . . . How can a liberal society avoid the Hobbesian abyss of a war of all against all? How is *e pluribus unum* possible?' (2005, pp. 248–50). Evensky, showing that *Homo economicus* theories are not strong enough to keep society from disruption, makes the following claim:

In sum, if a liberal society is to be cohesive and constructive, human beings must have 'mutual trust and confidence in the behavioral ethics of each other' because absent ethics, rent-seeking can run amuck. A society populated by *homo economicus* does not have the capacity to establish this prerequisite for social cohesion. (2005, p. 253)

The presence of something more than just *Homo economicus*, as Adam Smith tells us, and the risks of having models of human behaviour featuring only *Homo economicus*, as Evensky tells us, is also presented by Elinor Ostrom, in one of the essays contained in Gintis at al. (2005). Ostrom, presenting evidence from Public Goods games, claims:

Voluntary behavior is the result of what we have called the predisposition to contribute to a cooperative endeavor, contingent upon the cooperation of others. The monetary incentive to contribute destroys the cooperative nature of the task, and the threat of fining defectors may be perceived as being an unkind or hostile action (especially if the fine is imposed by agents who have an antagonistic relationship with group members). The crowding out of voluntary cooperation and altruistic punishment occurs because the preconditions for the operation of strong reciprocity are removed when explicit material incentives are applied to the task. (Ostrom, 2005, p. 20)

A final point can be addressed to show further how Adam Smith can be used in the experimental literature. While Evensky attributes to Smith the notion that 'Human nature is constant (we are not "better" than our predecessors), but human character evolves along with human institutions' (2001, p. 504), experimental results show that the predisposition to cooperate may be universal, but what is recognized as an appropriate locus for cooperation varies with time and place. That is to say, as Smith does, that norms of fairness and nature of punishment vary with cultures.

In 2000, Joseph Henrich started a series of field experiments across the globe using members of small-scale societies with a broad variety of economic and cultural conditions as subjects. His results, and the results of his colleagues, are different from the homogeneous results of industrialized countries (Henrich et al., 2004). Fairness seems to vary cross-culturally. The modal Ultimatum Game offers from the sample of the 15 foraging societies studied ranged from 15 to 50 per cent; what is most interesting is that rejection rates are much lower than those observed with undergraduate students. Trying to control for possible explanatory variables, Henrich et al. found that two variables account for a significant part (47 per cent) of the variation between groups.

These variables are 'market integration' (that is, do people engage frequently in market exchange?) and 'cooperation in production' (that is, what are the potential benefits to cooperative as opposed to solitary or family-based productive activities?). The higher the level of market integration, the higher the level of cooperation and sharing in the experimental games.

One study included in Henrich et al. (2004) deserves particular attention. Jean Ensminger ran Ultimatum, Dictator and Public Goods experiments in the Orma society in East Africa. Her results stray widely from what is observed in industrialized countries. She offers the following explanation:

> Both cognitive and psychological explanations can help us understand how even self-interested individuals could exhibit fairness in one-shot games and also how behavior designed primarily to promote reputation could emerge there. But it is quite likely that something more profound is surfacing in these data that points to the internalization of fairness norms in more market-oriented societies. Such internalization would require that fairness is learned in the course of the market exchange and we have evidence that this is the case across the developmental life cycle. Camerer and Thaler (1995) agree that norms of fairness are learned, noting that kindergarteners are most selfish in economic experiments, while by the sixth grade, more fair behavior towards one's peers emerges. (Ensminger, 2004, p. 358)

And while Ensminger looks at Albert Hirschman (1982) for an historical explanation of the effects of commerce on civil society, Maria Pia Paganelli (2007) points her finger to Adam Smith and his scholarship. Adam Smith describes the civilizing effects of commerce in many ways. One, famously recognized by Nathan Rosenberg (1990) and Dennis Rasmussen (2006), is that the introduction of commerce and manufacture brings along 'order and good government, and with them, the liberty and security of individuals . . . This, though is has been the least observed, is by far the most important of all their effect' (WN III.iv.4, p. 412). The 'regular administration of justice' is generated by commerce and is the foundation of commercial prosperity. Young (1992) also points to some of the civilizing effects of commerce described by Smith: the practice of abandoning unwanted children decreases with the increase in wealth brought about by commerce, and honesty increases with the decrease of dependency and the increase of interdependency brought about by commerce. In Smith's words, as cited in Young (p. 80): 'Nothing tends so much to corrupt mankind as dependency, while interdependency still increases the honesty of the people. The establishment of commerce and manufactures, which brings about this interdependency, is the best police for preventing crimes [LJB 205; WN III.iv.4]'.

To conclude, I would like to call attention to what Ashraf et al. (2005) say about Smith's TMS: 'Adam Smith's *Theory of Moral Sentiments* is not only packed with insights that presage developments in contemporary behavioural economics, but also with promising leads that have yet to be pursued' (p. 140). The richness of Adam Smith indeed is proving to be a powerful tool for explaining and understanding some otherwise puzzling results of economic experiments. Adam Smith is increasingly being read by experimental, behavioural and neuro-economists. He still has a lot to offer all of us.

Note

*   Thanks to Jeffrey Young for inviting this chapter and for helping me improve it with his suggestions. Thanks also to Tyler Cowen and David Levy for useful comments and encouragement. All mistakes remain mine.

References

Ashraf, Nava, Colin Camerer and George Loewenstein (2005), 'Adam Smith, behavioral economist', *Journal of Economic Perspectives*, **19** (3), 131–45.
Benhabib, Jess and Alberto Bisin (2005), 'Modelling internal commitment mechanisms and self-control: a neuroeconomics approach to consumption-saving decisions', *Games and Economic Behavior*, **52** (2), 460–92.
Berg, Joyce, John Dickhaut and Kevin McCabe (1995), 'Trust, reciprocity, and social history', *Games and Economic Behavior*, **10**, 122–42.
Bernheim, Douglas and Antonio Rangel (2004) 'Addiction and cue-triggered decision processes', *American Economic Review*, **94** (5), 1558–90.
Blount, Sally (1995), 'When social outcomes aren't fair: the effects of causal attributions on preferences', *Organizational Behavior and Human Decision Processes*, **63** (2), 131–44.
Camerer, Colin (1997), 'Progress in behavioral game theory', *Journal of Economic Perspectives*, **11** (4), 167–88.
Camerer, Colin and George Loewenstein (2004), 'Behavioral economics: past, present, future', in Colin Camerer, George Loewenstein and Mathew Rabin (eds), *Advances in Behavioral Economics*, New York: Russell Sage, pp. 3–51.
Camerer, Colin and Richard Thaler (1995), 'Anomalies: ultimatums, dictators, and manners', *Journal of Economic Perspectives*, **9** (2), 209–19.
Damasio, Antonio (1994), *Descartes' Error: Emotion, Reason, and the Human Brain*, New York: Putnam.
Ensminger, Jean (2004), 'Market integration and fairness: evidence from ultimatum, dictator, and public goods experiments in East Africa', in J. Henrich, R. Boyd, S. Bowles, C. Camerer, E. Fehr and H. Gintis (eds) *Foundations of Human Sociability: Economic Experiments and Ethnographic Evidence from Fifteen Small-Scale Societies*, Oxford, UK and New York, USA: Oxford University Press, pp. 356–81.
Evensky, Jerry (2001), 'Adam Smith's lost legacy', *Southern Economic Journal*, **67** (3), 497–517.
Evensky, Jerry (2005), *Adam Smith's Moral Philosophy: A Historical and Contemporary Perspective on Markets, Law, Ethics, and Culture*, New York: Cambridge University Press.
Fehr, Ernst, Georg Kirchsteiger and Arno Reidl (1993), 'Does fairness prevent market clearing?' *Quarterly Journal of Economics*, **108** (2), 437–59.
Forsythe, Robert, Joel L. Horowitz, N.E. Savin and Martin Sefton (1994), 'Fairness in simple bargaining experiments', *Games and Economic Behavior*, **6** (3), 347–69.
Fudenberg, Drew and David Levine (2004), 'A dual self model of impulse control', Working Paper.
Gintis, Herbert, Samuel Bowles, Robert Boyd and Ernst Fehr (eds) (2005), *Moral Sentiments and Material Interests: The Foundations of Cooperation in Economic Life*, Cambridge, MA and London, UK: MIT Press.
Guth, Werner and Reinhard Tietz (1990), 'Ultimatum bargaining behavior: a survey and comparison of experimental results', *Journal of Economic Psychology*, **11**, 417–49.
Henrich, Joseph, Robert Boyd, Samuel Bowles, Colin Camerer, Ernst Fehr and Herbert Gintis (eds) (2004), *Foundations of Human Sociability: Economic Experiments and Ethnographic Evidence from Fifteen Small-Scale Societies*, Oxford, UK and New York, USA: Oxford University Press.
Hirschman, Albert (1982), 'Rival interpretations of market societies: civilizing, destructive, or feeble', *Journal of Economic Literature*, **20**, 1463–84.
Kirkpatrick, Lee and Seymour Epstein (1992), 'Cognitive-experimental self-theory and subjective probability: further evidence for two conceptual systems', *Journal of Personality and Social Psychology*, **63** (4), 534–44.
Le Doux, Joseph (1996), *The Emotional Brain: The Mysterious Underpinning of Emotional Life*, New York: Simon & Schuster.
Levy, David (1992), *The Economic Ideas of Ordinary People: from Preferences to Trade*, London, UK and New York, USA: Routledge.
Loewenstein George and Ted O'Donoghue (2004), 'Animal spirits: affective and deliberative influences of economic behavior', Working Paper.
Metcaft, Janet and Walter Mischel (1999), 'A hot/cool-system analysis of delay gratification: dynamics of willpower', *Psychological Review*, **106** (1), 3–19.
Ostrom, Elinor (2005), 'Policies that crowd out reciprocity and collective action' in H. Gintis, S. Bowles, R. Boyd and E. Fehr (eds) (2005), *Moral Sentiments and Material Interests: The Foundations of Cooperation in Economic Life*, Cambridge, MA and London, UK: MIT Press, pp. 253–76.
Paganelli, Maria Pia (2007), 'The same face of the two Smiths', presented at the 2007 History of Economics Society Meeting.
Panksepp, Jaak (1998), *Affective Neuroscience*, Oxford: Oxford University Press.
Rabin, Mathew (1993), 'Incorporating fairness into game theory and economics', *American Economic Review*, **83**, 1281–302.
Rasmussen, Dennis (2006), 'Does "bettering our condition" really make us better off? Adam Smith on progress and happiness', *American Political Science Review*, **100** (3), 309–18.

Rosenberg, Nathan (1990), 'Adam Smith and the stock of moral capital', *History of Political Economy*, **22** (1), 1–17.
Roth, Alvin, Vensa Prasnikar, Masahiro Okuno Fujiwara and Shmuel Zamir (1991), 'Bargaining and market behavior in Jerusalem, Ljubljana, Pittsburgh, and Tokyo: an experimental study', *American Economic Review*, **81** (5), 1068–95.
Sloman, Steven (1996), 'The empirical case for two systems of reasoning', *Psychological Bulletin*, **119** (1), 5–16.
Smith, Adam (1759), *The Theory of Moral Sentiments*, 6th edn (1984), Indianapolis, IN: Liberty Fund (TMS).
Smith, Adam (1766), *Lectures on Jurisprudence*, R.L. Meek, D.D. Raphael and L.G. Stein (eds) (1982), Indianapolis, IN: Liberty Fund.
Smith, Adam (1776), *An Inquiry into the Nature and Causes of the Wealth of Nations*, Edwin Cannan (ed.) (1981), Indianapolis, IN: Liberty Fund (WN).
Smith, Vernon (1998), 'The two faces of Adam Smith', *Southern Economic Journal*, **65** (1), 1–19.
Smith, Vernon (2003), 'Constructivist and ecological rationality in economics', *American Economic Review*, **93** (3), 465–508.
Young, Jeffrey (1992), 'Natural morality and the ideal impartial spectator in Adam Smith', *International Journal of Social Economics*, **19** (10–12), 71–82.
Young, Jeffrey (1997), *Economic as a Moral Science: The Political Economy of Adam Smith*, Cheltenham, UK and Lyme, USA: Edward Elgar.
Young, Jeffrey (2001), 'Adam Smith's two views of the market', in P.L. Porta, R. Scazzieri and A. Skinner (eds), *Knowledge and Social Institutions and the Division of Labor*, Cheltenham, UK and Northampton, MA, USA: Edward Elgar, pp. 95–110.
Young, Jeffrey (2005), 'Unintended order and intervention: Adam Smith's theory of the role of the state', *History of Political Economy*, **37** (supplement), 91–119.

PART III

APPLICATIONS AND POLICY ANALYSIS

11 The invisible hand
Warren J. Samuels

Interest in and use of the concept of the invisible hand arises in three contexts: the meaning attributed to it by Adam Smith, the different meanings adduced either to Smith or to the concept *per se* by interpreters, and as a technique of analysing, positively, ontologically and normatively, the real-world economy.

The concept of an 'invisible hand' is widely held to be a foundation of modern economics and the invisible hand itself a foundation of the modern economic system. The concept is so protean and its uses so diverse, however, that every aspect of the concept is given multiple formulation, magnified by the recursive nature of many of the concept's topics. Other results include ubiquitous selective perception and ambiguity, and the centrality of the concept to numerous important controversies. Nonetheless, the concept has engendered diverse hypotheses for theoretical and empirical study, and has thereby facilitated and oriented numerous inquiries into other fundamental concepts, economic processes, adjustment mechanisms, and so on. The concept has given many economists confidence in the systemic nature of the economy, even though they disagree as to why. Ambiguity can therefore be reckoned to be a weakness or a strength. Another result, however, is that the concept is inconclusive with regard to its intended purposes; and only with additional a priori premises can one elevate one interpretation over others. Finally, it is inconclusive whether there is an 'invisible hand'; and, if so, what it is, what it does, and on what basis, other than apriorism, we know the foregoing. Some economists embrace the concept, as they understand it; some use the concept as a vehicle of communication; some reject it; and some use it, in one way or another, at arm's length.

This chapter is not concerned with what Smith 'really meant' by the invisible hand, nor with the correctness of the interpretations and usages made since Smith, nor with solving the problems raised by usage, nor with taking a position on key issues. It is devoted to understanding the concept's multiple usages by Smith and others, identifying problems with those usages, and fostering clear thinking about the concept, for example, the topics on which assumptions must be made to reach conclusions. The story is in the details. It is a very wide-ranging and complex story, so the details – most of which must go unremarked – are mountainous.

The principal questions raised by the concept are: What is the invisible hand, or invisible hand story, all about? What is the invisible hand? What are the functions of the invisible hand, or what does it do or signify? What are the connections between the identity of the invisible hand and its functions? From where does the invisible hand come? What are, first, the conceptual and, second, the substantive ramifications and complications of the uses of the concept? One problem is that multiple answers have been given to these questions and multiple positions taken on the issues they raise. The subject is not neat and tidy. It is possibly unsurpassed in messiness in economics, though such has not precluded the continued foundational status of the concept. Part of the problem is that many invisible hand arguments overreach and convey more about the arguers than the economy. They tell stories that suggest much more than they state, and state or suggest more than they can properly handle or prove. Part of the problem is that no independent test exists for choosing between alternative interpretations. Another part of the problem is that the concept of the invisible hand is itself part of the process of working out the economy whose explanation, in part, it is the purpose of the concept to provide.

Adam Smith's three uses
Adam Smith is the principal source of the use of the concept in economics. He used it thrice in written materials available to posterity. In *The History of Astronomy* he ascribes irregular natural events to 'the invisible hand of Jupiter' and his favour or anger (Smith, 1980, III.2, pp. 49–50). This use is typically noted and put aside as a curiosity. Smith called it 'the lowest and most pusillanimous superstition' (III.2, p. 50).

In *The Theory of Moral Sentiments*, Smith argues that spending by the rich gives employment to the poor, in effect making the distribution of consumption more equal than the distribution of wealth. Though the 'rich only select . . . what is most precious and agreeable', they 'consume little more than the poor'. Though they seek only

> the gratification of their own vain and insatiable desires, they divide with the poor the produce of all their improvements. They are led by an invisible hand to make nearly the same distribution of the necessaries of life . . . had the earth been divided into equal portions . . . and thus without intending it, without knowing it, advance the interest of the society. (Smith, 1976 [1759], IV.I.10, pp. 184–5)

Four characteristics may be remarked: Smith says 'is led', not 'as if led' – literal rather than metaphoric language. The individual behaviour of the rich is said to promote the interest of society. The language of 'without intending it, without knowing it' is that of the principle of unintended and unforeseen consequences, seen by some as *the* invisible hand mechanism or process. The argument about spending by the rich and employment to the poor is interpretable as the trickle-down theory.

In the *Wealth of Nations* Smith discusses how the study by an individual seeking 'the most advantageous employment' for his capital 'necessarily leads him to prefer that employment . . . most advantageous to the society'. A businessman's added concern about the insecurity of investment abroad will lead to increased domestic investment and thus more domestic income and employment:

> As every individual, therefore, endeavours as much as he can both to employ his capital in the support of domestic industry, and so to direct that industry that its produce may be of the greatest value; every individual necessarily labours to render the annual revenue of the society as great as he can. He generally, indeed, neither intends to promote the public interest, nor knows how much he is promoting it. By preferring the support of domestic to that of foreign industry, he intends only his own security; and by directing that industry in such a manner as its produce may be of the greatest value, he intends only his own gain, and he is in this, as in many other cases, led by an invisible hand to promote an end which was no part of his intention. Nor is it always the worse for the society that it was no part of it. By pursuing his own interest he frequently promotes that of the society more effectually than when he really intends to promote it. (Smith, 1976 [1776], IV.ii.9, pp. 455–6)

Smith again writes 'is led', not 'as if led'. The principle of unintended and unforeseen consequences is again present through the treatment of intentions and knowledge. An internal conflict exists between the use of 'necessarily', on the one hand, and 'generally', 'in this, as in many other cases' and 'frequently', on the other.

The principal use of the invisible hand is that in *The Wealth of Nations*; it is seen to be broader-ranging and the foundational basis of the concept in economics. The use in *The Theory of Moral Sentiments* is conventionally taken to be coordinate with it but its context is narrower.

The identity of the invisible hand

What is the invisible hand? The invisible hand has been given several dozen more or less different identities. These include the market, the price system; the competitive market–price system; and competition. These are among the most common identifications, along with self-interest, the entrepreneur, the spontaneous order principle and God. The competitive market and Hayekian spontaneous order are, perhaps, the two present-day canonical identities. Several conceptual and substantive problems arise with particular putative identities. In the case of 'the market', for example: (1) Is the invisible hand a pure abstract conceptual market or actual markets, or both? (2) What about actual markets due to the institutions which form and operate through them? (3) Is the market a mechanism or an institution, or both? (4) Is the invisible hand the market *per se*, or the hand of the market, or market forces? (5) If the invisible hand is a metaphor, and if the market is a metaphor (following McCloskey), what results from identifying one metaphor by another? (6) Is the market *per se* the invisible hand or is it conditional upon some structural or other feature? (7) What of markets as both selection processes and results of selection, for example, Coase's theories of firm and market? (8) 'Competition' can be defined in a number of conflicting ways, with the putative evidence of competition for one definition constituting evidence of the absence of competition for another definition.

Further identity candidates are: choice in a market; self-interest; the profit motive; private, or free, enterprise; and private property. The last four, perhaps especially the second and third, may be substitutable, hence synonymous. The candidacy of 'self-interest' is examined below; in invisible hand matters, it raises complex and important issues. 'Private property' may refer to: (1) the institution of property (undefined or the existing institution) or particular rights; or (2) continuity or change of rights, each of which has different implications for the use of the concept of the invisible hand.

The identity of the invisible hand as 'the entrepreneur' is rendered complicated by different views on: (1) whether a function or a particular group or an aspect of the behaviour of all persons is meant; (2) what makes any activity 'entrepreneurial'; (3) whether the entrepreneur is an active or a passive agent of change (that is, creating or finding niches); and (4) whether the meaning and defence of capitalism involves a system dominated by capitalists or entrepreneurs or a market system of economic agents without such domination.

Other candidates for the identity of the invisible hand found in the literature include: the economic system *per se* or system of natural liberty; interactive system-adjustment process; specifically informational system; spontaneous order principle; invisible hand mechanism or process; natural selection; intersubjectivity; condition bettering; status emulation; the deception that wealth is important; sympathy; division of labour – specialization; propensity to truck, barter and exchange; labour; exchange; consumer sovereignty; credit system; Walrasian auctioneer; capital accumulation; technology;

historical process; positive externalities, or good results and beneficial outcomes; final causes; nature; God; institutions, including government; covert power at a distance.

All of the candidates for identity of the invisible hand raise comparable problems. First, spontaneous order can connote either the identity or the function of the invisible hand. It always operates within the system of moral and legal rules, and is at least partly produced by them, and inasmuch as rules are subject to change and are themselves sometimes seen as governed by the spontaneous order principle, they therefore are subjects of controversy. Spontaneous order is sometimes understood in terms of institutions that arise and develop non-deliberatively. Yet, given the task of every generation to critique and possibly reform received institutions, eventually all institutions will be mixes of deliberative and non-deliberative institutions. This, too, is dealt with in more detail below. Second, the identification of institutions, especially government and law, as the invisible hand is ironic inasmuch as many uses of the concept seek to deny an activist role to government. Third, the invisible hand identified as externalities seems to embrace numerous other identities. When identified as positive externalities, questions arise as to the origin of negative externalities and of the possibility of tautology.

The foregoing identities may be classified into six groups: control mechanisms, adjustment mechanisms, generalized externalities (principle of unintended and unforeseen consequences), driving forces, processes *per se*, and invisible hand explanations. But the questions remain: Is there an invisible hand? In what sense is there an invisible hand? Is there one or more than one? Is any invisible hand proposition an assumption or a conclusion? Is there an independent test of any invisible hand proposition? Different authors respond differently, perhaps every statement made by one author being contradicted by another author.

What does the invisible hand do or signify?
The question of what the invisible hand does – its function – or signifies also has complications. Is the function always performed, or only sometimes or conditionally? Is it problematic, are there limits? Does structure affect performance and if so, how? What is the context of the function: production, exchange and/or distribution? Does the function have both empirical and normative status, and on what grounds? Again, different interpreters reach different conclusions.

The principal functions attributed to the invisible hand include: order; automatic self-regulation and adjustment; coordination; equilibrium; general harmony and beneficence; harmony among or of self-interests; Pareto optimality; harmony of self-interests with the social interest and welfare; economic performance; and so on. The difficulties encountered with each are important: 'order' is a subjective concept and often a matter of projection; so also are 'harmony' and 'beneficence'. 'Automaticity' is rarely if ever solely that, and self-regulation can give effect to, and signify, the status quo power structure. 'Equilibrium' has multiple definitions. It may be a definition of economic reality or an analytical or modelling tool. Significantly different identities of the invisible hand are said to generate equilibrium, for example, the market, the price mechanism, the auctioneer and institutions. While most economic theorists have been concerned with the existence, stability, uniqueness and optimality of equilibrium positions, some emphasizing tight prior equilibrium, others have treated equilibrium as an emergent process, with equilibrium *per se* never actually achieved, and still others emphasizing disequilibrium.

'Self-interests' have been defined as those of individuals, classes, sections, nations and groups. Pareto optimality involves maximizing and exhausting gains from trade and generating harmony among individuals, and is often equated with unanimity, consent, voluntarism, freedom and consensus, all of which have their critics as well as nuanced differences. Harmony among self-interested parties is not, or not necessarily, the same as harmony of self-interests with the social interest and welfare, which is Smith's explicit usage.

All of which engenders questions, questions that elicit conflicting answers: What is the substance of social welfare, and how is it known? Is society an independent entity? What are the directional flows of meaning: from individual to society or from society to individuals, or both? Is the social interest the sum of private interests, something given, or something to be worked out? The substance of economic performance has been defined differently: satisfaction, utility, production, value of output, welfare, happiness, wealth, and so on. The test of economic performance, whatever the substance, likewise has been variously identified: efficiency (by one definition or another), growth, most productive, Pareto optimality, stability, progress (by one definition or another), distribution, and so on. Efficiency, for example, can be defined in terms of exhausting gains from trade, or maximum or optimum production.

The idea that modern theory has got to the bottom of and refined Smith's vague idea is both widespread and problematic, and has involved increasingly technical and narrow terms. 'Refinement' has generally been defined in formal rather than substantive terms. It has also involved what is for some the curious role of the Walrasian auctioneer, which may, or may not, be a metaphor for the Hayekian spontaneous-order process.

On the technical economic side, the function of the invisible hand is typically seen to generate market-clearing prices, thus helping organize the allocation of resources (efficient in some sense) and the general operation of the economy, thus helping to achieve general economic performance (however defined), and thereby increasing the wealth of nations.

On the non-technical side, the function of the invisible hand is also seen to organize social cooperation and performance achievement, to synchronize social values, to give effect to but also to contribute to the organization of social and economic relations, including the society of nations, and to attain a rational identity or harmonization of interests.

Conflicting usages further abound with regard to: (1) diverse combinations of functions, for example, order and harmony, equilibrium and self-regulation, order and equilibrium, coordination and equilibrium; (2) diverse combinations of identity and function, for example, the market, or the entrepreneur, or private property and coordination or optimality or harmony; and (3) diverse identity-function relationships, especially recursive ones, and so on.

Conceptual ramifications and implications
The multiplicity of positions on the identity and function of the invisible hand are not the only interpretive problems. A number of conceptual problems confront the interpreter of Smith and those who would either develop their own use of the concept or interpret and critique others. As with the foregoing sources of multiplicity, an author must somehow choose their standpoint. Having done so, they assert their use notwithstanding the facts

that almost no one undertakes comparative analysis and that no independent test or meta-criteria exist.

Those who would understand and interpret Smith must confront three situations. First, Smith is silent on many questions that modern economists would like to have had him answer, such as: What is the invisible hand? What do you mean as between 'necessarily' and 'frequently'? When are you giving your own belief and when the beliefs of others? One source of this situation is that Smith was writing for contemporaries he had reason to believe would know what he meant. Another source is the methodology of his *History of Astronomy* in which he posits the use of rhetoric to allay the tumult of the imagination and to serve to achieve social recognition and moral approbation. The use of ambiguous language may have been intended to mask his uncertainty toward the truth of the matter; or it may reflect his not having an editor directing pointed questions to him; or his seeking to avoid criticism by religious antagonists.

Second, Smith posited a tripartite science of society, his synoptic and synthetic, recursive combination of the three worlds of the moral sentiments, the market, and government and law. He strongly tends in his writings and lectures to have treated them largely, albeit not entirely, independent of each other. This has led numerous interpreters to adopt one or the other of the three as primary and largely to subordinate and thereby effectively ignore the other two. The so-called 'Adam Smith problem', that sympathy is the central concept of *The Theory of Moral Sentiments* and self-interest of the *Wealth of Nations*, evaporates when one recognizes their respective positions in his tripartite model. Similarly with those who would jump from Smith's criticisms of Mercantilism to a supposed, narrowly defined laissez-faire theory of the economic role of government, especially in light of the *Lectures on Jurisprudence*.

Third, Smith partook of multiple paradigms in his work. These paradigms included naturalism, supernaturalism, pragmatism (utilitarianism), empiricism, historicism, secularism, materialism, nationalism, individualism, and so on. It is not clear how far he went in each paradigm. As a result, Smith's ideas appear differently to those who emphasize one or another of these paradigms, especially supernaturalism and individualism. To one mind, the invisible hand is God; to another, it may be the market, the entrepreneur, private property, competition or self-interest.

To the objective scholar not committed to one position, most if not all of these positions on the key questions should be included in a complete model of how the economy works. But most users of the concept of the invisible hand are not so ecumenical; they prefer their own position.

Closely related is the tendency to interpret Smith with an eye to the Enlightenment, especially the Scottish Enlightenment, but not with a single vision. The Enlightenment has meant different things to different people. To many it connotes a belief in progress; to others, the dissolution of the idea of a divinely concerned universe. Other meanings include rational study and choice uncontaminated by religious and monarchical politics, rational scepticism, factuality, scientific objectivity, empiricism, materialism, and so on.

Inasmuch as the Enlightenment then meant different things to different people, the foregoing meanings could and did coexist with religion and theology; indeed, the revolutionary doctrines of the Enlightenment both influenced and were influenced by religion and theology. Individuals could be sceptical about some matters but accepting of others. None of this should be surprising: the eighteenth century was more like its past than its future, but clear conflicts then existed between old and new value systems; between supernaturalism and most if not all other paradigms; and between old aristocratic and absolutist monarchical systems of government on the one hand, and the principles of democracy and equality on the other. A further tension existed between those with a desire for the apolitical and those who recognized and gave effect to a policy consciousness, to wit, that society was not part of the natural order of things but, however incrementally, socially constructed.

The concept of the invisible hand was tied up with several major social processes, processes which themselves could be examined using invisible hand mechanisms and processes (of whatever sort). The processes are those of the social mythological system, the social symbolic system, and the social ideological system. All three perform the functions of social control and social change.

Every society has its mythological constructs that, combined, provide an idealized image of that society. The social mythological system serves a psychic balm function, setting minds at rest about whatever is important in that society, and a further social control function, legitimizing the institutions, power structure and incentive system of that society, and altogether protecting the dominant belief system of that society. The concept of the invisible hand is, on the one hand, a projection of a desire for transcendental security, order, harmony and so on, and on the other, a projection of Western civilization's self-perception of individualism nested in a facilitative system. Karl Popper wrote that: 'Science must begin with myths – and with the criticism of myths'. The history of the use of the invisible hand suggests while it is always difficult for persons in any society to transcend or hold at arm's length the fundamental myths of that society, some people do so whereas others do not. Myths serve the functions of social control and psychic balm, the latter (at least) setting minds at rest.

The same is true of the social symbolic system. Every society has its symbols which selectively project that which is selectively attributed to them. These symbols have the same psychic balm and social control functions as does the social mythological system.

The concept of the invisible hand belongs to both the mythological and symbolic systems of Western society. The concept very likely originated in the domain of religion and, involved stories pertaining to God. Religion has shared the concept with economics.

More familiar to economists is the social ideological system. Ideology in Western economies and societies gives effect to and legitimizes the business or middle-class view of the world. It presents a defence of the capitalist market economy and, selectively, its institutional details. The business creed has had two major strands. The dominant strand stresses individualism, another stresses the socially beneficent power of management. The concept of the invisible hand is much more prominent in the former than in the latter. One putative function of the concept is to obfuscate and otherwise finesse the power of business, both as a system and as individual enterprises. The managerialist strand affirms that power; it does not need the obfuscating role of the invisible hand.

The question of self-reflexivity arises, as to whether objective thinking about an economy is possible by a person within that economy. Also, the multiplicity of identifications of invisible hand and other formulations raises the problem akin to that of philosophical realism: when (arguably) everyone accepts the reality of the invisible hand but differs as to its identity, the result is ambiguity and inconclusiveness.

The term 'invisible hand' is also part of the system of language. It is part of a sociolinguistic tradition of usage centring on invisibility and the mystical nature of the unseen. It elicits a sense of the transcendental, of something beyond the capacity of most if not all people to comprehend, of something that grabs the imagination. The realm of the invisible can be some ultimate transcendental force or being, some operative adjustment mechanism, even the working rules of morals, law, and athletic and card games.

The concept of an invisible hand has spawned an array of copycat uses, whose functions seem to be to capture attention and the imagination and to make a point using some variation on visibility or invisibility of the hand or another body part. These include: the palsied hand, the grabbing hand, the vanishing hand, the visible hand, a hand that has a green thumb, a hand that can be tracked, the invisible (or visible) fist, the invisible foot, the invisible handshake, and so on. Hegel's 'cunning of history' may, or may not, be an example of the invisible hand.

Some people likely consider the term 'invisible hand' a cliché. Nevertheless, the question arises as to what, precisely, the term is as a matter of language. The common practice is to label the term a figure of speech and within that category either a metaphor or, much less common, a simile. A metaphor involves an implicit comparison (for example, 'You are my sunshine'). A simile makes an explicit comparison, a comparison with a specific attribute and a specification of the object compared with (for example, 'You are red as a beetroot').

But perhaps the term is not intended to be a figure of speech. Perhaps it is intended to be literal. Smith did not label the term; he did not call it a figure of speech, nor a metaphor, nor a simile. He said 'is led' and not 'as if led'. Interestingly, 'as if' is used, erroneously, by many commentators.

But convention seems to warrant calling the term a figure of speech. Some users, however, undoubtedly intend it to be taken literally and others believe they are using a metaphor, simile or something else. Perhaps the term represents a mode of abstraction, or a rhetorical stratagem, and not a figure of speech. Can some uses, otherwise identical, be a metaphor and others a simile, and others a statement literally about reality, and so on? If the term (either in one use or all uses) is a metaphor, for what is it a metaphor? If it is a simile, with regard to what? Whatever figure of speech is involved, it may misidentify, by focusing on one aspect erroneously or to the neglect of other aspects. (It is not clear to this author that metaphor and simile are different in their application to 'invisible hand'. The usual formulation, that a simile involves 'like', either explicitly or implicitly, is not convincing.)

The term may be a convenient fiction; such terms are used in both economics and law. (Economics, accordingly, would be 'science fiction', in part because, firstly, it is necessarily incomplete and, secondly, it uses fictional terms.) That economists have provided a name for whatever they mean by it does not guarantee its literal existence. Language, following Peirce and Wittgenstein, and Smith himself, is a set of signs but not necessarily of something 'real'.

The category of figure of speech is not yet exhausted. The term 'invisible hand' has been called an analogy, meaning thereby partial similarity or resemblance, or explanation by comparison, or the process by which new constructions conform to more familiar and often unrelated ones. It has been called a euphemism, meaning an attempt to see things, or have things seen, not as they are but as we wish them to be seen (for example, a euphemism for obfuscated power structure). Another label has been that of synecdoche, in which part of a referent is used to stand for the whole (for example, 'All hands on deck'). A trope is another label, signifying the stylistic and/or substantive effects created by the choice of words – close to sign or signification, also akin to myth or symbol.

The term 'invisible hand' could also be called a primitive term – a term that is undefined by the user but whose definition and meaning is in practice supplied by readers and/or auditors. Not only the invisible hand could be so designated; many terms used in its discussion – such as human nature, self-interest, rationality, competition, nature, God, order – are primitive terms, general conceptual categories with variable selective definitions and nested meaning. The content of natural theology is a function of meaning attributed to both nature and status quo society – elastic, a priori, and a function of selective perception. Such parallels the utopian literature: different utopias and dystopias constructed on the basis of the same society, due to different perspectives; and also 'natural order', on the basis of selective perception, interpretation, reification and projection of the status quo (that is, different Platonic idealizations).

Many uses of the concept of the invisible hand are entangled with notions of the 'individual', 'self-interest' and the 'social'. The first two will be considered below.

Although much economic theory and most economists posit methodological individualism, the use of 'social' and thereby of methodological collectivism can hardly be avoided. Smith himself, it will be recalled, writes of 'society', 'public good' and 'public interest' in his discussion of the invisible hand in the *Wealth of Nations*. Society can be comprehended as (or a metaphor for) the sum of all individuals, an entity, or a process. The term is widely used to mean more than any one of the three. The nub of most such discussions ends up with an affirmation of institutional individualism, a notion that individuals are a product of socialization (societization) and societies are the result of the summation – the interaction and aggregation – of socialized individuals; in other words, a dual flow of meaning – from individual to society and from society to individual – a recursive system.

Three final conceptual problems have already been intimated above. The first problem has to do with the ontological and epistemological (in contrast with the linguistic) nature of invisible hand reasoning. Much such reasoning seems to have posited that it is a definition of reality and thereby involves the category of truth. An alternative view posits that such reasoning is conducted within, and itself comprises, a system of belief, with no necessary relation to reality and truth. A third alternative is to posit such reasoning as a mode of discourse, independent of belief system. A fourth alternative is to treat the invisible hand as a tool of analysis, perhaps no more than a methodological assumption, more technical and substantive than a mode of discourse and less commanding than a system of belief. Finally, the concept might only be 'words', words resembling a mode of discourse but, in allaying the tumult of the imagination, serving the functions of psychic balm and social control.

The second problem is that of naturalism. The first problem applies to it. The eighteenth century was arguably the first century in Western civilization in which naturalism – along with secularism and materialism – seriously challenged supernaturalism. However, naturalism and nature were given a variety of different meanings; even Smith used nature and naturalism in a number of different ways. Among the issues and positions are: natural versus artificial; nature as compelling mankind versus man in control of nature; nature as good, to be followed, versus nature as bad, to be overcome. Other considerations also pertain: natural law is not just any natural law; it strongly tends to be that derivable from the particular status quo system in which a thinker lives (see above re multiple utopias and multiple Platonic idealizations). Naturalism involves selective reification and projection. Man is part of nature. And the naturalistic fallacy is to treat what is of local human social construction as an absolute, universal and transcendental.

The third problem is that of supernaturalism and it here has at least two major parts. One is the question of Smith's personal position on organized religion and theology. The other is the set of impacts of religion and theology on the use, and on the analysis of the use, of the concept of the invisible hand. Both encompass many of the same questions and issues, including: belief in God; God in relation to nature; the status of deism in theistic Christianity; God as having designed and set the world going but thereafter a passive observer versus God as still active in the world (possibly including a personal God); organized religion versus natural religion.

Whether or not Smith believed in God is a continuing and likely perpetual mystery. Among the factors requiring study are: Smith's reaction to the treatments accorded Hutcheson and Hume; what he does not say about theology, as well as what he does say; his status as a sociologist of religion studying the secular origins of the moral rules against the background of the principles of approbation and disapprobation; the then-contemporary meaning and treatment of deism as religion and morality (already or to be) developed using reason and not revelation, a position close to that of natural religion and treated by some theists as a proxy for atheism; the meaning and scope of Smith's use of 'superstition' in the *Wealth of Nations* and the significance of his related affirmation there of a multiplicity of religious sects; whether Smith had two positions: his private views of God, theology/ontology, and organized religion, and his arm's length analysis of God, organized relation, established Churches, sectarianism and moral sentiments in relation to moral rules; whether his theological position was that of theodicy (in part, the relation, if any, of scarcity to the problem of Job, that is, if mankind's world has been designed, why do problems, including tragedies, exist?).

Different perspectives on all these conceptual matters yield different uses and different interpretations of the use of the concept of the invisible hand. Especially intriguing is the question: What is the significance of his *History of Astronomy* argument that the role of science = philosophy is to 'allay this tumult of the imagination' by placing rhetoric in the service of social recognition, moral approbation and setting minds at rest? Does that question finesse another, namely, 'What is the ontological or epistemological meaning of the concept of the invisible hand?'

Substantive ramifications and complications

Three substantive topics need to be considered. All three are important and enormously wide ranging and complicated.

One topic has to do with 'problems'. In light of there putatively being an invisible hand and in light of the honorific functions performed by the invisible hand, why are there costs? Or, what theory of cost is followed? Why is there economic instability, unemployment and waste? Why are there externality and public good problems? Why is self-interest sometimes dysfunctionally formed?

The second topic, enormously expansive and therefore highly compromising of any easy solution apposite to the use of the concept of the invisible hand, concerns self-interest and related matters. Self-interest is one of a group of cognate concepts also including methodological individualism (supra) and rationality (infra). At the very least, self-interest enters the use and discussion of the invisible hand because of Smith's use of it in the *Wealth of Nations*, both in general and in his own use of the invisible hand (for example, 'By pursuing his own interest . . .'). Self-interest is enormously expansive because it is enormously complex, the result being that any invisible hand discussion using self-interest – and it is almost impossible to avoid using it – renders the invisible hand highly contingent and problematic.

Among the principal difficulties and contingencies are the following, each of which is much more complicated than can be examined here:

1. Self-interest is frequently identified as the invisible hand. It is also frequently identified as a driving force that is the object of control by the invisible hand.
2. Competition may be identified as competition among self-interested economic agents but that is only one definition of competition and, again, here self-interest is not the invisible hand, it is competition.
3. Self-interest is sometimes given as a definition of reality, that is, people do pursue their self-interest. But it is also sometimes identified as a methodological limiting assumption to facilitate analysis, that is, as a modelling strategy.
4. As a definition of reality, self-interest may be given as the actual reality or as an idealized version of reality; that is, how people do act vis-à-vis a romanticized or ideal-type version of how they should act.
5. As either a definition of reality or a methodologically limiting assumption, self-interest may be an empty formalism or have particular substantive content. If the former, it amounts to a tautology; and as such it amplifies the tautology consequent to so defining efficiency (optimality) that only individual preferences count. If the latter, it may, in order to counter objections that the substance of self-interest is only material gain, expand the definitional domain of self-interest to include non-material gain plus social preferences, the result again being a tautology. Expansion of conceptual or substantive domain leads to tautology and to explaining everything and thereby nothing. The reliance on pattern models in such matters is not prevalent among economists. These considerations also apply to the substitution of 'enlightened self-interest' for 'self-interest' *per se*.
6. For self-interest either substantive or procedural rationality may be substituted. Much the same difficulties and contingencies arise with the use of rationality that arise with self-interest. Additional problems include: variations within economics in the definition of rationality; variations consequent to the import of psychology into economics, including experimental economics, and so on, the result of which is to render the notion of rationality even more complex and contingent; to the category of 'economic' rationality are juxtaposed other forms of rationality, such as social and administrative as well as pragmatic; and so on.
7. All arguments or assumptions can be given in strong or weak forms and in sophisticated or naive forms.
8. Whether self-interest and/or rationality functions as a definition of reality or a methodologically limiting assumption, some or much is ignored and/or neglected thereby.

9. The assumptions of self-interest and/or rationality may be products of the systemic environment, derivative of the self-perceptions of a particular type of culture and society.
10. In addition to the irony that self-interest is identified as both the invisible hand and a driving force requiring control by the invisible hand, a second irony arises. Concepts of the invisible hand and of self-interest are often invoked to counter – or, actually, to channel – social control, but exist within the system of legal and non-legal social controls of a particular type of culture and society.

As if the foregoing difficulties were not enough to render problematic and inconclusive any invisible hand discussion utilizing self-interest and/or rationality, the following complexities and contingencies greatly amplify the problematicity and inconclusiveness, again so as to render non-dispositive the purpose(s) for which the invisible hand concept is used:

11. Advocates of the self-interest assumption or its maximizing or optimizing equivalent in terms of rationality, whether adopting the assumption as a definition of reality or a methodologically limiting assumption, tend to treat it as systemically appropriate behaviour. An extreme formulation is to make the point by defining self-interest in terms of greed. The problem is that in Western culture self-interest is both applauded and condemned; and its condemnation typically is voiced as rejection of greed, excessive greed, avarice, cupidity, venality, rapacity, and so on. The condemnation may be associated with antipathy to the modern economic system or with the application of moral and legal principles to behaviour deemed disreputable. The psychological definitions of egomania, narcissism, megalomania and sociopathic or psychopathic behaviour are not all that different from popular understandings of business's pursuit of the 'bottom line'. In the Old Testament, the 'All is vanity' message of Ecclesiastes is juxtaposed to a universalist and messianic utopian message of Isaiah.
12. In Smith's and others' models of human nature and behaviour, often two models are combined, approximating sympathy (empathy due to a sense of common feeling) and self-interest, signifying that human psychology is too complex to be reduced to a simple unidirectional or single-valued notion.
13. If a theory of psychology or of social psychology is to be used, the problem arises as to which theory is to be used. *Inter alia*, there are conflicting theories of mind, consciousness, subtleties of human nature, non-rational and irrational behaviour, and intentionality. With respect to intentionality, for example, among the divisive issues are: passive versus active; behaviour as constituting compliance, withdrawal and/or aggression; problems of responsibility; and so on.
14. Among economists, in addition to adherents of the variations noted or hinted at above, are those who, like Stigler and Becker, define behaviour as a function of relative prices (broadly defined), and those who, like Coase and North, define behaviour as a function of institutions (either via relative prices or directly).
15. A central process bearing on self-interest and related topics is socialization, to wit, the individual as a social construction. Some interpreters of Smith consider the impartial spectator (process) to be a metaphor for socialization (some call it conscience or the internalization of moral rules).

16. Socialization is accompanied by individualization, that is, the formation of one's (sense of) identity and self-image, including the attachment of the individual to particular objects as an aspect of individualization. This is the problem of the 'self' in self-interest. Smith's theory of approbation and disapprobation encompasses the individual looking favourably upon themself and being looked upon favourably by others. Here is where Smith's use of status emulation comes in: other-directedness in the formation of self-identity and in preference formation, in part through achievement of moral approval and social recognition.
17. For both Smith and the arguably more objective modern analysts and interpreters, the foregoing is recursive, not unidirectional: socialization is a function of learning and learning is a function of socialization. Individualization takes place within society and society is a function of the individuals who comprise and are produced by it. Selective perception is a function of socialization and individualization, and socialization and individualization are a function of selective perception.
18. 'Society' is not the only relevant concept juxtaposed to 'self' or 'individual'. Another is 'community', relating to: (a) inclusion and exclusion of who benefits and who loses, or is seen to benefit or lose; and (b) the formation and dissolution of civil society.
19. The role of structure is critical. It governs whose identities, whose attachments, whose preferences and whose selective perceptions count.
20. Other dualisms are also important. Economists take positions on them, too, in part in discussions of the invisible hand, trying either to make sense of the concept or to advance a particular theory of it. The recognition or failure to recognize these dualisms affects, among other things, notions of cause and consequence. Some economists emphasize one-way direction; others emphasize cumulative causation, recursive relationships and overdetermination. The dualisms include: free will versus determinism (to which many of the others reduce); self-interest as a governing or governed variable; individual decisions and choice versus culture and institutions, and/or mind versus genetics, or some combination of the two; the individual versus environment; nature versus nurture (human nature versus socialization); mind and genetics versus control through human interaction and/or social control by legal and moral institutions. Genetic ability operates within culture and institutions, including medical practice, and culture and institutions, including medical practice, operate within the genetic base.
21. Individuals' self-interests are formed. Discussions which incorporate and reveal complexities and problematics (including recursive relationships in both regards) include those on: socialization, or institutional individualism; given preferences versus chosen preferences versus formed preferences; the individual as passive responder to market and other signals and external stimuli versus being an active agent of choice and change; social preferences; the formation of expectations; the relative roles of deliberative and non-deliberative decision-making by the individual; the formation of expectations; principal–agent relations and problems; incentive systems; expansibility of wants; learning; path-dependency; differential responses to the same experience; habit; routine; and so on. Similar factors and forces operate on firms' objective functions to which is added jockeying for position among those in a position to do so. (The tendency of many mainstream economists when con-

fronted with a difficulty is to postulate a market. For example, firms require objective functions; they may be worked out through the market for control.)

The third topic is the Hayekian theory of spontaneous order. It includes the theory of the spontaneous development of institutions and the principle of unforeseen and unintended consequences, hence also a theory of deliberative and non-deliberative decision-making. 'Spontaneous order' can refer to an invisible hand process, to the identity of the invisible hand, or to a function of the invisible hand. On the one hand, 'spontaneous' order has an air of mystery about it, like the concept of the invisible hand itself; on the other hand, unlike all other usages of the concept of the invisible hand, spontaneous order has the air of a jeremiad – a strongly critical view of deliberative decision-making.

Notwithstanding the foregoing, the elements of spontaneous order are clear and unimposing. About the principle of unintended and unforeseen consequences it can be said, first, that the consequences are due to such processes as interaction and aggregation of behaviour and choices; and, second, that the consequences can be positive or negative, good or bad, although devotees of the principle tend to emphasize the negative or bad consequences (of government). Actual institutions are the result of both non-deliberative and deliberative decision-making, and of both design and unintended and unforeseen consequences.

Carl Menger emphasized the social functionality of institutions that develop spontaneously but he also emphasized that each generation has as its 'calling' the task of critiquing and reforming such institutions. That is why actual institutions are the result of both deliberative and non-deliberative decision-making and both designed and unintended and unforeseen consequences. Spontaneous order deals not with two types of institutions but with two aspects of all institutions. This is so even though the Hayekian use of the theory is to laud the non-deliberative element and putatively non-deliberative institutions and to condemn activist deliberative decision-making. Actual institutions are partly deliberative almost from their beginning and Menger affirms an activist deliberative attitude as both necessary and ubiquitous. A complete and objective analysis of spontaneous order and the principle yield results which contradict the usual uses to which spontaneous order and the principle are put, namely, to discredit legal change; instead, deliberative legal change is made a fundamental social process – for some, the invisible hand.

Assume that an institution arises spontaneously in period one and continues in successive periods to develop spontaneously. Given Menger's calling, in every period after period one, deliberative critique and reform will take place and combine and interact with non-deliberative, spontaneous development, the latter being non-mysterious, the result of such processes as interaction and aggregation.

The conventional Menger–Hayek examples of spontaneous, non-deliberative development are language, the common law and money. Each, however, combines deliberative and non-deliberative decision-making. Language has prescriptive and permissive approaches and deliberative and non-deliberative decision-making with regard to new words, definitions, grammatical usage, pronunciation, and so on. The same is true of the common law. The evolution of precedent is unforeseen and unintended (though, as in all situations, not necessarily entirely universally so) but legal decisions are deliberative (the rule of law – Hayek's final emphasis – is not, or not completely, descriptive of reality) and once again legal change is underscored.

The theory of spontaneous order is not uniquely dispositive of the issues to which it is commonly put. Observation and study of the Hayek list identified disagreements about the following: (1) what Hayek's system would permit government to do; (2) what Hayek believed government should do; (3) the evolution of Hayek's ideas and positions; (4) Hayek as libertarian or not, and the meaning of libertarian; (5) soft versus hard Hayek; (6) interpretation (definition and evaluation) of the status quo; (7) the meaning of democracy and of democracy in relation to libertarianism, totalitarianism and authoritarianism; (8) soft versus hard Hayekians; (9) Hayek in relation to von Mises and others; and (10) Hayekian structure versus Hayekian results.

Natural selection may be either the mechanism identified as the invisible hand or the result of something else seen as the invisible hand. Evolution theory has similarities with spontaneous order and the principle of unintended and unforeseen consequences. However, the specification of the mechanism, the result, and the meaning of the evolutionary process vary among interpreters. Further difficulties arise from multiple specifications of evolution theory; fitness as a function of system-specificity, environmental factors, and position on continuity versus change; and the juxtaposition of the open-endedness of evolutionary theory to the principle of design in deism.

Two ironies apply. Firstly, the conventional rationality assumption of price theory – itself an identity of the invisible hand – conflicts with the Hayekian emphasis on non-deliberative decision-making, which would negate or greatly limit the possibility of rational choice, even though Hayekians think of the price system as illustrative of the principle of unintended and unforeseen consequences. Secondly, deliberative critique, following Menger, is applied to both past non-deliberative decision-making and past deliberative decision-making, thereby entering into the non-deliberative process of working things out.

The foregoing underscores the important roles of power structure and thus of concentrated power in such areas as the following:

1. Institutions and institutional change, especially institutions as both a dependent and independent variable – and here notably government and legal change – with regard to whose interest is to be given legal protection.
2. Multiple views of government and of the economic role of government enter the process of working things out, including: (a) negative versus positive results of government action; and (b) government as dysfunctional versus government (political markets – another metaphor?) as yielding optimal results – all with regard to whose view and whose interest is to be given legal effect and protection. (Politics and political externalities: selective analysis and inconclusive optimality and suboptimality.)
3. Government as a product, or not, of a self-organization process.
4. The definition of the economy as independent of government versus as a recursive, overdetermined process.
5. Spontaneity is always present within the system of moral and legal rules, and at least partly produced by them, rules which themselves are subject to deliberative and non-deliberative change.
6. The economy as a joint, recursive determination process: the working out of legal rights and the working out of allocative optimization.

Among the problems of self-interest being the invisible hand are:

1. Self-interest is often identified as the invisible hand but also as a driving force requiring control by the invisible hand.
2. 'Self-interest' can be a definition of reality or a limiting assumption; so too can 'rationality', a sometime substitute which itself has several different meanings; and both self-interest and rationality constitute for some only a modelling strategy.
3. Self-interest and rationality may be empty formalisms or have particular substantive content, in the latter case being products of environment, that is, society and societization.
4. Of what significance is the frequent condemnation of greed, avarice, cupidity, venality, rapacity and so on?
5. Of what significance are institutional individualism, social preferences, expectations, expansibility of wants, learning, habit and routine?

The idea of an invisible hand mechanism or process or explanation is found in many discussions of the basic concept. The core of the idea is that results are generated by behaviour, and by the interaction and aggregation of behaviours, by individuals who neither knew nor intended the results. A leading example of this is the combination of the principle of unintended and unforeseen consequences (seen above in the *Wealth of Nations* use of the Invisible Hand) and the theory of spontaneous order associated with the name of Friedrich Hayek.

References

Popper, Karl (1957), 'The philosophy of science: a personal report', in C.A. Mace (ed.), *British Philosophy in the Mid-Century*, London: George Allen & Unwin, pp. 155–91; 2nd edn, 1966.
Samuels, Warren J. (1999), 'Hayek from the perspective of an institutionalist historian of economic thought: an interpretive essay', *Journal des Economistes et des Etudes Humaines*, **9** (June–September), 279–90.
Smith, Adam (1976 [1759]), *The Theory of Moral Sentiments*, New York: Oxford University Press.
Smith, Adam (1976 [1776]), *An Inquiry into the Nature and Causes of the Wealth of Nations*, 2 vols, New York: Oxford University Press.
Smith, Adam (1978), *Lectures on Jurisprudence*, New York: Oxford University Press.
Smith, Adam (1980), *Essays on Philosophical Subjects*, W.P.D. Wightman and J.C. Bryce (eds), Oxford: Oxford University Press.

12 Adam Smith and economic development
*Salim Rashid**

Introduction

Any evaluation of Adam Smith's contribution to the question of economic development should begin by asking, what is economic development? To say that economic development deals with the growth of a poor economy is unsatisfactory because it does not serve to distinguish the subject from economic history. I will take economic development to be the study of continuous and rapid economic growth, combined with the vision that such growth is a real possibility for all. Furthermore, this chapter will focus upon those cases where rapid economic growth has been equitable and aimed at the common people; as a corollary, students of these phenomena will encourage the thought that poverty is not a permanent feature of the human condition. These are propositions of such enormous and universal significance that those who serve to illuminate them must rank among the benefactors of mankind. The economist who believes in economic development will not only show empathy for the common people, he will also, and primarily, have the responsibility of pointing out the obstacles – political, social and economic – which prevent or retard the achievement of economic development.

Adam Smith exhibited more sympathy for the poor than many of his contemporaries, so if Adam Smith falls short as a development economist it has to be for his analysis. According to Adam Smith, the primary and perhaps only obstacle to growth is government. He seldom notes that the primary instrument of economic growth is the ability of individuals to cooperate, and that government being one of the many forms of such cooperation, if perhaps the most prominent one, it has the potential of being the most potent instrument of economic growth. It follows, of course, that the very potency of government also makes it the most powerful potential brake upon economic growth, which is almost all that attracted Smith's attention. As to the possibilities for continuous and rapid growth, this is only indirectly addressed by Adam Smith. As such, beyond Smith's clear sympathies for the worker, the system of Adam Smith fails as a contribution to economic development. The burden of this chapter is to present the evidence for this case.[1]

One wants, in the first instance, to judge historical figures only by standards recognizably contemporary to them. Some scholars argue that just by arguing for good government and for reliance upon self-interest, the *Wealth of Nations* made a significant contribution. As the need for good government and the primacy of self-interested behaviour by merchants were well recognized by 1776, Smith's contribution in this regard can only be rhetorical and pedagogical. I will show below that many of Smith's contemporaries, writers from the 1720s onwards, were consciously addressing the main questions of economic development stated above. They were aware of the power and promise of continuous economic growth; they saw the need for government to intervene and supplement the market, not supplant it; Smith's contemporaries also were conscious that power had played its role in making England the world leader that it was by 1770; and that such power had led to an unjust treatment of Ireland.[2] Smith paid scant attention even to the developmental issues in his own Scotland; his approach to such policy issues can perhaps be described as 'ethereal'. The neglect of the central concerns of development economics, which had already arisen and were discussed in the century preceding the *Wealth of Nations* (hereafter, WN), made the economic system espoused in WN an unhappy landmark in the history of economic development.

Concern for the poor
How important was the welfare of the common man in Smith's estimation? What priorities did he suggest for economic policy so as to enrich and empower ordinary individuals? One can support workers negatively, by attacking those who have the power to oppress them. There are many passages in the WN where Smith sides with the worker when his interests conflict with those of the landlord or capitalist. But such instances of negative partiality for the worker are not all the evidence; there are several strong positive assertions:

> No society can surely be flourishing and happy, of which the far greater part of the members are poor and miserable. It is but equity, besides, that they who feed, cloath and lodge the whole body of the people, should have such a share of the produce of their own labour as to be themselves tolerably well fed, cloathed and lodged. (WN I.8.35)

In attacking legislation which hurt poor women who were spinners of domestic linen yarn, Smith wrote: 'It is the industry which is carried on for the benefit of the rich and the powerful that is principally encouraged by our mercantile system. That which is carried on for the benefit of the poor and the indigent is too often either neglected or oppressed' (WN IV.8.4).

These are but two of several instances which show Smith urging economic policy be directed towards the poor and there can be little doubt that he was partial to the workers. There were many mercantilist authors, Bernard Mandeville being perhaps the most readable of this group, who favoured policies treating workers as beasts of burden. Smith distanced himself from such taskmasters and urged that economic policy was to consider the happiness of the poor as a major concern.[3] But do such concerns direct the structure of the WN? I am afraid not. The instances of sympathy are forceful and vigorous when they appear, but they are not guiding concerns.[4] Smith was certainly partial to the poor, but his empathy has to be set in contrast with the views of George Berkeley on Ireland. In order to gain the proper perspective, a little history is in order, especially since Ireland also provides us the first example of a poor country systematically trying to work its way out of poverty.

Since the Cromwellian conquest of the mid-seventeenth century, Ireland had been treated as a subordinate colony, and one can well say that Ireland was the first victim of imperialism by a Western power. The sufferings of the Irish poor were made famous in the most morbid satire in the English language, Jonathan Swift's (1729) *Modest Proposal*. Over time, as the eighteenth century progressed, it is members of the Anglican hierarchy who felt impelled to protest at the policy of the English. Several members of this hierarchy devoted themselves to finding practical means to alleviate poverty and to analysing the methods by which a poor country like Ireland could grow. Archbishop King had already worried about such issues before 1720, but it was a circle of friends around George Berkeley who provided the most eloquent voice as well as the visible practical actions for poverty alleviation in Ireland. The circle who engaged in such good deeds were called the Dublin School and they collectively constitute the Irish School of Economic Development. Upon being posted as Bishop of Cloyne, one of the more remote and poor areas of Ireland, Berkeley turned the post to his advantage by engaging in many practical deeds to help the poor and in writing a profoundly philosophic pamphlet on the nature of wealth and how to obtain it. The *Querist* was written by George Berkeley (1948 [1735]) to gather together many years of concern about the poverty of Ireland. As is well known, the style of the *Querist* is unique. It consists of a series of rhetorical questions, and the queries are so carefully framed that the answer is not in doubt.

The dominant theories of economic prosperity focused upon foreign trade, and the state was supposed to follow a watchful, if not active, policy regarding exports and imports. In opposition, Berkeley engaged in a radical analysis and reminded everyone that it is hard work that makes a nation rich. The people have to be stimulated to work harder by having their desires aroused. The role of the state was that of organizing society so that hard work was seen as desirable and duly rewarded. Berkeley refined the argument in 1743 by emphasizing upon the intellectual qualities that need to be developed. In emphasizing the role of human capital in a sustained and sophisticated fashion Berkeley originated the idea that 'economic development is human development'.

The first five queries of the *Querist* set the message of the pamphlet in embryo:[5]

I. 1   Whether there ever was, is, or will be, an industrious nation poor, or an idle rich?
I. 2   Whether a people can be called poor, where the common sort are well fed, clothed, and lodged?
I. 3   Whether the drift and aim of ever wise State should not be, to encourage industry in its members? And whether those who employ neither heads nor hands for the common benefit deserve not to be expelled like drones out of a well-governed State?
I. 4   Whether the four elements, and man's labour therein, be not the true source of wealth?
I. 5   Whether money be not only so far useful, as it stirreth up industry, enabling men mutually to participate the fruits of each other's labour? (Berkeley 1948 [1735], pp. 3–4)

Queries 1, 3 and 5 stand together. It is hard work that makes a people rich; the state should encourage all its members to work hard; practically speaking, the most effective way to stimulate a people to hard work is through the use of a money economy and money is valuable to society only insofar as it continues to encourage industry. The fourth query can be considered a clarification of the earlier ones, in that it makes clear that any increase in wealth must come from production – 'the four elements, and man's labour therein'.

In queries 2 and 3, we come face to face with Berkeley's considerable originality. He defines the wealth of a nation to consist of the comforts of life, properly distributed. Berkeley cannot repeat this point with sufficient force. It is because the poor are important that Berkeley is so insistent on developing the home trade, so that the poor can improve their condition by using the resources close at hand. The responsibility for providing the poor with the chance to live decently lay with the rich. The industry of the people had to be aroused, and industry was stimulated by demand. The demand of the rich arose as conspicuous consumption while that of the poor had to be stimulated. Berkeley addressed the rich in two ways. On the one hand, he urged them to think more about the plight of Ireland; on the other hand, he realized that the upper classes would insist on distinguishing themselves by their manner of consumption. Why could they not do so using Irish goods – why not build well and live well on the plentitude of Irish materials? This constructive programme required a serious effort on the part of the Irish rich. Berkeley repeatedly tells them to think more, pay attention to education, to sound marriages, to pass better laws and to rid themselves of destructive fashions imported from abroad. Ultimately, it is the intelligence and virtue of people that gives rise to satisfactory development, both in the sense of a larger national product as well as one which would provide more happiness. Berkeley would appear to be the first economist who felt that economic development was really but one aspect of human development.

In view of this closely argued, widely read and practically implemented view of economic development, one can only consider Adam Smith as having provided new and effective knowledge by claiming that he had no knowledge of Ireland or the Dublin School or George Berkeley.[6] But this is a claim that is hard to sustain. Even if we discount the fact that Smith owned copies of both the *Querist* and Berkeley's collected works, there are many likely ways Berkeley's thoughts would have been familiar to Smith and it will be useful to list a few: Smith took tar-water around 1744 for a bout of depression, Berkeley's supposedly wonderful cure; the Dublin Society was emulated in both Scotland and England; he had copies of Dobbs and Prior in his personal library; and the Rev. Robert Wallace, the critic of David Hume's views on ancient population, made no secret of proclaiming Berkeley's pro-poor views in his writings (Wallace, 1758).[7]

System
Three axioms succinctly describe the economy as viewed by Adam Smith in the *Wealth of Nations*:[8]

(A1) All individuals desire to maximize wealth.
(A2) All individuals know better than Government what will maximize their wealth.
(A3) National wealth is the sum of individual wealth.

Axioms 1 and 2, in conjunction, prove that individual wealth is maximized when government leaves individuals alone. Axiom 3 then says that maximizing individual wealth suffices to maximize national wealth. If we describe the axioms loosely as greed, knowledge and additivity, then greedy and knowledgeable individuals surely do not need government in order to maximize their wealth and additivity suffices to assure us that, since the aggregate is the simple sum of the individuals, the aggregate also does not need government to maximize economic growth. Modern readers, familiar with externalities in the form of, say, pollution, will probably be most curious about the validity of axiom 3, but in most less developed countries (LDCs) axioms 1 and 2 are also worth questioning.[9]

Many modern supporters of Smith consider this too selective a reading of Smith. This is a trend whose modern source is a brilliant article of Jacob Viner, which I will consider in the next section.[10] Before going further, a methodological point has to be insisted upon. If a thinker says many contradictory things, then he is effectively telling us that anything can happen. This may be true, but then the thinker has effectively made theory redundant for policy purposes. If a thinker tells us of social phenomena that many widely different outcomes are possible, then, in order to legislate, one has to know so many particulars that practical men have quite as much authority as theorists. That Smith did believe himself as setting up a 'system' and saying something radical and important in the process, I consider the historical evidence to be quite unequivocal about. Viner himself left us in no doubt about where he stood:

> There is no possible room for doubt, however, that Smith in general believed that there was, to say the least, a strong presumption against government activity beyond its fundamental duties of protection against its foreign foes and maintenance of justice. (Viner, 1928, p. 140)

Insofar as Adam Smith had something of value to say, his ideas have to be judged primarily by the validity of a system based on greed, knowledge and additivity. The great power of these axioms is their simplicity. One is enabled to master the intricacies of economic policy without ever using a graph or following an equation. A theory of universal efficacy is proclaimed in simple and accessible language. One needs no knowledge of history, or politics, or culture, or religion. Economic truths are presented as impersonal, scientific and effective everywhere.

In foreign trade, the most important policy measure of Adam Smith's time would be bounties for infant industries, while in domestic trade the corresponding policy would be preventing speculation in food markets.[11] Smith was quite unequivocal about both. He rejected bounties for infant industries. He begins by noting that no one argues against natural advantages. 'The natural advantages which one country has over another in producing particular commodities are sometimes so great that it is acknowledged by all the world to be in vain to struggle with them' (WN IV.2.15). He goes on to illustrate this with his famous example of growing grapes in hothouses in Scotland. Then he transfers the argument in the blink of an eye to cases where there is no suggestion of natural advantage:

> Whether the advantages which one country has over another be natural or acquired is in this respect of no consequence. As long as the one country has those advantages, and the other wants them, it will always be more advantageous for the latter rather to buy of the former than to make. It is an acquired advantage only, which one artificer has over his neighbour, who exercises another trade; and yet they both find it more advantageous to buy of one another, than to make what does not belong to their particular trades. (WN IV.2.15)

This is just an evasion. If Swiss soil and climate enable them to grow the finest bananas, that is one thing, if no visible advantage makes the Swiss the best watchmakers, that is quite another. In the one case, there is no chance of competing successfully with Swiss bananas, in the other there is a very good chance. Paradoxically, this is one of the free trade policy measures that later neoclassicists have been willing to admit as consistent with free trade, 'properly understood'. Smith could have said that choosing which infant industries have promise requires too much knowledge and discrimination; or that such infants have a persistent tendency not to want to grow up. He does neither. So strong was his feeling on the matter that he simply bypassed the argument.

As to the need for preventing speculation in foodstuffs, Smith begins by assuring us that the interests of the consumer and the seller are identical:[12] 'The interest of the inland dealer, and that of the great body of the people, how opposite soever they may at first sight appear, are, even in years of the greatest scarcity, exactly the same' (WN IV.5.42). He goes on to admit that if a monopoly could be formed, it might be harmful to the public, but Smith scoffed at such a possibility. Indeed, if a famine had been suffered, Smith was sure it was because the government had attempted to regulate that which was properly left free:

> Whoever examines . . . the history of the dearths and famines which have afflicted any part of Europe . . . will find, I believe, that a dearth has *never* arisen from any combination among the inland dealers in corn, nor from any other cause but a real scarcity . . . and that a famine has *never* arisen from any other cause but the violence of government attempting, by improper means, to remedy the inconveniences of a dearth. (WN IV.5.44, emphasis added)

The proper course for the government therefore was to leave the corn trade completely unfettered at all times: 'The unlimited, unrestrained freedom of the corn trade, as it is the only effectual preventative of the miseries of a famine, so it is the best palliative of the inconvenience of a dearth' (WN IV.5.46).

The question is not whether free-market allocations should be acceptable during seasons of scarcity. It is to establish Adam Smith's unequivocal acceptance of such a policy. While many had argued for the freedom of all internal trades, foodstuffs were held to be an exception by all except a handful. Whenever there was fear of a deficient harvest, pamphlets immediately appeared attacking hoarders and speculators for driving up prices. Parliament did not ignore these popular fears and the statute books had laws prohibiting forestalling, regrating and engrossing – as the complex of activities involved in corn speculation were called. Of all the economic legislation of his time, none came in for stronger criticism from Adam Smith than the laws which were meant to prevent a monopoly of the distribution of the corn. 'The popular fear of engrossing and forestalling', Smith said, 'may be compared to the popular terrors and suspicions of witchcraft' (WN IV.5.65). The sheer importance of the food market in Adam Smith's day, and Smith's extreme stand on non-interference, should serve to demonstrate his abhorrence for intervention.[13]

This is one of the few points in the *Wealth of Nations* where the argument for a completely free trade is emphatically made, without any hint of a qualification. Indeed Smith even applies his advocacy of freedom in the corn trade unhesitatingly to India:

> The drought in Bengal, a few years ago, might probably have occasioned a very great dearth. Some improper regulations, some injudicious restrains imposed by the servants of the East India Company upon the rice trade, contributed, perhaps, to turn that dearth into a famine. (WN IV.5.45)

Smith provides no evidence to justify this assertion and it was a somewhat rash test of his theory considering that India had a poorer transportation system and a far less developed capitalistic structure than England. Smith's explicit reference to other European countries and to India as places where authorities had needlessly meddled, shows his belief in the policy of laissez-faire for the internal corn trade to be of universal applicability.[14] Since the WN took the strongest stand on each of the economic issues, domestic and foreign, that was of most importance to the public, his primary message is clear: the dominant and overwhelming need for leaving markets free.

Qualifications
One should not overlook the modifications an author makes to the content of one chapter at another chapter. In this sense, the primary difficulty in reading Smith carefully is Smith himself. Jacob Viner said it kindly when he described the WN: 'Traces of every conceivable sort of doctrine are to be found in that most catholic book, and an econo-

mist must have peculiar theories indeed who cannot quote from the Wealth of Nations to suit his special purposes' (Viner, 1928, p. 126).

This is a true characterization but it should not be seen as denying that Smith does have a definite economic system, and even the exceptions noted by Viner get exaggerated importance unless they are more carefully examined. Viner's long list of exceptions is misleading and the brilliance of his prose can easily mislead. Of the dozen or so cases listed on p. 130, the first eight deal with cases, such as the attempts of masters to oppress workers, which are irrelevant because such oppression has an effective remedy in competition. Two others, the payment of clerks and the 'eating up' of wages in old countries, are just flourishes of language. Despite his clear belief that Adam Smith supported free trade, Viner seems determined to provide a subtext where Smith was almost a German Cameralist. After wondering how Smith would respond to the success of German principalities in managing the public domain, Viner goes on to make the strong claim:[15]

> The modern advocate of laissez faire who objects to government participation in business on the grounds that it is an encroachment upon a field reserved by nature for private enterprise cannot find support for this argument in the *Wealth of Nations*. (Viner, 1928, p. 149)

Viner does not pursue this point seriously and since on the very next page we are reminded of Smith's absent-mindedness about natural liberty and how he frequently forgot his principles, it will be more to the point to look at some examples.

There are several cases, such as differential taxation of landlords, or taxing of small alehouses, which do question a libertarian position by using taxation to modify behaviour, but these are of minor quantitative importance. There are only two hard cases – usury and small notes. Smith claims that the Scotch bankers of his own day are myopic in issuing small notes to the public:[16]

> Had every particular banking company always understood and attended to its own particular interest, the circulation never could have been overstocked with paper money. But every particular banking company has not always understood or attended to its own particular interest, and the circulation has frequently been overstocked with paper money. (WN II.2.53)

As a consequence, Smith goes on to urge that the issue of small notes be prohibited:

> Such regulations may, no doubt, be considered as in some respect a violation of natural liberty. But those exertions of the natural liberty of a few individuals, which might endanger the security of the whole society, are, and ought to be, restrained by the laws of all governments, of the most free as well as of the most despotical. The obligation of building party walls, in order to prevent the communication of fire, is a violation of natural liberty, exactly of the same kind with the regulations of the banking trade which are here proposed. (WN II.2.94)

> According to the system of natural liberty, the sovereign has only three duties to attend to; three duties of great importance, indeed, but plain and intelligible to common understandings: first, the duty of protecting the society from the violence and invasion of other independent societies; secondly, the duty of protecting, as far as possible, every member of the society from the injustice and oppression of every other member of it, or the duty of establishing an exact administration of justice; and thirdly, the duty of erecting and maintaining certain publick works and certain public institutions, which it can never be for the interest of any individual, or small number of individuals, to erect and maintain; because the profit could never repay the

expence to any individual or small number of individuals, though it may frequently do much more than repay it to a great society. (WN IV.9.51)

This is a hard case because, in general, Smith asks us to trust selfinterest; how can we do this when the very people who deal with profit-making on a constant basis are capable of making 'systematic' mistakes about their own self-interest? The comparison with firewalls is forced, because a fire is an involuntary and accidental event while the pursuit of profit is the *raison d'être* of both bankers and borrowers. Much the same argument applies to Smith's acquiescence in the usury laws, for which he was attacked by Jeremy Bentham. Smith never replied to Bentham and this point begs for clarification. I would rather face up to these two inconsistencies as puzzles and conjecture that the case of small notes will receive a satisfactory explanation in terms of personal obligations if we ever get enough correspondence from this period. But too much has been made of several other remarks of Smith.

Consider Smith's approbation for laws prescribing a maximum for land owned in the American colonies.[17] One can praise this as prescient because it prevented monopoly and gave poor farmers a chance. But if government can prevent landlords from buying such large amounts of land for the good reasons stated, why can it not also dispossess them for the same good reasons? This brings us directly to the spate of legislation supporting land reform that took place in almost every LDC. Smith is on the verge of supporting intervention in the land market – only a slight extension of his argument will lead us there – but Smith stops carefully short. Before one concludes that land reform is a Smithian policy, we should emphasize that there is a considerable difference in laying down laws before the market begins to function and laying them down in an ongoing market – much as we have the right to decide the rules of a race, but not to change them during the race.

Or look at the tax on absentees that Smith favoured. Ireland figures mightily in any discussion of economic development, and Smith insists on the inequity whereby Irish absentee landlords can escape all taxes which maintain the Irish government by living abroad. Again, this is an imposition on property rights and freedom of movement. Smith appears sympathetic, but he is careful to say only that the measure is popular for good reasons. He does not say that he wants the tax to be imposed, nor does he relate it to any social duties the Irish landlords might owe their community or to the rate of growth of the Irish economy. And since the entire discussion is tucked away within a consideration of the benefits of a sales tax, one can hardly argue that Smith was suggesting some form of intervention. Insofar as it is valid to support a later book with quotes from an earlier one, it is appropriate to remember the following passage about a statesman respecting established powers in connection with the exceptions to free trade in the WN:

> He will accommodate, as well as he can, his public arrangements to the confirmed habits and prejudices of the people; and he will remedy as well as he can, the inconveniencies which may flow from the want of those regulations which the people are averse to submit to . . . like Solon, when he cannot establish the best system of laws, he will endeavour to establish the best that the people can bear. (TMS, VI.ii.2.16)

On the whole, the traditional view that Adam Smith justified only that economic development which arose through the market is correct.

The individual and the social

Perhaps the most persistent failure on Smith's part, at least where the needs of economic development are concerned, lay in his inability to focus on those issues where the social nature of man and the essential need for cooperation played primary roles. This can be best illustrated by looking at the division of labour, an issue of such importance to Adam Smith that we would expect him to give us his most comprehensive views on this question. We are emphatically told in Chapter 1 of Book I that the division of labour (DoL) is the most important reason for greater production and is the primary force leading to prosperity.[18] The famous example of pin making is used to provide illustrative proof that, on an average, therefore, each individual's productivity is increased 240-fold by the DoL – truly a momentous achievement.[19]

Three reasons are given why a concentration of effort upon a single task increases efficiency. Firstly, the skill of individual workers is much improved by specialization; secondly, workers save time and effort involved in having to switch from one operation to another; and finally, the division of labour facilitates the invention of machinery. The three reasons are most applicable only in manufacturing and Smith notes that agriculture is not suited to the division of labour, with the implication that one is not to expect much growth in that sector. Smith's analysis was most sharply disputed by one of his admirers, Dugald Stewart, who argued that the first two reasons, while real, are quantitatively unimportant. If, then, the division of labour is to explain the productivity of labour it must be by its influence upon the invention of machinery. Stewart doubts that workers themselves would engage in the invention of labour-saving machinery, as Smith had conjectured, because the effect of such improvements would not be to shorten the workday for the inventor and indeed might even lead to his being unemployed. Furthermore, Stewart argued that the effect of the division of labour was to fix attention on one simple operation while the improvement of machinery required knowledge of a great variety of operations.[20] Stewart's positive contribution consisted of two very significant innovations. Firstly, Stewart focused upon the separation of tasks into the simplest ones, thus drawing attention to those acts most easy to replace with machines; secondly, the entrepreneur is put at the centre of the stage by Stewart, since it is the capitalist who is driven by the lure of profits dissect the production process into individual actions, then to view each action in relation to the whole and thus to find ways to continually improve his machinery. E.G. Wakefield completed this far-reaching criticism by observing that every successful division of labour must be accompanied by a plan for its subsequent combination. 'The division of employments which takes place in a pin-factory, results from, and is wholly dependent on, the union, generally under one roof, of all the labour by which the pins are made' (Wakefield in Smith, 1843 [1776]), p. 25). Smith's one-sided emphasis upon division was misleading, because the successful division of labour presupposed its subsequent combination – an act of coordinating vision which took place in the mind of the entrepreneur. What is notable about Smith's prejudices is that he did not note the importance of coordination even for private enterprise. Smith cast much light on one aspect – the individualistic one – of the productive process but at the expense of throwing a shade on those features – such as the contributions of inventions, machinery and management – which require a coordinating vision and coordination, and which have proved of greater longer-run significance. The very eagerness with which Adam Smith's analysis of the division of labour in the pin factory was accepted makes it a good example of fine writing elevating inadequate logic.

As to larger or wider instances of social cooperation, there is not much material in the *Wealth of Nations*, and there is little reason to dispute Viner's assessment that: 'Though there is nowhere in Smith's writings a general discussion of the possibilities of voluntary co-operation, he makes clear that he did not hope for much good from it' (Viner, 1928, p. 153).

None of the three axioms of Smithian economic policy was new in content. But each had only been a working hypothesis before Smith. When he was not theorizing, Smith himself stated many exceptions to his axioms in the *Wealth of Nations* – not small exceptions, but fundamental ones. Does government have any functions at all? Yes, it has to maintain law and order and build canals, bridges and highways. Why rely on the government to build canals and bridges? If these benefit society, then this means that a suitably comprehensive view of costs and benefits would allow us to find that the canals and bridges produced a profit. Why do individuals not cooperate at the scale needed to build canals and bridges? Implicitly, Smith's answer is: because individual self-interest is too limited and markets are too weak to see distant benefits. How can we know beforehand the limits of self-interest in achieving the public good? Is this not a question that governments are to solve pragmatically through experience?

The important questions that the three Smithian axioms do not directly address are: What if the maximization of wealth requires that individuals coordinate their actions? Do the people have the 'sociability' to engage in such cooperative ventures? Or do they act as though life is a zero-sum game and thwart the common good? These are questions of immense importance to the development economist, as the recent attraction of the concept of 'social capital' testifies. Whether this coordination takes place through a specifically designed organization, such as a chamber of commerce, or by a special department of a general purpose organization – such as the state – is a subordinate matter. That such coordination is not an automatic event even in the most developed market system is clear from the observation of Paul Krugman regarding the centres of high technology in the United States, that is, Silicon Valley, California; Route 128, Massachusetts; and the Research Triangle, North Carolina. 'In general the new high technology clusters were the product less of intrepid individuals than of visionary bureaucrats (if that is not an oxymoron)' (Krugman, 1991, p. 64). This fundamental point about coordination is to reappear many times over in questions of economic development.[21]

Institutions and socialization
The three axioms on which Smithian economic policy are based are initially stated as though they apply to every single individual. But of course this is too strong a claim. Later Smith admits the possibility of some individuals not obeying these axioms; but this was not of major concern to Smith, since the great majority of individuals would be subject to the axioms. Let us explore the implications of the case which allows sway to the exceptions. We can now say:

1. Some individuals may not be greedy.
2. Some individuals may not be knowledgeable.
3. Some production may not allow additivity.

Ignoring concerns with additivity for the moment, let us ask: 'What if the property of the land is concentrated in the hands of those who are neither greedy nor knowledgeable? How will this generate economic growth, let alone economic development? In such cases, one would think that intervention was justified, and indeed, without putting the case in these words, such has been the implicit argument supporting land reform in LDCs during the 64 years since the Second World War. It poses the larger question: Can the process of economic development be given a vigorous jump start by designing institutions?[22]

We have just seen above a logical argument for redistributive land reform. Are there others? By asking that society see to the creation of greedy[23] and knowledgeable individuals who will then make the market work, we will have attained the proper perspective on economic development.

Let us examine Smith's response to the claim that workers worked harder when paid lower real wages, which would generate a backward-bending supply curve:

> In cheap years, it is pretended, workmen are generally more idle, and in dear ones more industrious than ordinary. A plentiful subsistence, therefore, it has been concluded, relaxes, and a scanty one quickens their industry. That a little more plenty than ordinary may render some workmen idle, cannot well be doubted; but that it should have this effect upon the greater part, or that men in general should work better when they are ill fed than when they are well fed, when they are disheartened than when they are in good spirits, when they are frequently sick than when they are generally in good health, seems not very probable. (WN I.8.44)

This direct assertion on Smith's part shows concern for the well-being of the worker, but it does not meet the factual objection. How real is the phenomenon?[24] And if it be as prevalent as contemporaries believed it to be, what was to be done?

The problem of a backward-bending supply curve would be most acute for those directly involved in trying to alleviate poverty. In seventeenth-century Ireland, the Dublin Society and George Berkeley were involved in just such an effort. Berkeley told the Irish poor that they were poor because they had reconciled themselves to poverty, thereby implicitly admitting the truth of the claim about backward-bending supply curves, diagnosing this as due to a want of 'desires' on the part of the Irish poor. In the *Querist*, Berkeley is forceful in advocating new wants among the poor in order to spur them to steady labour, cleanliness, and civilization:

> Query 20. Whether the creating of wants be not the likeliest way to produce industry in a people?
> Query 20. And whether, if our peasants were accustomed to eat beef and wear shoes, they would not be more industrious? (Berkeley, 1948 [1735], pp. 3–4)

Want more and you will get more, because your wants will lead you to work harder.[25] Smithian economists respond to such interventions by arguing that, if you give a native people enough time, they do respond to watches and bicycles and mirrors and movies. So the development of the 'work ethic' can be left to time. But one of the prime goals of development is speed. How long will it take for wants to grow by this method and what are we to do in the meantime?[26] Are there not peoples, such as some Native American tribes, who simply did not grow new tastes and modernize adequately? And how will population be kept at bay if preferences change very slowly? Will not the higher incomes produced by economic growth be diverted to larger families and thus halt the rise of per capita incomes so central to the definition of economic development?

Smith always asserted that the market could only function when law and order and legal regulations regarding property had been formulated and implemented. But he failed to assert with equal force that every economy is embedded in society and that the formation of individuals with market compatible beliefs is very much a task to be faced. Individuals are not born with just those beliefs and motivations needed for the market to function – society has to induce these. If economic development was an issue of importance to Smith he would have asked: How are people, in say, Egypt, socialized into the bourgeois virtues? What social institutions are needed to make them knowledgeable and profit-seeking? Under what circumstances can we expect private gain to also become social gain – when are negative externalities of concern? Smith lived at a time when many of the frequently voiced concerns were those we are also dealing with today – but he ignored them. Over time, the weight of his authority served to stifle the concerns of economic development. This led to a period when non-intervention acquired the force of a moral principle, a policy which has emerged again with a vengeance today.

Growth without end?

In an essay of 1721, written after the South Sea Bubble, Berkeley had noted that:

> There is still room for Invention or Improvement in most Trades and Manufacturers; and it is probable, that Premiums given on that account to ingenious Artists would soon be re-paid a hundred-fold to the Public. (Berkeley, 1948 [1721], p. 72)

This reflected a view of virtually all writers of this period: that the English economy had grown continually since the time of Elizabeth I, and the optimism of perhaps a majority that such growth could be expected to continue into the indefinite future.[27] Smith strongly admitted the truth of these propositions at one point. In a remarkable passage, Smith stated:[28]

> Since the time of Henry VIII, the wealth and revenue of the country have been continually advancing, and, in the course of their progress, their pace seems rather to have been gradually accelerated than retarded. *They seem, not only to have been going on, but to have been going on faster and faster.* The wages of labour have been continually increasing during the same period, and in the greater part of the different branches of trade and manufactures the profits of stock have been diminishing. (WN I.9.6, emphasis added)

If Smith truly felt for economic development as, say, the Irish did, this would give rise to some natural questions. How long can such growth continue? What are its human implications? Given Smith's belief that it is governments that repress growth and individual initiative that creates it, how have the roles of governments changed in the last 150 years both to allow continued growth and, indeed, to accelerate it? Unfortunately, none of these issues seem to attract his attention. Neither before nor after this wonderful claim do we find an extended discussion of the changes in the law, or in technology or in social organization that permitted such a wondrous period of growth to exist and indeed to continue 'faster and faster'.

Instead Adam Smith provides a 'history of economic policy' that seems to have been motivated by his desire to uphold free trade, and self-serving in that it portrayed past policy as being founded on elementary errors. There is no mention of the fact that England was the richest country in Europe by 1700 because it had dominated the international carrying trade by fighting three wars with the Dutch – wars designed substantially with commercial gains in view. Or that the tilt of Charles II towards the French and towards Catholicism raised a fear on the part of the Whigs that the trade with France was a means of furnishing Louis XIV with gold and silver, thereby not only enriching His Catholic Majesty but also providing France with the most potent means with which to prosecute wars. Instead, Adam Smith tells us in WN that earlier economic policy was largely based on the confusion between real wealth and the precious metals. Because of this error, economic policy was based on the obtaining a favourable balance of trade. One can only wonder why Smith would provide such a misleading account of past economic policy, when he had himself noted the correct state of affairs in his *Lectures*, or fail to correct himself when William Robertson noted the real import of the balance of trade in a letter to Adam Smith after the WN was published.

The theoretical concepts of the *Wealth of Nations* serve to make continuous and rapid growth an unlikely phenomenon. Adam Smith introduces the concept of a stationary state – perhaps the first among his contemporaries to do so:

> In a country which had acquired that full complement of riches which the nature of its soil and climate, and its situation with respect to other countries, allowed it to acquire; which could, therefore, advance no further, and which was not going backwards, both the wages of labour and the profits of stock would probably be very low. In a country fully peopled in proportion to what either its territory could maintain or its stock employ, the competition for employment would necessarily be so great as to reduce the wages of labour to what was barely sufficient to keep up the number of labourers, and, the country being already fully peopled, that number could never be augmented. In a country fully stocked in a proportion to all the business it had to transact, as great a quantity of stock would be employed in every particular branch as the nature and extent of the trade would admit. The competition, therefore, would everyw-here [sic] be as great, and consequently the ordinary profit as low as possible. (WN I.9.14)

The subsequent discussion of China is notable for the claim that China had reached the full complement of riches it could have with its current institutions. Smith allows that it could have been richer with a more Smithian set of institutions, but the crucial phrase we are seeking is that these new institutions would permit continual growth. Such a statement is missing.

Whereas many contemporaries viewed the growth of England as an ongoing process, Adam Smith only on occasion gives us such a view and indeed ensconces the passages on growth within theoretical constructs which suggest bounded growth. Accumulating capital, for example, serves to lower profit:[29] 'As capitals increase in any country, the profits which can be made by employing them necessarily diminish. It becomes gradually more and more difficult to find within the country a profitable method of employing any new capital' (WN II.4.8).

One can follow the strain of Smith's vision through several other discussions, such as his agricultural bias, which would again lead to a stationary state since agriculture was subject to diminishing returns, or his claim that profits and rents eat up wages in old settled countries, a phenomenon which implies steady or lower wages for the poor and does not give any hope of a steady accumulation of riches. Explicit statements are perhaps hard to find, but contemporaries wrote with the silent premise that steady continuous growth was part of the 'natural' state of mankind – such a premise is missing in the *Wealth of Nations*.

An important question that arises from the silent premise of Smith's contemporaries is whether poor countries would ever be able to catch up with rich ones. If asked, this question would lead into a discussion of the sources of rapid growth and its possible limits. Adam Smith quite neglected the question of 'catching-up'. The neglect is all the more surprising because the claim that 'Rich countries get richer' had been publicly debated and Smith himself had taken note of the debate in earlier writings.[30] The most prominent such public debate was that between David Hume, the philosopher, and the Rev. Josiah Tucker, Dean of Bristol and a well-known commentator on social and economic affairs. The origins of this debate are not of relevance here, but much of it was conducted in private correspondence around 1758 using Lord Kames as intermediary. As Smith was well known to both Kames and Hume, there is good reason to expect that Smith was familiar with the debate for some two decades prior to publishing the *Wealth of Nations*. Smith's library contained several of Tucker's works but Smith carefully avoided any mention of Tucker in his writings.

Tucker made public his views in 1774 in *Four Tracts*, a work which went through a third edition by 1776. The very first Tract posed the following vital question in its title:

> A solution of the important question, Whether a poor country, where raw materials and provisions are cheap, can supplant the Trade of a rich manufacturing country, where raw materials and provisions are dear, and the price of Labour high – with a postscript obviating objections. (Tucker, 1974 [1776])

The solution consisted of a set of arguments showing that the rich country had only itself and its policies to blame if it were surpassed; there were no economic grounds to expect that the poor country would ever necessarily catch up to the rich one.[31] It will suffice to provide only a listing of each of Tucker's brilliant points. Tucker noted that the rich country will have:

- Better commercial and transport and research infrastructure.
- More knowledge – the clarity of Tucker's argument bears quoting below.
- It will have greater capacity to innovate.
- Higher wages will induce more effort and ambition – even drawing out the genius of poor countries.
- Constant demands will permit greater division of labour.
- Greater competition will lead to greater efficiency.
- Lower interest will allow merchants to undersell poor countries.

In opposition to the Humean argument of manufactures seeking out cheap labour, Tucker asserts: 'It may be laid down as a general proposition, which very seldom fails, That operose or complicated manufactures are cheapest in rich countries; and raw materials in poor ones' (Tucker, 1974 [1776], p. 36). Tucker's words about the importance of knowledge and the possibility of its indefinite growth are so important that I quote them below:

> The richer Country is not only in Possession of the Things already made and settled, but also of superior Skill and Knowledge (acquired by long Habit and Experience) for inventing and

making of more. The importance of this will appear the greater, when we consider that no Man can pretend to set Bounds to the Progress that may yet be made both in Agriculture and Manufactures; for which can take upon him to affirm, that our Children cannot as far exceed us as we have exceeded our Gothic Forefathers? And is it not much more natural and reasonable to suppose, that we are rather at the Beginning only, and just got within the Threshold, than that we are arrived at the *ne plus ultra* of useful Discoveries? (Tucker, 1974 [1776], p. 30)

One has to wonder why someone who saw rapid and continuous economic growth as a real possibility would ignore such a debate as well as most of the arguments it raised to prominence.

Conclusion
How does Adam Smith rank for his contribution to economic development? Smith had considerable sympathy for the poor but – and this is a central qualification – not at the expense of market intervention. William Wilberforce noted with some pain Smith's response to a fund meant to provide fisheries for the Highlands poor:

Dr. Smith with a certain characteristic coolness, observed to me that he looked for no other consequences from the scheme than the entire loss of every shilling that should be expended on it, granting, however, with uncommon candour, that the public would be no great sufferer, because he believed the individuals meant to put their hands only in their own pockets. (Wilberforce, 1840, p. 177)

Contrast this with Berkeley, of whose works at Cloyne we read of in a letter:

Our spinning-school is in a thriving way. The children begin to find a pleasure in being paid in hard money; which I understand they will not give to their parents, but keep to buy clothes for themselves. Indeed I found it difficult and tedious to bring them to this; but I believe it will now do. I am building a workhouse for sturdy vagrants, and design to raise about two acres of hemp for employing them. Can you put me in a way of getting hempseed; or does your Society distribute any? It is hoped your flax-seed will come in time. (Fraser, 1871, p. 248)

Adam Smith was familiar with the writings of the Irish School, but failed to see how his own system was being challenged by Ireland – what if initial conditions were wrong? Should there be an initial land reform? What if some significant number of the wealthy were neither well informed nor maximizers? How should social institutions be devised to achieve the pre-conditions for a market?[32] Adam Smith was virtually unconcerned with Scotland as a distinct problem – Scottish economic growth was all part of the grand design for the prosperity of Great Britain. No special concern is visible for the Highlands in his writings. That they had different lifestyles was a commonplace, but it should have been made evident from the acts of military disobedience that occurred even into the 1770s.[33] Nor did he concern himself with the promise and potential for faster growth. This point needs emphasis if one is to understand the urgency of economic development: 7 per cent per capita growth means a doubling of one's real income every decade, or 16-fold increase in one's working lifetime of 40 years. How can the hopes and fears of such a person compare with those of someone who lives with 3 per cent per capita growth and can only hope for a little over doubling at the end of their working life? Tucker was more prescient on this.

I have emphasized the role of two clergymen, Berkeley and Tucker, because logic would suggest that they were the natural carriers of knowledge about economic development. Anglican clergymen were educated, many of them mingled with ordinary people, they administered poor relief, they christened, married and buried everyday folk. Their concern, education and social power made them natural conduits for the growth of beliefs about economic development. If the virtues of Berkeley and Tucker were proclaimed as loudly as those of Adam Smith have been, the history of economic development may well have been quite different. Berkeley stated it well when he justified his writings on economics in the preface to the second edition of the *Querist* (1948 [1735]): 'To feed the hungry and clothe the naked, by promoting an honest industry, will, perhaps, be deemed no improper employment for a clergyman who still thinks himself a member of the commonwealth.'

Overall, Adam Smith and his legacy has been a distinct brake on our understanding of economic development. We see the quaintness of the situation when we see Parliament repeatedly upholding the authority of Adam Smith as an economist, while referring to Ireland as beyond the laws of political economy:

> That it was mischievous to interfere with the regular course of supply and demand in the market was a principle no less generally recognized; but, so singular was the situation of Ireland, that this great principle of political economy must be violated. (Lord Lansdowne, quoted in Fetter, 1980, p. 59)

> The Irish government were endeavouring to give relief in every possible way; not with strict regard to the principles of political economy, for unhappily the case was one that compelled them to set all ordinary rules at defiance. (Sir Robert Peel, quoted in Fetter, op. cit., p. 59)

Notes

* I am grateful to Shahid Alam, Michael Perelman and M.G. Quibria for comments.
1. Without going into details, let me state that my priorities differ so considerably from some earlier commentators, such as Lord Robbins or Joseph Spengler, that I will not make direct reference to their works. It should be noted that I am concerned with per capita or intensive growth throughout.
2. Even in Scotland, which was not a colony, the need and the promise of government attention was widely recognized and accepted.
3. Heckscher (1955), Furniss (1965 [1920]).
4. Michael Perelman has pointed out that Smith seems to limit his sympathy for those who accept capitalism. He was not sympathetic to those who were not willing to harness their future to the market – self-sufficient farmers, rowdy urban workers (Perelman, 2000).
5. The following quotation and paragraphs are taken from Rashid (1988). I have tried to show the relevance of Berkeley today in Rashid (1999).
6. Andrew Skinner has pointed out that Sir James Steuart was also very concerned about the poor, especially during periods of transition. See Skinner (1979).
7. Smith (1987), pp. 103–5.
8. Wesley Mitchell first provided this compact and lucid characterization in Mitchell (1967), pp. 61–5. The supporting quotes are spread out over many pages of the WN, but are best found in Chapter 2 of Book IV of WN.
9. They were queried by contemporaries such as Mickle in the *Lusiad*, according to Jacob Viner in his Introduction to the reprint of John Rae's *Life of Adam Smith* (Viner, 1965).
10. See the recent papers of Jeffrey Young (2006) and of Medema and Samuels (Chapter 16 in this volume), both of which are thoughtful essays in this tradition. A useful review of the literature on Smith is in Vivienne Brown (1997).
11. The corn laws will run a close third.
12. All that follows is contained in four closely argued pages, 524–7, I will not give repeated references. More detail can be found in Rashid (1998).
13. Modern critics, such as E.P. Thompson (1991), have found Smith's long-run orientation to be wanting a 'moral imperative'. I am grateful to Andrew Skinner for this reference.

14. For a contrary approach, suggesting that Smith did not really mean to violate distributive justice in the strong fashion noted, see Barry Gordon and Jeffrey Young (1996).
15. Note the minimalist criterion for government participation – that it not lose money – is like saying that the bureaucracy should closely mimic a sustainable private firm.
16. Smith's argument is questionable. See an excellent review by Kevin Dowd (1990).
17. WN IV.vii.b.572 on land restrictions and V.ii.k.895 on absentee tax.
18. WN I.13.22. More details on the historical review can be found in Rashid (1998).
19. This example is especially interesting because the productivity increase involves no change in technique – it is purely a case of applying existing knowledge more efficiently. The next paragraphs draw upon Rashid (1998), Chapter 2.
20. Stewart (1877), pp. 315, 318, 319.
21. Its importance for economic development was noted by the Dutch economist Boeke in commenting upon Indonesia and later by Banfield (1953) in his study of the south of Italy.
22. US foreign policy got itself into an unedifying mess by supporting both land reform and the market in its efforts to stave off Communism after WWII. Rashid (1997).
23. Rather, the greed is innate, society can direct it.
24. Smith even quotes from a French author who substantiates the claim of a backward-bending supply curve of labour, but is unwilling to accept the evidence. Students of development economics have often wondered about Smith's attitude to facts. Thus, Smith attacked mercantilism, yet England had become a world power, both militarily and economically, under mercantilism. Was there no connection? Or should the observation be dismissed, with the theorists' claim that England would have grown even faster without mercantilism?
25. All societies arriving at 'modernization' have had to grapple with the question of backward-bending supply curves. So far was Berkeley from believing that work habits were natural that he was willing to force criminals into adopting good work habits.
26. The confidence with which the neoclassicists treat speed and automaticity is visible in the nature of the jump to the market proposed by so many after the demise of Communism. Their failure has led to a sort of mantra: 'Reform markets – if you cannot, then reform institutions, if you cannot, then reform cultures.'
27. Berkeley (1948), p. 72.
28. Smith (1776) seems to apply the idea to England since Elizabeth on pp. 365–7, and into the indefinite past.
29. When dealing with a micro context, the acquisition of wealth by individuals, Smith correctly notes that the hardest part is to get started (Smith, 1776, p. 104).
30. There is a marvellously erudite essay of Istvan Hont (1983) on this topic which is marred by Hont's claim that when Hume talked about money, he really meant riches; furthermore, that this error was committed by virtually all Hume's readers and that Hume himself failed to correct them. My disagreement with Hont's claim does not diminish my admiration for his scholarship.
31. Bernard Semmel (1970).
32. Smith is quite familiar with the non-capitalist mentality of landlords (Smith, 1776, p. 416).
33. Smith (1987), pp. 347–8. The point made by Perelman (2002) in note 4 above might explain his indifference to the Highlanders.

References

Banfield, E.C. (1953), *The Moral Basis of a Backward Society*, Glencoe: Free Press.
Berkeley, George (1948), *The Works of George Berkeley, Bishop of Cloyne*, edited by A.A. Luce and T.E. Jessup, London, Thomas Nelson, including *The Querist* (1735), *A Word to the Wise* (1721), *An Essay Toward Preventing the Ruine of Great Britain* (1749), all in Vol. 6.
Brown, V. (1997), '"Mere inventions of the imagination": a survey of recent literature on Adam Smith', *Economics and Philosophy*, 13, 281–312
Dowd, K. (1990), 'Did central banks evolve naturally? A review essay of Charles Goodhart's *The Evolution of Central Banks*', *Scottish Journal of Political Economy*, 37 (1), 97–104.
Fetter, F.W. (1980), *The Economist in Parliament, 1780–1868*, Durham, NC: Duke University Press.
Fraser, A.C. (1871), *Life and Letters of George Berkeley*, Oxford: Clarendon Press.
Furniss, E.S. (1965 [1920]), *The Position of the Laborer in a System of Nationalism; a Study in the Labor Theories of the Later English Mercantilists*, New York: Augustus Kelley.
Gordon, Barry and Jeffrey Young (1996), 'Distributive justice as a normative criterion in Adam Smith's political economy', *History of Political Economy*, 28 (1), Spring, 1–25.
Heckscher, Eli (1955), *Mercantilism*, Vol. 2, rev. edn, London: George Allen & Unwin.
Hont, Istvan (1983), 'The "rich country–poor country" debate in Scottish classical political economy',

in I. Hont and M. Ignatieff (eds), *Wealth and Virtue: The Shaping of Political Economy in the Scottish Enlightenment*, Cambridge: Cambridge University Press, pp. 271–316.

Krugman, Paul (1991), *Geography and Trade*, Cambridge, MA: MIT Press.

Mitchell, Wesley (1967), *Types of Economic Theory*, New York: Augustus Kelley.

Perelman, Michael (2000), *The Invention of Capitalism*, Durham, NC: Duke University Press.

Rashid, Salim (1988), 'The Irish School of economic development: 1720–1750', *Manchester School of Social and Economic Studies*, **56** (4), 345–69.

Rashid, Salim (1997), 'Is land reform viable under democratic capitalism?', Working Paper, University of Illinois.

Rashid, Salim (1998), *The Myth of Adam Smith*, Cheltenham, UK and Lyme, NH, USA: Edward Elgar.

Rashid, Salim (1999), 'Monetary economics and economic development in Berkeley's *Querist*', in G. Berkeley, *The Querist*, Düsseldorf: Verlag Wirtschaft und Finanzen, pp. 135–59.

Semmel, Bernard (1970), *The Rise of Free Trade Imperialism: Classical Political Economy, the Empire of Free Trade and Imperialism 1750–1850*, Cambridge: Cambridge University Press.

Skinner, Andrew S. (19790, *A System of Social Science: Papers Relating to Adam Smith*, Oxford: Oxford University Press.

Smith, Adam (1776), *An Inquiry into the Nature and Causes of the Wealth of Nations*, Edwin Cannan (ed.), http://www.econlib.org/library/Smith/smWN.html, WN.

Smith, Adam (1843 [1776]), *An Inquiry into the Nature and Causes of the Wealth of Nations: With Notes from Ricardo, McCulloch, Chambers and other Eminent Political Economists*, Edward Gibbon Wakefield (ed.), London: Charles Knight.

Smith, Adam (1976), *The Theory of Moral Sentiments*, D.D. Raphael and A.L. Macfie (eds), Oxford: Clarendon Press, TMS.

Smith, Adam (1978), *Lectures on Jurisprudence*, R.L. Meek, D.D. Raphael and P.G. Stein (eds), Oxford: Clarendon Press, LJ.

Smith, Adam (1980), *Essays on Philosophical Subjects*, W.P.D. Wightman and J.C. Bryce (eds), Oxford: Clarendon Press, *Astronomy*.

Smith, Adam (1987), *The Correspondence of Adam Smith*, Ian Simpson Ross (ed.), Oxford: Clarendon Press, Corr.

Stewart, Dugald (1877), *The Collected Works of Dugald Stewart*, Sir W.R. Milton (ed.), Edinburgh: Constable.

Swift, Jonathan (1729), *A Modest Proposal for Preparing the Children of Poor People from being a Burthen to their Parents or the Country, and for making them Beneficial to the Publick*, Dublin: Printed for S. Harding.

Thompson, E.P. (1991), *Customs in Common*, London: Merlin.

Tucker, Josiah (1974 [1776]), *Four Tracts on Political and Commercial Subjects*, New York: Augustus Kelley.

Viner, Jacob (1928), 'Adam Smith and *Laissez Faire*', in J.M. Clark et al. (eds), *Adam Smith, 1776–1926*, Chicago, IL: University of Chicago Press, pp. 116–55.

Viner, Jacob (1965), 'Introduction', in John Rae (ed.), *Life of Adam Smith*, New York: A.M. Kelley.

Wallace, Robert (1758), *Characteristics of the Present State of Great Britain*, London: Millar.

Wilberforce, William (1840), *The Correspondence of William Wilberforce*, Robert Isaac Wilberforce and Samuel Wilberforce (eds), London: J. Murray.

Young, Jeffrey (2006), 'Unintended Order and Intervention: Adam Smith's theory of the role of the state', in Peter Boettke and Steven Medema (eds), *History of Political Economy Supplement*, Volume 37, *The Role of Government in the History of Economic Thought*, pp. 91–119.

13 'In the heat of writing': polemics and the 'error of Adam Smith' in the matter of the corn bounty
Glenn Hueckel

The recognition that economic theory has indeed progressed should not be allowed to obscure the highly uneven rate of improvement which has typified the history of analytical progress in economics. General insights into the pure logic of the price system make their appearance embedded in a particular theoretical framework associated with the conditions and problems peculiar to the times . . . Propaganda and ideology are always there, but so is the discipline exerted by rules of scientific procedure built into economics by generations of practitioners: economics is forever catching up with the biases of yesterday. (Blaug, 1997b, pp. 4, 6)

Paradox

'The nature of things has stamped upon corn a real value that no human institution can alter'; so wrote Adam Smith in his famous attack on the corn bounty (WN ed. 1, IV.v.a.23), forming, thereby, a 'paradox' that has bedeviled his intellectual heirs for generations.[1] As Samuel Hollander put the question, how is it that so 'sophisticated' an economist as Smith seems to have 'neglected all the lessons that he himself had tried to expound' when he took up the question of the corn bounty? 'To deny the possibility of raising the relative profitability of agriculture by appropriate intervention is an extraordinary contention', particularly when that denial of the power of a corn export subsidy to stimulate grain production comes from an author whose exposition of the resource allocative function of the price mechanism is widely viewed as exhibiting a 'remarkable artistry' (Hollander, 1992, pp. 84–5, 322–3).

The discovery of yet another internal contradiction in Smith's work has, of course, long since lost the capacity to surprise his readers. Indeed, a flourishing cottage industry has arisen in Smith scholarship in which the various inconsistencies tucked away in his pages are searched out and lovingly dissected.[2] Nevertheless, while there can no longer be any doubt as to the presence of such conflicts in Smith's work, the evaluative weight we are to assign them remains a matter of uncertainty. Some would diminish that weight on the ground that 'consistency was never the central aim or virtue of eighteenth-century writers, especially of the Scottish sociological school. It certainly was not then the ark of the covenant that it is for our analysis-ridden age'. By this reading Smith and his intellectual compatriots 'were more concerned with giving a broad well balanced comprehensive picture seen from different points of view than with logical rigour' (Macfie, 1967, pp. 22, 126). Having now been well schooled by Blaug (1990 [1997a], 1999) in the importance of the distinction between 'rational' and 'historical reconstructions' of ancient texts, we can acknowledge the value of Macfie's warning that to apply modern standards of argument to the intellectual structures of the past is to fall into the error of anachronism.

Yet, try as we might to minimize the significance of Smith's occasionally troubling lapses, those internal contradictions carry undeniable consequences for the clarity and persuasive power of his argument. Though choosing to apply an apparently dismissive tone in describing those lapses as a 'conspicuous lack of that species of small-mindedness which makes a virtue of consistency', Coats (1975, p. 218) nevertheless cites this particular characteristic as among those 'features of Smith's style and mode of presentation [that] make it virtually impossible to determine the precise meaning and significance of his ideas'. Nor is it just within 'our analysis-ridden age' that the apparent inconsistencies in Smith's discourse have commanded attention. As Hollander (1997, p. 772) has observed elsewhere with regard to the particular policy matter at hand, Smith's 'irresponsibly rigid theorizing in the context of the Corn Export Bounty' offered a point of attack exploited by the two major criticisms of his work published during his lifetime – those of James Anderson (1968 [1777]) and Thomas Pownall (1987 [1776]). On those points where his analysis touched upon matters of current controversy, Smith's contemporaries were neither blind to apparent contradictions in his argument nor were they prepared to overlook them, though no doubt many, in agreement with one of Anderson's reviewers, would have seen them as no more than excusable errors, Smith having, perhaps 'through inadvertency . . . advanced arguments in one part of such a long work that are contradicted by his reasoning in other parts of it' (Anon, 1778, p. 365).

But the consequences of Smith's peculiar claims regarding the corn bounty extended beyond their risk to the power of his own argument to persuade his readers. To the extent that his fame prompted an uncritical acceptance of those claims, they sowed the seeds of error that would deflect the course of analytical advance undertaken by the generation to follow him. Smith's principle that the bounty can produce no change in the relative price of grain and thus no stimulus to grain output rested upon his conclusion that 'the money price of corn regulates that of all other commodities'. As we will see below, within the narrowly static confines of Smith's argument, a bounty-induced rise in the money price of corn is wholly passed through to money wages and thence to all other product prices. By this reasoning Smith insisted that the bounty could produce no more than a purely nominal shock: 'The real effect of the bounty is not so much to raise the real value of corn, as to degrade the real value of silver; or to make an equal quantity of it exchange for a smaller quantity, not only of corn, but of all other commodities' (WN ed.1, IV.v.a.11).

Now, it has been a staple of Ricardian commentary dating back to Jacob Hollander that Smith's principle of the 'regulating' character of the corn price constituted a 'vulnerable point in [Ricardo's] theory of the inverse relation between wages and profits', it being 'impossible to prove that a rise in wages was the exclusive cause of a fall in profits if it were true that a rise in wages necessarily occasioned a rise in prices' (Hollander, 1968 [1910], p. 83; cf. Sraffa, 'Introduction' to Ricardo 1951–73, Vol. I, pp. xxxiii–xxxiv). This reading has survived the changing fashions of Ricardian commentary right down to Samuel Hollander's massive re-evaluation of Ricardo's economics. Like his earlier namesake, the more recent Hollander identifies as Ricardo's 'fundamental conception' that inverse relationship between movements in real wage and profit rates, a principle that necessarily rests upon the presumption that 'capitalists are unable to pass on increased wage costs in the form of generally higher prices' and which, further, is to be understood as having been 'initially formulated as a direct challenge to received doctrine based upon Adam Smith's analysis whereby wage rate increases *are* passed on by capitalists' (Hollander, 1979, p. 7).

It is true that Hollander's reassessment of the earlier Sraffian vision of Ricardo's system has come under vigorous attack (see Peach, 1993, Chapter 1 for a brief survey of the issues and protagonists), but all parties are agreed that Smith's 'regulating' corn price provided the historical counterpoint prompting Ricardo's tortured journey into the mysteries of price determination, leading ultimately to his flirtation with a labor theory of value. Nor should this agreement come as a surprise, for we have as our guide Ricardo's own words in letters to James Mill, Malthus and McCulloch written in the midst of his struggle to compose the opening chapters of his *Principles*. It is in these where we first find him grappling with the problem posed for his own theory by 'those who maintain that an alteration in the value of corn will alter the value of all other things'. Such a view, which Ricardo himself had earlier held, could no longer be accepted since it denied the 'invariability of the value of the precious metals', which principle 'is the sheet anchor on which all [his] propositions are built' (30 December 1815, Ricardo, 1951–73, Vol. VI, pp. 348–9). That he understood this objectionable doctrine to derive from Smith is evident from his comment to McCulloch regarding the latter's *Essay on the Question of Reducing the Interest of the National Debt*: 'Your system proceeds upon the supposition that the price of corn regulates the price of all other things . . . but this I hold to be an erroneous system, although you have great authorities in your favour, no less than Adam Smith, Mr. Malthus, and M. Say' (4 December 1816, Ricardo, 1951–73, Vol. VII, p. 105).[3] Ricardo continued to confront that 'erroneous system' for the remainder of his life, the whole of Chapter 22 of his *Principles* being devoted to a criticism of Smith's bounty claims and giving special attention to this 'error of Adam Smith', which underlay those claims, and noting its subsequent recurrence in the work of Horner and Say. Hence, the 'paradox' of Smith's peculiar claim regarding the unique, 'price-regulating' character of corn continued to influence the development of value theory well beyond his own time.

'The heat of writing': the peril of polemic

How then are we to account for this paradox? In Smith we are faced with an author whose work could be praised by its reviewers 'for sagacity and penetration of mind, extent of views, accurate distinction, just and natural connection and dependence of parts', who had 'taken an extensive and connected view' of his subject, 'and from an happy union of fact and theory [had] deduced a system which . . . is on the whole more satisfactory, and rests on better grounds, than any which had before been offered to the Public' (*Annual Register*, 1776 and *Monthly Review*, 1776/77, reprinted in Mizuta, 2000, pp. 116, 165). Yet the author of that 'just and natural connection and dependence of parts', while opening his bounty chapter with the proposition that the 'effect of bounties, like that of all other expedients of the mercantile system, can only be to force the trade of a country into a channel much less advantageous than that in which it would naturally run of its own accord' (WN IV.v.a.2–3) – a statement that is in perfect harmony with his larger critique of those mercantile 'expedients' – could a few paragraphs later apparently contradict that opening proposition by insisting that a 'bounty upon the exportation of corn . . . can in no respect promote the raising of that particular commodity of which it was meant to encourage the production' (IV.v.a.24). The corn bounty is thus given a very peculiar aspect: like all mercantile 'expedients', it serves, 'by extraordinary encouragements, to draw towards a particular species of industry a greater share of the capital of the society than what would naturally go to it' (IV.ix.50, cf. IV.ii.3), but unique among those policy favors, the stimulus prompted by this particular subsidy, Smith insisted, is a purely nominal phenomenon, yielding nothing more than a rise in the general price level, with no gain in corn production (IV.v.a.9–15, 24). What are we to make of such a performance?

Smith himself provided a hint at an answer when he acknowledged in his letter to Andreas Holt that, in composing his first edition statement of the special, 'regulating' character of the corn price, his mode of 'expression was certainly too strong and had escaped [him] in the heat of Writing'. Indeed, it was, he admitted, James Anderson's criticism that prompted him to make in the second edition certain changes which he insisted 'corrected this careless expression' (*Corr.*, 208). Further adjustments were made to the bounty analysis in the third edition as well, but all these revisions taken together amount to little more than minor verbal alterations that do nothing to improve the substantive coherence of the argument (see Prendergast, 1987, pp. 394–6 for a catalogue of those modifications). Nevertheless, Smith's admission that he could be led, 'in the heat of writing', to press his case too far calls to mind another theme of Smithian commentary that is relevant to the question at hand – namely, the avowedly polemical tone and structure adopted in the *Wealth of Nations*. That Smith's most famous book is a work of polemic is, of course, no surprise, particularly in view of Smith's own description of the book in that letter to Holt as his 'very violent attack . . . upon the whole commercial system of Great Britain'. But the implications of that polemical intent for our understanding and assessment of his work has recently become the object of increasing attention among Smith's readers.

Among those implications is the matter of the weight to be assigned to those elements of his argument that appear to modern eyes as instances of analytical or historical error. O'Brien, for example, in cataloguing a number of objections to Smith's famous hierarchy of investment priorities, pronounces the entire argument 'an awful muddle'. Still, we are not to take these lapses as undermining the credibility of his larger theme. 'Smith', O'Brien assures us, 'was not a fool . . . what he was really concerned to do was to make an attack upon the forcing of capital into channels which it would not have entered, given an undistorted choice for the owners of that capital', and it is a mark of his success that he did 'in fact draw attention to this'. It is only 'unfortunate that he should have advanced a perfectly reasonable argument in terms which were not reasonable' (O'Brien, 2004, p. 251). Similarly, Skinner has observed that, as an exercise in historical reporting, Smith's recounting of the contemporary relations between Britain and her American colonies exhibits a number of 'apparent shortcomings'. But to focus on these is to miss the central point: in his treatment of the colonial trade: 'Smith's purpose was in part at least rhetorical', aimed at a 'critique of the mercantile fallacy' (Skinner, 1996, pp. 223–7; cf. Coats, 1975).

An appreciation of Smith's polemical aim also bears upon our assessment of his rhetorical structure, particularly as that structure encompasses an effective synthesis of theory and evidence. As we have seen from the *Monthly Review*'s admiration of the 'happy union of fact and theory' in the *Wealth of Nations*, this feature of Smith's discourse was frequently the subject of praise from his reviewers. The *Critical Review* likewise took note of Smith's 'abstract reasoning', which 'he never fails to illustrate and confirm by such apposite and familiar examples as place all propositions he deduces in the most striking and incontestible light' (Mizuta, 2000, p. 144). Even those who found fault with his conclusions expressed admiration for the structure of his argument. Pownall opened his long critique with the observation that Smith had:

by a truly philosophic and patient analysis, endeavoured to investigate *analytically* those principles by which nature . . . conducts the operations of man . . . And then, next, by application of these principles to fact, experience, and the institutions of men [Smith had] endeavoured to deduce *synthetically*, by the most precise and measured steps of demonstration, those important doctrines of practice. (Pownall, 1776 [1987], p. 337)

As these comments suggest, Smith's argument began with the 'abstract reasoning'; the appeals to historical events and institutional facts served only to 'illustrate and confirm', and thus to throw into 'the most striking and incontestible light' the propositions derived from his theory. Henry Buckle noticed this feature of Smith's rhetorical structure a century later, observing that Smith's frequent appeals to factual support 'are essentially subsequent to the argument. They make the argument more clear, but not more certain', for in the *Wealth of Nations*, 'every thing depends upon general principles' (Buckle, 1857–61 [1970], p. 285; quoted in part in Campbell and Skinner, 1976, p. 56). More recently, Smith's Glasgow editors gave this point its most memorable expression: Smith 'worked from the system to the facts not from the facts to the system', and when his facts diverged from the predictions derived from his system, 'Smith felt obliged to offer explanations of the divergence' (Campbell and Skinner, 1976, p. 56).

Nevertheless, those explanations and the facts themselves are all structured to serve the underlying polemical aim: Smith's 'very violent attack' on the mercantile institutions of his day. As Viner reminded us long ago, Smith's 'wider generalizations were invoked to support the attack on *these* political institutions. Everything else was to a large degree secondary' (Viner, 1927 [1958], p. 232). This means, of course, as the Glasgow editors acknowledge, that on matters related to that rhetorical objective, Smith's 'writing verges on propaganda, he uses evidence in ways which are not wholly convincing to those not committed to his system, and he presses interpretations of contemporary events to more extreme conclusions than may well be warranted' (Campbell and Skinner, 1976, p. 59). James Anderson was one of those who, being unpersuaded by Smith's system, found his arguments regarding the corn bounty to be an untenable plea for a favored hypothesis. In a pamphlet published a decade after Smith's death, and a quarter-century after the appearance of his first critique of Smith's bounty argument, Anderson delivered himself of the opinion that on no other question had Smith 'been so grievously misled as with regard to the influence of the corn-laws; concerning which he had formed a favourite hypothesis, which he cherished with that kind of pertinacity that is in general attached to every kind of bigotry'. It was, Anderson charged, this prior commitment to a preferred outcome that led Smith to a highly selective use of evidence: 'It is much to be lamented, that, when the mind is thus occupied with preconceived notions, many important facts are suffered to escape notice; and those only are deemed worthy of attention which serve to corroborate the favourite hypothesis' (Anderson, 1801, quoted in Hollander, 1979, p. 40). It was not only Smith's contemporary critics who complained so; the like reproach is echoed in the modern objection that Smith's 'procedure makes facts a convenient vehicle to carry one's theoretical views . . . As the facts are meant to illustrate, the potency of contrary facts will be denied' (Rashid, 1998, p. 58; cf. Bryson, 1945, pp. 85–6).

The echo of Smith's own acknowledgement that he could, in the 'heat of writing', be induced to press his case too far is likewise heard in his modern editors' assessment of his work as approaching 'propaganda'. This too is a feature of his discourse that has been noticed repeatedly. It is true that Dugald Stewart, his friend and first biographer, insisted that Smith's tendency 'to be too systematical and too much in extremes' was limited to 'his unpremeditated judgments' expressed 'in the society of his friends' (Stewart, 1794 [1980], V.15). However, David Buchanan, who published in 1814 a new edition of the *Wealth of Nations* together with his own extensive commentary, prefigured the appraisals of later editors when he tempered his praise of Smith's 'commanding reason' with the judgment that Smith had 'erred occasionally from too great a fondness for system. On some subjects his views are hasty, partial, and inaccurate; while on others, the truth and value of his doctrines seem to justify, and even to require farther explanation' (Buchanan, 1966 [1817], p. xi).

Finally, we have in Smith's admitted polemical intent a source of the acknowledged contradictions in the *Wealth of Nations*. That, at any rate, has been the judgment of his readers almost since the time of the book's appearance. Thus, by Anderson's telling, it was Smith's improper commitment to an untenable hypothesis that led his reasoning inexorably to its contradictory propositions:

> facts not being at all times easy to be reconciled to this hypothesis, the mind became, as it were, irritated, so as to catch at every appearance of an argument in its favour, wherever that occurred . . . It is to this circumstance alone that I am inclined to ascribe the many inconsistent, and even contradictory, remarks that occur respecting the corn-laws in various parts of his ingenious work. (Anderson, 1801, quoted in Hollander, 1979, p. 40)

Even his modern editors, though certainly more favorably inclined toward his 'system' than were his eighteenth-century critics, nevertheless acknowledge that the 'defects of Smith's [polemical] emphasis . . . may seem to justify the suggestion that he was never noted for his consistency'. But they temper the implied criticism with an important qualification: 'Paradoxically the inconsistency was often consistent because it rarely damaged the central analysis and was indeed usually introduced as a means of support for it . . . The inconsistencies appear only in the detail' (Campbell and Skinner, 1976, p. 59).

Argument 'from the system to the facts', the need to explain any divergence of those facts from the predictions of the system, 'too great a fondness for system' yielding a tendency to press the case too far, and 'consistent inconsistencies', all in service of his 'very violent attack' on the mercantile regulations of his day: all these are bound up in Smith's analysis of the corn bounty – an analysis whose peculiar claim that 'the money price of corn regulates that of all other commodities' has presented a 'paradox' for generations of readers. However, a reading of that analysis through the prism of Smith's polemical intent can carry us some way toward a resolution of that paradox. It is to that task that we now turn.

The problem of the bounty in Smith's polemic
In his assault on the array of political and institutional restraints on trade that comprised the 'mean and malignant expedients of the mercantile system' (WN IV.vii.c.56), Smith could not limit his attention to those 'expedients' alone. It was necessary also to confront the underlying conceptual error that provided the intellectual context for those policies. That conceptual context rested in the 'system . . . which represents national wealth as consisting in the abundance, and national poverty in the scarcity of gold and silver' (I.xi.n.1; see also IV.i.1–10). That erroneous concept of national wealth had given rise to the related 'popular notion' that inflation is an inevitable consequence (and therefore a

reliable indicator) of economic advance: 'as the quantity of silver naturally increases in every country with the increase of wealth, so its value diminishes as its quantity increases' (I.xi.e.30). It is in his effort to overturn this 'altogether groundless' claim that Smith found himself impeded by a widespread contemporary conviction that the corn bounty served to increase grain output and reduce its price. It is this received doctrine that Smith sought to overcome by his 'paradoxical' denial of the bounty's capacity to increase output. Hence, to appreciate fully the significance of Smith's bounty analysis, we must understand the function it was designed to serve within the larger context of his attack on that mercantilist 'popular notion'.

His first salvo in that attack was directed at the inability of that 'popular notion' to meet even the simple logic of the generally accepted principles of supply and demand. The demand for

> food is limited in every man by the narrow capacity of the human stomach; but the desire of the conveniencies and ornaments of building, dress, equipage, and household furniture, seems to have no limit or certain boundary . . . [Hence] . . . [t]hose . . . who have the command of more food than they themselves can consume, are always willing to exchange the surplus, or, what is the same thing, the price of it, for gratifications of this other kind. (WN, I.xi.c.7; cf. c.36)

Consequently, economic growth increases the demand for all other goods (including the money commodity) relative to that for food.[4] In the absence of increases in the world stock of specie, this growth-induced shift in demand will produce a falling, not a rising, silver price of food:

> The increasing abundance of food, in consequence of increasing improvement and cultivation, must necessarily increase the demand for every part of the produce of land which is not food, and which can be applied either to use or to ornament. In the whole progress of improvement, it might therefore be expected, there should be only one variation in the comparative values of those two different sorts of produce . . . As art and industry advance, the materials of cloathing and lodging, the useful fossils and minerals of the earth, the precious metals and the precious stones should gradually come to be more and more in demand, should gradually exchange for a greater and a greater quantity of food, or in other words, should gradually become dearer and dearer. (WN I.xi.d.1)

This is not to deny the mercantilist claim that the stock of precious metals rises with growth. It is true that 'a greater quantity of coin becomes necessary in order to circulate a greater quantity of commodities; and the people, as they can afford it, as they have more commodities to give for it, will naturally purchase a greater and a greater quantity of plate'. Hence, 'Gold and silver, like all other commodities, naturally seek the market where the best price is given for them, and the best price is commonly given for every thing in the country which can best afford it'. But the price of the monetary metals is simply the inverse of the money price of commodities: gold and silver 'are to be bought for a certain price like all other commodities, and as they are the price of all other commodities, so all other commodities are the price of those metals'. Consequently, the richest market, 'where the best price is given', will have the lowest, not the highest, money price of commodities. To argue, in accord with the mercantilist 'popular notion', that the money price of food rises in response to this growth-induced inflow of specie is tantamount to the ridiculous claim that luxury goods decline in relative price as wealth rises: 'as statuaries and painters are not likely to be worse rewarded in times of wealth and prosperity, than in times of poverty and depression, so gold and silver are not likely to be worse paid for' (WN I.xi.e.33–4, IV.i.11; the principle is repeated in varying contexts at I.xi.g.28; xi.i.2; xi.m.18–19; II.iii.24; IV.i.12–13). Hence, contrary to the 'popular notion', in the absence of offsetting changes in the world specie stock, we can be assured that economic advance will be associated with a *falling* money price of corn, as 'the precious metals ... gradually exchange for a greater and a greater quantity of food'.[5]

Here then is the purpose of Smith's long 'Digression concerning the variations in the value of silver': to test his hypothesis against the price trends produced by the acknowledged advance of European civilization over the previous four centuries. The hypothesis survives the test for the first of the three periods covered in the 'Digression'. By Smith's reading of the evidence: 'From about the middle of the fourteenth to the beginning of the sixteenth century, what was reckoned the ... ordinary or average price of wheat, seems to have sunk gradually [by] about one-half', and to have remained at that lower level 'till about 1570' (WN I.xi.e.8). The second period, running from 1570 to 1640, offers no test of the hypothesis since this was the time when, all agree, the newly discovered American mines produced a prolonged rise in the nominal price of corn. This long inflation ended, however, 'about 1636, [when] the effect of the discovery of the mines of America in reducing the value of silver, appears to have been compleated, and the value of that metal seems never to have sunk lower in proportion to that of corn than it was about that time' (I.xi.f, and g.1). With no further additions to the world stock of specie, continued economic growth after the first third of the seventeenth century should, by Smith's reasoning, have produced a decline in corn's nominal price; and Smith's data do indeed permit him to conclude that silver's purchasing power over corn 'seems to have risen somewhat in the course of the present century, and it had probably begun to do so even before the end of the last' (I.xi.g.1 and 6–11).

Those data do not, however, support the hypothesis for the seventeenth-century period. Over the last 64 years of that century, his series reveals a slight rise in the silver price of corn rather than the predicted decline. Here then Smith must offer an explanation for that discrepancy, and he does so by appeal to three extraordinary events: the civil war, which interrupted grain production through mid-century; the debasement of the coinage in the last years of the century, which raised the nominal price recorded in his sources; and the bounty on grain export, established in 1689, which, 'by encouraging the exportation of the surplus produce of every year, and thereby hindering the abundance of one year from compensating the scarcity of another, [served] to raise the price in the home-market'.[6] Finally, since the more recent decline in the corn price reported over the first two-thirds of his own century occurred in spite of the presumed tendency of the export subsidy to raise the domestic price, Smith insisted that the observed price decline 'must, in the same state of tillage, have been much more so, had it not been for this operation of the bounty' (WN I.xi.g.2–14).[7]

Breaching the bounty's defenses
The divergence of the price trend contained in Smith's data from that predicted by his 'system' was, then, to be explained in part by the effect of the bounty in redirecting domestic supplies to the export market. However, persuasive as it may be to modern eyes, a simple appeal to the allocative distortions of an export subsidy would carry no weight with Smith's opponents, as he was well aware:

it has been thought by many people that [the bounty] tends to encourage tillage, and that in two different ways; first, by opening a more extensive foreign market to the corn of the farmer, it tends, they imagine, to increase the demand for, and consequently the production of that commodity; and secondly, by securing to him a better price than he could otherwise expect in the actual state of tillage, it tends, they suppose, to encourage tillage. This double encouragement must, they imagine, in a long period of years, occasion such an increase in the production of corn, as may lower its price in the home market, much more than the bounty can raise it. (WN IV.v.a.7)

Smith was contending against that common confusion of cause and effect that every beginner in economic reasoning experiences as a confounding of movements along and shifts in supply curves. He would have had ample opportunity to encounter the fallacy in the work of his earlier namesake, Charles Smith, that 'ingenious and well-informed author' from whom he drew much of his information regarding the corn trade (for example, at WN, I.xi.f.4; IV.ii.20; v.a.4, and associated editorial notes). That earlier Smith repeatedly praised the legislature's wisdom in controlling the corn trade through the export subsidy and concurrent import tariffs, a set of regulations that, he insisted, ensured abundance and low prices:

The views of these Laws are most evidently no other than to give all possible encouragement to Agriculture and the growth of Corn, by opening to the Farmer a certain Market for his surplus, and assuring him at the same time that, in case of a failure in his Crop, foreign Corn shall not be imported on him till the necessity of the people requires it and the price is so far advanced as to put it in his power in some measure to make up his loss.

And the consequences have answered; for Agriculture hath been so much extended, and the art of husbandry so much better attended to and managed with so much more judgment and success, since the passing the above Laws, and under the protection and encouragement they give, than it was before that time; that, although large quantities of all sorts of Grain have been exported, and Wheat is much more generally used for Bread by the common people, yet the price thereof is considerably sunk. (Smith, 1766, p. 79)[8]

Indeed, the enormous importance which this earlier Smith attached to the role of exportation in ensuring a cheap and abundant domestic food supply is dramatized by an extraordinary 'short piece of history' said to be confirmed by 'an eye-witness of the facts', and offered to illustrate 'how far the farmer may by exportation, for which we give a bounty, be prompted to till, or by the prohibition thereof, . . . or by the fear of large importations, be discouraged from tillage'. We are told of a 'Grand Vizir' of Turkey, who 'suffered a more general exportation of corn . . . than any of his predecessors had done, insomuch that three hundred French vessels . . . were on one day seen to enter Smyrna Bay to load corn'. Yet in the face of these exports, 'wheat was then sold for less than seventeen pence English a bushel' (less than one-quarter the threshold for the cessation of the British export bounty). Unfortunately for the ruler, at the sight of these unprecedented exports, 'people took alarm, pretended that all the corn was going to be exported and that they, in consequence, must be starved', a conclusion which, naturally, caused them to grow 'so mutinous that they could not be appeased till the Vizir was strangled and his body thrown out to them'. The successor, taking 'particular care not to split on the same rock', prohibited grain export. But at this change of policy, 'many of the farmers, who looked on the exportation as their greatest demand neglected tillage', causing the corn price to rise, 'in less than three years', by more than four times; 'and the distress of the people was such that every bakehouse and magazine of corn was obliged to have a military guard' (Smith, 1766, p. 33n.). Smith evidently took the message to heart, for when he reissued his 1759 pamphlet in its 1766 edition, he rescinded a suggestion, advanced in the earlier version, that British agriculture had grown so strong under the bounty that the subsidy could be gradually withdrawn over a period of years. The intervening, 1764 edict of Louis XV freeing French grain exports and the reports of other observers that they would soon 'see as good a bounty given for corn exported from France as is given from England', convinced him that the earlier proposed repeal seems 'now in the year 1766 highly improper and that it would be wrong even to think of taking the bounty entirely off', lest Britain be inundated with grain from a resurgent French agriculture under its new export freedom (ibid., pp. 90–91).

This confidence that the bounty's operation was fundamental to the maintenance of an abundant national food supply underlay the extraordinary approbation accorded that policy by Adam Smith's contemporaries. He would have seen that his earlier namesake concluded a 1758 review of the laws regulating the external corn trade with the judgment that 'though some amendments may be made, we are bold to say, the general Plan cannot be improved' (Smith, 1766, p. 36). James Steuart's 1759 proposal for a national system of granaries was offered as one such 'amendment' to complement and complete the good offices of the bounty, in the conviction that 'by combining the two schemes of bounty-money and granary-making, the policy of grain may be brought under better regulations in England than it has hitherto been in any other nation' (Steuart, 1967 [1759, 1805], p. 359). There can be no doubt that in attacking the bounty Smith was taking on an institution that was held in nearly reverential esteem by his opponents. Francis Horner aptly characterized the intellectual context into which Smith ventured with that attack when, in looking back on the history of 'the law which gave a bounty on the exportation of corn' (upon the occasion of the renewal of the policy in 1804), he remarked that:

> the best writers and statesmen of England, throughout the first part of the last century . . . mentioned it always with admiration, as an institution that had been planned in wisdom, and the success of which was complete . . . an inseparable part of that peculiar system, to which England was indebted for her superiority over all other nations. (Horner, 1804 [1957], p. 97)

James Anderson, then, was simply expressing the common view when, in closing his critique of Smith's analysis, he insisted that: 'the operation of the bounty, and the other corn-laws, . . . is perhaps the wisest and best political institution that has ever graced the annals of any nation'. Indeed, it is chiefly to that enlightened policy that Britain owes her prosperity: 'Britain does not possess such a decided advantage over the nations around her in any other respect, as in what relates to her corn-laws; nor has perhaps any other circumstance contributed so much to her prosperity for a century past as this has done' (Anderson, 1968 [1777], pp. 294, 370).

One makes little headway against such views with the claim that the bounty will serve only to diminish national product through its effect, 'like that of all other expedients of the mercantile system', in producing a misallocation of the nation's capital. Indeed, Anderson was prepared to admit 'as a general rule that an unlimited freedom of commerce, without either encouragement or restraint, is the conduct that would be most highly beneficial to the state'. But an exception must be made for grain; the nation 'should be at all times provided with it in abundance: for it cannot be wanted for one day'. An 'excessive rise of [its] price is attended with infinitely more fatal consequences than a rise in the price of any other commodity. In other articles we trade merely for pleasure, or profit . . . in this we trade from necessity' (Anderson, 1968 [1777], pp. 338–9). In this too Anderson was only expressing the prevailing opinion. It was Smith's call to remove the grain market from the domain of constant government oversight that was considered the more radical position (Hont and Ignatieff, 1985, pp. 14–15).

That common view against which Smith had to contend understood the nation's grain stock as comprising a 'necessary' component and an unpredictable 'surplus', whose size depended upon the vagaries of the seasons. This perception is evident in Steuart's granary scheme, which was advanced as a means 'by which the legislature may be directed how to prevent, as far as possible, that part of every crop which is necessary for national subsistence, from being exported, or confounded with the surplus of grain, which is and must continue the object of foreign trade' (Steuart 1967 [1759, 1805], p. 354). Across the Channel, Jacques Necker, Turgot's successor as Controller General, worked diligently to establish a policy that was the reverse of that adopted in Britain ('in a country such as France, the prohibition to export corn ought to be fundamental law'). But Necker's prohibition of export was grounded in the same conception of the grain market that in Britain produced support for her export subsidy, though he added an additional consideration for charity:

> Every one would certainly consider an exportation as contrary to the public good which should deprive the inhabitants of France of part of the corn necessary for their subsistence, or which should carry out of the kingdom that quantity of the surplus which prevents the proprietors of corn from prescribing arbitrarily to those who stand in need of that corn to support life. (Necker, 1776, pp. 56, 345)

The claim of the bounty's apologists, that an export subsidy by raising the price received by the producer stimulates production and thereby reduces the price paid by the consumer, presents an obvious contradiction to the modern reader well schooled in distinguishing cause and effect. Smith, however, though he gave accurate expression to his opponents' argument, never pointed out for his readers its inconsistency. Another generation had to pass before that contradiction was recognized as an objection. We find that recognition in Horner's 1804 complaint that the bounty advocates persist in 'their opinion that the real price of corn will upon the whole be rendered cheaper to the consumers and that the same real price will be maintained permanently higher to the farmer; though these two positions are in direct terms contradictory of each other' (Horner, 1804 [1957], p. 106). The same objection is raised at greater length a decade later by Buchanan in his commentary on Smith's bounty chapter (Buchanan, 1966 [1817], pp. 151–2).

If he could not identify the internal contradiction contained in the claims advanced by the bounty's advocates, neither could Smith attack those claims by appeal to price data. It is, in this case at least, disingenuous to complain that Smith's 'procedure makes facts a convenient vehicle to carry one's theoretical views' (Rashid, 1998, p. 58) or that he was careful to employ only those which 'serve to corroborate the favourite hypothesis' (Anderson, 1801, quoted in Hollander 1979, p. 40). Given the rudimentary tools of empirical analysis available to him, this was not a question that Smith could resolve by appeal to facts alone. Writing from the perspective of the mid-nineteenth century, Buckle had a clear view of the methodological constraint under which Smith and his contemporaries operated: 'Such statistical facts were, in their origin, too complex to be generalized; especially as they could not be experimented upon, but could only be observed and arranged' (Buckle, 1857–61 [1970], p. 285). Moreover, those facts could be arranged to accord with a variety of hypotheses. In the matter of the bounty, Smith faced a problem analogous to that of which Hume famously complained in his essay 'Of the balance of trade': 'Every man, who has ever reasoned on this subject, has always proved his theory, whatever it was, by facts and calculations' (Hume, 1752 [1994], p. 137).

The bounty's advocates had their facts too, and they were undeterred by the fallacy of *post hoc ergo propter hoc*, which Horner noted in a gently stated censure of their method:

> The diminution of the average price and the progressive increase of exports, within the period at the beginning of which the bounty had been instituted, presented no doubt a very deceitful coincidence; and at a time when the analysis of national wealth was unknown, it was natural enough to believe that the cause of these curious facts could be no other but that remarkable law which just preceded their appearance. (1804 [1957], p. 97)[9]

Smith would have encountered the fallacy in his reading of the corn-trade pamphlets of his 'well-informed' earlier namesake, who, as we have seen, insisted that the bounty had stimulated an increase in both exports and domestic consumption of wheat and 'yet the price thereof is considerably sunk'. Elsewhere, that worthy offered as proof of the policy's efficacy the observation that: 'the Bounty was first given on the Exportation of Grain in the year 1689, now seventy years since; during which period, Grain hath in general been from fifteen to twenty *per cent* cheaper than for forty years before that time, which is a good proof of the utility of the Law by which it is ordered to be given' (Smith, 1766, p. 73).[10]

Arthur Young, that indefatigable defender of the agriculture interest, offered his own table showing a rise in wheat prices from 1594 through 1662 and a fall since 1688, which 'seems to be a plain proof that this sinking of the price was owing to the bounty'. The period from 1663 to 1687 is treated separately, 'because in that period a duty was first laid on the importation of corn ... the consequence of which is here visible in the price for wheat, which for many years before was rising, did at this time sink more than ten shillings a quarter'. From all this, he concluded: 'It is impossible that a stronger proof than this should be advanced of the certainty of the assertion I made before, viz. the exportation of corn gives plenty, and consequently cheapness at home; and now I may add, that preventing our receiving any from abroad is attended with the same effect' (Young, 1768, pp. 45–8). Finally, Smith was, of course, subjected to Anderson's criticism that not only was his 'reasoning ... about the pernicious tendency of the bounty ... unsatisfactory ... [but] he is still more unlucky with regard to the facts that ought to support it'. As to these, Anderson held that 'it is enough for our present purpose to rest barely upon the acknowledged depression in the price of grain that has taken place in England since the bounty was granted; as this alone seems to furnish an unanswerable argument against the hypothesis he has adopted' (Anderson, 1968 [1777], pp. 360–61). With arguments like these arrayed before him, it is no wonder that Smith pronounced himself as possessed of 'no great faith in political arithmetick' (WN IV.v.b.30; cf. *Corr.* 249).

Rent and the corn price: 'consistent inconsistency'

Facts alone, then, could not settle the issue. Further, Smith took no notice of the contradiction inherent in his opponents' claim that the bounty served both to raise the price to the farmer and to reduce that paid by the consumer. As we have seen, recognition of that flaw had to await the commentaries of Horner and Buchanan in the next generation. Nor was Smith in a position to insist that the acknowledged effect of the bounty in stimulating corn output is itself indicative of a rising price necessary to compensate a rising cost of production. His desire to adapt corn to serve his purposes as numeraire committed him to the principle that wheat output could be expanded 'in every different stage of improvement' at constant cost (WN I.xi.e.28; see Hueckel, 2000 for an expanded account).[11] With these lines of attack closed to him, Smith was left with just one channel by which the bounty could be said to raise the corn price: it must reduce the quantity available to the domestic market. That, of course, was the argument advanced: the subsidized exports, Smith insisted, drew product away from the home market 'in years of plenty' and, even when suspended 'in years of scarcity', aggravated the scarcity by reducing carry-over stocks (WN I.xi.g.12–13; IV.v.a.6). But to complete the argument, the bounty's alleged power to stimulate a potentially compensating rise in output had to be denied. As it happened, Smith's theory of rent could be interpreted to produce just such a result. Fortunately, the role of Smith's rent theory within his larger system of economic development has been described to varying levels of detail in other contexts (Brewer, 1995; Hollander, 1973, pp. 164–79, 1992, 82–84; Hueckel, 2000; O'Donnell, 1990, Chapter 5). We need only sketch the broad outlines of that story as it bears on Smith's dispute with the bounty's advocates.

Because 'food is always, more or less, in demand', and because wheat is, in Europe, the common food crop, 'Except in particular situations . . . the rent of corn land regulates in Europe that of all other cultivated land' (WN I.xi.b.1, 35; cf. xi.l.12). In other words, corn rents determine the opportunity cost which must be met if the land is to be turned to an alternative use.[12] Tilled land will be turned to animal products only 'when the price of cattle . . . rises so high that it is as profitable to cultivate land in order to raise food for them, as in order to raise food for man'. The mechanism of economic advance, then, involves a progressive expansion of the area of cultivation. At the beginning of the process, in countries 'almost waste, or but thinly inhabited', there is a preponderance of virgin land on which 'cattle, poultry, game of all kinds . . . are the spontaneous productions of nature' available 'in such profuse abundance, that they are of little or no value'. As society advances, the extension of cultivation reduces the quantity of waste land, thereby reducing that 'spontaneous' supply of meat animals, while at the same time, through the rise in grain production, increasing the demand for animal products. Hence, 'the extension of improvement and cultivation . . . necessarily raises more or less, in proportion to the price of corn, that of every sort of animal food' (I.xi.e.27; l.1–6; n.10; cf. xi.b.6–8).[13]

Other products of the land will likewise exhibit varying price trends depending upon the state of demand in their respective markets (which may be confined to a narrow locality for bulky goods, like building materials and coal – WN I.xi.c.5 and 17–19 – or which may extend 'to the whole commercial world', as in the case of wool and hides – I.xi.m.7) and upon the scope for efficiency gains (which systematically reduce, relative to that of corn, the price 'of every sort of vegetable food' – I.xi.n.10 – and 'of almost all manufactures' – I.xi.o.1–2). Nevertheless, at any particular 'period of improvement', each price must bear a specific ratio to that of corn by virtue of the latter's role as determining the opportunity cost of any alternative land use. Hence, a purely nominal change in the price of corn, maintaining the 'period of improvement' unchanged, must be communicated proportionately to all other prices. Furthermore, because the corn wage is constant within a particular state of development (though, of course, it varies as the nation moves from one state to the next), any change in the nominal price of corn must likewise be communicated proportionately to the money wage and thence to the prices of manufactured goods. By this reasoning, Smith is led to the principle which serves as the key weapon in his attack upon the bounty:

> the money price of corn regulates that of all other home-made commodities. It regulates the money price of labour, which must always be such as to enable the labourer to purchase a quantity of corn sufficient to maintain him and his family either in the liberal, moderate, or scanty manner in which the advancing, stationary or declining circumstances of the society oblige his employers to maintain him.
>
> It regulates the money price of all the other parts of the rude produce of land, which, in *every period of improvement*, must bear a *certain proportion* to that of corn, though this proportion is *different* in *different periods* . . . By regulating the money price of all the other parts of the rude produce of land, it regulates that of the materials of almost all manufactures.
>
> By regulating the money price of labour, it regulates that of manufacturing art and industry. And by regulating both, it regulates that of the compleat manufacture. The money price of labour, and of every thing that is the produce either of land or labour, must necessarily either rise or fall in proportion to the money price of corn. (IV.v.a.11–14; emphasis added)

Thus we arrive at the desired result: the capacity to increase output is denied to the bounty. 'The real effect of the bounty is not so much to raise the real value of corn, as to degrade the real value of silver' (WN IV.v.a.11). That is, subsidized corn exports produce, in the first instance, no more than a purely nominal effect, 'exactly in the same way as [that] absurd policy of Spain and Portugal', by which those nations seek an increased domestic specie stock by imposing restraints on its export (IV.v.a.19–20). This outcome is unique to corn. Preferences granted any other commodity raise the price of that commodity relative to that of labor, thus raising the 'real value' of producers' incomes as expressed in Smith's famous 'labor-commanded' unit and thereby enabling those producers to expand production of the favored commodity:

> When either by the monopoly of the home-market, or by a bounty upon exportation, you enable our woollen or linen manufacturers to sell their goods for somewhat a better price than they otherwise could get for them, you raise, not only the nominal, but the real price of those goods. You render them equivalent to a greater quantity of labour and subsistence, you encrease not only the nominal, but the real profit, the real wealth and revenue of those manufacturers, and you enable them either to live better themselves, or to employ a greater quantity of labour in those particular manufactures. You really encourage those manufactures, and direct towards them a greater quantity of the industry of the country, than what would probably go to them of its own accord.

In the case of corn, however, the introduction of a bounty can serve only to raise its nominal price. Since, within an *unchanging* 'period of improvement', prices of all other goods – including that of labor – must preserve their respective positions relative to that of corn, the labor-commanded value of producers' incomes is unaffected. Hence, by such a policy, 'you do not encourage the growth of corn, because you do not enable [producers] to maintain and employ more labourers in raising it' (WN IV.v.a.23).

Here then is that 'great and essential difference which nature has established between corn and almost every other sort of goods'. But the strictly static character of the argument must not be missed. The price of corn can be said to 'regulate' those of all other goods only within a particular 'period of improvement', or as Hollander (1973, p. 178) put it, only under 'given labour demand conditions'.[14] The principle cannot be applied to a dynamic context, for in that case – as the nation traverses several such 'periods' – the consequent changes in the real structure of the economy will alter the corresponding structure of relative prices. Nevertheless, judged within its narrowly static framework, Smith's peculiar denial of a bounty-induced stimulus to corn production can be seen as broadly consistent with his larger model of economic development; or, as Horner put it: 'Smith is quite consistent at least with himself' (Horner, 1804 [1957], p. 107). Indeed, for Hollander, it is this element of his analysis that 'establishes Smith as a genuine "model builder," for here he brings together a complex string of arguments' (Hollander, 1992, p. 83). However, it must be admitted that the assessment of his Glasgow editors is borne out here as well: Smith shows himself capable of pressing his argument beyond its limits, thereby introducing 'inconsistencies . . . in the detail'.

Inconsistencies in the detail
Smith's famous claim that a bounty-induced rise in the corn price is met by a proportionate rise in the money wage, leaving the corn wage unchanged, presents an obvious problem, which, while not recognized by his contemporaries, did become the object of comment a generation later. As we have seen, Smith's argument turned on the bounty's effect in reducing the quantity available to the home market. But, objected Buchanan, the corn wage must then decline to ration the deficient supply: 'the high price of provisions is a certain indication of a deficient supply and arises in the natural course of things for the purpose of retarding the consumption' to permit the 'smaller supply of food [to be] shared among the same number of consumers'. To argue for a proportionate rise in the money wage is to characterize 'nature as counteracting her own purposes – first raising the price of food to diminish the consumption, and afterwards raising wages to give the labourer the same supply as before'. Hence, there can be no question 'that in whatever degree the bounty raises the price of corn, it increases the farmer's profits and thus gives a real encouragement to agriculture' (Buchanan, 1966 [1817], pp. 59–60, 159). The same objection was raised by Ricardo in his *Principles*, where he praised 'the whole of Mr. Buchanan's arguments on this part of the subject of bounties [as] perfectly clear and satisfactory' (Ricardo, 1951–73, Vol. I, p. 315; cf., pp. 303–6).

Over a decade earlier, Horner too had observed that the result of the necessary decline in the corn wage 'will be a certain degree of new encouragement held out to husbandry'. However, Horner continued to hold without qualification to 'Smith's important doctrine that the variations of the money-price of corn are communicated ultimately to that of labour and other commodities', though he was careful to limit the principle to its properly static compass, reminding his reader that the result applies only 'while the general circumstances of the nation remain the same'. Given that condition, then, the decline in the corn wage following upon the introduction of an export bounty 'must be temporary; the wages of the labouring consumers had been adjusted before by competition, and the same principle will adjust them again to the same rate, by raising the money-price of labour, and through that, of other commodities, to the money price of corn'. Thus, in Horner's estimation, Smith's argument is to be faulted only in that it 'overlooked that *interval* which elapses . . . between the enhancement of the money-price of corn, and its communication to the money-price of labour and other commodities' (Horner [1805] 1957, pp. 101–6).

By Horner's reading, Smith's error derived from a *petitio principii*:

> in affirming that the quantity exported in every particular year, were it not for the bounty, would remain in the home market, he evidently takes for granted that this quantity, though there had been no bounty, would still have been grown. Now, this is the very question upon which he undertakes to prove his particular opinion. [Horner, 1804 [1957], p. 105]

The charge was directed at that comment, included in the long, eighth paragraph inserted with the other 1784 'Additions and Corrections', where Smith insisted:

> that whatever extension of the foreign market can be occasioned by the bounty, must, in every particular year, be altogether at the expence of the home market; as every bushel of corn which is exported by means of the bounty, and which would not have been exported without the bounty, would have remained in the home market to increase the consumption and to lower the price of that commodity. (WN, IV.v.a.8)

Horner's charge misses its mark, however, since the argument underlying Smith's conclusion denying the bounty's capacity to stimulate corn output does not simply assume that result at its outset but is, rather, a more complex sequence of inferences drawn from his larger theory of rent and the special role accorded corn within that theory. It is the added constraint that the argument is to be applied only under the condition of an unchanged structure of relative prices that ensures the peculiar outcome of that chain of reasoning. In this regard, Smith's bounty analysis is open to the same objection that has long been directed at the comparative statics reasoning that pervades economists' discourse: it fails to take due account of the dynamic process by which the market moves between the postulated equilibria states (for examples from other contexts, see Hueckel, 2004, pp. 272–6 and the references cited there, particularly Robinson, 1974 [2000], Hicks, 1976). Hence, Horner was closer to the mark when he characterized Smith's 'error' as having 'consisted in too hastily assuming . . . that a bounty on exportation would occasion *immediately* a rise of the money-price in the home-market' (Horner, 1804 [1957], p. 105).

For all his protestations, however, Horner's analysis was open to the like objection, for, as we have seen, although he acknowledged a disequilibrium output response in the economy's adjustment to the bounty, he refused to credit that response with the power to alter the characteristics of the postulated equilibrium state. Such, apparently, was his 'diffidence' in appearing to challenge 'the patient, circumspect, and comprehensive care' evident in 'the reasonings of that great author', that he could not bring himself to deny Smith's 'practical conclusion' regarding the corn bounty. 'Its complete and ultimate effect', agreed Horner, 'will always be found to be a corresponding rise of the money-price in the home market, both of corn, of labour, and of all commodities', a declaration that drew from Ricardo the complaint that Horner had 'imbibed the common error which has misled Dr. Smith' (Horner, 1804 [1957], p. 104; Ricardo, 1951–73, Vol. I, p. 302).

The claim that an export subsidy on corn can have no permanent effect beyond a general increase in money prices presented another problem: how is the rise in the price level to be financed? Although Horner gave no indication that he grasped the significance of this problem, Smith did at least allude to a proposed solution with his reference to the 'absurd policy of Spain and Portugal'. Apparently the subsidized grain exports are to be seen as the source of net specie inflows sufficient to finance the increase in prices (see O'Donnell, 1990, p. 108).[15] But such a claim raises a conflict with Smith's theory of international monetary flows. The appeal to Spain and Portugal is a false analogy: those nations obtain their specie from the mines, but the bounty supplies specie only through trade. If gold and silver 'naturally seek the market where the best price is given for them', then any bounty-induced rise in prices will be thwarted by specie outflows. This is the objection raised against the Smithian doctrine by Ricardo in his *Principles*, though with no mention of the associated conflict with Smith's treatment of specie flows. But Ricardo was not alone in recognizing the error. Even before Ricardo had composed his *Essay on Profits*, Lauderdale had grasped the significance of the objection and recognized the implied contradiction in Smith's analysis. In his private commentary (written about 1814) on Smith's claim (at IV.v.a.16–20) that the bounty produces only a 'degradation in the value of silver', Lauderdale observed: 'This is a circumstance which can never occur for Silver is a commodity so portable that it would be conveyed elsewhere the moment its value was in the least degraded, and such a scarcity would take place in the country from whence it was exported, as would immediately raise its value.' Then, in an assessment to be echoed by generations of later readers: 'Nothing but extreme eagerness to support a favourite theory could have induced the author to advance anything so contradictory to the sound doctrines he has elsewhere stated concerning the value of the precious metals' (Sugiyama, 1996, p. 131).

Although one might say with Horner that Smith's analysis of the corn bounty, for all its flaws, is nevertheless broadly 'consistent at least with himself' when it is confined to the strictly static domain for which it is structurally suited, Smith was unwilling to adhere to such a constraint. We find him instead extending his argument beyond the limit of its static framework to suggest a dynamic process by which the bounty is said to have a real effect in retarding the growth of corn output. In so doing, he introduced contradictions that serve only to blunt the force of his case. The precise channel of influence by which this retardation is supposed to occur differs across the editions. In the first two editions, the bounty operates solely through its effect in raising the domestic price level, which 'tends to discourage more or less every sort of industry which is carried on within [Britain] and to enable foreign nations, by furnishing almost all sorts of goods for a smaller quantity of silver than its own workmen can afford to do, to undersell them, not only in the foreign, but even in the home market'. This, together with the subsidy to foreign purchases of British corn, gives foreign 'industry a double advantage over our own' (WN IV.v.a.17, 20). Combining this terms-of-trade effect with the principle applied earlier in the Book III derivation of the famous investment hierarchy, that the agricultural and manufacturing sectors each serve as markets for the other, Smith could conclude that the bounty operates like any policy that 'tends to diminish in any country the number of artificers and manufacturers, tends to diminish the home market, the most important of all markets for the rude produce of the land, and thereby still further to discourage agriculture' (IV.ix.48; cf. III.i.1; iv.1–2).

Although all the elements of the argument are present in the first two editions, the claim of long-run harm to agriculture is there left implicit. The full argument is stated explicitly in those editions only in reverse form: the decline in the price level said to result from the actions of the grain importer to increase the domestic supply 'gives the industry of the country . . . some advantage in all foreign markets and thereby tends to encourage and increase that industry'. As domestic industry 'is the nearest and most convenient' and thus the 'most important market for corn', we are led to the remarkable conclusion that increased imports serve to stimulate domestic output in the import-competing industry (IV.v.b.32).

It is with the 1784 'Additions and Corrections' that Smith turned the argument explicitly on the bounty. But in doing so, he forgot his own principle that the bounty cannot alter the real wage, for we are told that the bounty-induced rise in the corn price imposes a 'very heavy . . . tax on the first necessary of life [which] must either reduce the subsistence of the labouring poor' or raise money wages proportionately. Here both alternatives are permitted real effects: the former 'to restrain the population of the country' and the latter to restrain employment. Consequently:

> the extraordinary exportation of corn . . . occasioned by the bounty . . . by restraining the population and industry of the country, its final tendency is to stunt and restrain the gradual extension of the home-market; and thereby, in the long run, rather to diminish, than to augment, the whole market and consumption of corn. (IV.v.a.8)

Thus, here we are led to the equally remarkable conclusion that export subsidies serve to restrain domestic production of the subsidized commodity.[16] Further, we encounter this result just three paragraphs before we are told that the bounty can have no effect but 'to degrade the real value of silver'.

Smith's inclination, 'in the heat of writing', to press his case beyond its logical limits posed no difficulty for Horner. He was able to resolve Smith's evident contradiction here by appeal to that presumed transitory period of disequilibrium adjustment. By Horner's reading, the necessary bounty-caused decline in the corn wage is limited to the interval of the money-wage adjustment lag; and the subsequent rise in money-wage simply returns the corn wage 'to its former level', leaving no permanent alteration in the rate of corn output (Horner, 1804 [1957], pp. 105–6). But in Horner, Smith had a particularly careful and sympathetic reader. For others, not so committed to his system of 'natural liberty', Smith's contradictions were likely not so easily dismissed.

It was the most flagrant of those contradictions that was seized upon by Smith's contemporary critics. All the objections raised to this point were noticed by authors writing in the generation after his death. His contemporary critics were content to exploit that point in his argument most vulnerable to attack, where Smith's own words could be employed against him. That point arose in his 'digression concerning the corn trade', where he was faced with conflicting polemical objectives. While obliged to maintain his denial of the bounty's capacity to encourage domestic agriculture, Smith sought also to contend against that 'popular odium' to which the corn trade was exposed and thereby to build the case for 'the liberal system of free exportation and free importation'.

The problem appeared where he took up the case of the grain exporter, for here Smith must reverse his field: he could no longer hold to his earlier claim that (subsidized) exports serve only to raise the general price level and, incongruously, to restrain the long-run growth of corn output. Instead, he must establish the reverse outcome. While he acknowledged that unrestricted grain export 'certainly does not contribute directly to the plentiful supply of the home market', he nevertheless insisted that 'it does so, however, indirectly'. In support of his case, Smith adopted both the reasoning and the phrasing of his bounty opponents. A 'plentiful' domestic supply can be ensured only by the existence in 'ordinary' years of a 'surplus' product over 'what is usually consumed'. That surplus serves as insurance against dearth in those inevitable periods when the vagaries of the seasons leave the farmer with poor yields. But the effect of such a surplus in reducing price means that unless it 'can, in all ordinary cases, be exported, the growers will be careful never to grow more, and the importers never to import more, than what the bare consumption of the home market requires'. Consequently, in the absence of free exports, the domestic market 'will generally be understocked, the people, whose business it is to supply it being generally afraid lest their goods should be left upon their hands' (WN IV.v.b.36).

But this is precisely the argument advanced by the bounty's supporters, and they gleefully turned Smith's words against him. After quoting in full the argument just described, Anderson commented as follows:

> But if the market would *in all ordinary cases* be under-stocked, would not the price of grain be *in all ordinary cases* enhanced by that circumstance? – It has, however, been already shown that grain *in ordinary cases* could not admit of being exported . . . unless it were for the bounty. It must, therefore, according to Dr Smith's own reasoning, tend in the most effectual manner to supply the home market abundantly at all times, and consequently to moderate the price. (Anderson, 1968 [1777], p. 338)

Pownall too leapt at the opening, quoting Smith's defense of the export merchant to demonstrate that his own argument indicated agreement with the principle that 'an assured constant vent by exportation of any surplus that should be raised' is necessary to the maintenance of such a surplus, concluding that 'this measure of a bounty on export is every way not only beneficial, but necessary', and again appealing to Smith's words for support: 'in this view you yourself find, that this trade of the corn merchant "will support the trade of the farmer, in the same manner as the wholesale dealer supports that of the manufacturer"' (Pownall, 1776 [1987], pp. 364–5; the last passage quoted from WN IV.v.b.18).

At least in the matter of the corn bounty then, the contradictions introduced by Smith's inclination to press his case beyond its logical bounds cannot be dismissed as mere 'inconsistencies only in the details'. His effort to deny to the bounty the power to influence grain production forced upon him positions that raised various points of conflict with his advocacy of that 'system of natural liberty' that lay at the core of his policy discourse. Yet for all its flaws, Smith's analysis of the corn bounty's distortions held its ground against the arguments raised in defense of that policy by Anderson and Pownall. To understand why, we turn finally to a brief survey of those defenses.

Smith and his critics
In his reaction to his two bounty critics, Smith stands accused, variously, of an 'almost complete silence and equanimity', considered puzzling in the circumstances, and of 'unpleasant responses to [Anderson's] criticism' (Teichgraeber, 1987, p. 354; Hollander,

1997, p. 772). However, the aptness of that reaction must be judged against the force of those criticisms; and, on that account, there seems little to question in Smith's conclusion that he had 'not thought it proper to make any direct answer to any of [his] adversaries' (*Corr.*, 208). Of those two critics, Thomas Pownall would have been considered the more influential at the time. Commonly accorded the honorific, 'Governor', in recognition of his service in that capacity for the Massachusetts colony, Pownall issued a pamphlet in the form of a letter in which he criticized Smith's views on a number of points, including the question of the bounty (Rae, 1965 [1895], pp. 318–19). On that matter, his views would have carried some weight with his contemporaries by virtue of his position as the Member of Parliament who, some four years earlier, had introduced the resolutions, eventually enacted, to reduce (from 48 shillings to 44 shillings per quarter) the threshold price at which the export subsidy was removed, a reduction which, when viewed against the subsequent rise in grain prices, came to be seen by a future generation as the 'virtual repeal' of the bounty (Barnes, 1961 [1930], pp. 42–4; Fay, 1932, pp. 30–31; Horner, 1804 [1957], p. 98). This was the Act that Smith was moved to notice in his first edition as 'an improvement upon the antient system', though disappointing for its introduction of a complete prohibition of export at the price at which the bounty ceased. Later, when he came to prepare his second edition, his view softened, perhaps in response to a mild reproach from Edmund Burke (Horner, 1804 [1957], p. 98; Rae, 1965 [1895], pp. 25–7). At any rate, in the later editions the Act was described slightly more favorably as 'though not the best in itself . . . the best which the interests, prejudices, and temper of the times would admit of' (WN IV.v.b.51–3).

Although they arrived at the conclusion by quite different paths, both of Smith's critics were agreed in the common opinion that a vigorous grain export was necessary to ensure that sufficient resources were devoted to domestic cultivation to guard against dearth in years of short crop yields, an opinion which, as we have seen, Smith too adopted in his defense of the grain exporter. Anderson's critique is contained in a larger work written as a series of letters urging a scheme to advance the prosperity of the Scottish Highlands through the introduction of fine woolen manufacture (Anderson, 1968 [1777], Letters III–IV; for a more complete treatment of Anderson's argument, see Prendergast, 1987). It was this desire to encourage industry that led him to his defense of the bounty, the chief virtue of which was, in Anderson's estimation, its effectiveness in stabilizing the price of grain: 'the great use of a bounty is to regulate the price of grain, and to keep it as moderate, and as steady, as the nature of things will admit of' (Anderson, 1968 [1777], 374–5).[17]

The great benefit of a stable grain price arises from the operation of a back-bending labor supply curve. Because:

> necessity alone induces men to work . . . when people can earn as much in one day as may maintain them for two, or more, they will then be more disposed to indulge their own inclinations, and work less than when the whole labour of the day is barely sufficient to supply the wants of nature; so that more labourers will be in the market in the last case than in the first. (Anderson, 1968 [1777], p. 277)

In this framework, both abundant and short harvests are disruptive to industry and social order. The former are to be avoided because, with the consequent low grain prices (and associated high corn-wage):

manufacturers would turn idle and insolent, commissions from abroad could not be executed in a proper time by our manufacturers, and foreign merchants would be obliged to apply to other markets for these goods; farmers would be unable to pay their rents; proprietors would be distressed for want of these, and the whole nation would be thrown into the most violent ferment that could be imagined.

Short harvests have at least the benefit of the 'temporary rise in the price of provisions . . . [which] must naturally produce a greater degree of industry among the labouring people', but there remains the problem that 'if this advanced price was to be long continued, the labourers finding themselves too much straitened in their circumstances, would either insist upon having more wages, or they would leave that country'. Anderson does not, however, tell us why this apparent ease of labor outmigration in periods of low real wages does not produce, in periods of abundance, a corresponding immigration sufficient to contradict his underlying assumption of a back-bending labor supply. We learn only of the possible outmigration, no doubt because that too threatens both the interests of the manufacturers and the social order: with rising wages and fewer workers, 'it becomes necessary to advance the price of manufactures in foreign markets; which slackens the demand for them, and is the cause of much uneasiness, that often ends in tumults and bloodshed at home' (ibid., pp. 293–6).

When we come to the bounty's effect on the agricultural sector, we find the case resting upon now familiar principles. Just as we saw in Smith's defense of the grain exporter, Anderson's farmers too require a 'certain and steady demand for a considerable quantity for exportation' to induce the investment of sufficient resources to maintain a surplus product in 'ordinary years'; which surplus, then, ensures against dearth 'in a year of scarcity, when the quantity that was destined for exportation comes to be naturally applied to make up the deficiency of that part of the crop which was originally destined for the home market'. Further, the assurance of that 'certain and steady demand' induces the adoption of productivity-enhancing techniques that serve to reduce society's vulnerability to the vagaries of the seasons:

> The bounty has a natural tendency to over-rule even the influence of bad seasons themselves . . . for as it gives the farmer perfect security . . . it necessarily occasions a more perfect culture of the soil; and every sensible farmer knows that a rich soil in a high degree of cultivation is far less liable to be affected by a variation of seasons. (Anderson, 1968 [1777], pp. 317–18, 327–32)

Evidently Smith's difference with Anderson over the desirability of the corn bounty did not arise from any disagreement as to the role of (unsubsidized) exports in stimulating domestic production. Their difference arose instead from conflicting views regarding the possibility of a privately managed intertemporal allocation of grain stocks on a scale sufficient to moderate the price variation arising from the vagaries of the weather. Smith, of course, advanced a thorough analysis of the inland corn trade to demonstrate that the unregulated market can be expected to ensure that the 'plenty of one year' will relieve the 'scarcity of another' (WN IV.v.b.1–26). Anderson, however, denied Smith's argument on this matter in its entirety on the ground that the high capital cost and the perishable nature of grain together with the risk of fire, riot and other calamities make private storage so costly that the mere suggestion of such an activity can be dismissed as 'extravagantly absurd'.[18] Hence, Anderson was left with the conclusion that the only means available to achieve this intertemporal transfer of product is through the bounty's power to promote a level of capacity capable of yielding a surplus in 'ordinary' years, which surplus is then available for redirection to domestic consumption in those inevitable years when the seasons turn unfavorable (Anderson, 1968 [1777], pp. 321–3).[19]

So far then as the analytical content of Anderson's bounty defense is concerned, there is little in the way of further response that Smith could have offered. That content differed from Smith's treatment chiefly in its presumptions concerning the labor supply relationship and the possibility of a market-directed system of grain storage, both topics on which Smith had already fully expressed himself. But if Anderson's bounty defense posed little theoretical challenge to Smith's position, Pownall's raised even less. Indeed, Smith must have read Pownall's argument with a particular exasperation, for it took as its opening premise that very 'popular notion' which Smith had already so strenuously sought to refute – namely that a 'country in that progressive state of improvement, by which England for near a century hath been rising, must have experienced a continued influx of riches; that continued influx must have and hath created a continued progressive rise of prices'.[20] The connection with the bounty comes with the addition of an assumed adjustment lag during which the relative price of corn and the real wage both decline: 'The relative proportion of the scale of prices being changed . . . and corn will be always last in the scale.' Although the corn price

> may and will rise, yet not rising in proportion to other things, and the rents of land and the wages of labour depending on the price of corn, the price of every other thing must not only rise before rent and wages can start in price, but must continue *so to forerun* in their rise that the landed man and labourer must be in a continued state of oppression and distress.

Consequently, the agriculturalist 'requires some adventitious force or spring to aid the velocity of the rise of the price of his commodity which he hath to sell', and the bounty serves as that 'spring'. In so doing it increases output, creating, by 'the high prices of the home market', a 'succession of surpluses' which 'keeps down the price taken in a general series of times' (Pownall, 1776 [1987], pp. 362–5). Thus, while the route differs, the destination is the same as that of other bounty supporters: the bounty assures the farmer a higher price which elicits a larger output than would be otherwise forthcoming, and that in turn yields (incongruously) a lower average price in the long run.

Apart, then, from the exploitation of the obvious and inevitable inconsistency between Smith's denial of the bounty's power to stimulate production and his defense of the export trade, the objections to his bounty analysis raised by his contemporary critics posed no theoretical challenge to the substance of that analysis. His critics failed to grasp the larger model of economic advance that supported and framed that analysis. Consequently, their remaining objections simply missed the mark. Anderson at least recognized that Smith's argument rested on his principle of the supposed 'regulating' character of the corn price, but he failed to appreciate the strictly static character of that principle. Because he understood Smith's maxim as intended for a dynamic context, he repeatedly saw error where none was present. He acknowledged, indeed, that:

> every difficulty would disappear, and that Dr Smith's reasoning would be here plain and consistent, if we were to suppose that the price of grain had such an immediate influence on that of all other commodities as necessarily to make the nominal price of each of these, on all occasions, to rise and fall with every fluctuation in the price of grain.

But such a 'supposition' was to be dismissed as 'so directly contrary to experience that it would be an insult on Dr Smith to suppose we should understand it in that way' (Anderson, 1968 [1777], p. 357n.). 'Insult' or no, this was precisely the meaning intended by Smith's limitation of his principle to a fixed 'period of improvement', as Horner understood.

Because of his misapprehension of Smith's principle, the several pages devoted by Anderson to criticism of that principle posed no threat to Smith's case that could not be deflected by a few expository adjustments. Thus, his objection that the corn price cannot 'regulate' the wage, as demonstrated by the observation that in the American colonies, 'the price of labour is very high, although the price of grain is extremely low' (Anderson, 1968 [1777], pp. 346–7), demonstrates nothing but Smith's conclusion that corn wages will be 'liberal, moderate, or scanty' depending upon the 'period of improvement'. Similarly irrelevant are the two quotations which Anderson drew together (ibid., pp. 359–61, in the 'long footnote' noticed by Prendergast, 1987, p. 394) to demonstrate his claim that Smith himself contradicted his own principle. The first of those quoted passages (from WN IV.ix.25) involves an import tax on manufactures (rather than corn), altering relative prices and, consequently, relative profit rates, producing thereby a reallocation of capital across sectors. Obviously the passage violates the static condition of the 'regulating' principle, which is defined only within a given structure of relative prices. Anderson's comment on the second of those quotations (from WN IV.ix.48) is no more than a misreading of the simple point that in trade between town and country, 'cheaper' produce is simply the inverse of 'dearer' manufactures, Anderson interpreting Smith's reference to 'cheap' produce as 'the money-price of corn'. Smith did make a one-word change to this passage in the second (1778) edition, presumably in response to Anderson's comment, altering the first edition phrase 'real value' to read 'exchangeable value' to make clear that the argument turns on the rate of exchange between commodities.

No doubt Anderson's repeated attempts to apply Smith's principle of the 'regulating' character of the corn price to contexts involving dynamic changes in the resource structure of the economy lay behind other small expository adjustments made to the later editions, chief of which being that change reported in his letter to Andreas Holt and made to the second edition to revise his 'careless expression' in the passage quoted at the opening of this essay, the 'corrected' expression describing corn's value as one that 'cannot be altered by merely altering its money price'. Since, in Smith's system, the bounty can, in the first instance, produce no more than a purely nominal shock, this simple adjustment was, he assured his correspondent, 'all that the argument required and all that I really meant'; and with it, he had taken 'away the foundation of the whole argument of Mr Anderson' (*Corr.*, 208). Apparently, however, he recalled his critics' objections some six years later, for we find that in the 1784 'Additions and Corrections' and third edition he has limited the application of his principle concerning the regulating character of the corn price to 'home-made' commodities only, no doubt in response to Anderson's (1968 [1777], p. 344) observation that if that principle is to hold, his 'manufactures must have been all worked up from materials the produce of his own country'.

We hear the echo of another misdirected critique in yet one more revision introduced in 'Additions and Corrections', and here the change must have struck Smith as doubly ironic. Anderson, whose own offers of empirical support amounted, as we have seen, to no more than repeated applications of the *post hoc* fallacy, objected that, in insisting that the acknowledged eighteenth-century decline in the corn price had occurred 'in spite of the bounty', Smith had 'contented himself with the bare assertion, instead of farther proof' (ibid., p. 336). Smith did, however, offer some evidence in support of his contention, repeating Necker's (1776, p. 271n.) earlier observation that the decline in grain prices had occurred in France as well, in spite of that nation's contrary policy prohibiting exports prior to 1764, a state of affairs which, Smith noted, made it 'somewhat difficult to suppose that nearly the same diminution of price which took place in one country, notwithstanding this prohibition, should in another be owing to the extraordinary encouragement given to exportation' (WN I.xi.g.15). To be sure, Smith's comment appeared, in the first edition, only in the digression on silver and was not repeated in the later chapter on bounties. Nevertheless, Pownall (1776 [1987], p. 361), who also was working from the first edition, did notice this 'decisive proof' and recognized its source in Necker. No doubt it was Anderson's criticism that prompted Smith to include in his 'Additions and Corrections', immediately after the passage that drew the complaint, a repetition of the earlier reference to the French experience (WN IV.v.a.5).

Only when they took explicit account of the relative price trends implied by Smith's larger growth theory did his critics manage objections that came closer to the mark. For his part, Pownall accepted Smith's conclusion that economic advance must produce a rise in animal product prices relative to that of corn, but he turned this principle against Smith's call for a removal of restraints on cattle imports, arguing that 'free importation . . . must derange this scale of natural prices and must arrest this progress of improvement in its course' (Pownall, 1776 [1987], p. 359). Smith, of course, understood the difference between a relative price rise resulting from demand growth and one produced by supply restraints; and he recognized further that it was larger, not smaller, quantities of feeding stock that contributed to improvement since 'the quantity of well-cultivated land must be in proportion to the quantity of manure which the farm itself produces' (WN I.xi.l.3).

Anderson too tried to turn one of Smith's relative price predictions against him but made a muddle of the attempt. Indeed, Anderson's failure to appreciate Smith's larger theoretical structure is revealed in his very premise: 'It will hardly be denied that the value of the precious metals hath decreased in Britain since the law granting a bounty on corn was enacted; and that, by consequence, the price of almost every commodity has risen proportionately in that period.' Smith, of course, had just devoted a great deal of effort to establish that such a claim can indeed be 'denied'. Moreover, in his next sentence, Anderson accepted the very piece of evidence to which Smith appealed in support of his own position, writing that 'corn, since that time has decreased even in its *nominal* value', concluding, thereby, that corn 'has therefore decreased in its *real* value in a much higher proportion' (Anderson, 1968 [1777], pp. 361–2). This he took as a refutation of Smith's claim that corn is imbued with an unalterable 'real value', apparently unaware that in Smith's system, a commodity's 'real value' is defined strictly in terms of its purchasing power over labor. All this must have struck Smith as profoundly ironic since he had likewise just devoted considerable effort to convince his readers that the nominal price of corn is a perfect index of 'the value of the precious metals'. Indeed, if his readers accept his assumption that the resource cost of corn production remains constant 'in all the different stages of wealth and improvement' they have no choice but to agree that 'the average or ordinary price of corn ... is regulated ... by the value of silver, by the richness or barrenness of the mines which supply the market with that metal' (WN I.v.16; xi.e.28; see Hueckel, 2000, pp. 333–8, for a fuller treatment). Hence, Smith would have taken Anderson's admission of a falling nominal price of corn as refutation of his own premise of a falling value of silver and proof of Smith's contrary claim.

Anderson, however, did not stop there. He argued further that the rise in the price of manufactures relative to that of corn occasioned by the observed decline in corn's nominal value undercuts Smith's famous claim that the source of the nation's prosperity is to be sought not in the operation of the bounty but rather in 'that security which the laws in Great Britain give to every man that he shall enjoy the fruits of his own labour' (WN, IV.v.b.43). This Anderson dismissed with the observation that such security of property right applied to manufacturing as well, where, by virtue of Smith's own recognition of a greater scope for the division of labor (I.i.4; IV.ix.35), that 'general security ... ought to have lowered the price of every other manufacture in a much higher proportion than that of grain', contrary to the trend which Anderson thought he saw all around him (Anderson, 1968 [1777], pp. 362–3).

But Smith had already demonstrated that the effect of economic advance on manufacturing price trends is more complex than Anderson's simple statement implies. Although 'it is the natural effect of improvement ... to diminish gradually the real price of almost all manufactures' through the discovery and application of labor-saving techniques, for 'a few manufactures' that tendency is reversed by the rise in the relative price of their raw materials. This is particularly true of the woodworking industries since wood's price must rise relative to that of corn with the extension of cultivation. The expected price decline apparently occurs to its greatest extent in the metal-working industries, but even in so important a sector as clothing manufacture there had 'been no such sensible reduction of price' over the previous two centuries, and perhaps even a rise over the previous quarter-century in 'superfine cloth'. But claims regarding trends in a commodity's price must be judged 'in proportion to quality', and quality being 'so very disputable a matter', Smith warned that we must 'look upon all information of this kind as somewhat uncertain' (I.xi.o.1–5). Hence, Smith would have found nothing to threaten his own analysis in Anderson's appeal to the supposed trend in manufacturing prices relative to that of corn; and, having already fully expressed himself on the matter, there was no point in continuing the dispute. It appears then that when judged against the substance of the criticisms he received, Smith's public response of 'almost complete silence and equanimity' is entirely unremarkable.[21]

Thus did Smith's peculiar denial of the capacity of an export subsidy to stimulate production remain largely untouched by the objections of his contemporary critics. Only with the passing of a generation do Horner, Buchanan, Ricardo, and their contemporaries see through the surface coherence to the inconsistencies below. By that time, though, the 'error of Adam Smith' had become so firmly established as to appear to Ricardo, at least, as an obstruction impeding the advance of his own theory.

Conclusion

It will by now be evident why Blaug's comment was chosen as the epigraph for this chapter. When considered at face value, Smith's denial of the power of an export subsidy to promote corn production is indeed a 'paradox'. But the mystery disappears when we heed Blaug's advice and return Smith's maxim to the role for which it was designed, as an element in his larger analysis of the process of economic growth serving a particular polemical purpose directed at a policy issue 'peculiar to the times'.

Indeed, Blaug's reference to the role of 'propaganda' takes on greater force when we notice the degree to which Smith's published position on the corn bounty had changed from that advanced in his earlier, jurisprudence lectures. There the bounty is condemned on the same grounds applied to all other mercantile 'expedients': it produced a misallocation of the nation's capital and thereby distorted the composition of output. According to his student scribe, Smith's class learned that, by virtue of the bounty, 'more ground has been turnd into corn and consequently less has been left for the production of grass', by which, 'the price of it necessarily rises and along with it the price of butcher meat'. Further, with the rise in the hay price, 'the maintenance of horses is therefore become much higher'; and 'the expense of transportation is increased and the inland commerce of the kingdom greatly embarrassed'. The dire consequences are traced out to great length indeed, and Smith apparently exposed his students to the same circular reasoning regarding the bounty's price effect that was found in the claims of so many of its defenders. At any rate, we find in the student's notes the peculiar comment: 'We see that the bounty on corn has sunk the price continually, the necessary consequence of which was that the rent of corn farms should sink also', a comment that was apparently repeated the following year. Yet, nowhere in these lectures do we find the paradoxical claim that the rate of corn output is uniquely immune to the effects of policy favors. On the contrary, Smith apparently told his students that the bounty 'encourages the raising of corn and makes in this manner an artificiall abundance' (LJ(A) vi.92–7; cf. (B) 234–5). That 'great and essential difference' imparted by 'nature' to corn alone, which was to become the point of attack by his critics and the source of consternation for even his most sympathetic readers, appeared only later, when in the course of his assault on the mercantilist 'popular notion' Smith was faced with the need 'to offer explanations of the divergence' he had found between his data and the predictions of his theory.

Blaug's admonition carries significance for the theorist as well as the historian of ideas. As the history of Smith's maxim demonstrates, the heat of polemic can introduce into the economist's discourse misconceptions that persist long after the controversy has been forgotten. Ricardo's struggle to overcome the 'error of Adam Smith' is one more illustration that future analytical work must be 'forever catching up with the biases [and errors] of yesterday'. The theorist who can identify the influences of past disputes on current doctrine will be better able to separate the nuggets of analytical insight from the dross of polemical excess. Had Ricardo and his contemporaries understood that Smith's maxim was derived as a strictly static principle employed to gain the polemical advantage over his mercantilist opponents, they would have recognized that it carried no relevance for the dynamic problem posed by Ricardo concerning the distributional consequences of a growing capital stock over a fixed endowment of land. In the event, however, Smith's dictum that the 'money-price of corn regulates that of all other commodities' was taken as a self-evident description of the dynamic reality, causing Ricardo that anguish he recorded in his letters as he struggled to overcome that misapprehension. One can only speculate how the development of value theory might have been altered had Smith's principle been understood for what it was.

Notes

1. Citations to Smith's works will employ the scheme adopted by the Glasgow edition, designating all relevant gradations – book, chapter, section, paragraph (or page number in original manuscript) – in the hope that readers will find helpful the larger contextual reference conveyed by that practice. The particular work to which the reference refers is indicated in the text by its title acronym (and the notation 'ed.1' where the citation refers to the first edition of WN, as distinct from the third edition copy text of the Glasgow volumes). References to the correspondence are indicated by the letter number in the *Correspondence*.
2. For examples see Blecker (1997), Bowles (1986), Mirowski (1982) or West (1997).
3. Just two days earlier, Ricardo had commented to James Mill that upon 'reading Adam Smith again, I find many opinions to question, all I believe founded on his original error respecting value. He is particularly faulty in the chapter on bounties' (Ricardo, 1951–73, Vol. VII, p. 100). See Peach (1993, pp. 145–54) for a brief exposition of Ricardo's early struggle against the 'error of Adam Smith' together with further quotations from the relevant correspondence.
4. Here we encounter one of those 'consistent inconsistencies' typical of Smith's discourse. In his *Lectures on Jurisprudence*, he sought to assure his students that while it may seem that the rich man consumes a larger share of the nation's produce than does the poor man, this is a matter of appearance only. Not only is it true that the rich man 'has not a larger stomach than any ordinary plowman', but even in his clothing, while certainly of a 'greater variety' than his workman, he nevertheless 'does not consume so much as an ordinary plowman'. This equality of consumption becomes apparent when we consider their respective life-time consumption patterns: the rich man 'never exposes [his clothes] to be spoiled by the weather or rubbed and torn by hard labour', and after he is finished with them, they are still fit for use by others, 'whereas the plowman who has his cloaths continually exposed to all sorts of destruction wears considerably more' (LJ(A) iii.135–6).

    This characterization of consumption levels as determined more by our common human condition than by income differences was retained in that famous passage in TMS (IV.1.10), where we read that 'the rich only select from the heap what is most precious and agreeable. They consume little more than the poor.' However, in WN (I.xi.c.7), where the argument requires that non-food items exhibit the greater income elasticity of demand, we are told that when we 'compare the spacious palace and great wardrobe of the one, with the hovel and the few rags of the other, [we] will be sensible that the difference between their cloathing, lodging and houshold furniture, is almost as great in quantity as it is in quality'. Apparently the differentially lower 'wear and tear' imposed on their possessions by the rich, so important to the argument of TMS, is in WN no longer considered sufficient to bring their non-food consumption into equality with that of the poor. Nevertheless, even in WN, when the argument requires it, Smith does not scruple to appeal to that very differential in rates of depreciation. In the discussion of capital accumulation, where the defining characteristic of capital is its durability, we are told that the 'man of fortune' whose 'expence had been chiefly in durable commodities' follows a 'mode of expence [that] is more favourable ... to the opulence of an individual ... [as it is] likewise to that of a nation' because 'the houses, the furniture, the cloathing of the rich, in a little time, become useful to the inferior and middling ranks of people' who purchase those goods 'when their superiors grow weary of them' (WN II.iii.38–9). Evidently, Smith's views regarding the relationship between consumption flows and income levels constituted one of those 'inconsistencies ... in the detail' that, as his Glasgow editors noted, were always consistent with the analytical needs of the moment.
5. When he came to compose his argument on this matter for publication, Smith's views had evidently changed significantly from those earlier expressed in his Glasgow lectures. There the issue turns not on the question of the relative income elasticities of demand for corn and for the precious metals but rather on a presumed difference in their respective supply response. The technical knowledge required to discover, mine and refine the precious metals is said to experience the more rapid advance over the course of economic improvement. Consequently, 'in a nation of savages', where 'the arts of working gold and silver and separating them from the ore are not to be expected', those metals are 'vastly rare and will purchase an immense quantity of goods'. However, 'when mankind are more improv'd, all the mines are carefully wrought and commerce brings in abundance of them, and they sink in their value'. Here then we find economic advance associated with a rising silver price of commodities – precisely the 'popular notion' that Smith would later seek to refute. Thus, according to the 1766 report, Smith told his students that 'from the fall of the Roman Empire to the discovery of the West Indies, the value of money was very high and continually encreasing. Since that latter period its value has decreased considerably.'

    It is true that there is a troubling inconsistency between the two lecture reports on this matter, the earlier report recording the reverse trend: 'From the fall of the Roman Empire till [the] discovery of the Span. West Indies prices continuall[y] rose, since which they have fallen.' However, as this contradicts the argument advanced in the immediately preceding sentences (and in the later report), it is likely that

the incongruity simply reflects the failure of the student scribe to distinguish the trend in 'prices' (of commodities) from that of the inverse – that is, the 'commodity price' of specie. See LJ(A) vi.133–5 and LJ(B) 253–4.
6. Modeled after an earlier Act of 1673 (apparently expiring in 1681), the 1689 Act (1 William and Mary, c.12) established a subsidy of 5 shillings per quarter of wheat exported when the price in the exporting port was below 48 shillings and the carrying vessel was British owned and at least two-thirds British crewed. Proportionate rates were also established for barley and rye. See Barnes (1961 [1930]), 10–11 and Gras (1967 [1915]), pp. 144–5.

The reported date of the Act presents some confusion due to the transition from the English old-style calendar. Smith dates the Act to 1688, though other histories place it in 1689. William and Mary were proclaimed regnant by Parliament in February 1689. However, on the English old-style calendar, the legal year ran to 24 March, a new year beginning with the Feast of the Annunciation, 25 March. Hence, the first 'regnal' year for William and Mary was recorded as running from February 1688. The Bounty Act received the royal assent in April 1689, but the Act did not specify a date upon which it was to take effect. In such instances, the practice was to date Acts from the first day of the Parliament, which in this case, since Parliament had opened prior to the old-style beginning of the new year on 25 March, was recorded in the parliamentary *Chronology* as 1688 (Fay, 1932, p. 12, n.1).
7. Smith's survey of the price history contains another of those points where his reading of the evidence seems to adjust itself to the needs of the current argument. In carrying that history up to his own time, Smith acknowledges that the 'high price of corn during these ten or twelve years past . . . has occasioned a suspicion that the real value of silver still continues to fall in the European market'. There follows a long discussion to convince the reader that this is a transitory event masking a continuing long-run fall in the price level produced by a 'gradual increase in the demand for silver' (WN I.xi.g.17, 23–35). Nevertheless, Smith is at this point able to muster no more than a highly qualified conclusion: 'That . . . the value of silver has, during the course of the present century, begun to rise somewhat in the European market, the facts and arguments which have been alleged above, dispose me to believe, or more properly to suspect and conjecture; for the best opinion which I can form upon this subject scarce, perhaps, deserves the name of belief' (I.xi.h.11; see also I.v.12 and I.xi.g.35 for similarly qualified statements). All these doubts and qualifications fall away, however, in the 'Conclusion of the digression', where the discussion returns to the polemic against the errors of the 'popular notion'. The 'high price of corn during these last ten or twelve years' is there summarily dismissed as 'sufficiently accounted for from the badness of the seasons, without supposing any degradation in the value of silver' (I.xi.n.6–7).
8. If Edward West's later assessment is correct, this early Smith was the first author to credit the corn bounty with the power to reduce price (West, 1815 [1934], p. 44).
9. Turning his attention to the renewal of the bounty in his own time, Horner lamented 'another coincidence of circumstances' by which, since the 'virtual repeal' of the bounty in 1773, the corn price had risen as the trade had shifted to a net import balance. With this reversal in those trends over the period of the bounty's suspension, those 'who have been moved in favour of the bounty by the first part of this experience . . . could not help feeling the second to be irresistible: if the original trial furnished a probable conclusion, this converse of the experiment, yielding the same result, seemed to establish it to demonstration' (1804 [1957], p. 98). See Buchanan (1966 [1817], p. 151) for a similar observation.
10. This passage was singled out for special attention by Edward West, who marshaled his own tables of price data in rebuttal, leading 'to a conclusion the very opposite to that which the advocates of the bounty have drawn'. The same fallacious appeal to price data marked Malthus's support of the bounty in the 1803 and 1806 editions of his *Essay*, which drew from West a like rebuttal (West, 1815 [1934], pp. 44–9). Perhaps it was criticisms like those received from West that induced Malthus to considerably restrain his support for the bounty in the 1817 edition, limiting its effect there to no more than a temporary, and transitory, output stimulus (cf. Malthus, 1803 [1989], Vol. I, pp. 411–12 and Vol. II, pp. 57–60; for a survey of Malthus's treatment of the bounty, see Prendergast, 1987, pp. 396–407).
11. It is true that Smith offered us in passing a tantalizing reference to diminishing marginal product on what would later become known as the Ricardian extensive margin in agriculture; but the principle carried none of the analytical burden of his larger system, serving only to illustrate Young's salutary reminder that the mere appearance in an early work of what appear as rudimentary statements of modern analytical concepts does not mean that the author 'would understand their importance and be able to integrate them into a logically consistent, complete body of theoretical statements' (WN I.ix.11; Young, 2001, p. 133; cf. Hollander, 1979, pp. 23–4).
12. The exceptions occur either when the land is incapable of alternative use (as in the case of rice land, 'a bog at all seasons', I.xi.b.38) or when demand forces disturb the 'natural proportion' (see I.vii.24; xi.b.10–14; or xi.b.29–34).
13. This result – that the meat–wheat price ratio necessarily rises with economic advance – provides Smith with a more generally applicable index of economic growth since, unlike the presumed growth-induced

decline in the money price of wheat, the rise in the meat–wheat price ratio is independent of changes in the world stock of specie (O'Donnell, 1990, pp. 76–9; Hueckel, 2000).

14. Although Hollander is careful to warn his readers that Smith's famous bounty analysis is properly understood as no more than a narrowly constrained exercise in comparative statics, that critical qualification seems to slip from his view when he comes to draw 'the fundamental implication of [Smith's] model', which he defines as the principle 'that an increase in the general money wage rate will be reflected in an increase in the prices of *manufactured* goods proportional to the labour input', while 'as for agriculture, the impact will be on rent, prices remaining unchanged' (1992, p. 84; cf. 1979, pp. 21–2; 1973, p. 179). This claim of a 'differential treatment accorded the determination of price in the manufacturing and agricultural sectors' cannot fail but to convey at least the appearance of non sequitur, following as it does immediately upon the quotation of the passages noted above, where Smith insists, within the confines of his bounty analysis, that a rise in the money wage occasioned by a rising corn price must be accompanied by increased prices 'of everything that is the produce of either land or labour'. Any unease the reader may feel with Hollander's argument on this point is well founded since that argument amounts to an attempt to cast Smith's dynamic principle of a secular decline in the profit rate as a conflation of the results obtained in two unrelated comparative-statics exercises: namely, his bounty analysis and his treatment of the incidence of a tax on wages. It is the tax analysis which, we are told, 'confirms' the presence of that supposed 'differential treatment' in the dynamic case (1973, pp. 179–80; 1979, pp. 24–5).

The particular 'confirming' texts offered in evidence are Smith's statements (WN V.ii.i.2 and V.ii.k.9) that since any tax-caused rise in wages is necessarily advanced by the capitalist, the manufacturer 'would both be entitled and obliged to charge it, with a profit, upon the price of his goods', while the farmer must 'pay less rent to the landlord'. But no notice is taken of the qualification, contained in the passage quoted, that the analysis presumes 'the demand for labour and the average price of provisions remained the same after the tax as before it'. Indeed, Hollander goes so far as to suggest that: 'there is no reason to believe that the secular rise in *per capita* wages in consequence of an increasing rate of capital accumulation was treated differently than a tax on wages or on wage goods', leading him to the inference that, in Smith's view, 'the increase in wage costs in [the growth] case too would be passed on in the form of higher [manufacturing] prices and reduced rents' (1973, pp. 180–81; see also 1979, p. 25).

But there is every reason to treat the two cases differently: a conclusion derived under conditions of a constant capital stock cannot necessarily be extended to the dynamic case of a rising capital stock. Indeed, when Smith, in his tax analysis, relaxed his confining assumption and permitted the tax to influence the rate of capital formation, the 'differential' in the outcomes felt by the two sectors is considerably reduced. 'Direct taxes upon the wages of labour', we are told in the paragraph following that quoted by Hollander, 'have generally occasioned a considerable fall in the demand for labour'. Consequently, it has been 'the declension of industry, the decrease of employment for the poor, the diminution of the annual produce of the land and labour of the country [that] have generally been the effects of such taxes' (WN V.ii.i.3). That unpleasant outcome is, of course, the inevitable result of capital's extraordinary mobility. Unlike the landlord, the capitalist 'is properly a citizen of the world' and can easily remove his capital from any employment in which it 'is exposed to a vexatious inquisition in order to be assessed to a burdensome tax'. Hence, far from maintaining the capital stock unchanged, any tax diminishing the capitalist's return would 'drive away stock from any particular country [and] would so far tend to dry up every source of revenue . . . Not only the profits of stock, but the rent of land and the wages of labour, would necessarily be more or less diminished by its removal' (V.ii.f.6).

There is, then, no mystery as to Smith's view regarding the distributional effects deriving from 'the secular rise in *per capita* wages in consequence of an increasing rate of capital accumulation', and there is certainly no need to rest our reading of that dynamic question upon inferences drawn from certain narrowly constrained Smithian exercises in comparative statics. Smith was, of course, quite explicit regarding the dynamic consequences of a rising capital stock: rents rise, wages rise so long as the capital growth exceeds that of the labor force, and profits fall (WN I.xi.p.1–10; I.viii; I.ix.2; II.iv.8; cf. Letiche, 1960, p. 68).

15. Here too the argument is confounded by contradiction. The bounty, we are told, not only encouraged exports in abundant years, but 'by hindering the plenty of one year from relieving the scarcity of another, it occasioned in years of scarcity a greater importation than would otherwise have been necessary' (IV.v.a.22; cf. IV.ii.20). Elsewhere we learn that the general rise in prices said to follow upon the bounty raises Britain's manufacturing prices and reduces those of its foreign competitors, giving the foreign commodities 'a double advantage over our own' (IV.v.a.20). Evidently, we are to understand that the corn bounty, in addition to its obvious encouragement of grain exports, served also to stimulate imports of both grain and manufactures. But how, then, are we to be sure that the outcome is a net specie inflow?

16. If the corn bounty harms the very group it is ostensibly intended to benefit, Smith's readers might well wonder how he accounts for its existence in the first place. The answer is the same as that given in other, similar contexts: the agriculturalists simply do not understand the consequences of their political action in seeking the bounty. Of course, this appeal to ignorance to explain apparently irrational political behavior

raises yet another troubling contradiction, in this case with Smith's fundamental principle that 'the law ought always to trust people with the care of their own interest, as in their local situations they must generally be able to judge better of it than the legislator can do' (WN IV.v.b.16; cf. IV.ii.10).

There is, however, a reassuring consistency in this inconsistency in that the rather dimwitted nature of Smith's 'country gentlemen' reveals the power of market incentives. Because those gentlemen receive their income with 'neither labour nor care', they have grown indolent, which 'renders them too often, not only ignorant, but incapable of that application of mind which is necessary in order to foresee and understand the consequences of any publick regulation' (WN I.xi.p.8). As in other areas of public policy, they have in the matter of the bounty been misled by the actions of the merchants. While, in seeking the bounty, the landlords 'acted in imitation of [the] merchants and manufacturers, they did not act with that compleat comprehension of their own interest which commonly directs the conduct of those two other orders of people'. Their error, of course, lay in their failure to grasp the character of corn's 'great and essential difference' (IV.v.a.23–4; cf. I.xi.p.10; IV.i.10).

17. Although Anderson credited the bounty with the capacity to 'moderate' the corn price, he cannot be justly charged with the circular reasoning evident in the claims advanced by other bounty supporters who promised both higher prices to the farmer and lower prices to the consumer. Anderson's desire to minimize the price effects of the inevitable variation in weather conditions is more properly described as an early effort to resolve the problem of a lagged supply response, later to become familiar as the cobweb theorem. The achievement of greater price stability would reduce the farmer's market risk, thereby inducing greater investment in agriculture and thus diminishing the average price over time (Anderson, 1968 [1777], pp. 310–27). Neither can he be charged with inconsistency in joining his advocacy of the bounty with his very clear statement of 'Ricardian rent' as an intra-marginal surplus arising from outward movements of the extensive margin on land of diminishing productivity. He was quite aware that bounty-induced increments in output under such conditions are obtained only at rising cost. His goal was national self-sufficiency in food, which was to be achieved by a corn export subsidy set so as 'to fix the average price of grain at a rate high enough to enable the farmer to cultivate so much of those unfertile fields as will be sufficient to furnish grain to supply the whole inhabitants with food in the scarcest years' (pp. 376–7).

18. It should be noted that Anderson's objection here amounted to no more than a denial of the possibility of significant storage under existing technology. At the more fundamental, analytical level, he raised no objection to Smith's larger defense of an unrestricted domestic trade in grain. Indeed, he closed his long critique of Smith's bounty analysis with the assurance that he was 'happy ... to be able to concur entirely with this very sensible author, with regard to the very great utility of an unlimited freedom on all occasions to the internal commerce of grain'. Those remaining laws which served 'in the most distant manner to cramp the internal commerce of grain', were, he insisted, 'badges of the ignorance of our forefathers', which, he hoped, 'as soon as possible, to bury in oblivion' (Anderson, 1968 [1777], p. 370).

19. In his defense of the inland corn trade Smith was in complete agreement with that other bounty supporter – his earlier, 'very well-informed' namesake. Indeed, the content and structure of the earlier Smith's analysis reappears nearly intact in Adam Smith's more famous treatment. Even the phrasing of the two authors is similar. Just as Adam Smith lamented 'the popular odium against a trade so beneficial to the publick', the earlier Smith was moved to defend the grain dealers against the 'general opinion' which attributed the high price of corn to 'the avarice of the farmers and iniquity of the factors ... and dealers in corn' (WN IV.v.b.9; Smith, 1766, p. 5). We find even the unmistakable shadow of the 'invisible hand' in the earlier Smith's defense of the farmer who, in time of scarcity, withholds his grain immediately after harvest: 'though he regards only himself, this conduct may be of public utility; for was he to supply the market in the beginning of the year with as much as in good years, too great a quantity might be exported and famine stare us in the face before next harvest' (Smith, 1766, pp. 26–7). The later Smith, when describing the same activity, simply adds the effective metaphor of the ship's captain: 'Without intending the interest of the people, he is necessarily led, by a regard to his own interest, to treat them, even in years of scarcity, pretty much in the same manner as the prudent master of a vessel is sometimes obliged to treat his crew.' When provisions are low, 'he puts them upon short allowance' (WN IV.v.b.3).

20. Anderson, to his credit, understood perfectly the Humean principles governing the distribution of specie amongst trading nations. See Anderson, 1968 [1777], pp. 277–84.

21. This is not to say that the objections raised by Smith's contemporary critics were widely dismissed by their readers. In reviewing Pownall's critique for the *Monthly Review*, William Enfield observed that this 'first direct attack upon [*The Wealth of Nations*], coming from a very respectable quarter, and being made with no inconsiderable degree of judgment and penetration, will doubtless engage the attention of the Public and will probably be thought not unworthy of notice by the Author of the Inquiry'. But as to Pownall's defense of the bounty, Enfield did not hesitate to reveal his own skepticism of the claim 'that the bounty on the exportation of corn is a judicious expedient to relieve the relative distress under which he apprehends (*on what grounds of reasoning or experience we do not clearly see*) that the owners of land and farmers must always labour' (Anon, 1777, pp. 117, 119; emphasis added; for authorship identification, see Nangle, 1934, pp. 15, 178).

Anderson's criticism of Smith's bounty analysis elicited a more favorable evaluation from his anonymous reviewer, who concluded that: 'it is incumbent on this ingenious author either to reconcile the seeming contradictions and inaccuracies of reasoning here pointed out, or to give up the argument entirely' (Anon, 1778, p. 365; also quoted in Rashid, 1998, p. 149). Nevertheless, as Anderson's theoretical objections arise entirely from misreadings of Smith's analytical structure, Smith's apparent effort to remove the sources of those misreadings through successive refinements to the exposition in subsequent editions seems a not unreasonable response.

References

Anderson, James (1968 [1777]), *Observations on the Means of Exciting a Spirit of National Industry*, New York: Augustus M. Kelley.
Anderson, James (1801), *A Calm Investigation of the Circumstances that Have Led to the Present Scarcity of Grain in Britain*, London: Printed for John Cumming.
Anonymous (1777), 'Review of Pownall's *Letter to Adam Smith*', *Monthly Review; or, a Literary Journal*, **56** (February), 117–20.
Anonymous (1778), 'Review of Anderson's *Observations on the Means of Exciting a Spirit of National Industry*', *Monthly Review; or a Literary Journal*, **58** (May), 362–74.
Barnes, Donald G. (1961 [1930]), *A History of the English Corn Laws from 1660–1846*, New York: Augustus M. Kelley.
Blaug, Mark (1990), 'On the historiography of economics', *Journal of the History of Economic Thought*, **12** (Spring), 27–37; reprinted in Mark Blaug (1997a), *Not Only an Economist: Recent Essays*, Cheltenham, UK and Northampton, MA, USA: Edward Elgar, pp. 55–65.
Blaug, Mark (1997b), *Economic Theory in Retrospect*, Cambridge: Cambridge University Press.
Blaug, Mark (1999), 'Misunderstanding classical economics: the Sraffian interpretation of the surplus approach', *History of Political Economy*, **31** (Summer), 213–36.
Blecker, Robert A. (1997), 'The "unnatural and retrograde order": Adam Smith's theories of trade and development reconsidered', *Economica*, NS, **64** (August), 527–37.
Bowles, Paul (1986), 'Adam Smith and the "natural progress of opulence"', *Economica*, NS, **53** (February), 109–18.
Brewer, Anthony (1995), 'Rent and profit in the *Wealth of Nations*', *Scottish Journal of Political Economy*, **42** (May), 183–200.
Bryson, Gladys (1945), *Man and Society: The Scottish Inquiry of the Eighteenth Century*, Princeton, NJ: Princeton University Press.
Buchanan, David (1966 [1817]), *Observations on the Subjects Treated of in Dr. Smith's Inquiry into the Nature and Causes of the Wealth of Nations*, New York: Augustus M. Kelley.
Buckle, Henry T. (1857–61), *History of Civilization in England*; reprinted as *On Scotland and the Scotch Intellect*, H.J. Hanham (ed.) (1970), Chicago, IL: University of Chicago Press.
Campbell, R.H. and A.S. Skinner (1976), 'General introduction', to Adam Smith, *An Inquiry into the Nature and Causes of the Wealth of Nations*, Oxford: Oxford University Press.
Coats, A.W. (1975), 'Adam Smith and the mercantile system', in Andrew S. Skinner and Thomas Wilson (eds), *Essays on Adam Smith*, Oxford: Clarendon Press, pp. 218–36.
Fay, Charles R. (1932), *The Corn Laws of Social England*, Cambridge: Cambridge University Press.
Gras, Norman S.B. (1967 [1915]), *The Evolution of the English Corn Market, from the Twelfth to the Eighteenth Century*, New York: Russell & Russell.
Hicks, John R. (1976), 'Some questions of time in economics', in A.M. Tang, F.M. Westfield and J.S. Worley (eds), *Evolution, Welfare, and Time in Economics; Essays in Honor of Nicholas Georgescu-Roegen*, Lexington, MA and Toronto, Canada: Lexington Books, pp. 135–51.
Hollander, Jacob (1968 [1910]), *David Ricardo: A Centenary Estimate*, New York: Augustus M. Kelley.
Hollander, Samuel (1973), *The Economics of Adam Smith*, Toronto: University of Toronto Press.
Hollander, Samuel (1979), *The Economics of David Ricardo*, London: Heinemann Educational Books.
Hollander, Samuel (1992), *Classical Economics*, Toronto: University of Toronto Press.
Hollander, Samuel (1997), '*The Life of Adam Smith*, by Ian Simpson Ross', *Journal of Economic Literature*, **35** (June), 771–3.
Hont, Istvan and Michael Ignatieff (1985), *Wealth and Virtue: The Shaping of Political Economy in the Scottish Enlightenment*, Cambridge: Cambridge University Press.
Horner, Francis (1804), 'Observations on the bounty upon exported corn', *Edinburgh Review*, **5**; reprinted in Frank Fetter (ed.) (1957), *The Economic Writings of Francis Horner in the Edinburgh Review, 1802–6*, London: London School of Economics and Political Science, pp. 96–114.
Hueckel, Glenn (2000), 'On "the insurmountable difficulties, obscurity, and embarrassment" of Smith's fifth chapter', *History of Political Economy*, **32** (Summer), 317–45.

Hueckel, Glenn (2004), 'Walker's equilibrium: a review essay', in W.J. Samuels and J.E. Biddle (eds), *Research in the History of Economic Thought and Methodology*, 22-A, Amsterdam: JAI, pp. 259–90.
Hume, David (1752), 'Of the balance of trade', in Knud Haakonssen (ed.) (1994), *Political Essays*, Cambridge: Cambridge University Press, pp. 136–49.
Letiche, J.M. (1960), 'Adam Smith and David Ricardo on economic growth', in Bert F. Hoselitz (ed.), *Theories of Economic Growth*, New York: Free Press, pp. 65–88.
Macfie, A.L. (1967), *The Individual in Society: Papers on Adam Smith*, London: George Allen & Unwin.
Malthus, Thomas R. (1803), *Essay on the Principle of Population*, Patricia James (ed.) (1989), 2 vols, Cambridge: Cambridge University Press.
Mirowski, Philip (1982), 'Adam Smith, empiricism, and the rate of profit in eighteenth-century England', *History of Political Economy*, **14** (Summer), 178–98.
Mizuta, Hiroshi (ed.) (2000), *Adam Smith: Critical Responses*, Vol. 1: *Contemporary Response to the First of the Posthumous Works*, London: Routledge.
Nangle, Benjamin C. (1934), *The Monthly Review, First Series, 1749–1789; Indexes of Contributors and Articles*, Oxford: Clarendon Press.
Necker, Jacques (1776), *On the Legislation and the Commerce of Corn*, London: Printed for T. Longman.
O'Brien, D.P. (2004), *The Classical Economists Revisited*, Princeton, NJ: Princeton University Press.
O'Donnell, Rory (1990), *Adam Smith's Theory of Value and Distribution: a Reappraisal*, New York: St Martin's Press.
Peach, Terry (1993), *Interpreting Ricardo*, Cambridge: Cambridge University Press.
Pownall, Thomas (1776), *A Letter from Governor Pownall to Adam Smith*; reprinted as Appendix A in Smith (1987), pp. 337–76.
Prendergast, Renee (1987), 'James Anderson's political economy – His Influence on Smith and Malthus', *Scottish Journal of Political Economy*, **34** (November), 388–409.
Rae, John (1965 [1895]), *Life of Adam Smith*, New York: Augustus M. Kelley.
Rashid, Salim (1998), *The Myth of Adam Smith*, Cheltenham, UK and Lyme, NH, USA: Edward Elgar.
Ricardo, David (1951–73), *The Works and Correspondence of David Ricardo*, 11 vols, Piero Sraffra (ed.), Cambridge: Cambridge University Press.
Robinson, J. (1974), 'History versus equilibrium', *Indian Economic Journal*, **21** (January–March), 202–13; reprinted in Donald A. Walker (ed.) (2000), *Equilibrium*, Vol. I, pp. 160–71, Cheltenham, UK and Northampton, MA, USA: Edward Elgar, pp. 160–71.
Skinner, Andrew Stewart (1996), *A System of Social Science: Papers Relating to Adam Smith*, 2nd edn, Oxford: Clarendon Press.
Smith, Adam (1759), *The Theory of Moral Sentiments*, D.D. Raphael and A.L. Macfie (eds) (1976), Oxford: Clarendon Press, TMS.
Smith, Adam (1776), *An Inquiry into the Nature and Causes of the Wealth of Nations*, R.H. Campbell, A.S. Skinner and W.B. Todd (eds) (1976), Oxford: Clarendon Press, WN.
Smith, Adam (1978), *Lectures on Jurisprudence*, R.L. Meek, D.D. Raphael and P.G. Stein (eds) Oxford: Clarendon Press, LJ.
Smith, Adam (1987), *The Correspondence of Adam Smith*, 2nd edn, E.C. Mossner and I.S. Ross (eds), Oxford: Oxford University Press, Corr.
Smith, Charles (1766), *Three Tracts on the Corn Trade and Corn Laws*, London: J. Brotherton.
Steuart, James (1967 [1759, 1805]), *A Dissertation on the Policy of Grain*, in *The Works, Political, Metaphisical & Chronological of Sir James Steuart*, Vol. 5, New York: Augustus M. Kelley.
Stewart, Dugald (1980 [1794]), *Account of the Life and Writings of Adam Smith, L.L.D*; reprinted in Adam Smith (1795), *Essays on Philosophical Subjects*, W.P.D. Wrightman and J.C. Bryce (eds) (1980), Oxford: Oxford University Press.
Sugiyama, Chuhei (ed.) (1996), *Lauderdale's Notes on Adam Smith's Wealth of Nations*, London: Routledge.
Teichgraeber, Richard F., III (1987), '"Less abused than I had reason to expect": the reception of *The Wealth of Nations* in Britain, 1776–90', *Historical Journal*, **30** (2), 337–66.
Viner, Jacob (1927), 'Adam Smith and laissez faire', *Journal of Political Economy*, **35** (April), 198–232; reprinted in Jacob Viner (1958), *The Long View and the Short: Studies in Economic Theory and Policy*, Glencoe, IL: Free Press, pp. 213–45.
West, Edward (1815), *On the Application of Capital to Land*, Jacob Hollander (ed.) (1934), Baltimore, MD: Johns Hopkins University Press.
West, Edwin G. (1997), 'Adam Smith's support for money and banking regulation: a case of inconsistency', *Journal of Money Credit, and Banking*, **29** (February), 127–34.
Young, Arthur (1768), *The Farmer's Letters to the People of England*, London: printed for W. Nicoll.
Young, Jeffrey T. 2001, 'From Adam Smith to John Stuart Mill: Samuel Hollander and the classical economists', in Steven G. Medema and Warren J. Samuels (eds), *Historians of Economics and Economic Thought: The Construction of Disciplinary Memory*, London: Routledge, pp. 129–65.

14 The mercantile system
*Andrew S. Skinner**

Introduction

Mercantilism, or the 'system of commerce', to use Smith's term, was essentially policy-oriented, although even here it is necessary to avoid undue generalization. As the economic historian P.J. Thomas put it:

> Mercantilism has often been described as a definite and unified policy or doctrine, but that it has never been. In reality it was a shifting combination of tendencies which, although directed to a common aim – the increase of national power – seldom possessed a unified system of policy, or even a harmonious set of doctrines. (1926, p. 3)

A common view, associated with Gustav Schmoller's *The Mercantile System and its Historical Significance* (1896, p. 96), is that in its innermost kernel it is nothing but state-making. This view was echoed by Eli Hecksher in his classic study, *Mercantilism* (1955). Writing in the same vein, P.W. Buck observed: 'Regarded as economic strategy, aimed at the achievement of political objectives in a world of competing national states, the policies of mercantilism exhibit logical consistency' (1942, p. 35). A.W. Coates recently offered this summary of objectives as the means of attaining the desired end of an increase in national power:

- the accumulation of treasure;
- the promotion of national wealth and economic growth;
- securing a favourable balance of trade;
- maximization of employment;
- the protection of industry;
- the encouragement of population; and
- state unification (1993, p. 46; cf. Schumpeter, 1954, p. 143 and severally, pp. 143–55).

But it should be noted that if the strategy embraced a single end, the means of attaining it would inevitably vary with circumstances. The validity of the choice of policy has to be seen, therefore, against the historical circumstances which happened to prevail at the time. The strategy is consistent with regulation, but also with more liberal policies, depending on the situation confronted. Hecksher quotes a passage from Colbert, the great Minister of Finance in the reign of Louis XIV: 'His majesty has long been aware, on account of his great experience, that liberty is the soul of trade and desires that merchants should have complete freedom to do as they wish, that they may be induced to bring thither their foodstuffs and merchandise' (1955, Vol. 2, p. 274).

Smith's assessment of Colbert was that while 'a man of probity, of great industry and knowledge of detail', he had 'unfortunately embraced all the prejudices of the mercantile system, in its nature and essence a system of restraint and regulation, and such as could scarce fail to be agreeable to a laborious and plodding man of business' (WN IV.ix.3). Such a judgement lacks a degree of objectivity and is essentially ahistorical, in that Smith does not provide the reader with the means of judging the circumstances which Colbert actually confronted. As D.C. Coleman has noted, an 'understanding of the contemporary economic situation may be a better guide to contemporary recommendations than a criticism of policy'; a point echoed by A.V. Judges, writing in the same volume (Coleman, 1969, p. 15).

Smith did not in fact provide an analysis of the policies which might have been associated with the 'mercantilist' position in its international and historical setting. Rather, he made it clear in the introduction to Book IV of the *Wealth of Nations* that he intended to address the 'system of commerce' since it was 'the modern system, and is best understood in our own country and in our own times'. In short, Smith was concerned with contemporary evidence in the context of the experience of Great Britain.

The preoccupation with British experience was further confirmed in a letter to Andreas Holt, dated October 1780. Smith himself referred to 'the very violent attack I had made upon the whole commercial system of Great Britain' (*Corr.* 208), and the reader will find ample evidence in Book IV of *The Wealth of Nations*. For example, Smith drew attention to the key role of merchants in defining policy, referring to arguments 'addressed by merchants to Parliaments, and to the Councils of Princes . . . by those who were supposed to understand trade, to those who were conscious to themselves that they knew nothing about the matter' (IV.i.10). Elsewhere, Smith consistently drew attention to the pernicious effects of the mercantile interest, to its members' 'mean rapacity' and 'impertinent jealousy' (IV.iii.c.9).

A.W. Coates has recently suggested that even Smith's admirers have been embarrassed by the decidedly polemical tone of these sections of the *Wealth of Nations*, citing as an example Hecksher's judgement that the whole was 'an emphatic piece of free trade propaganda' (1993, p. 140). While there is some truth in these assertions, nonetheless this aspect of the WN is informative with respect to the message which Smith wished to convey.

The doctrines which Smith associated with the 'pretended doctors' of the system were, first, their alleged belief that wealth consisted in money, and second, the associated belief that the purposes of the state could best be secured by attaining a positive balance of trade. Smith dismissed the first thesis as 'ridiculous' (WN IV.i.17), and the doctrine of the positive balance as 'absurd' (WN IV.ii.c.2). Elsewhere he referred to 'that most insignificant object of modern policy, the balance of trade' (WN IV.vi.13). He concluded: 'National prejudice and animosity, prompted always by the private interests of particular traders, are the principles which generally direct our judgment upon all questions concerning it' (WN IV.iii.a.4). It was this prejudice and animosity which prevented France and Great Britain from enjoying the mutual benefits of free trade. Smith's argument, which echoes that associated with David Hume, had already been forcibly expressed in his *Lectures*:

> From the above considerations it appears that Great Britain should by all means be made a free port, that there should be no interruptions of any kind to foreign trade . . . and that free commerce and liberty of exchange should be allowed with all nations, and for all things. (LJ(B) 514)

In addressing the mercantile preoccupation with a positive balance of trade, Smith concluded that: 'Its two great engines, for enriching the country . . . were restraints upon importation, and encouragement to exportation' (WN IV.i.35). Smith then proceeded to discuss each of the instruments which could be used to support these objectives, adding in a significant passage:

> I shall consider each of them in a particular chapter, and without taking much further notice of their supposed tendency to bring money into the country, I shall examine chiefly what are likely to be the effects of each of them upon the annual produce of its industry. According as they tend either to increase or diminish the value of this annual produce, they must evidently tend either to increase or diminish the real wealth and revenue of the country. (WN IV.i.45)

The true purpose of Smith's argument was to demonstrate the dangers of regulation in so far as it involved distortion in the use of resources, while also affecting the rate of economic growth:

> No regulation of commerce can increase the quantity of industry in any society beyond what its capital can maintain. It can only divert a part of it into a direction into which it might not otherwise have gone: and it is by no means certain that this artificial direction is likely to be more advantageous to the society than that into which it would have gone of its own accord. (WN IV.ii.3)

In Smith's eyes, regulation is liable to 'that general objection which may be made to all the different expedients of the mercantile system; the objection of forcing some part of the industry of the country into a channel less advantageous than that in which it would run of its own accord' (WN IV.v.a.24). It was his emphatic belief that: 'All the different regulations of the mercantile system, necessarily derange more or less this natural and most advantageous distribution of stock' (WN IV.vii.c.87). The language recalls that of the *Lectures*, where Smith drew attention to the point that intervention with the economic system must disturb the 'natural balance of industry' and the 'natural connection of all trades in the stock' (LJ(B) 498–9). But in Book IV of *The Wealth of Nations*, the illustration of the dangers of intervention is offered in the context of two theses which were developed in Books II and III – the first being that the rate of growth would be affected by the area of investment to which a specific injection of capital was applied (WN II.v), and the second that the most natural order of development, and the one which would maximize the opportunities for economic growth, would feature investment in agriculture, manufactures and trade (domestic and foreign) in that order (WN III.i). It was these theses which were to be deployed in Smith's critique of the centrepiece of the mercantile system – the colonial relationship with America.

When Smith returned to London in 1773 to finish work on *The Wealth of Nations*, the delay in finishing the book was attributed by some, notably David Hume, to his growing preoccupation with the American problem. Hume wrote in February 1776 to complain: 'By all Accounts, your Book has been printed long ago; yet it has never yet been so much as advertised. What is the Reason? If you wait till the Fate of America be decided, you may wait long' (*Corr.* p. 185). That Smith's interest in the American question caused the delay is certainly plausible. The colonies are scarcely mentioned in the lectures delivered in 1762–63, but feature in what is almost a separate monograph in *The Wealth of Nations*, in the form of the long, three-part Chapter 7 of Book IV. In this place, Smith reviewed the options open to the British government during the mid-1770s, passages which led Hugh Blair to complain that Smith had given the issues involved: 'a representation etc. which I wish had been omitted, because it is too much like a publication for the present moment. In Subsequent editions when publick Measures come to be Settled, these pages will fall to be omitted or Altered' (*Corr.* p. 188).

But Smith's real purpose in *The Wealth of Nations* Book IV was to produce a searching critique of the mercantile system by exposing the inconsistencies of policy with regard to the American colonies. With this end in view, he offered an examination of the thinking behind the regulating Acts of trade and navigation before proceeding to explain why current policy must change at some point, offering a rational solution to the problems which were in due course bound to be exposed as well as to those which were unfolding as he sat in London. Smith's preferred solution, as we shall see, was union and the creation in effect of an Atlantic Economic Community.

The regulating Acts
In describing the objectives of colonial policy, Smith concentrated mainly on its economic aspects and duly reported on the extensive range of restrictions which Britain had imposed on trade and manufactures, domestic as well as American. To begin with, the regulating Acts of navigation required that trade between the colonies and Great Britain had to be carried on in British ships, and that certain classes of commodities were to be confined initially to the market of the mother country. These so-called 'enumerated' goods were of two types: those which were either the peculiar produce of America or were not produced in Britain, and those goods which were produced in Britain but in insufficient quantities to meet domestic demand. Examples of the first type were molasses, coffee and tobacco; of the second, naval stores, masts, pig-iron and copper. The first broad category of goods was not of a kind which could harm British industry, and here the object of policy, as reported by Smith, was to ensure that British merchants could buy cheaper in the colonies with a view to supplying other countries at higher prices, and at the same time establish a useful carrying trade. In the second case, the objective was to ensure essential supplies and, through the careful use of duties, to discourage imports from other countries 'with which the balance of trade was supposed to be unfavourable' (WN IV.vii.b.35). Smith also took notice of another feature of British policy, namely that the production of the more 'advanced or more refined manufactures' was discouraged in the colonies (WN IV.vii.b.40). Thus woollen manufactures were forbidden, and although they were encouraged to export pig-iron, the colonists were prevented from erecting more refined mills which might have led ultimately to the development of manufactures competitive with those of Great Britain. There was a certain ingenuity in these arrangements in that the colonial relationship could be seen to benefit both parties, at least in the short run. For example, the relationship with the colonies, as defined by the regulating Acts, had the effect of creating a self-supporting economic unit whose main components provided complementary markets for each others' products, and in addition helped to minimize gold flows abroad (WN IV.viii.15). By the same token, the colonial relationship gave Britain access to strategic materials, and also contributed to national defence, through the encouragement given to her mercantile marine.

Smith also argued that there were considerable opportunities for economic growth within the framework of the colonial relationship. In this connection he placed most emphasis on American experience, and drew attention to three factors which contributed to explain her rapid rate of expansion. First, Smith isolated what may be described as 'institutional' forces in pointing out that the colonies possessed political institutions derived from the British model, which encouraged economic activity by guaranteeing the security of the individual (WN IV.vii.b.51).

In the same way he pointed out that the colonists had brought to an underdeveloped territory the habit of subordination and a 'knowledge of agriculture and of other useful arts' (WN IV.vii.b.2); the legacy of the more developed economies from which they had often come. Smith also emphasized that certain features were absent from the colonies, of a kind which contributed to slow up the rate of growth in Europe: for example, high rents, tithes and taxes, together with legal arrangements such as laws of entail which hindered the sale of lands to those whose object was to improve them.

Secondly, he drew attention to the economic situation of the colonial territories in pointing out that: 'A new colony must always for some time be more under-stocked in proportion to the extent of territory, and more under-peopled in proportion to the extent of its stock, than the greater part of other countries' (WN I.ix.11). This meant that the rates of both wages and profits were likely to be high, thus contributing to a level of activity which explained the 'continual complaint of the scarcity of hands in North America. The demand for labourers, the funds destined for maintaining them, increase, it seems, still faster than they can find labourers to employ' (WN I.viii.23).

Thirdly, Smith argued that the legislative arrangements governing trade with the mother country had contributed most materially to colonial development even though this had not always been the motive behind them. In this connection he drew attention to the fact that 'the most perfect freedom of trade is permitted between the British colonies of America and the West Indies', thus providing a 'great and extensive market' for their products (WN IV.vii.b.39). In addition, the relative freedom of trade in non-enumerated commodities provided a further market for the primary products involved, while Britain also gave preferential treatment to American products which were confined to her own domestic market. Again, Britain provided a large European market (albeit indirectly) for the enumerated items – for example, goods like tobacco which were largely re-exported.

Taken as a whole, the colonial policy had the effect of encouraging what Smith described as 'Agriculture . . . the proper business of all new colonies; a business which the cheapness of land renders more advantageous than any other' (WN IV.vii.c.51). This point is of great importance, since on Smith's argument agriculture was the most productive of all forms of investment, capable of generating large surpluses which could sustain further growth. He even argued that the restrictions imposed on the introduction of manufactures had benefited the colonies by ensuring that they bought from the cheaper European markets and therefore avoided diverting any part of the available capital into less productive employments. He concluded:

> Unjust, however, as such prohibitions may be, they have not hitherto been very hurtful to the colonies. Land is still so cheap, and, consequently, labour so dear among them, that they can import from the mother country, almost all the more refined or more advanced manufactures cheaper than they could make them for themselves. Though they had not, therefore, been prohibited from establishing such manufactures, yet in their present state of improvement, a regard to their own interest would, probably, have prevented them from doing so. (WN IV.vii.44)

There is no doubt as to the buoyancy of Smith's tone in describing the growth rate of North America: a country where the benefits available, natural, artificial and accidental, were such as to prompt the conclusion that 'though North America is not yet so rich as England, it is much more thriving, and advancing with much greater rapidity to the further acquisition of riches' (WN I.viii.23).

At the same time, it cannot be said that Smith minimized the benefits to Britain from the standpoint of economic growth. In this connection he pointed out that Britain (together with her neighbours) had as a matter of fact acquired, through the control of the colonies, a 'new and inexhaustible market' which had given occasion to 'new divisions of labour and improvements of art'. Indeed, it can be said that Smith's assertion of benefit accruing to Great Britain as a result of the colonial relationship simply reflects his own grasp of the gains from trade (WN IV.i.32). Smith's argument seems designed to suggest that the colonial relationship had both contributed to, and proved compatible with, a relatively high rate of growth in both the colonies and the mother country.

The contradictions of the system

The relationship between the mother country and the colonies is thus represented as beneficial to the two parties, both as regards the politico-economic objectives of the regulating Acts and the stimulus given to economic growth. But at the same time Smith evidently believed that there were contradictions inherent in the colonial relationship which must begin to manifest themselves over time. For example, while Smith took pains to emphasize the great stimulus given to the growth of the colonies, he also pointed out that the high and rapid rate of growth which they had attained must ultimately come in conflict with the restrictions imposed on colonial trade and manufactures; restrictions which could be regarded as the 'principal badge of their dependency' (WN IV.vii.c.64) and as a 'manifest violation of one of the most sacred rights of mankind'. He also pointed out that:

> In their present state of improvement, those prohibitions, perhaps, without cramping their industry, or restraining it from any employment to which it would have gone of its own accord, are only impertinent badges of slavery . . . In a more advanced state they might be really oppressive and insupportable. (WN IV.vii.b.44)

Smith quite clearly considered that in the long run some change must come in the colonial relationship for the reason just stated, although he did place most emphasis on the more immediate problems faced by Britain herself, as providing the stimulus for change.

As far as Great Britain was concerned Smith contended that although the colony trade was 'upon the whole beneficial, and greatly beneficial' (WN IV.vii.c.47), still the rate of growth was necessarily lower than it would have been in the absence of the regulating Acts. He quite clearly believed that: 'If the manufactures of Great Britain . . . have been advanced, as they certainly have, by the colony trade, it has not been by means of the monopoly of that trade, but in spite of the monopoly' (WN IV.vii.c.55). Smith advanced a number of points in support of this contention. First, he suggested that the monopoly of the colony trade had inevitably increased the volume of business to be done by a relatively limited amount of British capital and, therefore, the prevailing rate of profit. In this connection he argued that high rates of profit would affect the improvement of land (WN IV.vii.c.58) and the frugality of the merchant classes (WN IV.vii.c.61) while ensuring that available capital would be partly drawn, and partly driven, from those trades where Britain lacked the monopoly (that is, drawn by the higher profits available in the colony trade, and driven from them by a poorer competitive position).

But Smith especially emphasized that the pattern of British trade had been altered in such a way that her manufactures,

> instead of being suited, as before the act of navigation, to the neighbouring market of Europe, or to the more distant one of the countries which lie round the Mediterranean sea, have, the greater part of them, been accommodated to the still more distant one of the colonies. (WN IV.vii.c.22)

Smith's point was that the existing legislation had drawn capital from trades carried on with a near market (Europe), and diverted it to trade carried on with a distant market (America), while forcing a certain amount of capital from a direct to an indirect foreign trade; with consequent effects, he alleged, on the rate of return, the employment of productive labour, and, therefore, the rate of economic growth.

Smith added that the pattern of British trade had been altered in such a way as to make her unduly dependent on a single (though large) market:

> Her commerce, instead of running in a great number of small channels, has been taught to run principally in one great channel. But the whole system of her industry and commerce has thereby been rendered less secure; the whole state of her body politick less healthful, than it otherwise would have been. In her present condition, Great Britain resembles one of those unwholesome bodies in which some of the vital parts are overgrown, and which, upon that account, are liable to many dangerous disorders scarce incident to those in which all the parts are more properly proportioned. (WN IV.vii.C.43)

But Smith's account of the problem facing Great Britain is largely dominated by that of fiscal need. In Smith's opinion Britain's needs seemed to be growing more rapidly than her resources, and he noted in this connection that by January 1775 the national debt had reached the then astronomical figure of £130 million (absorbing £4.5 million in interest charges), much of which was due to the acquisition of the colonial territories. This was a matter of some moment since it meant that a country whose rate of growth had been adversely affected by the colonial relationship had to face a large and probably growing tax burden which would itself affect the rate of economic expansion, and thus compound the problem.

Smith thus concluded that Great Britain must in the course of time either solve the fiscal problem or abandon it, in the latter case accommodating 'her future views and designs to the real mediocrity of her circumstances' (WN V.iii.92).

A rational solution: the project of empire
It was Smith's contention that:

> The rulers of Great Britain have, for more than a century past, amused the people with the imagination that they possessed a great empire on the west side of the Atlantic. This empire, however, has hitherto existed in imagination only. It has hitherto been, not an empire, but the project of an empire ... If the project cannot be completed, it ought to be given up. (WN V.iii.92)

Yet Smith believed that the project of empire could be completed and that the tensions actual and potential which were present in the existing colonial relationship could be resolved by the creation of an Atlantic Economic Community which would establish 'an immense internal market for every part of the produce of all its different provinces' (WN V.iii.72).

Smith made a number of important points in connection with this thesis. First, he argued that Great Britain both could and should tax the colonies, partly as a means of relief from the growing burden of the national debt and partly as a means of making the colonies pay for benefits received from the imperial connection. It is worth noting that Smith did not defend colonial taxation on the ground that Britain had planted the colonies; on the contrary, he pointed out that they had been originally peopled largely as the result of religious persecution (WN vii.b.61). Nor did he suggest that taxation was justified on the ground that the mother country had originally invested in their improvement; on the contrary, he insisted that policy to regulate the colonies had only been implemented after the original colonists had made significant economic progress (WN IV.vii.B.63). He added:

> It is not contrary to justice that both Ireland and America should contribute towards the discharge of the publick debt of Great Britain. That debt has been contracted in support of the government established by the Revolution, a government to which the protestants of Ireland owe, not only the whole authority which they at present enjoy in their own country, but every security which they possess for their liberty, their property, and their religion; a government to which several of the colonies of America owe their present charters, and consequently their present constitution, and to which all the colonies of America owe the liberty, security, and property which they have ever since enjoyed. That publick debt has been contracted in the defence, not of Great Britain alone, but of all the different provinces of the empire; the immense debt contracted in the late war in particular, and a great part of that contracted in the war before, were both properly contracted in defence of America. (WN V.iii.88)

Having made a point which commanded a good deal of support in contemporary Britain, Smith went on to consider how such a policy might be implemented and what its consequences might be. To begin with, he suggested that the colonies might be taxed by their own assemblies, a proposition no sooner stated than rejected on the ground that colonial assemblies cannot be supposed to be the proper judges of the needs of the empire as a whole (WN IV.vii.c.70). Secondly, he suggested that taxes might be levied by requisition, which was the current practice: 'the parliament of Great Britain determining the sum which each colony ought to pay, and the provincial assembly assessing and levying it in the way that suited best the circumstances of the province' (WN IV.vii.c.71). Such a system had some obvious advantages in Smith's opinion, especially in that it left the central and colonial governments with important and appropriate areas of control. But this solution too was rejected, partly because he felt that the mother country might face some difficulty in actually extracting the revenue required (a point confirmed by British experience during the war with France), and partly because central control of taxation might have adverse repercussions as a result of its political consequences in America itself. Taxation by requisition and without representation would, Smith felt, effectively reduce the power and status of the colonial assemblies and, therefore, that of:

> all the leading men of British America who like those of other countries, desire to preserve their own importance. They feel, or imagine, that if their assemblies, which they are fond of calling parliaments, and of considering as equal in authority to the parliament of Great Britain, should be so far degraded as to become the humble ministers and executive officers of that parliament, the greater part of their importance would be at an end.

Smith noted that the Americans 'have rejected therefore, the proposals of being taxed by parliamentary requisition, and like other ambitious and high-spirited men, have rather chosen to draw the sword in defence of their own importance' (WN IV.vii.c.74).

Smith concluded that the British government should retain the right of assessment but extend the British system of taxation to all the colonies. The concluding sections of *The Wealth of Nations* were largely concerned with the technical problems of this aspect of harmonization, and Smith saw no reason to suppose that the major British taxes (land tax, stamp duties, customs and excise) could not be successfully applied to both America and Ireland. He added that such a change of policy would require a form of union which would give the colonies representation in the British Parliament and in effect create a single state:

> This, however, could scarce, perhaps, be done, consistently with the principles of the British constitution, without admitting into the British parliament, or if you will into the states-general of the British Empire, a fair and equal representation of all those different provinces, that of each province bearing the same proportion to the produce of its taxes, as the representation of Great Britain might bear to the produce of the taxes levied upon Great Britain. (WN V.iii.68)

Indeed, Smith believed that:

> there is not the least probability that the British constitution would be hurt by the union of Great Britain with her colonies. That constitution, on the contrary, would be completed by it, and seems to be imperfect without it. The assembly which deliberates and decides concerning the affairs of every part of the empire, in order to be properly informed, ought certainly to have representatives from every part of it. (WN IV.vii.c.77)

As to the colonists:

> Instead of piddling for the little prizes which are to be found in what may be called the paltry raffle of colony faction; they might then hope, from the presumption which men naturally have in their own ability and good fortune, to draw some of the great prizes which sometimes come from the wheel of the great state lottery of British politicks. (WN IV.vii.c.75)

He added that union would also deliver the colonists:

> from those rancourous and virulent factions which are inseparable from small democracies . . . [and] which have so frequently divided the affections of their people, and disturbed the tranquillity of their governments, in their form so nearly democratical.

Indeed Smith believed that the colonists would regret the loss of this opportunity (*Corr.* p. 384).

What Smith had in mind was an incorporating union of the kind introduced by the Act of 1707 and which was later extended to Ireland. But the union which Smith envisaged was distinctive in that he foresaw the eventual transfer of power from Westminster to the former colonies. It was Smith's view that America's progress 'in wealth, population and improvement' had been, and would continue to be, so rapid that:

> in the course of little more than a century, perhaps, the produce of American might exceed that of British taxation. The seat of empire would then naturally remove itself to that part

of the empire which contributed most to the general defence and support of the whole. (WN IV.vii.c.79)

The belief that America would in the long run prove to be the dominant influence also attracted a good deal of support. Thomas Pownall, for example, had already noted that America would become the major partner in his proposed 'grant marine dominion' and so too had his friend Benjamin Franklin, both in his *Observations* and in correspondence with Lord Kames:

> Scotland and Ireland are differently circumstanced. Confined by the sea, they can scarcely increase in numbers, wealth and strength, so as to overbalance England. But America, an immense territory, favoured by Nature with all advantages of climate, soil, great navigable rivers, and lakes, etc. must become a great country, populous and mighty; and will, in less time than is generally conceived, be able to shake off any shackles that may be imposed on her, and perhaps place them on the imposers. (Ross, 1972, pp. 340–41)

The implications of this position began to attract the attention of economists in the early part of the nineteenth century (Romani, 1993).

In this political context Smith's preference for union raises some interesting questions. Did he have in mind a form of association which would create a single economic and political union; an enormous free trade area of the kind which a later generation was to envisage for Europe, but with the advantage of a common language and culture? Or was the union which he envisaged designed to generate a position of global dominance for an Anglo-American empire? Whatever the reason, by the time Smith published *The Wealth of Nations* an opportunity had been lost: 'We, on this side of the water, are afraid lest the multitude of American representatives should overturn the balance of the constitution', he wrote, while those 'on the other side of the water are afraid lest their distance from the seat of government might expose them to many oppressions' (WN IV.vii.c.78). His tone had hardened further in his 'Memorandum on the American War' in 1778: '[I]n their present elevation of spirits', he advised Wedderbum, 'the ulcerated minds of the Americans are not likely to consent to any union even upon terms the most advantageous to themselves' (*Corr*. p. 381, App. B). In Britain, he wrote, the plan of union 'seems not to be agreeable to any considerable party of men'. He concluded, sadly, that:

> The plan which, if it could be executed, would certainly tend most to the prosperity, to the splendour, and to the duration of the empire, if you except here and there a solitary philosopher like myself, seems scarce to have a single advocate. (*Corr*. 382)

Assessment
First, it should be noted that Smith's analysis of the economic performance of the colonies and of the mother country rests very heavily on his thesis of the natural progress of opulence and the consequent belief that any derangement of the natural balance of industry would slow down the rate of growth. In particular, it would appear that Smith made much of the point that the colonial trade transferred capital from a near to a distant market where the rate of return was slower, and that he relied heavily on the (relative) decline in Britain's taxable capacity, as the source of her problems. However, there is remarkably little by way of verification of these critical points. As Koebner had pointed out, Smith 'did not take the trouble to check' many of his suppositions (1961,

pp. 229–30), and a similar criticism was voiced by a contemporary of Smith's, Governor Pownall of Massachusetts. The Governor questioned Smith's assertion that the rate of return was slower in the American as compared to the European trade, and insisted that the matter of diversion of stock from Europe to America was 'a matter of fact, which must not be established by an argument *a priori* – but on an actual deduction of facts ... I did not find the latter in your book' (1776, p. 41; *Corr.* 369, App. A).

Pownall made an even shrewder point when he recognised that Smith was using theses established in earlier parts of the book (II and III) as proven principles in another. For example, he recognized the central importance of Smith's views on the productivities of investment:

> In that part, however, which explains the different effect of different employments of capital ... I will beg to arrest your steps for a moment, while we examine the ground whereon we tread: and the more so, as I find these propositions used in the second part of your work as data; whence you endeavour to prove, that the monopoly of the colony trade is a disadvantageous commercial institution. (1776, p. 23; *Corr.* 354)

The Governor also drew attention to the style of Smith's argument in the course of a discussion of Britain's potential losses arising from the colonial relationship:

> It strikes me as material, and I am sure, therefore, you will excuse me making in this place, one remark *on the manner* of your argument, and how you *stretch your reasoning nicely*. You in words advance upon the ground of *probable reasons for believing* only, you prove by probable suppositions only; yet most people who read your book, will think you mean to set up an absolute proof, and your conclusion is drawn as though you had. (1776, p. 40; *Corr.* 369)

Writing much later, Richard Koebner made a similar point in adverting to the fact that Smith often presents views on the colonial issue in such a way that they appear, at first sight, to be 'unavoidable inferences' from his argument as a whole. As Koebner remarked:

> Adam Smith took care to have his reflections on the American problem organically woven into the context of his great systematic work. They could appear at first sight as unavoidable inferences of [a] consistent and comprehensive argument. (1961, p. 227)

Pownall's assessment of this part of the WN was undoubtedly acute – especially when we recall that WN was published on 9 March 1776 and that Pownall's *Letter* was dated 15 September and produced in the same year. But at the same time it must be noted that Smith's treatment of the colonial relationship does not depend entirely on the theses which Pownell attacked. The crucial point, as noted above, was that the rate of growth in America had exceeded that of Great Britain and would continue to do so: 'though North America is not yet so rich as England, it is much more thriving and advancing with much greater rapidity to the further acquisition of riches' (WN I.viii.23).

Secondly, it is worth emphasizing that Smith did not regard the existing economic links as the source of immediate danger. He noted that current restrictions affecting the colonies 'in their present state of improvement' (WN IV.vii.44) were not disadvantageous; a point which may reflect Smith's understanding that the economic 'folly' of the present system was not an immediate but rather a long-term problem. Yet little was made of this point, perhaps on the ground that it would weaken his carefully articulated case.

Smith obscured the fact that regulations after 1763 marked a major shift from a mercantile policy based on trade regulation towards an imperial policy based upon territorial aggrandisement and control: 'imperialism not mercantilism . . . was the first cause of the eventual rupture' (Andrews, 1924 [1942, 1961], pp. 122, 128–9). Such a sentiment reflects American opinion at the time and is illustrated by the text of the Continental Association of 1774 whose members found that:

> the present unhappy situation of our affairs is occasioned by the ruinous system of colony administration, adopted by the British ministry about the year 1763, evidently calculated for enslaving these colonies, and with them, the British empire. (Morris, 1970, p. 135)

In addition it should be noted that the regulating Acts which were so marked a feature of mercantile policy and which were regarded by Smith as unjust violations of natural liberty, were not at the time seen in this light by the colonists themselves. As Franklin pointed out in his examination before the House of Commons: 'The authority of Parliament was allowed to be valid in all laws, except such as should lay internal taxes. It was never disputed in laying duties to regulate commerce.'

As David Stevens (1975) has noted: 'Even when the First Continental Congress convened in 1774, the delegates, whom Dr Johnson was to call "croaker of calamity" and "demigods of independence", showed little opposition to the "old system".' In Resolve No. 4 of the Suffolk Resolves, he continued, it was stated that:

> We cheerfully consent to the operation of such acts of the British Parliament as are bona fide, restrained to the regulation of our external commerce, for the purpose of securing the commercial advantage of the whole empire to the mother country, and the commercial benefits of its respective members, excluding every idea of taxation internal or external, for raising a revenue on the subjects without their consent. (Stevens 1975, p. 213; cf. Crowley, 1993, pp. 29, 30)

It is interesting to observe in this connection that neither the Declaration of Colonial Rights and Grievances nor the Declaration of Independence, which included a comprehensive indictment of British policy, contained any critical reference to the Acts of trade and navigation. As Oliver Dickerson has pointed out, colonial objections to British policy after 1763 were 'not because they were trade regulations but because they were not laws of that kind' (1951, p. 295).

Thirdly, there was a constitutional dimension to the debate. On the one hand there was the colonists' contention, shared by Smith, that there should be 'no taxation without representation'; a belief which was aptly illustrated by Franklin's evidence when he appeared before the House of Commons in 1766 where he stated the view of his colleagues in these terms: 'They understood it thus; by the same charter, and otherwise, they are entitled to all the privileges and liberties of Englishmen . . . that one of the privileges of English subjects is, that they are not to be taxed without their common consent' (Morris, 1970, p. 85).

On the other hand there were complications presented by the doctrine of Parliamentary sovereignty which Smith did not mention. As Beloff put it:

> there was a single tradition of opposition to arbitrary government which went back to the struggles of the seventeenth century. In Great Britain it had come to serve as the foundation for a

theory of parliamentary sovereignty, in America as the basis of a theory of limited government. (1949, p. 6; cf. Crowley, 1993, pp. 26–9)

The dilemma is illustrated by the terms of the Declaratory Act of 1766. This Act accompanied the repeal of the Stamp Act but took the opportunity to state, despite the repeal, that the King in Parliament: 'had, hath, and of right ought to have, full power and authority to make laws and statutes of sufficient force and validity to bind the colonies and people of America, subjects of the Crown of Great Britain, in all cases whatsoever' (Morris, 1970, p. 87).

It might even be suggested that the state of conflict with America confirmed a contradiction other than the one which Smith had identified, namely, the contradiction inherent in the dogma of parliamentary sovereignty which was to Britain affirmation of her freedom from arbitrary power and to the American colonists confirmation of their subjection to it. Smith's assertion in 1783 that, 'It is unnecessary, I apprehend, at present to say anything further, in order to expose the folly of a system, which fatal experience has now sufficiently exposed' (WN IV.viii), needs careful consideration and may qualify the success of his 'violent attack' on a key feature of current mercantile policy. The critique of regulation remains unscathed, in principle, however. But there was one political dimension which Smith did not neglect. Having rejected, with regret, the possibility of union and accepted the likelihood of military defeat, Smith suggested that a third option open to the British government was simplicity itself – voluntary withdrawal from the conflict and recognition of America as a separate state. The advantages of such a bold course were, in Smith's opinion, immense. At one stroke, Britain would be free of the crushing burden of expenditure needed to defend the colonies and could avoid further conflict with France and Spain, at least in the New World. As Smith wrote in *The Wealth of Nations*: 'By thus parting good friends, the natural affection of the colonies to the mother country, which, perhaps, our late dissensions have well nigh extinguished, would quickly revive' (WN IV.vii.c.66).

Even if the two countries were to part with some evidence of bad feeling, he advised Wedderburn, 'the similarity of language and manners would in most cases dispose the Americans to prefer our alliance to that of any other nation' (*Corr.* 333). Yet withdrawal from the conflict was unlikely:

> Such sacrifices, though they might frequently be agreeable to the interest, are always mortifying to the pride of every nation, and what is perhaps of still greater consequence, they are always contrary to the private interest of the governing part of it. (WN V.vii.c.66)

He further elaborated this point in his 'Memorandum' of 1778:

> [T]ho' this termination of the war might be really advantageous, it would not, in the eyes of Europe, appear honourable to Great Britain; and when her empire was so much curtailed, her power and dignity would be supposed to be proportionably diminished. What is of still greater importance, it could scarce fail to discredit the government in the eyes of our own people, who would probably impute to maladministration what might, perhaps, be no more than the unavoidable effect of the natural and necessary course of things. (*Corr.* 383)

He continued:

> A government which, in times of the most profound peace, of the highest public prosperity, when the people had scarce even the pretext of a single grievance to complain of, has not always

been able to make itself respected by them, would have everything to fear from their rage and indignation at the public disgrace and calamity, for such they would suppose it to be, of thus dismembering the empire. (*Corr.* 383)

An evocative phrase for a later generation. Once again, it appears that the impediment to a rational solution was not economic in character, but political, the constraint being that of public opinion both national and international.

An essay in persuasion?
As we have seen, there are two sides to Smith's treatment of the American question. The first relates to his comments on the events as they unfolded in the 1770s. The volume of this material in WN probably led Alexander Wedderburn to seek Smith's advice in the aftermath of Saratoga.

On the other hand there is the serious business of the critique of the mercantile system as illustrated by the most important aspect of Smith's handling of the American question. As we have seen, Smith's critique of the mercantile system, and his emphasis upon the inevitability of a change in policy at some stage, rests heavily on his deployment of these associated with his treatment of the natural progress of opulence and of the different productivities of capital. This approach is open to the kind of criticism voiced by writers as far apart as Pownall and Kroebner.

It is also evident that Smith's account of the colonial problem does not provide the economist as commentator with any real understanding of the fact that the immediate (as distinct from the long-run) source of the difficulty was not rooted in mercantile policy. And yet Smith could write in 1783, the year of the third edition of *The Wealth of Nations* and of peace with America, that, 'It is unnecessary, I apprehend, to say anything further in order to expose the folly of a system which fatal experience has now sufficiently exposed' (WN IV.viii.15). The inference is seemingly unavoidable, namely that Smith's critique of the mercantile system had been confirmed by the loss of the colonies. To paraphrase one aspect of the discussion of justice in the *Theory of Moral Sentiments* (TMS), the reader is in effect invited to judge 'by the event and not by the design' (TMS II.iii.3.2). The interpretation may suggest that Smith's purpose was in part at least rhetorical.

Although these two main sides of Smith's argument are not always linked with the precision we might expect, it is interesting to observe the degree of elaboration which each receives and the juxtaposition in which they are placed, for, by so doing, Smith lent additional weight to each. The analysis of the mercantile fallacy with its emphasis on the natural progress of opulence gains in plausibility from the existence of the difficulties currently faced by Great Britain, just as these difficulties gain an additional dimension from being presented as the inevitable consequence of the fallacy itself. Smith may, in short, have written to persuade by producing an argument cast in such a way 'that the several parts, being thus connected, gain a considerable strength by the appearance of probability and connection' (LRBL ii.205–6). It would seem to be entirely possible that Smith's analysis, developed as it is in terms of a gradually changing focus, was organized in such a way as to attract the agreement of the reader in the manner of some advocate appealing to the jury. Smith may be seen to have presented his case in such a way that

> though he can bring proof of very few particulars, yet the connection there is makes them easily comprehended and consequently agreeable, so that when the adversary tries to contradict any

of these particulars it is pulling down a fabric with which we are generally pleased and are very unwilling to give up. (LRBL ii.196)

If this conclusion seems somewhat finely drawn, two points should be borne in mind. First, Smith was the author of a sophisticated series of lectures on rhetoric which were designed to illustrate the powers of the human mind and the manner in which we organize discourse in order to appeal to those whom we wish to teach. Secondly, it may be recalled that Smith was acutely aware of the fact that the connection with America had brought the mercantile system a degree of 'splendour and glory which it could never otherwise have attained to' (WN IV.vii.c.81). This key fact is not denied, so that even if Smith did regard mercantile policy as but the reflection of the mean and parochial habits of second-rate shopkeepers he may well have recognized, writing in the early 1770s, that it was necessary to rely on more convincing arguments in disposing of its claims. If Smith did delay publication in order to add to or modify his section on America, it is little wonder. He may well have perceived the exciting possibility of using the difficulties of the moment to 'confirm' the 'truth' of his own principles while at the same time striking a telling blow where he believed it was most needed. In 1776 Smith was still seeking to persuade and still on the offensive. By 1783, he could write as if his case had been confirmed by events, and with a degree of confidence which would have been inappropriate ten years earlier when he was in London.

America, in short, has acquired the status of an experiment which 'confirmed' Smith's theses; one which could be allowed to remain in *The Wealth of Nations* as a kind of permanent exhibit. Of course, no such conclusion can be established beyond a shadow of doubt, but if the case is plausible it counsels caution in the interpretation of this part of Smith's work.

Note
* This chapter draws upon four previous attempts, all with different emphases (Skinner, 1990, 1996, 1999, 2001). References to Smith's works follow the usages of the Glasgow edition.

Bibliography
Andrews, C.M. (1924), *The Colonial Background of the American Revolution*, New Haven, CT: Yale University Press; revised 1942 and 1961.
Beer, G.L. (1933), *British Colonial Policy, 1754–1765*, New York: Macmillan.
Beloff, M. (1949), *The Debate on the American Revolution 1761–1783*, London: Nicholas Kaye.
Benians, E.A. (1925), 'Adam Smith's project of an empire', *Cambridge Historical Journal*, **1** (3), 249–83.
Buck, P.W. (1942), *The Politics of Mercantilism*, New York: Holt.
Coates, A.W. (1975), 'Adam Smith and the mercantile system', in Andrew Skinner and Thomas Wilson (eds), *Essays on Adam Smith*, Oxford: Clarendon Press, pp. 218–36.
Coates, A.W. (1993), *On the History of Economic Thought: British and American Essays*, London: Routledge.
Coleman, D.C. (ed.) (1969), *Revisions in Mercantilism*, London: Methuen & Co.
Crowley, J.E. (1993), *The Privileges of Independence: Neomercantilism and the American Revolution*, Baltimore, MD: Johns Hopkins University Press.
Dickerson, E. (1951), *The Navigation Acts and the American Revolution*, Philadelphia, PA: University of Pennsylvania Press.
Fay, C.R. (1934), 'Adam Smith and the doctrinal defeat of the mercantile system', *Quarterly Journal of Economics*, **48** (1), 304–16.
Furniss, E. (1920), *The Position of the Labourer in a System of Nationalism*, New York: Houghton Mifflin.
Guttridge, G.H. (1933), 'Adam Smith on the American Revolution', *American Historical Review*, **38** (3), 714–20.
Hecksher, E. (1955), *Mercantilism*, rev. edn, London: George Allen & Unwin.

Howell, W.S. (1975), 'Adam Smith's *Lectures on Rhetoric*: An historical assessment', in Andrew Skinner and Thomas Wilson (eds.), *Essays on Adam Smith*, Oxford: Clarendon Press, pp. 11–43.
Koebner, R. (1961), *Empire*, Cambridge: Cambridge University Press.
Livingston, D.W. (1990), 'Hume, English barbarism and American independence', in R.B. Sher and J.R. Smitten (eds), *Scotland and America in the Age of Enlightenment*, Edinburgh: Edinburgh University Press, pp. 136–42.
Morris, R.B. (ed.) (1970), *The American Revolution 1763–1783*, London: Harper and Row.
Pownall, R. (1776), *A Letter from Governor Pownall to Adam Smith*, reprinted in Ian Simpson Ross (ed.) (1987), *The Correspondence of Adam Smith*, Appendix A, Oxford: Clarendon Press.
Rashid, S. (1998), *The Myth of Adam Smith*, Cheltenham, UK and Lyme, NH, US: Edward Elgar.
Raynor, D. and A.S. Skinner (1994), 'Sir James Steuart: nine letters on the American conflict, 1775–1778', *William and Mary Quarterly*, Third Series **51** (4), 755–76.
Reid, G. (2008), *Adam Smith*, London: Macmillan.
Romani, R. (1993), 'Early nineteenth-century European views on American growth: the Smithian legacy', unpublished paper delivered at the Colloque 'Adam Smith et l'economic coloniale', Paris.
Ross, I.S. (1972), *Lord Kames and the Scotland of his Day*, Oxford: Oxford University Press.
Rutman, D.B. (1971), *The Morning of America 1603–1789*, Boston, MA: Houghton Mifflin.
Schmoller, G. (1896), *The Mercantile System and its Historical Significance*, London: Macmillan
Schumpeter, J.A. (1954), *History of Economic Analysis*, New York: Oxford University Press.
Skinner, A.S. (1990), 'Adam Smith and America: the political economy of conflict', in R.B. Sher and J.R. Smitten (eds), *Scotland and America in the Age of Enlightenment*, Edinburgh: Edinburgh University Press, pp. 148–62.
Skinner, A.S. (1996), *A System of Social Science*, Oxford: Oxford University Press.
Skinner, A.S. (ed.) (1999), *The Wealth of Nations*, Bks IV–V, London, UK and New York, USA: Penguin Books.
Skinner, A.S. (2001), 'Adam Smith on the Mercantile System: the unnecessary loss of America?' in Michael Leaney (ed.), *Economist with a Public Purpose: Essays in Honour of J.K. Galbraith*, London: Routledge, pp. 247–66.
Smith, Adam (1759), *The Theory of Moral Sentiments*, D.D. Raphael and A.L. Macfie (eds) (1976), Oxford: Clarendon Press, TMS.
Smith, Adam (1776), *An Inquiry into the Nature and Causes of the Wealth of Nations*, R.H. Campbell, A.S. Skinner and W.B. Todd (eds) (1976), Oxford: Clarendon Press, WN.
Smith, Adam (1795), *Essays on Philosophical Subjects*, W.P.D. Wightman and J.C. Bryce (eds) (1980), Oxford: Clarendon Press, EPS.
Smith, Adam (1983), *Lectures on Rhetoric and Belles Lettres*, J.C. Bryce (ed.), Oxford: Clarendon Press, LRBL.
Smith, Adam (1978), *Lectures on Jurisprudence*, R. Meek, D.D. Raphael and P.G. Stein (eds), Oxford: Clarendon Press, LJ.
Smith, Adam (1977), *Correspondence of Adam Smith*, E.C. Mossner and I.S. Ross (eds), Oxford: Clarendon Press, Corr.
Stevens, D. (1975), 'Adam Smith and the colonial disturbances', in Andrew Skinner and Thomas Wilson (eds.), *Essays on Adam Smith*, Oxford: Clarendon Press, pp. 202–17.
Thomas, P. J. (1926), *Mercantilism and the East India Trade*, London: P.S. King & Son.
Viner, J. (1930), 'English theories of foreign trade before Adam Smith', *Journal of Political Economy*, **38** (2), 249–301.
Winch, D. (1961), *Classical Political Economy and the Colonies*, Cambridge, MA: Harvard University Press.
Winch, D. (1978), *Adam Smith's Politics: An Essay in Historiographic Revision*, Cambridge: Cambridge University Press.

15 Jeremy Bentham and Adam Smith on the usury laws: a 'Smithian' reply to Bentham and a new problem
Samuel Hollander

Authors are not much disposed to alter the opinions they have once published. (Adam Smith, 26 October 1780 (Mossner and Ross, 1977, p. 250))

Introduction
Adam Smith justified the contemporary usury laws which imposed a maximum of 5 per cent on private loans, as a means of preventing 'prodigals and projectors' from cornering the supply of loans. Bentham protested to Smith in a 'letter' of 1787 on the following grounds.

First, Smith had discouraged genuine innovation by applying a 'stamp of indiscriminate reprobation' upon the term 'projects and projectors', which encompassed for him 'all such persons as, in the pursuit of wealth, strike out into any new channel, and more especially into any channel of invention' (Bentham, 1787 [1952], pp. 168–9); for '[h]igh and extraordinary rates of interest . . . are certainly, as you very justly observe, particularly adapted to the situation of the projector:[1] not however to that of the imprudent projector only, nor even to his case more than another's, but to that of the prudent and well-grounded projector, if the existence of such a being were to be supposed' (p. 170). Smith therefore countenanced loans only 'to the situation which the sort of trader is in, whose trade runs in the old channels, and to the best security which such channels can afford'.[2] But it was an error to believe that lenders sought out good projects, at the legal maximum: 'a prudent man . . . will not meddle with projects at all. He will pick out old-fashioned trades from all sorts of projects, good and bad; for with a new project, be it ever so promising, he will never have any thing to do' (p. 171). The regulation thus gave a monopoly to the 'oldest and best-established' borrowers (p. 179), wholly against Smith's own dictum (Smith, 1976, p. 456) that '[t]o give the monopoly of the home-market to the produce of domestick industry, in any particular art or manufacture, is in some measure to direct private people in what manner they ought to employ their capitals, and must, in almost all cases, be either a useless or a hurtful regulation'.

Second, whereas at the interest-rate maximum lenders do not select good and avoid bad projects but avoid projects entirely, this is not the case in a free market having regard to '*the benefit of discussion*' (Bentham, 1787 [1952], p. 181). For the lender would add his critical evaluation of a proposal to 'the inventor's own partial affection . . . [T]here are, in this case, two wits, set to sift into the merits of the project . . . and of these two there is one, whose prejudices are certainly not most likely to be on the favourable side'.

Third, at the most general level Bentham saw Smith's position as conflicting with his own principle of liberty – his declaration, in the context of the sumptuary laws and import control, that '[i]t is the highest impertinence and presumption . . . in kings and ministers, to *pretend to watch over the oeconomy of private people*' (p. 176, citing Smith, 1976, p. 346; emphasis Bentham's). Indeed, if it was impertinent to control prodigality, it was all the more so to interfere with 'bad management' since prodigality was widespread and projection less so; moreover, whereas all prodigals were socially nefarious, this was not true of all projectors (pp. 176–7). Smith was proposing to replace 'the most perfect and minute knowledge and information, which interest, the whole interest of a man's reputation and fortune, can ensure', with the 'most perfect ignorance' of the legislator (p. 178), again quite against his own rule: '"What is the species of domestick industry which his capital can employ, and of which the produce is likely to be of the greatest value, every individual" (you say), "it is evident, can, in his local situation, judge much better than any statesman or lawgiver can do for him"' (citing Smith, 1976, p. 456).

Fourth, even in retrospect, projects that turn out to be failures would not have justified legislative interference. In the case of what Bentham calls 'the mine-lottery, the privateering-lottery, and so many other lotteries' – which Smith wrote of unfavourably – no good at all results from individual failure, and yet Smith did not call for their proscription; whereas from 'invention-lottery' – which Smith effectively proscribed – society might benefit even should the individuals initially involved (the inventor or his creditor) go under (Bentham, 1787 [1952], p. 182).

Fifth, I find no reference in Bentham's letter to Smith to evasion of the law. But this theme is much in evidence in his Letter VI: 'Mischiefs of the anti-usurious laws' and, particularly, in Letter VII: 'Efficacy of anti-usurious Laws'. In fact, Bentham there cites Smith's own statement that because of evasion:

> No law can reduce the common rate of interest below the lowest ordinary market rate at the time when that law is made. Notwithstanding the edict of 1766, by which the French king attempted to reduce the rate of interest from five to four per cent., money continued to be lent in France at five per cent., the law being evaded in several different ways. (p. 147, citing Smith, 1976, pp. 357–8)

Bentham protested that in all cases where a maximum is imposed the problem of evasion arises (p. 148). And he points out that Smith himself had elaborated on the practice of 'drawing and re-drawing [bills of exchange]' entailing sometimes effective rates as high as 13–14 per cent (p. 150).

Most modern writers are equally critical of Smith; bemused might be a better word. Lord Robbins found his position wholly anomalous; his support for a legal maximum interest rate must, he concluded, have occurred 'in an incautious moment' (Robbins, 1968, p. 86). George Stigler describes his position as an 'aberration' (Stigler, 1975, p. 41), and 'a strange argument' which 'seems to assume that lenders would pay no attention to the probability of being repaid, but only to the promised interest rate. Surely it was inconsistent with Smith's basic theory of sensible economic behaviour; here the lenders are being foolishly shortsighted' (Stigler, 1988, p. 208). John Rae, Smith's biographer, believed that Smith surrendered to Bentham's challenge (Rae, 1965 [1895], p. 423).[3] But Stigler relates Smith's silence in his final edition of *Wealth of Nations* (1789) 'to his continued belief in the essential validity of his views' – his erroneous views – illustrating a general phenomenon that 'the able economist . . . seldom admits or corrects a mistake' (Stigler, 1988, p. 208).

Keynes did not join the chorus of hypercritical opinion: 'Even Adam Smith was extremely moderate in his attitude of the usury laws . . . he defended [their] moderate application' (Keynes, 1936, p. 352). Keynes did not specify wherein precisely lay Smith's moderation. But it will be our argument that there is merit to his evaluation. *Pace* Bentham, Smith did not intend to squeeze out loan financing of all 'risky' ventures and give a 'monopoly' to safe, old-fashioned investments. In the first place, by keeping an eye on eighteenth-century economic history, we avoid overestimating both the risk attached to innovation and invention and the role of credit in finance. Bentham's objection that the usury laws imposed a severe break on innovation proves to be exaggerated. Apart from this, it was precisely to the end of partially accommodating risky ventures that Smith recommended a maximum somewhat exceeding the rate appropriate for the 'very best' loans. (It must be emphasized that all 'long-term' financing was to derive from private not bank credit, partly on the grounds that banks were incapable of evaluating risk properly.) As for ventures which though 'sober' were yet of a degree of riskiness rendering loan finance unavailable at the legal maximum interest rate, Smith recommended equity financing and allowed even for the social rewarding of successful undertakings. Finally, Bentham's complaint that Smith neglected the potential emergence of black credit markets does not hold water, for he explains why potential excess demand at the appropriately set maximum is contained, in contrast with the illegal trades that would emerge at an inappropriately low maximum.

Yet there remains a serious problem. I refer to the destructive implications for Smith's case flowing from a marked rise in the rate at which governments borrowed from 3–3.5 per cent to 5 per cent in the late 1770s. The justification of a 5 per cent maximum was thereby rendered a dead letter. That Smith did not alter his second edition of 1778, may perhaps be excused (but see below); but he remained mute in the third edition of 1784 and in the fourth of 1786. His silence in the last edition of 1789 in the face of Bentham's letter of 1787 has been the focus of scholarly debate, whereas the problem in fact lies much deeper, since he ought to have modified his position years earlier – at the least recommending an upward adjustment of the maximum – quite independently of Bentham's criticism.

Smith's case reviewed
Smith commended government policy respecting the usury laws; the series of statutory regulations lowering the legal maximum – these extended over two centuries from 10 per cent (1571–1623) to 8 per cent (1624–60) to 6 per cent (1660–1713), and thereafter to the ruling 5 per cent – are said 'to have been made with great propriety', in that they followed downward movements in, while always remaining marginally higher than, 'the rate at which people of good credit usually borrowed' (Smith, 1976, p. 106).[4] Thus, '[i]n a country, such as Great Britain, where money is lent to government at three per cent., and to private people upon good security at four, and four and a half, per cent., the present legal rate, five per cent., is, perhaps, as proper as any'; for the legal rate 'though it ought to be somewhat above, ought not to be much above the lowest market rate' (p. 357).[5] The justification for a maximum which somewhat exceeds the range of rates appropriate for private borrowers with high credit ratings (our 'prime rates') is made carefully:

> In countries where interest is permitted, the law, in order to prevent the extortion of usury, generally fixes the highest rate which can be taken without incurring a penalty. This rate ought

always to be somewhat above the lowest market rate, or the price which is commonly paid for the use of money by those who can give the most undoubted security. If this legal rate should be fixed below the lowest market rate, the effects of this fixation must be nearly the same as those of a total prohibition of interest. The creditor will not lend his money for less than the use of it is worth, and the debtor must pay him for the risk which he runs by accepting the full value of that use. If it is fixed precisely at the lowest market price, it ruins with honest people, who respect the laws of their country, the credit of all those who cannot give the very best security, and obliges them to have recourse to exorbitant usurers. (pp. 356–7)[6]

Smith thus justified loans albeit of less than the 'most undoubted' quality, and intended to preclude only transactions involving borrowers of relatively poor credit rating who would be prepared to pay interest much exceeding 5 per cent in a freely operating market:

The legal rate, it is to be observed, though it ought to be somewhat above, ought not to be much above the lowest market rate. If the legal rate of interest in Great Britain, for example, was fixed so high as eight or ten per cent., the greater part of the money which was to be lent, would be lent to prodigals and projectors, who alone would be willing to give this high interest. Sober people, who will give for the use of money no more than a part of what they are likely to make by the use of it, would not venture into the competition. A great part of the capital of the country would thus be kept out of the hands which were most likely to make a profitable and advantageous use of it, and thrown into those which were most likely to waste and destroy it. Where the legal rate of interest, on the contrary, is fixed but a very little above the lowest market rate, sober people are universally preferred, as borrowers, to prodigals and projectors. The person who lends money gets nearly as much interest from the former as he dares to take from the latter, and his money is much safer in the hands of the one set of people, than in those of the other. A great part of the capital of the country is thus thrown into the hands in which it is most likely to be employed with advantage. (p. 357)[7]

Where 'high' interest rates are available Smith thus attributed to lenders a bias favouring high-risk loans rather than a roughly equal distribution of preference across the spectrum of opportunities. Smith, therefore, denied that – faced with such opportunities – lenders would impose control over purely speculative ventures; and since lenders are thus prejudiced in favour of riskiness, there would not be that 'benefit of discussion' that Bentham relied on.[8] Stigler's objection appears valid, since the vast majority of Smith's lenders are represented as preferring to engage in high-risk lending should the opportunity present itself.[9] The bias is, however, reversed at a legal maximum rate of interest 'fixed but a very little above the lowest market rate', for then 'sober people are universally preferred, as borrowers, to prodigals and projectors'. That is the gist of his argument.[10]

The lack of concern with the emergence of a black credit market at the appropriate legal maximum, contrasts sharply with the assumed inevitability of such an outcome in the event of a total prohibition of loans at interest: 'Many people must borrow, and nobody will lend without a consideration for the use of their money as is suitable, not only to what can be made by the use of it, but to the difficulty and danger of evading the law' (p. 112); similarly, proscribing interest altogether 'instead of preventing, has been found from experience to increase the evil of usury; the debtor being obliged to pay, not only for the use of the money, but for the risk which his creditor runs by accepting a compensation for that use. He is obliged, if one may say so, to insure his creditor from the penalties of usury' (p. 356).[11] Smith also spelled out the problem of illegal trades –

'recourse to exorbitant usurers' – in the event that a maximum is set too low relative to the prime rate. More specifically: 'No law can reduce the common rate of interest below the lowest ordinary market rate at the time the law was made' (pp. 357–8). That he gave no similar caution in the case of the 5 per cent maximum, suggests that he presumed the effectiveness of such a maximum. This position reflects an assumed empirical reality (see pp. 288–91), but he in effect accounted for it by the argument that at the appropriate legal maximum lenders engage in an effective rationing process whereby 'prodigals and projectors' are excluded in favour of 'sober' borrowers, thereby containing excess-demand pressures.

The contrast between the behaviour of lenders who at the 5 per cent maximum seek out 'sober' borrowers, and the overwhelming bias towards high-risk loans should the legal maximum be set too high (or, by extension, where high interest rates are freely available), requires explanation. Smith's portrayal can be accounted for in terms of his general preoccupation with irresponsibility engendered by the promise of excessive returns. Thus for example: 'The high rate of profit seems every where to destroy that parsimony which in other circumstances is natural to the character of the merchant. When profits are high, that sober virtue seems to be superfluous, and expensive luxury to suit better the affluence of his situation' (p. 612). Furthermore, '[w]hen the profits of trade happen to be greater than ordinary, over-trading becomes a general error both among great and small traders' (p. 438). Regarding 'the situation' of the great landowner, he writes that it 'naturally disposes him to attend rather to ornament which pleases his fancy, than to profit for which he has so little occasion' (p. 385). Where profits are high, agricultural employers are prone to adopt inefficient methods: 'The planting of sugar and tobacco can afford the expence of slave-cultivation' (p. 388). Smith points to careless consumption behaviour should an item absorb only a small fraction of the budget (see Hollander, 1973, pp. 118–19). And most generally, '[i]n publick, as well as in private expences, great wealth may, perhaps, frequently be admitted as an apology for great folly' (Smith, 1976, p. 523, added in 1784 edition). A corresponding carelessness is ascribed to the labour market in cases where individuals work part-time so that their salary constitutes a fraction only of total earnings (p. 131).

Spencer Pack has maintained that Smith 'does not address Aristotle's fear that the use of money to make money generates the cancerous growth of avarice in society' (Pack, 1997, p. 128); 'Aristotle's fear that commercial society will unleash the passions of avarice and greed is nowhere addressed by Smith' (p. 135). Our case points to the contrary conclusion: to allow a high interest is unacceptable to Smith precisely because it does unleash avarice to the social disadvantage. But though tight markets – a hoped-for result of 'competition' – engender careful calculation, there are limits. For (as we have seen) legal interest rates set too low entail massive excess demand pressures on the part even of 'sober' borrowers that cannot be contained.

Smith and risk

Smith's case for a controlled credit market is more easily appreciated if we keep in mind his broad concern with a 'universal' (and unjustifiable) risk tolerance:

> The over-weening conceit which the greater part of men have of their own abilities, is an antient evil remarked by the philosophers and moralists of all ages. Their absurd presumption in their

own good fortune, has been less taken notice of. It is, however, if possible, still more universal. There is no man living who, when in tolerable health and spirits, has not some share of it. *The chance of gain is by every man more or less over-valued, and the chance of loss is by most men under-valued, and by scarce any man, who is in tolerable health and spirits, valued more than it is worth.* (Smith, 1976, pp. 124–5; emphasis added)

Smith illustrates the overvaluation of the chance of gain by observing that even the 'soberest people' were subject to the 'vain hope of gaining some of the great prizes' offered by lotteries; that the chance of loss was 'frequently under-valued' was revealed by the 'very moderate profit of insurance', people typically unwilling to pay the relatively low premiums available (p. 125). Though some shipping companies might not take out insurance finding it prudent to spread prospective loss over several ships, 'in most cases' the failure to insure ships (or houses) was not a matter of 'nice calculation, but of *mere thoughtless rashness and presumptuous contempt of the risk*' (p. 126; emphasis added). Indeed, so pervasive was the bias in question that the entire profit rate structure tended to be skewed, as proven by the incidence of bankruptcy and illustrated by the case of smuggling:

> Bankruptcies are most frequent in the most hazardous trades. The most hazardous of all trades, that of the smuggler, though when the adventure succeeds it is likewise the most profitable, is the infallible road to bankruptcy. *The presumptuous hope of success seems to act here as upon all other occasions, and to entice so many adventurers into those hazardous trades, that their competition reduces the profit below what is sufficient to compensate the risk* . . . [I]f the common returns were sufficient for all this, bankruptcies would not be more frequent in these than in other trades. (p.128; emphasis added)[12]

What, then, to make of the celebrated declarations pointing towards an apparently universal predominance of good conduct, particularly the assertion that 'seldom' can the 'circumstances of a great nation . . . be much affected either by the prodigality or misconduct of individuals' – referring by 'misconduct' to 'injudicious and unsuccessful' projection – 'the profusion or improvidence of some being always more than compensated by the frugality and good conduct of others' (p. 341)? As for 'good conduct', 'the number of prudent and successful undertakings is every where much greater than that of injudicious and unsuccessful ones' (p. 342). Smith concluded famously that: Great nations are never impoverished by private . . . prodigality and misconduct.' Similarly: 'In the midst of all the exactions of government . . . capital has been silently and gradually accumulated by the private frugality and good conduct of individuals, by their universal, continual, and uninterrupted effort to better their own condition' (p. 345).

Were it Smith's unconditional position that injudicious investment was relatively inconsequential, one would have to wonder at the enthusiasm for an interest-rate maximum to curtail typically irresponsible ventures. The question is answered if we understand Smith as taking for granted, in the course of his optimistic declarations, a maximum interest rate in consequence of which responsible behaviour predominates. In fact, Smith is explicit about the issue. The problem of lenders' high-risk preference is overcome, provided 'gross usury' is ruled out:

> The man who borrows in order to spend will soon be ruined, and he who lends to him will generally have occasion to repent of his folly. To borrow or to lend for such a purpose therefore,

is in all cases, where gross usury is out of the question, contrary to the interest of both parties ... Ask any rich man of common prudence, to which of the two sorts of people he has lent the greater part of his stock, to those who, he thinks, will employ it profitably, or to those who will spend it idly, and he will laugh at you for proposing the question. Even among borrowers, therefore, not the people of the world most famous for prodigality, the number of the frugal and industrious surpasses considerably that of the prodigal and idle. (p. 350; emphasis added)

One notes that the weight of emphasis is placed on the lender; it is the lender's responsible behaviour engendered by the interest-rate maximum that rations loans in a manner avoiding irresponsible borrowers; and although the particular context is limited to prodigality there can be little doubt that Smith's position extends to other forms of irresponsibility – specifically, to irresponsible projection, the two being so frequently spoken of together. That the rationing is imposed by the responsible lender – his responsibility engendered by the interest-rate maximum – is also apparent at other points in the narrative, especially the material at pp. 356–7.

I conclude then that when Smith writes of the powerful savings propensity that 'this effort, *protected by law* and allowed by liberty to exert itself in the manner that is most advantageous ... has maintained the progress of England towards opulence and improvement in almost all former times, and ... it is to be hoped, will do so in all future times' (p. 345; emphasis added), he intends by 'protected by law' to include not only security of contract and the like, but also interest-rate regulation.[13] In brief, the price system appropriately modified is itself part of the desirable institutional framework within which enterprise is to be allowed free reign.[14] This position does not necessarily imply that Smith 'defend[ed] the competence of an authority to direct the investor', – as Bentham complained; he may better be seen as 'defending a rule' not inconsistent with the position 'that government officials have no role to play in the direction of private resources' (Levy, 1987, p. 399).

Mention may also be made here of Smith's declaration of confidence that any outflow of precious metals due to note issue would be employed responsibly, that is, in the purchase of investment goods rather than in prodigal expenditure:

That the greater part of the gold and silver which, being forced abroad by those operations of banking, is employed in purchasing foreign goods for home consumption, is and must be employed in purchasing those of this second kind [referring to 'materials, tools, and provisions ... to maintain and employ an additional number of industrious people' rather than 'goods as are likely to be consumed by idle people who produce nothing'], seems not only probable but almost unavoidable. Though some particular men may sometimes increase their expence very considerably though their revenue does not increase at all, we may be assured that no class or order of men ever does so; because, though the principles of common prudence do not always govern the conduct of every individual, they always influence that of the majority of every class or order. (Smith, 1976, p. 295)

Smith so often links together 'prodigality' and 'projection', that the small likelihood here attached to the former may very well extend to the latter. In that case, considering his express concern with irresponsible risk-taking, one must again suppose that his confidence assumes an interest-rate maximum with the positive results expected to follow therefrom.

Also to be understood conditionally may be some of Smith's statements relating to the principal–agent problem. Thus the exemption of general stockholders by the limited-liability arrangement 'from trouble and from risk, beyond a limited sum, encourages many people to become adventurers in joint stock companies, who would, upon no account, hazard their fortunes in any private copartnery' (p. 741). Smith's editors see here a qualification of the idea that 'the chance of loss is frequently undervalued'. This is so, if the qualification presumes a ruling interest-rate maximum and the consequential prudential behaviour engendered thereby which dissuades investors from 'hazard[ing] their fortunes in any private copartnery'.

A 'Smithian' reply to Bentham
Pesciarelli finds the main difference between Bentham and Smith to lie in different conceptions of economic development: Bentham's characterized by discontinuous changes determined by improvements, and 'susceptible to a non-linear trend'; and Smith's which is 'slow, gradual, uniform and not susceptible to sudden variation' (Pesciarelli, 1989, p. 535). This view of Smithian 'undertaking' is in line with that portrayed by Spengler (1959) and Koebner (1959). Can Smith's justification of the usury laws be said then to reflect such minimization of the contribution by 'Schumpeterian' innovation? To the extent that this is the case, the element of risk would not be a major consideration at either the inventive or innovative stage and accordingly an interest-rate maximum would not greatly impede growth. We shall consider this matter here and below, pp. 288–91.

Certainly a picture of economic growth consistent with the Spengler–Koebner perspective is to be found in the *Wealth of Nations*, where the flow of improvements is frequently taken for granted in almost the same way that one may forecast cost reductions due simply to the overcoming of indivisibilities at a large scale.[15] Yet Smith did not ignore costly and risky innovatory investment. And he was by no means critical, legitimate projection figuring especially in his account of agriculture. He recommended that care be taken to choose those forms of land taxation least likely to affect the profits yielded by 'improvements' including draining and enclosure (Smith, 1976, p. 927), and condemned the church tithe because it reduced the motive for 'expensive improvements' (p. 837; also p. 390); increased land values due to improvements should be exempt from taxation for a fixed term of several years (p. 833; see also p. 927 for further warning against changes to the system of taxation which might threaten the return on landlord's investments). In the same context Smith recognized the expense and risk attached to inventive activity; it is only the wealthy landlord who can afford to undertake risky experiments: 'The landlord can afford to try experiments, and is generally disposed to do so. His unsuccessful experiments occasion only a moderate loss to himself. His successful ones contribute to the improvement and better cultivation of the whole country' (p. 832). Smith had in mind here the new commercial landowners, writing approvingly of them as 'bold undertakers' willing to make large innovatory expenditures: 'A merchant is commonly a bold; a country gentleman, a timid undertaker. The one is not afraid to lay out at once a large capital upon the improvement of his land, when he has a probable prospect of raising the value of it in proportion to the expense' (p. 411). But the allowance for legitimate projection extends more generally. As Pesciarelli reminds us (Pesciarelli, 1989, p. 524) Smith had this to say of the merchant class:

> It is the stock that is employed for the sake of profit, which puts into motion the greater part of the useful labour of every society. The *plans and projects* of the employers of stock regulate

and direct all the most important operations of labour, and profit is the end proposed by all those plans and projects . . . Merchants and master manufacturers are . . . the two classes of people who commonly employ the largest capitals, and who by their wealth draw to themselves the greatest share of the publick consideration. As during their whole lives they are engaged in *plans and projects*, they have frequently more acuteness of understanding than the greater part of country gentlemen. (Smith, 1976, p. 266; emphasis added)

Smith was moreover explicit that true innovatory investment, undertaken with the prospect of extraordinary returns in the face of risk, might turn out to be successful. This outcome too is a central feature of the growth process itself:

The establishment of any new manufacture, of any new branch of commerce, or of any new practice in agriculture, is always a speculation, from which the projector promises himself extraordinary profits. These profits sometimes are very great, and sometimes, more frequently, perhaps, are quite otherwise . . . If the project succeeds, they are commonly very high. When the trade or practice becomes thoroughly established and well known, the competition reduces them to the level of other trades. (pp. 131–2)

Thus just as unsuccessful projection constituted a loss of capital and a loss to society – 'Every injudicious and unsuccessful project in agriculture, mines, fisheries, trade, or manufactures, tends . . . to diminish the funds destined for the maintenance of productive labour' (p. 341) – so every successful projection is taken as in part responsible for economic growth. There is perhaps a presumption that the 'injudiciousness' of investment and failure go hand in hand, and correspondingly 'judiciousness' and success, but this was not a hard and fast rule, since even 'sober' investments – the context is 'overtrading' and complaints of 'scarce money' – sometimes run into difficulty:

Sober men, whose projects have been disproportionate to their capitals, are as likely to have neither wherewithall to buy money, nor credit to borrow it, as prodigals whose expence has been disproportionate to their revenue. Before their projects can be brought to bear, their stock is gone, and their credit with it. (pp. 437–8)[16]

Bentham, we conclude, exaggerated when he charged that Smith identified the antisocial consequences of 'projection' and of 'misconduct', neglecting that bankruptcy might reflect failure that cannot reasonably be termed 'misconduct'.

What though of the financing of risky innovative investment? Equity finance is taken for granted in the discussion of 'bold undertakers' engaged in agricultural improvement. Moreover, if the undertaking required particularly heavy capital conscription (as with banks, insurance companies, canals and water-works) an argument could be made for joint-stock organization, notwithstanding a general minimization of the profit-making potentialities of such organization (p. 756). In fact, if successful, a joint-stock trading company – formed to finance a risky and expensive venture – might even be accorded a temporary monopoly, on the same grounds that justified the patenting of machinery and copyright protection:

When a company of merchants undertake, *at their own risk and expence*, to establish a new trade with some remote and barbarous nation, it may not be unreasonable to incorporate them into a joint stock company, and to grant them, in case of their success, a monopoly of the trade for a certain number of years. *It is the easiest and most natural way in which the state can recompense them for hazarding a dangerous and expensive experiment, of which the public is afterwards to reap the benefit.* A temporary monopoly of this kind may be vindicated upon the same principles upon which a like monopoly of a new machine is granted to its inventor, and that of a new book to its author. (p. 754; emphasis added)

But beyond these allowances for equity financing there is the credit market, for Smith did not intend by his support of the usury laws to obstruct the loan financing of 'legitimate and socially advisable' – Keynes's terms – though risky projects. To the contrary, as we know he insisted that the maximum rate must exceed the rate appropriate for the 'very best' loans precisely in order to provide leeway for such ventures – a feature that might account for Keynes's description of the case for a maximum as 'moderate'. It is specifically the bank financing of long-term, capital-intensive projects to which Smith objected:

> The returns of the fixed capital are in almost all cases much slower than those of the circulating capital; and such expences, even when laid out with the greatest prudence and judgment, very seldom return to the undertaker till after a period of many years, a period by far too distant to suit the convenience of a bank. *Traders and other undertakers may, no doubt, with great propriety, carry on a very considerable part of their projects with borrowed money.* In justice to their creditors, however, their own capital ought in this case, to be sufficient to ensure, if I may say so, the capital of those creditors; or to render it extremely improbable that those creditors should incur any loss, even though the success of the project should fall very much short of the expectation of the projectors. *Even with this precaution too, the money which is borrowed, and which it is meant should not be repaid till after a period of several years, ought not to be borrowed of a bank, but ought to be borrowed upon bond or mortgage, of such private people as propose to live upon the interest of their money, without taking the trouble themselves to employ the capital; and who are upon that account willing to lend that capital to such people of good credit as are likely to keep it for several years.* (p. 307; emphasis added)

It will be noted that the various 'precautions' specified above would tend to reduce the lender's risk of loss due to a failure of the project, and accordingly the interest demanded (presumably within legal bounds). Such precautions Smith believed could better be taken by private creditors than by banks who are represented – he focused on the Ayr Bank – as unable to evaluate properly the credit-worthiness of their clients and thus fall into accommodating 'chimerical projectors' and 'extravagant undertakings' (p. 316).[17] By contrast:

> The sober and frugal debtors of private persons . . . would be more likely to employ the money borrowed in sober undertakings which were proportioned to their capitals, and which, though they might have less of the grand and the marvellous, would have more of the solid and the profitable, which would repay with a large profit whatever had been laid out upon them, and which would thus afford a fund capable of maintaining a much greater quantity of labour than which had been employed about them. (pp. 316–17)

Again, it emerges that private lenders are to be relied upon to impose the appropriate control – presumably at interest constrained by the 5 per cent upper limit.

We can also appreciate in these terms various striking allowances for effective interest rates exceeding the 5 per cent maximum. (Recall Bentham's surprise at Smith's recognition of such illegal rates.) It was the allegedly faulty discounting policy of the banks that was ultimately responsible, Smith pointing especially at the Scottish bankers who extended loans on liberal terms of repayment and without mortgage or guarantee (p. 299).[18] He refers here to the various devices of obtaining credit at enormous expence initiated in Scotland but adopted also in England during the war of 1756–63 'when the high profits of trade afforded a great temptation to over-trading' (p. 308), for example, the device of 'drawing and redrawing' of bills of exchange discounted by the banks which entailed loans at an effective interest rate far exceeding the 5 per cent legal maximum (p. 310).[19]

The practice frequently entailed bank financing of 'vast and extensive' projects in their entirety – thus breaking the Smithian rules of safe discounting – in ignorance of what in effect was occurring:

> The paper which was issued upon those circulating bills of exchange, amounted, upon many occasions, to the whole fund destined for carrying on *some vast and extensive project* of agriculture, commerce, or manufactures . . . It was a capital which those *projectors* had very artfully contrived to draw from those banks, not only without their knowledge or deliberate consent, but for some time, perhaps, without their having the most distant suspicion that they had really advanced it. (p. 311; emphasis added)

Smith's account reveals great hostility towards the projectors who aggressively misrepresented their private interest as the national interest at a time when at least some bankers were belatedly attempting to correct their excessive lending:

> Their own distress, of which this prudent and necessary reserve of the banks, was, no doubt, the immediate occasion, they called the distress of the country; and this distress of the country, they said, was altogether owing to the ignorance, pusillanimity, and bad conduct of the banks, which did not give a sufficiently liberal aid to the *spirited undertakings* of those who exerted themselves in order to *beautify*, *improve* and *enrich* the country.[20] It was the duty of the banks, they seemed to think, to lend for as long a time, and to as great an extent as they might wish to borrow. The banks, however, by refusing in this manner to give more credit to those, to whom they had already given a great deal too much, took the only method by which it was now possible to save either their own credit, or the publick credit of the country. (p. 312; emphasis added)[21]

As for the Ayr Bank, originally set up for the express purpose of relieving the distress of the country, it had been 'more liberal than any other had ever been, both in granting cash accounts, and in discounting bills of exchange' (p. 313). By advancing 'upon any reasonable security, the whole capital which was to be employed in those improvements of which the returns are the most slow and distant, such as the improvements of land', it:

> no doubt, gave some temporary relief to those projectors, and enabled them to carry on their projects for about two years longer than they could otherwise have done. But it thereby only enabled them to get so much deeper into debt, so that when ruin came, it fell so much the heavier both upon them and upon their creditors. The operations of this bank, therefore, instead of relieving, in reality aggravated in the long-run the distress which those projectors had brought upon themselves and upon their country. (pp. 313–15)

Smith, we have seen, was largely unconcerned about the emergence of a black market in illegal lending to high-risk borrowers. This generalization must obviously be qualified in the light of the foregoing account. Experience had taught him that banks were unable to calculate objectively the risk-worthiness of their clients, and accordingly financed irresponsible projects at the 5 per cent maximum. Not only that, their incompetence was such that they themselves borrowed at effective rates far exceeding 5 per cent, allowance made for compounding and costly commissions of different sorts. We are dealing with a major example of an alleged failure of self-interest: 'Had every particular banking company always understood its own particular interest, the circulation never could have been overstocked with paper money' due to inappropriate discounting (p. 302). And 'bold projectors' had taken full advantage; indeed 'the over-trading of bold projectors in both parts of the united kingdom, was the original cause of the excessive circulation of paper money' (p. 304). The hoped-for control to be exercised by lenders had thus failed. But were banks to limit discounting to so-called 'real bills' this particular weakness of the system would be closed off.[22]

Aspects of the contemporary economy: a corroboratory exercise
Smith's support for the usury laws may, to some extent, be better appreciated by keeping track of various conspicuous aspects of the contemporary economy. Those general features of the economy to which we can appeal on Smith's behalf include the contemporary industry structure and business finance, the risks attached to innovation, and the speculative mood.

It has been pretty well established that:

> During the classic period of the industrial revolution [1760–1830], it *is* realistic to think in terms of the individual entrepreneur, the man (or small group of men) of 'wit and resource' who organized, managed, and controlled the affairs of a unit that combined the factor of production for the supply of goods and services. (Payne, 1978, p. 182)

Individual proprietorship, or partnership, can be seen in part as the product of risk avoidance, for 'even if potential managers were apparently honest and sober, the assessment of their ability, wisdom, and integrity involved considerable uncertainty, and their employment necessitated avoidable expense' (p. 192).[23] The typical one-man firm or small partnership, moreover, expected to finance their undertakings with 'funds of their own or those of relatives and friends borrowed on their own responsibility' (p. 181).[24]

Consistent with this picture of small-scale and self-financing is Pressnell's observation that the interest rate – at least the long-term interest rate – would probably have been of relatively small import:

> Much investment was internally financed or came from local or family sources with limited sensitivity to interest rates. Moreover the investment process was not always so long, nor the expected returns so low, as in the public utilities or in agriculture. Long-term interest costs might not therefore bulk so large, and short-term rates ranked for closer consideration. (Pressnell, 1960, p. 195)

In Smith's day the creation of joint-stock companies with transferable shares and corporate status was difficult and expensive, requiring Acts of Parliament. But in any event there was no real need to depart from the traditional organization, for either financial or technical reasons:

> The practice of self-financing, coupled with a growing reliance on an increasingly sensitive network of monetary intermediaries, was able to meet the capital requirements of most firms.

The essential simplicity of so many of the productive processes, characterized as they were by a growth pattern involving simply the multiplication of units, rather than by radical reorganization, permitted continued direction by the single entrepreneur or by the small group of enterprises far bigger than had once been thought feasible. These factors enabled manufacturing and trading firms to grow without recourse to the joint-stock form.[25]

Smith might, therefore, have defended himself against Bentham's charges by insisting that, in practice, his support of the usury laws did not imply that investment – innovatory or otherwise – would be starved of funding.

There is, too, a related body of evidence to which Smith might have had recourse suggesting that the risks of contemporary 'innovation' should not be exaggerated in the Bentham manner. While the term 'entrepreneur' is nowadays often identified with the Schumpeterian-type creative innovator, it has been argued that 'the vast majority of entrepreneurs appear to have been imitative, even (one might argue, especially) during the period of the industrial revolution' (Payne, 1978, p. 184). Innovating entrepreneurs 'constitute special cases'; 'the great army of entrepreneurs were followers, dependent for their prosperity, even for their survival, on good management rather than innovation'. Moreover, risk was constrained considering the buoyancy of domestic and foreign markets, especially the former:

> fundamental to any understanding of the expansion of this [the cotton] and the other industries that experienced accelerated growth is that 'the home market for manufacturers was growing, thanks to improving communications, increase in population, high and rising average income, a buying pattern favourable to solid, standardized, moderately priced products, and unhampered commercial enterprise'. (p. 186, citing Landes, 1965, p. 285)

And 'the large number of business failures is not necessarily evidence of praiseworthy adventurousness (an interpretation denied to the Victorians) but may have been the consequence of sheer incompetence' (p. 187).

Payne takes account too of Rosenberg's observation 'that most mechanical productive processes throw off signals of a sort which are both compelling and fairly obvious; indeed, these processes when sufficiently complex and inter-dependent . . . create internal compulsions and pressure which, in turn, initiate exploratory activity in particular directions' (Rosenberg, 1969, p. 3, cited by Payne, 1978, p. 191). This perspective, according to Payne, applies not only to the early cotton industry, but to 'the innumerable minor improvements and modifications of machinery, methods, and organization which are less dramatic and consequently less well documented in this and in other industries'. And it implies 'that the risks involved in the adoption of technological improvement, during the classic period of the industrial revolution, were perhaps less than have hitherto been believed'.

All in all, this brief survey suggests that Bentham overemphasized 'praiseworthy adventurousness' of the Schumpeterian kind. And to the extent that this is so – particularly to the extent that riskiness was relatively moderate – there would be some justification for Smith's more balanced position that a moderate excess of the interest-rate maximum over the 'prime' rate could at least accommodate the desirable credit requirements relating to innovatory investment.

Smith also had some empirical justification for his confidence in the correction of excess demand by credit rationing on the part of lenders (setting aside the bankers).

Thus Ashton has maintained that 'though evasion [of the usury laws] was by no means unknown, the penalties were high, and the law generally respected' (Ashton, 1966, p. 28); 'there is a good deal of evidence that the usury law was generally respected' (Ashton, 1959, p. 175).[26] All this, however, changes during the American War, as we shall see below.

There is, more generally, considerable empirical justification for Smith's great concern with irresponsible speculation, for his was notoriously 'a century of speculation':

> A large number of companies were promoted, and trading was active in their shares. Insurance became a popular means of gambling on ships and on lives. State loans with lotteries attached were the rule; from 1694 to 1784 there were forty-two state lotteries. They facilitated the floatation of a large national debt. Life annuities introduced another element of chance. (Homer and Sylla, 1996, p. 153)

Even after the South Sea episode[27] speculative promotion continued throughout the century, much of it in government stock (p. 154). All of this would help account for Smith's suspicion of the 'chimerical', the 'grand' and the 'marvellous', and his lamentation that the 'splendid, but visionary ideas which are set forth in [Law's *Money and Trade Considered* of 1705] . . . and some other works upon the same principles, still continue to make an impression upon some people, and have, perhaps, in part, contributed to that excess of banking, which has late been complained of in Scotland and in other places' (Smith, 1976, pp. 317–18).

Smith himself expressed a particular concern with agricultural projectors who 'have within these few years amused the public with the most magnificent accounts of the profits to be made by the cultivation and improvement of land' (p. 374). Yet it is unlikely that his concerns were limited to agriculture. After all, he also wrote: 'Of all those expensive and uncertain projects . . . which bring bankruptcy upon the greater part of the people who engage in them, there is none perhaps more perfectly ruinous than the search after new silver and gold mines' (p. 562). And all his concerns underlying his support of the usury laws point to the entire range of projects, even if agriculture was the primary focus.[28]

It is revealing to place this against the background provided by Hamilton in his study of the failure of the Ayr Bank in 1772.[29] In that year:

> All the indications of over-trading were present. Indeed, the whole economy was caught up in the optimism of the times. In agriculture, in overseas trade and in the great schemes of capital investment, there is evidence of confidence in the future. Expectation of continuing profits intensified the demand for finance which the Ayr Bank was always ready to meet. Thus the economy was kept going and its very success engendered optimism and promoted enterprise. (Hamilton, 1956, p. 411)

Hamilton points also to the 'rage for agricultural improvements' encouraged by easy credit conditions during the late 1760s. Even some Ayr Bank directors 'were alarmed at the number of cash accounts, which, it was said, were becoming "burdensome and likely to be unprofitable, many being more used as loans than in the proper operations of business"'. Again: 'The Scots economy had become highly speculative', as the chartered banks – including the Bank of England – recognized (p. 413). And this speculative activity of 1770–71 contained within itself the seeds of collapse. Over trading and the too liberal, if not extravagant, creation of credit by the Ayr Bank undermined confidence in London and in Edinburgh. When this happened the boom was bound to burst. The failure of the Ayr Bank followed inevitably and this completed the destruction of high hopes and optimistic expectations. (p. 417)

Until the recovery in 1774.[30] It is precisely on the general speculative mood and the aggravating role of the Ayr Bank that Adam Smith focused, as we have seen.

The problem
It has been my argument that the criticism of Smith for maintaining a position on the usury laws to the detriment of innovatory investment has been overdone. He can claim to have made out a 'moderate' case, as Keynes opined, to the extent that the maximum had historically followed the market rate downward with a margin allowing for credit demands to satisfy a moderate degree of innovatory investment. He was positively not calling for a maximum below the 'market' rate on government loans or even one below the prime rate, which he believed would be unsustainable. This 'defence' of Smith I have supported by reference to aspects of the contemporary economy. Yet I now must raise serious questions regarding Smith's specific support of a 5 per cent maximum, considering the course of interest rates in the late 1770s and early 1780s. Here I see a true Smith problem.

From the early 1730s to 1745 the annual average yield on 3 per cent Funds[31] hovered around 3 per cent; from 1746 to 1748 it rose to 3.5 per cent, but from 1749 until the outbreak of war in 1756 returned to the vicinity of 3 per cent.[32] During the war of 1756–62 the average yield again rose to 3.6 per cent and thereafter remained between 3.3 per cent and 3.6 per cent until 1776. Despite the upward movement in the late 1750s the yield rarely exceeded 4 per cent (June and July 1759, and in 1762). But the average annual return rose to 4.9 per cent in 1779 and thereafter remained at an average of 5.1 per cent until 1785, falling to 4.5 per cent in 1786 and hovering around 4 per cent until 1790. The yield on new government long-term issues followed a similar pattern. The trend falls, steeply from a range of 8–9 per cent in the early years of the century to about 3.5 per cent in the late 1720s. Thereafter, the estimated effective yield remains at about 3 per cent until the mid-1770s with some exceptional highs of 4 per cent or more in the late 1740s, and again during the Seven Years War (one loan was made at 5 per cent). The 3 per cent pattern re-emerges in 1766 lasting until 1776; but the yield on the 1777 loan is 4.2 per cent, that of 1778 4.5 per cent and until 1785 well above 5 per cent (Table 15.1).[33]

Now in developing his case for a legal maximum of 5 per cent (above, pp. 6–8), Smith made much of the fact that before the Seven Years War (1756–63), the government borrowed at 3 per cent

> Since the time of Queen Anne [1713], five per cent. seems to have been rather above than below the market rate. Before the late war, the government borrowed at three per cent.; and people of good credit in the capital, and in many other parts of the kingdom, at three and a half, four, and four and a half per cent. (Smith, 1976, p. 106)

There might be some justification for his ignoring, in the 1776 edition, the wartime upward adjustment itself, since it was reversed thereafter. What is more striking is the failure in later editions to mention the post-1777 pattern and propose an upward revision of the legal maximum.

Table 15.1 Year and estimated effective yield, %

Year	%
1777	4.2
1778	4.5
1779	5.2
1780	5.7
1781	5.5
1782	6.8
1783	4.6
1784	5.2–5.4
1785 [conversion]	5.6

Source: Homer and Sylla (1996), p. 157, Table 12.

We have alluded to the general effectiveness of credit rationing at the legal maximum during much of the century (see p. 289). Now credit rationing was still the only legal means of proceeding when the market rate had risen to 5 per cent, as Feavearyear has pointed out with particular reference to Bank of England discounting:

> Throughout the greater part of the eighteenth century the market rate of interest had been below 4 per cent. and had therefore not conflicted with the legal maximum. The Bank had discounted, generally at market rate, as many bills as it could, after the Government's needs were supplied and having regard to its own safety. If it wished to improve its position it would refuse to discount fresh bills except at slightly higher rates. In 1773, however, the standard rate was fixed at 5 per cent., and remained there until 1822. When the maximum rate was reached it would send back, if it still wished to reduce its holding, a certain proportion of all the parcels of bills submitted. The Bank was always in the discount market. (Feavearyear, 1963, p. 243)

Pressnell makes the same point more generally: 'The long plateaux of virtually unchanged rates . . . reflect . . . a conservatism towards established rates – paralleled by the modern building society movement, for instance – that preferred to risk being starved of funds rather than disturb the status quo. This was unavoidable when the rate was already at the legal peak' (Pressnell, 1960, p. 192). And, similarly with an eye to changes in the value of money:

> Should the value of money change . . . lenders would not necessarily translate this into revised interest rates, They might prefer – like the borrowers on the other side of the fence – not to disturb settled rates; instead they might vary the intensity of credit rationing. To adopt Lord Keynes's illuminating concept, lenders undoubtedly acted upon the principle that at any rate of interest there was always a 'fringe of unsatisfied borrowers', which they widened or narrowed by varying their standards of eligibility [Keynes, 1930, II, pp. 364–7]. This was and still is characteristic of British banking and of British financial institutions in general. (p. 196)

The credit shortage was severely exacerbated by heavy government borrowing at or above 5 per cent during the American war: 'Our manufacturers, our traders, our farmers and even our landed gentlemen know to what a degree this expectation of Government premiums has affected them. Money cannot now be borrowed on mortgages, on the former terms' (William Pulteney, 1779; cited in Pressnell, 1960, p. 175).[34] The macroeconomic consequences of this deflection of funds to government is apparent from Ashton's account of the building sector (Ashton, 1959, pp. 86–7).[35] Indeed, the major depressions of 1761–2, 1778–84 and 1794–9 'seem to have been the direct result of upward movements in interest that cut off builders and contractors (their power of borrowing limited by the Usury Laws) from the market for funds' (p. 105). The problem, however, extended beyond the investment goods sector (p. 176). It is also clear that credit rationing did not always suffice to maintain the market rate at 5 per cent; evasions of one sort or another – some quite dramatic and not necessarily illegal – are apparent at periods of pressure:

> There were many ways in which money could become costly and more difficult to obtain without an overt variation in the rate of interest. When would-be borrowers . . . had to seek money elsewhere, the delay itself imposed an extra cost, since profits are a function of time. Equally, where assets had to be realized to raise money, a resultant capital loss was equivalent to a swingeing rate of interest. Those who failed to procure funds might swell the bankrupts' queue – it varied, after a lag, with interest rate movements – or enter the debtors' prison. (Pressnell, 1960, p. 197)

During the American war and later the Napoleonic Wars, those in need of money were sometimes 'driven to raise it by the sale of annuities at costly rates. Yet others, needing the money for themselves, would shoulder the capital loss of realizing assets (equivalent to a savage rate of interest)' (p. 184). The usury laws might also be 'quite legitimately short-circuited' by use of India bonds and other elements of the floating debt as means of payment the return on which calculated as a yield on their prices was free to fluctuate (p. 180). And the practice of granting trade credits and trade discounts provided indirect means of legally varying the cost of credit (pp. 197–201).

But whether during periods of heavy government borrowing credit was restricted by way of rationing at the maximum or by costly devices to circumvent the law, these implications of the maximum must have been patently apparent.[36] This was even the case on occasion during the earlier period of cheap money:

> From time to time landlords, farmers, and manufacturers were unable to obtain the resources they needed, not because savings had dried up, but because these had been directed to the state. Unable to raise money by the offer of higher rates of interest, men were forced to sell their assets for whatever these would fetch. The violence by which the century was marked is to be attributed less to the speculative tendencies or producers and traders than to the operation of the laws against usury. (Ashton, 1966, p. 29)

Let me summarize the problem that has now emerged. Smith's support for a 5 per cent legal interest-rate maximum breaks down in the late 1770s considering the major increase in the terms on new government borrowing to 5 per cent or more. Why did Smith not review his position, not by conceding the game to Bentham, but by recommending a significant upward adjustment of the legal maximum? After all, he so clearly explained that an appropriate minimum cannot be too low; that is, below – or even at – the 'lowest market rate': 'No law can reduce the common rate of interest below the lowest ordinary market rate at the time the law was made'; and he warned strongly that an inappropriately set maximum – even one coinciding with the 'lowest market price' – would oblige 'honest people . . . who cannot give the very best security . . . to have recourse to exorbitant usurers' (see also pp. 278, 280–81). He must then surely have realized that a 5 per cent legal maximum and a market rate exceeding 5 per cent are incompatible.

The problem can be restated: how is it that Smith neglected the 'crowding-out' effect exerted by government borrowing at 5 per cent and more, focusing entirely on the putative problem of the diversion of funds from 'sober' to irresponsible private ventures (and to conspicuous consumption)? After all, he took account of government borrowing at 3 per cent in his initial justification of the 5 per cent maximum. The picture is all the more extraordinary since Smith himself pointed out that even 'sober' businesses can run into liquidity problems.

There is one possible consideration. Smith had implied that financial crises result from 'overtrading' and undue extensions of credit:

> Even such general complaints of the scarcity of money do not always prove that the usual number of gold and silver pieces are not circulating in the country, but that many people want these pieces who have nothing to give for them. When the profits of trade happen to be greater than ordinary, overtrading becomes a general error both among great and small traders. They do not always send more money abroad than usual, but they buy upon credit both at home and abroad, an unusual quantity of goods, which they send to some distant market in hopes that the returns will come in before the demand for payment. The demand comes before the returns, and they have nothing at hand, with which they can either purchase money, or give solid security for borrowing. It is not any scarcity of gold and silver, but the difficulty which such people find in borrowing, and which the creditors find in getting payment, that occasions the general complaint of the scarcity of money. (Smith, 1976, p. 438)

It had been his major intention to prevent undue extensions of credit by the recommended checks on bank finance of long-term projects and lower limits on note denominations, as well as the hoped-for selectivity by private lenders at the legal maximum. He may, therefore, have allowed himself to be diverted from the problem of assuring accommodation for those in need of emergency credit, on the grounds that were these rules in place there would be less opportunity for overtrading in the first place, and thus less need for subsequent credit reduction. Nonetheless, all this is scarcely convincing in the circumstances of the American war, where complaints of 'scarce money' could legitimately be said to reflect heavy government competition for funding, not an earlier bout of speculative borrowing.

Concluding remarks
Smith's justification for a legal maximum interest rate in some respects resembles the rationalization of credit rationing by Stiglitz and Weiss (1981).[37] Their explanation of an equilibrium characterized by credit rationing at below the market clearing rate, turns on the hypothesis that bankers cannot stipulate (at least not costlessly) all the actions of a borrower that might affect the return to the loan, and consequently formulate the terms of the contract – including the interest rate – to the end of maximizing the expected return. Those terms are selected to screen potential borrowers in favour of those most likely to repay the loan, having in mind that a borrower's willingness to pay a high rate might reflect his perception that the probability of repayment is low; and/or to encourage borrowers to opt for safer projects, for 'higher interest rates induce firms to undertake projects with lower probability of success but higher payoffs when successful' (Stiglitz and Weiss, 1981, p. 393). Now both the 'selection' and 'incentive' effects are allowed for

by Smith. Certainly he ascribes to lenders faced by an excess demand a concern to select low-risk borrowers and a capacity to ration loans effectively, which prevents upward pressure on the interest rate. The second rationalization too has something of a Smithian flavour to it insofar as Smith associates the willingness to pay high interest specifically with rash projectors. There is, however, this important difference – that whereas the Stiglitz–Weiss solution has bankers imposing that interest rate (and other terms of the contract) which maximizes the expected return, Smith requires that the state undertake that function, removing a degree of freedom from lenders.

The deliberation with which Smith sets out his position leads me to doubt (with Pesciarelli, 1989) that he would have been convinced by Bentham's objections. We have reviewed various answers, both theoretical and empirical, to those objections. But even if Smith did not surrender to Bentham on matters of principle it remains possible that he accepted specific aspects of Bentham's position. Here I refer to a proposal by Bentham that has received little attention in the literature, namely his second-best solution should the legal maximum be retained, or 'the best means of relieving the projector from the load of discouragement laid on him by these [usury] laws, in so far as the pressure of them falls particularly upon him' (Bentham, 1787 [1952], p. 185). The proposal entails steps to pinpoint and exclude from the regulation genuine projects that have considerable promise:

> According to this idea, the object ... should be, to provide, in favour of projectors only, a dispensation from the rigour of the anti-usurious laws: such, for instance, as is enjoyed by persons engaged in the carrying trade, in virtue of the indulgence given to loans made on the footing of *respondentia* or bottomry. As to abuse, I see not why the danger of it should be greater in this case than in those. Whether a sum of money be embarked, or not embarked, in such or such a new manufacture on land, should not, in its own nature, be a fact much more difficult to ascertain, than whether it be embarked, or not embarked, in such or such a trading adventure by sea: and, in the one case as in the other, the payment of the interest, as well as the repayment of the principal, might be made to depend upon the success of the adventure. To confine the indulgence to new undertakings, the having obtained a patent for some invention, and the continuance of the term of the patent, might be made conditions of the allowance given to the bargain: to this might be added affidavits, expressive of the intended application, and bonds, with sureties, conditioned for the performance of the intention so declared; to be registered in one of the patent-offices or elsewhere. After this, affidavits once a year, or oftener, during the subsistence of the contract, declaring what has been done in execution of it. (pp. 185–6)[38]

I can see no reason why Smith, considering his allowances for the favourable treatment of successful joint-stock trading companies on a par with patent protection, would have objected to such a proposal. In fact, the informal indications of a fairly positive response on Smith's part towards Bentham (see above, note 3), might conceivably have related to this proposal.

But our main problem remains unanswered. Pesciarelli has pointed out that Smith 'would have had the time, if he had had the will, to change his opinions' in the last two editions of the *Wealth of Nations* (1789 and 1791) since he made significant revisions to the *Theory of Moral Sentiments* at this late period (Pesciarelli, 1989, pp. 535–6). Pesciarelli may well be right. But on our reading the problem is exacerbated, since much of Smith's case breaks down on empirical grounds after 1778, a full decade before the Bentham letter. Even were the 'indolence of old age' beginning to be a factor in

1785 – as Smith complained in November of that year (Mossner and Ross, 1977, p. 287) – the problem of heavy government borrowing with its damaging implications for the 5 per cent maximum set in much earlier. And despite major revisions to the third edition in 1784 he chose not to modify in any way his position on the usury laws.[39] Smith himself observed (to Andreas Holt) in October 1780, quite generally, that 'I have not thought it proper to make any direct answer to any of my adversaries' (p. 250).[40] But our question relates to a failure to respond to events, not to a critic. Smith's self-confessed practice of remaining silent in the face of criticism does not, therefore, help us. The difficulty is enhanced by the fact that a full-fledged retraction of this position was not called for, only a recommendation to adjust the minimum upwards to assure a level somewhat above the market rate.

One mundane solution would be that Smith considered the experience of the American War as temporary only and therefore not worth mentioning. However, in the early 1780s there was no way of knowing how long the conflict would last. It turned out that after the 1786 conversion loan with its effective yield of 5.6 per cent there was no new government borrowing during Smith's lifetime, while the yield on 3 per cent consuls fell from 5.4 per cent in 1785 to 4.5 per cent in 1786 and to 4.1 per cent thereafter. But here we recall that Smith's detailed case for the 5 per cent maximum was in fact based on rates of about 3 per cent on government issues ruling before 'the late [Seven Years] war'; thus his position was already somewhat dated even in 1776, since the range of rates did not fall markedly after the peace in 1762 (averaging 3.45 per cent in 1763–76, compared with 3.57 per cent in 1756–62). In brief, a yield of 4 per cent setting in after 1786 is still a full percentage point higher than the rates on which Smith based his initial case for a 5 per cent maximum.

Notes

1. As for 'prodigals', they were not a group who will demand money at high rates (Bentham, 1787 [1952], pp. 133–8).
2. Bentham claimed that there was no limit to the demand for loans at 5 per cent by 'old-established' concerns (Bentham, 1787 [1952], p. 171).
3. Rae opined that it was 'reasonable to think that if Smith had lived to publish another edition of his work, he would have modified his position on the rate of interest' (Rae, 1965 [1895], p. 424). Rae based himself on an alleged 'confession' by Smith of his conversion (to William Adam, MP) and reported by George Wilson to Bentham (4 December 1789, in Mossner and Ross, 1977, p. 387). Rae conceded that the 'admission' was only 'inferred by Adam from the general purport of the conversation'. And Bentham himself took nothing for granted, requesting of Smith, in late 1789 or early 1790, that he confirm 'the intelligence ... [since] the intimation did not come directly from you' (in Bentham, 1787 [1952], p. 188); also Bentham, 'Defence of a Maximum' (Bentham, 1801 [1952], p. 259; and Mossner and Ross, 1977, p. 402). Jacob Viner also was circumspect: 'from the information available' – this includes a presentation copy possibly of his *Theory of Moral Sentiments* that Smith sent to Bentham – 'all that can be safely inferred is that Smith bore Bentham no ill-will for his criticism and possibly did not deny that it had some force' (Viner, 1965, p. 19).
4. The penalty for breaking the law amounted to three times the capital involved and was imposed on lenders. The maximum did not apply to government loans.
5. See also Steuart (1767 [1998]), III, pp. 144–5.
6. See Smith's account of French experience, cited by Bentham (see above, p. 278).
7. Smith does not here formally weigh the merits of a free versus a controlled credit market, but focuses on alternative levels of the legal maximum. Nonetheless, since free-market rates would presumably rise above 8–10 per cent; it may be inferred that his argument applies *a fortiori* against a free credit market.
8. This concern was *a fortiori* true of bankers who, Smith believed, were incapable of arriving at a fair evaluation of proposals.
9. Walter Eltis points out to me that Smith in effect 'condemned what are nowadays described as junk

Jeremy Bentham and Adam Smith on the usury laws 297

bonds. And who can say he was wrong in view of the financial destruction they have often created' (communication, 25 June 1998).
10. In some respects Smith's language resembles Steuart's (see note 5 above). Locke (1968 [1691]), pp. 1–6, and Turgot (1963 [1770]), p. 74 opposed usury laws. Cantillon was non-committal (1931 [1755]), p. 221.
11. Smith ascribes the initiative to the lender, on which matter see above, p. 283.
12. Pesciarelli (1989), p. 253 implies that this citation relates specifically to Smith's 'adventurers' – those who, in Pesciarelli's terms, 'in the frenetic search for risk, spurred on by unrestrained confidence in success hazard their capital on the most difficult undertakings'. But there is a danger of downplaying Smith's concern with the pervasiveness of the character and an across-the-board failure of profit rates to reflect risk appropriately.
13. And various banking regulations, as we shall see.
14. For a wide discussion of appropriate institutional arrangements, see Rosenberg 1960.
15. For details, see Hollander (1973), Chapter 7.
16. Smith referred in correspondence of 1772 to 'Public calamities' involving Scottish businesses and banks in which various friends were involved: 'my attention has been a good deal occupied about the most proper method of extricating them' (to Pulteney, 3 September 1772; in Mossner and Ross 1977, pp. 163–4). In a letter from Edinburgh to Smith of 27 June, Hume had written of 'a very melancholy Situation: Continual Bankruptcies, universal Loss of Credit and endless Suspicions' regarding the stability even of major banking houses and a similar situation in London and the provinces; and he also had alluded to the Carron Company – the largest industrial company in Scotland: 'The Carron Company is reeling which is one of the greatest Calamities of the whole; as they gave employment to near 10,000 People. Do these Events any-wise affect your Theory?' (p. 162). Hume opined that '[on] the whole, I believe that the Check given to our exorbitant and ill grounded Credit will prove of Advantage in the long run, as it will reduce people to more solid and less sanguine Projects, and at the same time introduce Frugality among the Merchants and Manufacturers: What say you? Here is Food for your Speculation' (p. 163).
17. But see Hamilton (1956), p. 408, who represents the Ayr Bank not as a speculative enterprise, but as one founded in 1769 to overcome a shortage of working capital reflecting the conservatism of the chartered banks.
18. See Hamilton: 'By discounting bills and opening cash credits they put their notes into circulation often in districts far from their head office' (1956, p. 407).
19. Smith points out that the Ayr Bank itself was borrowing at effective rates exceeding 8 per cent, and lending at 5 per cent (Smith, 1976, p. 314). See on this Hamilton (1956), p. 408.
    On the irresponsible financing of the Carron Company, see Campbell (1961), pp. 125–32. From 1769 until the crises of 1772 the company was predominantly financed by the circulation of bills (p. 132).
20. See also Smith (1976), p. 308: despite liberal bank terms, 'traders and other undertakers' frequently complained that banks failed to meet their credit requirements, albeit dictated by expanding national trade, 'meaning, no doubt, by the extension of that trade the extension of their own projects beyond what they could carry on, either with their own capital, or with what they had credit to borrow of private people in the usual way of bond or mortgage'.
21. Hamilton (1956), pp. 407–8 observes that the chartered banks were alarmed, not other private banks such as the Ayr Bank.
22. Related to this is Smith's recommendation of lower limits to the denomination of paper money (Smith, 1976, p. 323). Here we recall the position that economic growth, to be successful, requires that it be 'protected by law' (see above, p. 283). To control of the interest rate by the state we must therefore add the various other restraints on bankers – a 'violation' of the 'natural liberty of a few individuals' in the interest of the 'security of the whole society' (p. 324). On the recommendation to limit the denomination of bank notes, see West (1977). West regards this recommendation – and other instances of support for money and banking regulation – as anomalous and inconsistent with Smith's general principles.
23. See also: 'The essence of the sole proprietorship or small partnership as a method of economic organization is that the decision-maker has sole property rights over his instruments of production; and by the unification of ownership and management, the partners who carry the risk also make the decisions determining its extent. It is important to recognize that one of the legitimate functions of the owner-manager was that of reducing risk to a minimum' (Payne, 1978, p. 184).
24. The 'offsetting disadvantage of owner-management was, of course, the restraint which it imposed on the scale of operation, a restraint deriving from the difficulties of delegation' (Payne, 1978, p. 192). But 'not until technological requirements made for an increase in size beyond that manageable by the partners, and capital requirements went beyond the resources of small, often related, groups of men, was it necessary to devise a new structure for the firm – not, in fact, until the second half of the nineteenth century' (pp. 192–3).
25. We should not though forget that some self-financing itself probably reflects the existence of usury laws and the rationing undertaken by lenders (Ashton, 1959, p. 86).

26. Ashton cites Thornton (1802 [1939]), p. 254, on which matter see also note 36 below.
27. For informal accounts of the atmosphere in 1720 on the collapse of the South Sea Company, see Plumb (1966), pp. 62–5; Ackroyd (1995), pp. 23, 35, 97.
28. In his 1762–63 lectures Smith justified the contemporary sanctions, extending to capital punishment, imposed on those convicted of fraud in bankruptcy proceedings on the grounds that 'there is no fraud which is more easily committed without being discovered' (Smith, 1978, p. 132). Similarly, in the 1766 lectures: 'Some frauds, however, on account of the facility and security with which they may be committed and the loss which they occasion, are justly subjected to capital punishment' (ibid., p. 483). I owe these references to Cabrillo (1986), pp. 40–41.
29. The previous year marked the climax of a period of economic progress dating back to the late 1740s (Hamilton, 1956, p. 405).
30. Joslin attributes the banking bankruptcies 1769–73 to 'rash speculation in commodities' and 'inexperience' (Joslin, 1962, pp. 346–7). See too Campbell (1961), p. 126, regarding bank speculation in stock.
31. Until 1752 on 3 per cent annuities, thereafter on 3 per cent consolidated stock.
32. See the data on long-term interest rates in Homer and Sylla (1996), pp. 155–63, and Ashton (1959), p. 187. Ashton points out (p. 88) that because government loans were not subject to the usury laws, the yield on government stock can be regarded as *the* rate of interest, all other rates – those on mortgages, bonds and bills – moving in line, at least within the limits imposed by the law.
33. All these new loans had lottery privileges attached to them. After 1785 there were no new loans until 1793.
34. Cited from Report of the Commons Select Committee on the Usury Laws, 1818, in BPP, 1845 (375/611), XII, Q.540.
35. Pressnell discusses the 'cramping' of existing or would-borrowers 'when the free market rate of interest, as registered in the stock markets, reached or passed the legal maximum' (1960, p. 183).
36. Ricardo argued in 1818 against the usury laws both on grounds of evasion and 'crowding out'; see Ricardo (1951–73), V, pp. 337–47. But Thornton had earlier presumed there was little evasion, and opposed the laws as creating an 'unnaturally low Interest of Money' and accordingly 'a much greater Disposition to borrow of the Bank at 5 per cent. than it might become the Bank to comply with', especially 'at the present Times' (evidence, 31 March 1797 in Thornton, 1802 [1962], p. 307). See also: 'The temptation to borrow, in time of war, too largely at the bank, arises . . . from the high rate of mercantile profit. Capital is then scarce, and the gain accruing from the employment of it is proportionably considerable' (p. 255).
37. The resemblance has been remarked on by Carr and Landa (1985), and Neihans (1994).
38. A further proposal is made, tongue-in-cheek: 'If the leading-string is not yet thought tight enough, boards of controul might be instituted to draw it tighter' (Bentham, 1787 [1952], p. 186).
39. For a convenient list of significant additions introduced between the second (1778) and the third (1784) editions of the *Wealth of Nations*, see Mossner and Ross (1977), p. 263n. Also their index, pp. 440–1.
40. Smith self-righteously claims that he 'had obviated' in his second edition various objections by Governor Pownall; that Pownall was not satisfied did not surprise him: 'Authors are not much disposed to alter the opinions they have once published' (Mossner and Ross, 1977, p. 250).

References

Ackroyd, P. (1995), *Blake*, London: Minerva.
Ashton, T.S. (1959), *Economic Fluctuations in England, 1700–1800*, Oxford: Clarendon Press.
Ashton, T.S. (1966), *An Economic History of England: The 18th Century*, London: Methuen.
Bentham, Jeremy (1787), *Defence of Usury*, reprinted in W. Stark (ed.) (1952), *Jeremy Bentham's Economic Writings*, Vol. I, London: George Allen & Unwin, pp. 123–207.
Bentham, Jeremy (1801), *Defence of a Maximum*, reprinted in W. Stark (ed.) (1952), *Jeremy Bentham's Economic Writings*, Vol. III, London: George Allen & Unwin, pp. 247–302.
Cabrillo, F. (1986), 'Adam Smith on bankruptcy law: "new" law and economics in the Glasgow Lectures', *History of Economics Society Bulletin*, **8** (Summer), 40–1.
Campbell, R.H. (1961), *Carron Company*, Edinburgh and London: Oliver & Boyd.
Cantillon, Richard (1931 [1755]). *Essai sur La Nature du Commerce en Général*, H. Higgs (ed.), London: Macmillan.
Carr, J. and J. Landa (1985), 'The Economics of Usury Laws', Manuscript, University of Toronto.
Feavearyear, A. (1963), *The Pound Sterling: A History of English Money*, 2nd edn, Oxford: Clarendon Press.
Hamilton, H. (1956), 'The failure of the Ayr Bank, 1772', *Economic History Review*, **8**, 405–17.
Hollander, S. (1973), *The Economics of Adam Smith*, Toronto: University of Toronto Press.
Homer, S. and R. Sylla (1996), *A History of Interest Rates*, 3rd edn, New Brunswick, NJ: Rutgers Unversity Press.

Joslin, D.M. (1962), 'London Private Bankers, 1720–1785', in E.M. Carus-Wilson (ed.), *Essays in Economic History*, Vol. II, London: Edward Arnold, pp. 340–59.
Keynes, J.M. (1930), *A Treatise on Money*, London: Macmillan.
Keynes, J.M. (1936), *The General Theory of Employment, Interest and Money*, London: Macmillan.
Koebner, R. (1959), 'Adam Smith and the Industrial Revolution', *Economic History Review*, **11**, 381–91.
Landes, D.S. (1965), 'Technological change and development in Western Europe, 1750–1914', in H.J. Habakkuk and M. Postan (eds), *Cambridge Economic History of Europe*, Vol. VI, Cambridge: Cambridge University Press, pp. 274–601.
Law, J. (1705), *Money and Trade Considered*, Edinburgh: Andrew Anderson.
Levy, D. (1987), 'Adam Smith's case for usury laws', *History of Political Economy*, **19** (Fall), 387–400.
Locke, John (1968 [1691]), *Some Considerations of the Consequences of the Lowering of Interest, and Raising the Value of Money*, New York: Kelley.
Mossner, E.C. and I.S. Ross (1977), *The Correspondence of Adam Smith*, Oxford: Clarendon Press.
Neihans, J. (1994), 'Adam Smith and the welfare cost of optimisim', University of Munich: Centre for Economic Studies, Working Paper No. 62.
Pack, S.J. (1997), 'Adam Smith and the virtues: a partial resolution of the Adam Smith problem', *Journal of the History of Economic Thought*, **19** (Spring), 127–40.
Payne, P.L. (1978), 'Industrial Entrepreneurship and Management in Great Britain', in Peter Mathias and M. Postan (eds), *The Cambridge Economic History of Europe*, Vol. VII, Cambridge: Cambridge University Press, pp. 180–230.
Pesciarelli, E. (1989), 'Smith, Bentham, and the development of contrasting ideas on entrepreneurship', *History of Political Economy*, **21** (Fall), 521–36.
Plumb, J.H. (1966), *The First Four Georges*, London: Collins.
Pressnell, L.S. (1960), 'The rate of interest in the eighteenth century', in L.S. Pressnell (ed.), *Studies in the Industrial Revolution*, London: Athlone Press, pp. 178–214.
Pulteney, W. (1779), *Considerations on the Present State of Public Affairs*, London: J. Dodsley and T. Cadell.
Rae, John (1965 [1895]), *Life of Adam Smith*, New York: Kelley.
Ricardo, David (1951–73), *Speeches and Evidence*, in P. Sraffa (ed.), *Works and Correspondence of David Ricardo*, Vol. V, Cambridge: Cambridge University Press, pp. 337–47.
Robbins, L.C. (1968), *The Theory of Economic Development in the History of Economic Thought*, London: Macmillan.
Rosenberg, N. (1960). 'Some institutional aspects of the *Wealth of Nations*', *Journal of Political Economy*, **68** (December), 557–70.
Rosenberg, N. (1969). 'The direction of technological change: inducement mechanisms and focusing devices', *Economic Development and Cultural Changes*, **18** (October), 1–24.
Smith, Adam (1976), *An Inquiry into the Nature and Causes of the Wealth of Nations*, W.B. Todd (ed.), Oxford: Clarendon Press.
Smith, Adam (1978). *Lectures on Jurisprudence*, R.L. Meek, D.D. Raphael and P.G. Stein (eds), Oxford: Clarendon Press.
Spengler, J.J. (1959), 'Adam Smith's theory of economic growth – Part II', *Southern Economic Journal*, **26** (July), 1–12.
Steuart, Sir James (1767), *An Inquiry into the Principles of Political Economy*; reprinted in A.S. Skinner (ed.) (1998), London: Pickering & Chatto.
Stigler, G.J. (1975), *The Citizen and the State: Essays on Regulation*, Chicago, IL: University of Chicago Press.
Stigler, G.J. (1988), *Memoirs of an Unregulated Economist*, New York: Basic Books.
Stiglitz J. and A. Weiss (1981), 'Credit rationing in markets with imperfect information', *American Economic Review*, **71** (June), 393–410.
Thornton, Henry (1802), *An Enquiry into the Nature and Effects of the Paper Credit of Great Britain*; reprinted in F.A. von Hayek (ed.) (1939), London: George Allen and Unwin Ltd.
Turgot, A.R.J. (1963 [1770]), *Reflections on the Formation and Distribution of Riches*, New York: Kelley.
Viner, J. (1965), *Guide to John Rae's Life of Adam Smith*, in Rae (1965 [1895]), *Life of Adam* Smith, New York: Kelley, pp. 5–145.
West, E.G. (1977), 'Adam Smith's support for money and banking regulation: a case of inconsistency', *Journal of Money, Credit and Banking*, **29** (February), 127–34.

16 'Only three duties': Adam Smith on the economic role of government
Steven G. Medema and Warren J. Samuels

Introduction

What Adam Smith meant to be understood as saying about the economic role of government is one of the great interpretive questions in the history of economic thought. Smith's view of the appropriate role for government within the economic system is usually summarized via his 'only three duties' – national defence, the administration of justice and the provision of certain public works – statement at the end of Book IV of the *Wealth of Nations*, and his subsequent elaboration of the content of these duties in Book V. Yet, his broad-based and nuanced treatment of these issues belies any claims of simplicity of interpretation. Moreover, Smith's views regarding the role of government go well beyond those elaborated in Book V or even in the *Wealth of Nations* as a whole.

Not only is the issue of what Smith meant to convey itself a great interpretive question, but it raises a number of other such questions, such as, how a theory of social control itself became part of the system of social control, how a small group of specific texts can be given divergent and contradictory interpretations, how the unsaid but taken-for-granted drives a body of theory, and how the social construction of legal-economic reality takes place.

The thread common to all such matters can be expressed thus: Assume that an object of inquiry, X, is in fact a function of variables A, B and C. So $X = f(A, B, C)$. If B and C are excluded from the analysis, then X is interpreted, understood, and analyzed solely as a function of A, and all that B and C might contribute to understanding X is lost; similarly with excluding A and B or A and C. But these formulations not only demonstrate what is lost in each case, they also indicate how X can be given multiple, conflicting interpretations. When students of X do not in fact know that $X = f(A, B, C)$, their accounts – their stories – vary with their perspective. Different perspectives see connections differently and assign different weights to evidence.

In the case of Adam Smith, the foregoing exercise applies to no less than three domains: Smith's tripartite model of society; the treatment of law and government in his three major works inclusive of his lectures on jurisprudence; and the several different and conflicting paradigms in which he more or less simultaneously moved. By adopting and working within only or largely one of the three models, or only one of the paradigms, or only one of his major works, an interpreter can readily neglect the others in producing what, upon reflection of their relevant totality, is an undernourished and abbreviated formulation.

Smith grounded his work in multiple paradigms, including naturalism, supernaturalism, pragmatism (utilitarianism), empiricism, historicism, secularism, materialism, nationalism, individualism, and so on. Smith's ideas appear differently to those who emphasize one or another of these paradigms. Those who focus on his naturalism or supernaturalism or on his individualism tend to discuss his ideas on the economic role of government in terms of definitive closure, hence minimal legal change. Those who focus on his pragmatism, empiricism, secularism and historicism tend to discuss his ideas on economic policy more open-endedly. Combinations are readily achieved: an emphasis on final causes, or on a deistic divinity who designed and established society, can support the social construction of moral rules and assign their ultimate genesis to the design of human beings on the basis of the principles of approbation and disapprobation. Conflict is also readily present. Historicism, especially evolutionism, can be denigrated because of the lack of scriptural identification or it can be accepted, if not applauded, as the mode through which design operates. The point is, again, that diverse interpretations can be grounded on different paradigmatic elements in Smith. Likewise, they can be grounded on different treatments of his tripartite model of society and on his own different treatments of law and government in his three relevant works.

Smith's tripartite model of society is in effect his system of social science. It was comprised of three modes of social control – of coordinating relations within society: moral rules, law and the market. Each worked in its own way to channel individual behaviour into directions socially apprehended. To understand Smith's system, then, requires coming to grips with the roles that these social control mechanisms play in social interaction as well as the forces that generate their evolution over time – both collectively and in terms of their relative import or extent.

In his *Theory of Moral Sentiments* (1976 [1759]) Smith addresses the operation of the principles of approbation and disapprobation in the working-out of the substantive content of moral rules. Individuals want to look good in the minds of others and in their own minds. They seek the moral approval and social recognition of others. In the process moral rules are formed and internalized in the 'impartial spectator' process, a process in which moral rules are also contested and changed. Smith is more interested in the process than in their (changing) substantive content. In this magisterial volume Smith presents his theory of moral rules as social control. If one were to consider it alone, then the other two domains would be excluded. Smith, however, concludes the volume with the announcement:

> I shall in another discourse endeavour to give an account of the general principles of law and government, and of the different revolutions they have undergone in the different ages and periods of society, not only in what concerns justice, but in what concerns police, revenue, and arms, and whatever else is the object of law. I shall not, therefore, at present enter into any further detail concerning the history of jurisprudence. (Smith, 1976 [1759], VII.iv.37, 342)

This volume he did not produce;[1] in its stead we have two sets of notes taken by students in his course on that subject, one of which was brought to light by Edwin Cannan in 1896[2] and both of which were published in 1978 as his *Lectures on Jurisprudence*. He did write, however, *An Inquiry into the Nature and Causes of the Wealth of Nations*, in which he articulates the spirit of and analyses what has come to be called the market economy, what he called the obvious and simple system of natural liberty.

The legal–economic nexus
Several interpretive problems have emerged from Smith's procedure in the *Wealth of Nations*, in part in juxtaposition to the world his monumental volume helped create. One

is that his specific opposition to mercantilism could be extended to general criticism of government as a whole, leading to a seemingly negative and minimalist agenda for government. Against this, however, we have Lionel Robbins going so far as to suggest that Smith's 'invisible hand' is actually government itself, stating that it 'is not the hand of some god or some natural agency independent of human effort; it is the hand of the lawgiver, the hand which withdraws from the sphere of the pursuit of self-interest those possibilities which do not harmonize with the public good' (Robbins, 1952, p. 56). Robbins may or may not be correct; the point here is that Smith does have a place for government that is both ubiquitous and important, though this ubiquity is perhaps more implicit in the *Wealth of Nations* and more explicit in the *Lectures on Jurisprudence*.

The Wealth of Nations
Smith is highly critical of the uses made of governments by ruling elites. Yet, he also states as a given that civil government is indispensably necessary for the security of property, that is, for the structure of power embedded in and given effect by the law of property. The former is expressed by Smith – forcefully – as follows:

> People of the same trade seldom meet together, even for merriment and diversion, but the conversation ends in a conspiracy against the public, or in some contrivance to raise prices. It is impossible indeed to prevent such meetings, by any law which either could be executed, or would be consistent with liberty and justice. But though the law cannot hinder people of the same trade from sometimes assembling together, it ought to do nothing to facilitate such assemblies; much less to render them necessary. (1776, I.10.82)

> The interest of the dealers, however, in any particular branch of trade or manufactures, is always in some respects different from, and even opposite to, that of the public. To widen the market and to narrow the competition, is always the interest of the dealers. To widen the market may frequently be agreeable enough to the interest of the public; but to narrow the competition must always be against it, and can serve only to enable the dealers, by raising their profits above what they naturally would be, to levy, for their own benefit, an absurd tax upon the rest of their fellow-citizens. The proposal of any new law or regulation of commerce which comes from this order, ought always to be listened to with great precaution, and ought never to be adopted till after having been long and carefully examined, not only with the most scrupulous, but with the most suspicious attention. It comes from an order of men, whose interest is never exactly the same with that of the public, who have generally an interest to deceive and even to oppress the public, and who accordingly have, upon many occasions, both deceived and oppressed it. (1776, I.11.264)

Note that, in both of these statements, Smith expresses a fairly dim view of businessmen and their motivations, but he also points up how the law plays a vital role in determining the extent to which businessmen can operate in ways contrary to the interests of consumers. Businessmen will attempt to use law – that is, government – to further their own interests. The alert reader will see here Smith's warning of actions that now go by the name of rent-seeking. Government, then, can facilitate these activities or inhibit them, as it chooses. In its ongoing attempts to reconcile these competing interests, legal change through government occupies a central place within Smith's system.

Smith presents a nice illustration of the impact of differential legal rules on market outcomes in his discussion of the exercise of monopsony power on the part of collusive employers as against the attempts by workers to assert some monopoly power through combinations of their own in an age when such unionization activity on the part of workers was illegal:

> We have no acts of parliament against combining to lower the price of work; but many against combining to raise it. In all such disputes the masters can hold out much longer. . . .
> We rarely hear, it has been said, of the combinations of masters, though frequently of those of workmen. But whoever imagines, upon this account, that masters rarely combine, is as ignorant of the world as of the subject. Masters are always and every where in a sort of tacit, but constant and uniform combination, not to raise the wages of labour above their actual rate. To violate this combination is every where a most unpopular action, and a sort of reproach to a master among his neighbours and equals. We seldom, indeed, hear of this combination, because it is the usual, and one may say, the natural state of things which nobody ever hears of. Masters too sometimes enter into particular combinations to sink the wages of labour even below this rate. These are always conducted with the utmost silence and secrecy, till the moment of execution, and when the workmen yield, as they sometimes do, without resistance, though severely felt by them, they are never heard of by other people. Such combinations, however, are frequently resisted by a contrary defensive combination of the workmen; who sometimes too, without any provocation of this kind, combine of their own accord to raise the price of their labour. Their usual pretences are, sometimes the high price of provisions; sometimes the great profit which their masters make by their work. But whether their combinations be offensive or defensive, they are always abundantly heard of. In order to bring the point to a speedy decision, they have always recourse to the loudest clamour, and sometimes to the most shocking violence and outrage. They are desperate, and act with the folly and extravagance of desperate men, who must either starve, or frighten their masters into an immediate compliance with their demands. The masters upon these occasions are just as clamorous upon the other side, and never cease to call aloud for the assistance of the civil magistrate, and the rigorous execution of those laws which have been enacted with so much severity against the combinations of servants, labourers, and journeymen. The workmen, accordingly, very seldom derive any advantage from the violence of those tumultuous combinations, which, partly from the interposition of the civil magistrate, partly from the superior steadiness of the masters, partly from the necessity which the greater part of the workmen are under of submitting for the sake of present subsistence, generally end in nothing, but the punishment or ruin of the ringleaders. (I.8.12–13)

The latter is stated, in part, as follows, in two passages that at times almost seem to exhibit shades of Marx:

> Men may live together in society with some tolerable degree of security, though there is no civil magistrate to protect them from the injustice of those passions. But avarice and ambition in the rich, in the poor the hatred of labour and the love of present ease and enjoyment, are the passions which prompt to invade property, passions much more steady in their operation, and much more universal in their influence. Wherever there is great property there is great inequality. For one very rich man there must be at least five hundred poor, and the affluence of the few supposes the indigence of the many. The affluence of the rich excites the indignation of the poor, who are often both driven by want, and prompted by envy, to invade his possessions. It is only under the shelter of the civil magistrate that the owner of that valuable property, which is acquired by the labour of many years, or perhaps of many successive generations, can sleep a single night in security. He is at all times surrounded by unknown enemies, whom, though he never provoked, he can never appease, and from whose injustice he can be protected only by the powerful arm of the civil magistrate continually held up to chastise it. The acquisition of valuable and extensive property, therefore, necessarily requires the establishment of civil government. Where there is no property, or at least none that exceeds the value of two or three days labour, civil government is not so necessary.
> Civil government supposes a certain subordination. But as the necessity of civil government gradually grows up with the acquisition of valuable property, so the principal causes which

naturally introduce subordination gradually grow up with the growth of that valuable property.

The causes or circumstances which naturally introduce subordination, or which naturally, and antecedent to any civil institution, give some men some superiority over the greater part of their brethren, seem to be four in number. (1776, V.1.45–7)

Smith continues by making explicit how these economic conditions give rise to pressures for law and legal change:

It is in the age of shepherds, in the second period of society, that the inequality of fortune first begins to take place, and introduces among men a degree of authority and subordination which could not possibly exist before. It thereby introduces some degree of that civil government which is indispensably necessary for its own preservation: and it seems to do this naturally, and even independent of the consideration of that necessity. The consideration of that necessity comes no doubt afterwards to contribute very much to maintain and secure that authority and subordination. The rich, in particular, are necessarily interested to support that order of things which can alone secure them in the possession of their own advantages. Men of inferior wealth combine to defend those of superior wealth in the possession of their property, in order that men of superior wealth may combine to defend them in the possession of theirs. All the inferior shepherds and herdsmen feel that the security of their own herds and flocks depends upon the security of those of the great shepherd or herdsman; that the maintenance of their lesser authority depends upon that of his greater authority, and that upon their subordination to him depends his power of keeping their inferiors in subordination to them. They constitute a sort of little nobility, who feel themselves interested to defend the property and to support the authority of their own little sovereign in order that he may be able to defend their property and to support their authority. Civil government, so far as it is instituted for the security of property, is in reality instituted for the defence of the rich against the poor, or of those who have some property against those who have none at all. (1776, V.1.55)

While it may be more easy to sympathize with 'security of property' than with attempts by businessmen to extract additional profits out of consumers, Smith's treatment of these issues makes it clear that in both cases pressures are being brought to bear for particular forms of law that will facilitate certain interests and impede others.

The result is that Smith both takes as a given the existing system of law and government, and criticizes some elements of that system. Both points are important. The three stated duties of government, read narrowly, do not exhaust the economic role of government. Criticism of the existing system points to the continuing process in which existing law is made subject to critique and reform. Smith clearly intended his work to be a contribution to that process of legal change. But it can, when read narrowly in the context of the argument of the *Wealth of Nations*, be interpreted as advocacy of both minimal government and of minimal legal change. The irony is that Smith clearly understood the ubiquity and importance of law and his argument in favour of 'the obvious and simple system of natural liberty' actually constituted a revolutionary doctrine in terms of introducing legal change. All this is made clear when one pays attention, first, to what Smith has to say (as above) about government and property, and the machinations of special interests; and, second, to the treatment of law and government, as well as property, in the *Lectures on Jurisprudence* (1978). In particular, government itself is not exogenous to the system, government is due to and to a large extent the instrument of the propertied, of those, that is, who use government to cement and institutionalize their systemic social power. As Smith says, 'Till there be property there can be no government, the very end of which is to secure wealth and to defend the rich from the poor' (Smith, 1978, LJB, 404). Social control through law must be understood through attention given to social structure.

Other aspects of the problem of interpretation include the following. Firstly, Smith was writing for a particular audience who, he could expect, took with him certain things (including certain publications) for granted, and likely did so about public, or legal, institutions. Smith cited John Locke in both of his major published works and in his lectures; Smith could assume his readers did not need him to elaborately ground his allusions to Locke. Like most people writing on the economic role of government, Smith typically took the regnant legal system and body of law as a given background. Also like most people, he did not hesitate to criticize either the legal system or the law. In other words, he was selective in what he implicitly accepted. Secondly, Smith concentrated on only what he deemed necessary for his present purpose. In the case of the three listed duties of government, the principal focus of discussion is how to raise the revenue with which to finance the expenses of government. Thirdly, the terminology of 'the obvious and simple system of natural liberty' is a good example of the interpretive predicament that Smith worked within several different and conflicting paradigms. Fourthly, he recognized as crucial the process of legal change. As already noted, Smith clearly intended his work to be a contribution to that process. Fifthly, Smith did not elaborate on his intended meaning of such terms as 'the obvious and simple system of natural liberty' and the 'invisible hand', leaving people to read into each whatever they interpreted it to mean, that is, to treat it as an undefined, primitive term. Sixthly, an important part of Smith's analysis in the *Wealth of Nations* and in his lectures on jurisprudence is his reliance on his stages theory of history. On the one hand, these stages are in large part defined in terms of their respective systems of law and government. One implication is the ubiquity and importance of legal social control. Another implication is that such points to what he took for granted. On the other hand, changes in stages involve changes in law and government. One implication is that legal change is due to changes both within a stage and between stages, each of which involves the need to choose between received rights and new claims of rights.

Smith's relative silence in the *Wealth of Nations* on topics of the structure and content of law, perhaps especially concerning property, should not be surprising. The United States Constitution deals with the structure and powers of government. Although it provides in Amendments V and XIV that no person shall 'be deprived of life, liberty, or property, without due process of law', and the former also providing that private property not 'be taken for public use, without just compensation', the Constitution silently takes for granted the existence of private property and the common law as the process through which the institution of private property is reformulated. It says nothing about either those points, or the elasticity of interpretation of the due process and takings clauses, or that those clauses do not apply to the courts themselves. In Smith's case, he was lecturing on law and government, and planning, at least early, on writing a volume on law and government. Both taking the status quo institution of property as a given, and ignoring the ways in which it has changed in the past, has the effect of tending to reify the existing property structure and leads to myopic interpretation and analysis.

Alexis de Tocqueville provides another example, either of identifying the widespread non-perception of government or of committing it himself. Gary Wills quotes the famous passage:

> Nothing is more striking to a European traveller in the United States than the absence of what we term government, or the administration. Written laws exist in America, and one sees the daily execution of them; but although everything moves regularly, the mover can nowhere be discovered. The administrative power in the United States presents nothing either centralized or hierarchical in its constitution; this accounts for its passing unperceived.

Wills says that de Tocqueville 'let the lack of trappings for what he recognized as government convince him that Americans had no government', and was therefore 'A man for whom government was invisible' (Wills, 2004, p. 53). This may be a wrong interpretation; de Tocqueville may be making the point of taking government for granted. Interpretation is complicated by de Tocqueville's different treatment of government and law. The operation of law is seen, but not the government. One might say it is the reverse.

Lectures on Jurisprudence

Smith's most elaborate treatment of government and law was given, not surprisingly, in his lectures on jurisprudence. The modern editors of the lectures quote the account of them given by John Millar, to the effect that Smith lectured on justice as a branch of morality, its gradual progress between stages or ages, the effect of changes in technology ('those arts which contribute to subsistence') and the accumulation of property in generating legal change ('in producing correspondent improvements or alterations in law and government'), and lastly 'those political regulations which are founded, not upon the principle of *justice*, but that of *expediency*, and which are calculated to increase the riches, the power, and the prosperity of a State' ('Editors' introduction', Smith, 1978, p. 3). Accordingly, it is clear from the editors' list of topics discussed in the lectures (ibid., pp. 24–7) that Smith covered under 'public jurisprudence' the organization of government and the rights of subjects; under 'domestic law', the relative rights of family members and of slaves and others; under 'private law', property and its transfer, and injury to person, reputation and property; and under 'police', a short discussion of cleanliness and security and a lengthy discussion of cheapness or plenty, that is, of the kinds of policies and theoretical topics also discussed in the *Wealth of Nations*.

In the *Lectures on Jurisprudence* Smith takes for granted the importance of his subject and concentrates on details and themes he considers important. He balances two conflicting views of government. These stem from the idealism–realism dualism that he struggled with in the *History of Astronomy* (1795 [1980]) and elsewhere. He identifies the ideal 'ought' of both government and the study of jurisprudence. He also grounds his discussion in the reality of social control and the exercise of power. This arises particularly in his discussions about the methods of transferring property. Each nation has developed its own methods of defining the procedures by which title is transferred, in addition to defining what can be transferred. Additional areas where the dualism arises are in his discussion of 'justice' and the impartial spectator. Although the lectures do not go into any depth on the concept of the impartial spectator, he does discuss fair play and the absence of injury as part of a social definition of justice. There is an ideal to be strived for regarding conduct, but simultaneously there exists a social reality of rules and regulations requiring an extensive process of working out adjustments amongst changing members of society.

Another topic is the strain between the 'historical' and 'ahistorical' approaches to defining rights. This is the evolutionary–creation conflict in rights and property definitions. Historical processes generate overall classes of rights and properties that are path-dependent on the social system. Differing societies passing through these stages have similar series of concerns regarding transitions of social classes. Ahistorical approaches to jurisprudence can use Smith's arguments about the universality of human socialization to work toward definitions of justice. Social changes are reflective of social definitions of humanity. Society makes changes based on individual choices regarding notions of what would best make a 'just system'. Smith acknowledges the possibility of making poor choices. Two side-by-side systems, each confronted with identical conditions, problems and assumptions about agents, could select two different governmental systems.

The lectures suggest that in working out pragmatic resolutions to conflicts over property, through changing the law society, that is, government and law, was involved in more than a simplistic administration of justice: government was involved in the continuing revision of the legal foundations of the economic system. The lectures have an empirical facet, indicating that he appreciates both the ideal justicial and material economic facets of legal change. Systems of law are constantly working toward what they 'ought to be' and it is only through experience and observation that policy-makers can make decisions. Once a law is tried and fails to fulfil (or no longer fulfils) the social need it was intended for, new laws are tried. This process is repeatedly discussed in Smith's works, appearing in discussions of property origins, secondary forms, transference, tax systems, voting systems, citizenship definitions, and so on.

If government and law seem anathema in the *Wealth of Nations*, they are part of Smith's obvious and simple system of natural liberty, that is, of the natural order of things. Combining both the *Lectures* and the *Wealth of Nations*, not only are law and government part of Smith's system and not only is legal change also part of Smith's system, but relative to the mercantilist agenda he opposes, his system includes what established interests could and in fact did oppose as revolutionary.

Market and state in *The Wealth of Nations*
Smith's discussion in the *Wealth of Nations* was in part intended counter the practice of mercantilism with its array of monopolies, special promotions and special prohibitions disbursed and deployed upon the whim of a reigning monarch or legislature. His analysis of the economic role of government must be understood against that background as well as that of the larger philosophical issues that will be treated below. He argued that the wealth of a nation consisted in the value of its produce and that the role for government within the economic system was to facilitate the growth of national wealth, so defined. In this sense, Smith demonstrated an important commonality with the mercantilist and physiocratic writers, but the accomplishment of the goal of maximizing the value of output required a very different role for government.

Smith's critiques of mercantilism and physiocracy were similar in that both promoted a flow of resources to favoured sectors of the economy in amounts greater than one would see in the absence of such policies. Smith's argument was that this is contrary to the interests of society, pointing out that: 'Every individual is constantly exerting himself to find out the most advantageous employment for whatever capital he can command', and that 'the study of his own advantage naturally, or rather necessarily leads him to prefer that employment which is most advantageous to society' (Smith, 1776, IV.2.4). This, of course, is where Smith's 'invisible hand' (IV.2.9) comes into the picture. In contrast:

> The statesman who should attempt to direct private people in what manner they ought to employ their capitals would not only load himself with a most unnecessary attention, but assume an authority which could safely be trusted, not only to no single person, but to no council or senate whatever, and which would nowhere be so dangerous as in the hands of a man who had folly and presumption enough to fancy himself fit to exercise it. (IV.2.10)

It is not simply a matter of government officials being incompetent or incapable; Smith believes that the market system does not require such overt direction:

> every system which endeavours, either by extraordinary encouragements to draw towards a particular species of industry a greater share of the capital of the society than what would naturally go to it, or, by extraordinary restraints, to force from a particular species of industry some share of the capital which would otherwise have been employed in it is in reality subversive of the great purpose which it means to promote. It retards, instead of accelerating, the progress of the society towards real wealth and greatness; and diminishes, instead of increasing, the real value of the annual produce of its land and labour. (IV.9.50)

For example, to produce at home that which could be produced more cheaply abroad – as promoted by mercantilist policies – reduces the value of the nation's output and enriches the businessmen who benefit from the protection while harming the interests of society as a whole.

It is at this point that Smith begins to lay out the basic framework for a government intending to promote national wealth under the system of natural liberty:

> Every man, as long as he does not violate the laws of justice, is left perfectly free to pursue his own interest his own way, and to bring both his industry and his capital into competition with those of any other man, or order of men. The sovereign is completely discharged from a duty, in the attempting to perform which he must always be exposed to innumerable delusions, and for the proper performance of which no human wisdom or knowledge could ever be sufficient; the duty of superintending the industry of private people, and of directing it towards the employments most suitable to the interest of society. (IV.9.51)

What, then, is the appropriate role for government here?

> According to the system of natural liberty, the sovereign has only three duties to attend to; three duties of great importance, indeed, but plain and intelligible to common understandings: first, the duty of protecting society from the violence and invasion of other independent societies; secondly, the duty of protecting, as far as possible, every member of the society from the injustice or oppression of every other member of it, or the duty of establishing an exact administration of justice; and, thirdly, the duty of erecting and maintaining certain public works and certain public institutions, which it can never be for the interest of any individual, or small number of individuals, to erect and maintain; because the profit could never repay the expence to any individual or small number of individuals, though it may frequently do much more than repay it to a great society. (IV.9.51)

As with so many interpretive questions, the issue is the substantive content Smith gives to each of these duties.

The defence of a society against the aggression of other societies is clear enough –

although his analysis is not sufficiently broad to capture the practice of mutual aggression in various forms of imperialism that has characterized both tribal societies and modern nation states, a situation of which he disapproves (IV.7).

Not so clear is what the protection, 'as far as possible', of 'every member of the society from the injustice or oppression of every other member of it' does and does not cover, or how the preceding language equates with or is amplified by 'the duty of establishing an exact administration of justice'. Such protection in practice will depend in part on the definitions of injustice and of oppression, and of the evidence thereof. His model provides for such a function, or duty, of government but seemingly leaves it up to society to work out the details.

Similarly elastic is the notion of public works and institutions that comprises the third duty. These 'public works' and 'public institutions' include, for Smith, the standard roads, bridges, canals, and harbours – which serve to facilitate commerce – but also education, to counteract what he saw as the mind-numbing effects of the division of labour, temporary monopolies given to joint stock companies to facilitate new trade avenues, and religious instruction for clergy.[3] Smith also allows for exceptions to his generally free-trade attitude to encourage and protect industries essential to national defence and to level the playing field for domestic products subject to tax at home, and he allows that retaliatory tariffs will be beneficial if they induce other countries to lower their trade barriers.

Smith was, on the one hand, in favour of doing away with the trade restrictions of the mercantilists, apprenticeship and settlement laws (which inhibited the free flow of labour), legal monopoly, and the laws of succession that impeded free trade in land. But yet, in addition to the basic governmental functions noted above, he also supported regulations dealing with public hygiene, legal ceilings on interest rates (to prevent excessive flows of financial capital into high-risk ventures), light duties on imports of manufactured goods, the mandating of quality certifications on linen and plate, certain banking and currency regulations to promote a stable monetary system, and the discouragement of the spread of drinking establishments through taxes on liquor (this being one of various regulations Smith advocated to compensate for the imperfect knowledge – or diminished telescopic faculty – of individuals).[4] That is, Smith was not a doctrinaire advocate of laissez-faire.

Indeed, someone paging through Book V of the *Wealth of Nations* cannot help but be struck by the expansive set of tasks elaborated by someone who is considered the godfather of laissez-faire. He had an inherent suspicion of the ability of government to manage economic affairs properly, but he also recognized that there were various policy actions that could improve the national welfare. His position is not that government needs to stay out of the way and let individual enterprise reign; rather, he lays out a specific (and lengthy) set of activities for government to undertake if it wishes to promote the national wealth. What it is, though, is a very different set of tasks from those undertaken by a mercantile government.

The role of the state, for Smith, was about more than just the tasks to be delegated to government; it was also about how government should carry them out. For example, he understood that certain useful public projects could give rise to incentives that dilute their effectiveness in various ways, and he saw financing methods as important mechanisms for adjusting incentives facing producers, consumers and politicians in ways conducive to enhanced performance. Thus, he advocated that professors be paid out of student fees in order to stimulate professorial diligence and that bridges and roads be financed through tolls in order to help ensure that they are constructed only where they are needed. In the case of tolls, he also argued for local administration on the grounds that national politicians would be likely to use the toll revenue otherwise than to keep the public works that generated them in good repair (V.1.71–89; V.1.130–89). Thus, while some might be inclined to see the system of natural liberty providing the context within which the invisible hand turns private interest into social interest, we see here how Smith situates government as an important player within that process.

At least as important, though, was Smith's recognition that the market does not operate in the absence of government; indeed, Smith calls political economy 'a branch of the science of a statesman or legislator' (IV.Introduction.1), making it, in part at least, a branch of jurisprudence. Smith found in the system of natural liberty a regulating mechanism that previous commentators had been unable to discern – a coordinating force that would keep self-interest from becoming totally destructive. Yet, he also understood that governmental action supplies the legal-institutional process through and within which markets function. It was not government that Smith was opposed to. He understood fully, as evidenced in both the *Wealth of Nations* and his *Lectures on Jurisprudence*, the integral relationship between government and economy. What Smith was after was not no government policy or intervention, but rather the appropriate set of policies to facilitate the growth of national wealth. And while Smith's writings have a natural-law flavour to them, his views on the appropriate role for government are not so much derived from a broad set of general principles as from the examination of specific circumstances and problems.

Smith and the market-plus-framework approach
Much of the foregoing is placed in focus by the market-plus-framework approach to the theory of economic policy in English classical political economy.[5] In this model, the market is a function of firm decision-making and of the institutions constituting the framework, namely, law and morals. Markets operate within frameworks of moral and legal rules that structure and operate through the markets they help form. The model gives effect to both private choice and social control. Changing the law seems to some people like substituting law for the market, whereas it is only a change in the interests whose protection comprises, in part, the framework function of government. The market, in whatever form it exists, exists in part because of government; changing the interests to which government lends its support is neither the replacement of the market nor the intrusion of government into an area in which government hitherto has been absent. Problems inevitably arise over the substance of the rules, the mode of determining rules, relative reliance upon and relation between moral and legal rules, and changing the rules. The model postulates joint processes: optimizing market resource allocation, and reforming the framework within which optimization takes place.

In the market-plus-framework model, two matters are clear: law is a fundamental part of the system, ubiquitous and important; and legal change is also, as technology, values, power structure and other variables change.

We thus can comprehend Smith's joint emphasis on the allocation of resources through (competitive) markets, on the roles of legal and moral rules, and the process of legal change. We can also appreciate Smith's analyses to be dealing with the problem of

Adam Smith on the economic role of government 311

working out the agenda of civil government in an age in which representative government was gradually replacing monarchical and aristocratic regimes; in which the values of virtue, valour and religion were being replaced by those reduced to money in the commercial marketplace; in which religious disputes were also disputes about government; in which new religious movements, notably deism, constituted challenges to orthodox religion as social control; and in which all the foregoing were complicated by perennial rivalry, and conflict, between Scotland and England. And we can understand how interpreters could themselves emphasize one or another of Smith's emphases, some emphasizing the making of government responsive to all people and some emphasizing limited, minimalist legal change; some selectively challenging social myths and some selectively adopting Smithian themes while transforming them into new social myths. Thus did the ideas of Adam Smith, the student of social control, eventually, long after his death in 1790, became part of the system of social control and its definition of reality, its belief system and its system of discourse.

Also clear are two further implications of the market-plus-framework model, especially in light of his overall tripartite model. One implication is that his tripartite model gives rise to three systems of value: that presided over by the market, that by moral rules and that by legal rules. The other implication is inevitable tension between the three domains and their respective systems of value. For example, there will be tension between framework-changing activities of government, on the one hand, and reliance on existing market structures (and their legal foundations), on the other. Changing the legal framework of the market will appear to some as substituting law for the market, and to others as only changing the legal foundations of the market, hence from one market form to another, with the market presiding over resource allocation through its value structure. (This inevitable tension is akin to that between levels of government and between branches of government, as in the United States.)

For reasons given above, the market-plus-framework approach is not the only interpretation of Smith on the economic role of government, though it has the advantage of encompassing all of Smith's works, his two great books and his lectures on law and government. The approach has defects, however. It does not yield conclusive solutions to problems of policy, which some find unsatisfying for various reasons – including those ideological. 'Framework-filling' activities and 'particular interventions' are subjective categories. No unequivocal solution is provided for resolving conflicts over the substance of the rules, the mode of determining rules, relative reliance upon and relation between moral and legal rules, and changing the rules. The model postulates joint processes: optimizing market resource allocation, and reforming the framework within which optimization takes place – and no unequivocal solution is provided to the problem of which is to take precedence and when.

Nor, however, does any other large-scale approach provide conclusive solutions to problems of policy. Jeremy Bentham's principle of the 'greatest happiness for the greatest number' is a case in point. The principle can be pursued in terms of maximizing the happiness of those most largely made happy or of the number of people made happy – the intensive versus the extensive margin. Thus there is a Benthamite Left and a Benthamite Right.[6] And Bentham is the father of both British individualism and British collectivism: the father of British individualism inasmuch and insofar as he wanted all individuals to count in the making of policy, and of British collectivism in the sense that once the masses acquired the right to vote, the resulting legislation was given the designation 'welfare state', as a collectivist concept.

If the Smithian–English classical market-plus-framework approach does not provide conclusively unequivocal results to problems of policy, the Smithian tripartite model does, for many interpreters, point to the process of working things out between morals and law, and markets and the other two, as well as between conflicting formulations of each.

Smith himself provided examples of grand simplification on both sides of the issue of legal change = regulation. On the negative side, for example, we have already seen Smith's (1776, IV.9.51) statement to the effect that the system of natural liberty functions to promote best the growth of national wealth and, in doing so, frees the statesman from the need overtly to direct the flow of resources in society and thereby leaves individuals free to pursue their own interests in the use of their labour and capital. Yet, it will be noticed that even here 'the obvious and simple system of natural liberty' and the 'perfectly free' pursuit of one's interest both presume the 'laws of justice'. On the affirmative side, we read:

> To restrain private people, it may be said, from receiving in payment the promissory notes of a banker, for any sum whether great or small, when they themselves are willing to receive them, or to restrain a banker from issuing such notes, when all his neighbours are willing to accept of them, is a manifest violation of that natural liberty which it is the proper business of law not to infringe, but to support. Such regulations may, no doubt, be considered as in some respects a violation of natural liberty. But those exertions of the natural liberty of a few individuals, which might endanger the security of the whole society, are, and ought to be, restrained by the laws of all governments, of the most free as well as of the most despotical. The obligation of building party walls, in order to prevent the communication of fire, is a violation of natural liberty exactly of the same kind with the regulations of the banking trade which are here proposed. (1776, II.2.94)

Here regulation is intended to support the system of natural liberty. Smith does not necessarily class relief of private oppression with the extraordinary restraints and extraordinary privileges 'once granted by reckless kings to favorite courtiers' (Ross, 1893, p. 732; referring to the conception of monopoly held by the Duke of Argyll). Liberty in Smith's system is multidimensional; courts and legislatures had to decide, for example, between rival claimants of interest, whether freedom of trade was compatible with factory legislation (protective legislation), and whether corporations and unions (labour relations legislation) were compatible with a Smithian economy.[7] The practical import of this was illustrated in the early stages of transition from plan to market economy, when the Russian government, abetted and hurried by some US economists, 'did not envision a role for the state in creating market-supporting institutions', resulting 'in a dearth of several key institutions critical for free enterprise' (McFaul, 1995, pp. 236, 237).[8] These institutions can be seen as freedom-enhancing or freedom-limiting; the operative point, though, is that certain legal limits and enhancements are necessary for markets to function in the various ways deemed socially beneficial, including the generation of national income and wealth.

Conclusion
We will not argue that Smith's view of the economic role of government is unambiguous. Among the rivals to the market-plus-framework approach to the interpretation of

Smith are interpretations which portray a more activist economic role of government; some of which suggest not a strict laissez-faire approach by Smith but a laissez-faire-with-exceptions approach, in which the exceptions are very important and sometimes rather broad-based;[9] and the minimalist interpretation, which claims that Adam Smith stands for the themes of laissez-faire, non-interventionism and minimal government – a dominant theme in economics and elsewhere, including among those critical of the laissez-faire position.[10] As the above analysis should make clear, however, minimalist or highly individualist interpretations of Smith are particularly difficult to sustain when set against the corpus of Smith's writings. That such interpretations have such currency in certain quarters is illustrative of our opening point about the problems that can arise from partial readings.

Notes

1. However, Smith did say in the 'Advertisement' inserted at the beginning of the sixth edition of *The Theory of Moral Sentiments* that in the *Wealth of Nations* he had 'partly executed this promise' of a volume on 'the general principles of law and government'.
2. *Lectures on Justice, Police, Revenue and Arms*, edited by Edwin Cannan (1896).
3. Smith's governmental functions are virtually identical to those set forth by Sir William Petty (1662 [1899, 1986]), except for the social safety net – perhaps because of Smith's belief in the ability of labour markets to clear relatively quickly and thereby eliminate involuntary unemployment.
4. See Viner (1927 [1991]) and Skinner (1996) for two excellent elaborations of Smith's rather broad-based conception of the appropriate functions for the state.
5. See, for example, Robbins (1952), Samuels (1966), Rothschild (2001) and Pack (1991).
6. On this point, see Samuel Fleischacker (2004).
7. This view is a partial confirmation of the market-plus-framework approach – and also of Max Weber's conception of the economy, in which he rejects the liberalist notion of a depoliticization of the economy because of harmony of interests due to natural law or an invisible hand (Palonen, 1999, p. 531).
8. 'All developed capitalist economies have a complex network of institutions that supports and facilitates market functions. The invisible hand is aided by visible institutions. Guided by neoliberal philosophies about the market, Russia's first postcommunist government assumed that these supporting institutions would emerge spontaneously. They have not. As a result, the absence of market-supporting institutions has added yet another impediment to the development of profit-maximizing privately owned firms' (McFaul, 1995, p. 237).
9. See, for example, Viner (1927 [1991]).
10. See, for example, Stigler (1965, p. 1), West (1990, p. 14), Samuelson (1962, p. 17) and Rosen (2002, pp. 5–6).

References

Cannan, Edwin (1896), *Lectures on Justice, Police, Revenue, and Arms*, Oxford: Clarendon Press.
Coats, A.W. (ed.) (1971), *The Classical Economists and Economic Policy*, London: Methuen.
Fleischacker, Samuel (2004), *On Adam Smith's Wealth of Nations: A Philosophical Companion*, Princeton, NJ: Princeton University Press.
McFaul, Michael (1995), 'State power, institutional change, and the politics of privatization in Russia', *World Politics*, **47** (January), 210–43.
Pack, Spencer J. (1991), *Capitalism as a Moral System: Adam Smith's Critique of the Free Market Economy*, Aldershot, UK: Edward Elgar.
Palonen, Kari (1999), 'Max Weber's reconceptualization of freedom', *Political Theory*, **27** (August), 523–44.
Petty, Sir William (1662), *A Treatise of Taxes and Contributions*, in Charles Henry Hull (ed.) (1899), *The Economic Writings of Sir William Petty*, Cambridge: Cambridge University Press; reprinted (1986) Fairfield, NJ: Augustus M. Kelley.
Robbins, Lionel (1952), *The Theory of Economic Policy in English Classical Political Economy*, London: Macmillan.
Rosen, Harvey S. (2002), *Public Finance*, 6th edn, New York: Irwin/McGraw-Hill.
Ross, Edward A. (1893), 'The unseen foundations of society', *Political Science Quarterly*, **8** (December), 722–32.

Rothschild, Emma (2001), *Economic Sentiments: Adam Smith, Condorcet, and the Enlightenment*, Cambridge, MA: Harvard University Press.
Samuels, Warren J. (1966), *The Classical Theory of Economic Policy*, Cleveland, OH: World.
Samuelson, Paul A. (1962), 'Economists and the history of ideas', *American Economic Review*, **52** (March), 1–18.
Skinner, Andrew S. (1996), 'The role of the state', *A System of Social Science: Papers Relating to Adam Smith*, 2nd edn, Oxford: Oxford University Press.
Smith, Adam (1976 [1759]), *The Theory of Moral Sentiments*, Oxford: Oxford University Press.
Smith, Adam (1776), *An Inquiry into the Nature and Causes of the Wealth of Nations*, Edwin Cannan (ed.), http://www.econlib.org/library/Smith/smWN.html.
Smith, Adam (1795), 'History of Astronomy', in W.P.D. Wightman and J.C. Bryce (eds) (1980), *Essays on Philosophical Subjects*, Oxford: Oxford University Press.
Smith, Adam (1978), *Lectures on Jurisprudence*, Oxford: Oxford University Press.
Stigler, George J. (1965), 'The economist and the state', *American Economic Review*, **55** (March), 1–18.
Viner, Jacob (1927), 'Adam Smith and laissez faire', *Journal of Political Economy*, **35** (April), 198–232; reprinted in Jacob Viner (1991), *Essays on the Intellectual History of Economics*, Princeton, NJ: Princeton University Press, pp. 85–113.
West, Edwin G. (1990), *Adam Smith and Modern Economics: From Market Behaviour to Public Choice*, Aldershot: Edward Elgar.
Wills, Garry (2004), 'Did Tocqueville "get" America?' *New York Review of Books*, 29 April, pp. 52–6.

17 Adam Smith on the standing army versus militia issue: wealth over virtue?
*Leonidas Montes**

Introduction

One aim of Pocock's influential *Machiavellian Moment* (1975) is to trace the intellectual development of the idea of 'virtue' from the revival of the Greco-Roman tradition in *quattrocento* Florence up to the American Revolution. Pocock investigates the concept of 'virtue', not only as the correlative antagonist of *fortuna* (a crucial term in Machiavelli's narrative), but also as an independent term with its own richly defined content. A central tenet of Pocock's argument is that virtue 'cannot be satisfactorily reduced to the status of right or assimilated to the vocabulary of jurisprudence' (Pocock, 1985, p. 41). The jurisprudential tradition is focused on rights, and society would be the association of private individuals. Civic humanism emphasizes duties, and following Aristotle's conception of *zoon politikon*, society would be a political community of social beings. Using Isaiah Berlin's famous distinction, the former would pursue 'liberty from' authority, and the latter 'liberty to' participate in public life (Berlin, 2000 [1958]). However this picture might overlook the fact that there was some interaction between the two traditions.[1] This chapter will show how Adam Smith's account of the militia issue is a good example of this interaction. Although both traditions are irreducible to any common discourse, reflecting a potential opposition between 'republicanism' and 'liberalism', Adam Smith's approach to the standing army issue reflects an attempt of finding means of reconciliation. What happened, how it happened and why it happened are wonderful examples of the tension and interaction between civic humanism and a jurisprudential approach, between commercial progress and morality, or between 'wealth and virtue'.[2] If Smith apparently epitomizes the economics of the militia issue, its underlying ethic is martial virtue.

This chapter begins with a brief analysis about what is classical republicanism and the importance of the militia for this political set of ideas. It then discusses how the militia debate was brought about in Scotland, underlining some crucial writings of Andrew Fletcher and Adam Ferguson. The next section investigates why and how Adam Smith apparently changed his mind on the standing army–militia debate, tracking the context and some possible reasons for this supposed change of mind. Smith's position on the militia, ranging from his *Correspondence*,[3] *Lectures on Jurisprudence* (LJ) and his published legacy in *The Theory of Moral Sentiments* (TMS) and *Wealth of Nations* (WN), will be discussed in some detail. I argue that although Smith clearly supported a professional army in WN, traces of civic humanism can still be found throughout his narrative. Finally I briefly conclude that if the father of economics might represent the twilight of a republican tradition, he does not preclude some crucial aspects of civic humanism.

Republicanism and the militia cause

Republicanism in context

Since the Greco-Roman tradition the militia issue, in terms of how it relates to the best form of government, has had a prominent and long-standing influence in modern political thought. The importance of martial spirit, and the search for some political reasons behind the rise and fall of the Roman Republic, inspired classical works that were revived during the Renaissance. Relying on these classic sources, intellectuals like Dante, Machiavelli, Erasmus and More, to name a few, gave rise to what has been broadly termed as classical republicanism. From the revival of the Greco-Roman tradition in *quattrocento* Florence up to the American Revolution, the cause of a citizen's militia was a fundamental topic of political discussion. In particular the republican tradition supported the militia against a professional army of mercenaries as an important political feature to preserve liberty. An army of mercenaries was deemed as a causal explanation for the decline of a republic.

In England republicanism was paramount. Within the context of the Glorious Revolution of 1688, which resulted in the abdication of James II and the succession of William III and Mary II, the debate on the standing army issue acquired renewed prominence and importance. Following James Harrington's *Commonwealth of Oceana* (1656), many intellectuals considered the militia as a crucial institution to preserve liberty. The memory of Cromwell's rule and the political discourses in support of an absolute monarchy (principally Sir Robert Filmer's *Patriarcha*, 1680) represented an imminent risk faced by members of this republican tradition. The radical Whigs who professed a republican ideology were most notably represented in England by John Milton (1608–74), James Harrington (1611–77), his friend Henry Neville (1620–94)[4] and their martyr Algernon Sidney (1622–83).[5] Their concern was not only about theoretical history, mainly characterized by the decline and fall of the Roman Republic: it was a real threat very much alive. If Harrington put forward a causal relationship between distribution of property and a form of government, proposing distribution of land as the key to create a republic, this political arrangement also demanded an obligation to serve in arms. Harrington's agrarian society represented Oceana as the English republic, in which the citizen's obligation to participate in the militia was for the sake of liberty. But this influential book was only part of a rich intellectual tradition known as republicanism, represented by what has been termed civic humanism, in which classical sources play a relevant role.

Republicanism was not an exclusive English political phenomenon. It was also an active intellectual force in Scotland. Before the Act of Union in 1707, the militia question was hotly discussed in Scotland. Taking into account Scotland's martial heritage and patriotic culture, the militia debate was an important issue for those who opposed the union with England. Andrew Fletcher of Saltoun was a notable voice against the creation of Great Britain. He fervently campaigned for an independent Scottish militia.

During the eighteenth century, commercial progress in Scotland motivated significant social and political changes. But the militia discourse, as part of a broader context of classical republicanism, with its emphasis on the corruption of society, was very much alive. Within the Scottish Enlightenment, Adam Ferguson was a key figure in this debate. In 1756 he wrote a pamphlet about the militia (*Reflections Previous to the Establishment of a Militia*), and his writings evince many of the preoccupations already highlighted by

English republicans. Moreover, the Poker Club was so named by Ferguson because its function was 'to stir up the question of a Scottish militia' (Ross, 1995, p. 341; see also Rae, 1965 [1895], pp. 137–8). Adam Smith was a member of this club, and there is some evidence that he supported this cause. But in his WN he supported a professional army, not only disappointing his friend Adam Ferguson and other members of the Poker Club, but also, according to some interpreters, changing his mind in what could easily be termed as another 'Das Adam Smith Problem'. This chapter will investigate this context, arguing that if Smith ended up defending a standing army for sound economic and political reasons, his narrative is still pervaded by civic humanist overtones. This might reflect Smith's early involvement in the militia cause and his possible, but not at all clear, sympathies for republicanism.

What is republicanism?
As research on the political tradition of republicanism is rapidly growing, this fascinating intellectual context might seem to any impartial spectator so ingrained in the history of ideas, that one could presume that it represents a long-standing and well-established research programme. However, its most inspiring works are quite recent.[6] Harrington's influence has long been widely acknowledged, but research on classical republicanism mainly began with Zera Fink's path-breaking *The Classical Republicans* (1945). Although Fink was especially interested in Milton, his politically charged narrative allowed her to identify a group of English republicans whose work was deeply influenced by classical sources. Fink immediately came to the conclusion that this reliance on some classical authors was not only ideological; it had a practical purpose for politically minded republicans like Milton, Harrington, Neville and Sidney. Then it was Hans Baron who delved into the Florentine concept of civic humanism with his classic *The Crisis of the Early Italian Renaissance* (1955). Baron analysed the important link between the classics, *quattrocento* Florence, and the English republicans. If both works are the foundations of this intellectual tradition, John G.A. Pocock and Quentin Skinner wrote two influential books that have triggered a rapidly growing line of research. Pocock's *Machiavellian Moment* (1975) investigated the civic humanist framework which, based on Aristotle, was recovered by the Florentines and humanists up to the American Revolution. Quentin Skinner not only developed an influential linguistic methodology,[7] but in his classic *The Foundations of Modern Political Thought* (1978) he focused on *quattrocento* Florence, the humanists and the Reformation, with its reliance on the Roman tradition (mainly Cicero).[8] If Pocock considered it an Aristotelian tradition, Skinner describes civic humanism as a neo-Roman political ideology.[9]

The civic humanist tradition, which will be conflated to what was originally labelled as classical republicanism,[10] has a particular moral grounding that understands citizens as part of a political community. In the republic, free participation is fundamental to guarantee public life. According to Pocock, following Aristotle's definition of the *zoon politikon* that considers human beings as essentially social or political beings, civic humanists viewed political life and public virtue as essential to our existence.[11] Within the institutional and material conditions that determine a republic, in which public virtue is the citizen's aim and liberty flourishes, the militia cause was inherent to the moral character of a republican. The complex concept of *virtù* plays a fundamental role within this historiographic paradigm as its all-encompassing meaning is related to public life in many aspects. In particular its etymological link to virility reflects the importance of martial valour.

In the Greek tradition we find important evidence regarding the concept of 'virtue' (*areté*) in the *Iliad* and the *Odyssey*. Anyone familiar with the Homeric legacy will understand the importance of martial virtues. This cultural understanding of martial prowess persisted for hundreds of years throughout the Greeks and the Romans, and it was then revived by classical republicans. As Werner Jaeger argued, 'in the city-state courage was called manliness, a clear reminiscence of the Homeric identification of courage with manly *areté*' (Jaeger, 1965 [1939], pp. 6–7) and 'the word *areté* had originally meant warlike prowess' (ibid., p. 8). Therefore originally virtue was also related to war, which was eminently a manly business, initiating a 'manliness tradition' that considers courage as a cardinal virtue (see Montes, 2004, Chapter 3). But just as the Greeks had the cardinal virtue of courage (*andreía*), the Romans coined the Latin word *virtus* from *vir*, also meaning 'man'. Cicero summarized this cultural tradition of virtue–manliness–courage when he wrote: 'it is from the word for man that the word virtue is derived; but man's chief quality is fortitude' (Cicero, 1966, pp. 194–5). Some 150 years later, Plutarch referred to Roman martial prowess and wrote, in Greek, that evidence for its importance 'may be found in the only Latin word for virtue, which signifies really manly valour' (Plutarch, 1968, p. 121). If virtue was needed to participate in public affairs, by simple extension the *vir virtutis* character of *virtù* (Skinner, 1978, Vol. 1, p. 87 and *passim*) was an expression of an autonomous citizen fighting for political liberty. If it is true that in Roman political philosophy the ideal of the citizen soldier is bound up with the overriding commitment to glory and imperial expansion, and the Greeks preserve glory without imperial ambitions, the concept of glory and martial virtue pervades both traditions. But liberty was a prerequisite of glory, and glory is related to martial spirit.[12] Hence the importance of a citizen's militia for any republican.

Although personal autonomy, also in economic terms, was fundamental to pursue public virtue, commercial progress was generally deemed dangerous by this classical republican tradition. The republican concept of corruption (*corruzione*), from Polybius, Machiavelli and up to the American Revolution, is also very important to understand the spirit of this political position that also entails a particular moral framework. If the discourse about corruption acquired its modern material connotation linking it exclusively to the selfish pursuit of money, originally this concept had a broader and more general sense. It meant pursuing private interest (not necessarily material) even in those cases when it conflicted with public interest. When commercial society showed its benefits, especially during the eighteenth century, the discourse of corruption entailed this contrast between material progress and a decline in morals. This narrative remained influential in England and Scotland, and during the Enlightenment we can see some nostalgic remnants of this tradition.[13] As will be argued below, even for Adam Smith, who epitomizes the ascendancy of political economy over politics, the triumph of self-interest over public virtue retains some traces of this civic humanist tradition. The standing army versus militia issue is a good example to appreciate how Smith acknowledged the rise of political economy within a fading civic humanist discourse.[14]

The humanists despised mercenaries. Following Petrarch, Machiavelli famously criticized their use. The so-called father of modern political science warns the Prince regarding the need of *virtù* to defend the principality against *fortuna*. At the end of Chapter 25 of *The Prince*, Machiavelli concludes: 'fortune is a woman, and if you want to control her, it is necessary to treat her roughly' (Machiavelli, 1988 [1532], p. 87), establishing the feminine character of *fortuna* that must be subdued by *virtù*'s manly character. Such *virtù* could only express itself through a citizens' militia under the Prince's command, and not through mercenaries who 'are useless and dangerous' (Machiavelli, 1988 [1532], p. 43). Mercenaries, as predecessors of a standing army, entailed two main political risks: fighting for money is not the same as fighting for one's own republic and, moreover, relying on them was detrimental to the republic. Within the republican tradition any standing army meant in political terms transferring power to an absolute monarch. This power would mean the loss of liberty. For this practical reason it was dangerous to the republic. The civic ideal of republican thought required the participation of the political community in the defence of the republic. If there was a pragmatic political stance against a professional army, the most entrenched rebuttal of a standing army was actually a moral question that entailed the virtuous character of the citizen. Public virtues were first and foremost represented by martial virtue. Defending the republic was an essential duty of a citizen, who would put the public interest above his own life. Therefore throughout the narrative of civic humanism contempt for an effeminate character and lack of valour are pervasive.

The militia debate in Scotland
Almost a decade after the Glorious Revolution, the so-called 'standing army controversy' of 1697–98 called for a militia along the lines of a civic tradition.[15] In England, most notably John Trenchard (1662–1723) published *An Argument Shewing that a Standing Army is Inconsistent with a Free Government, and then Absolutely Destructive to the Constitution of the English Monarchy* (1697),[16] and then *A Short History of Standing Armies* (1698). Together with Thomas Gordon (?–1750), concealing their identity, they published several articles now compiled as *Cato's Letters* (Trenchard and Gordon, 1995 [1720–23]). They followed Harringtonian principles, using the name of the republican martyr Cato the Younger as their referent for defending the militia cause. If Julius Caesar represented a base epicurean political approach that put his hedonist interest above those of the republic, Cato was seen as the republican martyr who, in a Stoic manner, gave his life for the republic.[17]

The corruption debate can also be seen as a political and philosophical struggle between Epicureanism and Stoicism, between wealth and virtue. On the one hand the latter represented the moral character defended by Shaftesbury. This moral character was related to politics. In this sense, the underlying idea of a republican call for civic duty was pervasive during the shaping of commercial society. On the other hand, being referred to as 'Epicurean' or 'Hobbist' simply meant political and moral degeneration. These epithets contained a severe pejorative sense that incited public disapproval during the eighteenth century. They also reflect the ethical overtones of the debate.

If classical republicanism was mainly an English political phenomenon, Scotland was not precluded from its political implications, especially regarding the militia. Scotland combined a remarkable martial history with a proud national identity that created a fertile context for debating the militia issue. Therefore it is not surprising that the militia issue was a very important topic to be discussed before the Act of Union of 1707.

Andrew Fletcher
A fascinating Scottish figure, Andrew Fletcher of Saltoun (1653–1716), published in Edinburgh *A Discourse of Government with relation to Militias* (1698).[18] This notable piece evinces the danger of a standing army through a historical analysis in which the corruption debate plays a significant role. Fletcher firmly believed that a national militia was a school of virtue. Just before the union with England, he turned into a fierce opponent of it. However, his challenge to the union was based on a civic humanist discourse that called for a revival of Scottish martial virtues. His strong advocacy of the militia not only evoked the distinctive martial heritage of the Scots, but also the ideology of classical republicanism.

Fletcher begins *A Discourse of Government with relation to Militias* (1698) with a plea to return to 'those excellent rules and examples of government which the ancient have left us' as they would allow citizens 'to discover all such abuses and corruptions as tend to the ruin of public societies' (Daiches, 1979, p. 2). After a brief historical account, he complains about 'how precarious our liberties are' (ibid., p. 11) and goes on to criticize the standing army. Fletcher, who was described by his tutor as 'a most violent republican' (quoted in Daiches, 1979, p. vii), strongly believed that mercenary armies are 'calculated to enslave a nation' (ibid., p. 12). The republican discourse of mercenaries and loss of liberty, despising those who make a trade of war, led Fletcher to declare that a militia 'is the chief part of the constitution of any free government' (ibid., p. 18). Through a scheme of camps, Fletcher proposed a rather Spartan regime for the young citizens in which punishments ranked very highly.[19] He concludes by contrasting the pride and glory of Britain with the situation in France, where reliance on mercenaries has tended to 'foment luxury of a court' (p. 26).[20]

If the Act of Union was a clear defeat for Fletcher, the pervasiveness of the militia issue debate was his triumph. The Act of Union meant the loss of the Scottish Assembly with political power mainly centralized in England. Moreover, Scotland became part of Britain, but not necessarily North Britain. Indeed, there was a strong nationalistic feeling within the Scots. Even though they were part of Britain, the South Britons still generally referred to themselves as English, maintaining a distinction with the Scottish. Smith was a great supporter of the 1707 Act of Union,[21] but when he refers dismissively to Oxford (WN V.i.f.8, p. 761) we should not only reflect on the quality of Scottish universities. This context matters here. If significant social, institutional and cultural changes followed in Scotland after the union, one clear reflection of this divide was language. The Scots had to learn English. Adam Smith's success in attracting an audience for his 1746–48 Lectures at Edinburgh (published as *Lectures on Rhetoric and Belles Letters*), was partly due to his six previous years at Oxford. Good English reflected good manners and 'propriety' for the Scottish elite. It is noteworthy that in the preface of the first number of the *Edinburgh Review* (1755), it is stated that: 'Two considerable obstacles have long obstructed the progress of science. One is, the difficulty of a proper expression in a country where there is either no standard of language, or at least one very remote' (EPS, p. 229).[22]

In this setting, with Scotland striving to become a polite commercial society, the militia issue reacquired political prominence as a matter of nationhood. The contrast between a civilized Lowland Scotland and the Highlands of clanship was a clear representation of progress, of the new ascendancy of commercial society over barbarism. During the Jacobite Rebellion those forces clashed. The Edinburgh town militia ran away when Highlanders and Jacobites approached. This evinced the importance of proper military training, so pervasive in the militia debate. Finally, with the defeat at the Battle of Culloden in 1746, the disintegration of the Highland army was seen as the collapse of those forces against civilization. But it could also be interpreted as a triumph for the professional army cause. Regardless of the latter, the debate about the militia was not exhausted. If political stability and economic progress were the hallmarks after the union, national identity and issues about future security, especially considering the turbulent period before the American Revolution and then the French Revolution, brought back once again the discussion about a citizen's militia.

Adam Ferguson
As the Scottish Enlightenment evolved, the militia issue was still debated. Adam Ferguson, most notably, published in 1756 a pamphlet entitled *Reflections Previous to the Establishment of a Militia*. Although he recognized commercial progress, and was a supporter of the union, Ferguson firmly believed in a society that should 'mix the military Spirit with our civil and commercial Policy' (Ferguson, 1756, p. 3). More cautious than his predecessor Fletcher, Ferguson was aware of the difficulties of imposing a militia, but also found historical evidence supporting the militia cause: 'The Examples of many an Age in *Europe*, the more recent Instances of a Militia opposed with Success even to regular Armies, will prove that what is proposed, and appears to be earnestly desired by this nation, is not impractible' (ibid., p. 5).

Ferguson, reflecting on the corruption debate, repeatedly regrets the loss of 'Honour and Glory' (ibid., p. 10) and the 'Decline of our martial Disposition' (ibid., p. 11). He is aware of the social and political changes,[23] but is also optimistic about his cause: 'Our People are remarkable for Public Spirit' (ibid., p. 13). Throughout his works, published and unpublished, he exposes the tension between commercial society and civic humanism. He attempts to reach a balance between Stoic austerity and progress, combining Presbyterianism with an spontaneous social order arrangement. Therefore it is not negligible that Ferguson fostered the human action–human design Hayekian concern:

> Every step and every movement of the multitude, even in what are termed enlightened ages, are made with equal blindness to the future; and nations stumble upon establishments, which are indeed *the result of human action, but not the execution of any human design*. (Ferguson, 1995 [1767], p. 119, emphasis added)

But for Ferguson the institution of a militia is the best way to restore civic virtue without sacrificing the advantages of commercial society (on all these themes, see Hill, 2006).[24]

His hope that 'our Militia would soon become a Strength to the Country' (Ferguson, 1995 [1767], p. 18), as a reflection of republican spirit, purposefully contrasts the dismal picture of 'a Time of Corruption, may come, when Ideas of a Constitution of Liberty, and of Independence, will cease to operate in the Minds of our People: that in such a Conjuncture personal Attachment will divide them; a *Caesar* will raise' (ibid., p. 26). This is a classic republican statement about the corruption debate: commercial progress would foster self-interest and this will eradicate public spirit with a serious blow to liberty. Ferguson views the militia as a citizen's duty, and as 'Honour be the most natural Principle of military Virtue' (ibid., p. 42), the militia is seen as an important foundation of public virtue.[25]

Although Smith and Ferguson were born in the same year, Ferguson outlived Smith for 26 years, and remained concerned about the militia issue throughout his whole life.[26] He lived for witnessing the compulsory militia established in 1797, which was far from his vision of a sort of 'Legion of Honour'. Even his own son, James Ferguson, prepared to serve his country following the example of his father's convictions (Sher, 1989, p. 262). If Ferguson saw the benefits of prosperity for society, he always remained committed to a militia.

Adam Smith and the militia issue
Smith was one of the founders, or at least one of the original members, of the Edinburgh Poker Club established in 1762. The club got its name in analogy to 'stirring' the establishment of a Scottish militia.[27] Adam Ferguson and Alexander Carlyle were the most animated promoters of this cause, although other notable members included the Duke of Buccleuch, Henry Dundas, David Hume,[28] John Home and James Steuart, among others. It seems that Smith remained in the club until its demise in 1784.[29] But Smith did not become a member of the newly established Younger Poker Club in 1786, perhaps due to his endorsement of the standing army in WN. Ferguson declared that the club was founded 'upon the principle of zeal for a militia and a conviction that there could be no lasting security for the freedom and independence of these islands but in the valour and patriotism of an armed people' (quoted in Rae, 1965 [1895], pp. 137–8), but there are divergent views on Smith's position regarding the militia issue. They range from Smith's endorsement of this republican cause, a change of mind, or an interpretation that simply leaves this issue as an open question.[30]

It is important to understand Smith's own position and his sources in this debate. However, it will be argued that on the standing army–militia issue, Smith shows a realistic approach consistent with those concerns that were crucial to classical republicanism. Before expanding on this conclusion, some traces of the civic humanist narrative in TMS and WN will be underlined. Then Smith's position on the standing army–militia issue will be traced through his correspondence, and his LJ. Finally his most developed and important account in Book V of WN will be briefly analysed.

A brief account of civic humanist narrative in TMS and WN
In TMS there are no explicit references to the standing army–militia issue.[31] However in TMS there are several passages that reflect Smith's concern with the corruption debate, especially regarding martial virtue. In Montes (2004) I have pinpointed some of these, and the possible connections that can be made between self-command and what can be termed as the *vir virtutis* discourse. It is important to recall some of these passages, as this narrative is significant to the argument of this chapter.

The idea of 'heroic valour' (TMS I.iii.2.5, p. 54) appears with important nuances. For example Smith gives the image of 'the patriot who lays down his life for the safety, or when for the vain-glory of this society, appears to act with the most exact propriety', concluding that 'his conduct, therefore, excites not only our entire approbation, but our highest wonder and admiration, and seems to merit all the applause which can be due to the most heroic virtue' (TMS VI.ii.2.2, p. 228). Then, when he explores his four chief virtues (prudence, justice, beneficence and self-command), Smith concludes that 'the most *heroic valour* may be employed indifferently in the cause either of justice or of injustice; and though it is no doubt much more loved and admired in the former case, it still appears a great and respectable quality even in the latter' (TMS VI.concl.6, p. 264, emphasis added). We admire the *vir virtutis* character of self-command, even if it has unintended negative consequences.

Let us recall Machiavelli's advice about *fortuna* and how she must be treated by the Prince. This tradition of the goddess Fortune as a woman, against manly courage, and the combination of fortune and courage, is also present throughout some passages of TMS. For example talking about Pompey and Lucullus, Smith refers to 'fortune and valour' (TMS II.iii.2.3, p. 99), much resembling a republican reading of Machiavelli. In addition, the many notable references in Smith to the cardinal virtue of 'courage' (*andreía*) and his contempt for the effeminate, as a reflection of cowardice, are noteworthy. For Smith the effeminate character 'forebodes ruin to the individual' (TMS IV.2.1, p. 187) and 'no character is more contemptible than that of a coward' (TMS VI.iii.17, p. 244). In WN he also refers, in a pejorative manner, to 'the effeminate and ill-exercised militia of the great Persian empire' (WN V.i.a.29, p. 702).[32] This opposes the manly *virtù*. Within the corruption debate the effeminate would correspond to the luxurious, and the martial character, to a republican concept of *virtus*. Therefore it is no surprise that in LJ he is reported to have conflated 'luxury' and 'effeminacy' (LJ, pp. 189, 202).

In WN we also find several references to 'courage' and 'valour',[33] but in this respect Smith's language in his famous account of the proto-Marxist concept of alienation is no doubt worth remembering. Smith grumbles that a man performing a few simple operations 'generally becomes as stupid and ignorant as it is possible for a human creature to become', rendering him 'incapable of defending his own country in war' (WN V.i.f.50, p. 782). He goes even further, claiming that: '[h]is dexterity at his own particular trade seems, in this manner, to be acquired at the expence of his intellectual, social, and *martial virtues*' (ibid., emphasis added), calling for government intervention through education. Economic progress entailed a new set of secondary virtues such as parsimony, frugality, commercial probity and punctuality, but they are far below the cardinal virtues, which include the *virtù* of courage.

The militia issue and Smith's correspondence

If Smith, especially after the agitations of 1759–60 in Scotland, does not make an explicit reference in his TMS and its successive editions (1760, 1767, 1774, 1781, 1790) about his position on the militia issue, he takes sides in his private correspondence. In April 1760, just when the militia bill was debated at the House of Commons, Smith wrote a letter to his publisher William Strahan. This letter was written just a few months after Carlyle's pamphlet demanded a militia for Scotland (published in January 1760)[34] and only a couple of years before Smith had become a member of the Poker Club (in 1762), where Carlyle was an important and active figure promoting the militia cause. Referring to the recently published memories of the Irish Jacobite Nathaniel Hooke,[35] Smith writes that this book, 'by no means well written', is 'published at an unlucky time, and may throw a damp upon our militia' (*Corr.*, p. 68).

Although soon after, on 15 April 1760, the militia bill was defeated by a conclusive vote of 194 to 84, exacerbating a nationalistic feeling (see Roberston, 1985, pp. 98–114), Smith appears like a supporter of the militia cause. He affectionately refers to 'our militia'. But this remark cannot be taken as conclusive evidence. It might simply reflect the fact that he shared this patriotic attitude that involved anti-English feelings in a pro-English political setting. Then we have Smith's grand tour with the Duke of Buccleuch (1764–66), which was followed by his ten years' retirement to work on his WN in his birth town of Kirkcaldy.

Just after WN was published, Adam Ferguson, the indisputable leader of the militia cause among the Edinburgh literati, after praising Smith's book, wrote in April 1776: 'You have provoked, it is true, the church, the universities, and the merchants, against all of whom I am willing to take your part; but you have likewise provoked the militia, and there I must be against you' (*Corr.*, pp. 193–4). Ferguson's tone is clear. After suggesting that 'gentlemen and peasants of this country do not need the authority of philosophers', he invites Smith to a further discussion by saying 'of this more at Phillipi'.[36] But Smith's clear dismissal of the militia cause was not left aside. Early in 1778 Alexander Carlyle anonymously published *A Letter to His Grace the Duke of Buccleugh, on National Defence; With Some Remarks on Dr Smith's Chapter on that Subject, in his Book entitled An Inquiry into the Nature and Causes of the Wealth of Nations*. In this pamphlet the tension between commercial progress (as luxury) and military virtue (as manliness), is clear: 'it is surely better to be a little less rich and commercial, than by ceasing to be men ... we become so luxurious or effeminate, as to leave the use of arms to strangers and mercenaries' (quoted in Sher, 1989, p. 247).

The contrast between *fortuna* – the effeminate – and *virtù* – manly courage – à la Machiavelli, is striking. But the fact that this pamphlet was addressed to the Duke of Buccleuch, who also was a member of the Poker Club, is not negligible. It certainly touched Smith, who had been the duke's grand tour tutor during 1764–66. In a letter to Andreas Holt, dated October 1780, Smith refers explicitly to this pamphlet:

> The anonymous author of a pamphlet concerning national defense, who I have been told is a Gentleman of the name of Douglas, has Written against Me. When he Wrote his book, he had not read mine to the end. He fancies that because I insist that a Militia is in all cases inferior to a well regulated and well disciplined standing Army, that I disapprove of Militias altogether. With regard to that subject, he and I happened to be precisely of the same opinion. This Gentleman, if I am rightly informed of his name, is a man of parts and one of my acquaintance, so that I was a little surprised at his attack upon Me, and still more at the mode of it. (*Corr.*, p. 251)

First, it is rather curious that Smith was not aware that the real author was precisely Alexander Carlyle, as surely Ferguson and other members of their intellectual circle knew. Second, as Sher points out, 'it was, in fact, Smith who had not read his critic's work to the end' (1989, p. 247), as the pamphlet not only praised, but cited Smith's call for promoting martial spirit. Therefore, as Sher (1989) asks, what reaction would Smith have expected from Ferguson?[37] This question is pertinent in my view, because Smith was a member of the Poker Club, and remained attached to it. At least it can be concluded that Ferguson, and his friend Carlyle, took the militia cause as a matter of principle. Now we will turn to see what Smith thought about this issue.

The militia issue and Smith's Lectures on Jurisprudence
We have seen that by 1762 Adam Smith was a member of the Poker Club, but this membership is far from proving his support for militias. For example, in his LJ, which were given in the two academic years before his grand tour with the Duke of Buccleuch

in 1764,[38] conclusive evidence about Smith's support for a militia cannot be found. But some suggestive passages are notable for their ambivalence in terms of maintaining some republican overtones.

In LJ(A), Smith is reported introducing his course on moral philosophy:

> It is therefore requisite that an armed force should be maintained, as well to defend the state against externall injuries as to obtain satisfaction for any that have been committed. In treating of this subject we shall consider the various species of armed forces that have been in use in antient and modern states; the different sorts of militias and train'd bands; and observe how far they were suited to the different natures of the governments. (LJ, p. 7)

When Smith analyses this issue he is very pragmatic, but well aware of the republican argument immersed in the corruption debate. Embedded within Smith's distinctive conjectural history, the discussion is always strictly related to the four stages theory of society in his LJ, and also in WN. For Smith, if 'arts and improvement' will increase population, 'the number of fighting people will be very small' (LJ, p. 229). The reason is simple economics: in commercial society 'a smith or a weaver' cannot leave his trade without a personal opportunity cost, which also implies a cost for society. In terms of defence, this situation means that 'improvement of arts and commerce must make a great declension in the force and power of the republick in all cases' (LJ, p. 231). But soon after, considering the effect of slavery in the classical world, Smith anticipates his famous passage about the consequences of the division of labour in WN (see WN V.i.f.50, p. 782), declaring that: 'they considered, and I believe with justice, that every sort of constant labour hurt the shape and rendered him less fit for military exercise, which made the chief view of all lawgivers at that time' (LJ, p. 231). He then explains what happened in the Italian republics, 'as soon as arts, etc. were imporvd, there was an intire decradation [*sic*] and loss of courage in the whole state' prompting, for example, the 'decay of Florence' (ibid.). The corruption debate is pervasive in Smith's pragmatic explanation. For example he repeatedly lectured that 'luxury comes in after commerce and arts' (LJ, p. 232), with serious consequences for a citizens' militia. He sums up this argument: 'Whenever therefore arts and commerce engage the citizens, either as artisans or as master trades men, the strength and force of the city must be very much diminished' (ibid.).

Then he gives another argument that comes up again in WN: 'the improvement of the military art' will also attract only 'lower ranks to make up the armies' (LJ, p. 233) in a conquering republic. This reality reflects the republican argument that would explain the fall of the Roman Republic. For Smith the decline of a republic is viewed as a natural process of loss of strength. Luxury, in its pejorative sense as effeminacy, is the main cause of this decline. But there is a possibility of establishing a standing army in commercial societies offsetting the risk of filling up the army with 'lower ranks'. Only if they 'fear their officers, who are still gentlemen, more than the enemy' (LJ, p. 266), will a good standing army not be dangerous to the country. The pragmatic Smith goes on to lecture that 'this institution has therefore taken place in all countries where arts and luxury are established' (LJ, p. 266).

In LJ(B) he repeats all these arguments. History has given us some lessons, therefore: 'As the citizens of Greece thought it below them to bear arms, and entrusted the republic to mercenaries, their military force was diminished and consequently a means was provided for the fall of the government' (LJ, p. 412). But Smith explores another cause of their decline, 'the improvement of the art of war' (ibid.) as a consequence of specialization. The latter is reassessed in WN, when Smith explains the two causes that make impossible a militia: 'the progress of manufactures, and the improvement in the art of war' (WN V.i.a.8, p. 694), giving rise to a more developed argument in terms of the division of labour.

In a brief special section entitled 'On arms', it is explained, in a rather Smithian passage, how martial virtue and luxury are both faces of the same human coin in different circumstances:

> But when arts and manufactures encreased and were thought worthy of attention, and men found that they could rise in dignity by applying to them, and it became inconvenient for the rich to go out to war, from a principle of avarice, these arts which were at first despised by the active and ambitious soon came to claim their whole attention. (LJ, p. 542)

The causal explanation for a standing army over a militia is not only about the division of labour, it is also about public approbation. Circumstances are relevant to explain social phenomena for Smith. In different stages of society people would behave differently: 'The merchant who can make 2 or 3000£ at home will not incline to go out to war. But it was an amusement to an ancient knight who had nothing else ado' (ibid.). In sum, 'manly courage we so much boast of depends upon external circumstances' (ibid., p. 543).

More ambivalent, and with a republican longing for a militia, is the following passage:

> However much standing armys may be exclaimed against, in a certain period of society they must be introduced. A militia commanded by landed gentlemen in possession of the public offices of the nation can never have any prospect of sacrificing the liberties of the country for any person whatever. *Such a militia would no doubt be the best security against the standing army of another nation.* (LJ, p. 543, emphasis added)[39]

Another important argument that is repeated in WN, is that: 'Yet on some occasions a standing army has proved dangerous to the liberties of the people ... This would never be the case if a proper militia were established. In Sweden, where it takes place, they are in no danger' (LJ, p. 544). The example of Sweden and the Swiss were widely used by those who defended the militia. Ferguson, for example, also deeply admired the Swiss militia (Sher, 1989, p. 260).[40]

The militia issue and The Wealth of Nations
In his WN Adam Smith develops and polishes up the main arguments that he had reportedly wielded in his *Lectures on Jurisprudence*. The militia debate is principally undertaken within the first part of Book V, in the part 'Of the expence of defence', which precedes the other two roles of government: 'Of the expence of justice', and 'Of the expence of publick works and publick institutions'. However, it is interesting to link this analysis to the classical republican and jurisprudential approach. At this stage WN's last book is entitled 'Of the revenue of the Sovereign or Commonwealth', and its first chapter 'Of the expences of the Sovereign or Commonwealth'. The Smithian 'Commonwealth', a word with clear republican etymological overtones, relates to economics, not to politics. Those titles entail a purpose. It is about 'expences', a positive issue. It is not about normative

issues related to what government should do. WN does not directly discuss the duties of government, or the roles of the state, but analyses how those duties emerge from economic reasoning. This is a simple signalling to understand how political economy can be seen as the twilight of a republican tradition. Economics appears to have taken over politics in its classical meaning. Smith's support for a standing army, as lectured by Smith in his LJ, was no exception in this setting, but has some important nuances.

Yet what bothered Ferguson, and those who supported the militia cause, was that in WN Smith publicly and bluntly declared that 'a well-regulated standing army is superior to every militia' (WN V.i.a.39, p. 705; see also V.i.a.25, p. 700). Smith's justification for defending this thesis, also within the conjectural history of the four stages of society, is mainly based on the progress of commercial society rather than on any anti-republican ideological grounds. Indeed, Smith is aware that '[m]en of republican principles have been jealous of a standing army as dangerous to liberty' (WN V.i.a.41, p. 706). After that he immediately adds:

> It certainly is so, wherever the interest of the general and that of the principal officers are not necessarily connected with the support of the constitution of the state. The standing army of Caesar destroyed the Roman republick. The standing army of Cromwell turned the long parliament out of doors. But where the sovereign is himself the general, and the principal nobility and gentry of the country the chief officers of the army; where the military force is placed under the command of those who have the greatest interest in the support of the civil authority, because they have themselves the greatest share of that authority, a standing army can never be dangerous to liberty. On the contrary, it may in some cases be favourable to liberty. (see WN V.i.a.41, pp. 706–7)

Repeating an idea already developed in his LJ, Smith argues that the structure of a standing army is too relevant not to be discussed. Yet Smith's debate is not only confined to economics.[41] On what might be termed as 'the lower-rank problem' (a standing army attracting only lower ranks), as a signal of the degradation of the army due to commercial progress, Smith develops further what he discussed in his LJ. In WN Smith demands that those generals and chief officers (who, according to Smith, should be the 'principal nobility and gentry of the country') have 'the greatest interest in the support of the civil authority'. This is a basic concern which is at the core of those who criticized mercenaries and defended the militia. It is not about a simple army of mercenaries, but a standing army composed of people from the 'high ranks' who would serve as an example and motivation for those engaged in a military career.[42] Duty towards the country is the political as well as moral cornerstone that underpins the first duty of the sovereign and those responsible citizens involved in the professional army. With this republican demand for those in command, resembling those reasons for defending the militia against an army of mercenaries, Smith argues that a standing army can never be dangerous to liberty. On the contrary, in some cases it can be favourable to it. This was a serious blow for those republicans defending a militia of citizens. In this sense, there is a difference between a merely professional standing army, and Smith's well-regulated standing army. The latter is commanded by those few who share the spirit of a republican commitment to the *politeia*.

The republican language is pervasive within his defence of a standing army:

> That in the progress of improvement the practice of military exercises, unless government takes proper pains to support it, goes gradually to decay, and, together with it, the martial spirit of

the great body of the people, the example of modern Europe sufficiently demonstrates. But the security of every society must always depend, more or less, upon the martial spirit of the great body of the people. In the present times, indeed, that martial spirit alone, and unsupported by a well-disciplined standing army, would not, perhaps, be sufficient for the defence and security of any society. But where every citizen had the spirit of a soldier, a smaller standing army would surely be requisite. That spirit, besides, would necessarily diminish very much the dangers to liberty, whether real or imaginary, which are commonly apprehended from a standing army. (WN V.i.f.59, pp. 786–7)

This passage reflects again Smith's intentions, conceding to Ferguson's argument. If Smith supports a standing army, it is not just any standing army. It is one in which citizens maintain the manly virtues, a community that praises courage, a country which sympathizes with the cardinal virtue of courage. Soon after Smith scorns a coward: 'A man, without proper use of the intellectual faculties of a man, is, if possible, more contemptible than even a coward, and seems to be mutilated and deformed in a still more essential part of the character of human nature' (WN V.i.f.61, p. 788).

This approach to the standing army debate is an excellent example of the dialogue between virtue and commerce that I have been trying to uncover. In WN we witness the emergence of the triumph of economic progress within a *vir virtutis* atmosphere. In brief, Smith does not fully delegate defence to professional soldiers, as he does not necessarily wish to deprive the citizen of martial virtue. On the contrary, the classical *virtus* of the Greco-Roman tradition interact with the fundamental condition for economic progress, that is, the division of labour, and specifically the need for labour as the source of wealth. Economic progress does not eradicate the moral foundations of classical republicanism, in particular the moral character of manly courage.

Smith's undertaking combines the 'stubborn facts' of a rapidly developing economic society with the civic humanist tradition. The father of economics is a turning point in what Pocock has appropriately termed as 'commercial humanism' (Pocock, 1985, pp. 50, 194). If Ferguson remains a civic humanist, and his defence of a militia will reach the nineteenth century, Smith's realistic support of a standing army constitutes an example of the nuanced twilight of civic humanism. Some sunny spells remain: Smith's position on the standing army debate is still carried out within the conceptual framework of the civic tradition. In my view, we can still find important vestiges of a republican narrative.

Conclusions
Adam Ferguson and Adam Smith represent two apparently divergent positions on the militia issue. Both are good examples to understand the crucial tension between classical republicanism and a jurisprudential approach, between wealth and virtue. Both savants reflected different stances on the corruption debate, which epitomizes the trade-off perceived and stressed by republicans between commercial progress and moral decline. If Ferguson's clear and permanent defence of a militia might seem a priori too different from Smith's position, the context of the standing army–militia debate is more complex and has some nuances. Smith defended the standing army as a political economist, but we can still hear a republican consciousness in his narrative. Smith's republican understanding of courage, his open contempt for cowardliness and derision of effeminacy, combines with the advantages of commercial society. The corruption debate of wealth against virtue is not over with the publication of WN.

Within the Scottish Enlightenment the jurisprudential tradition initiated by Grotius, and followed by his ablest disciple Pufendorf, was certainly relevant. Carmichael was fundamental in disseminating this jurisprudential tradition, and certainly Adam Smith was notably well acquainted with this framework, and also much influenced by it. His legacy testifies to a fact about the Scottish Enlightenment: the enormous influence of the jurisprudential approach. However, acknowledging its undeniable relevance does not mean simply dismissing civic humanism as non-existent. Vivienne Brown declared that: 'the language of rights and markets seems to lie uneasily beside the language of virtue and corruption in spite of a number of attempts to straddle both interpretative paradigms' (Brown, 1994, pp. 101–2). Recently James Alvey, following Harpham (1984), rejects 'the civic humanist interpretation of Smith' (Alvey, 2003, p. 133), but he also acknowledges 'certain *traces* of civic humanism' (ibid., p. 212, n. 72, emphasis in the original). The latter is crucial, as this chapter has attempted to sustain.

Few problems are more ideologically charged than the 'wealth and virtues' debate on Adam Smith. There is a political issue at stake, and Smith is not easy to fit into any political framework, not even during his time.[43] Jeffrey Young (1997) argues that: 'public spirit, or civic virtue was, for Smith, a vitally important aspect of the public life of a happy and prosperous community' (p. 163). This is undeniable, and then he suggests that Smith's concept of justice 'is couched in the language and categories of this tradition [civic humanism]' (ibid., n. 76). This has been disputed by those who follow a different interpretation of Smith's concept of justice.

As I have tried to argue in this chapter, in Smith we can still perceive traces of an important civic humanist narrative. By analysing what Smith actually wrote on the militia issue, why he wrote it, and how he wrote it, new aspects on the apparent ambiguities on Smith's position have emerged. The militia issue, although relatively neglected, is a rich source to discuss the tensions and interactions between the jurisprudential approach and civic humanism. Perhaps, considering that Smith does not fit neatly in any of these categories, we should start looking at Smith with new eyes.

Notes

*   I am much indebted to Ryan Hanley, Jerry Evensky, Peter Kennedy, Eric Nelson, James Otteson, Eric Schliesser and Craig Smith, for their very helpful comments on this chapter. Special gratitude is due to Jeff Young for his helpful and professional comments to improve it. Usual caveats apply.
1. It has commonly been argued that there is a jurisprudential tradition which is not only different, but even incompatible with civic humanism. I am much indebted to a personal correspondence with John Pocock (2 August 2006) in which he clarifies his own position in this issue. Recently Sullivan (2004) argues that classical republicans were not hostile to liberalism, but that many of the foremost British representatives of this tradition contributed to the formation of a 'liberal republicanism'.
2. The debate between the jurisprudential approach and civic humanism is well reflected in some essays of the collection edited by Hont and Ignatieff (1983), aptly entitled *Wealth and Virtues: The Shaping of Political Economy in the Scottish Enlightenment*. On the jurisprudential approach, Forbes (1976) and Haakonssen (1981) are paramount. On Smith and civic humanism, research includes Pocock's own work (1975, 1983, 1985, 1999), Dwyer (1987, 1990, 1992), Robertson (1983a, 1983b, 1985, 1987), Phillipson (1983) Teichgraeber (1981), Dickey (1986), McNamara (1997) and Evensky (1989). Although Winch (1978, 1996) makes use of the political discourse of civic humanism, in Winch (1983) some reservations about its methodology can be found. Phillipson (1983, p. 200, n. 89) briefly provides a taste of the debate in question. Harpham (1984) gives a powerful critique of Winch's (1978) approach to Smith, calling for a better understanding of liberalism, and in Harpham (2000) he investigates Smith's concept of liberty, questioning any republican interpretation. Stimson (1989) also criticizes any republican interpretation of Smith by suggesting that we cannot find a coherent Smithian theory of politics.
3. In this chapter I shall refer to the six standard books of *The Glasgow Edition of the Works and*

Correspondence of Adam Smith by their abbreviations for references and quotations: *The Theory of Moral Sentiments* (TMS), *An Inquiry into the Nature and Causes of the Wealth of Nations* (WN), *Essays on Philosophical Subjects* (EPS), *Lectures on Jurisprudence* (LJ), *Lectures on Rhetoric and Belles Lettres* (LRBL), and *Correspondence of Adam Smith* (*Corr.*).

4. Henry Neville, who incidentally had translated some of Machiavelli's works, was an influential republican figure in the political debate on the maintenance of a standing army without parliamentary approval.
5. Sidney was a colleague and second cousin of Neville. After being accused, on shaky evidence, of participating in the Rye House plot to kill Charles II and James, Duke of York, he was sentenced to decapitation. In his statement at the block, Sidney wrote that he died for 'that Old Cause in which I was from my youth engaged'.
6. For an introduction to this tradition, and its present state of the art, see Scott (2004, pp. 1–40).
7. Quentin Skinner's influential 'Meaning and Understanding in the History of Ideas' was originally published in 1969. For an interesting debate on his methodological position see Tully (1988). An extensively revised version of this influential essay, plus other of his important contributions on methodological issues, can be found in the first volume of the recently published collection of his works (*Visions of Politics: Regarding Method*, 2002).
8. If both authors follow the same intellectual tradition, they differ on the classic sources that gave rise to republicanism (Roman versus Aristotelian in Skinner (1978) and Pocock (1975), respectively). Recently Nelson (2004) has challenged many held views, recovering the role of *eudaimonia* and Platonic justice as also fundamental tenets within republicanism. But his underlying thesis clarifies a Roman versus a Greek republican theory, avoiding any conflation of both traditions as 'classical republicanism'. The first values independence, private property and glory. The second values a natural or harmonious political order and wealth distribution. This dichotomy would pose, according to Nelson (2006), serious questions on the origins of republicanism and its current ideologically charged interpretations. In other words, understanding republicanism and its historiography is fundamental for political theory.
9. Skinner argues that civic humanist roots are found already in thirteenth-century Italy, not during the Florence–Milan propaganda war of c. 1400, as previously suggested by Baron (1955).
10. I am aware that using both labels interchangeably is problematic, as this conflation involves too many issues. But broadly speaking civic humanism emphasizes active citizenship as the key to moral achievement. More generally, classical republicanism might refer to any republican position derived from classical sources.
11. However, it has been argued that Pocock (1975) misrepresents civic humanism as a form of Aristotelianism. Furthermore, he concludes that this form of civic humanism was the only form of republicanism in early modern political thought.
12. The Roman term *gloria* derives from the Greek *kléos*, which relates to public recognition and reputation. As *kléos* has the same root as *klúo*, 'to hear', *kléos* is literally what is heard about somebody (see Nelson, 2006). This tradition of glory might relate to Smith's ethics in his TMS, as sympathy and the impartial spectator are supported by a social underpinning that relates to moral recognition.
13. Of course Rousseau occupies a special place here. Smith gives a very interesting account of Rousseau's second *Discourse* arguing that it is a Platonic extension of Mandeville's *Fable of the Bees*. With unique subtlety Smith remarks that Rousseau is a 'republican carried a little too far' (EPS, p. 251).
14. On Smith and the militia issue see Sher (1989) and Winch (1978, pp. 103–20; 1996, p. 55, pp. 114–23). According to Winch's interpretation, Smith continued to support militias. See also Hont and Ignatieff (1984, pp. 7–8) and Robertson (1985, pp. 201–32) for Smith's justification of a standing army.
15. Schwoerer (1974) is a good source for this debate. On the standing army debate see also Western (1965). The best account on the militia and Scotland remains Robertson (1985).
16. An immediate reaction was Daniel Defoe's *An Argument Shewing that a Standing Army, with Consent of Parliament, is Not Inconsistent with a Free Government* (1698).
17. Note that Smith refers to Cato's previous moments, before giving his life, as 'arming himself with *manly fortitude*' (TMS I.iii.I.13, p. 48, emphasis added). On Smith's important opinions about Cato see also TMS (VI.iii.30, p. 252 and VII:ii.I.32, p. 286).
18. This was a modified version for a Scottish audience of his earliest published writing addressed to English readers, published in London: *A Discourse concerning Militias and Standing Armies; with relation to the Past and Present Governments of Europe and of England in particular* (1697). As mentioned before, Robertson (1985) is a very good source to understand this debate, and his exposition about Fletcher's influence is excellent.
19. For example, he asserted that 'no woman should be suffered to come within the camp, and the crimes of abusing their own bodies any manner of way, punished with death' (Daiches, 1979, p. 22). In this narrative the idea of the 'effeminate' against *virtù* is also embedded in the martial spirit of the cardinal virtue of courage. In Machiavellian terms, as it has already been argued, the prince has to tame *fortuna*, who is a woman.

20. The concept of 'luxury' was also paramount to the civic discourse of corruption. It resembles the effeminate against the manly courage, and also material progress against moral decline.
21. After giving evidence of his support for a militia, Smith wrote to his publisher William Strahan that: 'The Union was a measure from which infinite Good has been derived to this country' (*Corr.*, p. 68). In WN he also refers to its positive consequences for 'the middling and inferior ranks of people in Scotland' (WN V.iii.89, p. 944), and to its economic effects increasing the price of meat (WN I.xi.b.8, p. 165) and decreasing the price of wool (WN I.xi.m.13, p. 252).
22. In the same first number of the *Edinburgh Review*, Smith contributes with a review of Johnson's *Dictionary*. Based on that, John Bryce, editor of LRBL, suggests that Smith might have contributed to the preface just quoted. On the short-lived project of the *Edinburgh Review*, see Ross (1995, pp. 143–5).
23. Cf. 'The Manners of a Nation shift by Degrees, and the State of civil Policy, and of Commerce, at which we arrived, have greatly affected our Manners in this Particular' (Ferguson, 1756, p. 8).
24. At the same time as this chapter was prepared, Lisa Hill's (2006) *The Passionate Society: The Social, Political and Moral Thought of Adam Ferguson* was in press. I am indebted to Lisa as I could benefit from her research by reading some of her chapters before publication.
25. Ferguson's rhetoric reaches some notable peaks, for example: 'The Feeling of a Man unaccustomed to use a Weapon, is a Fear that it may hurt himself; that of a Man familiar with the Use of it, is a Confidence that it will hurt his Enemy' (Ferguson, 1756, p. 15).
26. Sher (1989) brilliantly shows that Ferguson's lectures on moral philosophy at Edinburgh (after the publication of WN), plus his correspondence and some unpublished manuscripts, can also be read as a dialogue between Ferguson and Smith's position on the militia issue. Analysing Ferguson's lectures, his personal correspondence and some unpublished writings, he also argues, *pace* Robertson (1985), that Ferguson remained faithful during his whole life to the militia cause.
27. On Smith and the Poker Club see especially Rae (1965 [1895], pp. 134–40). For other sources on this club, related to Smith and the militia see Ross (1995, pp. 141–2, pp. 346–8, p. 282 and p. 288), Robertson (1985, pp. 200–232) and Winch (1978, pp. 103–20).
28. Hume's relationship to the militia is difficult to assess. Although at times he flirts with the militia cause (see note 40), the most provocative link would come from the pamphlet *Sister Peg*. David Raynor (1982) suggests that this piece was actually written by Hume. If so, it could be interesting to help us unveil Hume's thoughts on the militia. This idea has some ground. For example, Alexander Carlyle refers in his *Autobiography* to Peggy as Hume's maid (Carlyle, 1866, p. 223).
29. Apparently Smith attended Poker Club meetings even after the publication of WN. Winch believes that Smith left the Poker Club in 1774 (Winch, 1978, p. 104), but Sher (1989, p. 261) found evidence that he attended meetings up to 1784.
30. Winch (1978) has argued that on the standing army and militia issue, 'Smith's position has been misunderstood . . . he continued to support militias; hence his views do not appear to have undergone a change between the *Lectures* and the *Wealth of Nations*' (p. 106). For Ross, Smith's 'realism drove him to the conclusion that, though citizens would benefit from training in martial arts, a professional corps would defeat militiamen' (p. 141). Halevy (1966 [1901], pp. 141–2) points out that Smith, in defending the standing army, would be incurring in another political inconsistency. John Rae is more prudent, claiming: 'I have no means of deciding' (1965 [1895], p. 137) what happened regarding Smith's supposed change of mind.
31. Given that TMS was first published in 1759 while the militia issue was hotly debated in Scotland during the agitations of 1759–60, the fact that Smith does not discuss this issue in TMS is not inimical for my argument. TMS is a book about ethics, and furthermore, Smith's omission about this particularly controversial political issue is understandable. Moreover, it does not preclude him of using a civic humanist narrative.
32. On 'effeminate', see also WN (V.i.g.1, p. 789).
33. Most notably WN (V.i.a.38, p. 705; V.i.a.27, p. 701; V.i.a.38, p. 705).
34. *The Question Relating to a Scots Militia Considered. In a Letter to the Lords and Gentlemen who have concerted a form of law for that establishment* (1760).
35. The title of this book was *The Secret History of Colonel Hooke's Negotiations in Scotland, in Favour of the Pretender; in 1707* (London, 1760). Hooke was a loyal servant of James II, and converted to Roman Catholicism. After all the Jacobite intrigues described in this volume, he practically retired, playing no role in the Rebellion of 1715.
36. Sher (1989, p. 246) suggests that 'Philippi' would be a place for a club meeting, but it would be also suggestive to recall that this was the place for Brutus's defeat in 42 BC. Although the context of Ferguson's letter does not necessarily lead to the latter, it would be a subtle republican remark from Ferguson.
37. Smith and Ferguson's relationship was not without some friction (see Ross, 1995, pp. 404, 230 and 288).
38. LJ(A) corresponds to session 1762–63, and LJ(B) to session 1763–64 (also known as 'Report' dated 1766).

39. Note that there seems to be a nostalgic claim when Smith reportedly lectured that after 'arts and commerce . . . it falls to the meanest to defend the state. This is our present condition in Great Britain' (LJ, p. 542).
40. Hume in 'Idea of a Perfect Commonwealth' briefly refers to the republican fear of a standing army under a monarch, and also to the Swiss militia (Hume, 1985, p. 520). But in some editions of this essay he praised a combination of militia and standing army: 'I must, however, confess, that *Sweden* seems, in some measure, to have remedied this inconvenience, and to have a militia, with its limited monarchy, as well as a standing army, which is less dangerous than the *British*' (ibid., p. 647). The Swiss model was a paradigm for militia supporters. The cantons that made up the Swiss confederation used their own militias for mutual defence. This citizens' army was quite successful against foreign enemies. All able-bodied males were liable to military service and regular training. Adam Smith also refers to the Swiss militia as an exception in Europe (see WN V.i.f.60, p. 787). In Ferguson's view the Swiss combined a militia with commercial progress. In a 1780 letter to William Eden, Ferguson refers to 'the only People in Europe who are regularly armed . . . are the most industrious and Peaceable Citizens' (quoted in Sher, 1989, p. 60).
41. It is worth mentioning, however, that when Smith refers to unproductive labour, in Book II, he directly refers to 'army and navy' (see WN II.iii.2, pp. 330–31).
42. Machiavelli would include the sovereign.
43. See our introduction to Montes and Schliesser (2006).

References

Alvey, J.E. (2003), *Adam Smith: Optimist or Pessimist?* Aldershot: Ashgate Publishing Limited.
Baron, H. (1955), *The Crisis of the Early Italian Rennaisance: Civic Humanism and Republican Liberty in an Age of Classicism and Tyranny*, Princeton, NJ: Princeton University Press.
Berlin, I. (2000 [1958]), 'Two concepts of liberty', in H. Hardy and R. Hausheer (eds), *The Proper Study of Mankind: An Anthology of Essays*, New York: Farrar, Straus & Giroux, pp. 191–242.
Brown, V. (1994), *Adam Smith's Discourse; Canonicity, Commerce and Conscience*, London: Routledge.
Carlyle, A. (1866), *Autobiography of the Reverend Dr. Alexander Carlyle, Minister of Inveresk, containing Memorials of the Men and Events of his Time*, Boston, MA: Ticknor & Fields.
Cicero (1966), *Tusculan Disputations*, ed. T.E. Page, Harvard: Loeb Classical Library.
Daiches, D. (1979), *Andrew Fletcher of Saltoun: Selected Political Writings and Speeches*, Edinburgh: Scottish Academic Press.
Dickey, L. (1986), 'Historicizing the "Adam Smith problem": conceptual, historiographical, and textual issues', *Journal of Modern History*, **58** (September), 579–609.
Dwyer, J. (1987), *Virtuous Discourse: Sensibility and Community in Late Eighteenth-Century Scotland*, Edinburgh: John Donald Publishers.
Dwyer, J. (1990), 'The imperative of sociability: moral culture in the late Scottish Enlightenment', *British Journal for Eighteenth-Century Studies*, **13** (2), 169–84.
Dwyer, J. (1992), 'Virtue and improvement: the civic world of Adam Smith', in P. Jones and A.S. Skinner (eds.), *Adam Smith Reviewed*, Edinburgh: Edinburgh University Press, pp. 190–216.
Evensky, J. (1989), 'The evolution of Adam Smith's views on political economy', *History of Political Economy*, **21** (1), 123–45.
Ferguson, A. (1756), *Reflections Previous to the Establishment of a Militia*, London: Printed for R. & J. Dodsley.
Ferguson, A. (1995 [1767]), *An Essay on the History of Civil Society*, Cambridge: Cambridge University Press.
Fink, Z.S. (1945), *The Classical Republicans: An Essay in the Recovery of a Pattern of Thought in Seventeenth-Century England*, Evanston, IL: Northwestern University Press.
Forbes, D. (1976), *Sceptical Whiggism, Commerce and Liberty*, Oxford: Clarendon Press.
Haakonssen, K. (1981), *The Science of a Legislator. The Natural Jurisprudence of David Hume and Adam Smith*, Cambridge: Cambridge University Press.
Halevy, E. (1966 [1901]), *The Growth of Philosophic Radicalism*, Boston, MA: Beacon Press.
Harpham, E.J. (1984), 'Liberalism, civic humanism, and the case of Adam Smith', *American Political Science Review*, **78** (3), 764–74.
Harpham, E.J. (2000), 'The problem of liberty in the thought of Adam Smith', *Journal of the History of Economic Thought*, **22** (2), 215–37.
Hill, L. (2006), *The Passionate Society: The Social, Political and Moral Thought of Adam Ferguson*, Dordrecht: Springer.
Hume, D. (1985), *Essays Moral, Political and Literary*, E.F. Miller (ed.), Indianapolis, IN: Liberty Fund.
Hont, I. and M. Ignatieff (1983), *Wealth and Virtue: The Shaping of Political Economy in the Scottish Enlightenment*, Cambridge: Cambridge University Press.
Jaeger, W. (1965 [1939]), *Paideia: The Ideas of Greek Culture*. Oxford: Oxford University Press.

Machiavelli, N. (1988 [1532]), *The Prince*, Q. Skinner and R. Price (eds.), Cambridge: Cambridge University Press.
McNamara, P. (1997), *Political Economy and Statesmanship: Smith, Hamilton and the Foundation of the Commercial Republic*, DeKalb, IL: Northern Illinois University Press.
Montes, L. (2004), *Adam Smith in Context: A Critical Reassessment of some Central Components of His Thought*, London: Palgrave-Macmillan.
Montes, L. and E. Schliesser (2006), *New Voices on Adam Smith*, London: Routledge.
Nelson, E. (2004), *The Greek Tradition in Republican Thought*, Cambridge: Cambridge University Press.
Nelson, E. (2006), 'Republican visions', in John Dryzek, Bonnie Honog and Anne Phillips (eds), *The Oxford Handbook of Political Theory*, Oxford: Oxford University Press, pp. 193–210.
Phillipson, N. (1983), 'Adam Smith as civic moralist', in Istvan Hont and Michael Ignatieff (eds), *Wealth and Virtues: The Shaping of Political Economy in the Scottish Enlightenment*, Cambridge: Cambridge University Press, pp. 179–202.
Plutarch (1968), *Lives*, E.H. Warmington (ed.), Cambridge, MA: Harvard University Press.
Pocock, J.G.A. (1975), *The Machiavellian Moment*, Princeton, NJ: Princeton University Press.
Pocock, J.G.A. (1983), 'Cambridge paradigms and Scotch philosophers: a study of the relations between the civic humanist and the civil jurisprudential interpretation of eighteenth-century social thought', in Istvan Hont and Michael Ignatieff (eds), *Wealth and Virtues: The Shaping of Political Economy in the Scottish Enlightenment*, Cambridge: Cambridge University Press, pp. 235–52.
Pocock, J.G.A. (1985), *Virtue, Commerce, and History: Essays on Political Thought and History, Chiefly in the Eighteenth Century*, Cambridge: Cambridge University Press.
Pocock, J.G.A. (1999), *Barbarism and Religion: Narratives of Civil Government*, Cambridge: Cambridge University Press.
Rae, J. (1965 [1895]), *Life of Adam Smith*, New York: Augustus M. Kelley.
Raynor, D.R. (1982), *Sister Peg. A Pamphlet Hitherto Unknown by David Hume*, Cambridge: Cambridge University Press.
Robertson, J. (1983a), 'Scottish political economy beyond the civic tradition: government and economic development in the *Wealth of Nations*', *History of Political Thought*, **4** (3), 451–82.
Robertson, J. (1983b), 'The Scottish Enlightenment at the limits of the civic tradition', in Istvan Hont and Michael Ignatieff (eds), *Wealth and Virtues: The Shaping of Political Economy in the Scottish Enlightenment*, Cambridge: Cambridge University Press, pp. 137–78.
Robertson, J. (1985), *The Scottish Enlightenment and the Militia Issue*, Edinburgh: John Donald Publishers.
Robertson, J. (1987), 'Andrew Fletcher's vision of union', in R.A. Mason (ed.), *Scotland and England 1286–1815*, Edinburgh: John Donald Publishers, pp. 203–25.
Ross, I.S. (1995), *The Life of Adam Smith*, Oxford: Clarendon Press.
Scott, J. (2004), *Commonwealth Principles: Republican Writing of the English Revolution*, Cambridge: Cambridge University Press.
Schwoerer, L.G. (1974), *No Standing Armies! The Antiarmy Ideology in Seventeenth-Century England*, Baltimore, MD: Johns Hopkins University Press.
Sher, R.B. (1989), 'Adam Ferguson, Adam Smith, and the Problem of National Defense', *Journal of Modern History*, **61** (1), 240–68.
Skinner, Q. (1978), *The Foundations of Modern Political Thought*, 2 vols, Cambridge: Cambridge University Press.
Skinner, Q. (2002), *Visions of Politics: Regarding Method*, Cambridge: Cambridge University Press.
Smith, A. (1981 [1776]), *An Inquiry into the Nature and Causes of the Wealth of Nations*, Indianapolis, IN: Liberty Fund, WN.
Smith, A. (1982), *Lectures on Jurisprudence*, Indianapolis, IN: Liberty Fund, LJ.
Smith, A. (1984 [1759]), *The Theory of Moral Sentiments*, Indianapolis, IN: Liberty Fund, TMS.
Smith, A. (1985), *Lectures on Rhetoric and Belles Lettres*, Indianapolis, IN: Liberty Fund, LRBL.
Smith, A. (1987), *Correspondence of Adam Smith*, Indianapolis, IN: Liberty Fund, Corr.
Stimson, S.C. (1989) 'Republicanism and the recovery of the political in Adam Smith', in M. Milgate and C. Welch (eds), *Critical Issues in Social Thought*, London: Academic Press, pp. 91–112.
Sullivan, V.B. (2004), *Machiavelli, Hobbes, and the Formation of a Liberal Republicanism in England*, Cambridge: Cambridge University Press.
Teichgraeber, R.F. (1981), 'Rethinking das Adam Smith Problem', *Journal of British Studies*, **20** (2), 106–23.
Tully, J. (ed.) (1988), *Meaning and Context: Quentin Skinner and his Critics*, Princeton, NJ: Princeton University Press.
Trenchard, J. and T. Gordon (1995 [1720–23]), *Cato's Letters or Essays on Liberty, Civil and Religious and Other Important Subjects*, R. Hamowy (ed.), Indianapolis, IN: Liberty Fund.
Western, J.R. (1965), *The English Militia in the Eighteenth Century: The Story of a Political Issue 1660–1802*, London: Routledge & Kegan Paul.

Winch, D. (1978), *Adam Smith's Politics: An Essay in Historiographic Revision*, Cambridge: Cambridge University Press.
Winch, D. (1983), *Adam Smith's 'Enduring Particular Result': A Political and Cosmopolitan Perspective*, Cambridge: Cambridge University Press.
Winch, D. (1996), *Riches and Poverty: An Intellectual History of Political Economy in Britain 1750–1834*, Cambridge: Cambridge University Press.
Young, J.T. (1997), *Economics as a Moral Science: The Political Economy of Adam Smith*, Cheltenham, UK and Lyme, NH, USA: Edward Elgar.

18 Adam Smith and the place of faction
*David M. Levy and Sandra J. Peart**

Introduction

If we know only one characteristic of Adam Smith's work, it must be the emphasis on individualism. At the same time, Smith warned us about 'faction', how it is that the 'masters of men' are everywhere and always in combination to the detriment of those outside the faction. In fact, groups play a significant role in Smith's two great works. The problem of factions is a longstanding one in political philosophy, so it might be instructive to see what Smith, who has a reputation of an anti-political philosopher (Cropsey, 1963 [1987], p. 635), makes of groups with unitary goals. In what follows, we examine the nature and role of 'factions' in Smith. The question of interest is how Smith moved from a recognition and appreciation of cooperative behavior, to the realization that cooperation might produce deleterious results, as in the case of employers, 'masters of men'. We shall argue that, for Smith, cooperation is a natural outcome for men who come together desiring approbation; deleterious outcomes are the result not so much of the actions or sentiments of men as the institutions that frame their actions. And, if the outcomes are deleterious, this is a sign that the institutions are in need of reform.

Smith used many words to describe groups with unitary goals. Some appear in only one of his great books. 'Cabal' is found only in the *Theory of Moral Sentiments* (TMS); 'corporation' and 'monopoly', often used to describe a group that controls a market, are used only in the *Wealth of Nations* (WN).[1] Smith used 'combination' to describe a group of people many times in the WN but only once in TMS. The word 'faction' is used often in both TMS and WN and so this is the word we use to mean groups in Smith with unitary goals.

Factions raise two important questions, the answers to which provide insight into how Smith justifies institutional reform. First, how does Smith come to believe that small groups have the ability to function with unitary goals? How does a monopoly, a group of unrelated agents with a special privilege, hold together? If they function effectively then how do these small groups fit into an explanation of the encompassing society comprised of individual actors and their judgments (for example, Morrow, 1923, p. 40)? Second, what judgment does Smith make about factions? It is in the context of faction that we find the seeming paradox of virtuous (vicious) behavior of individuals combined with deleterious (beneficent) consequences. This paradox, we argue, is central to Smith's justification of reform: when virtuous action produces deleterious outcomes, the institution that framed the action itself is judged to be deleterious, in need of reform.

Our approach to faction focuses on Smith's account of the interrelation between social distance and small group cohesion. We make the case that social distance is not necessarily constant in Smith's system. As social distance shrinks, sympathy becomes more habitual and the affection we have for others increases (Peart and Levy, 2005b). Factions reduce social distance, and this gives them power and makes them dangerous. By modifying social distance, they create a disconnect between behavior of which we approve (cooperation) and consequences of which we disapprove. It is in this context that we find virtuous behavior with deleterious consequences. The identification of 'corruption' with faction is emphasized in Young (1997, pp. 157–8). We take the additional step of connecting the identification to the conclusion that the institution that allows corrupt actions to flourish is in need of reform.

Economists will be familiar with the argument that, when self-interested behavior does not produce good social consequences, there is a problem with the institution. Rosenberg's 1960 'Some institutional aspects of the *Wealth of Nations*' located Smith in this argumentative enterprise. Rosenberg presupposed that Smith participates in the larger utilitarian tradition in which the social consequence of action is all-important. Bittermann's two-part article (Bittermann, 1940) is perhaps the most careful statement of this reading.

As scholars from other disciplines have taken an interest in Smith, a range of interpretations of his normative framework has emerged. Indeed, reading Smith's system in terms of an ethic of virtue has become important (for example, Fleischacker, 2004). This non-economic approach leaves open the question of whether Smith's attention to the virtue of people's behavior (virtue ethics) can be linked to considerations of the happiness of nations (utilitarianism). Cropsey, a student of economics before he turned to political philosophy, gives us the helpful clue to reading Smith: 'The question, What is virtue? is never distinct from the question, What deserves approbation? Approbation and disapprobation are bestowed upon actions' (Cropsey, 1963 [1987], p. 636).

To this, we would add that people also approve and disapprove of consequences. Indeed, in what follows we focus on the context in which the approval of the action and disapproval of the consequences takes place. We do not find this paradoxical; rather, that the judgment is formed by a person suggests a failure of what Rawls (1971) called 'reflective equilibrium'. If a person looks at an action and consequence and approves of the action but disapproves of the consequence, then there is something at fault with the institution in which the action has occurred. We refer to this as reflective disequilibrium. If a person's judgment about the action and consequences is carefully calculated, then because human nature can be assumed to be a fixed quality (Peart and Levy, 2005b), blame for the deleterious consequences must rest on the institutional framework that governs the action.

We address two examples of factions in some detail below. The first case is one in which social distance is influenced by regulation. This speaks to the question of how factions are held together. It also relates to the discussion of Smith among the Justices of the US Supreme Court in a recent case. Secondly, if factions are so powerful, what might destroy them? Here, we argue that while factions are robust against external enemies, they are vulnerable to the character flaws ('corruption') which are encouraged by the indulgence that accompanies reduced social distance (Paganelli, 2007). In this light, we reread Smith's account of the passing of the feudal lords, where Smith reports that corruption eventually resulted in good consequences. This is what we mean by institutions being out of reflective equilibrium. Before turning to these examples in some detail, however, we begin with the role of 'place' and social distance.

Place and social distance
The inevitability of some forms of social distance, exemplified by parents and children or country and citizen, led Smith to criticize the doctrine of the Stoic philosophers he

so admired (Levy and Peart, 2008b). In a Stoic system, social distance is a part of the concept of place, which along with time, void and sayables, comprise the four incorporeals. For the Stoics, since only body moves body, an incorporeal such as place has no (justifiable) motivational impact. As Smith quotes Epictetus, the Stoics held that we should lament no more nor less for the death of our child than for the death of any other child.[2] Smith sought to modify Stoicism by taking some types of social distance as inevitable. In his system, place thus attains motivational force and becomes corporeal. The inevitable types of social distance are given both motivational and normative weight and are described by the term 'natural' (Waterman, 2002).

Some reductions in social distance are the result of historical events. In such contexts, social distance shrinks and the moral constraints upon behavior are attenuated: parents, for instance, may indulge, while more distant acquaintances subject children to more stern moral judgment. Factions indulge the misbehavior of those inside the group. For Smith, the faction presents the greatest danger to civil order because it violates all moral constraints toward those outside the group.[3] Even peaceful factions distinguish sharply between approved behavior toward those inside and those outside the group.[4]

Social distance can also be influenced by policy. One example of importance to the economics of anti-trust law is how the tacit collusion of employers creates a group in which masters see themselves as closer to each other than to those they employ. Although the motivational impact of these artificial forms of social distance is real enough, the normative claims are suspect. In the context of faction Smith is cosmopolitan, identifying the well-being of the workers with the happiness of the nation (for example, Levy, 1995; Rothschild, 2001; Fleischacker, 2004; Peart and Levy, 2005a, 2005b; Schliesser, 2008). Beyond the majoritarianism that underscores this identification, Smith stressed that the norms internal to factions have the consequence of suppressing the 'great stoical maxim', the no-harm principle.[5] Judgments of actions are particularly interesting in the case of factions because virtuous actions of faction members, that is, actions that would be worthy of praise, can have evil consequences and vicious actions can have good consequences.

Smith singles out religious factions for particular attention because these cause us to doubt whether religious doctrine supports the imperatives of impartial justice. This casts doubt on the very stability of the larger society, so, not surprisingly, religious factions have received some attention (for example, Levy, 1978; Anderson, 1988; Brubaker, 2006; Levy and Peart, 2008b). But most factions are not of this nature, and so we focus on how factions serve to reduce social distance among actors.

Monopoly as unitary actor

Gordon Tullock once began an article with the claim that every sentence in the *Wealth of Nations* would eventually launch a book. The book in evidence, Adolf Berle and Gardiner Means's *Modern Corporation and Private Property* (1932 [1991]), became the subject of 75-year debate in economics.[6] 'Faction' appears in Smith's stimulating sentence. The opposing sides of the Berle and Means debate agree on little save that factions have no behavioral role to play for Adam Smith.[7]

Smith describes a monopoly in much the same way he would describe a faction, as a group characterized by a willingness to use violence to attain its interests:

To expect, indeed, that the freedom of trade should ever be entirely restored in Great Britain is as absurd as to expect that an Oceana or Utopia should ever be established in it. Not only the prejudices of the public, but what is much more unconquerable, the private interests of many individuals, irresistibly oppose it. Were the officers of the army to oppose with the same zeal and unanimity any reduction in the numbers of forces with which master manufacturers set themselves against every law that is likely to increase the number of their rivals in the home-market; were the former to animate their soldiers in the same manner as the latter enflame their workmen to attack with violence and outrage the proposers of any such regulation, to attempt to reduce the army would be as dangerous as it has now become to attempt to diminish in any respect the monopoly which our manufacturers have obtained against us. This monopoly has so much increased the number of some particular tribes of them that, like an overgrown standing army, they have become formidable to the government, and upon many occasions intimidate the legislature. (WN IV.ii.43)

Smith discusses the costs and benefits of monopoly in terms of a smaller group, which benefits at the expense of a larger group: 'It is thus that the single advantage which the monopoly procures to a single order of men is in many different ways hurtful to the general interest of the country' (WN IV.vii.148).

According to Smith, 'country gentlemen and farmers', not being 'subject to the wretched spirit of monopoly', share knowledge and information willingly (WN IV.ii.21). Social distance is influenced by physical distance:

Country gentlemen and farmers, dispersed in different parts of the country, cannot so easily combine as merchants and manufacturers, who, being collected into towns, and accustomed to that exclusive corporation spirit which prevails in them, naturally endeavour to obtain against all their countrymen the same exclusive privilege which they generally possess against the inhabitants of their respective towns. They accordingly seem to have been the original inventors of those restraints upon the importation of foreign goods which secure to them the monopoly of the home-market. It was probably in imitation of them, and to put themselves upon a level with those who, they found, were disposed to oppress them, that the country gentlemen and farmers of Great Britain in so far forgot the generosity which is natural to their station as to demand the exclusive privilege of supplying their countrymen with corn and butcher's-meat. They did not perhaps take time to consider how much less their interest could be affected by the freedom of trade than that of the people whose example they followed. (WN IV.ii.21)

Indeed, Smith defends a temporary monopoly in terms of a risk-bearing reciprocity between different parts of society:

When a company of merchants undertake, at their own risk and expence, to establish a new trade with some remote and barbarous nation, it may not be unreasonable to incorporate them into a joint stock company, and to grant them, in case of their success, a monopoly of the trade for a certain number of years. It is the easiest and most natural way in which the state can recompense them for hazarding a dangerous and expensive experiment, of which the public is afterwards to reap the benefit. A temporary monopoly of this kind may be vindicated upon the same principles upon which a like monopoly of a new machine is granted to its inventor, and that of a new book to its author. (WN V.i.119)

The temporary monopoly is a prize in a game that is open to all. We now turn to the world of special privilege.

Monopoly and social distance
The case of *Bell Atlantic* v. *Twombly* (550 US 2007) is noteworthy (Levy and Peart, 2008a), because Justice Stevens quoted the first sentence of this paragraph from the *Wealth of Nations*:

> People of the same trade seldom meet together, even for merriment and diversion, but the conversation ends in a conspiracy against the public, or in some contrivance to raise prices. It is impossible indeed to prevent such meetings, by any law which either could be executed, or would be consistent with liberty and justice. But though the law cannot hinder people of the same trade from sometimes assembling together, it ought to do nothing to facilitate such assemblies; much less to render them necessary. (WN I.x.82)

As the argument unfolds in the *Wealth of Nations*, Smith takes pains to explain how the connections mandated by regulation can change the social distance of people within a trade. Before the regulation they might be strangers, but not afterwards:

> A regulation which obliges all those of the same trade in a particular town to enter their names and places of abode in a public register, facilitates such assemblies. It connects individuals who might never otherwise be known to one another, and gives every man of the trade a direction where to find every other man of it. (WN I.x.83)

Regulation builds a community among the tradesmen: 'A regulation which enables those of the same trade to tax themselves in order to provide for their poor, their sick, their widows and orphans, by giving them a common interest to manage, renders such assemblies necessary' (WN I.x.84). All of this takes place in the dimension of social distance. Then Smith offers an explanation in terms of the enforcement of agreement:

> An incorporation not only renders them necessary, but makes the act of the majority binding upon the whole. In a free trade an effectual combination cannot be established but by the unanimous consent of every single trader, and it cannot last longer than every single trader continues of the same mind. The majority of a corporation can enact a bye-law with proper penalties, which will limit the competition more effectually and more durably than any voluntary combination whatever. (WN I.x.85)

In *Bell Atlantic* v *Twombly* Justice Stevens quoted a 'curious statement' to the effect that 'encroaching on a fellow incumbent's territory "might be a good way to turn a quick dollar but that doesn't make it right"' (Levy and Peart, 2008a). Supposing Smith did in fact see cooperative behavior as some sort of norm, how was cooperation (or collusion) enforced in his system? Today, economists might answer the latter question by presuming a punishment system is in force with repeated interactions. Expected pay-offs to cheating alter with repetition, making it no longer profitable to renege on cooperative agreements. All is handled in terms of expected monetary rewards. 'Right' actions are determined by the highest expected pay-off. We suggest that Smith thought otherwise.

When 'right' is wrong
Consider first cooperative behavior among the masters. Cooperation can of course be good for society. But when small groups cooperate at the expense of large groups, a problem that greatly troubled Smith, the outcome is less happy. That Smith believed the masters were 'always and everywhere' in a combination is readily apparent in the *Wealth*

of Nations. There, he considered the problem of wage determination in various societies, supposing a group bargaining situation with masters pitted against workmen. The combination of masters is, he wrote, 'the natural state of things':

> We rarely hear, it has been said, of the combinations of masters, though frequently of those of workmen. But whoever imagines, upon this account, that masters rarely combine, is as ignorant of the world as of the subject. Masters are always and every where in a sort of tacit, but constant and uniform combination, not to raise the wages of labour above their actual rate. *To violate this combination is every where a most unpopular action, and a sort of reproach to a master among his neighbours and equals.* We seldom, indeed, hear of this combination, because it is the usual, and one may say, the natural state of things which nobody ever hears of. (WN I.xiii.13, emphasis added)

The problem of small groups exploiting large ones is precisely the problem of factions. In the paragraph above, we emphasize that masters regard one another as 'neighbours and equals'. Social distance among faction members has shrunk as a result of regulation.

The question that follows is how is the faction maintained when there may be monetary rewards to cheating? Smith's answer was that rewards accrue in two incommensurate dimensions, money and approbation, and people like both money and approbation. People interact using language. These interactions yield two sets of rewards: money, and approbation, which is carried by language. Approbation results from following a norm of reciprocity (from not cheating on agreed-upon actions); disapprobation results from violating it (from cheating). Thus, the rewards to cooperation are augmented by the approbation that results when a person follows the group norm. For individuals who desire both approbation and income, cooperation satisfies what we have called 'katallactic rationality' (Peart and Levy, 2005b).

This provides the solution to Justice Stevens's puzzle. While a master might earn a bit more money if he were to deviate from his agreement with the masters, he would suffer their disapproval and be shunned by the group to which he belongs. So, the masters who cooperate are rewarded by the approval of their equals; their conduct would be approved, that is, said to be 'right'. Of course, when we take the larger group into account, this 'right' conduct might well be bad for society as a whole. The problem of factions is that the cooperation of the small group occurs at the expense of a larger group.

In Smith's account, it is unclear whether the combination of masters will succeed or not. What we do know is that the masters have a considerable advantage in his view because they are fewer and richer than the workmen (WN I.xiii.12). At the same time, combinations might not survive growth in the demand for labor. In America, Smith finds that the continual increase in the demand for labor makes employer collusion impossible so that the condition of the working class improves dramatically.

This raises the obvious question. If the workers' condition improves but that of the masters deteriorates, is society better or worse off? One way to decide is to count those helped and those harmed and to appeal to the reader as impartial spectator:

> Is this improvement in the circumstances of the lower ranks of the people to be regarded as an advantage or as an inconveniency to the society? The answer seems at first sight abundantly plain. Servants, labourers and workmen of different kinds, make up the far greater part of every great political society. But what improves the circumstances of the greater part can never be regarded as an inconveniency to the whole. No society can surely be flourishing and happy, of

which the far greater part of the members are poor and miserable. It is but equity, besides, that they who feed, cloath and lodge the whole body of the people, should have such a share of the produce of their own labour as to be themselves tolerably well fed, cloathed and lodged. (WN I.xiii.35)

Smith goes on to emphasize the importance of economic growth for the well-being of the children of the poor (WN I.xiii.36) and the influence of children on judgment.

'All for ourselves and nothing for other people'

How do we destroy a faction that has deleterious consequences? Smith is clear that factions are the testing ground for leadership.[8] He credits the factional violence of the ancient world with the creation of the stoicism as a philosophy of life (Levy and Peart, 2008b). Once the faction has succeeded in disposing of its enemies, it tends to indulge. From indulgence, selfishness follows. The masters of mankind are the most selfish of all humans. But selfishness makes a faction vulnerable. The greatest example, in Smith's telling, is the downfall of the feudal lords. Feudalism was a stable system, save for the selfishness fostered by intra-faction indulgence.

For Smith, dining together is one way to reduce social distance. Sharing a meal reduces physical distance and helps establish a connection among the diners. The stability of the feudal society depended upon an institutional set-up in which hierarchy reduced social distance. Commercial society reduced hierarchy at the same time as social distance widened. The social distance of the feudal lords and men collapsed relative to what Smith's readers would have known because the lords had no other way to spend their income than hospitality. We quote at length:

> In a country which has neither foreign commerce, nor any of the finer manufactures, a great proprietor, having nothing for which he can exchange the greater part of the produce of his lands which is over and above the maintenance of the cultivators, consumes the whole in rustic hospitality at home. If this surplus produce is sufficient to maintain a hundred or a thousand men, he can make use of it in no other way than by maintaining a hundred or a thousand men. He is at all times, therefore, surrounded with a multitude of retainers and dependants, who, having no equivalent to give in return for their maintenance, but being fed entirely by his bounty, must obey him, for the same reason that soldiers must obey the prince who pays them.

Smith paints an unforgettable picture of the 'rustic hospitality' of the feudal era:

> Before the extension of commerce and manufacture in Europe, the hospitality of the rich, and the great, from the sovereign down to the smallest baron, exceeded everything which in the present times we can easily form a notion of. Westminster Hall was the dining-room of William Rufus, and might frequently, perhaps, not be too large for his company. It was reckoned a piece of magnificence in Thomas Becket that he strewed the floor of his hall with clean hay or rushes in the season, in order that the knights and squires who could not get seats might not spoil their fine clothes when they sat down on the floor to eat their dinner. The great Earl of Warwick is said to have entertained every day at his different manors thirty thousand people, and though the number here may have been exaggerated, it must, however, have been very great to admit of such exaggeration. It seems to be common in all nations to whom commerce and manufactures are little known. (WN III.iv.5)

Their expenditure on hospitality was the basis of their power.

What brought an end to this state of things? The faction was robust against outside attack:

> The introduction of the feudal law, so far from extending, may be regarded as an attempt to moderate the authority of the great allodial lords . . . But though this institution necessarily tended to strengthen the authority of the king, and to weaken that of the great proprietors, it could not do either sufficiently for establishing order and good government among the inhabitants of the country, because it could not alter sufficiently that state of property and manners from which the disorders arose. The authority of government still continued to be, as before, too weak in the head and too strong in the inferior members, and the excessive strength of the inferior members was the cause of the weakness of the head. After the institution of feudal subordination, the king was as incapable of restraining the violence of the great lords as before. (WN III.iv.9)

It was, however, vulnerable against betrayal from within. The feudal system survived only as long as the social distance between master and man was constricted. The emergence of new commodities in the marketplace changed this by appealing to the vanity of the lords:

> But what all the violence of the feudal institutions could never have effected, the silent and insensible operation of foreign commerce and manufactures gradually brought about. These gradually furnished the great proprietors with something for which they could exchange the whole surplus produce of their lands, and which they could consume themselves without sharing it either with tenants or retainers. All for ourselves and nothing for other people, seems, in every age of the world, to have been the vile maxim of the masters of mankind. As soon, therefore, as they could find a method of consuming the whole value of their rents themselves, they had no disposition to share them with any other persons. For a pair of diamond buckles, perhaps, or for something as frivolous and useless, they exchanged the maintenance, or what is the same thing, the price of the maintenance of a thousand men for a year, and with it the whole weight and authority which it could give them. The buckles, however, were to be all their own, and no other human creature was to have any share of them; whereas in the more ancient method of expence they must have shared with at least a thousand people. With the judges that were to determine the preference this difference was perfectly decisive; and thus, for the gratification of the most childish, the meanest, and the most sordid of all vanities, they gradually bartered their whole power and authority. (WN III.iv.10)

The excesses that resulted served to undermine the feudal system, producing a public 'revolution' in happiness:

> A revolution of the greatest importance to the public happiness was in this manner brought about by two different orders of people who had not the least intention to serve the public. To gratify the most childish vanity was the sole motive of the great proprietors. The merchants and artificers, much less ridiculous, acted merely from a view to their own interest, and in pursuit of their own pedlar principle of turning a penny wherever a penny was to be got. Neither of them had either knowledge or foresight of that great revolution which the folly of the one, and the industry of the other, was gradually bringing about. (WN III.iv.17)

Conclusion

The spectator who approves of 'right' action and disapproves of deleterious consequences on the happiness of people will learn from Smith that there is something disturbing about a faction. When 'virtuous' action has dreadful consequences, the institution governing the action has failed.

The reflective disequilibrium in Smith results when judgments concerning actions conflict with judgments about consequences. It is important to reiterate that Smith's framework attends to both actions and consequences. Failing to take account of both actions and consequences strips away the possibility of a reflective disequilibrium, with the further consequence that we fail to see how Smith's argument for institutional reform unfolds.

Suppose the spectator concludes that an institutional change is praiseworthy. Does that in and of itself provide motivational force? Smith granted motivational force to moral philosophy in general and to Stoicism in particular. The cosmopolitanism which Stoicism teaches speaks to our conscience:

> The judgments of the man within the breast, however, might be a good deal affected by those reasonings, and that great inmate might be taught by them to attempt to overawe all our private, partial, and selfish affections into a more or less perfect tranquillity. To direct the judgments of this inmate is the great purpose of all systems of morality. That the Stoical philosophy had very great influence upon the character and conduct of its followers, cannot be doubted; and that though it might sometimes incite them to unnecessary violence, its general tendency was to animate them to actions of the most heroic magnanimity and most extensive benevolence. (TMS VII.ii.51)

At the same time, Smith is pessimistic about the possibility of reform, whether free inland trade (WN IV.ii.43) or the possibility of a peaceful end to slavery (WN III.ii.10). His ideas about reform seem to have been more powerful than he himself believed they would be (Peart and Levy, 2007).

Notes

* We are grateful to Jeffrey Young for the invitation to contribute to the volume. We would like to thank the Pierre F. and Enid Goodrich Foundation for their support.
1. Here are two examples among many: 'the oppression of the poor must establish the monopoly of the rich, who, by engrossing the whole trade to themselves, will be able to make very large profits' (WN I.ix.15); 'To give the monopoly of the home-market to the produce of domestic industry, in any particular art or manufacture, is in some measure to direct private people in what manner they ought to employ their capitals, and must, in almost all cases, be either a useless or a hurtful regulation' (WN IV.ii.11).
2. 'When our neighbour', says Epictetus, 'loses his wife, or his son, there is nobody who is not sensible that this is a human calamity, a natural event altogether according to the ordinary course of things; but, when the same thing happens to ourselves, then we cry out, as if we had suffered the most dreadful misfortune. We ought, however, to remember how we were affected when this accident happened to another, and such as we were in his case, such ought we to be in our own' (TMS III.i.53).
3. 'The animosity of hostile factions, whether civil or ecclesiastical, is often still more furious than that of hostile nations; and their conduct towards one another is often still more atrocious. What may be called the laws of faction have often been laid down by grave authors with still less regard to the rules of justice than what are called the laws of nations. The most ferocious patriot never stated it as a serious question, Whether faith ought to be kept with public enemies? – Whether faith ought to be kept with rebels? Whether faith ought to be kept with heretics? are questions which have been often furiously agitated by celebrated doctors both civil and ecclesiastical. It is needless to observe, I presume, that both rebels and heretics are those unlucky persons, who, when things have come to a certain degree of violence, have the misfortune to be of the weaker party' (TMS III.i.85).
4. Thus, Smith singles out one group of scholars that he thinks is exempt from faction: 'Mathematicians and natural philosophers, from their independency upon the public opinion, have little temptation to form themselves into factions and cabals, either for the support of their own reputation, or for the depression of that of their rivals. They are almost always men of the most amiable simplicity of manners, who live in good harmony with one another, are the friends of one another's reputation, enter into no intrigue in order to secure the public applause, but are pleased when their works are approved of, without being either much vexed or very angry when they are neglected' (TMS III.i.29).

5. 'One individual must never prefer himself so much even to any other individual, as to hurt or injure that other, in order to benefit himself, though the benefit to the one should be much greater than the hurt or injury to the other . . . There is no commonly honest man . . . who does not inwardly feel the truth of that great stoical maxim, that for one man to deprive another unjustly of any thing, or unjustly to promote his own advantage by the loss or disadvantage of another, is more contrary to nature, than death, than poverty, than pain, than all the misfortunes which can affect him, either in his body, or in his external circumstances' (TMS III.i.48).
6. Tullock (1969, p. 287): 'One of the more immutable of the immutable economic laws is that every sentence in the *Wealth of Nations* will eventually become a book.'
7. 'The trade of a joint stock company is always managed by a court of directors. This court, indeed, is frequently subject, in many respects, to the control of a general court of proprietors. But the greater part of those proprietors seldom pretend to understand anything of the business of the company, *and when the spirit of faction happens not to prevail among them*, give themselves no trouble about it, but receive contentedly such half-yearly or yearly dividend as the directors think proper to make to them' (WN V.i.107) (emphasis added). Smith is cited as the authority who supposes factions carry no behavioral consequence in Berle and Means (1932, pp. 303–4). The resulting Smith–Berle–Means theory of the corporation is named by Tullock (1969, p. 287), defended by Galbraith (1979 [2002], pp. 156–7) and attacked by Stigler and Friedland (1983, p. 240). Others who quote the sentence and have supposed factions have no impact include Rosenberg (1960, p. 562), Anderson and Tollison (1982, p. 1241) and Radner (1992, p. 1405). A factional theory of corporate governance is sketched by Hayek (1960 [1967]) and elaborated upon by Morck and Steier (2005).
8. 'Under the boisterous and stormy sky of war and faction, of public tumult and confusion, the sturdy severity of self-command prospers the most, and can be the most successfully cultivated. But, in such situations, the strongest suggestions of humanity must frequently be stifled or neglected; and every such neglect necessarily tends to weaken the principle of humanity' (TMS III.i.79).

References

Anderson, Gary M. (1988), 'Mr. Smith and the preachers: the economics of religion in the *Wealth of Nations*', *Journal of Political Economy*, **96**, 1066–88.
Anderson, Gary M. and Robert D. Tollison (1982), 'Adam Smith's analysis of joint-stock companies', *Journal of Political Economy*, **90**, 1237–56.
Berle, Adolf A. and Gardiner C. Means (1932), *Modern Corporation and Private Property*; reprinted (1991), New York: Transaction Publishers.
Bittermann, Henry J. (1940), 'Adam Smith's empiricism and the law of nature', *Journal of Political Economy*, **48**, 487–520, 703–34.
Brubaker, Lauren (2006), 'Does the "wisdom of Nature" need help?' in Leonidas Montes and Eric Schliesser (eds), *New Voices on Adam Smith*, New York: Routledge, pp. 277–315.
Cropsey, Joseph (1963), 'Adam Smith 1723–1790', in Leo Strauss and Joseph Cropsey (eds) (1987), *History of Political Philosophy*, Chicago, IL: University of Chicago Press, pp. 635–58.
Fleischacker, Samuel (2004), *On Adam Smith's Wealth of Nations: A Philosophical Companion*, Princeton, NJ: Princeton University Press.
Hayek, F.A. (1960), 'The corporation in a democratic society: in whose interest ought it to and will it be run?' in F.A. Hayek (1967), *Studies in Philosophy, Politics and Economics*, Chicago, IL: University of Chicago Press, pp. 300–312.
Galbraith, John Kenneth (1979), 'The founding faith: Adam Smith's *Wealth of Nations*', in John Kenneth Galbraith (2002), *The Essential Galbraith*, New York: Houghton Mifflin, pp. 153–68.
Levy, David M. (1978), 'Adam Smith, "the law of nature", and contractual society', *Journal of the History of Ideas*, **39**, 665–74.
Levy, David M. (1995), 'The partial spectator in the *Wealth of Nations*: a robust utilitarianism', *European Journal of the History of Economic Thought*, **2**, 299–326.
Levy, David M. and Sandra J. Peart (2008a), 'Adam Smith, collusion and "right" at the Supreme Court', *Supreme Court Economic Review*, **16**, 159–63.
Levy, David M. and Sandra J. Peart (2008b), 'The Evil of Independence: Stoic Sources for Adam Smith', *Adam Smith Review*, **4**, Autumn, 57–87.
Morck, Randall K. and Lloyd Steier (2005), 'A global history of corporate governance: an introduction', in Randall Morck (ed.), *A History of Corporate Governance around the World: Family Business Groups to Professional Managers*, National Bureau of Economic Research Conference Report, Chicago, IL: University of Chicago Press, pp. 1–64.
Morrow, Glenn R. (1923), *The Ethical and Economic Theories of Adam Smith: A Study in the Social Philosophy of the Eighteenth Century*, Cornell Studies in Philosophy, New York: Longmans, Green.

Paganelli, Maria Pia (2007), 'Distance in Adam Smith: the moralizing function of commerce in the *Theory of Moral Sentiments*', presented at the Summer Institute for the Preservation of the History of Economics, Fairfax, VA.

Peart, Sandra J. and David M. Levy (2005a), 'A discipline without sympathy: from median well-being to mean well-being', *Canadian Journal of Economics*, **38**, 937–54.

Peart, Sandra J. and David M. Levy (2005b), *The 'Vanity of the Philosopher': From Hierarchy to Equality in Post-Classical Economics*, Ann Arbor, MI: University of Michigan Press.

Peart, Sandra J. and David M. Levy (2007), 'Adam Smith on leadership, equity, and the distinction of ranks', Presented at the International Leadership Association, Vancouver.

Radner, Roy (1992), 'Hierarchy: the economics of managing', *Journal of Economic Literature*, **30**, 1382–1415.

Rawls, John (1971), *A Theory of Justice*, Cambridge, MA: Harvard University Press.

Rosenberg, Nathan (1960), 'Some institutional aspects of the *Wealth of Nations*', *Journal of Political Economy*, **68**, 557–70.

Rothschild, Emma (2001), *Economic Sentiments: Adam Smith, Condorcet, and the Enlightenment*, Cambridge, MA: Harvard University Press.

Schliesser, Eric (2008), 'The measure of real price: Adam Smith's science of equity', in Sandra J. Peart and David M. Levy (eds), *The Street Porter and the Philosopher: Conversations on Analytical Egalitarianism*, Ann Arbor, MI: University of Michigan Press, pp. 228–36.

Stigler, George J. and Claire Friedland (1983), 'The literature of economics: the case of Berle and Means', *Journal of Law and Economics*, **26**, 237–68.

Smith, Adam (1759), *The Theory of Moral Sentiments*, 6th edn (2002), http://www.econlib.org/library/Smith/smMS.html, TMS.

Smith, Adam (1776), *An Inquiry into the Nature and Causes of the Wealth of Nations*, Edwin Cannan (ed.), http://www.econlib.org/library/Smith/smWN.html, WN.

Tullock, Gordon (1969), 'The new theory of corporations', in Erich W. Streissler (ed.), *Roads to Freedom: Essays in Honour of Friedrich A. Von Hayek*, London: Routledge, pp. 287–308.

Waterman, A.M.C. (2002), 'Economics as theology: Adam Smith's *Wealth of Nations*', *Southern Economic Journal*, **68**, 907–21.

Young, Jeffrey T. (1997), *Economics as a Moral Science: The Political Economy of Adam Smith*, Cheltenham, UK and Lyme, NH, USA: Edward Elgar.

19 Adam Smith and the Chicago School
Steven G. Medema*

Introduction

Adam Smith's discussion of the system of natural liberty, its effects on the functioning of the market system, and the resultant implications for the economic role of the state has formed the basis for much of the subsequent economic literature analyzing the interplay of market and state. That there is no settled interpretation of this and any number of other aspects of Smith's work is clear; what is equally clear is that Smith's ideas have, via particular interpretive turns, been used to support the development of theories and frameworks for the analysis of economic policy. This is interesting for the interpretation given to Smith's ideas, the uses made of them in light of that, and how both of these factors influence the larger professional (and even popular) view of Smith. The present essay examines what may be the most fertile of these uses of Smith in the twentieth century: that associated with the Chicago School.

George Stigler opened his banquet speech at the Glasgow *Wealth of Nations* bicentennial conference by saying: 'I bring you greetings from Adam Smith, who is alive and well and living in Chicago' (Meek, 1977, p. 3). This 'genial proprietary claim', as Ronald Meek calls it, was not pulled out of thin air. For, while Smith is shared by virtually all economists, it would be hard to argue that the association of his name with any subset of them since the classical period is as strong as that with the Chicago School. There is also no question that the Chicago School has both claimed and evidenced a close affinity with Smith – directly or indirectly – for three-quarters of a century. Frank Knight, who is rightly considered a central figure behind the establishment of the Chicago School, did a great deal to help cement the place of Smith within the Chicago tradition. While the Cambridge school and the American institutionalists, for example, were distancing themselves in important ways from Smith and the larger classical tradition,[1] Knight embraced Smith. He considered *The Wealth of Nations* 'a work in which wisdom, learning, and the power of analysis are joined to an extraordinary degree' (1951a, p. 8). The same can be said for Jacob Viner, another prominent member of the early Chicago School, who had a tremendous passion for the history of ideas, perhaps going beyond that of any other prominent member of the Chicago School.[2] Viner wrote extensively on Smith, and in very positive, although not hagiographic, terms.

This strong interest in Smith continued in the second generation of the Chicago School, where George Stigler, Milton Friedman and Ronald Coase figure so prominently. Coase, for example, held Smith in extremely high regard, saying that *The Wealth of Nations* is a book that he 'contemplates with awe', and that: 'In keenness of analysis and in its range it surpasses any other book on economics' (1977, p. 325). But it is George Stigler, Adam Smith's best friend in the estimation of some, who has probably done more than anyone else to cement the professional tendency to associate Smith with the Chicago tradition. Stigler calls Smith 'the premier economist of all time' and 'as great an economist as has ever lived' (1976a, p. 351; 1976b, p. 1200). A major reason for this is that, according to

Stigler: 'Perhaps no other economist has ever fully shared Smith's immense understanding of the forces that govern the structure and development of economies' (1952, p. 206). In surveying the broad contours of the history of economic thought in his essay on 'The Economist as Preacher', Stigler makes it very clear that Smith is one set apart when he says that:

> All but one of the economists I quote were highly intelligent, disciplined men whose views on subjects related to economics deserve your attention and thoughtful consideration, but no more. One, Adam Smith, is differently placed: if on first hearing a passage of his you are inclined to disagree, you are reacting inefficiently; the correct response is to say to yourself: I wonder where I went amiss? (1981 [1982], p. 4)

Beyond suggesting that Smith is more likely to be correct than any modern who disagrees with him (and Stigler may well be on solid footing here), Stigler is in one sense, at least, putting Ricardo, Mill, Marx, Jevons and Marshall on one plane, and Smith above them all – a fact perhaps as remarkable for the status Stigler gives to Marx as for that given to Smith.[3]

One gets a strong sense from Stigler's writings on Smith that he does associate Smith with economics 'properly done', and he repeatedly emphasizes the lessons that economists of the present day can draw from Smith's work.[4] Given the extent to which Smith's ideas, especially those regarding the efficacy of markets, were being called into question within the profession at large, Stigler's position on the perils of disagreeing with Smith is not innocuous. And in light of Stigler's view that the Chicago approach is superior to the neoclassical orthodoxy on a number of fronts, it would not be stretching things to suggest that Stigler's suggestion of particular affinity between Smith and Chicago was something more than tongue-in-cheek.

The standard depiction of the Chicago approach to economics is that it seizes on two aspects of Smith's thought – the efficacy of the system of natural liberty and the dim view of the abilities of the state to improve on the outcomes associated with natural liberty – and pushes them to the limit in its elaboration of a model of a competitive market system in which government is an impediment to, rather than a facilitator of, economic efficiency. And, like most caricatures, this one has elements of truth to it. The minimalist view of Smith has long pervaded the Chicago tradition, as well as the Virginia school tradition that in many ways sprang out of Chicago. However, the Chicago School's discussion and use of Smith is not homogeneous, and the differences are reflected in the distinctions one can see between what McCloskey has labeled 'the Good Old Chicago School' of, for example, Frank Knight, Jacob Viner and Ronald Coase, and the 'new' Chicago School of, for example, George Stigler, Gary Becker and Richard Posner. The latter group has given us the man Jerry Evensky (2005) has named 'Chicago Smith', a Smith read in Benthamite terms and whose work thus corresponds rather closely to their own rational choice-based analysis of competitive market structures in an a-institutional context. The former group, in contrast, paints a picture rather closer to what Evensky calls 'Kirkaldy Smith' – a Smith who is grounded in the Scottish Enlightenment mentality. This Smith is a bit harder to pin down and is more overtly attuned to the import of what Coase has called 'the institutional structure of production' and the role played by government within that structure.[5]

The purpose of this chapter is not to get into a lengthy debate over the merits of the different Chicago interpretations of Smith as against each other or against other interpretations of Smith extant in the literature. Rather, we want to draw out the features of these Chicago views of Smith and, resisting all but the most basic commentary, leave it to the reader of this *Companion* to contrast the Chicago views with each other and with other perspectives on Smith and his work.

George Stigler and the construction of 'Chicago Smith'

To understand the context for the 'new' Chicago School's view of Smith, it is useful to begin with Melvin Reder's (1987, p. 413) identification of the 'two main characteristics' of the Chicago School. The first of these characteristics is the 'belief in the power of neoclassical price theory to explain observed economic behavior'. The second characteristic is the 'belief in the efficacy of free markets to allocate resources and distribute income'. And, Reder says, correlative with the second is 'a tropism for minimizing the role of the state in economic activity'. It seems natural, then, that one finds two major threads in the political economy of 'Chicago Smith': (1) the construction of economic theory founded upon the principle of self-interest; and (2) a demonstration of the efficacy of a competitive market system and an elaboration of the resultant implications for the role of government vis-à-vis the market in economic activity.

It would surprise no one to hear the Chicago School's approach to economics described as 'a stupendous palace erected upon the granite of self-interest'. This phrase was not used to describe the Chicago School, however, but Smith's *Wealth of Nations*, and the person doing the describing was none other than George Stigler (1971 [1982], p. 136).[6] For Stigler, Smith's 'one overwhelmingly important triumph' was that 'he put into the center of economics the systematic analysis of the behavior of individuals pursuing their self-interest under conditions of competition' (1976b, p. 1201). Indeed, such is the primacy of the concept in Smith's system, on Stigler's reading, that he questions whether *The Theory of Moral Sentiments* (1976 [1759]) bears any relationship at all to Smith's economics (1960, p. 44). Self-interest is not only central here, it is almost miraculous in its impact on national wellbeing. In *The Wealth of Nations*, Stigler argues, Smith shows us that: 'The immensely powerful force of self-interest guides resources to their most efficient uses ... in short, it orders and enriches the nation which gives it free rein. Indeed, if self-interest is given even a loose rein, it will perform prodigies' (Stigler 1971 [1982], p. 136).[7] So, on Stigler's reading, Smith considered the self-interested behavior that inevitably characterizes economic activity, channeled through a competitive system, as a recipe for efficient outcomes.

The centrality of self-interested behavior in the work of this 'Chicago Smith' led Stigler, circa 1971, to label Smith 'the premier scholar of self-interest' (1971 [1982], p. 139) and to call his aspect of Smith's work 'the crown jewel' of *The Wealth of Nations* (1976b, p. 1201). We do not know whether the maturation of Gary Becker caused Stigler to change his opinion on Smith's relative status among scholars of self-interest, but we do know that Stigler sees an essential continuity between what he considers Smith's model of self-interested behavior under competitive conditions and present-day economics. This continuity is evidenced in Stigler's view that Smith's approach 'remains to this day ... the foundation of the theory of the allocation of resources' (1976b, p. 1201).[8]

In fact much of the reason for Smith's greatness seems to rest, for Stigler, in Smith's 'modern-ness'. Stigler sees the analytics that underpin and undergird Smith's positions carried through in modern economics, and this goes well beyond the basic notion of self-interested behavior in the economic realm. Stigler goes so far as to link up Smith's approach with contemporary economics imperialism, characterizing Smith as giving us 'a theorem of almost unlimited power on the behavior of man' that is 'Newtonian in its universality' (1976b, p. 1212). This 'always and everywhere' gravitational allusion is not accidental, but rather reflects what Stigler sees as the pervasiveness of self-interested behavior throughout human life.[9] Such is its generality, he says, that: 'we today are busily extending this construct into areas of economic and social behavior to which Smith himself gave only unsystematic study', and this, in turn, 'is tribute to both the grandeur and the durability of his achievement' (1976b, p. 1212).[10] There are other examples of modern-ness as well, such as when Stigler asserts that, for Smith, the 'negatively sloping demand curve was already axiomatic' (1950, p. 308).[11] He also points to Smith's argument that, '*as a matter of demonstrable economic analysis* . . . the individual in seeking his own betterment will put his resources where they yield the most to him, and that as a rule the resources then yield the most to society' (1965a, p. 2, emphasis added). In doing so here and elsewhere,[12] Stigler equates Smith's statements about increased national wealth with the much more modern (and precise) notion of 'efficiency'.

Stigler's portrait of a Smithian system in which self-interest reigns has a normative component, too. Stigler's Smith believed that self-interested behavior, channeled through the market, is likely to generate desirable social outcomes as long as government does not interfere with its operation. As Stigler noted in his 1964 Presidential Address to the American Economic Association, 'The main burden of Smith's advice . . . was that the conduct of economic affairs is best left to private citizens – that the state will be doing remarkably well if it succeeds in its unavoidable tasks of winning wars, preserving justice, and maintaining the various highways of commerce' (1965a, p. 1).[13] One would have to search hard to find a more apt depiction of what most would consider the Chicago view – of Smith or of the world.

Milton Friedman's (1978) bicentennial essay on 'Adam Smith's relevance for 1976', while exhibiting neither the breadth nor depth of Stigler's extensive Smith scholarship, evidences the same minimalist view we find in the above-quoted passage from Stigler's AEA Presidential Address. Friedman seems to espouse a spontaneous order view of Smith, noting that: 'The market, with each individual going his own way, with no central authority setting social priorities, avoiding duplication, and coordinating activities, looks like chaos to untutored eyes.' Yet, he says, 'through Smith's eyes we see that it is a finely ordered and effectively tuned system, one which arises out of men's individually motivated actions, yet is not deliberately created by men' (1978, p. 17).[14] The associated implications for the economic role of government are straightforward, says Friedman, consisting of 'those elementary functions' of government – defense, justice, and certain public works – 'that Smith regarded as alone compatible with the "obvious and simple system of natural liberty"' (1978, p. 7). In like manner, Edward Lazear (2000) – writing on economic imperialism, as it happens – tells us that Smith gave us 'a positive theory of the economy, with limited or no role for the state'.

Of course, Stigler did not go so far as to suggest that there is no role for the state in Smith's system. In fact, he says: 'When the individual does not know, or does not have the power to advance, his own interests, Smith feels remarkably free to have the state intervene' (1965a, p. 3). Yet, Stigler seems to think that, for Smith, such instances are rather limited, and he sees Smith's preference for 'private economic activity' deriving from two sources. The first was Smith's 'belief in the efficiency of the system of natural liberty' (1965a, p. 2). For example, Stigler says, *The Wealth of Nations* contains a lot of preaching in its later pages, but Smith addresses little of it toward the private behavior of individuals (1981 [1982], pp. 4, 6). He cites Smith's attacks on protectionism as an illustration of the benefits of the system of natural liberty in that, in Stigler's view, they 'rested squarely on his theory of competitive prices'. That is, in Smith, according to Stigler, the 'crucial argument for unfettered individual choice in public policy was the efficiency property of competition' (1976b, p. 1201).[15]

The second source that Stigler finds for Smith's preference for private sector outcomes is that Smith 'deeply distrusted the state' – mostly because of its propensity to be captured by special interests (1965a, p. 3).[16] Smith's disparaging remarks about government officials are well known and need not be repeated here. What is worth noting, however, is Stigler's attitude toward Smith's discussion of political agents. Stigler contends that Smith 'implicitly locates the most numerous and consistent failures of self-interest in guiding people's behavior' in the political arena (1971 [1982], pp. 144–5).[17] Yet, he says, Smith's 'attitude toward political behavior was not dissimilar to that of a parent toward a child: the child was often mistaken and sometimes perverse, but normally it would improve in conduct if properly instructed' (1971 [1982], p. 142). The centrality of self-interest in Stigler's view of Smith comes through very clearly here, as he chastises Smith for failing to realize that political agents are self-interested in their behavior. In essence, Stigler is criticizing Smith for not being a prototype public choice economist. Nor is Stigler willing to allow that Smith's failure here could be explained by the fact that everyone else in that era, too, looked at political behavior in non-self-interested terms; Smith, he says, 'is a better man than everyone else' (1971 [1982], p. 143), and so should be above such slip-ups.

Recovering 'Kirkaldy Smith'? The 'Good Old Chicago School'
So far, the Chicago version of Adam Smith sounds pretty much as expected: his ideas correspond almost exactly to Reder's description of the Chicago approach. But there is a different Smith evidenced in the Chicago School literature – the Adam Smith of McCloskey's 'Good Old Chicago School' – and this Dr. Smith sounds a bit more eclectic and pragmatic than the 'Chicago Smith' of Stigler et al.

McCloskey has said that the 'Good Old Chicago School' is the legacy of Smith and the new Chicago School is that of Bentham – and thus the latter gives us a Smith read in Benthamite terms. We can see some evidence for McCloskey's position in that the part of 'Chicago Smith' that sees a world consisting of rational maximizers of self-interest promoting the general welfare within a framework of competition is somewhat difficult to find in the Smith portrayed by the Good Old Chicago School of Knight, Viner and Coase. For starters, Smith's man looks a lot less like *homo economicus* in the 'Good Old' depictions, and we certainly do not find the case for economics imperialism in this view of Smith. In fact, quite the opposite. In a market context, says Viner: 'The social sentiments are not aroused to action, and [Smith's] man behaves in response to calculating, rational self-interest' (1960, p. 60). However, things are rather different in other areas of life: 'For the social system as a whole, excluding its market aspects, the beneficial outcome of laissez faire, according to Smith, results from the social instincts embedded in human nature, as well as from the "moral sentiments"', including sympathy, desire for approval, conscience and benevolence (1960, p. 60). We find a similar perspective expressed by Coase, who argues that Smith's view of man is not economic man with his rational, single-minded pursuit of his self-interest. Indeed, he says:

> Adam Smith would not have thought it sensible to treat man as a rational utility-maximiser. He thinks of man as he is – dominated, it is true, by self-love but not without some concern for others, able to reason but not necessarily in such a way as to reach the right conclusion, seeing the outcomes of his actions but through a veil of self-delusion. (Coase, 1976, pp. 545–6)[18]

The point, according to Coase, is that Smith saw that benevolence cannot serve as a coordinating force in a market context. It will work in certain small, close economic contexts – for example, within the family, or among certain business associates – but in modern society we must 'rely on the market, with its motive force, self-interest'.[19] Outside of this context though, behavior, for Smith, is rather more multifaceted.

This more complex characterization of Smith can be found in other areas as well. Consider, for example, the case of the invisible hand and private–social harmony. Viner does not reject the notion that Smith sees a correspondence between the pursuit of private interests and the promotion of the larger interests of society. He allows that both *The Theory of Moral Sentiments* and *The Wealth of Nations* find Smith postulating a harmonious order of nature within which man, in the course of pursuing his own interest, serves the larger interests of society (for example, 1927, pp. 208–10). But he is also convinced that 'the significance of the natural order in Smith's economic doctrines has been grossly exaggerated' (1927, pp. 219–20). In contrast to Stigler's portrait of a Smith who expresses virtually unlimited optimism regarding the working of self-interest, Viner argues that Smith saw the linkage between self-interest and societal interests as 'partial and imperfect' in the economic realm. Self-interest and competition, he says, were for Smith 'sometimes treacherous to the public interest they were supposed to serve' (1927, pp. 208, 231–2). Knight, too, dismisses the view that Smith 'believed in a universal harmony of interests among men', calling this 'merely one discouraging example of what passes widely in learned circles for history and discussion' (1951b, p. 267). To style Smith as 'the "apostle of self-interest"', he says, leaves out a great deal of the story, particularly given that Smith 'took no pains to conceal his dislike for some of the forms in which self-interest manifests itself in trade and industry' (1951a, p. 9).

Even if human nature does exhibit the sort of harmony that some read into Smith, Coase (1976, p. 543) says that this 'does not imply that no government action is required to achieve the appropriate institutional structure for economic activity'. This, of course, is more or less the explanation for Lionel Robbins's (1952) identification of the state as the invisible hand. But problems with the harmonization process carry the case for government action well beyond this. And, because self-interest works only imperfectly to promote the greater social interest, Smith was certainly not averse to what Viner calls 'government interference with private interests' if the effects of such interference were likely to be socially beneficial (Viner, 1927, p. 217; Knight, 1951a, p. 9).

One can see a significant break between the earlier and later Chicago views of Smith here, both in the extent of government action considered socially beneficial and in the rationale for perceived limits on state action. On the first of these subjects – the appropriate extent of government action – both Knight and Viner saw a basic preference for non-interference in Smith, but they were also clear about the extent to which exceptions to this principle can be found in *The Wealth of Nations*. Speaking of the classical period generally, Knight points out that: 'The laisser-faire economists of the straightest sect made exceptions of a sort which opened the way to much wider departures from the principle when and as changed conditions might seem to demand', and, he argues, this 'applies particularly to the great apostle of the movement, Adam Smith' (1947, p. 50). Viner makes a similar point when he says that: 'If Smith had adopted the term "laissez faire" as an appropriate label for his own policy views, he undoubtedly would not have interpreted it literally as a condemnation of all government interference with the activities of private individuals' (1968 [1991], p. 259).[20] In fact, says Viner, while Smith's 'one deliberate and comprehensive generalization' regarding the proper functions of the state would 'narrowly restrain' its activities, the actual range of activities pointed to by Smith was so extensive that, if Smith 'had been brought face to face with a complete list of the modifications to the principle of laissez faire to which he at one place or another had granted his approval, I have no doubt that he would have been astounded at his own moderation' (1927, pp. 218–19). So, it seems, would Stigler and Friedman.

As regards the rationale for the limits on state action, recall that, in making the case for a minimalist Smith, Stigler put the efficacy of private actions and the system of natural liberty on at least equal footing with the pitfalls of state actors and actions. Knight, in contrast, did not see Smith as one who advocated individual or private activity as inherently beneficial. For him, the case for the market in Smith rests largely on 'the stupidity of governments rather than the competence of individuals' (1947, p. 2). In that vein, Knight seems particularly fond of Smith's remark concerning 'that insidious and crafty animal vulgarly called a statesman or politician', to which he refers on multiple occasions (see, for example, 1951a, p. 23). In like manner, Viner views Smith's antipathy toward government intervention not as a commentary on government *per se*, but on the relative magnitude of the flaws associated with untrammeled private action on the one hand and with government incompetence and corruption on the other. Many of the activities required an assumption that government knew better than the individual what was in his interest, and that, says Viner, was something Smith could not concede (1927, p. 221). Coase sees the matter in virtually the same pragmatic way, suggesting that Smith was opposed to many forms of government action not just because he considered them unnecessary, but because he felt that 'government action would usually make matters worse' – an artifact of governments lacking 'both the knowledge and the motivation to do a satisfactory job in regulating an economic system' (1977, p. 319).

On Viner's reading, Smith saw government, even though inept, as the best option in some cases (1927, pp. 231–2), and Smith was willing to give government a wide berth 'where, by exception, good government made its appearance' (1927, p. 227).[21] While Stigler, as we have already seen, was quick to criticize Smith for seeming to assume that politicians were more or less immune from the self-interest that he ostensibly attributed to most other forms of human behavior, we see no such criticism from Viner. Viner, in fact, seems very pleased with the non-doctrinaire nature of Smith's belief that government could show that it was 'entitled to wider responsibilities' if it improved 'its standards of competence, honesty, and public spirit' (1927, p. 231).

Beyond the greater optimism about government in the Good Old Chicago interpretation, we also see here a Smith who claims less for market outcomes than does the Smith of the 'new' Chicago view. Against Stigler's efficiency-oriented view, Viner contends that: 'It is not clear that Adam Smith believed that laissez faire would carry the wealth of a nation to some kind of theoretically-conceivable maximum'. What is clear, according to Viner, is that Smith believed that, 'subject to a vague and in part logically inconsistent list of qualifications . . . economic society left to its autonomous operation would produce a higher level of economic welfare than would accrue if government, inefficient, ignorant, and profligate as in practice it was, should try to direct or regulate or operate it' (1960, p. 60).[22] This same 'it's better than the alternative' perspective can be found in Knight, who says that Smith showed how the 'apparent chaos of competition' is actually 'an orderly system of economic cooperation' where 'individual freedom' rather than 'central direction' leads not to some 'maximum', but simply to increased national wealth and want satisfaction as compared with the alternative (1951a, p. 9).

This last point is reflective of the fact that the tightly analytical, 'axiomatic', and even determinate aspect of 'Chicago Smith' is largely absent in the Good Old Chicago School interpretation. Knight saw Smith's approach evidencing 'hard common sense' – mixed with 'genial humanity' – rather than 'rigorous analysis' (1947, p. 3). This last sentiment is echoed by Viner, who notes that Smith extensively qualified his statements with words like 'perhaps', 'generally' and 'in most cases', as a result of which 'his models are not tight or rigorous' (1968 [1991], p. 257).[23] The Good Old Chicago Smith is more circumspect and provisional than the new Chicago Smith. Moreover, both Viner and Coase laud the lack of a priorism in Smith's analysis, and one of the things that Coase finds so important about Smith's analysis in *The Wealth of Nations* is 'its careful observations on economic life' (Coase, 1977, p. 309). Likewise, Viner points out on several occasions that Smith's analysis is 'built up by detailed inference from specific data and by examination of specific problems' (1927, p. 210).[24] This includes Smith's generalizations about the appropriate role for the state and even his assessment of which specific governmental functions are consistent with the natural order – the latter being that group of functions which promote the general welfare, as revealed empirically (1927, p. 220). What we have, in Viner and Coase, is an almost Marshallian Smith – a Smith in keeping with the affinity for Marshall so amply evident in their respective works.

Conclusion

In the Chicago School, then, we meet two contrasting views of Smith. One is rather straightforward and well defined, the other more nuanced. One sounds a great deal like a neoclassical economist, the other more pluralistic. One is something of a champion of laissez-faire, the other evidences a more broad-based role for government within the economic system. Neither of these distinctions should be surprising. In the first instance, Stigler, Becker and other members of the new Chicago School are rational-choice theorists, writing at the time of its ascendancy, whereas Knight and Viner were writing during a much more pluralistic period. The assumption of self-interested behavior meant something very different in the second half of the twentieth century than it did in the first half, and so is likely to have different content and meaning given to it across these epochs.

As for the market versus government question, it is true that both the Good Old Chicago School and the new Chicago School give us a fairly non-interventionist Smith, although a strong case can be made that the Smith of the Good Old Chicago School has a stronger interventionist streak. The new Chicago view offers us a Smith who believes in private cum market success and government failure, the combination of which leaves little room for useful intervention by the state. The Good Old Chicago School view is one where private cum market failure is somewhat more widespread, but where government failure is common, too. The choice, from this perspective, is between two imperfect options, and the implications for government action are less clear cut, a priori.

So we have elements of continuity over time, but also, and especially, significant differences of interpretation. This, of course, is to be expected in the literature on Smith. As Viner so accurately pointed out: 'Traces of every conceivable doctrine are to be found in that most catholic book, and an economist must have peculiar theories indeed who cannot quote from the *Wealth of Nations* to support his special purposes' (1927, p. 207). Of course, Viner's point here was not that Smith should be used for such purposes, but that there are lessons to be drawn from the eclectic, pragmatic and provisional nature of Smith's work. As he says in closing out his famous article, 'Adam Smith and laissez faire':

> In these days of contending schools, each of them with deep, though momentary, conviction that it, and it alone, knows the one and only path to economic truth, how refreshing it is to return to *The Wealth of Nations*, with its eclecticism, its good temper, its common sense, and its willingness to grant that those who saw things differently from itself were only partly wrong. (1927, p. 232)

Notes

* I would like to thank Jeffrey Young, Ross Emmett, Jerry Evensky, Dan Hammond, David Levy, Alain Marciano, Deirdre McCloskey, David Mitch, Leon Montes, Malcolm Rutherford, Amos Witztum, and participants in seminars at the University of Reims Champagne Ardenne, the 2006 meeting of the European Society for the History of Economic Thought, and the 2006 Summer Institute for the Preservation of the Study of the History of Economic Thought at George Mason University for their comments as this project unfolded.

1. On Cambridge, see, for example, Pigou (1932) and the discussion in Shackle (1967); within institutionalism, see, for example, Mitchell (1967, pp. 166–7), Clark (1926) and the discussion in Rutherford (2005).
2. The main challenger would be Stigler, but Stigler was much more of a historian of economic theory as against Viner's broader intellectual history perspective. See Stigler (1941, 1965b).
3. While Stigler certainly had an appreciation for Ricardo's analytical approach, he says that 'Ricardo had neither Smith's genius for isolating fundamental empirical relationships nor his supreme common sense' (1952, p. 205).
4. The same is true for Coase, who repeatedly laments how little economists have advanced upon Smith's work over the last two centuries. See, for example, Coase (1977).
5. This distinction is perhaps nowhere more evident than in the meanings attributed to 'The Problem of Social Cost' by Coase and by Stigler, each of whom sees himself working squarely in the tradition of Smith. On this point see, for example, Medema (1996) and McCloskey (1998), who point out that Stigler's emphasis on the Coase theorem as the central message of 'The Problem of Social Cost', is diametrically opposed to Coase's own view that: (a) the article is about the need for comparative institutional analysis (which the Coase theorem would render unnecessary); and that (b) the Coase theorem is merely a fiction to debunk Pigovian externality theory.

    One might be tempted to conclude that these differences between old and new Chicago are generational, but, as the subsequent discussion will make clear, it is methodological issues that are at the heart of many of the differences of interpretation, perhaps even including those related to the economic role of the state.
6. In support of this, Stigler cites Smith's statement that: 'though the principles of common prudence do not always govern the conduct of every individual, they always influence that of the majority of every class and order' (Smith, 1976 [1776], II.2.36).
7. Citing Smith to the effect that: 'The natural effort of every individual to better his own condition, when suffered to exert itself with freedom and security, is so powerful a principle, that it is alone, and without any assistance, not only capable of carrying on the society to wealth and prosperity, but of surmounting a hundred impertinent obstructions with which the folly of human laws too often incumbers its operations;

though the effect of these obstructions is always more or less either to encroach upon its freedom, or to diminish its security' (Smith, 1976 [1776], IV.5.82).
8. See also Becker (1976, 1981).
9. Both Stigler and Becker see evidenced in Smith the idea of fixed tastes and preferences that influence behavior across the spectrum of human behavior. See, for example, Stigler (1981 [1982], p. 6) and Becker (1976, p. 282).
10. Beyond Stigler's general reference to the origins of economics imperialism in Smith, Becker (1975) links his human capital theory very explicitly to Smith's discussion in *The Wealth of Nations*.
11. Citing Smith's statement that: 'A competition will immediately begin among [the buyers when an abnormally small supply is available], and the market price will rise more or less above the natural price' (Smith 1976 [1776], I.7.9).
12. See Stigler (1971 [1982], p. 136).
13. Elsewhere, Stigler (1976b, p. 1201) argues that: 'The crucial argument [of Smith's] for unfettered individual choice in public policy was the efficiency property of competition'.
14. Friedman says that 'Adam Smith's invisible hand' gives rise to 'the possibility of cooperation without coercion' (http://www.econlib.org/library/Essays/rdPncl1.html).
15. Stigler here quotes Smith's famous passage that: 'Every individual is continually exerting himself to find out the most advantageous employment for whatever capital he can command. It is his own advantage, indeed, and not that of the society which he has in view. But the study of his own advantage naturally, or rather necessarily leads him to prefer that employment which is most advantageous to the society' (Smith, 1976 [1776], IV.2.4).
16. Citing Smith's remarks about legislatures being influenced by 'the clamorous importunity of partial interests' (Smith 1976 [1776], IV.2.44).
17. Stigler points to incomplete information, agency and public good problems mentioned by Smith, as other instances of the failure of self-interest to comport with the social interest, but Stigler is of the mind that most of these were 'nonexistent or of negligible magnitude' for Smith (1971 [1982], pp. 144–5)
18. In discussing Smith's treatment of the American Revolution in *The Wealth of Nations*, Coase agrees that self-interested behavior likely explains at least some of the motivation of the revolutionary leaders, as Smith suggests. Yet, he says, it does not seem to be an adequate explanation for 'why the American leaders had followers' (Coase 1977, p. 324). Coase finds the explanation in *The Theory of Moral Sentiments* and the ideas, expressed by Smith, that: 'The great mob of mankind are the admirers and worshippers, and, what may seem more extraordinary, most frequently the disinterested admirers and worshippers of wealth and greatness' (Coase, 1977, p. 324). This explanation of human motivation falls far closer to the Veblenian status emulation than to 'economic man'.
19. Coase goes on to opine that: 'If man were so constituted that he only responded to feelings of benevolence, we would still be living in caves with lives "nasty, brutish and short"' (Coase, 1977, p. 315).

    Coase's perspective on the scope of benevolence vis-à-vis the market contains a particularly Coasean twist, as the following two quotations illustrate.

    'We just do not have the time to learn who the people are who gain from our labors or to learn their circumstances, and so we cannot feel benevolence towards them even if benevolence would be justified were we to be fully informed' (Coase, 1977, p. 314).

    'Again, the observance of moral codes must very greatly reduce the cost of doing business with others and must therefore facilitate market transactions' (Coase, 1976, p. 545).

    What we see here is essentially a transaction cost explanation for the functioning of benevolence. In the former instance, the transaction costs associated with forming close relationships are sufficiently high to render the formation of such relationships either impossible or prohibitively costly. In the latter instance the observance of moral codes serves to reduce the transaction costs associated with market exchange. One might even say that, from this perspective, the impartial spectator, who regulates the interaction of benevolence and self-interest, is a transaction cost minimizer.
20. Viner goes on to list a string of activities that Smith sees as appropriate for the state.
21. Viner cites Smith's statement that: 'The ordinary, vigilant, and parsimonious administration of such aristocracies as those of Venice and Amsterdam, is extremely proper, it appears from experience, for the management of a mercantile project of this kind. But whether such a government as that of England; which, whatever may be its virtues, has never been famous for good oeconomy; which, in time of peace, has generally conducted itself with the slothful and negligent profusion that is perhaps natural to monarchies; and in time of war has constantly acted with all the thoughtless extravagance that democracies are apt to fall into; could safely be trusted with the management of such a project, must at least be a good deal more doubtful' (Smith, 1976 [1776], V.2.5).
22. In a swipe at the circa-1920s mantra of 'social control' as against those who parroted 'demand and supply', Viner suggested that Smith's words regarding the 'impertinence and presumption . . . in kings and ministers, to pretend to watch over the oeconomy of private people' had present import: 'If the standards

of public administration are low, progress from a life regulated by the law of demand and supply to life under the realm of social control may be progress from the discomforts of the frying pan to the agonies of the fire' (1927, p. 221). See Smith (1976 [1776], II.3.36).
23. Here Viner cites the same passage that Stigler cites to justify his view of a more straight-on self-interest motive in Smith. See note 6 above, and Smith (1976 [1776], II.2.36).
24. This is not surprising, coming from Viner, who encouraged the development of quantitative analysis at Chicago, as against Knight's more purely theoretical approach and outright resistance to the quantitative turn in economic analysis. See, for example, Reder (1982, 1987). Stigler (1952, p. 205), too, appreciated Smith's empirical and commonsensical bent as against, say, Ricardo, but was far more taken with Smith's analytical efforts and what they ultimately gave us for the present.

References

Becker, Gary S. (1975), *Human Capital*, 2nd edn, New York: NBER and Columbia University Press.
Becker, Gary S. (1976), *The Economic Approach to Human Behavior*, Chicago, IL: University of Chicago Press.
Becker, Gary S. (1981), *A Treatise on the Family*, Cambridge, MA: Harvard University Press.
Clark, John M. (1926), *Social Control of Business*, Chicago, IL: University of Chicago Press.
Coase, Ronald H. (1976), 'Adam Smith's view of man', *Journal of Law and Economics*, **19** (October), 529–46.
Coase, Ronald H. (1977), '*The Wealth of Nations*', *Economic Inquiry*, **15** (3), 309–25.
Evensky, Jerry (2005), '"Chicago Smith" versus "Kirkaldy Smith"', *History of Political Economy*, **37** (Summer), 197–203.
Friedman, Milton (1978), 'Adam Smith's relevance for 1976', in Fred R. Glahe (ed.), *Adam Smith and The Wealth of Nations: 1776–1976 Bicentennial Essays,* Boulder, CO: Colorado Associated University Press, pp. 7–20.
Knight, Frank H. (1947), *Freedom and Reform*, New York: Harper & Brothers.
Knight, Frank H. (1951a), 'Economics', in *Encyclopaedia Britannica*, reprinted (1956) in *On the History and Method of Economics: Selected Essays*, Chicago, IL: University of Chicago Press, pp. 3–33.
Knight, Frank H. (1951b), 'The role of principles in economics and politics', *American Economic Review*, **41** (March), 1–29; reprinted in *On the History and Method of Economics: Selected Essays*, Chicago, IL: University of Chicago Press, 1956, pp. 251–81.
Lazear, Edward P. (2000), 'Economic imperialism', *Quarterly Journal of Economics*, **115** (February), 96–146.
McCloskey, Deirdre N. (1998), 'The good old Coase theorem and the Good Old Chicago School: a comment on Zerbe and Medema', in Steven G. Medema (ed.), *Coasean Economics: Law and Economics and the New Institutional Economics*, Boston, MA: Kluwer, pp. 239–48.
Medema, Steven G. (1996), 'Of Pangloss, Pigouvians, and pragmatism: Ronald Coase on social cost analysis', *Journal of the History of Economic Thought*, **18** (Spring), 96–114.
Meek, Ronald L. (1977), 'Smith and Marx', in *Smith, Marx, and After: Ten Essays in the Development of Economic Thought*, London: Chapman & Hall.
Mitchell, Wesley C. (1967), *Types of Economic Theory: From Mercantilism to Institutionalism*, Joseph Dorfman (ed.), New York: Augustus M. Kelley.
Pigou, A.C. (1932), *The Economics of Welfare*, 4th edn, London: Macmillan.
Reder, Melvin W. (1982), 'Chicago economics: permanence and change', *Journal of Economic Literature*, **20** (March), 1–38.
Reder, Melvin W. (1987), 'Chicago School', in Jon Eatwell, Murray Milgate and Peter Newman (eds), *The New Palgrave: A Dictionary of Economics*, Vol. 1, New York: Stockton Press, pp. 413–18.
Robbins, Lionel (1952), *The Theory of Economic Policy in English Classical Political Economy*, London: Macmillan.
Rutherford, Malcolm (2005), 'Walton H. Hamilton and the public control of business', in Steven G. Medema and Peter Boettke (eds), *The Role of Government in the History of Economic Thought*, Annual Supplement to Volume 37, *History of Political Economy*, Durham, NC: Duke University Press, pp. 234–73.
Shackle, G.L.S. (1967), *The Years of High Theory: Invention and Tradition in Economic Thought, 1926–39*, Cambridge: Cambridge University Press.
Smith, Adam (1976 [1759]), *The Theory of Moral Sentiments*, Oxford: Oxford University Press.
Smith, Adam (1976 [1776]), *An Inquiry into the Nature and Causes of The Wealth of Nations*, Oxford: Oxford University Press.
Stigler, George J. (1941), *Production and Distribution Theories*, New York: Macmillan.
Stigler, George J. (1950), 'The development of utility theory I', *Journal of Political Economy*, **58** (August), 307–27.
Stigler, George J. (1952), 'The Ricardian theory of value and distribution', *Journal of Political Economy*, **60** (June), 187–207.

Stigler, George J. (1960), 'The influence of events and policies on economic theory', *American Economic Review*, **50** (May), 36–45.
Stigler, George J. (1965a), 'The economist and the state', *American Economic Review*, **55** (March), 1–18.
Stigler, George J. (1965b), *Essays in the History of Economics*, Chicago, IL: University of Chicago Press.
Stigler, George J. (1971), 'Smith's travels on the ship of state', *History of Political Economy*, **3** (Fall), 265–77; reprinted (1982) in *The Economist as Preacher and Other Essays*, Chicago, IL: University of Chicago Press, pp. 136–45.
Stigler, George J. (1976a), 'Do economists matter?' *Southern Economic Journal*, **42** (January), 347–54.
Stigler, George J. (1976b), 'The successes and failures of Professor Smith', *Journal of Political Economy*, **84** (December), 1199–1213.
Stigler, George J. (1981), 'The economist as preacher', *The Tanner Lectures on Human Values*, Vol. 2, Salt Lake City, UT: University of Utah Press; reprinted (1982) in *The Economist as Preacher and Other Essays*, Chicago, IL: University of Chicago Press, pp. 3–13.
Viner, Jacob (1927), 'Adam Smith and laissez faire', *Journal of Political Economy*, **35** (April), 198–232.
Viner, Jacob (1960), 'The intellectual history of laissez faire', *Journal of Law and Economics*, **3** (October), 45–69.
Viner, Jacob (1968), 'Adam Smith', in David L. Sills (ed.), *The International Encyclopedia of the Social Sciences*, Vol. 14, New York: Macmillan and Free Press, pp. 322–9; reprinted in Douglas A. Irwin (ed.) (1991), *Essays on the Intellectual History of Economics*, Princeton, NJ: Princeton University Press, pp. 248–61.

Index

'abstract reasoning' of Smith 233
accumulation 152, 153, 157, 159
action and motive 59
Act of Union 1707 316, 319
   loss of Scottish Assembly 320
Adam and Eve, as historical characters, Smith belief 91
additivity 220, 221
aesthetic appeal of systems 107
affection of the heart 59
agape, absence of 20
agency, issue of, in Smith's works 52
   central to his economic theory 69
   central to his moral philosophy 69
'agent' as 'moral agent' and 'economic agent' 52
agent-causation and free will 56
aggregate value increase 179
agnosticism, Smith on 84
agricultural bias of Smith 223
agricultural employers, slave cultivation sugar and tobacco planting 281
agricultural improvements on credit conditions 289–90
agricultural sector, corn bounty effect on 249
agriculture
   and commerce 115
   in new American colonies, Smith's encouragement 265
   long-run harm to 245, 246
   most productive application of capital 126
   safe investments in 5
allocation of resources 179
altruism–egoism 53
altruism or self-interest 187
ambiguity, a weakness or strength 195
American colonies
   cheap land, and cheap labour from Britain 265
   searching critique of mercantile system 264, 275
American goods, molasses, coffee and tobacco confinement to market of mother country 264
American independence
   global dominance for Anglo-American empire 269–70
American problem, Smith's interest in 263
American Psychological Association
   Character Strengths and Virtue 8

American war, Napoleonic Wars 295
   sales of annuities at costly rates 293
America's contribution to discharge of Britain's public debt
   Smith suggestion for taxation 268
analytical error, Smith 232
ancients, study of, in Renaissance 35
Anderson, James
   criticism of Smith on the corn bounty in his lifetime 230–33, 240, 247, 250–52
   ineffectiveness of his critique of Smith's bounty analysis 250–53
   praise of corn bounty 238–9
   substance of his bounty analysis 248–50
Anglican clergymen, carriers of knowledge about economic development 226
animal products, increase in demand through rise in grain production 241
animals as property of individuals 121
anti-hierarchism of Stoic philosophers opposed to Roman society 28
apprenticeship and settlement laws, Smith against 309
Aquinas, St Thomas, Seven Virtues 5, 7, 8, 13
   Smith not a close student of 13–14
Aristotelian encyclopaedia, new subjects 25
Aristotelian family model
   basis for legitimized relationship of power 34, 39
Aristotelianism, Smith as enemy 14
Aristotelian studies, expansion, 1500–1560 26
Aristotle
   and Adam Smith 25–48
   concept of *phronesis*, practical wisdom, ability to choose 38
   dependence of workers 38
   fear of avarice in society 281
   golden mean 9
   Middle Ages 25
   Middle Stoicism 27–30
   'secular' in Italy 25
   translations in Italy, sixteenth century 26
   zoon politikon, humans as social or political beings 315, 317
art of war, improvement 326
astronomy
   evolving ideas, Smith's historical approach 104

mathematics, Jesuit interest 26
  Smith's study in *History of Astronomy* 101–2
asymmetry in Smithian model, workers and capitalists 146
atheism of Smith 73, 83
Atlantic Economic Community 268
  Smith's preferred solution 264
atonement, Smith's deletion of 87–9
authority, divine, regal and paternal 29
authority, necessity of 304
automatic self-regulation 198

backward-bending supply curve 221
balance of trade, positive 262
bank financing of long-term projects 288
  Smith objection 286, 287
Bank of England discounting 292
bankruptcies 282
Battle of Culloden, 1746 321
behaviour-evolutionary theory principle 144–5
behaviour regulation to avoid extremes 33
belief derived from experience 101
belief in God 204
Bell Atlantic v. *Twombly* case (550 US 2007) 339
  quote from *Wealth of Nations* 339
benefits to Britain from the American colonies 266
benevolence 7, 14, 15, 79
  justice and self-love, human progress in 118
  market context 351
  self-interest 53
  Smith's vision of human perfection 84
Bentham, Jeremy 3, 218, 350
  A Fragment of Government 4
  'greatest happiness for the greatest number' 311
  proposal 295
  on usury laws 277–98
Berkeley, George
  addressing the rich of Ireland 212, 214
  on economic development 226
  on invention 222
  poverty alleviation in Ireland, Dublin School 213
  Querist, rhetorical questions 213, 221
  spinning school, Ireland 225
Berlin, Isaiah, on liberty 4, 315
blameworthiness, man's dread of 186–7
borrowing to spend, Smith disapproval of 282–3
bounties for infant industries, Smith rejection 215
bounty-caused decline in the corn wage
  money-wage adjustment lag 246

bounty-induced rise in corn price
  proportionate rise in money wage 243
British and French law, safety in London and Paris 124
British collectivism, Jeremy Bentham 311
British individualism, Jeremy Bentham 311
British public debt, from British mercantile empire 129
Buchanan, David
  criticism of Smith's 'fondness for system' 234
  on error of bounty supporters 239
  on error in Smith's bounty analysis 243
Buckle, Henry T., *History of Civilisation in England* 53
  on Smith's achievement 68–9
  on Smith's use of data 233, 240
businessmen's motivations, suspect by Smith 302
Butler, Bishop Joseph
  on people being unjust to themselves 17

capital accumulation 121, 125, 148
'capital'
  and 'revenue' 67
  as engine for growth, *Wealth of Nations* 115
  diminishment by prodigality 67
  employed in agriculture, America
    cause of wealth in American colonies 63
  increase by parsimony 67
  investment possibilities, economic interests 68
capitalists' surplus 159
capital stock 126
capital use for domestic industry, production industry 196
care of self and family property 34
caring ethic 18
Carlyle, Alexander 323, 324
Castiglione, Baldassare, *Il Cortegiano* 34
casuistry, Smith's attacks on 19
Catholicism and Presbyterianism
  struggle for supremacy in Scotland 101
Catholicism, extreme, opposed by Smith 20
cattle in Scotland, price rise of
  cause of improvements in low country 62
  raising value of highland estates 62
causality role 58–61
causal relations
  of economic system, individual interpretation 65
  significance for study of society 57
causation, Hume and Hobbes 56–7, 101
'causes' of wealth of nations 62
  multicausal analysis in *Wealth of Nations* 63
charity to the poor 54

Chicago School and Adam Smith 346–56
China
    growth 223
    Smith, on material riches and poverty of many 125
choice in a market, as invisible hand 197
Christian commitment of Smith 84
Christian ethical system
    Golden Rule, love of neighbour as self 84
Christian faith and ancients 35
Christianity 14
    Calvinistic, opposed by Smith 20, 73
Christian references 90
Christian revelation
    and human natural sentiments 89
    Smith's belief in 91
Christian revelatory theology 92
Christian Scripture
    references to scripture, in Smith 75
Christian theism of Smith's day 77–8
Christian theology, Minowitz's narrow understanding 74
Christian virtues 8, 10
church tithe, Smith condemnation 284
Cicero, *De Officiis*
    decorum as 'moral beauty' 33
    manual for education of ruling classes 28
    revival of interest in sixteenth century 33
    Stoic approach, redolent of Aristotelianism 41
city-state, organization of 27
civic ethics 124
in Great Britain 126
    and progress of opulence 123
civic humanism 26–7, 35, 130, 328
    and duties 315
    and militia issue 329
    leaders 129
    narrative 322–3
    tradition 317
civil freedom 74
civil government 122, 302
    for imposition of subordination 303–4
civilizing effects of commerce
    increase in wealth 190
classical economics 141
    output maximization and growth 144
classical political economy 310
classical republicanism, importance of militia 315
Coase, Ronald, Chicago School, and Smith 346
coincidence of wants 143, 144, 147
Colbertism, French form of mercantilism 135
colonial policy, economic aspects 264
colonial problem, Smith's account 274

colonial relationship 271
    British access to strategic materials 264
    national defence 264
colonial trade 232
commerce and independence 125
commerce, civilizing effect
    'order and good government' 190
commercialization 105
commercial progress as dangerous
    in classical republican tradition 318
commercial progress as luxury
    military virtue as manliness 324
commercial society
    and civic humanism, tension, militia issue 321
    for wealth and consumption 119
commercial system of Great Britain
    Smith's attack on 262
commonsense philosophy of Thomas Reid 101
commutative justice 123–4
    material production 122
competition 143
    as invisible hand 197
competitive market-price system, as invisible hand 197
competitive market structures, increasing returns 173, 178
competitiveness 175
'condition bettering' (*Moral Sentiments*) 66–7
'condition bettering' (*Wealth of Nations*) 66–7
consumer preferences for diversity 176
consumption 159
    level among working class, liberal plan for humankind 119
    levels, characterization of 255
    'luxurious' 161–2
    purpose of production 128
contempt for effeminate, as cowardice, Smith 323
contractarian theories, Hobbes, Thomas, Jean-Jacques Rousseau, John Locke 3
controlled credit market, Smith's case 281–2
conventional virtue 32
cooperation, predisposition for 189
cooperative behaviour among masters 339–41
    keeping wages down 340
coordination 142
    of actions in business 220
corn bounty
    Adam Smith's attack on 229–59
    error in argument of supporters 239
    its purely nominal effect in Smith 242
    post hoc/propter hoc fallacy 240
    praise of 237–40
    Smith's rent theory and 241–2

static nature of Smith's analysis 243
    thought to reduce corn price 237
corn bounty and loss of grass
    rising price of butcher meat 254
corn export 237
corn laws of England
    advantage over other nations, James
        Anderson 238
corn prices 236, 240
corn trade, freedom of 216
corruption and faction 336
corruption, as selfish pursuit of money 318
corruption debate 321–2, 325
cost theory 204
cotton industry 289
courage as manliness
    virtus (*vir*), Roman-coined Latin word 318
courage, cardinal pagan virtue 9
court system, evolution of 124
credit 286, 292
    rationalization of, Stiglitz and Weiss 294–5
critics of Smith, on the corn trade 246–7
Cromwellian conquest of Ireland 212

decision-making, deliberative and non-deliberative 208–9
Declaratory Act of 1766
    Americans as subjects of British Crown 273
decorum 34
    and behaviour 33–5
    and propriety 32
    honestum, moderation, beauty and good,
        Aristotle's and Cicero's views 35
deductivist theory 107, 109
demand for surplus reproduction, Smith 162–3
demand structure 159
demand with fixed current needs and wants 165
dependence and corruption 125
dependency decrease, honesty increase 190
Descartes, René, *cogito ergo sum*, principle
    contemplation and classical logic 109
    theory of fluxion 102
'desires', want of, in Irish poor 221
'determine', use of
    in *Moral Sentiments* 64–5
    in *Wealth of Nations* 64–5
de Toqueville, Alexis
    absence of government in United States 305–6
dialogic and monologic discourse 12
Dialogues Concerning Natural Religion
    (Hume), Smith's objections 80–81
Dictator Game 181
    Sender and Receiver 186

distribution theory 174
distributive justice, Aristotelian concept 34
diversity, preferences for 176–7
divine benevolence 77
divine ground of justice and punishment 88
Divine Justice and atonement 88
divine names, classifications of, in Smith 85–6
division of labour 107, 109, 141, 145, 148, 325
    agriculture not suited to 219
    consequence of propensity to barter 65
    in economics 108
    helped by religious rules 121
    invention of machinery facilitated 219
    skill improved by specialization 219
    time saver 219
domestic and foreign markets, buoyancy 289
dualisms
    choice versus culture and institutions 207
    free will versus determinism 207
    human nature versus socialization 207
    individual versus environment 207
duties of sovereign
    erecting and maintaining public works 308–9
    protection of members of society from oppression 308–9
    protection of society from invaders 308–9
duty and social order 118
duty, sense of 117

eclipse of sun and moon, Smith on 103
economic activity other than agriculture 27
economic affairs, and private citizens 349
economic system 66
    employment of money 68
economic agent, owner of capital 67
economic analysis
    history of 142
    in *Wealth of Nations* 62
economic axioms, Adam Smith 215
economic behaviours
    causal relations of economic system 67
economic development
    and Adam Smith 211–27
    'human development', George Berkeley 213
economic growth in food
    increase in demand for other goods 235
economic methodology of Smith 100–110
economic organization 106–7
    hunting, pasturage, farming and commerce 105
economic policy of Smith, axioms 220
economic progress theory, Smith 173
economic role of government, Adam Smith 300–313, 304, 307
economics

moral science 101
   and self-interest 348
   Smith's historical approach 105
economic situation of colonial territories 265
economic system, *Wealth of Nations* 65
   causal properties, analysis of 66
   'economic agency' concept 66
economic thought 100
economies of scale 175, 177
economists in twentieth century 15
economy a private concern, classical philosophers' view 40
Edinburgh Review, Scottish literary magazine 83
   Hume, policy of exclusion from 80
effective demand 147, 163
effects of progress (division of labour) 158
effeminacy, cause of decline of republic 325
egalitarian inclinations of Smith 14, 37
egalitarianism of original Stoicism, opposed to Roman society 28
egoism of Mandeville's system, *Fable of the Bee* 53
employer collusion 340
employment of capital 139
English judicial system
   'advance' by chance and circumstance 124
Enlightenment 20
   ethical theories 3
   Smith's interpretation, Scottish Enlightenment 200
entrepreneur, as invisible hand 197, 289
Epictetus 10
   'neighbour' argument 41
   Smith, a disciple 79
Epicureanism, Hellenistic philosophy 27
Epicureanism and Stoicism struggle wealth and virtue 319
equality, liberty and justice for humankind 119
equilibrium 159, 168, 198
equity finance 285–6
Erasmus, *De Civilitate* 33
ethics 3
   as interpersonal relations 18
   lecture series 88
   rational basis 4, 7
Euler's theorem 175
European educational reform and Aristotle's philosophy 25–6
evasion problem, in tax laws 278
evolution theory 209
'exchange, fair and deliberate' 188
   the origins of 173–4
experimental economics literature
   use of Adam Smith's work in 181–90

experimental method of Smith 109
experimental system, and deductivist system 110
Exportation of Grain, 1689 240
export subsidy on corn 245
external economies, concept of 176

'faction' 335, 337, 341
fairness, learning of, in market exchange 190
faith, hope and transcendent love
   in human philosophical psychology 21
   loss of, in Smith, evidence against 90
family love, Smith's view 9
family structure, Aristotelian type 41
family property and political office 34
farmers ('productive workers') cultivation of land 135–6
Ferguson, Adam
   divergence from Adam Smith on militia issue 328
   leader of militia cause 324
   Reflections Previous to the Establishment of a Militia 321–2
feudalism 115
   downfall of the feudal lords 341–2
feudal system 38
   undermining of 342
financial crises, resulting from overtrading 294
financing mechanisms 309
financing of risking investment 285
Fink, Zera, *The Classical Republicans* 317
fiscal need in Britain 267
Fletcher, Andrew of Saltoun (1653–1716)
   Discourse of Government with relation to Militias 315, 316, 320
Florence, *quattrocentro* 316–17
food markets, preventing speculation 215–16
foreign trade and economic prosperity 213, 215
foreign trade for Great Britain 262
foreign trade of consumption 126
fortuna (Machiavelli's term) 324
   goddess Fortune as a woman 323
Franciscan ideal of poverty 27
Franklin, Benjamin 270
   on 'no taxation without representation' 272
free enterprise, as invisible hand 197
free-market allocations 216
free markets, efficacy of 348
free trade advocation 216
free will and motives to action 56
French Enlightenment, deductivist theory 109
Friedman, Milton, Chicago School
   'Adam Smith's relevance for 1976' 346, 349
fundamentalist religion, Smith an enemy 13

gain and loss chances 282
general equilibrium theory 100, 110, 141–8, 164
   differences between Smith and neoclassical economics 168
generalized increasing returns 179
   welfare implications 178–80
Glorious Revolution of 1688
   abdication of James II 316
God as first person of Trinity, father 84
God as invisible hand 197
God-sovereign head of family triad in Middle Ages 29
gold and silver 63–4
golden mean 14, 38, 39, 117
   definition of 36
Golden Rule, love of neighbour as self 84
Good 12, 14
goodness and moral sense 79
goods
   features of 177
   produced in Britain, naval stores, masts, pig-iron, copper 264
   stochastic, not stable demands 178
government activity, administrative aspect 40
government
   as obstacle to growth, Adam Smith 211
   borrowing 294
      during American war, credit shortage 292–3
   expenses, revenue raising 305
government functions
   build highways, canals and bridges 220
   law and order maintenance 220
government policies for growth of national wealth 310
grain export, necessity of 248
grain prices, stable, back-bending labor supply curve 248
grain stock of England, Steuart's granary scheme 239
gravitation, principles of, Isaac Newton 102, 108
Greco-Roman world and Christian theology 77
Greek, humanistic-Renaissance interest in 26
gross output 149
Grotius, Hugo 329
groups with unitary goals
   corporation, monopoly, combination, faction 335

Harrington, James (1611–77) 317
   republican Whig 316
harvests, disruptive to industry and social order
   James Anderson's claim 248–9

Hayekian theory of spontaneous order 208–9
hay price rise, horse maintenance higher 254
'heroic valour' 322–3
hierarchical structure of family and state 29
hierarchy
   and egalitarianism 37
   family relationships, Aristotelian relation to other hierarchies 34
   reduction by commercial society 341
historical approach of Smith 114–15
Hobbes, Thomas, on the Good 14
Homeric legacy, martial virtues 318
home trade development, Berkeley 213
home trade, secure and quickest 126
home-versus-market model 179
homo economicus 89, 181, 188
honesty 20, 21
honesty, admired by Americans 7
Hooker, Richard, on human life 20
hope and faith, Christian, unwelcome to *philosophes* 20
Horner, Francis
   on error of bounty's supporters 239
   on error of Smith's bounty analysis 244
   on praise of corn bounty 238
household (economic) model, application to political economy 42
household model of state management 40
human action model
   in *Moral Sentiments* 65
   in *Wealth of Nations* 65
human agency, theory of 55, 69
human beings as social creatures 61
human condition and moral philosophy 113
human foundations of Smith's moral philosophy 116–20
'human frailty' 113
human institutions 115–16
humanism 34
humanists' contempt for mercenaries 318
humankind, evolution 114
human nature
   Hume's theory of sentiment (passion) and imagination, sympathy 101
   natural sentiments, construction of, by Divine Architect 92
   self-regarding and other-regarding 183
human need for transcendence 21
human sentiments
   self-love, justice and beneficence 116
Hume, David 4
   Dialogues Concerning Natural Religion 81–2
   Enquiry into Human Understanding 57–8
   'Idea of a Perfect Commonwealth' 329
   'Of the balance of trade' 240

Treatise on Human Nature 57
  belief in existence, prior to reason 101
  death, Smith's words on 79
  on the Good 14
  influence on Smith 101
  philosophy founded on reason, French Enlightenment 101
  'reconciling project' 55
  serious atheist, religious sceptic 79
  Smith's relationship with 79
humility 5
hunter-gatherers, response to mysteries of nature 120
Hutcheson, Francis, influence on Smith 79, 101

idealism–realism dualism, *History of Astronomy* 306
imagination
  central role of 103
  Hume's view 58
  power of 102
  reasoning ability, 'human frailty' 113
imitative arts (IM) 90
impartial spectator, engagement with 61–2
improved productivity 153
incentives for enhanced performance 309, 310
incompatibilities of wants 144
increase in output, decrease in cost 175
increasing returns 177
  aggregate output 175–6
independence, deliberative
  importance for model of human agency 62
independence of America, Smith's suggestion 273–4
independent judgment 61
independent Scottish militia 316
individual and social 219–20
individualism 200, 301
  emphasis in Smith 335–43
individualization
  in society 207
individual proprietorship, partnership risk avoidance 288
industry output 176
influence 60
influence of Smith on Hume's appointment
  Logic Chair at Glasgow 79–80
impartial spectator 36
institutional individualism 207
institution of civil government 123
institutions and socialization 220–22
institutions, role of
  humankind's evolution 120–25
insurance gambling 290
interdependence 144, 150, 190

across sectors, Smith 153
  in production 147
interest rate, maximum, Smith's justification 294–5
interest-rate regulation 283
international trade, theory 176
intra-personal specialization 177
intuition of virtuous man, versus scientific measures 32
invention, human capacity for 109
investment behaviour 68
investment in agriculture 263
invisible hand 200, 201, 204
  foundation of modern economics 195–210
  government 302
  hand of lawgiver 302
  identity of 197–8
  list of possible candidates 197–8
  the market 197
  meaning of 202–3
  principal functions 198
  Smith's use in economics 196
  The Theory of Moral Sentiments 146
Ireland after Cromwellian conquest
  victim of imperialism 212
Ireland's contribution to discharge of Britain's public debt
  Smith suggestion for taxation 268
Irish School of economic development 213

Jacobite Rebellion 320–21
joint-stock organization 285–6
judgement of merit 59
judgement of property 61
judgement of propriety 59
judgment and *phronesis* 37
Jupiter, invisible hand of, in favour or anger 196
jurisprudence lectures
  Adam Smith 306
  theological grounding 90
jurisprudential tradition
  in Scottish Enlightenment, initiated Grotius and Pufendorf 329
  on rights 315
jury system, evolution of 124
just benevolence towards self 17
justice
  admired by Smith 9
  common 118
  commutative and distributive 31
  fundamental values 34
  instead of love, Immanuel Kant 15
  institutions of 124
  security and 120

Smith's analysis of 116–17
virtue 5, 8, 20
justification of usury laws, Smith 284

Kant, Immanuel 3, 4
Keynes, John Maynard 286
  on Smith's view of usury laws 279
King Henry II and King Edward I
  Smith, on their success in judicial system 130
Knight, Frank, Chicago School, and Smith 346
knowledge, development of
  motivation from human nature 102
knowledge industry
  in Marshallian explanatory model 176

labour
  demand for 65
  division of 90
  money price of 65
  promotion of labourer's independence 37–8
  theory of value 231
labourers
  needs 159
  wages 151–2
laissez-faire principle 352
  Smith not a doctrinaire advocate 309
  with-exceptions approach by Smith 313
land cultivation and need for machines
  country and town cooperation 153
land owned in American colonies
  Smith's prescribed maximum 218
land reform, redistributive 221
land taxation 284
Latin's important role 26
Lauderdale, 8th Earl
  inconsistency in Smith's bounty analysis 245
law and property 121
leadership with vision, necessity of 130, 131
legal and moral rules 310
legal–economic nexus 301–7
legislative government, emergence of, property rights 122
legitimization of social hierarchy 31
lender's responsible behaviour 283
lending, high-risk 280
liberal plan for humankind 114
liberal vision of Smith 127
libertarian ideas in political philosophy 17
libertarians (Hume), 'reconciling project' 55–6
liberty as chaos 116
liberty of conscience, Shaftesbury (3rd Earl) 91
life annuities 290
literary genre, treatises on family and civil life 34

Locke, John, uncommitted to religious tradition 91
logic and metaphysics 30
Logic Chair at Glasgow 83
  Smith's views on his nomination 78–80
lotteries 290
love as Smithian virtue, *agape*, *philia* or *eros* 19, 34
  balanced with pluralism 15
love of one's neighbour, golden rule 73
love, virtue of, under many headings 20

Machiavelli, Niccolò, *The Prince*
  '*fortuna* is a woman' 318–19
  virtu of the Prince 4
macroeconomic considerations 179
majoritarianism 337
Mandeville, Bernard, *Fable of the Bees* 53, 67
manufacture, investment in 263
manufacturers and merchant class, labour of unproductive class of workers 136
market and state in *Wealth of Nations* 307–10
market as invisible hand 197
market behaviour, Smith's analysis 106, 110
market evaluation, objective measures of welfare 179
market exchange as social activity 183
market functioning and society 222
market integration 190
market interaction networks 177
market-plus-framework approach 312–13
  Smith, Adam 310–12
  tripartite model 311
market price equilibrium 68, 147
Marshallian external economies 175–8
martial virtues 322
masters and employees, social distance 337
masters and workmen, Smith on 303
materialism 203, 300
mathematics and astronomy, Jesuit interest 25
mediocritas, mediocrity 32, 35
  awareness of limits 34
  decorum and, Smith on 35–6
'mediocrity' of Adam Smith
  Aristotelian themes 34–9
'mediocrity', used disparagingly in *Wealth of Nations* 38–9
Mencius (372–289 BC), opposer of utilitarianism 7
Menger, Carl, on institutions 208
Menger–Hayek spontaneous development 208
mercantile fallacy, Smith's critique of 232
mercantile institutions, attacks on, by Smith 233

mercantile interests in Britain 129
　Smith's views on its domination 127, 130
mercantile policy to imperial policy, America 272
mercantile system,
　'system of commerce' (Smith) 261–75
　Smith's critique, confirmed by loss of colonies 274
　Wealth of Nations, Book IV 264
mercantilism 141, 262
　policy or doctrine, increase of national power, common aim 261
　Smith's criticism of 200, 307
mercenaries 316, 319, 325
merchant class, Smith on 284–5
Mercier de la Rivière, *L'ordre naturel et essentiel des sociétés politiques* 137
metals, use of, as money 65–6
militia bill defeat 323
militia debate in Scotland, standing army issue 319–22
　Smith support for standing army 315–32
　Lectures on Jurisprudence 324–6
Milton, John (1608–74), republican Whig 316, 317
　Paradise Lost, Adam and Eve, sentiments of 91
　references to scripture, in Smith 75
Mirabeau, Marquis de, *Philosophie rurale* 137
misinterpretation, Smith's paranoia about 89
Mitchell, Wesley 226, 354
Modern Corporation and Private Property (Berle and Means, 1932) 337
monetary incentives 189
monetary metals, price 235–6
monetary theory, Hume and Smith 106
money
　and approbation, results of human interaction 340
　and banking systems, Hume and Smith on 106
　employment of 67–8
money price of corn 230, 234, 243, 251
monopoly
　colony trade 266
　mercantile interests 128
　social distance 339
　unitary actor 337–41
moral agent 62
　independent stance required by moral judgment 62
moral approbation and disapprobation 107
　sentiment of affection 58–9
moral approval 207
'moral beauty' (*kalon*), Cicero's *honestum* 33

moral hierarchy, owing much to Stoics 62
　Adam Smith 52
moral judgment and sympathy 54, 61
　resting on feeling 57
moral philosophy 4, 12, 103, 107, 112–14
　vision of Smith 114–16
'Moral saints' by Susan Wolf
　altruistic definition of virtue 16–17
moral science and economics 103
moral side of human nature 183
moral sympathy in Smith 18
moral universe in Europe 5
moral virtues, beneficence 11
moral wisdom (prudence) 20
motivations of economic agency 66
motives to action in Smith texts 52, 55–60
multiple effects of analysis, *Wealth of Nations* 62
multiple equilibria 161
multisectoral analysis 147
myths in society, Karl Popper on 201

national debt 231
　in Britain 267
national defence 309
nationalism 21, 300
national power, increase in
　employment maximization 261
　favourable balance of trade 261
　industry protection 261
　population encouragement 261
　promotion of national wealth 261
　state unification 261
　treasure accumulation 261
national wealth
　erroneous concept 234
　sum of individual wealth 214
　under natural liberty, Smith on 308
natural advantage 215
natural course, human disturbance of 115
natural events, irregular
　The History of Astronomy (Smith) 196
naturalism 300
　and supernaturalism 203, 204
natural law philosophy 105–6
　refusal to homogenize family and state 39
　theory of, born to rule or born to obey 39
natural liberty 105, 141, 143, 159, 197, 307, 312
　duties of sovereign 308
　and market system 346
natural order for human nature 113
natural philosophy
　Smith, on Sir Isaac Newton's discovery of gravity 113
natural religion 76–7, 89

natural selection 115, 197, 209
natural theology 91
   and Christian theology 78
   Hume's rejection 83
   Smith on deist and Stoic influences 92
     in *The Wealth of Nations* 92
   of society 92
Nature's Truth, 'behind the scenes' 112
Nature, theological reading 85–6
'necessary connexion' 55–6
necessitarians (Hume), 'reconciling project' 55–7
Necker, Jacques
   observation on grain price decline cited by Smith 252
   prohibition of grain export from France 239
negative reciprocity 184
neoclassical analysis 144
neoclassical equilibrium 175
neoclassical paradigm, welfare implications 173
neoclassical price theory 348
net surplus and maximum growth 154–7
Newtonian methodology 30
Newton, Sir Isaac
   experimental philosophy, influence 105
   planetary motion 107
   scientific method of analysis and synthesis 105
Nichomachean Ethics, Aristotle 26, 31
non-interference by government 37
non-interventionism 313
notion of system, regularity from human nature 106
Nozick, Robert, on ethics 17–18

Old Testament, references to scripture, in Smith 75
ordination seeking in Christian faith 78
outputs and inputs, value of 174
over-trading, and circulation of paper money 62
overtrading as reason for scarcity of money 63, 294
own surpluses 151

Panaetius of Rhodes 29
   harmony with Roman *nobilitas* 28, 29
   inspiration for *De Officiis* 28
paper money, Smith on
   issue of small notes 217–18
paradigms, Smith's work in multiple 200–201, 300
Pareto optimality 18, 178–80, 198–9

parliamentary sovereignty of Britain in America 273
parsimony, not industry 14, 15
   cause of increase in capital 63
partial and general equilibrium 164, 166
passion for present employment (Smith) 163
passions and humankind 104
patriarchal theories transferred to state 39
peace and order in society, subordination, necessity of 37
perception, versus scientific knowledge 32
perfect equilibrium, inner state 33
perfection, deviation from 36
perfection of virtue 32
performance achievement 199
persuasion of knowledge 108
philosophical background of Smith 100–112
   Scottish Enlightenment 100
philosophy and science in Scottish education 104
phronesis, Adam Smith's 'judgment' 37
Physiocracy
   Adam Smith's views on, in *Wealth of Nations* 135–40, 307
   influence on Smith's economic vocabulary and analysis 138
   Smith's sympathetic, critical account 136–7
piety, attack on 20–21
pin factory metaphor 173–4
   in *Wealth of Nations* 108
Pinker, Steven, modern evolutionary psychologist 19
place and social distance 336–7
planetary motion, notion of 102
Plato 25, 27
   Republic, stay in one's own place 31
   Smith's exposition of 8
Pocock, John G.A., *Machiavellian Moment* 316–17
Poker Club, Edinburgh, named by Ferguson
   militia for Scotland 323
   stir up militia question 317, 322
polemic, *Wealth of Nations* as 232
political economy 3, 135
   laws of 54
politicians, Smith's view of
   antipathy to government intervention 352
poor, Smith's concern for 211–12, 225
population of colonies, result of religious persecution 268
positive law, and progress of opulence 123
positivism 15
possessors of money as economic agents 68
poverty alleviation in Ireland, Dublin School
   Berkeley, George, on Ireland 221

power structure, role of government and institutions 209
Pownall, Thomas
　critic of Smith in his lifetime 230, 247, 250, 252
　criticism of Smith on corn bounty 247
　ineffectiveness of critique 250
　influential critic 248
　praise of Smith's system 233
　on Smith's views on investment in colonial relationship 271
practical and theoretical knowledge
　Cicero on Aristotelian dichotomy between 38
pragmatism 300, 301
praiseworthiness, man's desire for 186–7
praxis, Aristotelian philosophy 26
precious metals, outflow
　Smith, on their success in judicial system 283
preferences, other-regarding 181
preferential treatment to American products 265
Presbyterianism and social order arrangement 321
price and conditioning expansion paths 160
price determination 231
price level of corn, rise, financing of 245
price of commodities, rent, wages and profits 64
prices 159
　and wages of labourers 249
price system as invisible hand 197
price theory 209
principal–agent problem 283–4
principles, nature and role, influence of Newton 108
private creditors 286
private enterprise as invisible hand 197
private interest against public interest 318
private morality 54
private ownership and worker subsistence 146
private profit as sole motive 68
private property 121
　as invisible hand 197
private virtue of individual 35
prodigality 67
producers and consumers, simultaneous 177
production function, constant returns
　ratio between input and output value 175
productive powers of labour, effect of division of labour 125
productivity increase 152
product of land and labour of country 66
professional army, supported by Smith 317

professors paid out of student fees
　for stimulation of professorial diligence 310
profit motive as invisible hand 197
profit, pursuit of
　systematic economic analysis 68
propaganda role 254
property
　civil government defining laws 122–3
　individual 27
　and inequality 303
　law 305
　rights 121, 183
property transference, power exercise 306
proprietors' expenditure to improve land 135
propriety 14
　and Aristotle's golden mean 31
　rules about 18
protectionism, Smith's attacks on 350
protectionist policies or mercantilists 127
prudence 8
　admired by Smith 9
　and justice, fundamental values 34
　and mediocrity 34
　as virtue 4, 5, 10, 14, 17, 34, 38
public debate on 'catching-up' 224
public institutions 309
public policy 54
Pufendorf, Samuel von 329
puritans 91

quality of virtues, errors of, reduction of ethics to taste 15
quantity of virtues, errors of 15

radicalism fear 3
rates of interest 280
rationalism
　approach, Hobbes and Locke 106
　behaviour 145
Rational Choice prediction 184
　prudence 145
　theology 81
real net surplus 163
reason and ethics 16
reasoning ability 113
reciprocity 188
　in human nature 183, 185
reflective disequilibrium 343
reflective equilibrium 336
'regulate', causal meaning of 65
regulation 339
　of commerce 263
　of price of other goods, by price of corn 243
regulations supported by Smith 309

Reid, Thomas
  Essays on the Active Powers of Man 56
  successor to Adam Smith, as Professor of Moral Philosophy, Glasgow University 56
relation between cause and effect 63–4
religion
  conventional virtue in 20
  human institution, rules of morality 120
  moral framework for social intercourse 121
religious factions 337
religious fanaticism in Scottish Kirk 20, 80
religious instruction for clergy 309
religious movements, deism
  challenges to orthodox religion 311
religious scepticism of Hume, tension with Smith over 79
religious superstition 20
religious views of Smith 73
Renaissance Aristotelianism 25
rent and corn price 241–3
rent-seeking 302
rent, wages and profits
  and price of commodities 64
representative government
  replacing monarchical and aristocratic regimes 311
reproduction and luxurious consumption
  dependence on prices and accumulation 164
reproduction in *Wealth of Nations*, crucial 163
republicanism
  argument 325
  classical 317
  and militia cause 316–19
  Scotland 316
republic, decline of, loss of strength 325
restraint, sense of
  in *decorum* and temperance 35
Revelation
  references to scripture, in Smith 75
revelation, access to non-baptized 89
rewards for hard work 213
rhetoric
  exercise in persuasion 102–3
  Smith lectures on 275
Ricardo, David
  on the 'error of Adam Smith' 230–31
  Ricardian logic 173–4
rich and poor countries
  Rev. Josiah Tucker on success of rich 224–5
rich, spending by, employment for poor 196
'righteousness' and 'propriety' 7–8
rights and duties in society
  rules of dress, precedence 34
rights and property definitions 307

rigoristic attitude of Stoic philosophers, moderation of 28
risk element 284
risk limiting to landowners 284
role of prices 159
Roman Catholic clergy, Smith against 74
Roman law and civic ethics contrasted with Greek, by Smith 123
rules and maxims, Smith against 19
rules of behaviour, established 61
ruling classes, status
  preserved by treatises on family life 34
Russell, Bertrand
  lack of ethical reasoning 16
  on values and cognitive life 16

safety and functioning of society 62
saving
  as accumulation of capital 67
  denial of consumption 67
scale economies 174
Scepticism
  Hellenistic philosophy 27
Schmoller, Gustav, *The Mercantile System and its Historical Significance* 261
scholasticism, revolt against 13, 26
'Schumpeterian innovation' 284
Schumpeter, Joseph, economist 15, 16
science, anti-Aristotelian
  reaction against Middle Ages and scholasticism 25
science of political economy, Henry Buckle on 54
science of society, tripartite
  moral sentiments, market, government and law 200
scientific methods
  theological synthesis 26
  traditional authority 26
scientific revolution 25
Scotch banking companies, terms of repayment
  trade of these companies 62
Scotland and England, rivalry 311
Scotland's martial history 319
Scottish Enlightenment 100, 107
  Adam Ferguson a key figure in militia discourse 316
  'experimental' approach 109
Scottish Enlightenment philosophy
  connections with continental Europe 101
Scottish Historical, 'analytical history' 105
Scottish union with England, challenge to Scottish nationhood 101
scriptures, authoritative for Christianity 91

secular and pagan virtues 13
secularism of Smith 203, 300
   Joseph Cropsey's view 74
'secure tranquility', Smith, peace of mind 120
Self and Other 17
self-approbation and self-disapprobation, Smith 108
self-deception of man 103
self-gain and invisible hand 196
self-interest 53, 199, 207, 218
   benevolence and 53
   competition 204
   driving force 204, 205
   economics and 348–9
   greed 206
   invisible hand 197, 210
   motive force for market 351
   public good and 220
   rationality 204, 205
   selfishness and 54
self-interest and good government argument *Wealth of Nations* contribution 211
selfishness 53
selflessness, unjust or egalitarian 17
self-love 10
   impartial spectator within us 186
   other humans, Smith on 118
   specialized version of Christian love 15
self-preservation
   role for self-advancement and self-love 92
self-reflexivity 61, 201
self-regarding preferences 15, 181, 182, 187
self-regulated conduct of life 36
self-shaping temperance, chief theme of TMS 18
'sense and feeling', versus reason 32
sense of duty 62
sentiment or affection 59
Seven Primary Virtues 5, 6, 8, 12
Seven Years War, government borrowing 291
Shaftesbury, Earl of, 1713, on private or self-good 17
   system of natural religion 91
shepherding stage of society, complexity increase 121
signification of invisible hand 198–9
silver and gold mines, search after, Smith against 290
   in America, cause of diminution of silver value 62
Smith, Adam, a classical liberal
   'Adam Smith problem' 52, 55, 58, 69, 93, 182, 200, 317
   'Additions and Corrections' 251

'Digression concerning the variation in the value of silver', corn bounty, 1784 236
History of Astronomy, rhetoric, use of, Smith posited 200
Lectures in Jurisprudence 40, 90, 105, 123–4,
Lectures on Rhetoric and Belles Lettres (LRBL) 100
The Theory of Moral Sentiments 3, 30–31, 52, 58, 100, 103, 146
   criticism of Christianity of Hutcheson 10, 11, 15
   divergent views on religion in 74
   on metaphysical implications of 56
   psychological perspective in 182
Wealth of Nations 4, 5, 11–12, 52, 302–6
   anti-Christian work, rejection of Christian God 74
   capital as fuel for opulence 125
   divergent views on religion in 74
   identifying causal relations 62, 69
   and Aristotle 30–39
   behavioural axiom, on objects of trade 183
   and Bentham, different conceptions of economic development 284–8
   on Colbert, Louis XIV's Minister of Finance 261–2
   critics 247–53
   defence of corn exports as opening for critics 246–7
   on Descartes 103
   economic role of government 300–313
   economic thought, moral and philosophical frame 113
   egalitarianism in *Wealth of Nations* 37
   elements of Stoic philosophy, less radical in 41–2
   'equality, liberty and justice' 129
   eulogy on Hume's death, James Boswell's comments 82–3
   father of economics, *homo economicus* 181
   inconsistencies in bounty analysis
      corn wages 243
      dynamic consequences 245–6
      specie flows 245
   key weapon in his attack on bounty 242
   lapsed Christian, convert to Stoicism 76
   lecture topics 306
   legacy of 226
   non-causal approach to action 61
   moral agency, moral deliberation 69
   obsessive editor 89
   politics, working people and right to vote 31
   presumption against government activity 215
   use of data 233, 239–40
   usury laws 277–98

5 per cent maximum, a problem 291–4
  view of a monopoly 337–8
  work of polemic 232
Smith, Charles
  praise of corn bounty 237, 240
  praise of corn dealers 258
Smith corpus, references to scripture 75–6
Smithian axioms
  individual greed 220
  individual knowledge 220
Smithian model of general equilibrium 141–71
smuggling as hazardous trade 282
social and political institutions, constructive role 120
social cohesion, mutual trust and confidence in ethics 189
social consensus of rules 32
social contract, Smith against 40
social control through law 311
social distance 335–7
social distance among faction members 340–41
social exchange 183–4
social ideological system 201
socialism 21
socialization 207
  accommodation of behaviour 117
  importance for model of human agency 62
  learning 207
social mythological system 201
social norms, inculcation of 61
social, political and economic conditions 119
social symbolic system 201
societal construct, production of materials for society 119
society as association of private individuals 315
society as distortion of liberal plan 115
solidarity with lower classes, Smith 37
sophia/sapientia, phronesis/prudentia
  Cicero 38
South Sea Bubble 222
  speculation in government stock 290
sovereign power, grounding on authority and utility 40
specialization and trade, productivity of 173
speculation and risk 285, 290
speculation, irresponsible, Smith's concern for 290
Spengler–Koebler perspective of economic growth 284
spontaneous order principle 208–9
  as invisible hand 197
standing army–militia issue 315, 322, 326
state, Smith's distrust of 350
stationary state concept, Adam Smith 223
status maintenance in society 34

Stewart, Dugald 66, 94, 106, 115, 135, 219, 227, 233, 234
Stigler, George, and construction of 'Chicago Smith' 348–50
Stigler, George, Chicago School, on Smith 346–7
stochastic demand 177
  and extent of the market 173–80
Stoicism
  Adam Smith's relationship to 41–2
  admiration of temperance 9
  Aristotelian philosophy and 27
  attitude to suicide 11
  described by Smith 10–11, 13
  Hellenistic philosophy 27
  'manly' character 337
  Smith as convert to 76–7
Stoic moral hierarchy 69
Stoic references, in names 87
Stoic theory and Aristotle
  on grading of human relationships 30
  Stoic tradition and Plato 5
Stoic virtues 4, 8, 14
stylized competitive equilibrium
  non-optimal 178
subordination, necessity of 304
suicide, Stoic attitude to 11
Sunday School movement, Smith support 78
superfluous consumption 161
supernaturalism 200, 300
  belief in God 204
superstition as polytheistic religions 120
superstition, religion as
  simplistic view on Smith by Minowitz 74
surplus and profit
  determined by actions of workers 146
surplus creation, as heart of economic system Smith, Adam 148
surplus, proper use of 145, 158
superintendence of others' conduct 92
Swift, Jonathan, *Modest Proposal*
  satire on treatment of Irish 212
sympathy
  and self-interest 54, 200
  motive to action 54, 56
  role of, in society 103
sympathy–selfishness 53
systems as machines, Smith's metaphor 107

Tableau économique (Quesnay) 137
taxation of the colonies 268–9
taxes, prohibition and trade restrictions 128–9
tax incidence analysis, Physiocrats 137
tax on absentee landlords, favoured by Smith 218

technological improvements, risks 289
technology
   effect of changes 306
   improved 158
temperance 5, 11
   admired by Smith 9
   (self-control) 20
   virtue 5
theft, argument against, in Stoic formula 41–2
theism of Adam Smith 73–95, 77, 92–3
   in his written work 83
theistic superstition, religion as
   simplistic view on Smith by Minowitz 74
theological naturalism 85–6, 89–90
theological virtues 14
theology and moral questions 26
theology in Smith's work 77, 204
   in lost manuscript discovered 88
theory of value 147
thrift 5
time and uncertainty
   in general equilibrium theory 145
tolls for roads and bridges 310
trade, and merchandisers, Smith's anger 127–8
trade, British
   unduly dependent on large market (colonies) 267
trade, domestic and foreign 263
trade freedom between British colonies of America and West Indies 265
trade or exchange, Smithean logic 173
trade restrictions of mercantilists, Smith against 309
trading and specialization for gains 173
trading opportunities, Scotland and America 101
transcendence, faith in a past, hope and love 8, 21
trickle-down theory of Smith 159–96
tripartite model of society 301
Tucker, Rev. Josiah 225
   on economic development 226
   on social and economic affairs 224
Turgot, A.R.J. and Adam Smith
   on use and employment of capital 139
   views on, in *Wealth of Nations* 135–40
Turgot's economic writings
   influence on *Wealth of Nations* 137
Trust Game 181

Ultimatum Game 181, 184, 189
   rejection of unfair offers 185
   Sender and Receiver 185–6

uniform rate of profit, uniformity 147
unionization activity, illegal on part of workers 303
unique equilibrium 162
unitary goals 335
United States Constitution
   structure and powers of government 305
university curricula in Italy, science 26
usury laws, maximum of 5% on private loans 277–98
usury laws, government policy 279
usury laws, Smith's support for 288–9
utilitarianism 4, 7, 300
utility-maximizing behaviour 188

valued inputs and valued outputs 175
Viner, Jacob, on *Wealth of Nations* 216–17
virility and martial valour 318
virtue and vice 113
'virtue' concept, *fortuna* (Machiavelli's term) 315
virtue ethicist 9–15, 18, 336
'virtue', in *Iliad* and *Odyssey*, martial virtues 318
virtue or vice of action 59
virtues and moral values, exercise of
   transformed by Christianity 34
virtues, core characteristics 8
virtues, peoples' opinions 7
virtù, manly character 319, 323–4
virtuous action motives for 53
virtuous behaviour
   determination by feeling, not reason 42
voluntary behaviour 189
vox populi, existence of 32

wage determination 340
wage-fund doctrine 147
wage increase and price increase 63
wages of labour, Smith on 303
Walrasian general equilibrium 142–3, 145
wants and growth, coincidence of 146
wars, England with Dutch, by 1700
   for commercial gains 223
wealth
   as money 262
   from hard work 213
   inferior and superior 304
   maximization 214
   of nation, annual produce of 66–7
   pursuit of, detoxification by Smith 19
   value of produce 307
   'wealth and virtues' debate on Adam Smith 315–32
welfare economics, mutual benefit 17

welfare of common man
   Smith, attacks on power of oppressors 212
welfare state, collectivist concept 312
Westminster Confession 78
Wilberforce, William, on Smith and Highlands' poor 225
William III and Mary II, succession to English throne 316
wise man, as self-governor, Stoicism 29
woodworking industries 253
woollen manufactures, forbidden in American colonies 264
'work ethic' development 221
work for the working classes 54

Young, Arthur, defender of agricultural interest
   praise of corn bounty 240
   table on rise in wheat prices, 1594 on 240